The

CHAOS

of

EMPIRE

THE BRITISH RAJ *and the* CONQUEST OF INDIA

JON WILSON

PUBLICAFFAIRS
New York

Published in the United States by PublicAffairs™, an imprint of Perseus Books, LLC, a subsidiary of Hachette Book Group, Inc.

PublicAffairs books are available at special discounts for bulk purchases in the U.S. by corporations, institutions, and other organizations. For more information, please contact the Special Markets Department at the Perseus Books Group, 2300 Chestnut Street, Suite 200, Philadelphia, PA 19103, call (800) 810-4145, ext. 5000, or e-mail special.markets@perseusbooks.com.

Typeset in Bembo by M Rules

A CIP catalog record for this book is available from the Library of Congress.

LCCN: 2016944891
ISBN 978-1-61039-293-8 (hardcover)
ISBN 978-1-61039-294-5 (e-book)

First published in the United Kingdom in 2016 by Simon and Schuster UK Ltd.
UK ISBN 978-1-4711-0125-0

First Edition

10 9 8 7 6 5 4 3 2 1

'The total character of the world is . . . in all eternity chaos.'

Friedrich Nietzsche, *The Gay Science*

'Power cannot be made secure only against power, it also must be made secure against the weak; for there lies the peril of its losing balance.'

Rabindranath Tagore, 'A Cry for Peace'

for Delilah and Elsie

CONTENTS

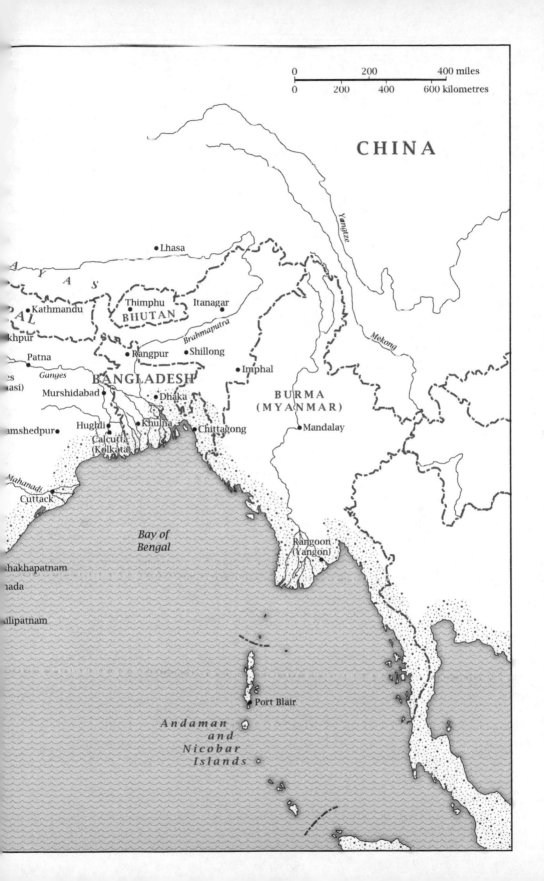

CHINA

Lhasa

Kathmandu
Thimphu
BHUTAN
Itanagar

khpur

Patna

Ganges

Rangpur
Shillong

Brahmaputra

Imphal

BANGLADESH

asi)

Murshidabad

Dhaka

BURMA
(MYANMAR)

amshedpur

Hughli
Khulna
Chittagong

Mandalay

Calcutta
(Kolkata)

Mahanadi

Cuttack

Bay of
Bengal

Rangoon
(Yangon)

hakhapatnam

ıada

ılipatnam

Port Blair

Andaman
and
Nicobar
Islands

Yangtze

Mekong

0   200   400 miles

0   200   400   600 kilometres

Preface

FACTS ON THE GROUND

While turning Bombay's home for old European sailors into a legislative assembly in January 1928, labourers came across patches of red dust. The dust was the disintegrated remains of the city's first English residents. Now 200 metres inland, workers had dug into a graveyard that once stood on the desolate promontory of Mendham's Point, looking out over crashing waves and shipwrecks. There, senior English officers had been buried in elaborate tombs, but the bones of clerks and soldiers, the ordinary English functionaries of empire, were thrown in a shallow grave under a big slab of stone. Corpses were quickly dug out by jackals 'burrowing in the ground like rabbits', according to one account. Even the clergy were buried in common graves, with Bombay's first five priests thrown together in one hole. The cemetery was 'more terrible to a sick Bombaian than the Inquisition to a heretic', one observer wrote. By 1928, the cemetery had been entirely forgotten.[1]

The English ruled territory in India from the 1650s. Britain was the supreme political force in the subcontinent that stretches from Iran to Thailand, from the Himalayas to the sea, from at least 1800 until 1947. These years of conquest and empire left remains that survived in South Asia's soil, sometimes until today. Perhaps a quarter of a million Europeans are still buried in more than a thousand 'cities of the dead', as the British explorer Richard Burton called them in 1847, scattered through the countries that once made up British-ruled India – India, Bangladesh, Pakistan and Burma.

These graves trace the geography of British power during those years, marking the processes and places from which imperial authority was asserted. The earliest are in ports and forts like Bombay, Calcutta and Madras. There, tiny groups of British merchants sheltered behind thick stone walls, with white-skinned soldiers and gunners to protect them from people they tried to make money from. The largest numbers are close to British-built courts and tax offices, near blocky churches built quickly by army engineers as Britain's conquests extended power through every part of India in the early nineteenth century. Some, like the graves every few miles on India's grand trunk road between Calcutta and Delhi, are by highways, marking the death of Europeans travelling or laying roads. Others, like the hilltop cemetery at Khandala three hours' train ride from Bombay, cling to slopes above railway tunnels built at the expense of many Indian and a few European lives, as the British asserted their power by cutting lines of steel into Indian soil from the late nineteenth century on. From the early 1800s the largest single group of graves were those of children, 'little angels', as the tombstones often described them, killed by disease in their first years before they could be shipped back to Britain to boarding school. One hundred and fifty-one of the nearly 400 gravestones in the cantonment town of Bellary marked the death of children under the age of seven. All these graves mark the death of Britons who intended to return home.[2]

There is little sense of imperial celebration in the inscriptions on these gravestones. More often, the words on tombs convey a sense of distance and failure. Epitaphs describe men and women retreating into small worlds cut off from Indian society who died unhappily distant from their homes. Very few mention any connection to the people they ruled. What mattered was their sense of private virtue and the esteem of British friends and family, close by or

thousands of miles back in Britain or Ireland. Shearman Bird, dead
in Chittagong at forty-one, 'was a bright example of duty, affection,
strength of principle and unshakeable fidelity', his gravestone says.
'His converse with this world contaminated not his genuine worth.'
Richard Becher, dead at Calcutta in 1782, was buried '[u]nder the
pang of disappointment / and the pressure of the climate'. Graves
like Bird's and Becher's were not those of a triumphant race, but the
tombstones of 'a people scattered by their wars and affairs over the
face of the whole earth, and homesick to a man', as the American
Ralph Waldo Emerson wrote of the English.[3]

There are 1,349 recorded British graveyards in South Asia. Now
they are quiet and still, the only signs of life coming from the visits
of grass cutters or tourists. But other imperial remains in modern
South Asia are full of activity.[4] South Asia's independent states have
moved into the institutions of British rule, many close to the centres of present-day public power. The architecture of old Indian
city centres usually conforms roughly to imperial plans, with sites
of administration standing aloof from the centres of commercial
activity, in quiet, green, low-rise compounds, with court buildings
and tax offices together with residences for senior officers. Through
the Indian subcontinent court cases are decided, taxes collected and
laws made in British-era buildings. Many of the jobs people do now
link back to British days. In many districts, the chief local administrator is still called the Collector. Local courts, treasuries, irrigation
offices and public works departments have boards listing their
chief officers which stretch back a century or more, suggesting an
unbroken continuity between the present and the imperial past. The
current manual to India's Public Works administration, published
in 2012, begins by noting that 'the present form' of the department
was inaugurated in 1854 by Lord Dalhousie, the Governor-General
whose actions instigated the great north Indian rebellion of 1857–8.
There is no mention that India became independent in 1947.[5]

Perhaps the most pervasive legacy of empire is the imperial system
of record keeping. At every place where there is some kind of official

activity, pre-paid taxi booths or airport security scanners, police
stations and licensed offices, details are written in pen in big lined
ledgers. India exports computer professionals by the thousand and
its government has put more data online than any other state. Yet
its filing schemes and administrative systems are little changed since
the days of the British empire. The latest edition of the Indian government's office manual has not altered much since the 1920s, the
most recent editions simply adding an extra line in the list of correspondence that can be processed by the state's departments: email.[6]

It is easy to imagine that these legacies are the remains of a
powerful and purposive regime. Colonial cemeteries, imperial-era
courts, grand railway stations and fat, rigid looking law codes seem
to indicate a regime that had a sense of purpose and power. They
allow many, Britons and some Indians, to look back on the 'Raj' as
a period of authority, a time when *Pax Britannica* imposed reason
and order on Indian society and corruption or violence were less
rife than now.

This book shows how those perceptions are wrong. They are,
rather, the projections of British imperial administrators with a
vested interest in asserting that they ruled a stable and authoritative
regime. From Robert Clive to Louis Mountbatten, the Britons who
governed in India were desperate to convince themselves and the
public that they ruled a regime with the power to shape the course
of events. In fact, each of them scrabbled to project a sense of their
authority in the face of circumstances they could not control. Their
words were designed to evade their reliance on Indians they rarely
felt they could trust. They used rhetoric to give verbal stability to
what they and many around them castigated as the chaotic exercise
of power. But too many historians and writers assume the anxious
protestations of imperial bureaucrats were accurate depictions of a
stable structure of authority. The result is a mistaken view of empire.
We end up with an 'image of empire as a sort of machine operated
by a crew who know only how to decide but not to doubt', as historian Ranajit Guha describes it.[7]

In practice the British imperial regime in India was ruled by doubt and anxiety from beginning to end. The institutions mistaken as means of effective power were ad hoc measures to assuage British fear. Most of the time, the actions of British imperial administrators were driven by irrational passions rather than calculated plans. Force was rarely efficient. The assertion of violent power usually exceeded the demands of any particular commercial or political interest.

Britain's interest in India began in the 1600s with the efforts of English merchants to make money by shipping Asian goods to Europe. At the start, traders who did not use force made more money. Isolated, lonely, desperate to prove their worth to compatriots back home, Britons believed they could only profit with recourse to violence. An empire of commerce quickly became an empire of forts and armies, comfortably capable of engaging in acts of conquest. Even then violence was rarely driven by any clear purpose. Most of the time, it was instigated when British profit and authority seemed under challenge. It was driven on paranoia, by the desire of men standing with weapons to look powerful in the face of both their Indian interlocutors and the British public at home. But violence did not create power. Most of the time it only temporarily upheld the illusion of authority.

From the middle of the nineteenth century, as more Britons arrived to rule India, the imperial regime seemed more stable. The fiction of power was sustained by its ability to manipulate the world of things as much as to commit acts of violence. Authority began to be built in stone, in the construction of ornate imperial follies like Frederick Stevens' Royal Alfred Sailor's Home, the elaborate Bombay gothic construction built on the site of Bombay's first European cemetery in 1876, or Edwin Lutyens' massive Viceroy's Palace in New Delhi. In a more prosaic way, the British tried to assert their power on the surface of the earth, in roads, telegraphs, railway lines, survey boundary markers. In each case they used their capacity to re-engineer the physical fabric of India as a surrogate for their failure to create an ordered imperial society.

The British used paper as a surrogate for authority, too, asserting power in census reports and judicial decisions, regulations
and surveys. By 1940 more than 400 different ledgers were being
maintained in each district office in the province of Bengal, and
that number does not include the register of things like birth, death
and company directorships held by other departments. British
administrators created a form of government that reduced the lives
of people to lines in accounting books as if they were goods to be
traded. Once official writing could be reproduced by printing and
typewriters, the British civil service in India became a massive
publishing house. Asserting power in reams of writing was a way
to mitigate the chaos that British policies and interests had created
by creating order in a small realm that was closest to hand. It also
cut the British off from the messy entanglement with Indians they
believed might endanger British rule. In practice, British engagement with the complex reality of Indian life was limited and brief.
Judging in court or demarcating agrarian boundaries were cursory
acts, involving as little conversation with the subjects of empire as
could be managed, before officials retreated back into comfortable
European worlds, their home, the club, their minds. Whether using
guns or cannons, railway lines or survey sticks, the techniques used
to assert British power shared a common effort to rule without
engaging with the people being ruled. As long as they could get on
with their job (whatever that job was) Britons in India were rarely
interested in the people among whom they lived.

Imperial rule in India was not driven by a consistent desire to
dominate Indian society. The British were rarely seized by any
great effort to change India. There was no 'civilizing mission'.
The first, often the only, purpose of British power in India was to
defend the fact of Britain's presence on Indian ground. Through the
seventeenth to twentieth centuries, India was a place where good
livelihoods for individual members of Britain's middle and upper
classes were made. 'The East is a career', as the British politician Sir
Henry Coningsby said in Benjamin Disraeli's novel *Tancred*. When

he said that he did not mean it was worthwhile. Coningsby's point was that politics in Britain was the only proper pursuit for a gentleman, and that empire in India was a romantic distraction. In real life 'India' was a career that did not link to any great national or social purpose. The most important thing for those Britons who chose it was the retention of personal dignity (in a world that offered great scope for humiliation) and to return home relatively young with a good pension.[8]

Careers in the British Indian government were often transmitted from father to son. Some British elite families had four or five generations holding government office. Take the Stracheys, whose most famous son, the Edwardian writer Lytton, wrote a coruscating attack on the hypocrisy of Victorian values. Strachey's *Eminent Victorians*, published in 1918, criticized the previous two generations' combination of high-mindedness with imperial violence. The Victorians praised God yet built a 'system by which it sought to settle international disputes by force', Strachey noted. Strachey was writing about his own family. Over four generations, members of the Strachey dynasty traced every turn in the patterns of British power in India. Lytton Strachey's great-grandfather was Robert Clive's private secretary. His grandfather and great-uncle were district magistrates in Bengal. He was named after the Earl of Lytton, Viceroy of India between 1876 and 1880. His uncle was an imperial bureaucrat who wrote the 'standard reference for the facts of Indian politics and economics', published in 1888. His father was an irrigation engineer, the first secretary of British India's public works department, and a pioneer of cost-benefit accounting. Strachey's brother ended up as chief engineer on the East Indian Railways. His cousin was the judge in Bombay who tried and convicted the Indian nationalist Bal Gangadhar Tilak in 1897, in the process widening the definition of sedition to include any text not actively positive about British rule. For each generation, the greatest concern was to maintain the institutions that supported the family business of empire.

With his family's life so deeply immersed in talk of empire, Strachey was no anti-imperialist. He spent his early twenties writing a 400-page thesis on Warren Hastings, a work which saw its subject as 'the one great figure of his time'. Strachey's critique was that empire was banal, lonely, purposeless. There was no grand imperial mission; the British were merely 'policemen and railway makers'. Strachey was filled with pity for his relatives, seized by a sense of 'the horror of the solicitude and the wretchedness of every single [English] creature out there and the degrading influences of so many years away from civilization'. India was a place to try and 'go away and be a great man', but Warren Hastings would have been more use to the world if he had stayed at home and become a great Greek scholar.[9]

For the centuries of its existence, there was something self-justifying and circular about the reasoning Britons used to justify the family business of imperial rule. The empire's few grand statements of principle came when the livelihood of British officers seemed under the greatest threat. Then, political leaders responded with exaggerated rhetoric, but that rhetoric often meant little in practice. In 1922, David Lloyd George described the elite civil service as India's 'steel frame'. Lloyd George's words came in a parliamentary debate in which MPs complained about the low morale and declining pay of British officers in Asia. After the First World War, the British faced a fiscal crisis and a revival in opposition from Indian nationalists. The government felt it had no choice but to allow Indians to start sharing power with their masters, not least to part justify the claim that the First World War had been fought to defend liberty against autocratic powers. In response to a demand for reassurance that positions in the business of empire would not contract, Lloyd George offered fine words but few promises. His metaphor of the 'steel frame' was part of an anxious tirade asserting the centrality of the civil servant to Britain's rapidly collapsing empire. Official unease continued to intensify, accelerating the process in which the British handed over positions of power.

We tend to see empires as systems of effective economic and intellectual power, as structures aiming to subordinate as much of the world as they can to their commercial power and values. The context to Lloyd George's words shows that empire is not what we now often think it is. In fact, in India, the British empire was never a project or system. It was something far more anxious and chaotic. From beginning to end, it was ruled by individual self-interest, by a desire for glory and a mood of fear, by deeply ingrained habits of command and rarely any grand public reason. It consisted of fiercely guarded outposts of British sovereign power; it did not possess a machinery able to impose British authority evenly across Indian land. To see the real life of Britain's strange imperial state at work, we need to look beneath the abstract statements of great imperial officers trying to persuade their peers of their power and virtue. We need to tell the story instead of how British and Indian lives became entangled, often fractiously, sometimes violently, on Asian soil.

1

SOCIETY OF SOCIETIES

The Indian subcontinent is the fastest moving place on earth, geologically speaking. It was formed when a massive chunk of the great southern continent of Gondwana sheared off 100 million years ago, sped through the Indian Ocean at the lightning speed of twenty centimetres per year and then slammed into the Eurasian landmass. The violence of the split created a 1000-metre-high escarpment, and caused the subcontinent to tilt downhill from west to east. Those cliffs are now the Western Ghats, a mountain range less than a hundred miles from India's west coast. The subcontinent's tilt causes the flow of water from west to east across nearly all of South Asia's landmass. To the north, the shock of collision is still creating the world's highest mountain range, the Himalayas, most of whose meltwaters drain out through the massive Ganges river delta in the east.

India's violent geological origins shaped the movement of people to and in the subcontinent. They forged a landmass divided into different ecological zones, each repelling or attracting men and women searching for a better livelihood or striving for power. At the far north of the subcontinent the Himalayas and Hindu Kush mountain ranges form a 3000-kilometre border which blocks the route to China and Central Asia, apart, that is, from a few valleys, the Khyber Pass being the most famous. For thousands of years their grassy foothills fed cattle and horses which hill-dwellers took back and forth to India's plains. Often, they joined armies battling for control of the central north of the subcontinent: Punjab, Rajasthan, the Delhi plain and then the plain which stretches east around the Ganges. These flat, wheat-growing lands formed the heartland of the empires that governed much of India in historic times.[1]

Further south, the Deccan plateau rises up and spreads out in a raised triangle sloping west to east, reaching a kilometre at its highest point, and extending to India's far south. The plateau is dotted with rocky protuberances which provide the foundations for hundreds of forts, surveying, defending and threatening the surrounding countryside. It has always been hard to persuade the Deccan's black, hard soil to produce edible crops, but the land is good for growing cotton. Until the slave plantations of the American South expanded cultivation in the last years of the eighteenth century, the Deccan was the world's greatest source of cotton fibre. But cotton has never been enough to sustain an entire community's livelihood. Unable to feed conquering armies, the Deccan has been the graveyard of empires. In the late nineteenth century it was scene of the British regime's worst ever famines.[2]

For millennia from the Deccan plateau people have migrated to wetter lands to the west and the east. Until relatively recently, they largely failed to dominate the thin coastal strip between the subcontinent's great western escarpment and the Arabian Sea. This lush, undulating stretch of land extends from Bombay to Kerala. It is cut through with rivers which carry water from the monsoon rains quickly to the sea. The difficulty of moving on land through this wet, hilly, undulating landscape meant settlements were less prone to the encroachment of raiding armies or tax collectors from the interior. The climate is good for growing spices, cinnamon, nutmeg and, above all, pepper. Before good roads and railways cut permanent lines up though the hills, India's west coast was often better connected to the Middle East or Africa than the Indian interior; it

was 'long-guarded by tight-fisted foreigners', as one seventeenth-
century chronicler put it. This is where Christianity and Islam first
took root. It is also where European fleets initially landed.[3]

Land to the east was easier to access and conquer. Here an arc
of territory sweeps down from the far east of Bengal to the south
of the Indian landmass merging with the sea in a series of flat,
convoluted, ever-shifting river deltas. The Himalayas' waters drain
through the Ganges and Brahmaputra rivers into the Bengal delta,
merging and splitting into the distributary channels that now dominate the landscape of Bangladesh, the Jamuna and Padma. Further
south, water flows in narrow streams through the Deccan plain
and discharges into the sea through a succession of river deltas: the
Mahanadi, Godavari, Krishna, Penna, Cauvery. India's eastern
coast and rivers are rich, well-watered rice-growing alluvial land
where a family can live with relatively little labour. Household
industries grew quickly, with large numbers of people making a
living spinning and weaving cotton and silk, for example. This is a
region whose towns and villages are quickly reached on horseback,
on foot, or by boat. Until the middle of the nineteenth century it
attracted migrants and raiders from across the subcontinent. It was
here that the English fought their first battles and first conquered
land.[4]

These geographical differences shaped the politics of India,
helping mould the variety of units in which India's population
ruled themselves for centuries. Along India's south-west coastline,
the difficulty of transportation created small settlements ruled by
warrior-peasants proud of their refusal to submit to outside power,
called Nairs in the far south, Bunts further north. Decisions were
made in meetings premised on the capacity of each member to have
their say. In the Deccan and India's northern plain, the idea of military brotherhood was important, too, but greater mobility meant it
was easier for villagers to be integrated into larger political units. In
Gujarat in coastal western India the village leader or Patidar, often
also given the surname Patel, was supposed both to communicate

between villagers and regional officials or kings. In Maharashtra, to the south and east, the right of individuals to cultivate particular plots of land was supposed to be agreed in assemblies of landholders, presided over by the local *deshmukhs* (literally heads of the land).

In India's deltaic east, the ease with which rice could be cultivated and distributed created larger political formations. From Bengal to Tamil-speaking country in the south, eastern India was dominated by little kingdoms that stretched for tens or hundreds of miles, ruled by leaders with titles like raja, reddy, palaiyakar or zamindar, the latter word meaning 'landholder' in Persian, the language of India's early modern ruling class. The politics of these places was no less dynamic or argumentative than the west, but power was shaped more through negotiation between kings and subjects than discussion among supposed equals. The prosperity of eastern India's rice-growing land meant, if conditions became difficult, the best option was often to move elsewhere rather than fight.

Friendship and union

In 1600, when the English East India Company started planning its first voyages, the Indian subcontinent was a society of little societies. Politics was driven by the effort of men and sometimes women to build power by creating a following. Authority was built in alliances between groups of people that had their own organization and identity. In their doomed effort to tell a single story about India, later British administrators gave the groups that formed from this process fixed labels. Some argued that it was caste that was crucial, but were not sure whether caste was defined by occupation or race. Others suggested it was the village that characterized the essence of Indian group life. In reality, India's little societies took thousands of different forms, varying according to political and particularly geographical conditions. Nicholas Dirks, a critic of European representations of Asia, puts it well: in India before the British the 'units of social identity were multiple', their trajectories 'part of a complex, conjunctural, constantly changing political world'.[5]

India had long been shaped by a continual process of overland circular migration. Beginning in the second millennium BCE people moved back and forth, as groups of herders drove their cattle down onto the plains, perhaps because of a succession of hard winters, bringing their horses, cattle, language and religion, but then returning to their original societies. The same process continued with less or more violence over the next three millennia. From the thirteenth century many of these warrior-adventurers were Muslims who travelled to India as part of the horse trade, selling steeds for use in transportation and battle. Some settled, becoming local lords or creating regimes that grew to rule large areas of Indian territory. They did so partly through the recruitment and management of soldiers and partly through their capacity to persuade enough of India's myriad little societies that it was in their interests to submit to their authority. They did not conquer as strangers, but imposed power over societies they had long had dealings with and knew well.

By 1600, the Mughal dynasty had ruled the northern Indian plain for eighty years and was extending its sway beyond. The empire was founded in the 1520s by descendants of Genghiz Khan and his Turko-Mongol successor Timur (Tamerlane to contemporary Europeans). The Mughal dynasty first ruled an area in Uzbekistan that had long been an important part of the silk route. A series of local conflicts forced them to look to territories beyond their homeland. Gaining control of Kabul the Mughals then pushed on to the more fertile lands beyond the Khyber Pass in the late 1520s, gaining supporters as they went. The first Mughal armies were relatively small, only 12,000 fighting at the Battle of Panipat in 1526, for example. They won initially by using cannon and matchlock rifles against Afghan and Rajput rulers who up to that point relied on mounted swordsmen.

The Mughals had adopted the language and political and religious culture of the Middle East's most stable and sophisticated empire, Persia. Their firepower came through Persia, too. But Central Asia's loose, nomadic style of government influenced the empire until the end: 'Mughal' is just the Persian word for Mongol. Just as their Central Asian ancestors sojourned in India for millennia, the empire's first two rulers, Babur and Humayun, journeyed back and forth along the diagonal route that cuts down from Central Asia through the Himalayas to the Ganges plain. Akbar (1556–1605), the emperor whose reign coincides almost exactly with that of Queen Elizabeth I of England (1558–1603), created a more stable structure. Movement was important to the way the Mughals did politics until the eighteenth century, and it was shaped by India's geography. From Akbar to Alamgir (who ruled between 1659 and 1707, and is also known by his birth-name Aurangzeb), the emperors resided in their capital city only four-tenths of the time, and the capital itself kept moving, between Delhi, Agra, Lahore and Fatehpur Sikri. When they were in the field, emperors moved to and fro, first travelling to conquer the lush rich lands of the east, then, under Alamgir, invading the dry Deccan to the south. Such constant movement was necessary so that people could see the splendour of authority close up. Local rulers needed to negotiate their submission to imperial power in person.

Mughal conquests were not about violence alone. Territories came under Mughal rule as local leaders were coaxed into shifting their allegiance to the new regime. Force was needed to demonstrate the potency of Mughal authority, but it was followed by affection. '[A]s soon as fear and aversion had worn away,' one Mughal noble said, describing the process during the eighteenth century, 'we see that dissimilarity and alienation have terminated in friendship and union, and that the two nations have come to coalesce together into one whole, like milk and sugar that have received a simmering.' For union to be possible, new subjects needed proof that the Mughals could protect and enhance people's livelihoods. That meant the regime was able to defend itself and its subjects from external threats, but also to support local agriculture and industry sufficiently to sustain decent living standards.[6]

Living from generation to generation on Indian soil, the Mughal regime nonetheless created a distinct Persian-speaking administrative cadre. The work of this highly trained class of men was governed by practices which defined their existence as a separate, skilled elite class: hunting, falconry, particular forms of music and Persian literature. Their formal status was defined by an empire-wide system of numerical ranking. The emperor moved senior Mughal officers from region to region to ensure they did not get too close to local society. But the Mughal elite's intention was not to impose the will of a centralized state through every part of Indian society.

Mughal officers defined their task as to keep an ordered balance between the different forces which constituted Indian society. Long before the British emphasized the diversity of India's castes, regions and religions, Mughal political leaders recognized India as a society of societies, cut through with social, cultural and religious differences; there could be no such thing as Mughal nationalism. The Mughal political order was based first on submission to the personal authority of the emperor, then on fostering harmony between different groups rather than imposing homogeneity or enforcing compliance. Mughal governors left decision-making to local leaders they trusted. Disputes between merchants were adjudicated by local merchant corporations; villagers and townsfolk were left to govern their own societies. Even under Emperor Alamgir, often seen as an Islamic zealot, the Mughal regime recognized India's different religious practices and institutions, making little effort to convert non-Muslims or force them to accord with Islamic law. When Hindu temples were destroyed it was because they belonged to rulers who refused to submit to the emperor's authority, not because they symbolized religious difference. The Mughal elite thought their power was best sustained if different groups retained their distinct characteristics, and it tried to maintain a harmonious balance between each.[7]

The scope for local autonomy meant politics in Mughal India was a talkative, argumentative, often rebellious enterprise. There were millions of public spaces in villages, towns and cities where the acts and beliefs of the powerful could be debated and challenged. India before British rule was not a particularly deferential society. It was not unusual for the preacher in a mosque to be interrupted in the middle of a sermon and be challenged to a debate, nor for disciples to correct their masters, or subjects to challenge sovereigns in their courts. Ordinary people were continually part of public debate in the street, in bazaars and at fairs. Early eighteenth-century Delhi had street corners set aside for public speeches. An English traveller described sweet shops ('the coffee house of India!') as places 'where all subjects except that of the ladies, are treated with freedom', where conversation occurred without the 'refinement of language, as among politicians of an European capital', yet with 'equal fervour and strength of voice'. The scope for ordinary people to criticize meant resistance was common, and had to be heeded by those in power. In Ahmedabad, capital of the province of Gujarat, throughout the late 1600s officers were routinely pelted with stones when they tried to increase prices. In the Mughal empire's biggest port of nearby Surat, traders frequently shut up shop and refused to do business unless the government met their requests, on a few occasions forcing the town's governor to be sacked, to be replaced by someone more sympathetic to their interests. Another tactic was for crowds to halt prayers being said in mosques. The emperor's name was read out at each sermon, so preventing prayers was a way of challenging the empire's legitimacy.[8]

Early modern India was a highly literate society, where economic and political life was documented by meticulous record keeping. Every small society had its office, or *kachchari*, staffed by managers, administrators and clerks who kept tabs on who owned what. The 1600s saw the rise of the scribe, of men belonging to communities which had cultivated writing and accountancy as hereditary skills such as Kayasthas in eastern India or Chitpavan

Brahmins in the west. Scattered through the archives of present-day South Asia are millions of documents produced by these men, a vast and underused record of the social history of India before British rule.[9]

The increase of paperwork in Mughal India did not lead to the growth of centralized governments that tried to control every detail of local society. Writing was a way of recording the complex details of local circumstances, not assimilating them to a single set of rules. Often, local records were simply an extension of the documents that households used to manage their finances. Records were often hidden or burnt when central officers came to inspect them, because they indicated the presence of taxable resources. Their seizure by agents of the state, before and during British rule, was fiercely resisted. In 1780 the Rani of Rajshahi in Bengal condemned East India Company officers for beating up her servants because they would not hand over accounts.[10]

Authority in Mughal India was based on the balance between trusting personal relationships and violence. Despite the flow of information on paper, face-to-face contact was crucial. Coming into the physical presence of the *hakim* (the ruler) was the central source of Mughal power. The exchange of gifts between rulers and subjects built and cemented reciprocal relationships. Important subjects gave gifts that ranged from coins to elephants, and were dressed by the ruler with a *khil'at*, or *sir-o-pa* (Arabic for dress, or Persian for head to foot). These were full sets of silk clothes which enacted their incorporation into the body politic. In this world written agreements, in Persian called *parwanas*, *firmans*, *sanads* and *razenames*, were used, but 'most of the time, judgment' in disputes that came before the ruler was 'delivered only verbally and [is] not recorded in writing'. The East India Company's later insistence on fixing its trading privileges in writing challenged the essentially oral nature of social relations in the subcontinent.[11]

Hard country

The decentralized, continually contestable character of politics created space for challengers to grow within the political structures of Mughal government. Rebellion was ever-present in the Mughal empire. It was not rare for insurgent local lords to ally themselves with the emperor's rivals in court to try to loosen his grasp on central power. The fate of a regime depended on its capacity to create a broad but authoritative base of support, enticing potentially recalcitrant supporters with political and financial opportunity while demonstrating power by crushing out-and-out rivals. Emperors did not see it as beneath them to haggle over the terms on which a minor landholder would submit. In this fluid, argumentative political world there were few permanent alliances. Friendship, maintained by continual favours and constant conversation, was the only way to make sure someone stayed onside.

The greatest challenge to Mughal power came from a group of lower-caste peasant-warriors originally from the hilly regions of western Maharashtra. The Marathas started off as military contractors, guarding and raiding the trade routes which transported goods, particularly cotton, between the Deccan plain and the coast; commerce with Europe was significant in the initial build-up of Maratha power. Shahji Bhonsle, born in around 1600, built an army of perhaps 20,000 men as a sub-contractor of the Muslim Sultanates which ruled land south of Mughal territory in the Deccan. His son Shivaji built his own independent authority in the hills around Pune from the 1650s. With tactics honed in their home landscape, the Marathas avoided confronting enemies in battle, raiding their supply trains to strip them of food, then leaving them to starve in the dry Deccan before retreating to the mountains. '[E]ven the steed of unimaginable exertion is too weak to gallop over this hard country,' Shivaji wrote to the Emperor Alamgir. 'My home', he said, 'is not situated on a spacious plain.'[12]

There was little to distinguish the Maratha style of conquest and politics from that of the Mughals, other than short-term military tactics. In fact, they continually negotiated with Mughal authorities, constantly seeking good terms on which to submit to Mughal power. Only a set of avoidable misunderstandings ensured negotiations continually broke down, and allowed the Marathas to have more independence than other political forces. Shivaji had initially written to the Emperor Alamgir asking for the Mughal empire to acknowledge his authority over his lands in return for sending 500 soldiers to the Mughal army. He demanded portions of the land tax from neighbouring regions called *cauth* (a quarter), paid in return for not unleashing devastation on a particular area, plus the one-tenth share which usually went to the local king; together making 35 per cent of local resources as, in effect, protection money.[13]

To deal with these claims Alamgir sent his uncle and leading military commander Shaista Khan to negotiate Shivaji's submission, offering the Maratha leader land grants but not giving in to his full demands. When negotiations broke down in 1663, Shivaji broke into the Mughal camp and killed Shaista's son. Alamgir sent more soldiers. Even then, talking continued, and a deal was briefly reached. Shivaji was invited, along with 250 of his troops, to the Mughal capital to discuss with the emperor his submission to Mughal power. But the Maratha leader was insulted about being treated like a mere landholder rather than a king; he refused to put on the ceremonial robes he was offered, stormed out of Alamgir's audience hall and fled back to Maharashtra. Even then, Shivaji agreed to peace, sending his son to Alamgir's court to be recognized as a Mughal official as well as a small army to join the emperor's main force.

Shivaji died in 1680. His last eleven years were spent in constant war with Mughal armies, leading to his eventual decision to have himself crowned as an independent Hindu king, an audacious act for a man who did not belong to the kingly Kshatriya caste. After his death, Shivaji's empire was divided between factions that wanted to ally with members of the Mughal ruling class and those that did not. The Maratha regime was driven back to a series of hilltop hideouts scattered throughout southern India, and was all but extinguished. It expanded after Alamgir's death in 1707, when weakened Mughal leaders sought the submission of Maratha generals on easier terms. Eventually, in 1719, the Mughals granted them 35 per cent of all local resources in western India as a way of keeping the area under some form of Mughal authority. The Marathas went on to become the leading political force in eighteenth-century India, powerfully shaping the process by which British power emerged. But their growth took place as a vassal of the Mughal empire.[14]

An absolute externality

The Marathas were very much part of the pattern of early modern Indian politics, with its shifting alliances, constant negotiation and capacious political structures able to embrace radically different faiths, institutions and ways of life. Christian Europe was a different world altogether, often as much as ten months away by sea. Stepping ashore after thousands of miles at sea, the Portuguese, Dutch, French and English knew little of the country and were unknown quantities. Europeans saw themselves as, in the words of Ranajit Guha, an 'absolute externality' to Indian society, an attitude that was often reciprocated. A Sinhalese observer of the Portuguese in the 1500s described them as 'a race of white and very beautiful people, who wear boots and hats of iron and never stop in any place. They eat a sort of white stone and drink blood'.[15]

Since the days of the Roman empire, Europe had been connected to Asia, but it was linked by such an extensive chain of trading connections that the origins of communication were quickly lost. Gujarati merchants would buy spices and cloth, which they sold to Ottoman traders across the Arabian Sea, who in turn traded with Venetian merchants for widespread distribution throughout northern Europe. Some Europeans did travel to India but direct contact was limited.

The Portuguese nobleman Vasco da Gama led the first European ships to sail around the African coast, landing near Calicut in the summer of 1498. The plan was to open up the spice trade between India and Europe, and find isolated groups of Christians who would help the Portuguese challenge the Muslim Ottoman empire in Europe. The absence of everyday contact with Indian society meant the Portuguese were seen, and saw themselves, as strangers in a strange land. So great was their ignorance that Vasco returned to Europe believing that Kerala's Hindu temples were in fact the churches of a heterodox Christian sect. The next decade saw an average of fifteen ships a year arriving to conquer a succession of forts on India's south-west coast.[16]

The Portuguese would dominate the seaborne trade of this sliver of land for the next century. Their power was centred in Goa, half-way down the Indian peninsula. It spread by peppering the west coast of India with seventy sea forts. The Portuguese traded with a string of small principalities which were defended from the Mughals and Marathas by India's great escarpment, the Western Ghats. Western India's geography made it hard for land-based powers to interrupt their maritime activities, but it also stopped the Portuguese from having any impact on India's interior.

From the 1500s, Portugal had claimed to be 'lords of the sea' throughout Asia. The theoretical basis of their assertion lay in Pope Alexander VI's bequest of the trade of 'the eastern extremities of Asia' to Portugal in 1493. '[T]oo mad for the veriest visionary that ever played with the imagination', this was a claim Europe's Protestants fiercely contested. The Dutch philosopher Hugo Grotius calling it 'empty ostentation', but the Portuguese tried to make it a reality by installing a form of military bureaucracy in the sea lanes of western India. Concerned first of all to establish a monopoly on commerce in spices and then horses, the Portuguese found it more profitable to tax other people's trade. Heavily armed Portuguese ships forced every vessel sailing in the region to buy a pass, or *cartaz*, from them, and then to dock at Portuguese forts where they were required to pay customs duties.

Portuguese sea power was based on the fact that they, just like the Mughals, had bigger and better cannon than their rivals to begin with. Their naval artillery did not help the Portuguese control the trade in spices, horses or anything else, but it did ensure that their system for taxing other people's trade was effective, if 'not excessively irksome', as historian Michael Pearson puts it. As Pearson points out, local Indian regimes could have invested in better cannon and ships to defeat the Portuguese. A concerted effort by land-based powers would have overcome the barrier of the Western Ghats and driven them into the sea. But it was cheaper for Indian merchants simply to buy Portuguese passports and pay their taxes. By 1600 a European power had a foot in India, but it was a hold which had little impact on the rest of the subcontinent. 'Wars by sea are merchants' affairs', said one ruler of Gujarat, 'and of no concern to the prestige of kings.'[17]

The Portuguese presence on India's west coast was challenged by a rival European maritime state, in the shape of the Netherlands. Merchant adventurers from republican, Protestant Holland sent dozens of fleets in the 1590s to challenge Catholic Iberian control of the spice trade. In 1601 sixty-five ships left for the Indian Ocean. The following year the Dutch East India Company was founded to merge and coordinate the actions of competing Dutch traders and provide an effective military challenge against Portugal's fleets and forts. It always focused more on Indonesia than India, but by the 1650s the Dutch Company had built a network of eleven forts, centred at Kochi in Kerala, and had a significant presence at the Mughal port of Hughli in eastern India. By then it had driven Portugal from her domination of the pepper trade on India's south-west coast, and had a good stake in the export of Indian silk and cotton from the subcontinent. The Dutch maintained their supremacy over European trade to South East Asia until the late 1700s; but from the 1680s their brief hegemony over trade with India was being challenged by a new power from the west, the English East India Company. The island of Bombay was handed by the Portuguese to England in 1661. Twenty-five years later the English had built a string of pepper forts in Kerala, too.

The rise of the English East India Company during the next century and a half was based on the exercise of violence on land more than sea. Robert Clive, the East India Company officer usually associated with Britain's first conquests in India, was a leader of armies not navies. The forces which conquered India were commanded by generals with military experience drawn from land wars in America or Europe, from Charles, Earl of Cornwallis, to Arthur Wellesley, later the Duke of Wellington, Francis, Marquess of Hastings to Sir Henry Havelock. The British were the first Europeans to build a landed empire in southern Asia. They were able to conquer on land because of transformations that occurred in the structure of India's great agrarian empires in the eighteenth century, not in the disposition of sea power. Those changes were wrought by invading forces that marched over land from Persia and Afghanistan.

Yet throughout the years when the power of the British grew they remained strangers from over the ocean. Invariably, Britons arrived after long sea voyages with little practical knowledge of the society from which they hoped to profit. Unlike Europe for their compatriots or India for Persians, for the British the path to India was not well-worn. In many places in the Indian subcontinent, British institutions grew from the wreckage of organizations created by European maritime powers. They used Portuguese scribes and soldiers, established trading bases where the Portuguese and Dutch had built theirs, and sometimes even used their language to communicate. Spending two months in Brazil on his first voyage to India, Robert Clive thought the most important thing he could do there was learn Portuguese. Like most other governors, however, he never learnt an Asian language.

Early modern England saw itself as a state which dominated the sea not the land, just like Portugal. Eighteenth-century Englishmen and women considered their empire 'maritime, commercial and free'. The difference in India was that the English East India Company sailed around the other side of Cape Comorin at the southern tip of India.[18]

While the Portuguese Estado da India stayed locked into the narrow coastal strip between the Western Ghats and the sea, the East India Company tried to profit from a terrain whose rivers took it quickly deep into the interior. The English Company was concerned with making money from trade with the rice-growing hinterland, buying and selling cotton, silk and saltpetre which could be transported along inland rivers, not just spices which grew on trees near the coast. In the same way as the Portuguese, the English tried to assert their power by building forts, creating pockets of absolute control rather than negotiating with the complex structures of Mughal authority, but they adopted the attitudes and tactics from maritime dominance and, over time, used them to build an empire on land.

2

TRADING WITH GHOSTS

Nawab Shaista Khan was busy at work one morning soon after the end of 1682's monsoon season, sitting under a red velvet canopy in his grand audience hall in the city of Dhaka. One of the Emperor Alamgir's most important officials, Shaista had been moved from western India after losing his son in a surprise defeat by the Maratha ruler Shivaji. Eighty-one years old, he had been governor of the Mughal empire's far eastern province of Bengal for sixteen of them.

One hundred and fifty years after Babur had first marched through the Khyber Pass, the Mughal empire was at the height of its authority yet there were many challenges. Most of Shaista's career had been spent driving Mughal power through South Asia, but a century after Bengal was conquered its power was still being challenged by smaller neighbours, from Assam to the north, and Arakan and Burma to the east. There was also the prospect of rebellion from lords closer to home. The provincial capital of Dhaka, a city then seventy years old, was surrounded by jungle. It still felt like a military camp. To survive, the empire needed to be in a constant state of movement. One moment governors were sending troops to fight, the next they were conciliating rival chiefs with promises of money and order. In his audience hall, Shaista Khan listened to information from spies and despatched instructions in response. On this day he was hearing news of defeat. An army from Assam had routed Mughal forces, compelling them to retreat 60 miles, and every one of the 600 Portuguese mercenaries fighting for Shaista Khan had fled the battlefield. The Anglo-Irish merchant sitting opposite was the least of his worries.[1]

After three-quarters of an hour, Shaista Khan turned to William Hedges, chief officer of the English East India Company's operation in Bengal. Hedges had been in Bengal for two months and Dhaka for two days. He had come with the intention of acquiring a guarantee that the English East India Company could trade without having to pay customs duties on the goods it exported to Europe. At their first meeting, however, it was Shaista Khan who asked the questions. How long was the sea journey from London? Had Hedges been to Germany? Where was Spain? Where did silver came from? Most importantly of all, Shaista Khan wanted to know about other English merchants in Bengal.

After a short initial conversation the two men met again two weeks later, during which the Mughal governor continued his interrogation. His big question was about the role of private English merchants exporting goods from Bengal. The Company had a monopoly on commerce between Britain and Asia and wanted to expel independent traders from India. In the 1680s the most important of these 'interlopers' was Thomas Pitt. Pitt's venture was eventually bought out by the East India Company. An incredibly able merchant, he went on to become Governor of Madras and was grandfather and great-grandfather to two British prime ministers. In 1682, however, the Company regarded him as little better than a pirate. From the Mughal empire's perspective, the East India Company's relationship with men like Pitt was a puzzle. The idea of a corporation banning its fellow countrymen from trading in a foreign land was odd to say the least. Shaista inquired whether it was usual for private English merchants to trade 'in these parts'? Hedges answered with a firm no, but was quickly contradicted by a Mughal nobleman, and nothing Hedges said could persuade the court that Thomas Pitt's conduct was wrong.[2]

William Hedges was treated well in Dhaka, but he demanded privileges which the Mughal empire could not grant him. Hedges wanted the Company's right to trade without paying taxes to be guaranteed in writing, but Mughal politics stressed the importance of face-to-face negotiation rather than written contracts. He demanded that the East India Company be favoured above independent English merchants like Thomas Pitt, but such preferential treatment would have corroded the Mughal empire's claim to be a neutral broker between different groups of its subjects. He wanted Mughal officers to treat the Company's merchants in exactly the same way in every part of Bengal, but local Mughal administrators governed with discretion, and were not controlled from Dhaka. These were the requests of a monopolizing maritime power, not compatible with a land empire held together by balance and negotiation. Hedges and the East India Company tried to assert a form of power that subverted the way the Mughal empire worked.

In the 1680s, the English presence in India was a small and anxious one. Company officers were scattered between twelve cities along the country's rivers and coastline, half a dozen or so in each. When it did not get its own way, this small band felt beleaguered and undermined and saw violence as the only solution to an impasse. Eventually, Hedges concluded that the Company's position in Bengal could only be guaranteed by war, the aim of which would be conquest: not the conquest of a country, but the capture of enough land to build a fort. The Company wanted a fortified base to allow it to trade without being 'harassed' by Mughal demands. But war wasn't driven by the minute calculation of financial advantage. It was a battle for status. The English felt humiliated, and saw force as the only way to restore their honour.[3]

Four years after William Hedges' audience with Shaista Khan the English sent an invasion fleet. Nineteen vessels, with 200 cannon and 600 soldiers sailed from Portsmouth. A second fleet followed in 1688. The force sailed with the intention of asserting England's power over the entire Bay of Bengal. It was instructed to attack the King of Siam (modern-day Thailand) because another group of interlopers was threatening to undermine the East India Company's commerce there as well. Its first port of call was Dhaka. A massive armada by contemporary standards, the combined Indian invasion fleet was the largest to sail to Asia before the 1790s. Robert Clive, the man whom most historians consider to have conquered Bengal seventy years later, did not have such a large body of British ships and troops under his command.[4]

This, the first of three wars between the East India Company and the Mughal empire, began the long cycle of violence that ended with the British conquest of South Asia. As with later conquests, its purpose was not to capture large areas of territory. The history of empire was a history of action in the heat of the moment, not of coherent plans and ideas. The British dominance of India grew from the cumulative response of passionate and often angry men to the situation they had put themselves in in India. What marked British actions in India from 1686 onwards was their effort to create invulnerable pockets of British power, followed by the reluctance of the Company's administrators and soldiers to negotiate. That reluctance allowed violence to grow over the next two and half centuries; without negotiation it was hard for the British to end wars. The result, by the 1850s, was that British armies had spread through every part of the Indian subcontinent. But as time went on other instruments were used to assert unchallengeable power, too: written rules, new technologies like railways, steamships or dams, bricks and mortar. All had the same purpose: to make Britain's power in India invulnerable to challenge from the multitudinous Indian forces the British needed to deal with to do their work. Of course, each of these initiatives failed on its own terms. But the British regime was built from its response to a succession of crises, from its catastrophic defeat in the Anglo-Mughal war of 1686–90, until it was finally forced out.

Why did this violent dynamic start? How did such a strangely bellicose institution as the East India Company emerge? To answer these questions, we need to explain how William Hedges reached Dhaka and what happened when he did. But before that, we must start with the origins of the East India Company, and tell the peculiar story of the way traders from London banded together to make money in Asia. The possibility of violence and conquest was present in the history of this particular organization from the very beginning.

Dealing with spirits

Like India at the same time, early modern England was a society of little societies. The East India Company was founded in a world that had many companies and corporations. The economy of seventeenth-century England was dominated by highly social traders who grouped together to maintain order, protect honour and nurture the habits of interaction that kept commerce going. After Henry VIII's dissolution of the monasteries, town and city corporations replaced churches at the centre of urban life. Different branches of enterprise were ruled by craft guilds, which allowed independent craftsmen to nurture the 'mysteries' of their trade. Even after Henry's Tudor revolution, the central state had limited control. An array of small corporate bodies was scattered throughout England's towns and cities. It was these organizations, not the central state, which performed most of the functions of government, keeping the peace, aiding the poor, regulating the economy and supporting commerce. Essential to this system was the free conviviality each association nurtured. As historian Philip J. Stern notes, 'by its very nature, to "traffic" was not only to truck and barter but to engage in intercourse and exchange'. English society was a commonwealth made up of 'little platoons', as Edmund Burke later called them. These were institutions where men (and a handful of women) met to talk and argue, often drunkenly, bound together by common rituals.

As a 1695 dictionary put it, the word 'society' denoted 'company, conversation, civil intercourse, fellowship'. England's companies were not corporations in the way we understand that word today, but social bodies dedicated to nurturing the conviviality necessary to sustain a commercial society.[5]

Yet there was something different about the East India Company from the start. The Company began life in exactly the kind of convivial conversations that ruled every other area of English commercial life in the seventeenth century. But discussion quickly turned to political power and violence. In the 1590s, merchants from the City of London talked especially about trading spices and cloth with Asia. Nutmeg, pepper, mace, cinnamon and cloves were popular, profitable products, but it was difficult and expensive to ship them from Asia. Black pepper is indigenous to India's south-western coast, Kerala and southern Karnataka. Other spices came from the Molucca Islands in South East Asia. Calico, or plain unbleached cotton fabric made on India's south-west coast, made the same journey. These goods had come through the Mediterranean to Venice, or around Africa to Lisbon, but in the late seventeenth century these routes were blocked. Venice's connections to Asia had been by war with the Ottoman empire in the 1570s. Portugal's route was halted by war between Spain and the Protestant powers of the north. In response, Amsterdam and London, two cities that were political allies but fierce commercial rivals, sent their own ships around the Cape of Good Hope. The Dutch fleet returned intact and quadrupled the money paid out to investors. All three ships from London were lost. The response to this crisis was the creation of a new Company with unique powers.[6]

Throughout 1599 and 1600, a group of London merchants petitioned Queen Elizabeth to let them create a company that could exclude rivals from trade with Asia, and then use force to defend English interests there if need be. Other trading companies existed, but they were associated with private merchants who subscribed together to share in the infrastructure needed to trade in Russia or Turkey, for example. But this new company would be more than an agglomeration of traders. From the start it was a political body with a single stock of money to hire ships, pay soldiers, build factories (as seventeenth-century merchants called their warehouses) and also to buy goods on its own account. It could even sign its own treaties with local rulers.

On the last day of the first year of the seventeenth century, 'The Governor and Company of Merchants of London trading into the East Indies' was created as 'one body corporate and politick', when the Queen issued its first charter. The first governor was Thomas Smythe, whose trading interests included America and Russia as well as India, a man who signalled his global interests by building a tomb for himself patterned with globes. The Queen gave the London Company a monopoly on trade with all parts of Asia not in the possession of 'a Christian prince'. Its royal charter meant that when it acted it did so with the command of the English state.[7]

The Company's fleet left Woolwich with five ships and 500 men in 1601, heading for the spice islands of Indonesia. By the 1630s, the Company was importing over a million pounds' worth of pepper, and had spread to Java, India and the Middle East, even briefly operating a base in Japan. Dutch dominance of South East Asia made London's breakthrough into the spice trade difficult, so the Company shifted to other markets, moving from Indonesia to India, starting to increase its purchase of textiles rather than spice. Madras, on the south-east coast of India, was founded as the East India Company's first self-contained settlement in India in 1639. Bombay became a Company possession in 1668. English operations began seriously in Bengal in the late 1660s, accelerating after 1676 when a warehouse was built at Hughli, then the second port in Mughal-ruled Bengal after the city of Chittagong.

From the beginning, the Company was controversial. From its foundation, England's political class debated whether this institution was compatible with the laws and traditions of a people proud of their liberty. Critics argued that the East India Company wielded an abstract, inhuman and unaccountable kind of power, acting like a tyrant rather than a trader. A particular moment of conflict occurred in 1683, the year after William Hedges arrived in Bengal. A private trader called Thomas Sandys sent a vessel to southern India, bought a shipload of cloth there and arrived back in the English Channel in January 1682. When his ship sailed up the Thames, East India Company officers seized it and tried to levy a fine. Instead of paying up, Sandys filed a suit in court, contesting the Company's right to interfere. Called 'the Great Case of Monopolies', the dispute became one of the late seventeenth century's most celebrated trials.

The case ended up at the Court of the King's Bench in Westminster Hall, and lasted two years. A huge, now empty space, the oldest part of the building where the two houses of parliament dwell, in the 1680s Westminster Hall was the centre of England's legal life, full of lawyers and litigants, spectators and witnesses, including a few willing to provide fake evidence for a fee. It was here that Guy Fawkes, Charles I and Warren Hastings were tried. The scene in 1683 was busy but ramshackle. The hall's three royal courts were not in separate rooms but sat behind different boarded enclosures, with spectators in one court able to hear what was happening in the next. The 'Great Case of Monopolies' brought in a good-sized audience, as one of England's most powerful institutions was being challenged, and some of the country's greatest political figures argued for or against.[8]

Thomas Sandys was defended by Henry Pollexfen. Pollexfen was a prominent Whig politician, a man whose legal career had been built on defending the right of citizens to freely gather together in corporations to collectively manage their own affairs. He had no problem with a corporation trading with Asia. He objected to a company that could command its employees to make money on behalf of anonymous stockholders in London, and then exclude everyone else from Indian commerce when it did so. Trust and sociability were central to his argument. For commerce to be possible, there had to be a reciprocal relationship between trading parties, and each to have a personality and a soul. Pollexfen's point was that you could only trust real, living people. 'I do not speak against Companies, nor regulating, nor managing trade,' he said. Regulation could be done 'virtuously and commendably'. But it should protect individual merchants who continued to 'trade upon their own particular stock and estates'. 'A Man should know with whom he dealt, who were his Debtors, and how to come to them.' From this Whig point of view, commerce was only good for society if it was rooted in the free and public conduct of individuals who had the power to govern their own lives. The Company's anonymous, bureaucratic structure corroded the social relations that allowed trade to flourish and be mutually beneficial. Commerce with a company that traded on its own account was 'a kind of dealing with Spirits'. Faced with such 'an Invisible Body', buying and selling goods from the Company was like trading with a ghost.[9]

Sharply at odds with the mainstreams of domestic commercial life, the East India Company's governors needed a theory to explain why they had created such a strange institution to trade with Asia. They did so by appealing to religion, and arguing that Asia was different. In 1682, this argument was made by Heneage Finch, the lawyer employed to defend the Company in the Sandys trial. Finch was a High-Church Tory, a believer in the absolute, divinely ordained power of the state to impose its authority on people's lives. Finch's tactic was to concede much of Pollexfen's argument. Thomas Sandys' lawyers were right, he said, up to a point. Since the days of Edward I, English merchants had had the freedom to trade as they pleased, but, Finch suggested, that right was based on the trust and friendship that came from contact with people who shared the same religion. Free trade existed because Europeans had created a civil society based on their common Christianity, he said. Non-Christians did not share the same civil laws and moral codes, so had to be treated as enemies. In India, the English were in a continual state of war, so trade in Asia needed to be specially regulated by the state, and protected by a corporation with despotic powers. Finch noted that the medieval law that Pollexfen used to defend free trade only gave Englishmen the freedom to trade with other Christians. Edward I had also expelled the Jews. If Jews were enemies, India's Hindus and Muslims were so even more.[10]

Thomas Sandys' supporters considered this chain of reasoning ridiculous, one calling it 'absurd, monkish, fantastical and fanatical'. The free merchants' point was that peace was possible with infidels. It was perfectly safe for private traders like Thomas Sandys and Thomas Pitt to trade in India. Asian governors like Shaista Khan were good business partners, as long as merchants were willing to negotiate and then submit themselves to Mughal authority.[11]

With its control of the vast bulk of trade with Asia, the Company managed to persuade large sections of London's elite that their claims were valid. Most importantly, England's new King, James II, became a strong supporter of the Company's rights. James' short-lived tenure on the thrones of England and Scotland was based on the divine right of kings, so the Company's use of arguments that strengthened monarchical authority helped sway their case. A gift of £10,000 a year from the Company's profits was persuasive as well. The connection was so close that the East India Company came to be seen as more than an organization of merchants with government sponsorship, but the agent of English royal power in Asia. The document which despatched English soldiers to fight the Mughal empire was signed by King James II.[12]

The East India Company's use of these absolutist arguments was, from one point of view, very surprising. Before James II came to the throne in 1685, the Company had been associated with a low-church, Whiggish kind of politics sceptical of claims about the sanctity of sovereign power. Josiah Child, a former beer supplier to the navy at Portsmouth, was the Company's leading director in these years. Child had been part of a network of dissenting traders whom James tried to exclude from government contracts before he became king. Child, certainly, was ideologically supple in the interests of profit. Men with ancestral wealth criticized the speed with which he accumulated a fortune, the diarist John Evelyn lambasting the splendour of his country estate in Epping Forest as the kind of place where the 'suddenly monied for the most part seat themselves'. Yet behind the twists and turns in their alliances and arguments, the men who led the East India Company were consistently committed to the development of an organization which offered the prospect of absolute and stable control from England over commerce with Asia. Throughout Child's writings one finds a steady concern about ensuring that prices were stable, interest rates were low and the constant stream of commodities from the subcontinent routine. Most important was the exclusion of rival private traders, whom Child thought might be in league with hostile powers to obstruct the regularity of Company trade. Child's ideal form of government was one which imposed the mechanical regularities of maritime commerce, with their seasons, their licences, passes and shipping timetables, upon the political life of the land. Under James II, it seemed that absolute monarchy offered the most suitable form of authority to support the Company's claim to control English capitalism in Asia.[13]

Interlopers

William Hedges left for Bengal only a few weeks before Child instigated proceedings against the 'interloper' Thomas Sandys. Born in Co. Cork in Ireland to a family of merchants, he started his career trading with the Ottoman empire. Like other Company traders, he had interests in different places, with a stake in the Royal African Company's slave trade as well as Turkey, the Levant and India. In his mid-thirties, he was the Levant Company's treasurer in Constantinople. In his forties, in the late 1670s, Hedges was living in one of the streets behind London's Guildhall, part of a community of merchants with Dutch and dissenting Protestant connections. Hedges' first wife Susannah was sister-in-law of Jeremy Sambrooke, the leader of a radical dissenting faction in the East India Company. It was through this network that Hedges quickly worked his way up the East India Company's hierarchy. His knowledge of Asia, albeit a different part of the continent, led to his appointment as the Company's chief in Bengal in September 1681.[14]

Hedges' task was particularly to suppress the trade of interlopers. He was sent to Bengal to replace Mathew Vincent, the previous chief of the Company's operations in 'the Bay', whose many crimes included trading with private merchants. Hedges' ship, the *Defence*, was shipping a small detachment of soldiers to imprison Vincent and seize other interlopers if need be. But from the beginning of his voyage, Hedges came across private merchants trading in defiance of the Company about whom he could do nothing. In January 1682, while waiting off the coast of Kent for his final instructions, he saw Thomas Sandys' *Expectation* shortly before it was seized by Company officers. Once he was on his way, Hedges spotted Thomas Pitt a few hundred miles off the coast of Brazil. They saluted each other and went their separate ways. When he landed at Baleswar on the coast in Orissa in July 1682, Hedges found that Pitt had been there for two weeks, had bought a house and was quickly buying up goods. Pitt was telling everyone the old East India Company had collapsed and 'a new Company erected', and marched through town with red-coated soldiers, music and flags to prove his point. Hedges protested, but to no avail.[15]

Hedges then sailed on to Hughli, where he took up his position as chief of the Company's presence in Bengal. Thirty miles upriver on one of the Ganges' tributaries from the spot of swampy ground where the city of Kolkata now lies, Hughli was one of India's busiest ports, in Bengal second only to the port of Chittagong on the province's eastern coast. It was a Mughal city of perhaps 100,000 people, home to thousands of merchants from across India, the Middle East and East Asia, as well as factories belonging to all the European trading powers. With its five English officers, the East India Company's factory was the centre of a network of English outposts scattered throughout the rivers of eastern India, the place where goods from a variety of suppliers were stockpiled before being

shipped to London. Saltpetre and rough cotton came from Patna, in
Bihar. Silk came from Malda and Kasimbazar. Finely woven muslin
came from Dhaka. All these commodities were put on to rowing
boats and sent downriver to Hughli. Until the 1690s, the uncharted
shoals and mud-banks of Bengal's delta meant ships' captains dared
not sail into the Ganges' estuaries. Goods were stored and repacked
at Hughli to be shipped and loaded again onto ocean-going vessels
at Baleswar, 200 miles south. At each of these places, the Company's
profits depended on a capacity to engage with Indian merchants
and manufacturers, and then to develop a productive relationship
with Indian political power. Such commercial relationships could
be tense and difficult, and it was precisely these that Thomas Pitt,
as well as the Dutch, Danish and French East India Companies, was
trying to undermine.

The Company's way of doing business was as controversial in
India as it had been in England. Company traders were usually more
aggressive and less conciliatory than Indian merchants. For example,
in the years before Hedges arrived, a group of Company merchants
at the silk-producing centre of Kasimbazar had tried to reduce the
prices they paid to weavers. Workers protested against the factory
chief Job Charnock's 'unjust and unworthy' dealings with them,
refused to work and appealed to the town's Muslim judge. Putting
Mughal ideas of justice into practice, the *kazi* called the parties
together to negotiate a compromise. Charnock refused to attend, so
the dispute ended up being dealt with by the provincial governor,
Shaista Khan. Once it reached Dhaka, a Company officer represented Charnock's point of view to the Nawab, but Shaista Khan
threw the English official out of his court, saying 'the English were
a company of base, quarrelling people and foul dealers'. Eventually,
Job Charnock had no choice but to agree to the arbitration of a
group of local traders.[16]

Soon after his arrival at Hughli, William Hedges' relationship
with Mughal officers became fractious and difficult. The city's
chief administrator was Parameshwar Das, a member of the

Hindu Kayashta community that for generations had supplied India's Mughal empire with bureaucrats. He, too, saw his task as ensuring a balance between Hughli's different interests, and that meant not favouring the East India Company in its conflict with private English traders. Parameshwar seems to have been well disposed to Thomas Pitt and his 'interloping' colleagues because they were more willing to support the Mughal regime than the Company. Pitt offered to pay 3 per cent customs duty to facilitate the flow of goods, while the Company insisted it had the right to pay nothing at all. The result was that consignments of Company goods were stopped and searched, shipments held back and taxes demanded.

Such 'harassment' did not make a big difference to the Company's profits. In fact, the late 1670s and early 1680s were good years for the Company's exports from Hughli. In these years, Bengal supplanted other East India Company centres as the main source of Asian goods sold in London for the first time. But Hedges and his colleagues had no way of calculating the Company's corporate profitability as a whole; their frustration and anger got the better of their capacity to judge the interests of the organization they worked for. A tiny group in a foreign city, they felt the Hughli administration's actions on a personal, visceral scale. Hedges insisted that the 'affronts, inso-lencies [sic] and abuses' inflicted on the Company were unbearable. Again and again Parameshwar Das invited Hedges to the negotiating table, but the English continually fled, frightened they would be ambushed at a meeting.[17]

It took a group of Indian merchants trading with the East India Company to get the two sides together. In October 1682, the Mughals and the English met on the waterfront at Hughli to try to negotiate a settlement. Parameshwar and Hedges strolled hand in hand, talking openly. Their meeting was intended to make public their desire to be friends, but also to demonstrate their ability to blow each other to pieces if need be. Parameshwar assured Hedges of his 'respect and friendship', but he was 'guarded by Peons and

Servants, and I [Hedges] by the soldiers and Peons of the Factory, with most of the Englishmen in town'.

The meeting was an encounter between two men in very different moods. Parameshwar had time on his hands. He wanted Hedges and the English to submit to his authority, to be a source of profit for the Mughal empire and to enrich himself if at all possible. He could only maintain good relations if Hedges remained in town to negotiate. The chief officer, on the other hand, was impatient. His instructions from London were to make sure goods were sent back on time. He worried that Mughal officials would hold the shipments back, and force vessels lying at anchor in the Bay of Bengal to wait before being loaded with cotton, silk and spices. He was further anxious that interference by Mughal officials would cause the Company to lose the race to get products to the market in Europe, and thus lose money. He did not believe that a conversation on Hughli's waterfront solved anything, so he decided to force his way to Dhaka to see Shaista Khan, the governor. The night after he had met Parameshwar, Hedges slipped out in the darkness, taking to the river in two heavily armed boats with 'two stout fellows', an Englishman and Spaniard, in charge of each. An armed Mughal customs boat tried to attack two hours after nightfall, but the Spanish mercenary fired his musket and 'we saw them no more', Hedges said. After rowing for ten days through 'the most pleasant country I have seen in my life', Hedges arrived in Dhaka.[18]

The encounter on the waterfront was a clash between two different styles of government and two different forms of power. The East India Company was not interested in creating authority or building an empire. In the 1680s, it was only concerned with making money, and this it was doing. But it was exclusive and belligerent, obsessed with its rights and desperate to control everything that threatened its success and survival. It wanted its position to be fixed and immutable, not vulnerable to the vicissitudes of local politics. By contrast Parameshwar Das and Shaista Khan were officers of an empire that ruled by negotiation and the flexible incorporation of potentially rival forces. The Mughal empire insisted its emperor and officials be recognized as supreme and was willing to fight those, like the Marathas in the 1660s, the Assamese in 1682 or the East India Company three years later, who threatened to deny their supremacy. But it sustained its authority by acknowledging the autonomy of different interests and nationalities, and that could include the English. Force was an important part of Mughal statecraft, but it was usually followed by some kind of attempt to negotiate as deals were struck between political leaders who had previously been rebellious or antagonistic.

Villainous tricks

The East India Company's strange tactics meant that Shaista Khan's court was divided in its opinion as to how to treat the English emissaries. Hedges' visit to Dhaka brought the debate to a head. Shaista Khan himself was all for being lenient towards this strange and argumentative organization. Global trade boomed during the 1670s, with a 30 per cent increase in ships returning from Asia to Europe compared to the previous decade. Shaista himself had benefited from European commerce, trading horses with western Asia in partnership with English merchants, for example. The governor felt there was room within the open structures of the Mughal polity to accommodate the Company's demands, but officers on the tax-collecting side of the Bengal administration saw the Company as an organization of tax avoiders trying to flout Mughal power rather than a source of wealth. In the 1680s, money was required to pay for the Mughal wars in Bengal and in the south of India. The Mughal empire's chief revenue officer in Bengal insisted the Company contribute by paying the fixed rate of 3 per cent customs duty. When Hedges suggested the Company would leave if the tax demand persisted, the Diwan answered simply that 'they might go if they pleased'. As ever, Shaista Khan tried to broker a compromise, but all he could do was write to the Emperor Alamgir asking if he would grant the Company a *firman* (or order) giving it the permanent right to tax-free trade, and then giving the Company an eight-month period of remission while they waited for a response from Delhi. The *firman* never arrived.[19]

It was their need to negotiate continually with Mughal officers at Hughli, not the 3 per cent tax rate, which caused the English so much anxiety. Hedges' visit to Dhaka did not end the 'harassment'. While the English chief was away his junior officers were arrested, and were in 'so great fear the Ships would not go away this year' that they paid 4000 rupees 'to let our goods pass to and fro without molestation'. When he got back to Hughli, Hedges complained that Parameshwar, as he put it, 'began to play his villainous tricks with us again'. With support from elements within the Mughal regime, Thomas Pitt managed to leave Bengal in the early autumn with ships stuffed with goods to sell in England. He reached England in February 1683 where the profits from his trade enabled him to buy a manor in Wiltshire, and then the parliamentary seat of Salisbury. By contrast, the Company's ships had sailed late in January in 1680 and 1681, and without a full cargo in 1682. Hedges did not manage any better in 1683 but he harried and cajoled, coming down to Baleswar to try to speed the *Defence* (the same ship in which he had sailed to Bengal) and two other vessels on their way. They left at the beginning of February, too late to get the best prices in Europe for the load of silk, cotton and saltpetre they carried.[20]

William Hedges' mission in Bengal had been a failure. He had not successfully established a monopoly for the East India Company over England's trade with Asia; the interlopers were still trading; he had gained no lasting concessions from the Mughal empire. Soon enough, orders came from London for him to be sacked, to be replaced by William Gyfford, a senior official based at Madras. Hedges became a renegade. Going into hiding in the Dutch East India Company's factory at Hughli, he then escaped back to England via a long overland route through Persia, Syria and the Mediterranean in order to avoid the Company's ships. He landed at Dover early in the morning of 4 April 1687, four years after the return of his nemesis Thomas Pitt, with no job or family but considerably more wealth than he started with. Hedges' wife and children had died during his travels (there is no reference as to when or how in his writings), but he returned with bales of cotton and silk to sell in London and the last pages of the diary he had maintained in order to justify his actions to his peers in London. That diary would play a part in turning the mood in London towards war.

The idea that the East India Company should conquer land in India did not begin in England. It started among officers in Bengal itself, frustrated about their fractious relationship with Mughal authorities. Hedges thought that the oscillation between 'friendship' and 'insult', the toing and froing between officials like Parameshwar Das and Shaista Khan, could not be sustained. The first half of Hedges' diary had been sent to London in January 1784, and contained a firm message that the Company needed a strong, defensible fort if it was to trade in Bengal. The Company needed to 'resolve to quarrel with these people', Hedges wrote. Despite squabbling among themselves, this was becoming the consensual view. William Gyfford, Hedges' replacement in Bengal, argued that 'the trade of this place could never be carried on, and managed to the Company's advantage, till [the Company] fell out with the Government, and could oblige them to grant better terms: which he thought very feasible'. The Company needed to achieve some kind of permanent, tax-free security. 'No good was to be done with these people without compulsion.'[21]

The notion of war was the response of merchants in Asia to pressures imposed from London. Initially, the Court of Directors was unwilling to follow through the implications of its rigid demands. Josiah Child and his colleagues in London were doubtful to begin with about the conquest plan, worrying that war would cost too much, and that it would antagonize their Dutch rivals. Some thought a strong base at the newly acquired port at Bombay would be a far better 'check' on the Mughals. No one doubted the Company needed to stand up to what they saw as humiliation by the Mughals. 'We are positively resolved', the Court said, 'to assert our right due to us. ... We shall never submit peaceably to the Custom demanded of us.' But instead of an invasion, London initially suggested that the Company make a scene, landing a band of foot soldiers 'with officers, drums, and colours' before marching to Dhaka to demand redress.

The anxious flow of messages between India and London in the second half of 1684 and 1685 changed the minds of the Company's London governors. Men debating in the Company's courts and councils started to panic, thinking the Dutch and interlopers were annihilating the East India Company's share of India's trade. They imagined that Shaista Khan 'took advantage of the unnaturall division betwixt the English themselves to oppress us all'. Talk was of frustration, dishonour and the increasing need to act quickly before things suddenly got worse. Increasingly war was proposed as a way to overcome the 'misery and thralldom' in which the English in Bengal were imagined to live. The Company asked its captains and officers what they thought and found that they:

> all do Concur in this Opinion (and to us seeming impregnant truth) viz/t that since this Gov[ernmen]t have by that unfortunate accident, and audacity of the Interlopers, got the knack of trampling upon us, and extorting what they please of our estates from us by the besieging of our factories, and stopped our Boates upon the Ganges, they will never forbear doing so, till we have made them as sensible of our Power

'[T]here must', the Court of Directors wrote, 'be some hostility used to set our privileges right again.' The target was the city of Chittagong, a place where there had long been a big Portuguese presence, and the only port the English believed could be defended from Mughal attack. The trouble was the Company in London had not the faintest idea where Chittagong was. The port directly opens onto the Bay of Bengal, but the Court of Directors worried whether a conquest fleet could 'get up the great Ganges as high as [Chittagong] without the aid of our pilots'.[22]

The 'quarrel' started in earnest when nineteen warships were hired in London in January 1686 and sent with six companies of soldiers. The first soldiers sent from England landed at Hughli, not Chittagong. Mughal troops were sent to the city in response. By then Job Charnock had taken over as chief of the Company's operations in Bengal, and complained that the Nawab 'ordered downe for the guard of this towne two or three hundred horses and three or four thousand Foot'. With Mughal troops flooding into Hughli tensions rose. War began in the middle of October as the result of an 'unhappy accident', when a fight broke out between three English soldiers and a larger group of Mughal sepoys in the bazaar and sparked a conflict between already edgy troops. Mughal forces burnt the East India Company's factory. The English tried to attack Hughli from the river. Their ships captured 'a Greate Mogull's ship, and kept firing and battering for most of the night and the next day'. Charnock described these acts of 'conquest' as a 'great victory', but the English had left 14,000 bags of saltpetre onshore. Commodities mattered more than revenge against the Mughals, so the Nawab's offer of peace was accepted. Writing home, Charnock's greatest concern was that the Dutch had managed to use the disturbance 'to make their markets' in time.[23]

Charnock then ordered English forces to Sutanati, a village forty-nine miles downriver from Hughli on the spot where the city of Kolkata now lies. He wanted to retreat to an isolated base distant from the Mughal army to load the ships and negotiate a treaty, while the Company had force at their disposal. The Company in London was not happy with this kind of 'timid' conduct. The Court of Directors wanted to stick to its guns, and 'undauntedly pursue the war against the Mogull until they'd conquered a fortified settlement'. Charnock was criticized for putting the Company's financial

interests before the honour of its institutions and the country: the
Company was very clear that honour came before profit. 'We
know', they wrote to Charnock,

> your interest leads you to returne as soon as you can to your
> Trades and getting of Money, and so, it may, our interest prompts
> us; but when the honour of our King and Country is at Stake we
> scorn more petty considerations and so should you.

Wishing Charnock 'were as good as soldier as he is ... a very
honest merchant', the English King and Company sent a new force
of fifteen ships.

Captain Heath, the commander who had first brought William
Hedges to Bengal, was sent back to lead the fight against the
Mughals from his ship the *Defence*. But Heath fared no better than
Charnock. He sent Shaista Khan a series of threatening letters, to
which Shaista responded by arresting the small English contingent
in Dhaka and keeping them in chains in the city's red fort from
March 1688. There they complained about being kept in 'insuffer-
able and tattered conditions', imprisoned 'like thiefs and murders'
until the end of June. Heath then bombarded the city of Baleswar,
'committing various outrages against friends as well as enemies'
as Job Charnock put it. He then sailed to Chittagong, but found
the city too heavily defended for his force to capture. The port's
Mughal governor sent a message asking the Company to stay and
talk, believing that the Company's ships might be useful for ferry-
ing their own soldiers to fight the neighbouring state of Arakan, if
terms with the English could be agreed. As usual, Indians wanted
to prolong negotiation, but the English were impatient, concerned
as ever about their markets. Heath fled back to Madras, arriving on
4 March 1689. With his retreat, England's first war with a state in
India came to an end.[24]

As well on this Side of India as the other

While Captain Heath's fleet was shambolically cruising around the Bay of Bengal, a similar series of political breakdowns led to an outbreak of war on India's west coast. The centre of conflict was the island of Bombay, still populated by Portuguese priests, Marathi toddy-tappers, merchants and mercenaries from many nations. Bombay had been English ever since the marriage of Catherine of Braganza to Charles II in 1661, and was the concern of the Company since Charles offloaded it on them in 1668. It did not become a major centre for the Company's operations until the late 1680s. As in Bengal, English commerce in western India began in a Mughal port, in this case Surat, the entrepôt of the Mughal empire. As also in Bengal, expanding trade led to fractious relations with the Mughals and caused Company officers to assert their power more decisively and to try to separate themselves from Indian society behind gun embankments and fortified walls. In Bombay (unlike Bengal) they got as far as retreating behind the bastions of such a fort, but they didn't survive there for long.

In theory, the English were sovereign over the island of Bombay in a way that they were sovereign over nowhere in Bengal. In practice, such sovereignty meant little as the island was enmeshed in a tight network of western Indian trade and politics, in which the Company played only a small part. The East India Company had no choice but to let Mughal and Maratha sailors and soldiers treat the island as their home.

In the 1680s ships belonging to Sidi Kasim wintered at Bombay. Sidi Kasim was a seafaring Ethiopian chieftain whose maritime force effectively acted as the Mughal navy. Tension between the Sidi's soldiers and the English led to violence. In May 1683, an English soldier was killed in a fight with Ethiopian sailors in the bazaar. Soon, after an English officer was thrown off one of the Sidi's ships when he tried to procure a slave girl for sex in a drunken late-night encounter. Sir John Child, the Company's governor (no relation to Sir Josiah), refused to seek revenge, arguing that any critical response would be 'like a tolling bell for us all'. A group of soldiers decided to take matters into their own hands, staging a coup in order to more effectively assert their 'honour' against Mughal power. Their rebellion did not last long, however, talking and drinking itself out of steam over a few months. But the rebels did evict Sidi Kasim's Mughal fleet from Bombay harbour and seriously corroded the relationship between the English and the Mughals in western India.[25]

There had been 'murmuring and complaint' as the customs on the Company's goods was raised from 2 to 3½ per cent in the Mughal port of Surat. As in Bengal, company officers complained about Mughal 'harassment'. Relations broke down so badly that, according to an English chaplain, customs were demanded on the gold buttons 'which the chief Factors wore upon their Cloaths' so 'in a short time the very Intrinsick Value of his Gold Buttons would be spent in Custom'. The English castigated the Mughals for siding with interlopers, and ended up issuing a list of thirty-five grievances to the Mughal Governor of Surat. Once war started in Bengal, Sir John Child switched from pusillanimity to violence. 'It will', he said, 'become us to Seize what we cann & draw the English sword, as well on this Side of India as the other.' The aim in the west was the same as in the east, to 'gaine a New Settlement'. Child captured a few small Mughal ships carrying provisions for Sidi Kasim's fleet on his way back from Surat and he wrote to the Sidi saying, 'should he dare to come with forces to *Bombay*, he would blow him off again with the wind of his bum'. The Sidi then demanded the return of his ships; if they were not returned he would occupy Bombay three days later. When they were not, he did just that.[26]

As in Bengal, in Bombay English hubris vastly outweighed its military capability. 'Buoyed with a strong opinion of their own Valour, and of the *Indian's* Pusillanimity', as one observer put it, the English in Bombay were rapidly overwhelmed by Sidi Kasim's troops. Company officers imagined that a show of English power would cause Indian soldiers to flee. In fact, it was the Company's troops who deserted, as 116 fled from the tiny English contingent, and officers ran so quickly they left behind ten chests of treasure and four of arms for the Mughals. 'On the Siddy's comeing on this your Island, the whole Inhabitants left us, hardly one struck a stroke in the defence of the Island,' Child wrote. The governor suggested the English were fighting alone, but the reality was very different. A militia of Koli fishermen was formed by the Parsi merchant Rustom Dorabji. The defence of Bombay depended particularly on Bhandaris, Marathas who made money by distilling alcohol but who had been driven out of Bombay by an increase in tax. Another group whom the British called 'Sevajees', possibly after Shivaji, also offered support. These various communities were part of the complex network of alliances that made up the Maratha polity. Conceivably, their loyalty to the Marathas led them to be hostile to Bombay's Mughal attackers.[27]

The Anglo–Maratha forces, no more than 2,500, were massively outnumbered by Sidi Kasim's invasion army of 20,000. In February 1689, the same month Heath was driven from Chittagong, the Sidi pushed the English into Bombay castle, using 'men enough to have eaten up all the Company's servants for breakfast'. They were besieged there for a year. Eventually, as supplies ran out and desertion made defence unsustainable, the Company had no choice but to sue for a humiliating peace.[28]

War was a financial disaster for the East India Company, weakening its position with its competitors. In 1689 eleven Dutch ships returned to Amsterdam stuffed with goods, but 'we have but one ship come, and that not rich laden' as one newswriter put it. Another thought 'most men conclude that the East India trade is all lost'. Tiny shipments came from Bengal between 1688 and 1696. Exports from Bombay dropped to a quarter of their value in the early 1680s, and did not recover until the last years of the 1690s. There was a rapid decline in the Company's stock price. With reports of English officers and troops being paraded in chains in the streets of Dhaka and Surat, of Company representatives kneeling and begging for mercy from the Emperor Alamgir with their hands tied behind their backs, it began to sink in that this was a moment of English humiliation as well as commercial loss. The East India Company's first attempt to challenge the Mughal empire had ended in cata-strophic disaster.[29]

In London, defeat in the first Anglo–Mughal war brought about the end of the Company's privileges. The Company's crisis coin-cided with the Glorious Revolution. In November 1688, William of Orange, the Dutch head of state, invaded England with the support of Protestant nobles and merchants opposed to King James' Catholicism and absolutism. Since Sir Josiah Child had stitched up James' backing for the East India Company, William's supporters included many fierce rivals of its corporate power, including many interlopers. Once William had taken the throne alongside his wife, Mary, their first response was to deregulate English commerce with India, passing an Act of Parliament that allowed free access to Asian trade in 1694. Next, in 1698, they created a new rival organization, 'the English Company trading to the East Indies' backed by King William and his supporters in Parliament.[30]

The first decade of the eighteenth century was a period of squab-bling and financial catastrophe, as rival groups of English traders in India competed for trade and favours from the Mughal empire. But despite a dramatically different political scenario, too many people had an interest in the existence of a single monopolistic company trading with Asia. Queen Anne's accession to the throne in 1702 brought with it an attempt to revive some of the institu-tions of Jacobean authority and create a more centralized form of power. One consequence was the union of the separate crowns and parliament of England and Scotland, creating the Kingdom of Great Britain. Another was the merger of England's rival East India Companies and the return of a single organization with a monop-oly on trade with Asia. These efforts to create unity allowed the Company's revival, but the humiliation of defeat by the Mughal empire created twenty years of crisis and instability in Britain's relationship with India.

The Company only survived in Britain because it had become an inextricable part of the economic lives of the country's political elite. It only survived in India because the Mughals thought it could benefit them, too. After 1690, the Company was the beneficiary of the classic Mughal tactic of offering friendship only once a rival had been defeated. For Alamgir and his ministers, the English were no different from any other group within the Mughal polity's patch-work of communities. They could prosper, Mughal officers argued, as long as they submitted to the authority of the emperor and did not too dramatically undermine the balance of power within the places they resided.

In Bengal, Shaista Khan returned to Delhi and was replaced by a new Nawab. Ibrahim Khan had been Governor of Patna, where he had been an 'old friend to [the Company's] affairs, and particularly known to the agent Charnock'. When he learnt that the East India Company had 'repent of their irregular proceedings' and submitted to Alamgir's authority, Ibrahim Khan wrote to the English asking them to return. Job Charnock came back to Bengal in 1690 to create a new settlement. Ibrahim Khan offered the Company a site two miles south of Hughli in order to keep the English close at hand. But, rather than choosing a settlement so close to a centre of Mughal authority, Charnock returned to the tract of land further south where he had first fled after the attack four years earlier. As usual, the English story about settlement was one which left out its Indian origins. Company officers in Madras complained that Charnock had settled in an empty swamp. His plan was 'contrary to all reason, or consent of the [Mughal] Government, who will neither permit building or factory'. In fact, the Company landed at a cluster of villages that was home to merchants, weavers and an important Kali temple. The name Sutanati, one of the villages, means cotton bale. It was a place where a group of five merchant families had created a market for selling textiles on a piece of land raised three or four metres above the river, with Portuguese traders just across the water.[31]

Charnock's decision was based on 'his feares of being seiz'd by some of the Government [of Bengal]'. His first step was to negotiate a deal with the Portuguese merchants to hire a frigate to defend the settlement. Like Captain Heath and the Court of Directors, Charnock believed the Company's commerce could only thrive if the English had a fortified base that it could defend against Mughal attack. Unlike them, however, Charnock's strategy was to conquer by stealth rather than open fighting. His aim was to create a settlement away from the centre of Mughal politics, avoiding messy entanglement with the Nawab. Building a fort at Sutanati was one of the first British attempts to create power by evading the negotiations that everyday Indian politics required.

To begin with, life in this new settlement was bleak for the English. The Nawab banned them from building in brick, so they lived in a 'wild unsettled condition', with only 'tents, huts and boats' and a retinue of soldiers. The traveller Alexander Hamilton worried that 'he could not have chosen a more unhealthful place on all the River'. In August 1691, there were said to be 1,000 residents, but Hamilton counted 460 burials listed in the clerk's book of mortality by the following January. One of those who succumbed was Job Charnock.[32]

The new settlement was only able to grow because the new Nawab of Bengal's troubles had started to multiply, and he needed the East India Company as an ally. The 1690s was a decade of war for the Mughal empire in Bengal once again. A rebellion of local landholders took advantage of the Mughal regime's concentration on war in the Deccan to take control of large swathes of the province's land, and by 1696 the rebels controlled half the province. Ibrahmin Khan saw an English fort in a peripheral part of the province as a cheap way of maintaining Mughal power. Chastened by their defeat, the East India Company would protect the interests of Mughal officers and merchants as well as English traders. In 1698

the governor even coerced local landholders to sell them land, in
the process giving the East India Company a small income to pay
the local cost of their new establishment.[33]

A town grew around the new fort, amid the trading villages of
Sutanati, Govindpur and Dahi-Kolkata, sustained by rent paid by
local farmers and the income from trade up and down the Hughli
river. This town grew into a city during the eighteenth century: it
became Calcutta, India's largest metropolis and the second city of
the British empire until the early twentieth century. The city can
trace many different points of origin, its expansion over two centuries fuelled by the movement of people and money from many
different places – Portuguese seafarers, Bengali traders from upriver,
Marwari merchants, Bihari labourers, Chinese opium sellers and
cooks, a famous Albanian nun and, most recently, computer pro-
grammers and call centre workers from Hindi-speaking northern
India. Until recently, Job Charnock, whose tomb still stands in Park
Street Cemetery, was celebrated as the city's founder. The association with this empire builder allowed the English to imagine that
this was 'a European city set down upon Asiatic soil', 'a monument
to the energy and achievement of our race', as Lord Curzon put
it. Rudyard Kipling was more down to earth: 'Power on silt', he
called it. In the last few years, patriotic Bengalis have challenged
such hubris. In the twenty-first century descendants of the landholders who sold their villages to the East India Company in 1698
appealed to the High Court for school history books to be changed.
After setting up a commission of scholars, the court declared that a
settlement existed before Job Charnock landed on 24 August 1690.
The city 'does not have a "birthday"', the court rightly pronounced.

Mughal chroniclers, however, told another more interesting
story, that is at least as true as the blustering British narratives.
According to them, the East India Company's house at Hughli
was washed away in a flood. Job Charnock started to build a new
dwelling two or three storeys high, 'so high that they may spy into
our homes and look upon our wives and daughters'. The governor

banned masons and carpenters from working on the building, and Charnock 'prepared to fight'. The English set fire to some houses. Hughli's Mughal governor tried to keep them there so they could be held to account, but Charnock and his band of men fled by ship to the Deccan where the Mughals were fighting. There, so the story goes, Charnock met Emperor Alamgir and offered to help the Mughal army in their wars in the south of India. Charnock's ships carried food to supply the Mughal military (just as we know Captain Heath was asked to do by Shaista Khan) and in some versions of the story led an army which helped defeat the Mughals' enemies.

The English feature first in this story as pirates and insurgents, as a community in rebellion against Mughal peace. But always believing enemies could become friends, the Mughals brought the English back into the fold once they had changed their ways. Having 'rendered loyal and good service' by feeding and fighting, showing that the English could be useful allies if they submitted to Mughal power, Job Charnock was given permission to trade in Bengal, to build a fort and thence found the great city of Calcutta.[34]

3

FORGOTTEN WARS

The capture of Katherine Cooke was an event which was closely entangled with the emergence of a new political order in India. Her father, Thomas, was an army captain and military engineer involved in the building of Fort William at Calcutta, one of hundreds of lower-middle-class European men who made a living as functionaries of the East India Company's enterprise. By 1709 he was struggling financially. Returning to Bengal from England, Thomas Cooke's ship stopped at Karwar, a port 200 miles south of Bombay. There, he gave his daughter's hand in marriage to the chief of the English settlement in return for a sum of money.

John Harvey was old and crippled but he was rich, with assets scattered across the Company's possessions in western India. Katherine, reputedly 'a most beautiful lady, not exceeding thirteen or fourteen years of age', spent the early months of their marriage helping her husband sort out his accounts and consolidate his wealth, in preparation for their return to Britain. Harvey died within a year, and Katherine soon married an attractive but penniless young officer by the name of Chown who had just arrived at Karwar. After a couple of years together the pair set off for Bombay to claim the money left to Katherine by the late John Harvey. Sailing to the seat of the Company's power in western India in November 1712, Katherine's ketch was attacked by a fleet of ships commanded by Kanhoji Angre, leader of the Maratha regime's sea force and one of the most powerful figures in western Indian politics. Katherine's new husband had an arm blown off by a cannonball and bled to death on deck in her arms. It was not the first time Katherine was widowed in India and nor would it be the last. She was taken prisoner and held at the Maratha fort of Kolaba for four months. Her release was surprisingly rapid, because her captor had a part to play in creating eighteenth-century India's greatest political power.[1]

In Katherine Cooke's life we can see many of the forces that shaped the British presence in India during the early eighteenth century. Her military engineer father practised a profession in great demand during the years after the Anglo-Mughal war, as the East India Company tried to defend itself with gun embankments and thick walls designed to protect Britons from the very society they made money from. Katherine's money came from John Harvey's trade in cotton with India's arid Deccan interior, a market which expanded quickly during the growing commercial prosperity of the early eighteenth century. Most importantly, the East India Company had to deal with a new kind of Indian power, with a series of regimes concerned more closely with the management of land, commerce and violence than the Mughal empire. These were decades when the Company's room for manoeuvre was closely circumscribed by Indian politics. Tension was all but continuous. In Bengal and in the south, around Calcutta and Madras, minor incidences of violence did not escalate into conflict, but on India's western seaboard the Company was involved in a succession of now long-forgotten wars.

The main Indian protagonist in those wars was Kanhoji Angre. The English considered him a pirate, in doing so castigating him as a force of illegitimate violence and chaos in contrast to the disciplined regularity they claimed to represent. The use of the word pirate was part of the East India Company's rhetoric in Britain; Britons were more likely to support retaliation against piracy than a war against a regular, legitimate state. In fact, Angre saw himself as a loyal servant of a legal power, an administrator imposing the authority of the Maratha state over sea lanes that were rightly his to control. Mrs Chown's vessel was attacked because it did not have the correct paperwork.[2]

Kanhoji thought the Company's insolence merited a violent rebuke, but he released Katherine quickly and with very little ransom demanded because a far more important visitor was on his way. For the past six years the Maratha regime had been fighting a civil war. Every force of significance in Maratha lands had been divided between two leaders who differed in the attitude they took to the Mughal empire. Tarabai, the widow of one of Shivaji's sons, had rebuilt the Maratha state after it was crushed by Mughal armies in the 1690s and 1700s, and was opposed to any submission to the empire. Her rival and nephew, Shahu, was the child of another of Shivaji's sons and favoured cooperation with the Mughal regime. Shahu had been captured by the Emperor Alamgir as a child, and grew up in luxurious imprisonment at the Mughal court. When Alamgir died in 1707, leading Mughal courtiers released Shahu with a force of fifty men, giving him rights to land revenue throughout western, central and southern India which Maratha leaders had long demanded. With the empire wracked by conflict over the succession to the 88-year-old emperor, Mughal officials thought that a friendly Maratha leader, better able to tax local lords and gather an army than their own officers, would be a useful ally.[3]

Over the next few years, Shahu defeated his aunt and established the basis for a stable Maratha regime that would endure for the next half-century as the undivided centre of political power in western India. Shahu's administration was based on a new kind of politics. Instead of building alliances with old, potentially fickle Maratha warlords, Shahu's regime centralized the control of resources. It depended particularly on a new class of administrators, mainly Brahmins, who combined their ability to lead troops in battle with skills in management and accountancy and a closer connection to commerce and banking.

The most important bureaucrat in Shahu's regime was Balaji Vishwanath, a member of the low-ranking coastal Chitpavan Brahmin community who started his career as a clerk in the salt works of Sidi Kasim at Janjira but became chief administrator of the city of Pune around 1700. Balaji decided to back Shahu early in the Maratha civil war. Along with the accounting aptitude learnt in the world of coastal commerce, Balaji brought negotiating skills, the capacity to lead men in battle and a network of Brahmin bureaucrats and bankers able to provide the administrative framework for Shahu's regime. He rose to be chief organizer of Shahu's armies in 1711, and was appointed chief administrator of Shahu's regime with the Persian title of Peshwa, or leader in 1713.[4]

Rumours that Balaji was marching an army down from Pune to the coast prompted Kanhoji Angre to free Katherine Chown. At the time Kanhoji was at war with the Portuguese and constantly battling a fleet led by Sidi Kasim. With the prospect of a war with Balaji's well-organized army, Kanhoji Angre had no desire to fight the East India Company as well. Thus he appealed to the Company for friendship, and the Company was surprised by the favourable terms he offered. Kanhoji returned the property he had seized earlier, promised never again to 'meddle with any English ships' and granted English merchants free use of his ports. Lieutenant Mackintosh, the English officer sent with 30,000 rupees in ransom to collect Katherine, described how she had 'most courageously withstood all Angre's base usage, and endured his insults beyond expectation'. There is, however, no evidence that she was treated badly at all.[5]

In fact, the rumours that Kanhoji had heard were wrong. Balaji Viswanath was coming to woo him rather that to fight, marching with the aim of enlisting Kanhoji as an ally within Shahu's expanding Mughal-sponsored Maratha regime. The two men met at Lonavala, the resting place halfway between Pune and Bombay where the road up from the sea meets the Deccan plain. Balaji's idea was to appeal to Kanhoji's Maratha patriotism and their common maritime homeland. Both men were loyal to the Maratha regime; they were also both from the same strip of coast between the sea and the Western Ghats, and shared a common dialect and sense of superiority over their landlocked compatriots. The plan worked. Kanhoji switched sides in the Maratha civil war, was given control of all the sea forts under Maratha control and allied his naval and financial clout with Shahu's land-based forces. It was as the leader of the Maratha state's seaborne forces that this 'pirate', once so desperate for the East India Company's friendship, became early eighteenth-century British India's greatest foe.

Economical states

The rebirth of the Maratha regime under Shahu, Kanhoji and Balaji was part of a broader set of changes which took place in India during the early eighteenth century, years which saw the reconfiguration of Mughal power. The network of alliances and Persian-speaking officials which had allowed the Mughal empire to exercise authority throughout India began to fragment. Effective government authority now moved to new regional states that claimed to govern in the name of the emperor, but administered on their own: Arcot and Hyderabad in the south and south-east, Bengal and Awadh to the east, the Marathas in the west. Each of these were autonomous regimes created by former members of the Mughal nobility. Each thrived by creating a more centralized form of administration in its own domain, based on a strong relationship with merchants and a close connection with the countryside. To the English, each seemed to offer new challenges to the East India Company's capacity to profit from India, ensuring the relationship was fractious, difficult and occasionally violent. They were certainly powerful enough to ensure the Company did not expand beyond its scattered outposts.

It was the death of the Emperor Alamgir at the age of eighty-eight in 1707 that triggered change in India. Rival camps had had decades to build their power. Bahadur Shah, Alamgir's son, won the first succession battle and created a stable but short-lived regime. He himself was an old man by the time his father died, and only lasted five years After 1713, infighting broke out, Delhi's authority weakened and Mughal officers began to leave the capital to build more stable forms of power in the provinces.

The new political order emerged as, following chaos in Delhi, the imperial centre failed to control the flow of cash. Alamgir had spent the last years of the seventeenth century 'seized with a passion for capturing forts' in the Deccan plateau. The Deccan wars were a testing ground for many of the Mughal leaders who rose to prominence in the early eighteenth century. But with soil that was so difficult to cultivate, the Deccan didn't bring land into the empire that could pay its way. The costs of these conquests made investment in the central power of the Mughals a bad deal. Money therefore began to flow to more productive, profitable places and it did not come back. Political power moved, too, out from the old Mughal capitals on India's northern plain to new regional centres: to Aurangzeb's old Deccan capital at Aurangabad and then to Hyderabad; to Lahore and Pune; to the newly built regional capital cities of Arcot in the south, Jaipur in Rajasthan, Lucknow in Awadh and Murshidabad in Bengal, as well as to the European companies' fortified port towns. The first forty years of the eighteenth century saw the flourishing of urban life in these dispersed court cities, with the growth of new styles of architecture and new forms of literature and music while the old Mughal capitals on India's northern plain declined.[6]

Alongside the growth of new cities, the early eighteenth century saw the rise of a new kind of imperial officer. This was the age of the administrator, of men such as the aforementioned Maratha Peshwa Balaji Vishwanath. Armies began more to be paid from each state's treasury rather than being mobilized by nobles, so leaders needed to combine accounting skills with the capacity to command men under arms. The Mughals had always relied on banking families to lend them money, but the relationship between capital and

government became far closer in these new provincial regimes. Like
the old Mughal empire, the new regimes combined military force
and negotiation to assert their authority. But they imposed Mughal
ideas of balancing power more systematically on the countryside.
With more money and a more compact territory to rule, the new
states sent their officers into the hinterland to negotiate with small
landholders in a way their predecessors could not. Leaders who tried
to build alternative centres of authority, whether 'rebel' zamindars
or European companies, were more easily subdued.[7]

One of the smallest examples of this new kind of state was
Savanur, the regime that provided the fortune made by Katherine
Chown's first husband, John Harvey. Harvey made money from
transporting cotton fibre and cloth grown and woven in the Deccan
down from the market town at Hubli to Karwar, then on to Bombay
and eventually Europe. Hubli's success as a commercial centre came
about because of the investment of the Savanur nawabs, a political
lineage founded by Afghan warriors who had moved to the region
in the seventeenth century, and consolidated their regime in the
confused conditions of the early eighteenth century. In the 1720s,
their ruler Nawab Abdul Majid Khan built a new town at Hubli,
named Majidpur after himself, to handle expanding trade. Savanur
was successful because its rulers were able to switch from war to
trade in the flourishing economic conditions of the eighteenth
century, and to establish a productive relationship with European
merchants.[8]

In Bengal a similar process took place but on a much larger
scale. The governor who held the greatest authority in Bengal was
Murshid Quli Khan. Born a Brahmin in the Deccan, he converted
to Islam and spent the early years of his life serving a Mughal officer
in Persia. Murshid Quli Khan's administrative skills were spotted by
Alamgir and he was appointed *diwan,* officer in charge of revenue,
over territory conquered in the Deccan. He then moved to take over
revenue collection in Bengal before becoming sole ruler of the province by 1717. The Bengal regime's power depended on commercial

connections. Murshid Quli Khan shifted his government from Shaista Khan's capital of Dhaka to the new city of Murshidabad, five miles south of the silk-producing centre of Kasimbazar. He consolidated his authority by intervening more directly in the countryside than had his predecessors. His regime built alliances with autonomous local landholders who supported the regime, but sent his own officials into the countryside to inspect, scrutinize and sometimes collect revenue directly when the relationship broke down. Sometimes that involved dispossessing local lords with the use of violence. The Nawab and his local allies built markets, roads, bridges and police stations to augment trade, and Murshid Quli Khan monitored the weekly price of grain, expanding the flow of information to the capital. The result was that revenue from land increased by 40 per cent in the twenty years after 1722.[9]

The new regime provided stability and support for commerce, allowing the East India Company's trade to grow. As Mughal chronicler Salimullah noted, Murshid Quli Khan was 'sensible that the prosperity of Bengal depended on its advantageous commerce [so] showed great indulgence to merchants of every description', including Europeans. Tension grew nonetheless. When the English tried to fortify their factories in order to defend themselves against a more powerful regime, Bengal's nawabs saw this act as the sign of a nation of supposedly peaceful traders that was prone to violence. In 1717, the Nawab's officers at Hughli pulled down a half-built British building. When they sought an explanation, the Company received a document condemning the Company's recurrent violence in Bengal, starting with Job Charnock for having 'plundered the whole city and then burnt it'. Peace was only restored after the complaints of Indian merchants saw the Company dragged to the negotiating table once again.[10]

In predominantly Tamil south-east India, the region close to the Company's port of Madras, Nawab Sa'adatullah Khan created a similar regime. Like Murshid Quli Khan, Sa'adatullah was another efficient administrator whose organizational talents were spotted and nurtured by Alamgir. Nicknamed *kifayat* (economical) Khan by the emperor, he used his control of finances to outmanoeuvre the regional governor, the fierce, dog-loving Afghan warrior Da'ud Khan Panni, to become Nawab himself. Under Sa'adatullah's rule, Arcot grew into a city of perhaps 100,000 people, with a vigorous textile industry and sophisticated literary culture. Sa'adatullah imposed his authority over the territory of the region more emphatically than his predecessors had done, subduing rival power centres with overwhelming force rather than enlisting them as allies.[11]

As in Bengal, the East India Company's response to the growing power of a neighbouring Indian state was to fortify. The fortifications of Madras were repaired and extended in the 1720s, and a new barracks and building for storing gunpowder built. Fort St David, the British outpost 120 miles south of Madras, was strengthened in 1725. The Court of Directors worried about the cost of new defences, but anxious Company servants in the subcontinent insisted that bigger forts were needed to protect them against malevolent Indian powers. In 1724 London tried to reduce spending in Madras by a third, thus bringing it in line with the figure paid in 1707, but officers in Madras simply refused to follow orders. The paymaster was particularly worried about cuts to the military and the gun room: 'the Gunner declares now he has barely any room to dry his powder,' he wrote. Eventually, the Company in London gave in. '[A]s at this distance we cannot see what has been done,' the Court of Directors admitted in 1730, 'we must rely on your integrity,' they wrote to Madras.

The Nawabi government saw the conduct of the East India Company as rebellious and arrogant. The growth of Madras's fortification, together with occasional English violence against Nawabi officials, fuelled Sa'adatullah Khan's desire to undermine the strength of the East India Company. Yet Sa'adatullah recognized that with 500 troops to protect a 'fortress defended by the sea', Madras was impregnable. Instead of attempting to subdue the Company with the use of force, he developed a different strategy. He planned to build a succession of port cities along the Tamil coast, enticing merchants trading with the British or French, as well as independent 'interloping' Europeans. The first new port, named Sa'adat Pattan, was inaugurated in 1719. But Sa'adatullah's plan failed; five years after the buildings were finished the new city's palace and fort were in a state of ruin, and fifty of the eighty new shops empty. Along with the nearby French town of Pondicherry, Madras had become too important in the region's trading networks to be undermined by an alternative commercial strategy. Sa'adatullah tried again, in 1728 inviting an Ethiopian from western India called Sidi Jauhar Khan to build a sea fortress, enticing merchants with the offer of exemption from customs for five years. This second port did not last either. In south-east India during the first half of the eighteenth century, European companies dominated the sea while compact and powerful states dominated the interior.[12]

A passion for conquering forts

The East India Company's relationship with its neighbours at Arcot and Bengal was dominated by fractious, fortified peace during the first half of the eighteenth century, with only sporadic outbursts of fighting. Things were different on India's western coast. There, the relationship between British and Indians was frequently ruptured. These tensions led to half a century of war with Maratha sea forces led by Kanhoji Angre, and smaller conflicts with independent rulers along the coast of western India further south. Historians today suggest that the 'first Anglo-Maratha War' began in 1775, but when Clement Downing published his *Compendious History of the Indian Wars* in 1739, it was conflict with the Maratha sea captain Kanhoji Angre that he was writing about. These forgotten wars sapped the Company's resources, costing the treasury in Bombay 80,000 rupees a year (£1.3 million in 2016 prices) during their height, in addition to ships and soldiers being sent from Britain. Such wars did not go well for the British: the Company failed to inflict a single defeat on the Marathas on land or sea.

Throughout the conflict, the East India Company battled a Maratha state which built a compact regional regime tied into the reconfigured structures of Mughal power. After convincing Kanhoji Angre to back Shahu in the Maratha civil war, Balaji Vishwanath's next success at the negotiating table was to persuade the Mughal emperor to put his relationship with the Marathas on a permanent footing. In May 1719, Balaji at last negotiated a stable relationship between the two powers. The Marathas would pay 100,000 rupees into the Mughal treasury and provide troops for the dominant faction at court in Delhi; in exchange, the Marathas would have absolute control over their heartland, and then have the right to collect 35 per cent of land revenue in a vast swathe of territory in the south of India beyond. The deal gave Shahu's regime unchallengeable legitimacy in the eyes of Marathi nobles and merchants, and allowed his government to centralize power within the administrative offices which Balaji Vishwanath established at Pune.

Shahu's regime consolidated power in the same way as other Mughal successor states in Bengal, Arcot and elsewhere, tightening control of land rights, deepening its relationship with regional trading networks and using military force more readily against rival centres of power. The difference was that the Marathas tried to assert dominion over the sea as well as the land; they, like the Portuguese before them, claimed to be lords of the sea. It was this claim that entangled Kanhoji's maritime forces closely with the affairs of the East India Company.

The Marathas used techniques learnt from the Portuguese to assert power over the ocean, filling the vacuum left by the decline of the Estado da India. By 1710, Kanhoji's sea force asserted its sovereignty from Goa to Surat by insisting every ship bought one of their passes in order to be allowed to sail and trade. The Maratha capacity to make this claim real was far greater than the Portuguese Estado da India's had been even at its peak. But, still, the reality was that a single force was unable to dominate India's western coast. The Marathas were willing to concede the export trade to foreigners, letting ships managed and owned by Europeans sail freely if they acknowledged their authority, insisting only Indian vessels pay customs duties. There was, in other words, plenty of scope for an accommodation with the East India Company. But English paranoia made peace difficult to sustain.[13]

Five years of peace followed Katherine Chown's capture and quick return, but fighting between the English and Kanhoji Angre broke out again in 1718. The cause this time was the Maratha admiral's capture of four ships. Kanhoji claimed they belonged to Indian merchants who were using the Company's flag to shield themselves from Maratha power, and had not paid customs. One, which the Company said belonged to a British merchant from Calcutta, had been sold to an Indian trading with Muscat. Another was the property of Trimbakji Maghi, a Marathi merchant travelling with goods belonging to traders from the Mughal port of Surat. Kanhoji claimed that Trimbakji was from Alibag on the Maratha mainland, so did not fall under the protection of the Company. The Company claimed he was a resident of Bombay and so was under their jurisdiction.

A succession of claims and counter-claims was made in a stream of letters between Kanhoji Angre and the British Governor of Bombay. They show how entangled British trade had become with the mercantile life of western India, and how difficult it was to map the flow of commodities on to national communities. In this fast-moving world of shifting identities, it was impossible to say what belonged to the Company and what did not. The exchange of goods between states could only be sustained if people were willing to talk, and give each other the benefit of the doubt. A big man with a reputation for talking plainly and simply, Kanhoji complained that the British did not treat him with respect or amity. Moments of tension were inevitable, Kanhoji said, but could be resolved if people were willing to trust one another. But the Company's officers treated him as someone who could only be dealt with through threats and bribes, Kanhoji complained, and let 'doubts and disputes' corrode their relationship. After one dispute, Kanhoji forbade the Company's ships from entering Maratha rivers and the British prepared for war.

Bombay's council issued a proclamation blocking Kanhoji's ships from British ports, sending troops with drums and trumpets to read it 'in a thousand places' throughout the island. The British then started raiding. They sent twenty small ships to seize vessels 'and if possible plunder his country'. In two such expeditions in May 1718, they 'destroyed some villages and cattle'. Panic inspired a wave of new fortification in Bombay, and the search for new sources of money to pay for it. To cover the extra costs, traders were charged additional duties, and an extra tax levied on the owners of houses within the fort. Eventually, on 1 November, a Company fleet of seven ships, two 'bomb ketches' and forty-eight rowing boats attacked Kanhoji's fort at Khanderi. The raid was a disaster. The ships could not get close enough to bombard the fort with cannon, and the soldiers who landed got stuck in marshy ground. Eventually the Company's force of 558 Indian troops refused to march into the relentless cannon and small arms fire coming out of Angre's fort, and the English had no choice but to return, defeated, to Bombay.[14]

In practice, the East India Company had neither the money, the men nor the strategy to defeat the powerful Maratha military at sea. The idea that Kanhoji could be subdued was yet another example of British hubris. But Company officers were driven by their mad rage against the 'pyratical' behaviour of Kanhoji Angre. Even when a peaceful settlement was possible, they were not willing to negotiate. After another humiliating defeat, their response was not to question the decision-making that led to the beginning of such a disastrous war, but to blame their failure on the supposedly treacherous action of Indian allies.[15]

Bombay in the 1710s and 1720s was a fast-growing settlement with a tiny English population trying, and usually failing, to impose authority over between 10,000 and 20,000 Indian inhabitants. As well as merchants, Parsis, Muslims and Brahmins, the island was populated by weavers and landholders, shopkeepers and fishermen, toddy-tappers, 'enemy' sailors and ships' captains. A tiny fraction of this population was engaged in the export trade to Europe, working as weavers, dyers, washers or beaters in the textile trade, for example. Most of Bombay's residents had nothing to do with the ostensible purpose of the Company as the supplier of an export market, but were attracted instead to live in a fortified city that was becoming a central node in western India's complicated networks of coastal trade. Beyond the tiny, half-mile-square enclave of Bombay fort, the Company did not establish anything like a rule of law. Robbery was a continual problem and the wealthy needed to employ their own guards. Taxes were collected through the same network of local intermediaries that the Portuguese had appointed. The East India Company did not even rule its own soldiers. Bombay's militia had over a thousand men under arms. They relied primarily on Portuguese and Brahmin brokers to recruit Bhandari troops. This was the same community that provided most of Kanhoji Angre's seafarers.[16]

The Company blamed one of these military recruiters for defeat at Khanderi. Rama Kamath was a wealthy Indian merchant who had long been an ally and commercial partner of the English. Kamath was a Gaudi Saraswati Brahmin, a member of a Hindu community that once flourished in Goa but was driven out when religious dogmatism made it harder for non-Christians to live under Portuguese rule; the Catholic Inquisition had spread to Goa in the 1560s. By 1686, Rama Kamath was living most of the year in Bombay, using his connections throughout the Brahmin diaspora to build a formidable trading network based primarily on the cultivation of tobacco. An 'old trusty servant of the Right Honourable Company', he helped during the war with the Mughals 'not only in procuring [troops] but encouraging them to fight the enemy'. Kamath was an important trading partner of John Harvey's predecessor as chief at Karwar, William Mildmay. In 1709, Kamath borrowed 10,000 rupees at what, by contemporary standards, was the very low interest rate of 9 per cent, proving there was a degree of trust between the two men.

Kamath used the money he earned to invest in the social life of Bombay, paying particularly for the construction of Hindu places of worship. In 1715 he funded the reconstruction of Walkeshwar Temple, an old site of Hindu piety on Bombay's Malabar Hill which had been demolished by the Portuguese. But Bombay's public life involved a degree of religious plurality. Kamath paid for Parsi institutions as well, and helped support the construction of the city's first British church, now St Thomas's Cathedral, next to Horniman Circle Gardens, completed in 1718. The church was consecrated on Christmas Day of that year, and the Company paid another 1,175 rupees for a festival that started with the baptism of a child and ended with drunken revelry. Kamath celebrated this moment 'with all his caste'. His entourage was 'so well pleased by the decency and regularity of the way of worship, that they stood outside it for the whole service'.[17]

Three months before those celebrations, it was Kamath who had recruited the soldiers sent into battle against Kanhoji's fort at Khanderi. Kamath was blamed for the fact that they refused to walk into blistering Maratha gunfire. In the year after the defeat, Governor Boone and his colleagues on the Bombay council began to prosecute this once staunch ally of English power in Bombay for treason. Kamath wasn't only accused of encouraging soldiers to mutiny, but also of informing Kanhoji Angre that the 'Bengal ship' sailing through Angre's waters with a Company flag didn't belong to a British merchant, and giving the Maratha admiral advance warning of English military actions.

Kamath had certainly broken with the East India Company's orders not to trade with the enemy, buying wool and turmeric from Kanhoji Angre during the war; but dividing commerce along national lines was always an impossibility in the multi-national city of Bombay. The remainder of the charges were pure fiction. The letters upon which the case against Kamath relied were forgeries;

witnesses had lied. But Governor Boone, who led the charge against Kamath and his servant Dalba Bhandari, wasn't deliberately making things up. He was furious about being defeated and extremely keen to find the simplest cause of British vulnerability in Bombay and purge it. The trial demonstrated the scale of British paranoia. Deeply enmeshed in political and commercial relationships they had little control over, Bombay's British residents saw plots and conspiracies everywhere when things did not go their way. 'The Angre was always on our brain then,' as one writer later commented.

Charged and convicted of treason, Rama Kamath was held in prison in Bombay fort until his death ten years later in 1728. The Company's paranoia nearly caused a full-scale rebellion at the fort. Uncertain who would be next arrested, angry merchants gathered and protested against the Company's government. Governor Boone quickly published 'a proclamation for quieting the minds of the people', and issued a full pardon for all but Rama Kamath and Dalba Bhanderi, also supposedly involved in the plot.

War between the Company and Kanhoji Angre continued. A British attack in October 1720 failed. In March 1721, the Company persuaded the Portuguese at Goa to collaborate with them, but their joint attack led to nothing more than the loss of a large ship. The Court of Directors in London sent reinforcements later that year. When a fleet of ships commanded by a Commodore Matthews arrived in September 1721, another combined attack with the Portuguese was rebuffed by Angre's boats and forts with the death of thirty-three British soldiers. In December, Kanhoji's navy was reinforced by an army of 6,000 Maratha troops sent by Shahu from the Deccan and the British were defeated again. Balaji Vishwanath had died in 1720, and his young son and successor as chief administrator of the Maratha empire tried to persuade the English to negotiate. The Marathas stuck to their argument, insisting on their sovereignty over the sea, and free trade for ships of all nationalities, a right which would have undermined the British offer of physical protection. Mindful of the humiliating war with the Mughals forty years earlier, London reminded the Company's officers that 'the Society whom you serve are a Company of Trading merchants and not Warriors', but fighting nonetheless continued throughout the 1730s and 1740s. The first British victory in its fifty-year sea war against the Marathas occurred in 1755 but by then Kanhoji Angre had died, and his sons had fallen out of favour with the Peshwa, the chief administrator of the Maratha regime. The Company only defeated the Angres because, by then, they fought as allies of the Maratha regime.[18]

Atop flows of trade

In the first half of the eighteenth century, conflict between the East India Company and Indian states was endemic. The anxious sensibility which ruled British actions in the subcontinent continually impelled the Company to war, but the Mughal empire's successor states were simply too powerful for the English East India Company to have any chance of defeating them militarily. The closest it came to conquering territory during the period was much further to the south, beyond the influence of Mughal power.

Katherine Chown once again found herself caught up in events. Soon after her release by Kanhoji Angre, she met the man who would become her third husband. He was 25-year-old William Gyfford, son of the senior officer who had succeeded William Hedges as chief of the Company in Bengal. Gyfford used his contacts, commercial skill and 'smooth tongue' to rise quickly in the Company's trading establishment. He was first given charge of Bombay market, and then managed the Company's trade with Mocha in the Middle East, all the while building a large private trading portfolio on the side. At the age of twenty-seven, in 1715, Gyfford took charge of the East India Company's fort and pepper-trading operations at Anjengo, eighty miles from the southern tip of the Indian subcontinent. There he was caught up in a moment of extraordinary violence.[19]

In the early eighteenth century, the authority of the Mughals and Marathas stopped at Goa, but the Kanara and the Malabar coast extended 600 miles further south. Until the middle of the century, the coast south of Goa was ruled by a shifting succession of small polities and principalities. Each ruler claimed authority over no more than a small section of coastline: the Keladi Nayakas, the queens of Gersuppo, the Zamorin of Calicut, the rajas of Cochin and then the rulers of Valluvanad, Kollam, Attingal and, at the far south of the subcontinent, the state of Travancore. Only Cochin and Travancore survived as 'native states' until the end of British rule, the rest coming under British power in the early nineteenth century. Along this coastal strip the Western Ghats blocked the expansion of larger, more settled regimes, 'shut[ting] Nayar country entirely out of the rest of India' as K. M. Panikkar put it in 1918. Here, with no great, settled regimes, there were always many overlapping political authorities, as rulers tried to stitch together temporary, shifting alliances with armed peasant-warriors that allowed them to survive in power.[20]

Money to fund these regimes came not from taxing these assertive bands of cultivators, but from each ruler's capacity to tap into the networks of global trade, in particular that of pepper. Pepper had always been a staple in Kerala. In Europe it was a high-value commodity for those merchants who could find suppliers and the search for a stable source of the spice dominated European interest in the region; the supply of pepper structured local politics. As historian Dilip Menon puts it, regimes 'sat atop the flows of trade', making their situation precarious. The result was a tense, argumentative but mutually dependent relationship with European companies and traders.[21]

The Company's fort at Anjengo was built in the middle of a fifty-mile stretch of territory ruled by the queens of the small state of Attingal. It was constructed in the 1680s when Queen Aswati invited the East India Company to trade in the region. Described by a Dutch observer as a woman 'of manly conduct, who makes herself much feared and respected', Queen Aswati was no absolute despot. Her authority was a continual balancing act, as she shared power with four princes who competed for the allegiances of Nayar villagers and a share of the pepper trade. Aswati had wanted to introduce the same principle into her relations with European traders. Worried that Dutch dominance would drive down pepper prices and limit her power, she invited the English to open a factory to provide a balance.[22]

The English, she said, were such loyal subjects, and 'have always been obedient to me', that in 1684 they were allowed to build a stone fort at Anjengo and 'abide there for ever'. But the creation of a small military base at Anjengo turned the Rani of Attingal's short overtures of friendship into a long story of petty violence. Just like Kanhoji Angre and the Mughal empire, Attingal treated the Company as a vassal with which she could negotiate. But the English didn't act like vassals. They built a solid, square bastion, housing a garrison of 120 European and Portuguese soldiers, and informed the queen that the fort was intended to keep the Dutch at bay. But its sixty guns were pointed inland, towards Attingal, as well as to sea.

The English built the fort because they were afraid of local warrior bands as much as other European companies. It gave them the belief that they could assert their autonomy from all local relationships, quite apart from the exchange of cash needed to buy pepper. This, they felt, was a land ruled by princes whose interests were 'various and uncertain'. John Wallis, a British resident throughout the 1720s, thought pepper only came forth 'when our weapons are good'. The reality, as ever, was that life for the British at Anjengo depended on their relationship with local rulers and merchants. Pepper only came when the British were on good terms with princes who could ensure supplies. Even Anjengo's water supply relied on local women being paid to walk more than 'a league' to the nearest wells.

These relationships sustained the private trading interests of Company servants as much as the Company's corporate accounts.

Much of the time, Anjengo seemed to act as the outpost for the private interests of English officials, whose defence was paid for by Company cash. The factory chief before William Gyfford, John Kyffen, worked with one prominent lord, Vanjamutta, to buy pepper privately, keeping the best to sell for himself and passing on the rest to the East India Company at a higher price. Wallis described Kyffen as a man who 'thought of little else than driving a private trade in pepper even to quarrel with the heads of the country government'. He was dismissed for undermining the Company's authority, but his successor, William Gyfford, continued in the same style.

Tension grew early in 1720 when a Company employee, the Portuguese trader Ignatius Malheiros, took over land supposed to belong in perpetuity to a Hindu temple, angering local peasant-warriors in the process. Employees of the Company shaved off the beard of a Nambudiri Brahmin, then members of Malheiros's household insulted a group of Muslim traders who had come to the fort to negotiate with Company merchants. They had come specifically to see Simon Cowse, a British Company servant who was also William Gyfford's commercial rival. It was Shrove Tuesday, when local Catholics threw coloured paint 'upon each other for pastime, and upon anybody else walking in the Street'. An intimate female companion of Malheiros daubed one of the merchants in paint. 'The man's passion was the sooner kindled even to have killed her', but his companions persuaded the merchant that he should appeal to William Gyfford for justice instead. Gyfford's private interests obscured his vision of the long-term interests of the settlement. The three men had recently chosen to sell pepper to Cowse rather than Gyfford, finding the chief's British rival, with his knowledge of local languages, a much better trading partner. Gyfford took his revenge by rejecting their complaint and dishonouring the men by breaking their swords on their head.

The mood among the British in Anjengo in the early 1720s was an anxious mix of dread and a desire for domination. Their behaviour seemed to display the small-minded psychology of the embattled bully. Men like Gyfford responded to their sense of vulnerability and inability to get their way, to the absence of strong relationships with local society, by asserting power through petty acts of humiliation. Company servants engaged in insulting behaviour that the East India Company's hierarchy, away from the scene, was embarrassed by. When officers elsewhere were critical, their intervention usually came too late.

Gyfford's insulting behaviour started a small war, instigating a cycle of violence in which different groups in the social patchwork of south-west India, Nayar warriors, Brahmin priests and Muslim descendants of Arab traders, joined forces to undo the humiliation Gyfford and his compatriots had caused. A mixed group of local residents tried to storm Anjengo fort. The pepper stored in the Company's outposts was burnt and a few officers killed, but soldiers at the fort itself repulsed the insurgents. Four Company ships arrived towards the end of 1720 from Kochi, a frightening move that Queen Amutambaran, Aswati's successor as Queen of Attingal said 'so terrify'd the inhabitants that they quitted their places and came to me'. She sent Vanjamutta to 'make up the differences between the English and the Inhabitants'. By now a trading partner of William Gyfford, Vanjamutta had every reason to patch things up. A combination of fear and contractual commitments maintained a fractious peace throughout the next year. Feeling safe behind their walls from the voices of local inhabitants as well as physical danger, Gyfford and his compatriots did not notice the growing tension beyond them.[23]

There was a period of calm in the first few months of 1721, then, in April, the East India Company's command at Anjengo decided to make a show of power by marching to the polity's capital in military formation to pay Queen Amutambaran the customary seventy-five pieces of gold due as rent for the fort. On 12 April, with 'all his best men', William Gyfford led 120 Company employees dressed in their finest uniforms, with arms and flags and a full trumpet band, up the hill to Attingal castle. Simon Cowse was anxious about rumours he had heard on the way, but Gyfford dismissed his fears.

Things took a turn for the worse when Gyfford learnt that his ally
Vanjamutta was drunk, and could not intercede on the Company's
behalf. Presents were handed over but when the Company's soldiers
tried to fire a ceremonial salvo they discovered their arms had been
tampered with. The gunpowder was damp. Gyfford managed to
send a note back to one of the few soldiers left guarding the fort: 'We
are dealt with treacherously', he said. 'Take care and don't frighten
the women, we are in no great danger.'

He was wrong. The British and their Indian employees were
massacred. All but a small group of soldiers were killed. Fourteen
Portuguese mercenaries from the 120 men who had left Anjengo
managed to hobble back 'miserably wounded, some with 16 cutts
and arrows in their bodyes to a lower number, but none without
any'. The Company's leaders were not simply despatched, their
bodies were violated and then dismembered. Gyfford's tongue, the
organ responsible for the verbal humiliation of his neighbours, was
cut out, his body nailed to a piece of wood and floated down the
river. Malheiros was chopped to pieces. Simon Cowse had a better
relationship with the men who ambushed the British detachment
and escaped the initial wave of ritualistic violence, but on his way
back to Anjengo fort he stumbled upon a merchant who owed him
money, who took advantage of the chaos to clear his debt by mur-
dering his creditor. With only English sources transcribed from the
panicked reports of fleeing Portuguese soldiers it is hard to determine precisely the motivation for the attack. But the nature of the
violence meted out on the bodies of the Company's men suggests
that honour played a crucial part. Mass murder and dismemberment
could be seen as an attempt to reassert the status of Indians against
a group of people who had walled themselves off from local society
and humiliated the people among whom they lived.

With only a handful of wounded European troops, six children,
three English women and a two dozen or so Portuguese mercenaries, the fort at Anjengo had a fight on its hands to survive.
Anjengo's inhabitants were besieged from April until October.

A concerted attempt from different groups of Attingal's inhabitants took a while to mobilize, which gave the Company time
to send two small ships from Kochi, followed by boats and men
from Calicut and Tellicherry. An attack on 24 June was beaten off.
Queen Amutambaran made it clear that the fighting was led by
local peasant-warriors rather than her; she was far too dependent on
the Company's access to pepper markets to challenge the English.
Amutambaran had 'fled into another's dominions' and pleaded with
the British to return with big guns to return her to her seat of power.

Eventually, a fleet arrived from Bombay to recapture the hinterland of Anjengo and raid the countryside. As John Wallis put it,
'a considerable acquisition of land was conquer'd from the natives'.
The British were driven by desire for revenge, to make 'a sufficient example ... of the murtherers'. The opportunity to acquire
a sizeable territory now presented itself, as well as one to protect
the Company's pepper trade and wreak revenge on the sources of
English humiliation. British officers wanted to hunt the 'murtherers'
and conquer land, to restore 'the honour of the English Nation'.
But this was the autumn of 1721, when the Company at Bombay
was building for another attack on Kanhoji Angre. The seizure of
land around the Company's small pepper factory at Attingal was
suspended, as the Company's council in Bombay called its ships
back north for the more important project of fighting the Marathas.
The British at Anjengo were left with a few troops, an old Dutch
pleasure boat and a 'mouldering fort' to defend them. The first thing
the new British chief of Anjengo did was to sign a new contract
for pepper with the queen. The relationship remained difficult.
Because of fractious dealings with local traders, the British pepper
trade at Anjengo declined and commerce moved to other Company
factories.[24]

Anjengo was the greatest disaster for British forces in India
between the Anglo-Mughal war of 1686–90 and the occupation
by Nawab Siraj-ad-Daula of Calcutta in 1756. The sequence of
events in this long-forgotten defeat followed the same pattern as

later moments of conquest. The Company's relationship with Indian rulers broke down as they failed to control the flow of money into their treasury. Driven by impatience and motivated by revenge, the Company's attempt to show its power with violence failed. Defeat was followed by a desire for revenge and for new lands to conquer. The difference between the disaster of Anjengo and later incidences of British conquest had nothing to do with the organization of the British, or even the scale of force at their disposal. Things changed because, in the years that followed the Anjengo war, forces over which the British had no control transformed India's political landscape.

Anjengo never became part of the East India Company's Raj but the war hastened the downfall of Attingal. The Anjengo war showed peasant-warriors in this part of Kerala that Queen Amutambaran and her lordly allies offered no protection to them, so they looked for other sovereigns with whom to ally themselves. The next decade saw conflict between the different regimes which bordered Attingal vying for the support of local inhabitants. Amutambaran's relative, the raja of the neighbouring state of Travancore, won those battles. His regime did what the others whose histories have been traced in this chapter did: it built an administration to control land and sea more intensively, particularly by allowing trade to flourish. Travancore maintained cordial relations with the English. Understanding the East India Company's desire for retribution, it presented itself as the best means to 'punish the enemies' of the East India Company, in 1731 giving the British a garden in compensation for the 'loss and damage' to English interests at Anjengo, for example. Travancore survived despite the growth of British power around it, retaining a strong sense of autonomy until 1947. Even then its rulers tried to maintain their power, making a brief attempt to prevent their state from being swallowed up by the independent state of India.[25]

Unlike the story of the state of Travancore, the lives of most of the British men and women discussed in this chapter ended in unhappiness and, usually, an early death. Thomas Chown and William Gyfford both died young, the victims of Indian fire-power. They were buried at Mendham's Point in Bombay. William Mildmay, Rama Kamath's trading partner, died on his way back to Britain still a young man. Each man's life was sacrificed in the Company's effort to assert absolute corporate authority over forces it could not control. Trying always to separate themselves from the Indians, they traded with guns and forts; their fate was wrapped up in the great delusion of British control.

Katherine Gyfford, née Cooke, survived the longest, but she was a victim of the same power. At Karwar and Bombay, she was celebrated as a heroine who represented pure and steadfast English womanhood against Indian avarice and chaos – or the perception of it. She briefly played the same role in Madras, as she fled the bru-tality of Anjengo in a small boat with the other Company servants' wives and children and a small bundle of papers. Such a heroic view of Katherine made sense only as long as she and her three husbands were seen as nothing more than the embodiment of the Company's power. In fact, William Gyfford's wealth came from his private dealings, sometimes at the expense of the Company's profits. Even as Katherine was negotiating her route back to London, the Company in Madras and then Calcutta insisted she pay back the 50,000 rupees they believed Gyfford owed them from his private trading. Katherine complained about her 'vast complication of misfortune', suggesting she 'cannot but think they have used me a little hard', particularly as her husband 'met his fate in performing his duty to his masters'. Officers in Madras claimed that Gyfford was responsible for his own death. Commodore Thomas Matthews, captain of the fleet sent from Britain to fight Kanhoji Angre, was ultimately the only Company official willing to take her side. Against the orders of his employers, he gave Mrs Gyfford passage back to Britain in autumn 1722 to flee her creditors. In Britain she spent the next few years battling the East India Company's lawyers for her share of her dead husband's assets, suing and being counter-sued in London's courts of law. By 1732 she'd had enough and accepted £500 'to put an end to the dispute between them and us'. For the rest of her life she journeyed back and forth, finding England too cold and expensive but India too dangerous. She and 'her black maid servant Anna' settled back in Madras in 1743; but she returned to spend the last years of her life in the Oxfordshire village of Nuffield where she was buried in 1771. By then the East India Company had gone from possessing a scattered string of forts to ruling large stretches of land.[26]

4

PASSIONS AT PLASSEY

Nader Shah was Mughal emperor for only fifty-seven days, in 1739, but those days created aftershocks that transformed India's politics. They broke existing centres of authority, massively shrinking the scope of Mughal power. They set loose bands of mounted warriors who ransacked the countryside seeking wealth from villages and towns. They pushed traders behind the walls of whichever power had the strongest forts. For a short period plunder, rather than negotiation, became the most effective tool for creating new centres of wealth. Those fifty-seven days laid the ground which allowed the East India Company to conquer territory in India for the first time.

Nader Shah was born a long way from India, but he was from the kind of background which for centuries had nurtured men attracted to India as a source of adventure and power. He began life as a mercenary on the southern edge of the Caucasus Mountains between Russia and Iran, recruiting a band of soldiers who seized power in Persia when the 200-year-old Safavid dynasty collapsed in the early 1730s. He reunited Persia and defended the country against invading Turks and Russians. Instead of restoring a Safavid monarch to the throne, in 1736, at the age of thirty-eight, he decided to take the Persian imperial crown himself. Concerned about the security of his authority in Persia, he then marched east in search of legitimacy. If he could be declared Mughal emperor, successor to great central Asian sovereigns like Timur, Babur and Akbar, Nader Shah believed his presently shaky grip on power in Persia itself would be secure.

By the 1730s Delhi had become the Mughal empire's weak point. Mughal authority, as we have seen, had been dispersed in a network of strong regional regimes. The capital became a centre of symbolic importance more than administrative or military power. So when Nader Shah marched through the Khyber pass into northern India, most 'Mughal' rulers stayed in their home provinces. An overwhelming Persian victory at Karnal on 24 February 1739 was followed by a choreographed ceremony in Delhi's gold-walled audience hall on 19 March, where Nader Shah took the formal sovereignty of the Mughal empire but left the existing emperor in practical charge. Nader Shah's aim was to make a name for himself as the conqueror of India but leave the existing political structure intact. But something went badly wrong.

As usual, tension began in the marketplace, the one arena where people from different places and with different assumptions were forced to interact. Nader Shah's troops were not used to the unruliness of the Indian mob. When they tried to fix the price of wheat, they were greeted by protests from Delhi merchants. When soldiers then tried to suppress the crowd, they were attacked. To begin with the new emperor trusted his new subjects more than his own troops, saying, 'some villain from my camp has falsely accused the men of Hindustan of this crime.' But when townsfolk fired upon Nader Shah himself, he concluded that only a massive show of violence could secure his new dignity and power. Unsheathing his sword on the roof of a mosque in Chandni Chowk, he signalled the beginning of a massacre, and 'remained there in a deep and silent gloom that none dared disturb' while the killing went on around him. The *kotwal*, or head of Delhi's police, estimated that 20,000 to 30,000 men and women died.[1]

After staying less than two months, Nader Shah left with silver, gold, 300 elephants, 10,000 horses and the famous jewelled Mughal Peacock Throne that would became the symbol of Persian sovereign power. On his way out, he placed the 'crown of Hindustan' on the head of Emperor Muhammad Shah, who 'offered' Kashmir and Sindh to be ruled by Persia in 'gratitude'. Ananda Ranga Pillai, a merchant and adviser to the French East India Company at the southern coastal city of Pondicherry, asked 'if such, indeed, be the fate that befell the Emperor of Delhi, need we wonder at the calamities which overtake ordinary men'. He added: 'Of what avail is the power and wealth of kings, on this earth.' Nader Shah's conquest taught that '[t]hese are perishable'.

Nader Shah's eruption did not dent eighteenth-century India's prosperity as most of the soldiers who helped him conquer Delhi spent their plunder in India. But the Persian conquest did corrode the systems which held together eighteenth-century India's polity. The Mughal empire's authority to arbitrate between rivals in India's provinces vanished, allowing civil war to proliferate. Credit networks temporarily disappeared, making it harder to transfer money from one place to another. The British found it difficult to remit money through Indian bankers from Surat to Calcutta for example; the banker they relied on in Bengal had begun 'withdrawing all his money from the Europeans as well as the natives' in response to the shock of Mughal decline. The collapse of public finances meant groups which felt they had a legitimate claim on the state's resources started harassing local populations to collect it, rather than asking at the treasury. A time of prosperity for some, the years after 1739 were a period of insurgency and disorder for others, as social groups who had previously been kept in check by the complex balance of Mughal politics asserted their autonomous power over India's small towns and the countryside. With its forts and armed forces, the East India Company was designed to protect itself against political violence. The chaos of the 1740s and 1750s was a time when it thrived. [2]

Self-assertion

Robert Clive was the greatest beneficiary of the transformation caused by Nader Shah's conquest. Clive was the eldest of thirteen children born to a well-connected lawyer and former Member of Parliament from the small town of Market Drayton in Shropshire. His background, as the member of an ambitious but not wealthy family of minor gentry, was typical of East India Company officials. Somehow or other though, it seems to have given him a peculiar gift for 'self-assertion', as the Bengali writer Nirad C. Chaudhuri put it. Clive is often thought responsible for the beginning of the Company's empire in southern India, and then for the Battle of Plassey, the first moment when a British army asserted military dominance over a large area of territory in India. But Clive's greatest talent was telling stories which put him at the centre of the action. In reality forces over which he had no control shaped the course of events.[3]

Clive first arrived in Madras as a 19-year-old in 1744. In the five years since Nader Shah had conquered and left, the politics of south-east India had been transformed by the invasion of Maratha armies marauding in search of money they could no longer collect from Mughal treasuries. Until 1739, the far south-east of India had been part of the Mughal province of Arcot, ruled by increasingly autonomous Nawabs; the area to the north, now the Indian states of Telengana and Andhra, was governed by the Viceroy of the Deccan, a man with the title Nizam ul-Mulk ('Regulator of the Realm'), who had authority over all the Mughal empire's territories in the south of India. But their deals with a succession of Mughal emperors let the Marathas claim 35 per cent of revenue throughout these lands. Until 1739, that money had reluctantly been paid directly from the Nawab or Nizam's treasuries. As the Nizam wrote, 'if I had the necessary strength to destroy them [the Marathas] and their homelands, I would not have asked for meetings, mutual consultations and united action.' But Nader Shah's invasion broke the credit networks and emptied the treasuries which sustained the political order of southern India. Instead of negotiating with regional states, the Marathas sent bands of horsemen to collect revenue directly from local leaders scattered throughout the region's towns and villages. By 1744, Arcot had seen five years of raiding by the Marathas, and the fracturing of political power into dozens of petty principalities and a myriad of fractious local powers. 'Every officer who had been entrusted with a petty government was introduced as a na[wab]', the Nizam said while travelling through the region. One day he is supposed to have exclaimed, 'I have seen, this day, eighteen nawabs in a country where there should be one, scourge the next fellow who comes with that title.'[4]

Robert Clive's English education gave him no inkling of the Mughal and Maratha politics which would shape his career. His childhood allowed him to imagine India as a place to make money quickly, perhaps also as a scene of Britain's ancient quarrel with France. Writing home in his first months, the homesick nineteen-year-old said his purpose was no more than 'to provide for myself & . . . being of service to my Relations'. His first fighting in the region was indeed driven by English conflict with France. When war broke out between the two European powers and Madras briefly occupied by the French in 1748, Clive managed to escape, enlist in the Company's army and then helped defend the second British force in the region, Fort St. David. But it was as part of a Company army allied to Indian forces that Clive made his name.

In the years after Nader Shah's invasion, groups of Indian nobles kept their valuables and more vulnerable family members in the strongest local forts. The paranoia and mutual animosity of the European Companies in the region ensured that Madras and, 100 miles to the south, the French town of Pondicherry were two of the region's best defended citadels. One claimant to the rule of the Arcot region, Chanda Saheb, sheltered with the French. His rival, the man recognized by the Mughal emperor as the Nawab of Arcot, became an ally of the English. Each enlisted the respective European

Company's army on their side, and in the late 1740s and early 1750s the French alliance was winning. By 1751 the Nawab Muhammad Ali Khan had been driven out of every part of southern India apart from Trichinopoly, a fort 210 miles south-west of Madras. In return for a 'a gratification adequate to the charges' – a tract of land twenty-five miles around Madras and a bill of exchange for 20,000 rupees – the Nawab enlisted the East India Company's army to reassert his control over the south.[5] Muhammad Ali Khan suggested the British recapture the province's capital city of Arcot. Getting control of the city's revenue-collecting offices would help the nawab to pay his debts to the Company. When Captain Rodolphus de Gingens, the British Commander-in-Chief in Madras, refused to help with the raid, Robert Clive was appointed as second choice. It was the siege of Arcot that began Robert Clive's career as a great martial hero.

With 210 soldiers, Clive left for Arcot on 26 August 1751. When he reached the city he found the garrison had been abandoned. Chanda Saheb's own finances were in a far worse state than the British or Muhammad Ali Khan imagined. The fragmentation of authority meant that even with the possession of the Nawab's capital, collecting revenue was impossible, so troops had not been paid and hence had abandoned the garrison. Upon his arrival, Clive hoisted two flags, one signifying that Arcot was now under Mughal authority, the other the flag of the nawab. In Clive's first military venture, there was not a Union flag to be seen; the Company was acting as mercenary for a Mughal ruler. His first action was to appoint revenue officers to collect money from lords in the surrounding countryside on behalf of the Nawab.

Shortly after Clive's arrival, Chanda Saheb's son appeared with a French detachment and some 2000 Indian soldiers and blockaded the fort. Clive strengthened the defences, displaying skill in placing British cannons so as to inflict maximum damage. Clive and his soldiers spent fifty days camped in Arcot fort while the French and their Indian allies blew the town to smithereens. Two-thirds of his troops were killed by enemy gunfire. But it wasn't Clive's military acumen or his soldiers' bravery which caused the siege to end. After ten hours of constant bombardment on 14 November, Chanda Saheb's forces stopped firing and abandoned the town at two o'clock in the morning. They fled so quickly that they left behind four large cannons and a sizeable stock of ammunition. What frightened them was the arrival of 6,000 Maratha soldiers come to support Clive, the Company and the Nawab.

In fact, while Clive was besieged at Arcot, the political situation had turned dramatically in favour of the Company's ally, Muhammad Ali Khan. The Nawab had been playing the old Mughal game of fear and friendship, enticing a growing band of supporters to join his alliance. The rulers of Mysore to the west supported him in exchange for a promise of territory south of Trichinopoly. The rajas of Tanjore, an offshoot of the Maratha ruling family, had been humiliated by Chanda Saheb a decade earlier and were keen to join the alliance, too. Most importantly, large Maratha armies based in central India had returned to the south, lured by the region's prosperous agriculture and commerce. In September 1750 the Maratha leader Raghuji Bhonsle sent his general Murari Rao to Arcot. Murari Rao's force had the full backing of the Maratha Peshwa Balaji Rao, grandson of Balaji Vishwanath. The Marathas decided to support Muhammad Ali Khan against Chanda Saheb and his French allies.[6]

'You would never believe', the French commander Dupleix wrote, 'that four or five hundred Marathas [he miscounted] would make M. Giupil determine to raise the siege.' After resting for two weeks Clive's small force marched to join the Maratha army. On 3 December, at Arni, twenty miles south of Arcot, a joint Anglo-Maratha army force of 1,000 men defeated Chanda Saheb's troops, also seizing 100,000 rupees in cash. This was Clive's first real battle. Here, he led English troops acting as an auxiliary in a Maratha action. Five months later, Chanda Sahib himself was killed in a fight with the combined forces of the Nawab of Arcot, the East

India Company, the rajas of Tanjore and Mysore and the Marathas. It was Maratha not British support which turned the tide in favour of the Company's Indian allies.[7]

These victories did not found a British empire in South Asia, but they did see the British change from being armed merchants to tax collectors in southern India. In return for lending soldiers and money to Indian rulers, the East India Company began to acquire property outside the vicinity of its forts for the first time. With little cash to pay the Company directly, the Nawab of Arcot handed the British a succession of rights over remunerative assets. In 1748, he gave the East India Company his share of the 50,000 pagodas (gold coins worth three rupees each) collected from pilgrims of the temple at Tirupati each year. Three years later, St Thomé, an old, abandoned Portuguese base along the Coromandel coast, together with a semi-circle of land twenty-five miles outside Madras, paid for the British presence at Trichinopoly and Arcot. The Nawab would stay an ally of the British, with steadily less and less power, until 1799. In addition, in 1759 the Company was handed 30,000 square miles of territory by the Nizam of Hyderabad to the north, in return for the Company's support against the French and other rivals; the grant was then confirmed by the Mughal emperor in 1765. These northern *sarkars* (districts) were made up of well-watered rice-growing land which included the Kistna and Godavari river deltas. They were the first significant territories to come under direct British command. The handover similarly cemented an alliance with the Nizam, and Hyderabad remained autonomous until 1947.[8]

Here and elsewhere, the British saw land as a financial asset and a way to fund their fortified outposts, rather than an opportunity to assert political power over large areas of territory. In the northern *sarkars*, at the temple of Tirupati and throughout the tranche of territory surrounding Madras, the Company acted as Indian rulers did when their financial commitments exceeded their political power: they sold revenue-collecting rights to tax farmers, often leaving them in charge of the same officers who governed them under the Nizam or Nawab. In the 1750s, the British did not want to extend their political leadership evenly over Indian territory. By now possessing theoretical sovereignty in some places, they were not interested in exercising effective political power.[9]

What honour is left?

It was in the eastern province of Bengal that the Company acquired control over their greatest stretch of land. Here, too, the Company's rise was shape by the forces that disrupted South Asian politics in the years after Nader Shah's arrival. The Nawab Shuja ud-din died five months after the Persian invasion, possibly from shock at the collapse of Mughal power. The old servant he sent to defend Bengal's western borders quickly seized power on his death, ruling as Alivardi Khan. Alivardi spent most of his reign battling invasions from Maratha forces which, as in southern India, claimed they had a right to collect a proportion of the province's total tax take. Raghuji Bhonsle led 20,000 soldiers on horseback in 1742, recruiting the same number again as he was joined by nobles from Bihar and Bengal who backed Alivardi Khan's rivals. The capital of Murshidabad was burnt to the ground and three million rupees (£46 million in 2016 prices) taken from the treasury. The new Nawab forced the Marathas to flee, but they returned six times over the next nine years.[10]

As elsewhere, the Marathas extended their influence by claiming to be the guardians of legitimate Mughal power. A Bengali poet writing about the invasions said the Marathas had come after the Mughal emperor and condemned the 'servant' Alivardi for overturning the natural Mughal hierarchy and seizing power. 'He has become very powerful, and does not pay me tax,' Emperor Muhammad Shah is supposed to have complained. 'I have no army.' The poet thought the Maratha invasions were divine punishment for the disorder that had engulfed Bengal since Alivardi took the throne at Murshidabad. Bengal had become a place where 'the people took pleasure with the wives of others. No one knew what might happen at any time,' he said.[11]

Unable to collect money from central state treasuries, the Marathas harassed and plundered small towns and villages as part of their usual bottom-up process of state formation. Their aim was to force local leaders to back them to preserve the peace, causing the existing regime to collapse. In some parts of the region ruled by the Nawab of Bengal, this strategy was successful. To stop them raiding Alivardi recognized the Marathas as rulers of the province of Orissa in 1751, which had perhaps a fifth of the population he governed. There, the Marathas stopped marauding and adopted Mughal forms of statecraft, governing through a process of negotiation with local rajas. As they supported the constellation of institutions which commercial society relied on, bridges, ferries and temples, markets and mosques, so Orissa's prosperity returned.

In Bengal and Bihar, the Nawab held on but the raids corroded the capacity of his regime to maintain a balance of power. In historian P. J. Marshall's words, 'the fabric of acquiescence on which the Nawab's governed rested was severely stretched'.[12] To pay for his swelling army Alivardi demanded money from landholders, local princes, and the European companies. 'Coming down with all His Excellency's cannon' to Hughli in 1752, the East India Company complained that Alivardi managed to 'bully' 300,000 rupees (£4.9 million in 2016 prices) from the Company. The French wrote about wanting 'to humble the pride of that man'. Robert Orme suggested to Clive that 't'would be a good deed to swinge the old dog'. But Alivardi was an old soldier who retained the loyalty of his army, and was skilful at ensuring potential opponents had no opportunity to unite. He died, of natural causes, aged over eighty, in April 1756.[13]

Through the years after Nader Shah, British officers thought their capacity to control the flow of commodities in Bengal was continually in danger. Raghuji Bhonsle's troops had attacked the

Company's boats on the Ganges in 1748. Other local lords took advantage of insecurity and seized Company goods through the 1740s and 1750s. In response the Company strengthened its forts in Bengal, building bigger walls and new gun emplacements around its settlement. A line of defences was dug around Calcutta in 1742, to protect the city from attack; it is still called the Maratha ditch. In the last years of Alivardi's reign the Company built new battlements to the north of Calcutta, ostensibly to defend against the French. Bengal's government complained that these defences increased their strength against the legitimate authority of the Nawab's regime, as much as the French or the Marathas.[14]

Alivardi was succeeded by Siraj-ad-Daula, the old Nawab's 21-year-old grandson who had been nurtured as heir since his late teens. The change of Nawab fractured the fragile peace which Alivardi had maintained. On taking the throne, Siraj found a province populated by armed groups of men trying to challenge his attempt to keep order. For example, land to the east was controlled by Rai Durlabh, a nobleman with strong independent power based around Dhaka; three of the biggest local lords in Bengal, the rajas of Birbhum, Burdwan and Nadia, refused to pay any revenue at all. Amid the chaos caused by Maratha incursions, the death of an effective local ruler left a polity at war with itself. And as in the south of India a decade earlier, the power of the East India Company was strengthened by the flight of merchants and nobles behind the walls of its fortified port. [15]

To Siraj-ad-Daula the flight of rival nobles to the British port made the fortified city an island of disorder, the most serious obstacle to his effort to maintain a balance of power throughout his land. Within two months of becoming Nawab, Siraj insisted the English 'fill up their ditch, raze their fortifications' and trade on the same terms as they had done under Murshid Quli Khan, otherwise he promised to 'expel them totally out of the country'.[16] Nobles in Siraj's entourage complained of the 'contumacy, usurpation and violence of the English', and urged him to act. To begin with the

Nawab tried to negotiate, sending an envoy to remonstrate with the East India Company when Rai Durlabh's son fled to Calcutta with a fortune of 5.3 million rupees, Siraj-ad-Daula sent an envoy. The emissary received a slap from a British officer and was expelled from the British city, returning to Murshidabad asking, 'What honour is left to us, when a few traders, who have not yet learnt to wash their bottoms reply to the ruler's order by expelling his envoy?' Eventually, with his nobles clamouring for action, Siraj-ad-Daula marched south and, in June 1756, occupied Calcutta.[17]

Gusts of passion

When Siraj-ad-Daula expelled the British from the capital of their operations in eastern India, Robert Clive's mind was on the Marathas not Bengal. Clive had been away in England for two years, but in 1755 he was appointed second in command of an expedition to join a Maratha campaign against the Nizam, then supported by a strong French army under the great general Marquis de Bussy-Castelnau. The plan was for a British force to arrive at Bombay, meet their Maratha friends at Pune and march together towards the Nizam's capital at Aurangabad, forcing the governor of central India to abandon his alliance with France forever. Clive was appointed lieutenant colonel and given the position of chief at the Company's subordinate base at Fort St David once the expedition was over. He saw the appointment as a chance to act out the life of a great military hero and return home with new glory.[18]

When he landed in Bombay, however, Clive was disappointed to find the Aurangabad invasion plans had been cancelled, falling foul of British indecision and doubt. After helping the Marathas recapture a string of forts from rebels along India's western coast instead, Clive sailed to take up his appointment at Fort St David. He imagined there was to be no more fighting. On his way, he wrote to the governor in Madras saying he had been reconciling himself to being 'happily seated at Fort St David, pleased with the thought of . . . my application to the civil branch of the Company's affairs and improving the investment'.[19]

Within a week of taking up his new post Clive learnt that an 'event which must be [of] the utmost consequence to [the Company's] trade' had occurred. The British had been driven from Calcutta. Most upsetting was the incident that found infamy as the Black Hole. After the Nawab's army captured Calcutta, the small number of British soldiers and officers who had not managed to escape were crammed into a tiny jail room in Fort William and left overnight. Many (historians dispute the exact number) suffocated to death. News of the capture caused intense passion at Madras and other English settlements. This was 'the greatest calamity that ever happened to the English nation in these parts', one of them said. 'Every breast seems filled with grief, horror and resentment', as Clive put it.[20] Rage was directed particularly at Siraj-ad-Daula, the conqueror of Calcutta and supposed murderer of their compatriots. But there was also a feeling of humiliation at the ease with which Calcutta had been captured, and a desire for recrimination among the British themselves. A notice was quickly put up at Falta, the village thirty miles south of Calcutta to which Company servants had fled, asking British officers to state 'what they think blameable concerning the unfortunate loss'. The mood was for the redemption of lost honour through violent revenge.[21]

Robert Clive was always conscious of the way his actions would be perceived by a hopefully admiring public back in Britain. The recapture of Calcutta was, he thought, his chance for glory, so he quickly put himself forward to lead the reconquering army. On hearing of the fall of Calcutta, he quickly travelled north to Madras to offer his services, pressing his friend Robert Orme, then a member of the Council, to make his case. Clive was appointed joint commander along with Admiral James Watson. 'This expedition', he wrote to his father, 'if attended with success may enable me to do great things. It is by far the grandest of my undertakings.'[22] In October 1756, he sailed north, accompanied by 'a fine

body of Europeans full of spirit and resentment': 784 in total. He
also had copies of certificates from the Mughal emperor giving
the Company the right to settle in Bengal. Like the Marathas,
the Company claimed its valiant actions were underwritten by
Mughal authority.[23]

Others less concerned with personal glory found ensuing events
hard to comprehend, and their perspective allows us to trace the
importance of passion and glory hunting in the unfolding drama.
John Corneille wrote a particularly illuminating narrative. A lieutenant in the Duke of Dorsetshire's regiment who fought alongside
Clive, Corneille sent a series of puzzled letters about the East India
Company's war with Siraj-ad-Daula to his father. For him, the
British war against Siraj was not a calculated effort by the British to
maximize their advantage. It was an event driven by 'the vicissitudes
of fortune', by luck and passion.[24]

The history of the British empire began for John Corneille
when he joined an army packed 'from the different regiments of
the kingdom of Ireland' into nine ships at Cork in 1755. Corneille
was a 'military man' whose vocation required him to be 'ready at
short warning to go wherever [his] duty might call him', be it India
or fighting the French in Europe. But by the time Corneille's ship
reached Madras in March 1756, war with France had been put on
hold. Instead, Corneille found himself a mercenary tax collector,
leading troops against local lords in Arcot who refused to pay
revenue to the Company's ally, Nawab Muhammad Ali Khan.
By July, he was back in Madras where 'everything was in a state
of tranquility'. The following month, stories about the capture of
Calcutta were circulating. Sharing a sense of outrage at Britain's
humiliation, Corneille was also hostile to the 'irresolution and
delays' of his commanders. When it finally headed north, his ship
sailed into bad weather and sprang a leak. With 225 soldiers on
board seriously seasick, Corneille's vessel only made it halfway up
the coast to Vizagapatam. There, the frustrated officer spent his days
wandering and shooting in the lush countryside, angry at missing

out as 800 European and 1000 Indian soldiers led by Clive and Watson recaptured Calcutta.[25]

Calcutta was reconquered on 2 January 1757. The Company's army carried on to Bengal's second biggest port of Hughli, twenty miles north, and 'made a prodigious slaughter' of the Nawab's army. Shortly afterwards, on 9 February, the Nawab of Bengal signed a treaty that gave the Company the right to trade without paying taxes, to mint coins and a promise of compensation for the cash lost in the occupation of Calcutta. After the signing of the treaty John Corneille wrote that 'the English after an eight months banishment were restored again to their settlement, and not only to the full enjoyment of their ancient rights and privileges but many more'.[26]

Clive and Watson believed Siraj decided to sign a peace treaty with the East India Company because he was cowed into submission by the British army. 'Arms', Admiral Watson wrote, 'are more to be dependent on, and I dare say will be much more prevalent than any treaties or negotiations.' In fact, Siraj's agreement to a peace treaty was shaped by circumstances beyond Bengal of which the British had only an inkling. In 1756 and early 1757, Delhi was in a state of political turmoil once again. Nader Shah's conquest of 1739 had started a sequence of western invasions, as northern India once again became a field for thousands of adventurers, warriors and empire-builders from Persia and Afghanistan. The greatest of these was Ahmad Shah Durrani, a Pashtun soldier from the Afghan city of Herat who began his military career in Nader Shah's army. Ahmad Shah invaded northern India seven times between 1748 and 1767, but perhaps the most devastating incursion occurred in the final months of 1756 and first part of 1757. Siraj-ad-Daula was concerned that warriors invading from the west were about to pour into Bengal, so at the beginning of February 1757 he believed that a quick agreement to the East India Company's demands might help enlist the British as allies.[27]

John Corneille thought the treaty with Siraj-ad-Daula would end the fighting for good, but then news that war had finally broken out with France reached India. The troops Corneille commanded became part of 'a scheme ... towards dispossessing [the French] out of their settlements in Bengal'. Corneille left Vizagapatam for Calcutta on 1 March 1757. His first action in Bengal was to take part in the British conquest of the East India French Company's small fort at the town of Chandernagore, fifteen miles north of Calcutta, an event that gave the lieutenant of the Devonshires his greatest sense of honour. With the defeat of the French the British had at last 'recovered that character which their pusillanimous behaviour at Calcutta had justly lost them, and were once more looked on as a great and powerful people', Corneille argued. Still keen on enlisting the English as partners against Ahmad Shah, Siraj-ad-Daula wrote to Clive of his 'inexpressible pleasure' at the British victory over their old rivals.[28]

Despite Siraj's clear interest in negotiating with the British, the months between March and June saw the relationship between the two finally collapse. The exchange of threats and insults, humiliation and revenge that had begun in June 1756 created a cycle of antagonism that neither side was able to step out of, despite the apparent willingness of both to do so.

Young, and with little experience in the practical arts of statecraft, Siraj-ad-Daula was a man ruled by a more passionate desire to seek speedy revenge than his predecessors had been. 'Siraj-ad-Daula was not the man to forget what he regarded as an insult,' Jean Law, French chief at Chandernagore observed. He had quickly become 'incensed against the English'. Richard Becher, one of the most thoughtful British observers, argued that Siraj had decided to occupy Calcutta to begin with in a 'sudden gust of passion'.

Yet even Siraj tried to move beyond the cycle of anxious violence. He knew the rules of Mughal statecraft, the politics of combining friendship with fear, even if he wasn't always experienced enough to put them into practice. Throughout his exchanges with the East India Company Siraj tried to play the part of the statesman, appealing to the British to act in the way appropriate for merchants. 'You have taken and plundered Hughli,' he wrote to Admiral Watson in March, 'and made war upon my subjects: those are not actions becoming merchants.' As traders and men sharing a common belief in the same God, he thought the British had a duty to keep their promises. In February, he compared them unfavourably to the Hindu Marathas. 'The Mahrattas are bound by no gospel, yet they are strict observers of treaties,' Siraj wrote. 'It will therefore be a matter of great astonishment and hard to be believed, if you, who are enlightened with the gospel, should not remain firm, and preserve the treaty you have ratified in the presence of God and Jesus Christ.'[29]

For their part, British officers ignored Siraj's allusion to prophets and scriptures. They spoke as if being merchants was inextricably linked to the use of military force. They believed that the honour of a merchant in Asia always depended on his capacity for violence. The British addressed the Nawab as a fellow warrior, believing that he shared with them a martial ethos. Clive and many of his compatriots thought anything other than an explicit admission of the Nawab's contrition an insult to their martial power.

Indian friends of the British tried to encourage a less aggressive tone. Commenting on one draft of a letter that Clive intended to send to Siraj, the Company's ally Manik Chandra complained that Clive used 'improper expressions'. Clive replied that it would not be consistent with his 'Duty to the Company or their honour' to write in submissive language. 'We are come to demand Satisfaction, not to entreat his favour.' 'I know you are a great Prince and a great warrior. I likewise for these past ten years have been consistently Fighting in these parts and it has pleased God Almighty always to make me successful,' he wrote to the Nawab.

While Siraj's unusually quick passion played some part in the breakdown, the anxious, prickly sense of honour the British carried with them in the subcontinent contributed the most to the escalation of conflict. As they had been in the run-up to the Anglo-Mughal war seventy years earlier, the Company's officers thought they could not achieve self-respect in the subcontinent without achieving total dominance over their rivals. As then, a concern with the profits of the East India Company underlaid British actions. But it was overlaid in turn by an anxious, often paranoid attitude which interpreted every possible slight as a major humiliation, and considered violence the only means of restoring honour.[30]

The difference was that the fractured political landscape of Bengal in the 1750s gave the British allies in their project of intended revenge. Since becoming Nawab, Siraj had failed to successfully enlist powerful magnates with sufficient offers of friendship, particularly alienating merchants and nobles from the commercial cities of Dhaka and Patna. In the spring of 1757, merchants from Patna had started talking about ousting Siraj. They reached out to Rai Durlabh, Governor of Dhaka, the man whose son had fled to Calcutta but who since then had maintained a fractious friendship with Siraj. They also enlisted traders and military commanders from the Nawab's capital at Murshidabad. Central to the conspiracy were the Jagat Seths, the biggest bankers in Bengal, who increasingly believed Siraj was incapable of providing the security needed for commerce to flourish. To begin with, the Company was not involved in the plot. With good reason as it turned out, Bengal's rebellious merchants and magnates worried that the East India Company would twist any situation to their own advantage, but the Company's possession of money and arms made them too useful an ally to ignore. In May 1757, the conspirators approached William Watts, the British agent in Murshidabad, and the Company asked to join the coalition against Siraj.[31]

The conspiracy to oust Siraj-ad-Daula would have happened even without the Company. The British march on Chandernagore and then Plassey would have happened without the conspiracy. The plot gave the British an alternative candidate with whom to replace the new Nawab. The plan which developed from the beginning of May 1757 was to replace Siraj-ad-Daula with his military paymaster,

Mir Jafar, a man whom Clive believed 'as general [sic] esteemed as the other was detested'. It also threatened to divide the Nawab's army, giving the Company a chance of military victory. After they 'weighed and debated' the proposal, Calcutta's council decided that 'a revolution in Government' would be good for the Company. Siraj-ad-Daula's 'word, honour and friendship' could no longer be trusted, so a new Nawab was needed in order for British interests to thrive. To set the plot in motion, Clive and Watson marched their troops north from Chandernagore on 19 June. John Corneille did not believe this confrontation to be the result of rational thought. The East India Company had already received everything it wanted from the Nawab. Corneille thought the decision to fight was an act of passion, driven by a desire for retribution more than profit. 'Thus situated', he wrote to his father, 'with minds still angered against the nabob the tempting opportunity of pursing further revenge could not be withstood.'[32]

The British army certainly seems to have been ruled by alternating fits of rage and fear. Cooler British minds had cautioned against fighting, saying violence would 'throw the country again into confusion'. But the 784 British soldiers (613 infantry and 171 artillery) in Clive's force of 3000 were driven on by a desire for 'satisfaction' at the affront they believed they had suffered when the Nawab drove them out of Calcutta. Troops marched to the small fortified settlement of Katwa, forty miles south of the capital of Bengal, and the town which Marathas soldiers had used as their base to conquer Bengal in the 1740s. The march north to Plassey had been hot-headed, but by the time the Company's army had trudged ninety miles north in the early monsoon rain, passions had cooled somewhat and the British were frightened about the possible consequences of their actions.

In the dark, wet night of 21 June that mood of fear overcame Clive and he was wracked by indecision. Sleep eluded him as he considered the prospects and risks of fighting Siraj. Only a few miles away from Siraj's army, the real limits of British power was apparent.

Clive did not know where his potential Indian allies were. He had no news of Mir Jafar and it was rumoured that a Maratha force was marching to Bengal again. Having failed to displace Alivardi Khan from Bengal, they thought they would have a better chance now that a younger, weaker successor was on the throne. Perhaps Clive should fortify his position, and wait for Maratha support, as he had done six years earlier at Arcot. Or perhaps the Nawab would come to terms. Clive had called a council of war the previous evening, a majority of whose members shared his mood. By a vote of twelve to six, the British decided to call off their march north and wait for the Marathas; unsurprisingly, Corneille voted against action. An hour after the meeting ended, however, Clive had changed his mind and decided to continue the march. But still he did nothing, and he did not sleep that night.[33]

Many biographers see this moment as a sign of Clive's erratic temperament, evidence of the tendency for destructive self-doubt that accompanied his capacity for brilliant action. Yet Clive's paralysis tells us more about the mood of empire than the mind of one man. Throughout their time in India, from the 1680s to the 1940s, British officers were impatient in trying to assert their command over circumstances. They used force to make money and secure their settlements, but also to prove to themselves that they were men of honour who could act decisively. As much as anything else, Clive's military exploits were driven by his desire to put himself in a heroic light in England. The same was true for British officers in India for more than a century. Yet their power in India was always limited by their reliance on allies they usually did not trust and often found difficult to understand. The British idea of power was always out of kilter with their true ability to act. This brought about a strange, indecisive state of mind, one that oscillated between violent action and profoundly paranoid paralysis.[34]

The following afternoon, after a day without rain, passions prevailed once again. Clive ordered his soldiers to march overnight the fifteen miles to the village of Palashi, a mile south of the Nawab's army. By three o'clock on the morning of 23 June, troops were in position opposite Siraj's forces in a mango grove. At first light Siraj-ad-Daula tried to surround the smaller British army, commencing with an artillery bombardment. But three of four sections of the great arc intended to annihilate the Company were commanded by Mir Jafar and his fellow plotters, and did not take part in the fighting. Clive's plan had been to hold on until sunset, then launch a surprise attack on Siraj-ad-Daula's camp at night. At midday it began to rain again. The Nawab's army had not kept their powder dry but the British army had. When they tried to charge, Siraj's forces were cut down by the Company's nine cannon. As Clive changed into dry clothes following the down-pour, his second in command launched a counter-attack. Initially angry that his authority had been usurped, Clive then joined the charge. Demoralized by the rain, and seeing that such a large part of his army refused to charge, Siraj-ad-Daula ordered his forces to retreat to Murshidabad to fight another day. Most of his army, however, fled in panic.[35]

Since 1757 historians have tended to play down the importance of 'the Battle of Plassey', as it became known. They have suggested it was the lucky result of political negotiations, 'the successful cul-mination of an intrigue' as Percival Spear put it, rather than a real fight. Such judgement depends on an unrealistic idea of what deter-mines the outcome of normal wars. There was nothing particularly unusual about the fact that Plassey was shaped by forces off the field. Until mass mechanized warfare, most battles were determined by who didn't fight rather than the capacity of those who did. Siraj lost because his forces reflected his own limited capacity to assert authority over the constituent parts of Bengali society. Defeat was a consequence of the breakdown of political authority caused by the social upheaval that followed the invasion of Nader Shah. In June 1757, the East India Company was better able to hold a fighting force together than its enemies. The important point, though, is that the real British ability to lead a small body of men on the battlefield did not give them the capacity to command the submission of the province's twenty million people afterwards. Plassey did not found an empire. It merely ensured that political chaos endured in Bengal far longer than it would have done otherwise.[36]

Insolence and interruptions

Clive's army marched on to the capital, Murshidabad, where Mir Jafar 'found himself in peaceful possession of the palace and city'. The new Nawab asked to be formally recognized by the force he believed had brought him to power. On 1 July, a week after Plassey, Clive escorted the new ruler onto the throne at Murshidabad. A day later, Siraj-ad-Daula was found and killed by the new Nawab's son. Clive imagined that these events meant Mir Jafar was 'firmly and durably seated on the throne'. '[T]he whole country has quietly submitted to him,' he optimistically wrote. With 25,000 'matchless seapoys . . . there shall be nothing wrong to make the country flourish and subjects happy', he insisted in a letter to the Mughal emperor in Delhi asking for Mir Jafar to be acknowledged as Bengal's new ruler. In Calcutta Britons celebrated the 'revolution' so vigorously that women danced until their feet were sore.[37] Clive later said Plassey was an act that acquired and delivered 'absolute power' to a regime governed by allies of the Company. In fact, it was a moment that handed power to no one.[38]

Many of Bengal's inhabitants experienced the beginning of the British-backed regime as a time of chaos. Merchants were particularly vulnerable to the collapse of authorities able to maintain a balance between different interests, and the undisciplined expansion of British power. For example, two weeks after Mir Jafar took the throne in Murshidabad the warehouse of the trader Mir Ashraf was raided. This took place in Patna, 300 miles west of and upstream from Bengal's capital on the River Ganges. Ashraf was one of this great Mughal city's merchant aristocrats, a man whose trade lay at the centre of an urbane, cultured civil society, which supported poetry and music, hospitals for the poor and centres of Muslim piety. With his brother Mir Ashraf ran a business that traded in potassium nitrate, otherwise known as saltpetre, the most important ingredient in gunpowder.[39]

The raid was led by Paul Pearkes, chief of the East India Company's factory at Patna, possessor of a large fortune made from private trade and owner of one of the biggest mansions on the Hughli river. Pearkes claimed Ashraf had been housing French goods. In fact, he had long been desperate to enrich himself from Patna's saltpetre trade; he wanted to use the Company's power to create his own private commercial empire. Until Plassey he had been unable to compete with Ashraf's efficient commercial operation. Pearkes' raid was an attempt to take advantage of the change in Bengal's balance of power and to undermine a commercial rival.

During the first half of the eighteenth century, the prosperity of Patna, like that of other commercial cities, had been secured by a network of urban organizations that mediated between rival interests, underwritten by a Mughal regime concerned with maintaining the local balance of power. These institutions allowed Patna's trade to grow even after Nader Shah's invasion. Patna, like Calcutta, was one of the few safe centres for commerce, a haven for merchants and money. The Europeans were a potentially violent presence, the East India Company having at least 170 soldiers to guard its factories and potentially harass its inhabitants. Yet fear of reprisals from the Nawab had prevented anything but small, violent clashes, until now. After Plassey, Ashraf found that the balance of power had changed drastically. He appealed to the city's merchants, and then to the Nawab's court in Patna, but to no effect. The commander of the British troops was sympathetic, but had no power over the chief of the Company's factory. Ashraf wanted only to trade in peace. 'God preserve the reign of the present nabob and that all may rest in quietness,' he wrote to Amir Chand.

Mir Ashraf eventually got his property back from Pearkes, but only after a personal appeal to Robert Clive. Ashraf saw that

Plassey brought about the speedy collapse of the institutions that had allowed trade to prosper in cities like Patna. Now the prosperity of individual merchants depended on a fragile chain of personal connections rather than a stable structure of power. Because of this, Mir Ashraf tried to create relationships with as many potential allies as he could, even if they were on opposite sides. By the beginning of 1759, he was helping the Shah Zada, son of the Mughal emperor Alamgir II, whose forces were then threatening to invade Bengal. He became a secret but 'firm friend' of the French. In 1763, he tried, unsuccessfully, to acquire land revenue rights from the Company, as land seemed a more secure basis on which to make a living than commerce in such troubles times. None of these tactics worked in the end. A decade after Plassey, Mir Ashraf's company had been taken over by an Indian merchant employed directly by the British. Eventually it was assimilated into the East India Company itself. Paul Pearkes didn't get his way, but the Compay encroached on the commerce of an independent Indian trader.

Throughout the whole of the Bengal presidency, from Patna to Dhaka, the years after Plassey were a chaotic time of mistrust and crisis. Indian businesses collapsed as marauding British traders and their Indian allies undermined the viability of Indian enterprise. The number of European merchants outside Calcutta quickly expanded. By May 1762, there were at least thirty-three British traders scattered through Bengal on 'private business', most working in partnership with East India Company officials buying and selling a range of commodities. These traders claimed immunity from taxes and believed they were not subject to the power of the Nawab. As in Patna in 1757, or when a party of soldiers 'killed one of the principal people' of Sylhet 'on account of a private dispute', they created disorder by enlisting the Company's violent capabilities in personal battles.[40]

In the long term it was revenue not trade that dominated British politics in Bengal. In eastern India this demand for revenue began as an insistence on land to compensate for the losses in Calcutta,

but ended up as an aim in its own right. The treaty signed with
Mir Jafar promised more than twelve million rupees (£158 million
in 2016 prices) in supposed recompense. Gifts of more than ten
million rupees were promised to British civil and military officers
'for their services'. Clive alone received two million. Military men,
including John Corneille, were given five million rupees in total.
The Company was promised land, too, 24 sub-districts to the south
of Calcutta, still called 24 Parganas and Clive was given an estate
that paid a further 300,000 rupees a year.

Despite these 'gifts' the Company was no more confident with
its new allies than the now murdered Siraj-ad-Daula had been.
With characteristic impatience it pressed Mir Jafar to pay money
that had been promised, often by violent means. In the days after
Plassey Clive deliberately kept his troops outside Murshidabad to
prevent them from plundering Bengal's capital, but officers sent to
investigate the condition of the town complained about the 'shuf-
fling and tricking' of Mir Jafar's new ministers, saying there was
far less money in the treasury than they expected. Clive decided
to march into Murshidabad with a 'guard' of 500 men to secure
the Company's share of Bengal's cash. Over the next twenty-four
hours at least two-thirds of its treasury was emptied and shipped
to Calcutta.

Undermined by the force used by his British sponsors Mir Jafar
did not last long as Nawab. The cash he needed to pay his army
was quickly depleted. The post-Plassey frenzy of private British
commerce led every trader, big and small, to claim he was doing
business on behalf of the East India Company and to take advantage
of the Company's tax-free trade privileges, so that tax revenues collapsed. Local lords used the weakness of the regime to assert their
autonomy, and refused to pay revenue. As Robert Clive's successor
as governor put it, 'the general disaffection of the people [meant]
the revenues of most parts of the province were withheld by the
Zemindars [sic]'. Commercial confidence in this recently prosperous province plummeted. The government's authority evaporated.

The Nawab's own army was unpaid and starving, 'their horses are mere skeletons, and the riders little better', as Warren Hastings, the Company's resident at Murshidabad noted. Eventually, hungry troops mutinied and barricaded Nawab Mir Jafar in his palace. Bengal's nobles began to organize themselves around alternative candidates to rule Bengal. Robert Clive was Mir Jafar's last British supporter. Mistrustful of yet still loyal to the man he had personally escorted onto the throne, Clive left India in February 1760, again apparently for the last time, tired and ill but with a fortune and a grand story to tell back home about his great deeds. Mir Jafar survived less than a year.[41]

The big issue during the next few months was the fate of Chittagong. Chittagong was Bengal's only seaport, a tough town to attack, the place the British had imagined would become the centre of their trading empire in the Bay of Bengal since the late seventeenth century. The lure of this great port had led the British to fight, and lose, a war with the Mughal empire in the 1680s. After the Battle of Plassey, the British demanded the new Nawab hand over the port and its district but Mir Jafar resisted. The city's governor even blocked the East India Company's attempt to open a factory there. Company officers suggested force was necessary. As one argued, Chittagong 'will require a season when we can command instead of requesting'. In a controversial move opposed by Robert Clive's allies, the new British governor in Bengal supported Mir Jafar's replacement by his son-in-law, Mir Qasin, when he promised to hand them the city along with the revenues of the districts of Burdwan and Midnapur. With no support from the Company's new governor and prominent nobles and bankers, Mir Jafar abdicated and fled to Calcutta. In October 1760, the new Nawab, Mir Kasim, arrived to find the city and throne of Murshidabad empty for the second time in three years.[42]

In these troubled times the physical occupation of an empty palace did not bring with it the right to rule. The Company could only collect revenue from Chittagong once four companies of

Company troops were sent to force the local governor to submit. In other districts local leaders fled to the hills, leaving no one for the British to collect revenue from, and no records of who was supposed to pay them anyway. The new Nawab thought he could only build his own authority if he checked the East India Company's power; Mir Kasim tried to put into practice the classic Mughal policy of balancing interests. To counter the British East India Company he backed the Dutch East India Company, and gave tax-free trade to all merchants. But with no revenue to pay troops needed to check the Company and maintain order, small instances of violence escalated throughout Bengal. The English factory in Dhaka complained of the 'general insolence of the natives, with interruptions put upon the trade in general', and prepared for battle. Local conflicts coalesced into full-scale war. The Company again marched to Murshidabad to evict a Nawab, but this time it was one they had themselves installed. Mir Kasim moved his army and capital west to the town of Monghyr in Bihar, and joined up with Shah Alam II, the newly crowned Mughal emperor on the borders of Bengal, capturing and killing East India Company officers as he did so.[43]

Pangs of hunger

'It is all very well', the poet Mir asked of the Mughal emperor in these days

> to be generous and charitable
> The question is whether the king can afford this?
> When he himself is living, hand to mouth
> And pangs of hunger have reduced him to a skeleton.[44]

These were years of crisis in the Mughal capital. Alamgir II had been emperor since 1754 but was killed by invading Afghans in 1759. Delhi was the scene of conflict between Afghans and the Marathas, each of whom was backed by rival groups of Mughal nobles. Maratha generals considered sending the Mughals into permanent exile and placing a Hindu, Maratha emperor on the throne. Instead, they decided to support Mughal authority, making Alamgir II's son emperor as Shah Alam II. He was duly crowned in December 1759. The Marathas then suffered a massive defeat when they took on the Afghans in 1761 at Panipat. Shah Alam II was supposed to be 'protector of the world', a sovereign who lit up the universe 'like the sun'. But he fled Delhi's chaos looking for support from whoever had the troops and money to bring order back to the Mughal capital.

For the first twelve years of his reign Shah Alam II was an emperor in exile, a man trying to build authority at the very moment when the Mughal empire was suffering its greatest eighteenth-century crisis. During these years the victories of British armies in Bengal seemed to demonstrate that the East India Company was a possible ally for the new emperor. In a series of letters to Clive and his successors, Shah Alam II offered the East India Company the position of imperial tax collector in Bengal, the famous office of *diwani*, in return for the use of the British army. The 'Delhi project', as historian G. J. Bryant calls it, appealed to British soldiers' ideal of heroic violence, forming the main subject of gossip 'from generals down to subalterns' for a few months. As one captain asked, 'Does anyone talk of a trip to Dely? Or are we to be D—d to a garrison life? No! that I cannot imagine while you have a king to put on the throne.' Company officers were enamoured with the idea of fighting to restore a legitimate monarch whom they could then manipulate. But the East India Company's concern for maintaining its own security and profitability trumped any romantic desire for martial glory. A Delhi trip would be expensive, and might involve a confrontation with the force Britons feared the most, the Marathas.[45]

Rather than the British, Shah Alam II was supported by the ruler of Bengal's western neighbour, the Nawab of Awadh, and the East India Company's latest enemy, the exiled Mir Kasim. The emperor, the recently ousted Nawab of Bengal and the ruler of Awadh threatened to march on Calcutta and oust the East India Company. The Company marched to meet them. The consequence was the Battle of Buxar, one of only three moments in the history of the British empire in India when Company soldiers directly fought troops commanded by the Mughal emperor. Unlike the first Anglo-Mughal war, this was a tough and even contest. At a massive cost in dead and injured (a quarter of the 7,000 troops who fought on the British side were killed or seriously wounded) the Company emerged victorious.

The defeated Shah Alam II once again offered the East India Company the office of *diwan*, revenue collector, in Bengal. This move was an attempt to put in play the classic Mughal tactic of assimilating an enemy into the polity as a privileged subject once again. It was the same tactic used in 1691, when the Mughals allowed the East India Company to settle in Calcutta after they were so humiliatingly defeated in the first Anglo-Mughal war. Realpolitik dictated that Shah Alam II had to concede far more than the right to build a small fort in a far-flung swamp; but even in defeat the emperor needed to retain his prestige. He could not present the grant of the office of *diwan* as a bargain made after a battle. It needed to be seen as the gift of an emperor made with full authority. It was not, for example, mentioned in the Treaty of Allahabad between the Company, Mir Kasim and the Nawab of Awadh but 'sealed and approved' in the presence of the emperor.

The British already had as much practical control over the revenues of Bengal as they wanted. But accepting the *diwani* gave their practical power legitimacy, and proved to critics in Britain and India that they were not interested in challenging more powerful forces in the Indian subcontinent. On his journey back to Asia for a third time, this time as Governor and Commander-in-Chief in Bengal, Robert Clive feared that if 'ideas of conquest were to be the rule of our conduct, I foresee that we should of necessity be led from acquisition to acquisition until we had the whole Empire against us'. That, of course, is exactly what happened in the end, as the passion for conquest outweighed the rational limits of British power. But in 1765 the *diwani* was acquired to prove to audiences in both Britain and India that the East India Company was interested only in trade and money not political power.

The *diwani* was seen as a reluctant necessity for both sides. There was little ceremony when it was granted, the emperor scaling the treaty seated on top of a bedframe in Clive's tent. 'Thus', one Indian observer wrote, 'a business of such magnitude ... was done in less time than would have been taken up for the sale of a jack-ass'.

Shah Alam II was to be given 2,600,000 rupees (£325,000) a year in tribute from the East India Company's expanded revenues. Clive hedged the Company's bets, and promised to pay his old allies the Marathas money from the Bengal revenues as well. These payments still theoretically left the Company 12,300,000 rupees (£1,355,000) each year from Bengal's revenue.[47] The *diwani* caused a quick bubble in the East India Company's stock price, but no new bonanza to British taxpayers. But it did not alter the Company's finances, as the costs of collecting cash increased as quickly as the Company's capacity to collect revenue. Its surpluses only, briefly, expanded in the early 1770s because the size of its military was scaled back, but the onset of new wars in the late 1770s more than soaked up the revenues gained from the *diwani*, pushing the Company into deficit. By 1780, this once profitable commercial organization was teetering on the edge of bankruptcy.[48]

East India Company, revenue and expenditure in India, 1762–1781.[49]

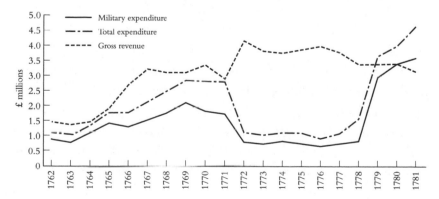

The meeting at Allahabad officially turned the Company into revenue collectors in Bengal and rulers of the northern *sarkars* in coastal Andhra. The Company also signed a treaty of mutual defence with the defeated Nawab of Awadh, allowing its great neighbour to the west to rely on British troops in exchange for cash and the right of British merchants to trade without paying taxes. Soon after Buxar, a British garrison was constructed in the city of Allahabad as a last line of defence for Bengal. In 1765, the British aim was still to protect the fortified enclaves from which they tried to control commerce and collect cash. Company politics were rooted in the sentiments of mistrust and impatience that had grown, in the eighty years since their defeat in the Anglo-Mughal war of 1686–90, within the paranoid, walled worlds of their forts and factories. But they had begun to imagine that those enclaves stretched throughout much of south India and extended from Calcutta halfway along the Ganges towards Delhi.

Come here to die

In a strange way the grant of the *diwani* saved the Mughal empire. It made it the East India Company's interest to uphold the prestige of the authority which gave the British such power in Bengal. As historian Robert Travers notes, the *diwani* also 'drew elite Britons into the courtly world of late Mughal governance', creating a brief moment when a collaborative form of Anglo-Indian polity seemed possible. Company officers sought Mughal titles and attended lavish dinners hosted by officers of Bengal's Nawab, just as in Arcot. In neither place was there any immediate desire to dispense with Indian institutions. The next few years saw British efforts to find and govern with Mughal India's 'ancient constitution'.[50]

But if Plassey, Buxar and the grant of the *diwani* did not bring the demise of the Mughal empire in Bengal, they did practically kill off Mughal techniques of statecraft. The polite tone of conversations which took place in the houses of Indian nobles did not last long once the British got down to talking business. Nor did it extend far beyond the Company's fortified citadels. The exercise of British power in India in the years after Plassey was marked by a refusal to engage in the kind of negotiation that had been so vital to the creation of Mughal authority and prosperity in practice. Perpetually impatient and prickly, the Company's officers usually saw any challenge as 'insolence', or as a humiliation that needed to be avenged, rather than an act which required conciliation. The constitutional niceties of Anglo-Mughal conversation did not alter the British assumption that their primary purpose in India, to make money, relied on their Company's capacity for violence. It was that deep-rooted instinct which corroded the possibility of any enduring form of partnership.

To collect cash from the new territories in Bengal acquired with the *diwani*, Robert Clive ordered ten companies of troops to march into the countryside and enforce payment. In his two last years as Governor of Bengal, 1766–7, Clive tried to focus the Company's servants' attention more emphatically on the goal of collecting revenue, banning officers from engaging in private trade and allowing them a commission on the Company's private trade instead of private profits. This met with much resistance, and Company servants continued to make fortunes from personal commerce for another twenty years. But the impatient focus on the collection of revenue at all costs undermined the capacity of political authorities in Bengal to respond to economic crises. The consequences were catastrophic.

The rains were light in 1768 and did not come at all in the summer of 1769. It was only in late November 1769 that the British started to take notice. '[T]he oldest inhabitants never remembered to have known anything like it,' Clive's successor Henry Verelst wrote. But even then, the 'calamity' which mattered most to the Company was the depletion of the Company's revenue supplies. By February 1770, 70 per cent of the largest of Bengal's three annual rice crops, usually harvested in December and January, had been lost. The Company's council in Calcutta optimistically remarked that 'we have not yet found any failure in the revenue'. But the price of rice had increased five times in some places and millions were starving. Historians debate how many people died in total, but a good estimate is that somewhere between 15 and 20 per cent of the province's population of perhaps twenty million perished in the famine of 1769–70.

The few Britons who wrote about it described the famine as a moment when the fragile power of human society to organize its subsistence was conquered by the malign forces of Indian nature. In these years, scavenging carnivores were everywhere in British minds. One observer described 'thousands falling daily in the streets and fields whose bodies, mangled by dogs, jackals, and vultures in that hot season (what at best the air is very infectious) made us dread the consequences of the plague'. John Shore, a later Governor-General, wrote in bad verse how 'in wild confusion dead and dying lie / hark to the jackal's yell and vulture's cry'. Company servants thought people had reverted to a state of natural barbarity, with descriptions by June 1770 of the living feeding on the bodies of the dead.[51]

Later British officers saw Bengal as a place peculiarly vulnerable to these malign natural forces. In reality, though, they found it very difficult to find evidence for such a devastating famine in Bengal's recent history. The last similar event occured in 1574, when the Mughal conquest of Bengal had only just begun. Between then and 1769, the back and forth of Mughal politics ensured ecological shocks did not cause human disasters. Good years created surpluses of food and money, which could then be redistributed to feed people in lean times. Bengal's little kings and Mughal rulers used their reserves to buy grain, to feed the poor, to accept the late payment of land revenue and lend money to farmers to get them started again if their crops were wiped out. This was not an economy with a high rate of growth, and living standards were poor by today's standards. But bad harvests, in 1737 and 1738 for example, did not create large mortality rates. India before the

British was, after all, a polity where power depended partly on consent, and resistance and flight were options for subjects who did not like the way a ruler behaved. Maintaining political authority needed political leaders to be sensitive to the needs of subjects when their livelihood was under threat. It was that sensitivity the British lacked.[52]

By 1769, twelve years after the 'conquest' of Plassey, the political conditions that prevented famine had evaporated. As the British themselves noted, the decline of commercial security and rise of local violence meant the bonds of trust that bound traders to each other had collapsed. In 1768, the Calcutta council warned of the 'danger of a complete breakdown in the commercial life of Bengal'. Next year, Richard Becher worried that 'this fine country, which flourished' even under what he imagined had been 'the most despotic and arbitrary government, is verging towards ruin'. 'Gentlemen in the Company's service' were blamed for making massive profits by hoarding grain. Desperate to feed the men needed to defend their forts, the Company seized rice from merchants' stores, giving it to builders and soldiers who threatened to desert unless they were fed. The biggest cause of death by famine was not the absence of grain but inflation, a rapid increase in the price of rice. Hardest hit were agricultural servants, weavers, boatmen, anyone who lived on their wages rather than the food they grew themselves.

Squeezed by British revenue collectors in lean years, local nobles could afford to distribute little to the starving. The Company itself offered almost no relief. One Company servant, whose account of the catastrophe was printed in a London newspaper, observed forty dead bodies within twenty yards of his window, 'besides hundreds laying in the agonies of death for want'. The anonymous officer sent his servant out to demand that the living 'move further off' for fear of contaminating his house. They refused, he said, shouting, 'Baba! Baba! My Father! My Father! This affliction comes from the hands of your countrymen, and I am come here to die, if it pleases God, in your presence.'[53]

The thousands who wearily walked to the British 'presence' in Calcutta and other towns and cities were animated by a memory of the way political authorities were meant to behave. Protection in bad times was the price rulers were supposed to pay for their subjects' submission, labour and cash. Those sad marches mark the recognition by Indians that the East India Company possessed some kind of sovereign authority, which should be held to account in the same way as other rulers. But the limited distribution of food, and the British insistence on a rigid revenue demand whatever the condition of the harvest, marked a clear breach of the mutual obligations which bound rulers to those they ruled. The Company's victories at Plassey and Buxar gave the British a right to demand tax, and also some kind of capacity to govern. But the East India Company evaded the responsibility that Indians (or, for that matter, the British in Britain) thought were a consequence of sovereign power. They would continue to do so in the years to come.

Heaven-born

In these years of turmoil and famine in Bengal, the citizens of London looking for something to do on a summer night might very well have paid sixpence to take a boat from Westminster. The boat would have taken them across and down the river to the Vauxhall Pleasure Gardens. There, they would join perhaps 1,000 others, far more on special occasions, to stroll, gossip and eat along tree-lined walks lit by hundreds of lamps. The English prided themselves that such 'entertainments' were conducted without a police force, and 'without tumult and disorder, which often disturb public diversions of France'. A French observer complained that the English there looked as glum as if they were at a bank. If they had taken dinner, our gloomy pleasure-seekers would have sat in a pavilion decorated with paintings by the artist Francis Hayman. The pictures Hayman painted in the 1740s were amusing distractions, of dancing milk-maids, girls playing badminton or scenes from Shakespeare. During the early 1760s the subjects became more serious. The gardens' proprietor asked Hayman for a series of six massive works commemorating British victories in the Seven Years War with France. One was of General Wolfe's victory in Quebec. Another, a scene without a Frenchman in sight, was of Robert Clive meeting a grateful Mir Jafar after the Battle of Plassey.[54]

When news of Plassey reached Britain in the autumn of 1757, the British were looking for a hero. War with France was going badly. 'We had lost our glory, honour and reputation everywhere,' Prime Minister William Pitt said in Parliament. 'But', Pitt went on, 'in India there the country had a heaven-born general who had never learnt the arts of war.' Soon after news of Plassey arrived, Clive's old friend and brother-in-law wrote to Mrs Clive that his 'health is drunk by as many as the King of Prussia's'. In July 1760, Clive landed in Britain with a fortune of perhaps £310,000. He was quickly given an Irish peerage, bought an estate in Shropshire and rented a large town house in London's Berkeley Square. Clive's intention was not only to enjoy his money but to establish himself as a man of great power. Recounting his great deeds in Bengal was vital to this, as was acting as a generous local benefactor offering prize money at the races, for example.[55]

But the heroic deeds of men who won wars in India could only be celebrated if the East India Company continued to be a stable source of income for prosperous Britons. Throughout the eighteenth century money-making was the Company's primary purpose. If the years after Plassey were a time of irrational hope about the possibility of massive riches being shipped back to Britain, they were also a time of financial crisis. Clive's personal stature suffered as his name became associated with the causes of the Company's diminishing returns. By 1761, when news of Mir Jafar's ousting reached London, the Company's stock had fallen to its lowest price for thirty years. Two years later, the Company had to borrow money from the Bank of England to stay afloat. Clive was blamed by many. His private income, most importantly the money from land he received from Mir Jafar, was seen as cash plundered from the Company's corporate assets. Clive was both the object and protagonist of infighting between the Company's proprietors. In 1763 he won a short-term victory in the battle of the councils, managing to persuade Prime Minister George Grenville that the only way to solve the Company's crisis was to send him to India again with complete civil and military powers. But the brief recovery in his status did not last.

Crisis was followed by a bubble and then another crash. News of Shah Alam II's grant of the *diwani* arrived in London in April 1766, causing the Company's stock price to quickly double in value. Clive's supporters in London told anyone who would listen that the Company was now 'in possession of the labour, industry and manufactures of twenty million of subjects'. The *diwani* would be the 'salvation of the Company'. Its directors demanded Clive quickly convert cash from Bengal into goods that could be sold in London, for 'if we do not find ways and means to bring our great acquisitions to centre in England neither the Company nor the nation will reap the expected benefit of them'.[56] But the massive imagined transfer of wealth failed to materialize. News of wars with new Indian enemies was received in London. In 1767, the British were fighting a state few Britons had previously heard of, the rapidly growing southern Indian sultanate of Mysore. Again, the Company needed to borrow money to stay afloat, this time from the government. For many, Clive became the symbol of the private greed that much of the British public associated with India. In the 1768 general election, he won the lowest number of votes in Shrewsbury, only keeping his seat by manoeuvring the winners out on appeal. The next six years saw him try to rebut continual efforts to take away his property and status, eventually pleading that the House of Commons should 'leave me my honour, take away my fortune'. In fact, the opposite happened. Clive kept his cash by buying support in Parliament, but his reputation collapsed. Tired, ill, disillusioned and angry about the failure of his personal empire, Robert Clive died in November 1774 at the age of forty-nine, from an overdose of opium. It is uncertain whether this was a suicide attempt or if the drug was taken to ease Clive's increasingly turbulent state of mind.

To begin, the stories Clive and his friends had told in London were received well in a world that valued such heroics. The public, as the painter Allan Ramsay wrote, had a 'passion for conquest and admiration of conquerors'. As the philosopher David Hume lamented, '[h]eroism, or military glory, is much admired by the generality of mankind'. Hume's point was that the public's desire for conquest allowed people to forget the uncertain consequences of heroic war, which as often as not were 'infinite confusions and disorders'. Britain's distance from India allowed the authors of violence to tell impressive stories about their imposition of power through conquest, which belied the reality of politics in Asia. In fact, Clive's fate in India was shaped by forces over which he had no control; by Nader Shah's invasion, by the power and tactics of the Marathas, by Shah Alam's need for allies. The actions of British officers in the subcontinent were accountable to nothing but the disconnected ideas of India propagated by rival gangs engaged in domestic political battles, and the fickle flow of commodities to London. The voice of Indian politics was mostly silent in Britain.[57]

The failure of British power in Asia was communicated in one blunt, inarticulate medium: money. Revenue did not follow rhetoric. The boom which accompanied stories about glorious moments of conquest was followed by a bust caused by the anarchy over which the Company presided. Brought down by the East India Company's stock price as much as anything else, Robert Clive was a victim of the delusory idea of power that he had helped to create. His life was governed by the effort to persuade people he was a man able to impose his authority on events, but in the end that effort merely heightened the gap between rhetoric and reality.

Francis Hayman's portrait of Clive did not depict the Bengal famine, but the viewer enjoying dinner on a pleasure trip to Vauxhall Gardens might have been touched by the painting's sense of uncertainty. The painting depicts Mir Jafar on a field spread with the carnage of war, beseeching Clive to support his claim to the throne. Mir Jafar's war elephant stands stately and subdued. Clive's horse is rearing, perhaps a symbol of the unbridled, unpredictable passion that lay beyond British force. The Union flag flutters above Clive's head, symbolizing British victory. Yet this is not the moment that founded an empire. Clive is the magnanimous champion, but he has his arms outstretched, too. The two men are engaged in a conversation, to which there has been no resolution. The painting does not portray a settled state. What the battle was fought for, and what victory would produce, seemed still very much in doubt.

5

NEW SYSTEMS

The last quarter of the eighteenth century was a time of revolutionary change across the globe. Patriots expelled the British from their thirteen North American colonies. Republicans executed the French king and then France's liberal state marched into every corner of Europe. Spain's American empire was divided between a succession of republics. On both sides of the Atlantic, ancient establishments and old elites were displaced. Land was taken over by new men wielding a different kind of power, by lawyers and officials with no capacity to command the loyalty of bands of men and women, but who possessed money and bureaucratic authority in its place.[1]

In India, in the lands which the East India Company had conquered in Robert Clive's wars, change was more subtle, but dispossession no less real. It was not revolutionary ideology or the desire for military authority that transformed Indian society in the territories the British conquered. Social change was wrought instead by forms of government that anxious East India Company's officials used to defend their new position. This was a profoundly conservative revolution, created as ideologies designed to prevent upheaval in Europe were put into practice in India to defend British power. In London the Anglo-Irish Whig Edmund Burke railed against the revolution in France for annihilating aristocratic grandeur. In

Asia, his ideas about land and property had the unintended effect of dispossessing old lords. It was the same kind of men as in France or America – clerks, revenue officers and accountants – who prospered at the expense of the old aristocracy.

The revolution occurred as the East India Company introduced a new system of government to the territory conquered during the middle of the eighteenth century, in particular to the arc which curves from the foothills of the Himalayas, through Bengal and Bihar along the northern Coromandel coast and Madras. These regions were prosperous and well governed under the rule of the Mughal empire and its Nawabi successors. Here, India's eighteenth-century regimes shared political authority with local leaders, with the men and women the Mughals demeaningly called zamindars. For the first twenty years after the Company's conquests, the British stayed in their fortified cities and trading posts, summoning land-holders and revenue collectors to negotiate the terms on which they would pay revenue and submit to the Company's power. Most of the time, these landholder-kings were left to rule with little challenge to their authority.

In the 1790s, a new system led to the spread of British officers from the Company's fortified port cities, from Bombay, Madras and Calcutta, to small settlements scattered throughout the Indian countryside where they set up their offices and tried to build a new kind of regime. The task of Company officers changed dramatically in these years. In the 1770s, only a fifth of the East India Company's 430 civil officers had been based outside the capitals of the East India Company's three provinces, the 'presidencies' of Calcutta, Madras and Bombay. Most were merchants. By the end of the 1790s, the British-born civil service had increased to more than 600. Almost half were scattered in the *mofussil*, the upcountry regions of India, as tax collectors and local judges. Throughout the East India Company's eastern lands, the rule of merchants and warriors had been replaced by the administration of bureaucrats.

The aim of the new system was to secure the Company's

collection of revenue without the need to negotiate with India's local elites. The Company was motivated by the same desire to have its relationship with Indian society fixed in writing which drove the first Anglo-Mughal war a hundred years before. Only now, fixity was being imposed on local landholders not great governors and kings. The idea was to replace face-to-face conversation with written rules. The rules insisted landholders paid a fixed amount of money each month with rigorous punctuality, and did not disturb the peace. In return their property rights were to be secured. The system was supposed to give the British stable allies to buttress the Company's power, in return for their being allowed to profit peacefully from their lands. But the system undermined the negotiation and face-to-face conversation which had been so essential to the politics of eighteenth-century India. As a result, it brought dispossession and the collapse of a once rich region's wealth.[2]

Refractory lords

Polavaram was one place transformed by the new system. Thirty miles inland in Telugu-speaking country 300 miles north of Madras, the Polavaram estate straddled the hills and plains at the point where the Godavari, India's second longest river, broadens out before spilling into the sea. The lowland portion of Polavaram was on well-watered soil rich in nutrients. The nearby town of Rajahmundry was an important Mughal trading centre, a place where cotton from the black, dry soil of the interior and textiles from weaving villages were exchanged for money and shipped throughout Asia and Europe. Attracted by the region's prosperity, the dynasty that ruled Polavaram had only moved to the region in the late 1600s. By the time the British arrived they had created a powerful local regime.[3]

This was a mobile world in which local rulers needed to negotiate hard to keep people with different interests on their land. The Raja of Polavaram could threaten peasants who did not pay with a visit from men armed with lathis, or big sticks. But peasants had a choice. With plenty of empty land and rival manufacturing centres, there were other possible livelihoods nearby. There was always the option of fleeing to the hills. The raja's power depended on a retinue of perhaps 1,000 armed men. But it also relied on the local lord paying for markets and travellers' rest houses, funding temples and schools, giving rice to people in need and lending money to pay for the rice plants sown each year. Their manipulation of the politics of investment and redistribution meant that, by the 1790s, the Polavaram rajas had built authority over more than a hundred villages, possessed four forts and a dozen temples. Authority was built up in the same way throughout India's eastern riverine and coastal region, in Bengal as well as the south.[4]

Landholders thought they should have a similar relationship of give and take with the government. Mangapati Devi Reddy, the Raja of Polavaram in the 1780s, maintained a friendly relationship with the East India Company in the first years after conquest. Every few years he travelled to meet British officials in their fortified enclaves at Madras or Masulipatam, negotiating the terms on which he would pay taxes to the Company. The deal was reciprocal. When family members tried to oust him in the early 1780s, the British backed Mangapati with troops, proclaiming that anyone who supported his rivals would be considered 'traitors and rebels' to both him and the British regime. But the coming of the new system transformed Mangapati's relationship with the Company.

Benjamin Branfill was the British officer who arrived, in 1794, to put the new system into practice. Branfill was from a typical East India Company family. His great-grandfather had been a sailor in Devon but made a fortune shipping slaves from Africa to the Caribbean around the time William Hedges was travelling in Bengal. He used his money to buy a mansion at Upminster, fifteen miles from London, starting a business that traded with Portugal. Eventually he sank its capital into the East India Company. Two generations later, income from the amoral activities of global commerce had been converted into the seeming security of a civil servant's salary. Branfill began his Indian career as a nineteen-year-old in Madras in 1780, the same year Mangapati Devi became Raja of Polavaram. Fourteen years later he was appointed to the new position of District Collector in the town of Rajahmundry, twenty miles south of Polavaram. He arrived with his wife, one British assistant, a small retinue of Indian officers, a pile of empty ledgers and account books and a set of rules defining how British officers were supposed to govern rural India for the first time.

The early 1790s had been years of heavy rains and bad harvests. The weather, together with disputes within the Polavaram Raja's family, made it difficult for Mangapati to collect rent from villagers. He got into debt, and complained to the new Collector that he could not afford the Company's revenue demands. Branfill did not know what to do. To begin with he pleaded with his superiors in Madras to let the landholder postpone his revenue payments. After all, Mangapati had been a good ally in previous years. But the new system prevented this kind of negotiation. Branfill's next request took the opposite tack, suggesting the Company violently dispossess the Raja and find another ally, waiting, though, until an armed force was available to do so.

In the stream of correspondence between Rajahmundry and Madras, Branfill began to write about Mangapati in the vocabulary typical of British officers when things did not go their way, describing him as a 'refractory' and 'contumacious' character. This condescending language was only a thin veil for Branfill's fears. Mangapati had marshalled a large force of armed men, of peasant-warriors as well as tribesmen from the nearby hills, and the rigid demands of the new system were alienating him. In his letters to Mangapati, Branfill postured and blustered, threatening that if revenue was not paid 'the Company would exterminate him, and his adherents wherever they take refuge'. In response, Mangapati prepared for a violent struggle, strengthening his fort and recruiting an army of peons to defend himself. With only a tiny garrison thirty miles away, the second half of 1799 was an anxious time for the small, new British enclave at Rajahmundry.[5]

Luckily for the British a detachment of East India Company soldiers was marching through the area on its way from fighting in the south. Branfill was given permission to use them and to 'proceed with vigour for subduing the rebel by force of arms'. Two hundred Bengal Volunteers captured Polavaram fort after a tougher fight than they expected, but still with only four soldiers injured. Mangapati fled. Fearing a counter-attack, Branfill sent soldiers into the hills in pursuit of Mangapati, hacking some of his followers down, burning the villages of allies on the plains.[6]

By the beginning of 1801, the Raja of Polavaram was on the run and his estate was up for sale. Over the next few years, the Polavaram estate passed from one owner to another. In the process, the authority needed to maintain its prosperity collapsed. A succession of Mangapati's relatives and neighbours briefly gained control but failed to persuade its villagers to pay them revenue. Eventually they were forced to sell. The man who eventually profited from decline and chaos was Koccharlakota Jaggayya, a locally-born Indian officer who worked for both the East India Company and the rajas collecting revenue and marshalling armed men. Jaggayya had been Branfill's most trusted official, a vital source of information about local society when the Collector first arrived. It was Jaggayya who led the British army's attack on Polavaram fort. Over the next decade he made enough money manipulating the district's accounts to buy what was left of the Polavaram estate, paying 43,210 rupees for it in 1813. This 'money was certainly made somewhat too rapidly', one British officer complained. Jaggayya's swift rise did not make him popular with local residents. He tried to enlist support by building temples on the plains, but his possession of Polavaram was resisted by its one-time subjects in the hills, over whom he never gained control. The hills remained a source of 'trouble' for the British throughout the nineteenth century. With no funding for irrigation work, and little money advanced to farmers during difficult economic times, Jaggayya's lands got poorer. Nonetheless, the new raja, as he styled himself, lived into old age.[7]

Benjamin Branfill fared less well. Madras had a new governor, Lord William Bentinck, a political Whig who preferred a more conciliatory approach to the Indian subjects of the East India Company. Branfill was castigated for undermining the reputation of the Company by using too much violence, marching to the hills 'to the destruction of the health of the soldiers and to the degradation in the eyes of the inhabitants of a military reputation'. The Company's policy, Governor Bentinck said, should always be 'to reclaim by gentle methods', and be careful of 'the religious prejudices' and 'ordinary customs and manners' of 'the natives'. Branfill thought that this softer approach would have left him dead.[8]

A commission led by Thomas Thackeray, uncle of the author of *Vanity Fair*, was sent to Rajahmundry to find out what had really happened. Thackeray believed the demise of Polavaram was caused by a plot of Indian officers against Mangapati. Collector Branfill had not noticed that Indian officials, including Jaggaya, had demanded large bribes from landholders to massage the revenue accounts. Mangapati only got into trouble when he stopped paying the bung. It was, Thackeray argued, 'partly through their intrigues that the Country was reduced to a state of anarchy, and the Zamindar harassed into rebellion'. By the spring of 1805, complaints against Branfill were making their way from India to London. Believing he had done everything possible to protect the honour and revenue of the Company, Branfill felt let down by this challenge. He returned to London and at the beginning of 1806 resigned from the East India Company's service.[9]

Benjamin Branfill, Mangapati Devi Reddy and the peasants of Polavaram were all victims of a system of government that replaced negotiation with written rules and thus made political power far less accountable in practice. The premise of the new system was that the judgement of British officers could not be trusted, so their conduct needed to be dictated by regulations and checked by a continual flow of correspondence up the chain of command. As the 'Examiner of Indian Correspondence' at the East India Company John Stuart Mill smugly put it a few years later, the 'great success of our Indian administration' was because it was 'carried on in writing'. The existence of detailed rules and the capacity to check every act performed by British officers 'was a greater security for good government than exists in almost any other government in the world'.[10]

In reality, the extraordinary flow of paper that Mill celebrated constructed a world of letters, ledgers and account books that had its own pristine order but could not comprehend or rule the forces which shaped rural society. Paperwork created new centres of British power, whether in Calcutta, Bombay, Madras or London, and these new centres created their own stories about the success or viability of British rule. But the new maze of paperwork blocked the creation of the public, reciprocal relationship between the state and local lords which political authority and economic prosperity had relied on before. It also meant that decisions were increasingly made behind closed doors. As the public places where Indians could hold officers to account were closed off, so the opportunities for intrigue and corruption expanded. The old lords were replaced by new men, good at manipulating the paperwork created by the new rules but with little inclination or capacity to create authority or order. In the early nineteenth century, institutions which had previously supported the local economy collapsed, corruption became rife in the Company's offices, district officers became ever more embattled and anxious. The new system meant that much of rural India ended up being ruled by chaos.

Perhaps none of this should surprise us. The new system was not designed to create a stable political order in the Indian countryside. Its aim was to defend the integrity of the East India Company from accusations in Britain of venality and vice. It began life as an effort to manage metropolitan moral anguish, not to handle the complaints of Indians about what Company officers were doing in India. Its ostensible purpose was to uphold the property of Indians as a block to the potentially corrupt power of British officers. But transmitted from the debating halls of London to the paranoid writing chambers of Calcutta and Madras, these intentions were twisted as they were turned into action. Paradoxically, a policy whose purpose was to protect existing rights caused a revolution in the social structure of Indian society.

Ancient constitutions

The origins of the new system lay in the relationship between the East India Company's fragile fortunes in India and the febrile political atmosphere of London. The 1770s and 1780s was a rare moment in which British politics mattered to the way India was ruled. The East India Company had come under venomous criticism from its opponents in London once again. Critics made the same arguments they had been making for a century: the Company wielded a wicked kind of despotic power, illegitimately combining trade and political authority, corroding the balance of interests which sustained Britain's polity. The Company had built its own 'common interest' in tension with the interests of both Britain and India, as the Company's greatest critic, Edmund Burke, put it. The Company was 'a kingdom of magistrates', 'separated both from the Country that sent them out and from the Country in which they are'. It was, in other words, a power no one could control.

A few opponents argued that Britain needed to sever entirely its connection with India. The Yorkshire MP Sir George Savile complained that the Company's commerce 'brought too great an increase in money, which would overturn the liberty of this country'. But the Company paid too much in duty to the British Treasury for the connection to be cut and 40 per cent of MPs held Company stocks. Instead of arguing for abolition, politicians in London called for the Company and its rapacious officers to be brought under greater scrutiny from politicians in Britain. 'The publick', Prime Minister Lord North argued, 'have a right to call to account all persons civil and military.' When the Company almost went bankrupt in 1772 British taxpayers lent the Company £1.5 million. In return, the Company had to agree to a Regulating Act which introduced new forms of scrutiny and gave Parliament the power to appoint the Company's chief officer. The Governor of Bengal was given a new title, Governor-General, and handed authority over the provinces of Madras and Bombay as well. The man given this office was the 41-year-old Company officer Warren Hastings.[11]

On his appointment Hastings was seen as a far more virtuous man than most of his compatriots in India, but his approach was fundamentally at odds with the clamour for more control from London. Hastings wanted Indian officers and Indian principles, not British MPs, to hold the East India Company to account. In particular he wanted to revive a Mughal style of government. A Company servant since 1750, Hastings spent his early career close to the centres of Mughal power in Bengal where he became unusually fluent in the languages of Indian government, particularly Persian and Urdu, and developed a rare sympathy for Mughal styles of rule. Hastings argued that the Company needed to assert its sovereignty aggressively over its Indian territories, creating 'one grand and systematic arrangement' to settle 'so divided and unsettled a society'. But British sovereignty would be exercised through Mughal officers and institutions. Hastings wanted Indian officials to be stationed in the districts of British-ruled India, who would then negotiate with Indian landholders. Justice would be secured by courts of law staffed by Indians, not British lawyers, administering Indian jurisprudence. To prove that India had a viable system of justice, Hastings commissioned a 'synod' of ten pandits to write a code of Hindu law which he sent to the Chief Justice, Lord Mansfield, in London.

But Bengal's years of chaos had corroded the Mughal system of government beyond repair. Since 1757 British traders believed the Company's armed power gave it licence to maraud and rampage in search of private profit and India's pre-colonial officials and institutions were too weak to offer a challenge. Hastings could not find Mughal officers of sufficient skill or grandeur to occupy positions in the countryside. There was no consensus about how a revived Mughal constitution would work. In practice, Hastings' Mughal constitution was nothing more than an intellectual fantasy. The Governor-General spent his years in office tired and demoralized, constantly battling British enemies in Calcutta who thought the Company should put in place different systems of accountability. The pressure to maintain a stable stream of cash into the Company's coffers meant he ended up selling the right to collect revenue to the highest bidder, a tactic employed by the Mughals and Marathas only in times of crisis.[12]

Hastings' reputation in London was not helped by the ease with which accusations of corruption could be levelled against him. During his time in India Hastings sent over £218,000 (£2.7 million in 2016 prices) in private wealth back to Britain, mostly in diamonds and bills of exchange, and spent lavishly. 'No man by all accounts takes less care of his money,' one critic said. In 1784, his German-born second wife, Marian, returned as a dazzling 'Indian princess' who paraded through elite society in brilliant clothes and jewels. The diarist Fanny Burney wondered if Marian adopting a 'modest & quiet appearance & demeanour' might have been better for Hastings' reputation. The money had, Hastings' accusers argued, been made by taking bribes and selling offices. For many politicians and sketch writers, Hastings became a symbol of the very British corruption in India that he had been sent to stamp out.[13]

Hastings' main accuser was Edmund Burke, the Anglo-Irish Whig politician most famous for his fervent critique of the French Revolution. Every prosperous, ordered society, Burke argued, was based on institutions that created bonds of trust between different classes in society. The submission of some people to others was, for Burke, a fact of life. But the institutions of modern civilization, the church, the law, the spread of refined manners and expansion of property rights, allowed submission to be enjoyed rather than suffered. By forcing rulers to act with moderation those institutions made 'power gentle, and obedience liberal', as Burke put it in *Reflections on the Revolution in France*. Burke was concerned that the desire to dominate, what he called the 'spirit of conquest', endangered the subtle balance between different social orders that prevented society from descending into anarchy. Burke's most important political interventions occurred where he saw this spirit of domination unchecked by other powers. Worried by the domineering attitude of the British towards American colonists, Burke had been in favour of conciliating rebels there. He saw the French Revolution as the ill-mannered effort of a few out-of-control lawyers to conquer France in the name of nothing but abstract principles; it would destroy every means French society possessed of keeping tyranny in check. Burke levelled the same accusations against Warren Hastings, only adding the charge of theft from Indians on a massive scale. He believed Hastings had confiscated 'all the landed property of Bengal upon strange pretences'. Land was handed over to men Burke described as 'black tyrants scattered through the Country' who annihilated the bonds which united rulers and the ruled. Aristocratic institutions were despoiled, wars against ancient monarchies prosecuted for private gain and India pushed, as a consequence, to the edge of anarchy. The worst thing, for Burke, was that Hastings' tyranny and corruption had brought dishonour to the British nation.[14]

Burke's attack on Warren Hastings began in 1781 and led to the East India Company's decision to recall their Governor-General in 1784. Two years after stepping ashore at Plymouth early in 1785, Burke managed to get Hastings impeached by the House of Commons. Hastings was prosecuted for using the Company as a vehicle for tyranny on the same spot in Westminster Hall where Thomas Sandys had been tried for breaking the Company's monopoly a hundred years before.

In fact, Burke and Hastings agreed about more than they realized; their rage marked a shared diagnosis of the problem facing

British rule in India. Both were concerned to find ways to discipline
the 'spirit of conquest' that had driven the East India Company's
military victories in India. Both men thought India had been
better governed before the British had conquered Indian land.
Neither thought it was possible to control British corruption from
Parliament. Each wanted to restore Indian institutions which could
check the power of East India Company officers. The disagreement
was only about how it was possible to do that. Hastings thought
accountability would return by reviving Mughal offices and officials
to check on British avarice. Burke, by contrast, believed it came
from restoring 'ancient' property rights, and giving power to landed
magnates who, he imagined, had natural and enduring roots in local
Indian society.[15]

Burke's championing of the principle of property allowed him
to win the debate easily. Hastings' arguments could too easily be
characterized as a defence of tyranny. On the other hand, Burke
offered an argument that connected to the British political class's fear
about the creeping power of central government, but also offered a
principle able to 'settle' the Company's relationship with India for
good. Burke's arguments were given practical life in two acts passed
to regulate the East India Company's government of its Indian territories, in 1784. Parliament's India Acts were intended to restore
order and put the Company's rule on a secure footing. The first
made the Governor-General a Crown appointment with absolute
power and created a Board of Control, made up of ministers selected
by Parliament, to monitor all the Company's correspondence with
India. The second mandated the Company to restore the rights of
different classes of men who owned land, and settle 'upon principles of moderation and justice, the permanent rule by which their
respective tributes and services shall in future be paid'. The property
of 'divers, rajas, zemindars ... and other native landholders' was to
act both as a bulwark against British avarice and a guarantee for the
East India Company's ability to collect revenue.[16]

The absolute and sacred power of government

The man sent to replace Warren Hastings as Governor-General and to put this new settlement into practice was Charles, Earl and then Marquess Cornwallis. Cornwallis was an aristocrat and a soldier, a stoical man 'firm in his purposes' and uncritical of his own thoughts. Like Burke, Cornwallis had Whiggish views about the need for a balance in which the power of kings was challenged by the rights of propertied social classes. But in practice he was used to being obeyed, and always able to project himself as a seat of authority and power. Cornwallis had been second in command of the British troops defeated by republicans in America. Cornwallis had surrendered British troops at Yorktown, yet he managed to avoid any blame for the collapse of Britain's North American empire. His task in India was to ensure a similar defeat did not happen there.

Cornwallis arrived in Calcutta in November 1786 in the middle of a financial crisis. 'The state of our finances is alarming, the difficulties are infinite,' he wrote. 'I feel that the whole may go to ruin in my hands.' Cornwallis's plan was to stop British corruption and stave off ruin by writing a new set of rules. Those rules, variously described by contemporaries as 'the Cornwallis Code', the 'new system' or the 'permanent settlement', were supposed to bind the fate of India's landed elites to the destiny of the Company. The rights and revenues of landholders were fixed in perpetuity. So long as they paid revenue in regular instalments, the Company withdrew from any pretence that it could govern rural society. Property rights were to be secured by new courts of law and new revenue offices that spread out through district capitals scattered across the East India Company's territories.

Edmund Burke had argued that the East India Company was 'a Commonwealth without a people' in which there were 'no people to control, to watch, to balance against the power of office'. Burke's aim had been to erect Indian property as the permanent counter-balance to the Company's power. But as the Burkean principles articulated by Parliament cascaded out into official practice in India they created an abstract, limited and silent state, obsessed by nothing more than its own security, whose influence worked above all to make the conditions of local prosperity more insecure. For the authors of the new system, power lay not with the convivial conversation between governor, landholder and tenant, as Burke imagined, but with the distant and abstract force of regulation. George Barlow, Cornwallis's closest colleague in Calcutta during these years, noted that the first aim of the new 'arrangements' was to ensure that '[t]he power of Government to make what Laws, or do what acts it may think proper must be held up to the people as absolute and sacred.' Barlow and Cornwallis believed corruption would be cleansed from the East India Company's official class by restricting the scope of individuals for local intervention and private deal-making. These were limitations not 'very agreeable to Englishmen' as Barlow noted, but necessary to ensure control was maintained over a distant empire. These restraints on the discretion of British officers consolidated the barrier of silence that separated Britons from Indian society. As historian D. H. A. Kolff puts it, 'the great virtue of the dispensation now deployed in India consisted of its aloofness.'[17]

A thorough John Bull

The new system meant a new generation of supposedly more virtuous Company officers, men such as Benjamin Branfill, were dispersed throughout the rural districts of India to put the new rules into practice. In the districts British work and settlement grew in places distant from existing Indian networks of power. A few collectorates, like Rajahmundry, were in old but declining Mughal centres of administration. Some, like Burdwan in Bengal, were in Mughal towns where prominent local lords had built their house and offices over the previous century. More commonly, though, the British created their district capitals in places where the East India

Company already had a military or commercial presence, but was distant from what they saw as the aggravation of Indian politics. In Barisal, in south-eastern Bengal, the Collector decided to move his office to a different town to get away from the influence of local power-brokers twenty miles away. At Bankura, they built around an old Company army camp. In every district capital, the Company's houses and offices were some distance from existing settlements, on cheap, open land where British buildings could sprawl into rural surroundings. In the ancient city of Benares, the British built their settlement two miles outside the old town. 'The crowded streets of an Asiatic town possess few attractions for Europeans,' one British observer stated in explanation as to why the British had 'insulated themselves in their own grounds'. Each of these new settlements consisting of a cluster of one-storey brick buildings, the collector-ate's offices, or *kachchari*, a treasury, a record room, a court, a few official residences, and perhaps also a cemetery and an ugly, army-built church.[18]

Life for the British in these small outposts of imperial power was very different from life in India's big cities. In the fortified port cities of Calcutta, Madras and Bombay, British behaviour was animated by a strong sense of racial distinction and social hierarchy, but a cosmopolitan existence grew up in which Europeans and Indians traded and sometimes socialized together. In the capital cities of Indian states like Delhi, Hyderabad or Gwalior, British officers could integrate themselves into the local political hierar-chy if they chose to. It was in the country's big Indian-ruled cities that the familiar imperial image of British life in early colonial India, with its white Mughals, its gossip, scandal and occasional moments of Anglo-Indian dialogue and even romance, could be a reality. But during the early nineteenth century most East India Company officers were collectors and judges stationed in small district towns, living with their wives and young children in tiny communities with three or four other European officers. In these scattered enclaves of British power Company servants transported the psychology of estrangement their predecessors had developed in the early days of the Company to new sites, trying to assert their embattled, isolated sense of power amidst an Indian population they did not trust and could barely communicate with.

Britons in the countryside tried to protect themselves from the rest of Indian society with their servants, their architecture, their domestic habits and procedures of office life. The *East India Vade Mecum*, an 1810 guide to British life in India, listed thirty-nine different kinds of domestic servant each officer needed to have. In his Company work, each judge or Collector had between thirty and fifty Indian officials working for him, ranging from senior accountants, translators and record-keepers to guards. British residences physically separated Europeans from the world beyond. The district officer's bungalow usually consisted of a square of nine rooms, surrounded by a veranda and enclosed green space, fusing the form of the Indian village hut and Palladian English villa into a style of architecture which provided a constant flow of air to remove supposedly bad Indian odours, and to defend the British against Indian sociability. Indian light was blocked out by Venetian blinds. Of course, absolute separation was impossible to maintain in practice. The Company's activities created new forms of Indian commercial life on their doorstep, for example the *kerani*, or clerk's bazaar, which opened in many Indian towns next to the Company's offices. Collectors and judges were heavily reliant on their Indian subordinates to do their job. But officers constantly struggled to assert their power over commercial connections and Indian staff while still trying to lead a quiet life, defending themselves through separation against what they saw as the incomprehensible disorder of Indian society. Boredom was staved off by solitary pursuits, by working on Company paperwork into the night, by reading Latin and Greek classics, gardening, inspecting local flora and fauna. Collecting insects and cataloguing plants were particularly popular pastimes.[19]

Perhaps most importantly, officials expressed their sense

of isolation in letters home. Later in his career, Mountstuart Elphinestone developed a public reputation for having good relations with Indians. Writing to his mother from the British station in Benares in the late 1790s, however, he offered no sense of connection with Indian society. His official duties, 'trifling criminal cases such as beating, abusive language, petty thefts', were banal. 'I only wish', he wrote, 'the time of my stay was out when I should return to England and never again be obliged to leave it.'[20]

Until the middle of the nineteenth century British officers rarely travelled beyond the towns where their offices were placed. British power was supposed to cascade out and down from the British officer in his district capital through a series of local Indian police and revenue offices into India's villages and petty principalities. But with no travel and no scrutiny, this system of authority only existed 'on paper', as the officer appointed to the newly created post of Police Commissioner in Bihar complained in 1839. The commissioner noted that he was only the second 'European officer of the Government' to visit the 'interior' of the district since 1793.[21]

When British officers did travel it was an unpleasant intrusion into the solipsistic routine of office work and domestic life. Julia and James Thomas were an unusually engaged and sociable couple, dining in the houses of Indian merchants in Madras, to the surprise of their compatriots. In 1836 Thomas was appointed judge to Rajahmundry, the town where Benjamin Branfill had been posted, and enjoyed the 'sweet country air', the occasional company of travelling British officers ('no troublesome company, yet always enough to prevent us from feeling lonely'), and the 'amusement' of short visits from the area's landholders. Unusually, they set up a school for local boys, and Julia learnt some Telegu verbs. But their desire to retreat to and stay in safe, comfortable and monolithically English spaces was typical of British officers throughout the first half of the nineteenth century. The Thomases built a home in Rajahmundry around their English objects and obsessions, gardening, reading, entomology and constant letter writing to Britain.

When he was invited to pay a visit to Rajahmundry's most prominent landholder-king, James Thomas needed to be persuaded by his more gregarious wife to accept. 'We should be "more quiet and comfortable at home",' the judge said. 'Such a thorough John Bull!' Julia complained.

In her letters home, Julia wrote up the trip as a stressful few days away from the quiet of life at their collectorate 'home'. On tour through the Raja's estate, the British couple constantly tried to find comfort amidst the 'heat, din and glare' of 'Hindoo hospitality', with its 'stinking torches', 'nautch' dances and 'crowds of spectators'. James Thomas was the most powerful government figure for hundreds of miles, yet he insisted on closing the door of his palanquin as they toured, only peeping at the people he ruled through shutters. His host needed to 'beg that [James] would do him the favour to keep it all open', to 'show himself to the multitude' and make visible his authority. British officials' instincts were to hide their power behind closed doors, making it less vulnerable but also less effective. The couple brought their books, their tea things and their drawing materials on the thirty-hour journey from their bungalow at Rajahmundry. At the end of each day they escaped to a room that 'looked as quiet and comfortable as at home'. The Thomases' Rajahmundry home didn't last long. Julia returned to England in December 1839 when their three-year-old daughter became seriously ill. James himself died the following year.[22]

In this new order, the Company officers' home and office in the district capital were fixed points surrounded by the constant movement of people and things. Landholders, peasants and merchants arrived with petitions asking for a job, or for the government's help in some dispute. British officers developed tactics to limit their exposure, only taking petitions during very short fixed hours, or pretending not to be at home. Officials were more friendly to travelling Europeans, whether civil servants or army staff. Julia Thomas noted the 'relays of stranger-company' her husband accommodated at their house in Rajahmundry, imagining their compound was an island of peace and order for Europeans travelling through a hostile and alien countryside. Most of all, though, the district office was a fixed point in the ceaseless flow of paperwork which kept the East India Company's administration going.[23]

The new system Cornwallis created replaced the movement of people with the circulation of paper. Travel and negotiation were supposed to be unnecessary because the government imagined 'all rights had been reduced to writing', as Cornwallis put it. The flow of paper was designed to give anxious officials in Madras or Calcutta the security that came from knowing what was going on in the districts. But it moved decision-making away from public view, making Indians anxious that decisions were being made over which they had no say. The hidden nature of British power, in contrast to the public display of authority under the Mughals, made many Indians extremely nervous. The Raja of Nadia was so concerned things were happening behind closed doors that he paid a Bengali clerk in the Collector's office to tell him what was written in letters exchanged between the district capital and Calcutta.

More than any other set of texts, the circulation of the East India Company's regulations was designed to give security to the British regime. Bengal's new code was enacted by the Governor-General's Council in thirty-eight regulations, printed on folio paper and sent out to officers throughout eastern India on 1 May 1793. Other areas used the Bengal code as a model, so similar volumes were sent to officers in the south and west of India over the following decades. The regulations claimed to provide a stable, fixed set of meanings which could be executed with no negotiation by district officials, regardless of the particular place or people they were applied to. Soon after these rules were passed, a thirty-ninth regulation was enacted which insisted that from then onwards, 'the same designations and terms were to be applied to the same descriptions of persons and things' in the English regulation, and that 'the same uniformity' used when they were translated into Bengali or Persian. But paper on its own offered very little guidance to the way officials were supposed to act in practice. The regulations created only an illusion of security, often merely disconnecting officers from the political circumstances that called upon them to make decisions in the first place. When they needed to act, the civil officers posted by the East India Company to British-ruled India during the first half of the nineteenth century were puzzled, diffident and usually anxious.

The two most important officers stationed throughout the districts of eastern India were the judge and the revenue collector.[24] The purpose of the Company's new law courts was to secure 'the preservation to the people of their own laws', and 'the security of their person and property'. Property cases were supposed to be determined by Hindu and Muslim legal traditions, and criminal cases governed by a modified version of Muslim law that Mughal officials had used. But British officers had no experience, rules or guidance for deciding what the relevant law was, or how property rights were defined. In practice even translations of Indian texts were too complicated to be used by officers who understood little about South Asia's traditions of jurisprudence and did not have the time or inclination to delve into details. More often, judges simply handed judicial decision-making over to Indian law officers, issuing their verdicts if they understood them, castigating them for inconstancy or corruption if they did not.[25]

Before British rule, disputes between Indians had been adjudicated in noisy courts where rulers heard the complaints of their subjects and everyone was entitled to voice their opinion. By contrast, the East India Company's new system of justice was supposed to be silent. Instead of long sessions cross-examining witnesses, subordinate officers were sent to ask questions of litigants and witnesses, and then British officers made decisions after scanning through the translations of their reports. As Ghulam Hussein Khan, a critic of the Company's effort to rule through writing, noted in the 1780s, the British hated 'appearing in public audiences, and whenever they come at all, it is to betray their extreme uneasiness, impatience, and anger, on seeing themselves surrounded by crowds, on hearing their complaints, and clamours'. Often, judges tried to avoid making decisions themselves, passing the entire case over to Indian law officers for a verdict. As Rammohan Roy, a former Indian Company officer, put it, each judge became so 'disheartened at seeing before him a file of causes which he can hardly hope to overtake', the Company's judicial officials were 'induced to transfer a great part of this business to his native officers'.[26] With their attempt to impose silence and their effort to make decisions behind closed doors, British judges seemed to betray the principles that guaranteed the virtue of Indian public life.[27]

In Calcutta and Madras there were a few moments when the court's attempt to wash its hands of decision-making sparked a major public debate. In 1793, a dispute arose about who was entitled to the profits from a temple icon in the city of Dhaka, two rival groups of holy men claiming the image of a Hindu deity. It ended up being 'taken up by almost all the Hindoos of the City, and parties were so violently inclined'. The Dhaka court's Hindu law officer gave a report 'so unsatisfactory as to perplex the business more than ever'. When the case ended up at Calcutta the judge forsook these elaborate arguments and decided with the most pragmatic consideration, declaring the land belonged to the side likely to commit the worst violence.[28] In 1816, the prominent journalist and newspaper editor Bhabanicharan Bandopadhyay tried to claim that property given by his father to a younger brother in fact belonged to him. The Hindu law experts in the Company's highest court in Bengal disagreed about the proper verdict again, so the judges called on pandits in other courts and colleges in Calcutta to give their opinion. The result was a major debate in the city's press and meeting halls. With no interest in taking part in the debate themselves, the British judges simply executed the view of the college pandits with no comment, and Bhabanicharan ended up gaining control of the land.[29]

Judicial officers found the behaviour of Indians in their courts puzzling, often complaining about their 'litigious' conduct. Some

went further, seeing the courtroom as the setting for the display of
the poor 'general moral character' of their subjects. The judge of
the district of Rangpur in northern Bengal, James Wordsworth,
described their character as 'pusillanimous, ungrateful, and not
uncommonly revengeful'. Another judge in Dhaka, J. D. Paterson,
thought 'their minds are totally uncultivated', and ruled by 'that
low cunning which generally accompanies depravity of heart'. The
myth was that British stability would eventually encourage Indians
to act more honourably, for the long-term.[30]

But it was probably the uncertain decision-making within the
British system of justice which encouraged people to act in the
short-term. The reluctance of British judges to make judgments left
decisions in the hands of unaccountable groups of Indian officers,
who could easily be cajoled and lobbied by powerful groups outside
the court. When they did impose their authority, British judges'
opinions were arbitrary, given for reasons that the judges did not
state and probably did not understand and then not efficiently put
into practice. When judges made decisions for random reasons litigants who otherwise didn't have a chance thought it was worth a
gamble to go to court. The 'litigious' conduct of Indians was perhaps a rational response to the way East India Company's officers
made decisions in court.[31]

British revenue collectors were similarly often perplexed about
how to act in practice. The logic of British power placed revenue
collection above secure property rights. Cornwallis's regulations
insisted that estates were sold if landholders did not pay the amount
due to the Company. British officers imagined that, where landholders could not pay, collectors would preside over the quick
and clinical transfer of an easily defined asset to its more efficient
owner. Landholders could 'guard against the exercise of the collector's powers by the punctual payment of revenue' according to
the documents they had agreed with the Company. Of course, this
was a fantasy.

The arrival of a newly rigid approach to revenue collection in the 1790s coincided with an economic downturn in many parts of India. The price of rice, sugar, silk and other goods fell, so land-holders found it hard to collect rent from producers reliant on the prices of these goods and often failed in their revenue payments. The result was the Company's attempt to dispossess defaulting proprie-tors. One auction after another was held in the open spaces outside the Collector's office, a process local lords found humiliating. Worse than the sale itself for many was the compilation of public inventor-ies of their private property and personal circumstances, as officers were sent to inquire into the landlords 'competence' to manage an estate. When the Collector of Birbhum criticized the district's young raja for 'living in a dissolute manner' the British officer criticized him for 'thus aspers[ing] my character to the people'. It was 'of no consequence', he argued, if estates were 'sold agreeably to the regulations to liquidate the balance due to government'. But he could not stand having his lifestyle disgraced in public. These kinds of inquiries and land sales challenged the authority of local landholder-lords, making it harder for them to collect rent, often precipitating the collapse of their principalities. In Birbhum the first sale of land occurred in December 1795, a few months after the Collector's public challenge to the local landlord. The Company's intervention undermined the prestige and financial viability of the estate, leading to sixteen auctions in quick succession, so that half the estate was lost in five years and the remainder broken up in ten.[32]

Nowhere where Cornwallis's system was put into practice was the old regime replaced by a stable new order of property. In fact, in the years after the East India Company's new regulations were introduced it became harder to identify who had control of which piece of land. To determine which villages needed to be sold and transferred for non-payment of revenue, each Collector required documents that only landholders possessed. The process of sale involved a struggle over the control of local records and local staff, as landholders and the British state battled to win the allegiance of the Indian officials who knew what was going on locally, and could help them gain or lose money by altering the accounts. Landlords about to be dispossessed only gave up their records 'with much trouble and delay', as William Massie, the Collector of Dhaka district, put it. In some case, they burnt down the district record office.

Landholder-lords sometimes won the struggle to retain authority over local resources, at least in the short term. With long-standing connections to the neighbourhood, landholders had far more local knowledge and power than the Company's district officers. They could exploit their relationship with local peasants and officials to stop anyone bidding for land, or prevent people who had paid good money getting near their land. For example, in the southern delta of Bengal, the Paniotty brothers, Greek merchants who made money on the silk route to Assam and China, tried to buy the old principality of Chandradwip ('moon island'), but found it impossible to break the bonds connecting the young raja with local society. The Chandradwip raja presided over civic bodies such as the region's Brahmin caste council. He was central to local networks of patronage, funding the Hindu temples which are still scattered through the countryside, mosques and a Portuguese church. The Paniotty brothers failed to collect rent, and failed to persuade the Company to send more than a handful of troops. 'We do not', they complained, 'purchase the Zumeendaree for after years, that it might be of use after our deaths.' The old landholder regained control and the Paniotty brothers abandoned their brief, unsuccessful foray into the land market, returning to trade.[33]

In the twenty years that followed the arrival of the new system in 1793 most of the great lords of Bengal, Bihar and the northern Coromandel coast lost their land. They were not for the most part replaced by merchants like the Paniottys, but by bureaucrats, clerks and revenue collectors who worked for the local lord or the Company. These men used a range of tactics to expand their portfolios. In Dinajpur, in northern Bengal, a group of Indian officials employed by the local principality misappropriated money due to the Company, causing large parts of the estate to be put on the market which they then bought.[34] Near Allahabad, the senior Indian revenue officer in the district spread the word that 'the collector was like a tiger' whose 'fearful presence' should be shunned, and the estate was sold when arrears built up. These were men who knew the countryside and the new system of British management and could use their knowledge to benefit from chaos.[35]

The new men did not purchase land 'for after years', as the Paniottys put it, but as a short-term investment in an increasingly unstable economic environment. They kept control of their assets by doing exactly the same as the East India Company did with theirs, by trying to secure a fixed return, ensuring they received the same sum of money month in, month out, irrespective of the condition of the land or its tenants. Risk was reduced as landholders outsourced the job of collecting revenue from peasants to middlemen. The only large principality to survive in Bengal, Burdwan, did so by introducing its own permanent settlement, in which revenue collectors were asked to pay a fixed amount of rent to the raja. If they could not they were summarily dispossessed.[36]

The consequences varied from region to region. In some places, where land was plentiful and the climate and ecology allowed peasants to farm without support from political authorities, the economy remained buoyant. Until the end of the nineteenth century there were still thousands of miles of jungle in the eastern districts of Bengal. Similarly, where the East India Company was fighting wars nearby, the economy flourished as revenue collected from other regions was funnelled to markets buying goods for soldiers. The region around Kanpur, a rapidly growing cantonment which supplied British armies throughout north and central India, was an island of wealth amid the depressed and anarchic condition of much of the rest of northern India. Even here, the East India Company's tax collection system broke down for a short while in 1807.[37]

Elsewhere the collapse of eastern India's old principalities together with the colonial regime's new insistence on the rigidity of its revenue demand had a bad, sometimes catastrophic impact on local livelihoods. Lords did not have the money to invest in the infrastructure needed to maintain local prosperity. As a result irrigation canals silted up, roads fell into disrepair, ferry men went out of business and markets declined. Production shrank in western Bengal and Bihar. But the greatest crisis took place on the northern Coromandel coast, the once wealthy tract of land which included Polavaram, where Mangapati Reddy had lost his estate. There, the effort of a succession of new landholders to extract from their tenants 'the utmost possible amount of present revenue' had stripped the land of resources. The region's infrastructure fell apart. To give one example, a few miles south-east of Rajahmundry, on the road to the old port city of Machilipatnam, the raja of the small village of Challipatam had cleared the jungle and erected inns, shops and places of worship, 'for the reception of travellers of all nations', planting 'coconut and other fruit gardens to render the place populous and comfortable'. The Company had insisted on a fixed revenue demand but was unable to protect the coconut glades from neighbouring landholders, so the road-stop fell into ruin, and the quality of the road itself started to deteriorate, too.[38]

As the institutions which sustained good living conditions collapsed in places like these, peasants fled to neighbouring areas even where there was much poorer soil, from the region around Challipatam to the lands governed by the Nizam of Hyderabad, for example. Local manufacturing collapsed: the weaving villages around Rajahmundry, where Benjamin Branfill had once been posted, had more than 7,000 looms in the 1780s, less than half that number fifty years later. A few years of low prices and bad harvests pushed the district over the edge into famine. In the same area, a fifth of the district's 740,000 population was lost to migration and death in the third and fourth decades of the nineteenth century.[39]

Cornwallis's 'new system' was intended to introduce financial stability and moral rectitude to the East India Company's government of its Indian territories for the first time. Later imperial ideologues imagined it did both. But Cornwallis's rules upheld the British sense of their virtue by diminishing the power and capacity for independent judgement of British officers, giving them little incentive and even less time to monitor the conduct of their Indian subordinates. The new regime still relied on corruption and violence, but it was pushed down, out of the sight of the enclaves where the Company's British covenanted servants lived; corruption was increasingly identified as a peculiar trait of Indian society. Unsurprisingly, Britons stationed in the countryside were prickly, defensive and profoundly protective of their status.

The new rules did not create a regime able to guarantee its own financial security. The collapse of the old principalities and the decline in the region's agrarian society meant the Company's collectors could rarely collect the revenue they demanded from landholders. The Company only survived because of a kind of accounting 'magic'. The cash collected from purchasers at land auctions was not separated from ordinary revenue collection in each district's accounts. The shortfall in revenue was made up from the proceeds of land sales. In Bengal, 9 per cent of the Company's land revenue came from the sale of land.[40] In Godavari district, where Mangapati Reddy was ousted as zamindar, 11 per cent was 'derived from the capital of strangers', as the official Henry Montgomery put it, rather than the capacity of landholders to collect revenue from each district's agrarian production. The Company's economic survival was dependent on the continual resale of an asset whose price was far higher than its real value.[41]

Eventually, though, land prices collapsed. In Bengal, the increase in cultivation of new crops for exports like indigo and opium kept land prices high in the short term, but the land market was glutted and collapsed in 1830. By then, financial institutions had started to invest in land, so the crash in the value of land in 1830 had catastrophic consequences for Calcutta's commercial economy, as banks went to the wall and agency houses collapsed. The East India Company only survived by borrowing money in Britain, by making massive cuts in its expenditure and by increasing its sale of narcotics, opium especially, to China.[42]

Meanwhile, new landholders had started to lobby the British to adjust their rules to help them hold onto their lands. Constantly harassed by the old lords they had replaced or by peasants and village leaders who refused to submit and pay revenue to their new masters, the new men needed strong backing from the East India Company if they had any chance of supplying the British with a stable stream of revenue. Time after time, British officers in the districts were faced with a quandary: whether to augment the power of a landholder in extracting cash from his tenants, or back the challenge by poorer inhabitants knowing this would curtail the Company's capacity to collect cash. Unsurprisingly, the tendency was to back the new local elite.[43]

Throughout the first three decades of the nineteenth century, the Company eliminated the checks and balances that had prevented landed elites from oppressing their subjects. Changes in the regulations made it far harder for peasants to use the Company's courts to limit landholders' ability to extract rent. The East India Company's violence was used more to protect landholders from their tenants. In Saran district in Bihar in 1842, for example, British officers called in the infantry to suppress a revolt by peasants who felt their rights were being trampled on by the local Raja of Hathwa. The incident created a bitter argument between British officers. The magistrate supported the tenants and the Collector backed the landholder. In this case, the local police commissioner waded in to the dispute and forced the magistrate to be investigated and then sacked. Incidents like these led to the corrosion of the idea of a justice system able to keep a check on the collection of revenue. By the 1850s, the functions of judge and collector had begun to be merged into a single officer whose interest it was to put order and revenue before any attempt to ensure the local balance of power. For their part, the threat of Company violence lifted pressure on landholders to gain the consent of local society, and removed the necessity of negotiating with peasants and members of the local gentry.[44]

One with the Englishmen

In Edmund Burke's tirade against Warren Hastings in the House of Lords, the most grotesque tale of brutality came from a story about events in the small Bengali town of Rangpur. Describing the actions of a revenue farmer called Raja Devi Singh who was appointed by Hastings, Burke spoke about wedges being driven into the joints of fingers, children being beaten and the houses of peasants burnt down. He culled these from official reports and added shocking (but entirely fictitious) accounts of sexual violence. The aim of Burke's catalogue of cruelty was to 'work up the popular senses' against Hastings, arousing the base 'mobbish' (as he put it) feelings of his audience. According to the trial reporter, Burke's descriptions of events in Rangpur were 'more vivid, more harrowing, and more horrific, than human utterance on either fact or fancy, perhaps, ever formed before'. The horrified response in London about events in Rangpur contributed to a dramatic change in the way this district of northern Bengal itself was ruled. But those changes transformed Rangpur in a way that would have horrified even Burke.[45]

With a population of perhaps half a million, located fifty miles south of the foothills of the Himalayas, Rangpur district was a prosperous area, a vital marketplace on the eastern silk route, trading goods between India, Bhutan and China. In Rangpur authority had been exercised by a handful of principalities originally created by officers of the Mughal state in the late seventeenth century. During the eighteenth century these officers laid out markets and built courts, creating seats of local power under the distant surveillance of the Mughal capital at Murshidabad, a hundred miles south-west, turning themselves into princes and rajas. Their descendants lived in brick forts in modest splendour. These landholder-kings spent most of their time going back and forth negotiating with peasants, weavers and traders, ensuring the continued prosperity of the region. Peasants' 'frequent migration from one village to another' meant landholders needed to attract them with low rents, and financial support for local civic institutions. It was the 'custom of the country' for peasants only to pay rent on crops they cut and sold, for example. British district officers were bemused by all the coming and going, imagining, wrongly, that prosperity only came with permanence. But the economic life of the district was enough to support the region's own currency, the narayani rupee, and this made an appointment to Rangpur one of the Company's most lucrative postings for British officers.[46]

From the late 1780s the East India Company's new system brought a British-style bureaucracy to Rangpur; before then the area had been governed from the old Mughal settlement of Ghoraghat. Rangpur was chosen because it was the site of a Company warehouse where goods were bought, sold and stored on the route to China. By the early nineteenth century a population of perhaps 15,000 were housed in 3,000 buildings made of mud and straw, and forty-two of brick. They were serviced by ten shops, seven Hindu temples and six mosques. The Company's practice of siting its administrative offices away from the marketplace or landholder's house meant that Rangpur was merely a cluster of administrative and commercial buildings separated by fields, a settlement without the civic life of a normal town.[47]

The British district officers who arrived in the 1790s tried to fix the rights of both farmers and landholders with new pieces of paper, insisting that the exact amount written down was paid every month. The new system cut the bonds of mutual obligation that connected peasant and lords and was resisted by all classes. Landholders complained about the new system in a collectively organized petition. The landholders' criticism was that unless the Company was more lenient in its revenue demands they would have to use violence to collect it, and that would cause peasants to flee. As they put it, 'to use any coercive measures to secure payment would cause a desertion among the Ryotts [peasants], and be productive of infinite losses.' The Company's new system meant 'our Estates have been subjected to sale and we are reduced to the distress of disposing of our effects and taking loans from bankers.' The District Collector was sympathetic, but the Board of Revenue refused to allow a deduction in the revenue demand. When the Collector tried to sell land, some landholders tried to resist by less polite means. Early one morning in October 1798, the Collector's office was burnt to the ground, 'with the whole of the records therein deposited'. With no records, British officers were unable to calculate how much land should be sold to pay arrears of revenue. Despite the protestations of the old landholders, auctions were held and land sold. Between 1793 and 1810, in sales that took place every month, large chunks of every one of Rangpur's twelve main estates were cut up and sold.[48]

Some of eastern India's great nineteenth-century families built their livelihoods by buying estates in Rangpur. Krishna Kanta Nandy was Warren Hastings' agent and bought an estate in the district to add to lands scattered throughout the rest of Bengal. Rai Danishmand Nityananda was a weaver who ended up as assistant to the Commercial Resident at Rangpur, and one of the region's great magnates. Darpanarayan Tagore was *diwan* to another British officer, grandfather of the merchant and political leader Prosanna Kumar Tagore. As the importance of landed families having a visible, political presence in the countryside died out, Rangpur's greatest landholders spent most of their time in the city of Calcutta. For these *bhadralok* (the word means polite people, and was used to refer to Bengal's elite) families, authority and prestige no longer came from being a leading figure in local society. Rather, it was about taking part in the cultural life of the province's metropolis. Landholders even started to pressure the government from the city, not the countryside. After the deaths of his grandfather and father, Prosanna Kumar Tagore was the largest landholder of Rangpur district and the driving force behind the Landholders' Association, a body for upholding landholders who had benefited from the permanent settlement; it was founded in 1838 in Calcutta. Prosanna Kumar became a lawyer and clerk to the Governor-General's council, and bequeathed some of his fortune to support a series of lectures in law. His son converted to Christianity, was disowned by his father and became India's first British-trained barrister, being called to the bar from Lincoln's Inn in 1862. For these men, buying real estate was simply a financial transaction, a sensible investment with a regular return according to rules written at the place where they thought power lay, Calcutta.[49]

One of the most fervent criticisms of the new system came from a man who had spent many years in Rangpur too. Rammohan Roy was perhaps nineteenth-century Bengal's most important intellectual, a translator, newspaper proprietor, political and religious reformer, described variously as 'the father of modern India' and India's first liberal. Rammohan was born in the 1770s, into the Brahmin family of a minor Mughal official and small-time landholder in western Bengal. In his late twenties he was employed as translator and broker for a succession of British officers, eventually working in Rangpur for the Collector John Digby from 1809. Digby worked closely with Rammohan for a decade, describing him as a man of 'industry, integrity and education', from a 'respectable family'.[50] He lobbied hard to have Rammohan appointed to the official position of *diwan*, the most senior Indian official in a district, and paid him privately when the Board of Revenue refused. Unusually for the times, their relationship was a reciprocal one. Digby enjoyed Rammohan's connections to Rangpur's Indian elite, and Rammohan learnt English and Greek, and began to read European political philosophy and works on religious reform with his employer.[51]

Rammohan moved to Calcutta when Digby retired in 1815. As the East India Company's monopoly on trade was abolished in 1813, and restrictions on press freedom lifted in 1818, these years saw the short-lived blossoming of a cosmopolitan civil and literary culture in the East India Company's capital city. Rammohan was at the centre of this liberal life. From the pages of his newspapers and the podium of Calcutta Town Hall he supported a succession of classically liberal causes: freedom of the press, free trade, the security of property held by both men and women and the spread of trial by jury. His arguments were designed to instil self-confidence in Indians, to create more space for them to rule themselves and to create better connections between wealthy Indians and the East India Company's bureaucracy which, Rammohan argued, treated Indians like strangers and did not understand the country or its people well.[52]

As a jealous observer from Bombay complained, these years saw rich Indians and Britons together create in Calcutta a 'community of feeling' which spawned a spate of Anglo-Indian 'societies, meetings, projections'. A 'current of healthy sympathy and sentiment seems to pervade the monied mass'. Like other members of his liberal political milieu, Rammohan was friends and collaborator with British traders, journalists and lawyers, a group who were interested in creating a life for themselves in India outside the rigid structures of the Company and who were equally keen to create of a free civil society in Bengal. His closest friend was Dwarkanath Tagore, grandfather of the poet Rabindranath and another Rangpur zamindar who created a firm to trade in coal in collaboration with a British merchant, John Palmer. Dwarkanath noted that British power was exercised differently in Calcutta compared with the countryside. It was their collaboration with 'merchants, agents and other independent English settlers' which made sure Indians who had moved to Calcutta were in a better condition than 'their countrymen in the mofussil', Dwarkanath argued. Both Rammohan and Dwarkanath saw one solution to Bengal's poverty as the migration of more Britons to India, a cause both men backed against opposition from both the East India Company and Indians more anxious about British power. Their argument was that the Company would take India's districts seriously if British citizens lived there; that British rule would no longer contribute to chaos and poverty if the physical distance separating ruler and ruled was broken down by European settlement.[53]

Rammohan travelled to Britain, in 1831, as an emissary of the Mughal emperor, Akbar II. By then, Akbar's world had shrunk to no more than an enclave surrounded by British officers in Delhi.

In Rammohan he had a man who understood both Indian politics
and the workings of the East India Company to make the case for a
larger subsidy before the King and ministers in London: Rammohan
spoke Persian and Arabic, as well as English, Sanskrit and Bengali.

In Britain, the East India Company blocked Rammohan's official
mission by claiming he was a British subject, so could not be an
official of the Mughal empire. But between his arrival at Liverpool
in April 1831 and his death at Bristol two and a half years later,
Rammohan was feted by radicals and royalty alike and made into
an exotic celebrity of whom everyone wanted to catch a glimpse.
Despite always insisting he was indeed a British subject, Rammohan
was seated with the foreign ambassadors at the coronation of
William IV. Despite the Company's misgivings, he was received as
the Mughal emperor's emissary by the new King.[54] The Whig politician Thomas Macaulay, soon to leave for a senior official position
in India himself, wrote of waiting until midnight for Rammohan
to arrive at a party before leaving 'in despair' when he failed to
show up. The aged utilitarian philosopher Jeremy Bentham suggested Rammohan stand as a Member of Parliament 'to subdue the
prejudices of colour', an option Rammohan seriously considered.[55]

During this brief moment of Anglo–Indian civility, Rammohan
articulated a thoroughgoing critique of the way British officers governed India. As historian C. A. Bayly noted, Rammohan thought
Cornwallis had enshrined 'a social contract between government
and incipient civil society'. In a series of submissions to the House of
Commons, Rammohan argued that the contract had been broken;
its breakdown had made the condition of India's rural poor deteriorate during the previous forty years. Rammohan's solution was
to force the Company's government out from its dark offices to be
visible and accountable to an Indian public sphere that extended into
the *mofussil*, into towns like Rangpur, as well as Calcutta.

Rammohan argued that India needed to return to its tradition
of justice being meted out in public. He was insistent that the
Company publicize its actions by printing and posting notices

across the countryside, at marketplaces, ferries and police offices. He argued that courts needed to be constructed for large numbers of people 'hearing and witnessing the whole proceedings' and the minutes published. Rammohan doubted the ability of British officers, troubled by 'the heat of the climate' and Indian languages they found difficult to understood, to make good judgements on their own. In reality, Rammohan argued, Indian officers were collecting revenue and deciding disputes. But low pay and no scrutiny meant it was hardly surprising corruption was rife. Rammohan wanted to Indianize the collection of revenue entirely, appointing distinguished local men as revenue officers at a third of the cost of Europeans and placing their actions in public view. Redundant British officers would be transferred to 'some other department, or allowed to retire on a suitable pension'. The only British officer to stay in the countryside would be the judge who would administer justice on a bench alongside two Indian assessors. Rammohan's challenge to the Company was that a stable and powerful British government in India needed to be visible and accountable to Indians, and give 'natives' positions of 'trust and responsibility' within the state. Rammohan's argument was that the system of government established in the 1790s had failed to enlist Indian allies.[56]

Rammohan's project was to civilize the Company's authoritarian style of rule by forcing it to share power with local Indian elites as well as British merchants, in the process spreading the propertied cosmopolitanism they had created in Calcutta into the countryside. Rammohan's plan echoed Warren Hastings' attempt to return to a Mughal constitution and limit British power by Indian officers. In Rammohan's own day, a few Britons tried to imagine greater political union with Indians. The Governor-General in post during Rammohan's last two years in India, Lord William Bentinck, spoke in a language suffused with talk of regenerating Indian public life. These were mere words. In fact, Bentinck spent most of his time dealing with the deficit caused by the collapse of Bengal's rural economy, most controversially cutting the pay of soldiers.

Nonetheless, when he left Bengal Bentinck was feted by educated Bengalis as 'the man who first taught us to forget the distinction between conquerors and conquered and to become, in heart and mind, in hopes and aspiration, one with Englishmen'.[57]

The everyday practice of empire beyond India's cosmopolitan capital cities still relied on precisely that distinction. For most of the East India Company's hierarchy, maintaining a separation between Britons and Indians was essential to the assertion of European power in a conquered society. For them, there could be no alliance even with the new men their system of government had created. British rule depended on distance even if that meant the Company sacrificed any chance of exercising effective power into the countryside.

The argument Rammohan made about creating a more inclusive regime was taken seriously in parliament and in London garden parties. But it always ran up against the anxieties of the colonial bureaucracy. In British India's districts, British officers were too keen to insist that every member of the local population subordinate themselves to the British hierarchy to listen to criticism. Symptomatic was the treatment meted to Rammohan when he passed the Collector of the district of Bhagalpur, Sir Frederick Hamilton, on 1 January 1809. Rammohan was in a closed palanquin, so didn't salute. The British officer stopped him, shouted at him for not paying proper respect to an imperial official, and then thrashed one of his servants. Rammohan wrote to the Governor-General complaining about being 'degraded by a representative of the supreme political power' and Hamilton was mildly reprimanded. But Rammohan's complaints to the Governor-General blocked his career in the Company's administration. In practice, Company officials were not even willing to negotiate with people who wanted to be their allies.[58]

6

THEATRES OF ANARCHY

In May 1799, 150 soldiers commanded by Raja Ravivarma Narasimha Domba Heggade destroyed the temple of Manjeshwar, removing its ornamental chariots and many sacks of gold. Situated in the Kanara region halfway between Bombay and the southern tip of India, the temple is a central shrine for the Gaudi Saraswati Brahmins, a mobile community of merchants and bureaucrats scattered along India's western coast. The destruction of Manjeshwar temple occurred a few days after a moment of British conquest supposed to bring peace and order to the area. The temple's destruction suggests British victory did not bring an end to fighting.

Ravivarma was the chief of Vittala, a fortified temple town twenty-five miles inland from Manjeshwar. For the last forty years of the eighteenth century this small kingdom, together with the rest of the area now forming the state of Karnataka, came under the rule of Mysore, the regime built by the brilliant generals Haidar Ali and his son Tipu Sultan after 1761 whose growth the British fought in a succession of wars between 1767 and 1799. Ravivarma's family had sporadically enlisted in Mysore's military projects, his great-uncle briefly embracing Islam as well as Haidar Ali's power. By the last Anglo-Mysore war Ravivarma was an ally of the British. His troops were supplied with British guns and those guns helped defeat Tipu

Sultan. But British conquest did not bring peace. The guns the
Company gave were turned first against Manjeshwar temple and,
eventually, against British power.

Historians usually see the period between 1798 and 1818 as
the final British conquest of India, a time when the East India
Company's domination was successfully asserted throughout the
subcontinent. These were indeed years when the Company subjected all the territory along India's great coastlines and rivers to
British power, leaving only a few regimes in the dry hinterland in
Indian hands. But to punctuate these two decades with the dates
of battles and assume they mark the history of the consolidation of
imperial rule is to mistake the Company's rhetoric for reality. The
British imagined peace only came with total domination, but that
was never possible. In reality, after every conquest British power
always seemed shaky and fragile.

Manjeshwar is part of the coastal strip of land along the sea which
stretches from Goa to the tip of India, and which has always been
hard for states to subdue. Just like the territory around Anjengo
further south, the Kanara region around Manjeshwar was a land of
assertive warrior-communities which successfully resisted invasions
of Mughal and Maratha armies for generations. The arts of violence
were finely cultivated; this was the home of kalarippayyatu, one of
the world's oldest martial arts. Yet by the 1790s, its elaborate swords
and shields had been replaced by muskets and cannons. Expensive
war between the British and Mysore had brought a far less civilized
form of conflict to the neighbourhood that lingered far longer than
the theoretical moment of British conquest.[1]

When the British expelled the Mysore regime from Kanara they
found a society up in arms. 'Everything is fear and distrust – a man
when a stranger asks him the road eyes him with suspicion, or
starts back and draws a knife to defend himself.' Lieutenant Colonel
Thomas Munro was sent to Kanara to settle the province and collect
revenue in the months after Tipu's defeat. Munro suggested that
men were armed 'not merely both with matchlocks and swords,

but with flintlocks which they have either purchased or received as allies of one of the various European settlements of the coast'. It was not rare for people to walk with unsheathed weapons in the street. Farmers tilled the soil with guns strapped to their backs. Munro thought local rulers like Ravivarma used the chaos of war to extend their own power. '[P]etty chiefs . . . look anxiously forward to times of confusion and weakness in order to render themselves masters of some district or other,' he wrote.[2]

That was exactly what Ravivarma tried to do. The warlord thought his alliance with the British meant he would be allowed to extend his control over local institutions, including temples. Perhaps he also felt challenged by centres of Hindu piety he could not control. Whether the British gave him tacit permission to raid the temple or not, the action brought an enraged response from local Brahmins who lobbied Thomas Munro to act. By the beginning of 1800, Munro believed Ravivarma's independence was a threat to the East India Company. He thought that British security depended on chiefs 'leaving the practice of arms' and instead taking up 'habits of order and industry'. When Munro asked Ravivarma to hand over his guns, he refused. Instead of acquiescing to a quiet life and a Company pension under the civil government of the British, Ravivarma joined up with other local leaders, sent emissaries to Kanara's village assemblies and called on peasants to gather and fight the British.

By April 1800, men commanded by this recent ally of the East India Company had driven the British out of a thirty-mile swathe of territory in every direction from Manjeshwar, capturing forts and collecting money from villagers. British forces pushed back. Munro eventually forced the insurgents to retreat to their fort at Vittala itself. Holed up in his home town, Ravivarma surrendered, believing that the Company would be lenient to its one-time ally. But Munro had other ideas. On 22 August, with three relations and five other men, Ravivarma was hanged from Light House Hill, the highest point in the nearby city of Mangalore. 'We may now, by making an example of him and his associates, secure [K]anara from internal disturbances in the future,' Munro argued.[3]

Munro's solution to chaos and violence was to introduce martial law, disarm the population and dispossess the local rajas. 'Till it is done,' he said, 'our Conquest is not complete.'[4] But there was a paradox. The British had no power to dispossess on their own. Their domination depended on the Company's ability to enlist new allies and support other Indian sources of power. The soldiers who defeated Ravivarma were not East India Company recruits but retainers of Kumar Heggade, a rival of Ravivarma's from the town of Bantwal, only twelve miles north of the rebel chief's base. Kumar had his own aims, which did not necessarily mesh with the Company's. Allying with the Company gave him money and the possibility of building his own independent authority in place of a local rival that might, in the future, allow him to confront British power.[5]

Tigers

Thomas Munro's description of anarchy in Kanara was written in a letter to the new Governor-General, Richard Wellesley. Wellesley arrived at Calcutta in 1798. There, he joined his younger brother, Arthur, later more famous as the Duke of Wellington. The sons of a Protestant Irish musician and politician, the Wellesleys were from a family whose everyday life was about the domination of people who had no formal power; but they had not made empire their destiny. Richard graduated from Christ Church, Oxford, before beginning a political career in Dublin and then Westminster. Arthur, nine years younger, went to a horse-riding school in France, before his elder brother bought him an army commission in Ireland. Growing up in an upper-class Protestant Irish family at a time of political turmoil gave them a keen sense of the fragility of political authority. Richard Wellesley only became Governor-General because the British government seemed under threat in his native, embattled Ireland. The Prime Minister, William Pitt, had originally wanted

Lord Cornwallis to return to the subcontinent, but the threat of revolution in Ireland led him to appoint the empire's greatest troubleshooter there instead, and to send Wellesley to India.

When he arrived in the subcontinent Wellesley consciously styled the office of Governor-General on that of the Lord Lieutenant of Ireland, building a grand new Palladian government house in Calcutta, putting the established Anglican church on display and creating a new college to instil a greater sense of discipline in Company officers. Designing a form of government that C. A. Bayly called 'proconsular despotism', Wellesley's aim was to subordinate Company India to a far more absolutist style of rule. In the process, he helped forge a new kind of Tory politics, flexible in religious dogma and economic doctrine but insistent that authority needed to be visibly asserted to stop society from breaking down. This way of thinking was pessimistic about the quick decay of all forms of order if power was openly challenged. The new Tory imperialism created a different form of government in newly conquered British territory compared to the Whig system of private property rights introduced to the East India Company's eastern lands.[6]

The French Revolution was critical to this mentality. France had degenerated into political violence when the Wellesleys were in their formative years, their teens and early twenties. The revolution seemed to prove how quickly the social order could collapse without a strong military elite. The Wellesleys learnt the need to be liberal on questions like free trade and religious toleration if political authority was to be maintained. Later, as the Duke of Wellington and briefly Prime Minister, Arthur Wellesley faced an onslaught from fellow Tories for giving Catholics the vote. But in Britain and India Wellesleyan politics was ruled by the belief that any diminution in the power of the state and the elite that ruled it would unleash anarchy.

In India the attitude of Richard and Arthur Wellesley quickly meshed with the views of a group of men of a militaristic disposition who had passed these tumultuous years fighting and trying to build British political power in India. At the centre of the Wellesley circle were Thomas Munro and John Malcolm, two soldiers who had been stationed in India since the 1780s and who worked closely with Arthur Wellesley in the aftermath of the Mysore war. Like the Wellesleys, Malcolm and Munro came from civilian families with little connection to empire. John Malcolm's father was a tenant farmer from the Scottish borders, Thomas Munro was the son of a Glasgow merchant who made money trading across the Atlantic Ocean but whose prospect of wealth was blocked by American independence. Instead of having its own tradition and ways of life, soldiering for these men was an instrument for imposing the power of the British state, as well as a way to make a name and some money. The Wellesleys, Munro and Malcolm all had fortunes to amass or to restore.

These men were connected with a younger group of civilian officers who articulated a less hawkish variation of the same set of ideas, among them Neil Edmonstone (son of a Scottish MP), Mounstuart Elphinestone (son of a Scottish laird) and Charles Metcalfe (the only one with previous Indian connections, from an Anglo-Irish family of Company soldiers). They shared a similar style, valuing quick action rather than contemplation or conversation, prizing blunt, frank and often forceful responses, guided by a strong sense of the imperilled nature of political power. They all thought British rule in India was based on violence and the display of violence; the Wellesley circle never imagined Indians would ever accept British rule by consent. As the by-then knighted Sir John Malcolm, political agent with Arthur Wellesley during the Maratha wars and later Governor of Bombay, wrote in 1832, 'our Eastern empire ... has been acquired, and must be maintained, by the sword'. '[W]e never can expect active support in the hour of danger from the mass of the population of India. A passive allegiance is all these will ever give to their foreign masters.'[7]

Richard Wellesley arrived as Governor-General in April 1798.

Within eight months, he put the East India Company's sword into action against the state of Mysore. Ruled by the Hindu Wodeyar family since the early seventeenth century, Mysore controlled a large swathe of territory as part of the Mughal political system. That role was broken when the brilliant leader of the Maratha army, Haidar Ali, staged a coup in 1761 and took control of the state. From the beginning, this expansionist military regime was seen as a threat to British interests in southern India. Particularly worrying was the possibility of an alliance with France.

French craftsmen had built the mechanism inside the famous life-size toy tiger that is now on display in London's Victoria and Albert Museum. The tiger, a symbol of the Mysore regime, has sunk its fangs into the throat of a prostrate European man, and it roars when it bites. Wellesley was worried that France and India would collaborate in more than symbolic craftwork, fearing particularly that the French navy would invade western India from its base at Mauritius to join up with Mysore and drive the British from southern India.

Even before he landed in Calcutta in May 1798, the new Governor-General Richard Wellesley decided the East India Company would only be safe if Haidar Ali's son and successor, Tipu Sultan, was drawn into war, defeated and forced to hand over at least the western coastal lands to the British. In February 1799 Wellesley organized a 26,000-strong army to march from Madras, to join 20,000 troops belonging to the Nizam of Hyderabad marching from the north and a British group of 4,000 from the west. The march was slower than anticipated because of the amount of equipment to be transported: battering machines and mining gear, thousands of bullocks loaded with rice and wheat as well as senior officers' luxurious tents and silver-plated table sets. The Company's armies arrived at Tipu's capital of Sriringapatam in April. The city survived a month's siege, but on 2 May the Company managed to blow a series of big holes in the walls of the fort and then, over the next two days, fought their way into the city. Tipu was seen shooting from the battlements with hunting rifles, but was killed in the fighting, his still warm body later found in a room full of corpses. Inside the palace, soldiers found Tipu's mechanical tiger, and three of the real beasts, caged and starving.[8]

Arthur Wellesley was appointed military governor of Tipu's lands. His first act was to shoot the tigers: '[T]here is no food for them, and nobody to attend them, and they are getting violent.' Unable to tame three angry big cats, Arthur Wellesley nonetheless acted as sovereign over this territory at a few strategic sites. A combination of punitive violence and attention to the interests of elites quickly secured peace and order in the towns of Mysore and Sriringapatam themselves. Soldiers patrolled the streets, looters were summarily hanged, court rituals were re-established and property secured. Wellesley went door to door to reassure prominent citizens of Mysore. Within four days, the bazaars had reopened and were stocked with goods.[9]

But these tactics could only work for short periods of time and over small areas. Beyond its capital, the East India Company's conquest of Mysore brought increased chaos and violence. British power imposed authority on a small enclave where trade, troops and officials were centred, and then only targeted forces that offered a major challenge to the East India Company's power beyond. The aim of victory was merely to restore 'the peace and safety of the British foundations of India', as Wellesley put it. There was no practical effort to protect the livelihoods of the people they ruled. Beyond the small zones the British controlled the situation was anarchic. Violence was fuelled by the dispersal of men with guns in both Mysore and the East India Company's army. Local chiefs like Ravivarma used this plentiful military labour force to build their own independent power, using their soldiers to violently subdue tracts of countryside. Beyond its ordered enclaves, British power oscillated inconsistently between anxious efforts to extirpate any potentially insurgent armed force, and the desperate attempt to cultivate alliances, between what the historian Mesrob Vartavarian calls 'terror tactics and strategic concessions'.[10]

Together, these conflicts involved greater violence and bigger armies than those which conquered large, stable states like Mysore or the Marathas. In northern Kerala, to the south of Kanara, Raja Pazhassi Varma gathered local Muslim and Hindu warriors (Nairs and Mapillas) and Pathans who had been disbanded from Tipu's army to challenge British power. They were eventually only suppressed after thousands of British troops chased them through forests in 1805.

The British response was often brutal, but was also shaped by the Company's limited power. The so-called 'Poligar wars' of 1799–1801 (poligar is a word from the Telugu *palegadu* or Tamil *palaiyakkarar*, or head of a military camp) saw the Company try to subdue chiefs who had captured castles and imposed their power over the local countryside around Tirulnelveli in the south-east.

The greatest poligar leader, Kattaboma Nayakkar, was hanged in October 1799 in front of an 'assembly' of other leaders. In the months afterwards British officers imagined this 'unparalleled triumph to the cause of order' had frightened forty-two poligars into demolishing their forts. The British wrote pompously celebrating their now absolute authority, the Collector of the region suggesting that 'the rebellions have been subdued ... the oppressed have been upheld and exalted ... and the extinction of divided authority has restored the fairest province of the Carnatic.' But with 20,000 poligar troops in arms against the British, the Company had little power to impose its will. Within two years of Kattaboma's death the Company was 'disconcerted' that forts once supposedly demolished had 'risen from the ground', 'as if by the wave of a magician's wand' and were being used against the Company in a second wave of rebellion.[11]

After spending eighteen months in Kanara, Thomas Munro was transferred to take charge of the Ceded Districts, a tract of land where once again the British capture of territory was followed by an uprising. Now the region of Andhra Pradesh called Rayalaseema, the Ceded Districts were 26,000 square miles of thin, dry, gravelly soil, which had been transferred from the Nizam of Hyderabad in compensation for the Company's help in defeating his enemy Tipu. As in Kanara and Tirulnelveli, local lords used the recent political turmoil to increase their power. Eighty poligars with perhaps 30,000 retainers refused to submit to the Company's government, engaging in what Munro described as 'predatory warfare'. They were joined by disbanded unpaid soldiers from the Nizam of Hyderabad's army.

Munro asked his superiors for military command of the region to put into practice the same strategy as in Kanara, to dispossess and then impose British power directly on village society by forcing villagers to pay rent directly to the Company. Again he wanted to use brute force against the poligars. 'I am convinced that it is possible to expel them all and to hang the great part of them,' he said. Munro was not made a general, so could not hang all those he wanted to, but he was assisted by thirty-six companies of soldiers, 'with a due proportion of guns and artillery', making a total of at least 5,000 troops with which to impose British power. They did so with highly visible displays of force. The fort of the old, blind chief of the village of Vemulakota was violently captured in May 1801. Six months later the fort of Ternakal was taken after two weeks of fighting. Together these two minor and forgotten moments of pacification saw greater casualties to the Company than the Battle of Plassey, with 233 Company troops lost. In response, some local chiefs did submit, and some were pensioned off. Others disappeared into the wilds or to the tribal districts of central India, and a few carried on fighting. Operations to suppress insurgency after the supposed moment of 'conquest' were more violent than conquest itself, and still left British authority shaky.[12]

Armed republics

Interspersed through this violence Munro led a team of British and Indian officers moving from village to village assessing how much tax each farmer needed to pay, hearing complaints and collecting cash. Thomas Munro was putting into practice a new style of rule, pioneered in Kanara and then developed in the Ceded Districts and beyond. This was the 'raiyatwar' system. Instead of using landlords to oversee taxation and maintain order, the system dispossessed local chiefs and then created new institutions for collecting revenue directly from peasants, or *raiyats*, hence the system's name.

Munro's system was a dramatic break with both pre-British practice and the way the East India Company did things in the early years. It relied on the deployment of military force on an unprecedented scale. It also involved the British employing a much larger cadre of Indian revenue officers to survey land and collect money directly from peasants. In each district, the Collector's job changed from distant oversight to the active, everyday assertion of British power. It relied on the Company's hierarchy giving district officers an unprecedented amount of discretion. As Munro put it in his usual ironic way, the system would only work if his superiors could 'trust my supposed skill in discerning what they were made of by catichising them on revenue and lanaterising their physiognomies'.[13]

Implausibly, Munro claimed these new armies of soldiers and bureaucrats were merely returning India to the norms of ancient Indian society. Here, Munro made an entirely novel set of arguments about the nature of landed society in India. In the reports he sent to Madras's Board of Revenue from Kanara, he argued that chiefs like Ravivarma Narasimha Domba Heggade were usurpers who had illegally seized land. The real owners, according to Munro, were the peasants who lived in homesteads scattered throughout Kanara's countryside, and who cultivated the soil. There were, Munro argued, documents proving that peasants had enjoyed secure property rights and paid a low, fixed rate of rent for 350 years before Mysore's invasion. Most of these 'black books' had been conveniently destroyed by Haidar Ali and Tipu Sultan, but Munro said enough of them survived to prove the point. In the Ceded Districts, there were no black books. But there, too, Munro claimed ancient precedent for his dispossession of local lords and the reconstruction of a social order based on the supposedly natural, quiet industry of peasant proprietors.

Munro's arguments about how an imperial power could govern the war-torn lands of southern India initiated one of the most powerful ideas about India, that India was a society of self-sufficient villages. As Munro's friend Sir Charles Metcalfe later wrote, 'village communities are like little republics, having nearly everything that they can want within themselves, and almost independent of any foreign relations'. 'They seem to last where nothing else lasts', Metcalfe continued. The notion that the real India lay in autonomous villages not towns would become one of the most powerful myths about South Asia, driving British policy in the late nineteenth century as well as the attitude of nationalists like M. K. Gandhi. In the early 1800s, it was an entirely new idea.[14]

This concept of village India emerged in very peculiar circumstances. It was an idea that described a society fractured by war. Peasants looked as if they led entirely 'independent' lives because they cut themselves off in times of crisis, retreating behind village walls to protect themselves from violence wrought by the marauding armies of the East India Company, Mysore or the Marathas. Officers like Munro mistook a peculiar practice for the permanent state of things. They did so conveniently, to justify a strategy which removed argumentative political intermediaries who seemed a dangerous threat to British power. The myth of village India depicted the country as a place without local political leaders, as an essentially unpolitical society inhabited by peasants who wanted nothing more than to cultivate their fields in peace. This was a picture not of India as it actually was but as the British wanted it to be.

But over the next thirty years, in fits and starts the raiyatwar system was introduced throughout the parts of southern and western India that the East India Company had recently conquered. A variation of the scheme developed by Charles Metcalfe in the conquered lands of the north, collected taxes from villages combining their resources together rather than individual peasants, and other versions were tried in different places. Wherever it was implemented, raiyatwar began as a form of military rule. Its spread was initially supported by soldier-administrators like Munro and political officers like Metcalfe, but was resisted by most of the East India Company's civilian officers. To them Munro's scheme was costly and time-consuming, dragging the British into unnecessary complications when they should simply have settled lands with land-holders and let go. Edward Strachey, a former judge in Bengal who later worked for the East India Company in London, was typically critical. He noted that the spread of raiyatwar was driven by the rising 'influence' of 'collectors and soldiers', and the decline in the influence of judges. For Strachey individuals like Munro were 'good and able men', but they 'don't like justice much'. '[O]ne must look with a jealous eye to everything that comes from such a quarter on such a subject.' These arguments were overcome because raiyatwar offered a convenient response to justify the projection of British power at a moment when the Company's authority seemed to be continually in crisis. Raiyatwar allowed the British to imagine they could dispense with troublesome local political leaders. Of course, in practice the idea that the British could govern India without intermediaries was a fantasy. In reality, the East India Company had no choice but to deal with Indian political authorities who could marshal men and resources and escalate what, to the British, seemed a frightening scale of violence.[15]

After the defeat of Tipu Sultan, the East India Company handed a diminished Mysore state back to the old Wodeyar family, and con-cerned itself with other threats to its presence in India. In the late 1790s, the British became increasingly paranoid about the fragmen-tation of the Maratha regime. The devastating defeat by the Afghans at the Battle of Panipat in 1761 had shattered Maratha unity. Over the next generation, Maratha power was rebuilt in capitals through-out west-central India, notably under the aegis of Mahadji Shinde at Gwalior, Raghoji II Bhonsle at Nagpur, Manaji Rao Gaekwad at Baroda and perhaps the most skilled Maratha administrator of her generation, Ahilyabhai Holkar, at Indore. These men and women were descendants of the new leaders who had created a strong, centralized Maratha state in the early eighteenth century. Half a century later, they rebuilt authority in ordered, prosperous states, but this time they did it in their own local capitals, undermining the capacity of any central leader to hold the Maratha regime together. The Peshwa, based at Pune, had once been the supreme Maratha political administrator but was now dramatically undermined by new centres of Maratha power. Peshwa Madhav Rao felt so constrained by these competing houses that he committed suicide in 1795.

The East India Company's paranoia escalated intra-Maratha conflict; the Company, again, was particularly worried about one or other Maratha politics allying with France. Troops from Shinde were already being trained and led by French mercenary officers, for example. Richard Wellesley's strategy was to entice as many Maratha leaders as he could into a grand alliance, offering to buy the support of Company troops. All five Maratha leaders resisted the British move to begin with. But after he was driven from Pune by more powerful rivals, the new Peshwa sought British help, and signed a treaty with the Company in exchange for British help in recapturing his capital. In exchange, the Company insisted on revenue from a third of the Peshwa's domains to pay for the troops. The four other Maratha chiefs were horrified at this submission of their one-time leader to British power, and prepared to fight. As the Pathan warlord Amir Khan, then an ally of Holkar, put it, the Peshwa's decision to submit to the Company showed he had 'taken leave of his senses' and deserved to be brought down. The Company and the majority of the Maratha houses prepared for war.

The key to victory for the British was to secure the supply of food and armaments to their army. In the two years running up to the beginning of the conflict, Arthur Wellesley spent much of his time harassing and cajoling British officers and Indian political leaders into sending supplies. These years saw massive bullock droves crossing central India, laden with rice: 32,000 bullocks were sent from Sriringapatam to the Company's northward marching armies in a single month, January 1803, for example.[16]

Belligerent as ever, Thomas Munro believed that conquest and the dispossession of local elites was the only way to put the Company's supply lines on a sound footing. By the beginning of 1803, when war with the Marathas seemed likely, he sent an increasingly excited stream of letters to Arthur and Richard Wellesley proposing the capture of territories that lay to the south of Pune in order to supply the army. His plan was to seize Dharwad, ten miles from Hubli and the largest fort between Mysore and Pune, and establish his raiyatwar system to allow the Company to tap the region's resources. Brought under British power, Dharwad would become a permanent centre of power and supplies, drawing rice from Kanara to 'be converted into a grand depot capable of subsisting the most numerous army for a whole campaign'.[17]

Arthur Wellesley and his political agent John Malcolm thought this project was mad. Rather than concocting impossibly hawkish invasion plans, their preparations involved a difficult process of bargaining with possible allies. Instead of dispossessing, Wellesley enticed. While marching from Sriringapatam to Pune in April 1803, he talked with a succession of chiefs, discussing the terms on which they would supply goods to the Company and support the campaign to reinstate the Peshwa at Pune. Most importantly, he negotiated to establish a series of markets to supply his army's route north. These chiefs had been strong allies of the Peshwa, so were inclined to support the old Pune regime, but they bargained hard. Wellesley and Malcolm worked out a series of deals, offering financial guarantees, promising protection in case other rulers attacked, negotiating a truce between rivals, and in the process constructed as broad an alliance as they could. Arriving at Pune in April 1803 with 20,000 troops under his own direct command and 20,000 recruited by six Maratha sirdars, the city was taken without a fight.[18]

The capture of Pune was followed by a chase throughout northern India, as Company armies tried to pin down those of

Shinde, Holkar and Nagpur. The British Commander-in-Chief, General Gerard Lake, commanded an army of 10,000, which left its garrison at Kanpur in northern India in August 1803. Lake's force then defeated Shinde's armies at Aligarh, Delhi and Laswari, in the process extending British domination of north India 300 miles north-west up the Jamuna and Ganges rivers. The East India Company's victory at Delhi 'liberated' the old, blind Mughal Emperor Shah Alam II from what Richard Wellesley called his 'abject condition' under the control of the Marathas. For the next fifty years, it was to be the British not Maratha soldiers who would act as the Mughal emperor's protectors and prison guards.[19]

Arthur Wellesley's southern army followed Maratha troops on a similar seek and destroy mission, starting from their base at Pune. Wellesley's force marched north-west. In June 1803, they captured the fort city of Ahmednagar in an attack which saw heavy casualties. Wellesley's army marched on in September, unexpectedly encountering Maratha forces 150 miles further north on 23 September. What followed was the savage Battle of Assaye, which Wellington would later describe as being tougher than Waterloo. The battle was fought between big guns on one side and horses on the other, as the Maratha army's technically advanced artillery tried to stop British cavalry charges. 'Nothing', one British artillery officer said, 'could surpass the skill or bravery displayed by their golumdauze [gunners].' Eventually, Wellesley managed to take Maratha forces by surprise, attacking while 'the bullocks of Shinde's artillery were away grazing and the men quite unprepared'. Company casualties were enormous, above all because the British misjudged their rivals: a third of Wellesley's army were either killed or seriously wounded. The 74th Infantry regiment was so badly decimated that it had to be temporarily dissolved. It took eight months for the wounded to be transported back to Bombay. As the Afghan warrior Amir Khan reported, 'there was an immense slaughter on both sides'. 'This', one British officer noted, 'was the only time I ever saw heads cleanly cut off.'[20]

Assaye was followed by Wellesley's capture of two more Maratha forts, and the nervy British defeat of Raghuji Bhonsle's army at Argaum. There was no complete victory. By the end of 1803, peace treaties with Shinde and Bhonsle reduced both states but still left them powerful. At Gwalior Shinde signed over land around the old Mughal capital that Lake had captured for the Company, but retained an army of 30,000 soldiers until as late as 1844. The Bhonsles of Nagpur gave Orissa to the East India Company, making the British rulers of the entire sweep of eastern India's coastline from Chittagong to Madras for the first time. But the Nagpur regime was still in control of most of central India. And Holkar, by 1803 the most powerful Maratha state, continued fighting. The Company's troops were defeated to the south of Delhi, when the Mughal emperor was very nearly freed from his British 'protection' in the old Mughal capital. Holkar had created an innovative way of fighting, in which light cavalry were supported by small, manoeuvrable artillery, allowing them to move quickly and still blow British infantry positions to pieces. Eventually, it was the British who sued for peace in 1805. Holkar was left in possession of lands throughout Rajasthan. Two years later, rumours began to circulate that Holkar's leader Yashwant Rao had recruited an army of 100,000 men to drive the British from India. Only his death prevented them from marching to Calcutta.

Nonetheless, their limited victories over the Marathas made the East India Company just about the strongest power in India. British authority and Company administrators had extended throughout every part of India for the first time. Victory was not the result of Britain's technological or tactical superiority over opponents. The East India Company won because it was much better at mobilizing money than its rivals. Here, the big difference was the Company's unrivalled ability to borrow money from global money markets. Revenue collection did not keep up with military demands, but the Company's fiscal gap was made up by bullion borrowed from London. Ostensibly, gold and silver were sent to fund the East India

Company's growing trade in tea with China; but in practice cash was siphoned off into the war effort. More than half of £1.3 million (£84 million in 2016 prices) in gold and silver shipped from China to India between 1792 and 1809 ended up buying guns not tea. In addition, the Company relied on money borrowed from Indian merchants and bankers around the rivers and deltas of eastern India, from Calcutta, and from the burgeoning commercial capital of Benares. In these years Company officers stationed in commercial towns also went door to door, trying to tap into the resources of mercantile corporations and families, getting Indian merchants to subscribe to the Company's loans at 5 or 7 per cent. None of the Company's rivals had such financial reach. When Shinde or Holkar ran out of cash, their only recourse was to send mounted soldiers into the countryside to extract payment from villagers. The Company's capacity for deficit financing allowed it to buy the supplies and allies needed to defeat its rivals.[21]

British expansion was funded by debt, but debt created animosity in London towards the Company's governors, leading to the downfall of Richard, by then first Marquess Wellesley. As conflict with the Marathas expanded, Wellesley demanded that the East India Company in London channel more and more cash to India to fuel wars that, he argued, were in Britain's national interests. His concern about Indian powers demanded intervention far more frequently than the Company in London was willing to countenance. By contrast, the Court of Directors thought money should fund trade not war. They still had their shareholders to think about.

By 1804 there was open hostility between the advocates of trade or war. Wellesley believed cutbacks would endanger British power; the Court of Directors believed the Governor-General saw himself as a despotic sovereign, not the leader of a mercantile corporation. The Company's dividend payments had dramatically diminished. In the end, it was the British government which had the power to decide. It supported Wellesley as long as his armies were successful. In 1805, the tide of victory had turned. The cost of war was growing but the Company's armies were finding Shinde's soldiers impossible to pin down. Prime Minister William Pitt admitted that Wellesley 'had acted most imprudently and illegally and that he could not be suffered to remain in the Government'. With no ministerial support, Wellesley decided to quit. When he left on 15 August 1805 his successor, the Marquess Cornwallis once again, was already on his way.[22]

Civilized Predatory Powers

The Wellesley brothers' wars eradicated the threat to the Company which came from the armies of early nineteenth-century India's great states. '[O]ur policy and our powers have reduced all the powers in India to the state of mere cyphers,' as Arthur Wellesley put it in the last days of 1804. Seen from the misleading perspective of global geopolitics, Britain's position in India seemed secure. But closer to the ground the picture was very different. The Marathas' defeat did not impose British order over newly conquered territories in the north and west, just as the conquest of Mysore had not brought peace to southern India. Paradoxically, military victory often weakened British authority because it freed soldiers and local lords to plunder and fight on their own terms. The British were no longer confronted by large standing armies, instead by dispersed clusters of violent Indian political power. The violence which confronted the East India Company had disaggregated and dispersed; but the British constantly worried it would organize into a full-scale onslaught.[23]

What happened was complicated and uneven, but local violence and the Company's response shaped the variegated political geography of north, west and central India in the nineteenth century and beyond. To explain the reality of conquest it is necessary to break down the story of British power into different elements, tracing the history of the Company's relationship with particular local regimes. It is impossible here to consider what happened everywhere. We can only offer a flavour of the process by showing how three independent chiefs were diminished, in different ways, by British power.

First, Amir Khan, the founder of a stable and successful princely state. Amir Khan was born in 1775 into an Afghan family living in Moradabad, in the Rohilkhand region of northern India where Afghans had settled since the days of Nader Shah. Like other Afghan chiefs in India, Amir Khan intended to live the honourable life of a gentleman within the Mughal polity, with land and a retinue of soldiers to guarantee his livelihood and status. The only way to achieve this ambition was through military service. He left home with a group of friends at the age of twelve and spent most of his youth in the army of the Afghan-ruled state of Bhopal. Amir Khan's commander noted his 'signs of high destiny' and tried to marry him off to his daughter, at which point he moved on. Before he left Bhopal, Amir Khan was earning perhaps ten to fifteen rupees a month commanding sixty troops. Over the next few years he served numerous different princes, building his own following of troops and acquiring scattered rights over land. By 1798, he commanded 1,500 men based at the fort of Fatehgarh.[24]

Amir Khan always saw himself as a territorial chief, the loyal, honourable ally of the ruler he was serving. He was quick to castigate those who arbitrarily switched allegiance. In 1798 he allied with Yashwant Rao, the Maratha ruler of Holkar, who granted him land in the town of Tonk in Rajasthan and the title of Nawab. Soon afterwards, Arthur Wellesley tried to 'gain over' Amir Khan, sending allies with credit notes for 60,000 rupees. In his own version of events, Amir Khan insisted on his loyalty to Yashwant Rao, tearing the notes up and saying he would not 'separate from the cause to which I am pledged' even if 'the sovereignty of the whole world' were offered him.

In 1803 Amir Khan was at Pune when the Peshwa fled, and then tracked Arthur Wellesley's force, but was too cautious to attack. Two years later, in the last months of the Maratha war, Amir Khan harassed the convoys of goods sending supplies to General Lake's army,

which was trying – and failing – to seize Holkar's fort at Bharatpur.
As he put it himself, Amir Khan was 'held in greater awe' than any
of the other Maratha chief by this time, playing a critical role in
forcing the East India Company to sue for peace. During these years
Amir Khan's army varied in size, but depending on the scale of the
opportunity numbered between 500 and perhaps 20,000 men: and
when he needed to he could call on 200 pieces of artillery. Sir John
Malcolm reported that his soldiers believed in the prophecy of a
'holy mendicant' that Amir Khan 'would be sovereign of Delhi'.[25]

By 1805 the life of an Afghan gentleman-soldier had become
difficult to sustain. With the British squeezing their sources of
cash, Maratha states found it harder to finance their wars. Instead
of being paid from state revenues or the plunder of military targets
such as Company supply trains, a warlord's income came from
'collections' (in other words extortion) his band of troops made
from the countryside through which they marched. In practice,
this mode of subsistence made it difficult for Amir Khan to keep
his army together. With no stable source of revenue, soldiers lived
from hand to mouth and were often unhappy. British officers noted
that his military targets were increasingly dictated by the demands
of troops, not by their leader's own strategy.

Driven by the demand of his troops for plunder Amir Khan
raided Indian states in Rajasthan and then, in 1809, made sorties
into territory 500 miles to the south-east, in Berar in central India.
Here he attacked the Company's factories and undermined the
British ability to collect revenue. As raiding proliferated, travel
throughout central and western India became more difficult.

The Company was uncertain whether 'marauders' like Amir
Khan were independent or being directed by Maratha chiefs. Amir
Khan himself 'sometimes advanced claims in Holkar's name' but
where he could prudently do so he tried to prevent Holkar from
being dragged into conflict with the East India Company. But tension was inevitable and British officers disagreed about the situation
they faced. In his *History of the Mahrattas*, James Grant Duff argued

that Amir Khan was an agent of the Holkar state, sent officially by a Maratha sovereign 'to collect or extort subsistence from the provinces'. Sir John Malcolm believed decentralized violence flourished as Maratha state power died, arising 'like masses of putrefaction in animal matter, out of the corruption of weak and expiring states'.

Whatever their disagreements about its causes, officials believed British authority needed to be asserted in order to check the breakdown of political order. The British were anxious about the absence of a stable, defensible border between their own realms and territory beyond their control. The violent fluidity of local politics made them anxious. As the Governor-General who arrived in 1813, the Earl of Moira, argued, the problem was the 'want of definition in our relations with the powers around us'.[26]

Moira was an Irish-born soldier who grew up in the same world as the Wellesley brothers. But in the first years of his tenure in India, British power had helped defeat Napoleon; the empire was newly confident it could also subordinate Indian rulers to British power.[27] Moira proposed a twofold strategy to make the British position secure. He argued that there needed to be a massive military operation against 'predatory' warlords like Amir Khan. But to create greater definition in the Company's relations with its neighbours he also proposed the incorporation of the different Maratha houses into a single 'confederation' in which the British government would be 'the principal power'. Moira insisted the five Maratha states promise not to fight each other, and also not to assist the bands of wandering horsemen he believed had caused such chaos. The only way to stop the violence would be for 'the native states to acknowledge a sort of feudal duty to us'. Moira dressed his scheme up in as much 'tact' as he could muster. Not surprisingly, Maratha rulers saw this for what it was, an effort to crush their autonomy, and resisted Moira's plans.

The Peshwa Baji Rao II, and the Maratha houses of Bhonsle and Holkar all quickly mobilized for war. During October 1817's Dassera festival, traditionally the start of the fighting season, Baji Rao II created a massive spectacle of Maratha military power in

Pune, sending a large detachment of Maratha cavalry charging towards the British garrison in the town, only wheeling away at the last minute. A month later his soldiers tried to drive the British out of Pune, attacking the residency and cantonment. But the Peshwa was almost bankrupt, as the lords within his dominions refused to pay revenue. With no money to pay his troops, the Peshwa's army was quickly defeated. The Peshwa's territory was taken under the direct administration of the East India Company.[28]

But the conflict between the Company and these reduced, bankrupt Maratha regimes was not the real fight. That was against western and central India's dispersed warrior bands led by men like Amir Khan, as well as the more loosely structured groups of armed men called Pindaris. From the beginning of 1817, the Company built the largest army it had ever assembled in India to suppress these 'predatory powers', enlisting 110,000 troops, including 20,000 irregular soldiers lent by its Indian allies, and more than 500 guns. It was an army not of conquest but of pacification. The idea was to encircle the Afghans and Pindaris from every direction, squeezing them into an ever-shrinking central area of territory so that they could be eliminated. In fact, the army did very little fighting.

The army in the north-west was commanded by Sir David Ochterlony, a Massachussets-born army officer who had previously been British Resident at Delhi, and was famous for adapting to the lifestyle of a Mughal courtier. Ochterlony was given the title of Nasir ad-daula, defender of the state, by Emperor Shah Alam II, and gave his own mixed-race daughters Persian names. He was comfortable in Indian dress, and was one of the few East India Company officials to show no desire to retire with a fortune and return to Britain. Ochterlony observed what he imagined to be Indian protocol in dealing with Indian sovereigns. These cultural proclivities probably helped him negotiate with Amir Khan.[29]

By the start of the fighting season in 1817, Amir Khan faced a continuous challenge from his own troops, unable to supply them with a decent means of subsistence. More than once he was imprisoned by soldiers who 'showed a disposition to mutiny for their arrears'. Many of those who did not rebel simply disappeared, faced with no chance of making a living and the looming prospect of Ochterlony's army. A number of his senior commanders started to defect and Amir Khan worried that 'his troops would seize him and deliver him up to the English, for many used to talk [so his autobiography tells us], of the great benefits of accommodating with that nation'. Shinde had agreed to the Company's terms. British armies were on the verge of defeating the Peshwa and Amir Khan's old allies at Holkar, and Bhonsle. Amir Khan began to negotiate with the Company, sending agents to Delhi to talk. He signing an agreement on 7 November, but waited until the East India Compamy had forced the Peshwa to submit before agreeing to ratify it.

Amir Khan finally submitted to British authority in a complicated ritual on 17 December 1817. Each surrounded by 500 troops, Amir Khan and Sir David Ochterlony approached each other mounted on elephants before joining hands. Ochterlony clearly enjoyed the ritual more than Amir Khan, the Afghan warlord shouting 'chalo, chalo', 'get a move on', midway through the ceremony. That afternoon Amir Khan argued over the details of the agreement, but overnight he decided to submit, telling Ochterlony the next morning that, 'unlike the infidels' (the Marathas), he had no intention of signing 'to answer a present purpose' only to violate it at a future date. His troops were not so easily disarmed. When Amir Khan urged them to hand over their weapons and live in peace he was so badly 'beset by the discontented rabble' that he was forced to a neighbouring lord's territory and barricaded himself in the fort. Ochterlony only managed to stop a full-scale rebellion by promising to enlist 3,000 of Amir Khan's best horsemen into the Company's army.[30]

In 1817 Amir Khan converted from being an enemy warlord into the ruler of a loyal 'native state'. His relationship with the British was governed by a treaty giving him the independent power to manage his own internal affairs, in return for relinquishing his capacity to exercise violence and handing control over foreign relations to the British. From the early nineteenth century until 1947, a third of India was ruled by semi-independent states of this kind, which ranged in size from the Nizam of Hyderabad's realm of 83,000 square miles in central India, to princes ruling a few fields in Gujarat. Amir Khan's principality was somewhere in between. From 1817 until his death in 1834, he lived peacefully as the Nawab of Tonk, the only Muslim-ruled princely state in Rajasthan, a position his descendants continued to hold until India's independence in 1947. Amir Khan himself was prosperous and respected, spending his time 'administering justice' and 'joining in social and instructive discourse with the learned and pious'. On a personal level, Amir Khan's aim of living as a noble warrior was sublimated into a life of private piety.

Despite Amir Khan's personal loyalty, Tonk was a place where arguments which viciously challenged British rule as oppressive and impious could be advanced. The city became a centre of Muslim religious revivalism, and was home to many Muslims who later believed they had a duty to fight against the idolatry of British rule. During the 1857–8 uprising the largest band of Muslim *ghazis* or martyrs who fought British troops right to the last were from Tonk.[31] But all this was far removed from the profile Amir Khan himself liked to project to the British. Visitors found a 'frank, affable and lively' man of wit and culture, 'ready in repartee' and keen to entertain with stories of his great deeds. When the Governor-General, Lord William Bentinck, visited in 1832 he was handed a manuscript telling the story of the warlord's own life: Amir Khan was one of the few Indian warriors to write an autobiography. H. T. Prinsep, Bentinck's secretary and translator, thought the contrast between his deeds as a warlord and his life after as a raconteur made Amir Khan 'the most finished actor and dissembler in India, and perhaps in the world'.[32]

Prinsep's unease with Amir Khan came from his failure to understand the different kinds of people who took part in the dispersed violence of the early nineteenth century. Amir Khan was often

accused of being a Pindari, but there were important differences.
For the East India Company, the Pindaris were the most threatening armed force roving central India during the early nineteenth
century. They were soldiers on horseback, usually armed with
spears. Like Amir Khan's Afghan troopers, their subsistence came
from whatever they could plunder and extort from the villages they
passed through. But their connections with Maratha governments
were more distant. Unlike the town-dwelling Afghans, Pindari
bands were recruited from the fringes of settled society, made up of
peasant-warriors from the forests and hills of central India, mobile
people who have since been ascribed 'tribal' ethnic identity. In the
1800s they had nothing but their short-term membership of fighting
bands to bind them together. It is uncertain even where the word
'Pindari' came from. Some British commentators claimed it derived
from the alcohol these fighters consumed before going into battle.
More likely, it comes from *pendha*, or bundle of straw, suggesting
that the Pindaris were recruited from wandering herdsmen.[33]

Our second independent chief, Chitu Khan was the most
important Pindari leader, but he did not come from these desolate, marginal tracts. He was born in Mewat in the heartland of
Hindustan only a day's gallop south of Delhi. But Chitu built up
bands of soldiers who came from marginal places and so was treated
with the same disdain as the men he enlisted. The Maratha ruling
houses regarded men like Chita as cheap, effective but dangerous
allies. Pindaris cost nothing because they lived off the land they
raided. They were quick, elusive and resourceful but as likely to
turn on their patrons when there was no other source of subsistence.
To begin with Maratha rulers tried to keep them at arm's length,
refusing to let Pindari leaders sit with them in public court. Between
1807 and 1811 Chitu was kept under house arrest by the leader of
Shinde, Daulat Rao.[34]

But as defeat by the East India Company corroded the Maratha
capacity to pay for their troops the Pindaris became more closely
bound up with the political life of the states that recruited them.

Daulat Rao saw them as the only way to enable Shinde to defend itself with force. By 1813 Chitu was given land, a Mughal title and a flag bearing the state's symbol of the snake. Such public acts of acknowledgement were controversial. When the two men met to plan how to counter the East India Company's growing supremacy, Yaswant Rao Holkar reproached Daulat Rao for recognizing such barbarous, untrustworthy men. But with little money and limited options, the Maratha princes had no choice but to rely on the Pindaris' fluid forces of decentralized violence. By 1814, Yaswant Rao himself was recruiting large numbers of Pindaris to protect Holkar's power.[35]

By then there were perhaps 30,000 Pindaris in central India, sometimes fighting for their Maratha employers, otherwise riding and extorting on their own account. From 1812 they seemed to the British to be systematically raiding Company territory, marching as far as Rajahmundry and Masulipatam in the south, Mirzapur to the east and Surat in the west. The Pindaris created panic in the Company's settlements. When a group of washermen wandered around on donkeys waving broomsticks, pretending to be Pindaris, a wave of fright swept throughout Madras. The Pindaris became the subject of numerous official memoranda, and an inquiry in Parliament. 'The extirpation', wrote a Captain Sydenham in 1809, 'of such a race of men would be not only a measure of policy, but a service to humanity itself.' Local officials built defences and sent troops to defend passes through which the Pindaris marched to make their 'depredations'. The Governor-General suggested that, in practice, the Company was already at war with them in 1814. Their ultimate eradication was the main aim of the East India Company's unprecedented deployment of troops in 1817–18.[36]

This, however, was a war of dispersal rather than elimination. 'No where', as Sir John Malcolm complained, did the Pindaris 'present any point of attack'. 'Their chief strength lay in their being intangible.' Faced with the slow, heavy British onslaught, most of the Pindaris simply disappeared, returning on horseback to scattered villages and forests, unpacking the small collection of loot when they arrived. Chitu himself briefly attempted to negotiate a settlement with the British and then fled to a tract of forest where thieves and mutinous soldiers found refuge. With support from local lords, Sir John Malcolm chased Chitu into the wild, tracking him 'like a hunted animal, through the jungles, by the prints of his horse's hoofs'. Chitu never submitted to the Company. In the end he was killed by a tiger, his body mauled, his head the only part left. It was found and handed to Malcolm by a local landholder.[37]

By 1818 Amir Khan and all five of the Maratha ruling houses had finally submitted. Chita was dead, the Pindaris dispersed and the British had occupied most of the lands ruled by the Marathas. The British soldiers and political officers who took part in these operations wrote their actions up quickly, rapidly publishing historical memoirs. First came H. T. Prinsep's authorized account of Lord Hastings' proceedings, then the *Memoirs* of John Malcolm, and the *History of the Mahrattas* of Grant Duff. These texts told a common story about the British introduction of order to a 'theatre of anarchy and rule', as one mid-ranking soldier-author described north and central India during the early nineteenth century. The British were particularly anxious about groups of unattached men whom William Sleeman later described as 'persons floating loosely upon society' with no respect or connection to any kind of regular government or social order. Their intention was to use force to reconnect these disordered atoms with the main body of India's population. With more than a little anxiety Malcolm wrote about the way Pindaris had become 'concealed' among the poor of central India's settled villages 'by the benefit which is derived from their labour in restoring trade and cultivation'. Another official, Adam White, suggested that by the end of 1818 30,000 men were 'compelled ... to begin a career more favourable to the interests of society'. 'At this proud moment, the British state had risen to a loftier pinnacle of wordly grandeur than it had ever yet attained.'[38]

Violence alone could not rebuild central India's war-torn society. A few thousand Afghan warriors were employed in the army; a few

Pindaris were given land and resettled. Others did give up fighting to scratch a living sowing coarse grains like jowar (sorghum), maize or wheat along the Narmada valley or in Awadh, but the Company was not able to create an alternative livelihood for very many. As historian Radhika Singha puts it, 'those who had swelled the ranks of various mercenary bands in Central India could as well take to the roads to rob travellers'. All British violence had done was to cut the connections between armed bands and political society. The Company's attempts at 'pacification' pushed violence further to the fringes of colonial society. Many Pindaris became bandits and highway robbers, and potential future rebels. In the process they created more fear among the British. No longer afraid of being driven into the sea by massive Indo-French armies, the new British concern was that thieves might strangle them in their beds, or, worse, that disordered elements might join up to became a great insurrectionary army.[39]

The Continuation of War

The year 1818 brought the beginning of British supremacy throughout the whole of India, but this was followed by neither domination nor peace. The British imagined they had created an India-wide confederation that subjected the entire subcontinent to their power, and held every insurgent force in check. If we end the story of conquest in that year, 1818 seems to mark the moment when the British turned from war to a very different, peaceful, kind of rule. 'The principal task', as historian Eric Stokes wrote in 1959, 'was now to devise an effective and economical administration for the vast areas suddenly annexed to the Company's territories.'[40]

Continuing the story for the next few years forces us to revise Eric Stokes' argument. Seen from the perspective of 1824 or 1828, 1818 seems to be a brief pause in the oscillation between conquest and resistance that surrounded the Company from its first arrival in India. It was a comma not a full stop, a moment of hiatus rather than the termination of a process. In fact, many of the acts that Stokes described as 'administration' look more like the continuation of war.

The Company's commanders thought they still operated in a hostile environment. The number of British-commanded (European and Indian) soldiers in India continued to rise after 1818; numbers rose from 195,472 to 244,064 between 1814 and 1818, but increased again by 1826 to 292,162. The Company's greatest expenditure on the military until the 1857–8 rebellion occured in 1826: £12.8 million out of the Company's £24.1 million (£1.8 billion in 2016 prices) total expenditure. It also saw the highest ever *proportion* of revenue spent on the armed forces after the end of the Maratha wars, with 61 per cent being spent on the army compared to only 57 per cent during the year of the mutiny itself.[41] 'Peace' in British India was a violent enterprise. After the last Maratha war, the submission of Indian leaders to the expansion of British money and violence was reluctant, edgy and conditional. The defeat of the Marathas did not mean conquest.[42]

East India Company, revenue and expenditure in India, 1782–1836.

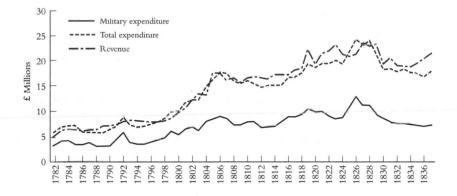

The year 1824 was particularly dangerous for the British. Amongst other things, it was the year when our third independent chief, the Queen of Kittur, was subjugated to British power. Halfway along the road between Bangalore and Pune, Kittur was a fortified village which acted as the capital of an 'ancient'

principality. By the turn of the nineteenth century it owed a loose kind of allegiance to the Maratha Peshwa and with that came loyalty to British power. Arthur Wellesley relied on the Desai of Kittur (Desai comes from the Sanskrit word for landlord) as a vital source of rice for the Company's army. Kittur sent 100 horsemen to capture Pune with the British in 1803, staying loyal to the Company for the next fifteen years.

When the Peshwa's land was taken over in 1818 the region came under the Company's rule, but there was no peace. Thousands of militiamen still wandered the countryside around Dharwad and Kittur, unpaid but loyal to enemies of the Company. British officers were anxious 'about the approach of any body of freebooters'. The Company's troops were themselves a source of disorder. Even shutting shops selling alcohol could not stop them looting and stealing cattle. No one seemed able to fix the price of anything that could be sold in the markets, so merchants found it impossible to trade and the Company could not collect taxes. In this fractious region, the fort of Kittur seemed a solitary source of stability.[43] Once again appointed to settle a territory after conquest, Thomas Munro decided to offer relaxed terms for the Desai of Kittur to sign up to the new order to keep the peace. The Desai of Kittur was exempted from paying revenue for three years in recognition of his 'fidelity and attachment to the British Government'.[44]

What kind of authority did the British government possess as Kittur's new master? That question was asked in earnest in 1824 when the Desai died childless. The British believed they had the right to approve an heir and appoint managers to run the estate. The court at Kittur, led by the Desai's aunt and his stepmother Chinnamma, did not consider that the Company had any such power so they wrote to the man who had taken over from Munro as Commissioner, St John Thackeray, announcing the adoption of a son. Thackeray despatched his surgeon to Kittur to investigate. The Desai's body, cold and stiff, indicated that he could not have approved the adoption before he died. The surgeon believed there was a plot afoot to deny the East India Company its right to manage the estate and worried that the treasury of Kittur was about to be plundered. St John Thackeray took a small team of officers and troops to guard the money in the fort. Arriving in mid-October, he worked on Kittur's accounts by day, sleeping in tents a few hundred yards outside the fort at night. The two women who managed the estate refused to see him and there were rumours that they had called for armed men to gather from the surrounding villages. On the morning of 23 October, the Company men found they had been locked out of the fort, and saw that its ramparts were occupied by hundreds of men with guns and spears. When Company artillery threatened to blow the gates open, British soldiers were shot up and then cut down by a rush of troops coming from inside. Thackeray believed he could command on horseback, leading from the front, but he was shot and hacked to pieces and his two British assistants captured and taken inside the fort.

Rani Chinnamma, the Queen of Kittur, then tried to negotiate. She condemned St John Thackeray's intervention in the affairs of the estate but offered to release the two prisoners if the British accepted her choice of heir. The 'rebel' leaders said they wanted to recreate the friendly relationship they had had with the Company in 1801 and 1817, but Wellesley and Munro had only conciliated Kittur because they thought they had to. In 1824, when war with the Marathas was long over, the British Collector in Kittur thought peace and order relied on Kittur's rulers prostrating themselves in front of the Company's sovereign power.

To oppose that power and take revenge for the death of Thackeray, six regiments of Company troops gathered to subject Kittur fort to the Company's power. Chinnamma released the two hostages in a desperate effort to get the Company to negotiate, but there was to be no talking now. The fort was stormed in a quick battle in late November, in which Thomas Munro's nephew and two other British soldiers were killed and twenty-three injured. The principality of Kittur was abolished, and its 286 villages placed under the direct government of British collectors and judges. Chinnamma was given a pension, but deprived of any authority. Even then, fighting did not stop. Some of Chinnamma's allies gathered armed men from Kittur's villages together to defend their homeland. The insurgency reached its height in 1830, when Company offices and treasuries were attacked. As one British army officer lamented, 'the insurgents had the sympathies of . . . the whole population of the province'. The rebel leader himself was captured and hanged from a banyan tree a few miles north of the fort where the insurgency had started.[45]

The condition of British institutions in India in 1824 'was not exempt from sources of uneasiness', as Horace Wilson later euphemistically wrote. It was not only Kittur. Wilson noted 'a general sentiment of discontent' throughout the whole of north India, and others assessed a similar mood in the west, east and south. The harvest was poor. Traders did not have confidence in the market to buy and sell. Squabbling about the eastern border of British India had led to war with Burma, and the Company began to ship ever larger quantities of food and manpower into the Burmese jungle without a sign of victory. At the end of May 1824, the Indian public had learnt of a humiliating British defeat. Looking back thirty years in 1858, Wilson thought the mood of hostility in these months was expressed only in 'acts of petty and predatory violence' that were easily suppressed by the Company's forces. But that was not how it felt for the British at the time. Throughout their enclaves and cantonments, British residents were afraid. They could not trust the Indian soldiers they paid to defend them, sometimes organizing their own militias, sometimes locking themselves up in the few forts they did control. From Delhi, Charles Metcalfe thought the public was filled with an 'expectation of our immediate downfall'. The Company's soldiers mutinied at Barrackpore, near Calcutta, and at Jaipur in Rajasthan. British authority evaporated through much of central India, as Shaikh Dalla, a notorious, never captured Pindari leader, started to rebuild his authority, linking up with some of the relatives of overthrown Marathas. At Bharatpur in Rajasthan, 140 miles south of Delhi, it took nine regiments of British troops just under a year to put a ruler who the British recognized as raja back on the throne. The combined result of these moments of resistance was more British officer casualties — 260 — than in any other single year over the previous twenty years of 'conquest'. Throughout India, thousands 'repeated with the most enthusiastic exultation, "The English reign is over!"'[46]

The events of 1824 illustrate the limited character of Indian submission to British rule, and the unstable nature of Britain's conquest. From Barrackpore to Bharatpur, Kolhapur to Kittur, resistance occurred when Indians felt humiliated by the way the Company asserted its power. In reality, stable authority depended on give and take. Each moment of insurgency began when British officers refused to negotiate when their power started to look precarious. Instead, they thought they were the sole judges of what was just and good, and tried, catastrophically, to impose their will without talking to those they ruled. It was their refusal to negotiate that made British power seem so vulnerable and fragile.[47]

Yet contact between Indian institutions and British power was not necessarily fatal. During these years, some Indian ways of life were able to flourish amid the East India Company's limited but chaotic and violent dominance. The early nineteenth century was a poor time for Indians who relied on networks that involved contact with British power. Old, mobile ways of life such as horse-breeding or cattle-droving, for example, died out. The greatest economic change during the first half of the nineteenth century was the retreat of artisans and traders, warriors and nomads to the villages, and to lifestyles that relied on the direct cultivation of the soil. Increasingly, India became 'a land of settled arable farming' as C. A. Bayly puts it. The complex, mobile meshing of commercial roles was replaced by 'the more homogeneous society of peasants and petty moneylenders'.[48]

In matters of religion Indians also found they could retreat from the vicissitudes of imperial power. There were always points of

contact with the imperial regime, but the British promise to leave
religious institutions unmolested enabled such places to thrive in
the early nineteenth century. Pilgrimages increased as British non-
interference was signalled by the abolition of pilgrim taxes. The
early nineteenth century was a boom time for centres of pilgrimage
such as Benares. Mosques and temples were rebuilt in many places.
In India, religious revivalism has often occurred at times of great
social upheaval. The ornate style of the new religious architecture
was not a sign of India's prosperity, but an indication that religious
institutions were one of the few places in which it was safe to invest.

There is a coda to the story of the sacking of Manjeshwar
temple with which this chapter began. The hanging of Ravivarma
Narasimha Domba Heggade, and the seizure of his property by the
British, led to the rebirth of the Antaneshwar temple on the site
of the old temple. Before the Company arrived in the region, the
existence of temples had been wrapped up with the vicissitudes of
local political authority. But to Kanara's inhabitants, the events of
1799 seemed to demonstrate that while political power was fickle
and vulnerable, religious authority was safe as long as it did not challenge British power. In 1804, the region's Gaudi Saraswati Brahmins
returned from exile and rebuilt the Manjeshwar temple with a new
image of the god Narasimha installed by a priest from Benares. The
modern temple was founded on that date. For the Hindus who have
prayed before the Narasimha image in the last 200 years it has been
a centre of social action, funding schools and cultural activities, but
never of political power.[49]

7

THE IDEA OF EMPIRE

Four years after the great rebellions of 1824, the after-effects of one particular pilgrimage seemed to threaten the end of the British empire in India once again. But this time the new danger took place in law courts and council rooms, not in battles in front of forts. The crisis was a dispute between different groups of Britons, not between the Company and Indian powers and armies. It created a fracas that seemed to demonstrate the unstable and fractured nature of British authority in India. At least one official thought it undermined the basis of British power altogether. John Malcolm, by then Governor of Bombay, believed 'there is more danger [in the dispute] than in the defeat of our armies or the loss of provinces'. It might force the East India Company to 'shut up shop' entirely if a solution was not quickly found, Malcolm said. The response was the first great reconfiguration of British rule in India.[1]

The crisis began as a dispute over who should pay the costs of a trip to the holy city of Benares. Pandoorang Dhamdhere was from a family of wealthy Maratha noblemen, important enough to send a few thousand troops to any war the Marathas were involved in. Warlords like him had travelled to Hinduism's holiest city for generations to sanctify their status as kings, turning the city of Kasi, as they called it, into a refuge for merchants and money escaping from their own troubled lands. Wealthy Marathas built the city's grandest temples. Pandoorang visited in 1816, journeying with an expensive armed guard through the ungoverned lands of central India to get there. The journey pushed Pandoorang almost half a million rupees into debt. He thought the money should be paid equally by all parts of his family, including the branch headed by his dead brother's grandson, a boy named Moro Raghunath. Pandoorang tried to split the family's extended family then collect half the cost from the boy's property. By 1824, he had persuaded the East India Company's courts in Pune, a city that had only been under British rule for six years, to order the boy to pay 245,762 rupees (£16,384 or £1.2 million in 2016 prices) to his great uncle. The boy was placed under house arrest until he paid. But there was another English court that took Moro Raghunath's side.[2]

Like Calcutta and Madras, Bombay had a tribunal staffed by English judges independent of the East India Company, called by various official titles but usually known simply as the King's court. It was supposed to put into practice the English principle of ensuring that the action of one authority was checked by another, so was entirely independent of the Company. In 1826, Moro Raghunath's father–in–law travelled ninety miles down through the steep passes that guard the Maratha highlands to the island of Bombay, to persuade the King's Court to free his son-in-law. By 1828 the court had been persuaded to issue a writ of habeas corpus, demanding Moro Raghunath be freed and brought before them. It was this act which seemed to radically challenge the basis of the East India Company's power.[3]

In Britain the decade after 1828 was one of reform. These years saw the great parliamentary Reform Act of 1832, the transformation of local government, the abolition of slavery and the inclusion of dissenters and Catholics in the polity for the first time. Economic depression connected to an escalating critique of old institutions throughout Britain and Ireland. Aristocrats realized they needed to appear as moral leaders, and include at least some of the voices of the marginalized if they were to survive. In India after 1828, reform was provoked by political crisis, too. British officers tried to restructure the institutions they had created in seventy years of haphazard conquest on more rational, systematic lines. But unlike reform in Britain, in India it emphatically excluded the population being governed from having any say in the way they were ruled. If the 1830s started Britain itself slowly on the road to democracy, in India they saw an attempt to consolidate a fragmented regime by creating a form of centralized, absolute power.[4]

In 1828, the British in India were divided between a chaotic conglomeration of different 'establishments'. There were four different kinds of regime, whose origin we have traced in the previous chapters. First, the old fortified ports of Madras, Calcutta and Bombay that dated from the 1600s. Second, the coasts and deltas of eastern India conquered in Robert Clive's wars, and ruled by Lord Cornwallis's new system of revenue collection and law. Third, territories conquered from Mysore and the Marathas which came under a more flexible but violent kind of martial law, where the Company dispossessed local lords where it could. Finally, there were cantonments and residencies in the capital cities of 'native states', which mostly ruled over arid and less profitable lands that could be left to be governed by Indian princes, such as Amir Khan's Tonk, Hyderabad, Mysore and Gwalior.

Conquest had created chaos. The messy process in which Britons extended their power in India had produced a fractured set of conflicting regimes whose legal basis was uncertain.[5] As one group of Calcutta judges complained in 1828, no one was clear who or what ruled where. Government happened with 'shreds and patches of law of every texture and hue'. Dozens of disputes like the Moro Raghunath case seemed to show that 'doubt and confusion' were rife.[6]

In response, in the 1830s the British tried to mould these disparate regimes into a more centralized state, creating a unified system of command over its fragmented territories and divided authorities. Under the new order, authority was supposed to cascade down from ministers in London to the Governor-General and council in India, then be evenly imposed by district officials through every square mile of Indian territory.[7] The British tried to take away the power of independent tribunals to challenge the Company's will; they attempted to eradicate the possibility of Indians or Britons outside the Company's hierarchy having a say in their own rule. They tried to use new technologies, from codified law to steamships, to more efficiently communicate orders and impose British command. In fact, though, British power remained fragile and fractured. Much of the imperial regime's efforts at centralization remained a fantasy. But in the 1830s an idea of centralized authority was imposed on India that would have alarmed the most autocratic Tory in Britain. It was justified with the same argument Britons in India had used for more than a century and a half: India needed to be treated differently, because British authority was in danger in Asia in a way it was never vulnerable in the British Isles.

Fighting with the judges

In Bombay and Pune one of the earliest architects of the reformed order was the arch-Tory John Malcolm. At the age of fifty-eight he had had a long career in western India and Persia and was looking forward to a parliamentary seat and a leisurely life in Britain. But in 1827 he was lured back to India with an offer of money and the idea of excitement. Ever the romantic, Malcolm wanted to be the swashbuckling warrior not the 'office man'. He thought he was returning to subdue the 'wild Rajahs and Thakoors' of central India, whose turbulence had partly caused Pandoorang Dhamdere's great debt. But when he landed, Malcolm was asked instead to take charge of the government of Bombay. There, quickly, he found his authority being challenged 'not by honest fellows with glittering sabres, but quibbling quill-driving lawyers'. 'I have been fighting with the judges', he wrote to his wife in August 1828, 'but hitherto have kept most of the commanding ground.' Battle was fought about the case of Moro Raghunath.[8]

The judges' argument was that India needed to be governed with the same institutions and laws as England. They claimed that the conquest of western India had made Pune 'part of the vast fabric of the English empire'. Conquest gave Indians the rights which all 'British subjects' (England and Britain blurred in their writings) had been given by Magna Carta in 1215, even if those rights clashed with the power of the East India Company's government. India was not different, which meant that Indians should be ruled by English institutions and English law. Indians viewed the court differently, as an independent centre of arbitration where Bombay's mixed community of merchants could resolve disputes in a practical ad hoc way. In court English legal procedures were fudged or forgotten when they did not suit local circumstances. But Bombay's merchants and British lawyers agreed that the East India Company should not have the power to lock people away without trial. 'False imprisonment', they argued, undermined commerce and civilized society.[9]

Malcolm was interested in preserving British power in India not resolving disputes. In 1828, he thought the East India Company was in a uniquely precarious position. To his mind, fractious forces in Britain's newly conquered Maratha lands were continually plotting the downfall of the Company. If Moro Raghunath were freed, 'appeals would have been made in a hundred other cases'. What's more the Company needed to retain the acquiescence of influential nobleman like Pandoorang Dhamdhere. If such individuals had their cases dismissed the Company would be brought to the point of collapse. The Raja of Satara, heir of the Maratha emperor Shivaji, had already requested a meeting with the King's Court's judges to bring his own claims against the Company. Princes in Gujarat were refusing to pay debts to the British. Malcolm reported that a Maratha Brahmin 'of some intelligence' told him that Pune's inhabitants spoke of the crisis as 'resembling the great division of interests' that tore the Maratha polity apart in the 1770s, when one group of Maratha lords had been ranged against another. 'Pure and disinterested lawyers' might try to 'check misrule and oppression',

Malcolm sardonically suggested but 'a knowledge of law and free-dom ... translated into Mahrattas, means litigation and sedition'. As historian Haruki Inagaki puts it, 'the government's anxiety was based on their perception that Indian society was always in a state of emergency.' Malcolm spoke about 'a secret war against our author-ity', of plots and conspiracies fermented by 'unseen hands'. In this kind of environment, Malcolm believed the law needed to be an instrument of command not a mechanism to contest state power. Anyhow, he argued, the case was based on a pack of lies. Moro Raghunath was not in prison at all. He 'was one of the most lively spectators at a Fancy Ball last night', Malcolm wrote in May 1828, reporting that the prisoner innocently asked the governor a series of difficult questions about European science.[10]

The King's Court threatened to call out Bombay town's local militia to free Moro Raghunath from this luxurious kind of con-finement. In response Malcolm enlisted the support of the vast majority of officers and politicians in India and Britain. The new Governor-General, Lord William Bentinck, had just arrived. Bentinck saw himself as a Whig reformer, but he backed the arch-Tory John Malcolm in his battle with the King's Court whole-heartedly. Malcolm was supported by the Privy Council in London, too. Despite receiving petitions from Bombay merchants and law-yers, including one signed by 4,000 people, the United Kingdom's senior law body decided that the Bombay court had exceeded the bounds of its jurisdiction and forced it to pull back.[11]

Other cases in these years seemed to demonstrate the danger-ously fractured character of British power, too. In one dispute after another heard before courts in Calcutta and Madras as well as Bombay the Company's authority was repeatedly challenged: convicts were released, property transferred, children were liber-ated from the hands of the guardians they had been assigned to by British officials. These controversies were built on the increasingly assertive attitude of Indian traders and their metropolitan European allies. Both groups wanted the rule of English city courts, not the

Company's authoritarian hierarchy, to extend into the countryside. The result was, as one Company officer complained, that 'a native of the snowy Himalaya' could be dragged 800 miles 'to the swamps and jungles and stifling heat of Bengal' merely to prove he was not subject to the King's Court's rule. A stream of increasingly anxious letters ricocheted around the Company's capitals in India, by 1830 feeding their way on to the Company's offices in Leadenhall Street and eventually to Parliament. Conflict between the law courts and the Company was getting get out of hand, 'feelings' were inflamed and British power seemed to be corroding. The slow speed of communication meant there was nothing anyone in London could do before a crisis got out of hand.[12]

The trail of correspondence which followed the Moro Raghunath case from Pune to Bombay and then London comprised 200 dense pages when it was printed by the House of Commons. The document describes how a minor incident escalated into a moment that changed the character of British rule in India. The legal disputes of the 1820s fused with British fear about the fragile basis of their regime, creating a debate about how the East India Company might assert its sovereign authority over every inch of British-ruled space in the subcontinent. Judges, Company officers and British politicians offered different answers, but their diagnosis of the problem was the same. Doubts about who had power over whom had caused 'alarm to our native governments, embarrassment to the local Governments, and discredit to our Country'. The law was disordered, vague, complicated and confused. It was hardly surprising that the East India Company's courts were more than 100,000 cases in arrears.[13]

The consequence was the 1833 Charter Act. Passed in the year between the first ever reform of Parliament and the abolition of the slave trade, the Act 'marked the beginning of a system of government for the whole of India'. It wound up almost all of the East India Company's trading functions. It centralized law-making and finance, giving absolute power over all British 'territories and revenue' to the 'Governor-General of India-in-Council'. It gave his council a new power to make laws that every court had to obey. It insisted that law in India was systematically restructured in a series of codes, which would define neatly and efficiently everyone's duties and rights. It directed the East India Company to appoint its officials by merit, assessed through competitive exams. Overall its purpose was to bring unity and order to the chaotic aggregation of institutions with which the British tried to rule India.

All-directing and leading rule

The effort to rationalize and codify is often traced to the influence of progressive European ideas. Writing in one of the most important books written in the twentieth century on the history of India, Eric Stokes saw the 1830s as a moment when imperial government was shaped by the 'utilitarian' ideas of Jeremy Bentham and his band of followers in London. 'It is remarkable', Stokes said, 'how many of the movements of English life tested their strength and fought their early battles upon the Indian question.' Written when Britain's empire was chaotically unravelling in the 1950s, Stokes' book projected the idea of a liberal, improving Britain onto the past. But his argument was wishful thinking. In fact, the paths that led the East India Company to assert its authority more systematically over India were far more unsteady and anxious than Stokes suggested. British officers read Bentham but the arguments of utilitarian philosophers did not persuade them to think new thoughts. British philosophy only helped them put their existing ideas into practice.[14]

The 1820s and 1830s were an age of anxiety in Britain. British society was undergoing a process of rapid industrial change. Many thought that the social relations which held society together were breaking down. The growth of factories, the rise of working-class protest, a new sense of the importance of middle-class opinion all created a moment of political and philosophical ferment. Utilitarianism was just one fairly insignificant response to Britain's relatively short-lived moment of crisis. It connected to the mentality of British government in India because it shared the same view of government and human nature.

Both the English utilitarians and British officials in India took a very bleak view of the chaotic and disordered state of society without systematic structures of command. English utilitarianism's starting point was a pessimistic understanding about how people would act if their conduct was not continually scrutinized. Jeremy Bentham and his main ally, James Mill, were venomously critical of invisible pockets of power where they thought fraud could thrive, in England as well as in India. The complexity of the English law was a particular target. With its arcane network of courts and titles, England's legal institutions seemed to be plagued by 'tautology, technicality, circuity, irregularity, inconsistency'. Words spoken in court did not mean what they seemed to. The law was ruled by 'the pestilential breath of fiction', as Bentham famously put it. This system of unaccountable power allowed lawyers to enrich themselves 'through bigotry and artifice', Bentham argued. The answer was to minimize discretion and define every act of government in clear rules.[15]

This critique of British institutions was based on the same almost visceral set of fears that had dominated the thinking of British administrators about India from the seventeenth century: of chaos, uncertainty, the possibility that bad things were happening beyond their sight. The utilitarians imagined that corruption (the word appeared 290 times in Bentham's *Constitutional Code*) was always rife unless exposed to the sanitizing scrutiny of an enlightened overseer. To suppress corruption and chaos, the utilitarians wanted to create a geometrical system of command in which power cascaded perfectly and evenly from a single authority. Bad government would only be done away with if the staff who worked in the different branches of the state had no freedom to act in their own interest. There needed to be, Bentham argued, an 'all-directing and leading rule – *minimize confidence*' in the subordinate officers of government. His was a 'system of distrust', which required authority to emanate from one all–seeing point.[16]

The connection between the utilitarian critique of English government and British rule in India began in 1806, when James Mill began to write his *History of British India*. Mill was a poor, embittered Scottish immigrant who arrived in London in 1802 to make his fortune. Four years later he was still trying to scrape together a living. Mill had trained for the clergy but failed to find a parish (he was a very poor preacher), and then took up work as a tutor to aristocratic children and a hack writer. A clever and charming man, Mill saw that India would become politically more important, and thought a book on the subject would be a route to prosperity and power. In 1806, knowledge about 'this scene of British action' was in a mess, 'scattered in a great variety of repositories', he noted. Mill thought that producing the first systematic account of the history of British India would get him a job. The gamble paid off. Mill was appointed as a senior official in the East India Company's officers in Leadenhall Street from 1818.[17]

Described by one popular publisher in 1857 as 'the beginning of sound thinking on the subject of India', Mill's *History* argued that India was, intrinsically, a land of chaos and disorder. This was particularly true of its government. In 'the skilful governments of Europe', Mill wrote, power was centralized at a single point. Officers dispersed throughout the land 'together act as connected and subordinate wheels in one complicated and artful machine'. But in India, Mill said, power was not exercised systematically. The authority of each king was fragmented among officers who squabbled, argued and fought. There was no regular system of law, so property was not secure. The disorder of government rested on the chaotic character of Indian society, particularly its religion, Mill argued. 'No people', he splenetically wrote,

> have ever drawn a more gross and disgusting picture of the universe than what is presented in the writings of the Hindus. In the

conception of it no coherence, wisdom, or beauty, ever appears: all is disorder, caprice, passion, contest, portents, prodigies, violence, and deformity.

Indian law books were 'all vagueness and darkness, incoherence, inconsistency, and confusion'. On page after page Mill repeated his main point, that there was no effort in India to govern life through rational, coherent systems. The solution was for the British to create a systematic body of law and a centralized and absolute structure of command.[18]

In reality, Mill was projecting the disordered character of British institutions onto Indian society. Here, Mill's *History* drew upon the sense of unease growing among Europeans in India about the unstable basis of their authority. Mill was meticulous in reading every report from British officers he could lay his hands on. His footnotes were full of references to judges and revenue collectors, clergymen and surveyors who complained about the disordered character of Indian social relations and the fragile grip of British power on Indian society. These were men whose experience of Indian society came from moments of fracture and breakdown, from arguments in court or disputes about who should pay revenue. Where they did travel, it was to investigate places that had recently been conquered. Mill's account of the poor state of Indian agriculture came from Francis Buchanan's description of Kanara in the aftermath of the Anglo-Mysore war, his account of property rights from a judicial official stationed in southern Bengal. Not surprisingly, his story emphasized political crisis and social breakdown, and failed to notice that the disorder they observed was brief, and exacerbated by British violence.[19]

With its angry critique of British institutions, utilitarianism was usually associated with political radicalism and the liberal politics of reform. But as Stokes pointed out, utilitarianism found its earliest echoes in India among officers from the Wellesleyan tradition of authoritarian imperialism, men like Mountstuart Elphinestone, Charles Metcalfe and John Malcolm whose approach to governing

India grew amidst the fighting of the Mysore and Maratha wars. In British politics these men were either Tories or conservative Whigs, interested most of all in preserving the established political order, particularly the authority of the aristocracy. The connection with utilitarianism came through Bentham and Mill's viscerally hostile rhetoric towards pockets of invisible power, and their unease about the fragmented, continually endangered character of government if everything was not visible. In Britain, those instincts opposed the political establishment. In India, they justified the more emphatic assertion of absolute British power.[20]

John Malcolm's predecessor as Governor of Bombay, Mountstuart Elphinstone, was one of the few people who enjoyed Jeremy Bentham's turgid prose. A man who otherwise read Greek, Latin or Persian before breakfast every day, Elphinstone suggested that this abstruse and abstract philosopher's arguments were simply common sense, and tried to put them into practice. When he became Governor of Bombay in 1819, Elphinstone concluded that an effort to transcribe and systematize Indian law in newly conquered Maratha territory was necessary. Indian law in western India was 'vague', 'unknown' and could easily be controlled by whoever had the most money, he argued, echoing the utilitarians' lack of faith in the virtue of officials and judges to act without every rule of conduct being precisely defined. As with many descriptions purporting to represent the enduring characteristics of Indian society, Elphinestone took the broken state of institutions in the immediate aftermath of conquest as the norm. He spoke fondly of Maratha *panchayats* (councils), but did not notice that, before the war, these bodies lay at the centre of sophisticated systems for adjudicating disputes. In their place, Elphinstone gathered a committee of Indian lawyers and British officers, instructing them to distil local customs and laws into a single book. The code was never finished, but Elphinstone did consolidate British regulations and create a complete body of criminal law.[21]

Similar efforts proliferated in other regions, in Bengal and the south-east of India, as well as Bombay. By the middle of the 1820s, printing presses were pouring out texts which purported to reduce the complexity of Indian law to a set of pithy rules: digests, codes, *Principles and Precedents*, translations of Indian law texts. Ostensibly, their efforts were driven by a desire to understand, sometimes even to preserve native Indian law. But they betray the belief that nothing had authority in India without the interposition of British power. With no faith in Indian institutions, the British thought only their own power could create certainty and order. Men like Elphinstone thought Indian judges were corrupt unless they made decisions under the scrutiny of British officers, and that scrutiny required the law to be translated into terms Britons could understand. The texts officials produced were thoroughly utilitarian in purpose. Their aim was to ensure that human actions were governed by a certain system of authority in which 'sovereignty was single and indivisible', as Stokes put it. But the motive of Elphinestone and Malcolm was neither 'improvement' or reform. It was to retain a grip on what seemed to them a fragmented and easily shocked system of power.

Until the late 1820s, this coalescence of Tory and utilitarian arguments was very controversial. For a large section of the British press and public opinion the East India Company was a despotic power which needed to be checked and challenged. Its authority was contested by radicals and Whigs who spoke the same language that had been used to criticize the East India Company's corporate power since the 1680s at least. Free traders won the argument in 1813, when the Company's monopoly was abolished in everything other than tea. But the Company could still be criticized as an essentially commercial organization acting as an accountable sovereign power, whose growing territories 'had become a constant burden and grievance to the nation'. In the 1810s India was only mentioned in the House of Commons when politicians praised British generals for their great victories over Marathas and Pindaris, or condemned the Company for its incompetent and despotic administration.[22]

Such criticism connected to the voice of non-official Britons and wealthy Indians in India who made common cause against the 'despotism' of the East India Company, and created a short-lived Anglo-Indian opposition movement in the cities of Bombay, Calcutta and Madras. This was the public which had celebrated the fall of Spanish and Turkish absolutism with raucous dinners, and thought a similar revolution could take place in the subcontinent. It was centred in the presidency towns' judicial institutions. In the mid-1820s it campaigned in favour of press freedom and trial by jury, and against the extension of taxation without representation. Freedom of speech was particularly important. The newspaper proprietor James Silk Buckingham was expelled from India for criticizing the East India Company's power; his defence of the freedom of the press in India became a liberal cause. European and Asian participants in these debates believed that the subjects of British rule should have the capacity and the power to hold the Government of India to account.

These liberal positions were articulated in the dominant languages of British politics. They emphasized the importance of historical precedent and the need for a balance of powers. In contrast to the utilitarian case for concentrating authority Indian political leaders like Rammohan Roy in Calcutta and Ram Raz in Madras suggested that the East India Company had violated the standards for dialogue and balance set by the Mughals and other pre-British rulers. European settlers and their supporters in Britain claimed the Company had undermined the spirit of British government, and violated the rights of freeborn Englishmen. The King's Court in Bombay defended its effort to free Moro Raghunath from the Company with reference to Magna Carta. In the same year, 1828, merchants in Calcutta condemned the Company's attempt to introduce a stamp duty in Calcutta as an encroachment on their historic liberties.

'[S]ince the days of the Norman Conquest,' John Crawfurd, a champion of Calcutta's merchants argued in 1828, 'language more presumptuous and revolting has never been addressed, by Englishmen in authority, to men of their own country.' He attacked the Company's 'corporation spirit, combined with the habitual contemplation and exercise of despotic power'. These arguments used mainstream language and were published in mainstream periodicals. Crawfurd's castigation of the Company was printed in the *Edinburgh Review*, the journal of self-styled philosophical Whigs interested in furthering a progressive, propertied social order based on a union between the commercial middle classes and Britain's historically dominant aristocracy. In the political climate of the 1810s and 1820s there was nothing particularly radical about attacking the East India Company's absolutist form of corporate power.[23]

Vent for manufactures

The onset of economic crisis changed the mood and made these Whig arguments untenable. After the years of austerity that followed the Napoleonic Wars, the mid-1820s saw a quick boom and rapid crash in both Britain and British Asia, causing the demise of ideas of Anglo-Indian commercial and political partnership, and consolidation of more absolutist ideas about imperial power.

The boom of the early 1820s was driven by the rapid construction of new cotton factories in the north of England, and the idea that easy money could be made from silver in newly developed mines in the independent Latin American republics. In India, money was cheap and the cost of labour relatively low, so speculation in indigo, coffee and cotton expanded. To fuel growth the government decided to reduce import duties rather than increase its surplus. Free-trading ideology was increasingly taking hold, fuelling a growing challenge to the Company's absolutism.[24]

The crash of 1825 was perhaps the world's firstly truly global financial crisis. The bubble in London burst in September of that year, just as the East India Company was facing increased costs because of the unexpected escalation of its war with Burma. To resolve their own financial difficulties, manufacturers from Britain flooded India with goods made in the mills of Manchester and ships from the dockyards of the north-east of England. The amount of cotton yarn imported to India expanded forty times in four years, to 4.6 million pounds. The import of British-made vessels annihilated the Bombay ship-building industry. Faced with this onslaught of cheap commodities from Europe, it was hard for traders to export from India. The Company and private European merchants could only make money by exporting silk and opium, the latter shipped in large quantities to China. Without an outlet for their commodities, British private merchants and Company officers tried to ship more and more of their money back to London. As their capital was withdrawn, a succession of banks, investment houses and indigo companies collapsed quickly in 1830. The price of raw materials in India sank, dramatically cutting the income of farmers. In the region around Madras peasants' income from selling rice fell by half between 1825 and 1831. Some regions fell victim to famine; many parts of India did not recover until the 1840s.[25]

Concern about the fractured character of British authority was heightened by these economic and financial crises. The capacity of British merchants to make money and the British Government of India's capacity to pay its costs seemed to have been endangered. In the five years before 1828, the Company's trading profits had been eaten up and the Company ran a deficit of £2.9 million each year. For Lord Ellenborough, President of the Board of Control in the Duke of Wellington's short-lived Tory government, the Company's dreadful finances were caused by 'disrespect and disobedience' to orders from London: 'nothing but a continuation of strict rule could bring India to subordination'. The deficit had, the Tories argued, been caused by 'great delays in the communication with India'. It took two and half years for instructions to be sent and receive a response. Ellenborough was optimistic that technology would allow greater control. Speaking to the British cabinet in November 1829 he suggested that a link by steamship would allow orders to be sent and replied to in sixty days.

The overlapping crises of the late 1820s disabled the Whig

opposition to the authoritarian approach proposed by Wellington's Tory government. Whig parliamentarians as well as 'progressive' journals such as the *Edinburgh Review* began to argue that India could only be ruled by an authoritarian regime that was anathema to English constitutional principles. One-time critics of the East India Company made peace with its 'corporation spirit' and supported the exercise of 'despotic power'. Others challenged the Company's right still to rule, suggesting the British state take over directly. The call, in particular, came from the beleaguered sites of British industry: Liverpool, Bristol, Manchester, once centres of radical arguments about reform in the subcontinent.

The shift is clear from looking at the changing arguments of those who wanted reform in the early 1820s. At Hull in 1822, the radical economist and entomologist William Spence condemned the Company's monopoly by arguing that its abolition would expand trade in both directions. At similar meetings in 1829 and 1830, Spence described India not as trading partner but as one-way 'vent for our manufactures', a place to offload the 'superabundant capital' of Britain. By late 1829, when he published a tract in favour of the free movement of people and goods between Britain and India, John Crawfurd had abandoned his critique of the exercise of 'despotic power' in India. He admitted that Britain 'holds our Indian empire by the power of the sword'. The British should, Crawfurd said, emulate the practice of authoritarian states like Russia and Spain in encouraging the investment of money and migration of people to conquered countries. The priority was no longer the involvement of private traders and Indian elites in government, but the creation of a form of rule able to smash open new markets.

The export of capital and goods formed an important part of the argument Thomas Macaulay made for transforming the nature of British rule in India. Son of the missionary and anti-slavery activist Zachary Macaulay, Thomas Macaulay combined a particular interest in empire with a growing role as a Whig historian and philosopher. After being elected to Parliament in 1832, Macaulay became spokesman on India for the new Whig government in the House of Commons. It was he who gave the centrepiece speech in defence of the government's Charter Act in 1833. The speech was an eloquent case of the need for India to be governed by British despotism. Absolute power was needed to maintain order and ensure the 'diffusion of European civilization amongst the vast population of the East'. But despotism had to create consumers of British goods, Macaulay said. There was no point in establishing imperial rule if Indians were 'performing their salams [sic] to English collectors and English magistrates, but were too ignorant to value, or too poor to buy, English manufactures'. At a moment of economic crisis, Macaulay was most interested in diffusing European habits of consumption.[26]

In 1828, Macaulay had written a coruscating defence of the principle of political balance against the dry rationalism of Mill's 'Essay in Government'.[27] When he rose to defend a new charter for the East India Company in July 1833, he adopted all of James Mill's proposals for the Government of India: opening India to free trade; retaining the East India Company as an institution of rule; forming a single legislative council to bring all of British India's disparate territories into a single unit of command; creating a code of law which applied equally to all subjects of British power. To the cold authoritarianism of James Mill's utilitarianism Macaulay added one liberal flourish. He insisted on adding a 'noble clause' to the new charter which promised that all public appointments were open to Indians as well as Europeans. With the anxious, mistrustful attitude British officers had towards Indians in positions of public office, it was a meaningless gesture, which had no effect for a generation.[28]

Macaulay and Mill differed in their language and attitude not their intentions. Both wished to centralize power, to place all subjects under a single authority, to remove the power Indians had over their own government and reduce discretion by codifying law. But they cast the changes they proposed in a dramatically different light.

Mill wrote with an air of desperation as if catastrophe beckoned about the need to create order from chaos and corruption. His language was saturated with the anxiety of his age: this was a time of rapid industrial change, political unrest and seeming continual imperial crisis.

Macaulay's success came from his ability to hold this anxiety back. He took Mill's arguments and shoehorned them into an optimistic narrative about enlightenment and the progress of civilization. His greatest literary achievement was *The History of England*, published from 1840 onwards. Long before then his political attitude was ruled by the logic of the storyteller, the romantic historian, skilful at placing the fragmented actions of fallible beings into a heroic story about great men creating progressive social change. Macaulay's genius was to persuade contemporaries that a panicked response to economic and political crisis was a deliberate act of improvement; that an authoritarian effort to shore up the East India Company's creaking structures of power was a moment of liberal, enlightened reform. As historian Robert Sullivan put it 'above all, Macaulay sold the British empire'.[29]

Beneath Macaulay's poetry, the future of the East India Company was determined in a series of prosaic and sordid negotiations. The East India Company's proprietors gave up their commercial privileges for a fixed income and a vague idea of their power. The Company had lost its monopoly over British trade with India in 1813. But its institutional strength allowed it to compete effectively with private traders until the depression of the 1820s. The economic crash meant the Company could be easily convinced to give up its commercial privileges. It was Sir John Malcolm, just returned after his three-year stint in Bombay, who did the persuading. According to the deal Malcolm negotiated, Company stockholders exchanged their income from India's beleaguered export trade for an annuity paid at 10½ per cent per annum guaranteed by the British state. As straightforward as they were, the negotiations seem to have killed Malcolm. The influenza epidemic gripped his stressed body in the spring of 1833. He collapsed while giving a speech to the East India Company and died in May, at the age of sixty-four.[30]

The Charter Act did not, though, kill the East India Company or

its way of working. It ended the Company as a financial interest separate from the British state. But the loss of its commercial functions
was a victory for the East India Company's way of doing business. In
1833 the Company merged with the British state, and won the battle
over how India should be ruled. Representative government and a
balance of power were not admitted as a valid way to govern the
'anomalous' circumstances of India. Instead the East India Company
was able to stand forth with an unashamedly absolutist form of government, an 'enlightened and paternal despotism', as Macaulay put it.
The Charter Act of 1833 marked the transformation of the idioms of
power which had ruled the Company since the 1690s into a new idea
of imperial authority. Rather than being conceived as a collection of
different political authorities India began to be seen as a single terrain
on which the consistent and unaccountable exercise of British power
began to be imagined.[31]

Legislating for a conquered race

In the 1830s there were a proliferation of British projects which had
the aim of making this idea of imperial power a reality. Most of them
were unsuccessful. Some were never implemented. Others were only
put into practice after long delays. But their growth tells us something important about the changing character of British rule. From
the 1830s Britain's leading officers in India developed projects at a
great distance from the point at which they would be put into practice. These schemes took many forms: making new laws, surveying
land, building canals, roads and eventually railways. What they had
in common was their abstract character, particularly their effort to
circumvent the need for a relationship with or knowledge about local
political circumstances. They created an idea of imperial domination
that was very real in the minds of its authors, but always seemed out
of kilter with what was happening in reality. In the process India
became a land of unprecedented possibility and disappointment, of
social and technological fantasy as well as recurrent crisis.

The most important project was the attempt to create a new set of laws for India. British observers universally observed that law in India was chaotic and arbitrary and thought certainty and uniformity ('where it was possible') were vital for securing British power. In his 1833 speech to Parliament, Macaulay repeated common complaints about major areas of law left uncertain. He had, he said, asked a senior civil servant what a judge would do if an enslaved dancing girl ran away from her master. 'Some judges', he said, 'send the girl back. Others set her at liberty. The whole is a mere matter of chance.' Macaulay imagined that Britain's absolute power would make the compilation of a new code of law an easy task. A 'quiet knot of veteran jurists' could quickly do what a 'large popular assembly', with its factions, debates and need to be publicly accountable could not, he thought.[32]

The 'quiet knot' deputed to write India's new law was led by Macaulay himself. In 1834 he resigned his parliamentary seat telling his constituents in Leeds that he was sailing to 'legislat[e] for a conquered race, to whom the blessings of our constitution cannot as yet be safely extended'. Macaulay had been offered the position of chief lawmaker of the new Indian Legislative Council. The salary was large enough to ensure he would be financially secure for the rest of his life. But Macaulay's elation at securing a decent livelihood was combined with an elevated sense of imperial purpose. There was, he wrote, 'no nobler field than that which our Indian empire presents to a statesman' than legislation.[33]

During his three years in India, Macaulay cut himself off from Indian life, ensuring nothing would challenge this sense of authoritarian purpose. 'We are strangers here,' he insisted, and he wanted to keep it that way. He saw the world outside the high-walled palace in which he lived as corrupt and chaotic, a place of threat, turmoil and danger. When his residence was being renovated he was forced to spend a short stretch in a smaller dwelling, and there complained about being 'deafened by the clang of native musical instruments and poisoned with the steams of native cookery'. In theory, Macaulay was willing to concede to 'the feelings of the natives of India' in his work, but had no way of communicating to gauge what they were. The laws he wrote during his isolated sojourn were works of detached rationalist abstraction. His Code of Criminal Law was a body of jurisprudence written for everyone and no one, which had no relationship to previous Indian laws or any other form of government at all. As the Law Commission insisted, 'no existing system has furnished us even with a ground-work'.[34]

In Parliament Macaulay promised that India's newly centralized, absolute government would sweep away the confused mass of British–Indian jurisprudence with a series of rational codes. Most important was the reduction of the religiously-rooted Hindu and Muslim law which British judges used to govern inheritance disputes into a systematic, written form. Suspicious as ever of their Indian interlocutors, all but a few British judges saw the traditions of legal practice which governed property before their arrival incomprehensible. Despite occasional flourishes of radical language from Macaulay, the British government was too worried to engage in any serious reform. Efforts to alter existing practices were rare and only occurred once officials convinced themselves that change would be popular, or conformed to authentic Indian customs and laws. The iconic and solitary instance of British social engineering in Lord William Bentinck's period as Governor-General was the decision to ban sati, or the practice of Hindu women being burnt alongside their dead husbands. Here legislation was only passed after a decade of trying to regulate the practice failed. Bentinck only outlawed sati once he was convinced that it was not an authentic Hindu rite.

Macaulay and his three fellow law commissioners finished their Code of Penal Law in 1837 but it sat unread and unenacted for twenty-four years. The intention to codify Hindu and Muslim law was seen as too difficult even to start. As chaotic as the existing system seemed, judges and officials throughout British India were worried that change would create opposition. Instead, judicial officers sponsored the printing of yet more unofficial codes and guides: Theobald's *Acts of the Legislative Council*, Morley's *Analytical Digest of Cases*, Beaufort's *Digest of Criminal Law*, Harrison's *Code of Bombay Regulation*, for example. In the 1830s and 1840s, the law was not reshaped by the explicit authority of the central state. This was an era of manuals and guidebooks, as officials and judges moulded the practice of law for themselves by printing books which reduced legal complexity to simple rules without the official sanction of the Governor-General.

The perseverance of the boiling kettle

Macaulay's legal reforms were intended to pull distant places together and bring scattered centres of British authority within a single orbit of command. Their purpose was to subjugate the actions of British officers under a single set of rules, and so make the empire whole and united. Their success relied on the existence of physical means of communication that could disperse orders and rules from the centre of authority to its satellites. Along with legal reform the 1830s was a time in which projects to improve transportation proliferated. Roads and steamboats came first. After the years of Lord Bentinck's savage expenditure cuts, investment in public works increased after 1837. But even on the most liberal calculation, until the mid-1840s public works took a fractional 2 per cent of British India's £20–£25 million total expenditure.[35] Most of this money was spent on roads which connected district capitals, or extended a few miles out from the Collector's office to ease the transport of cash from landholders to the Company's treasuries. Still, by the end of the 1830s, the empire's road network was fragile and left the British in a constant state of danger. Even on the Grand Trunk Road that connected Calcutta to Delhi and beyond raids were frequent. Vehicles carrying British goods needed to keep together in the Government Bullock Train, a heavily armed convoy of animals and carts, to have a good chance of getting through to their destination.[36]

Most of all, though, it was the regular throb of water-borne steam engines which British officers imagined would allow them to consolidate their power throughout India. In the 1830s British entrepreneurs developed scheme after scheme for steamboats. To begin with, interest from the British who ruled India was slow. The first commercial steam vessels in Britain began to operate in 1811. By 1820 steam was a familiar presence on European and American coasts and rivers, but it was the Indian ruler of Awadh, Amjad Ghazi-ud-din Haidar, who brought the first steamboat to India in 1819, not the Company. The Nawab of Awadh also laid India's first metalled road. In 1823, a committee of merchants was formed in Calcutta to lobby for a steam connection between London and Bengal. It was granted 20,000 rupees by the Company, but given no other support. It was only when steam seemed a viable tool of government that the authorities became enthusiastic.[37]

The first steamboat to be put to use by the imperial government arrived by accident. The captain of the *Diana*, a vessel chugging its way from London to Guangzhou in China, became ill so ended his journey in Bengal. The boat was originally intended to push the opium trade through China's rivers. British anxiety about hurting 'Chinese sentiments' compounded by the loss of the captain led the boat to stay in Calcutta. The Company turned down the offer of buying the boat when it was first offered for sale at 60,000 rupees. It became more interested when war broke out with Burma. The Burmese were pushing the Company's army back down the Irrawaddy river, and the government was desperate to buy anything that might give it an advantage. In April 1824, the *Diana* was purchased for 20,000 rupees more than the original price. It began to steam its way up and down the Irrawaddy towing gunboats. It was not long before Britons began to write as if their victory was made inevitable by their possession of the irresistible power of steam. As one commentator wrote sixteen years later, on the river 'the muscles and sinews of men would not hold out against the perseverance of the boiling kettle'. The war seemed to demonstrate that steam 'may become an element in reclaiming barbarians'. But the eventual British defeat of Burma was a close-run thing, and certainly not based on European technological advantage.[38]

The Company first commissioned steamships as vessels of war. After the *Diana*'s success, engines to fit two Calcutta-built boats, the *Hughli* and *Berhampore*, arrived from London in 1828. Both were intended to consolidate British power along the Brahmaputra river, where the conquest of Assam from Burma needed to be secured. The *Berhampore* set about this task, chugging its way to the north-east of India. But the newly arrived, technology-obsessed Governor-General, Lord William Bentinck, wanted to see a steamship service open up along the Ganges between Calcutta and Allahabad. As a result, the *Hughli* was sent on an experimental jour-ney up the river. In its twenty-day voyage from Calcutta to Benares, the steering failed and the vessel continually ran aground. The *Hughli*'s accommodation was too smelly and too noisy for any but the most junior officer to put up with, and the cost was extortionate. But the mere physical fact of a steamboat making its way 700 miles upriver allowed the experiment to be deemed a success. In other ways Bentinck's government was desperate to cut costs, but along the Ganges it started to build the elaborate infrastructure necessary for a permanent steamboat service, commissioning engines to be shipped from London, finding stocks of coal and laying them out at coal depots, hiring boatmen and pilots to staff every one of the twenty-eight stations between Calcutta and Allahabad. By 1836, there was a fully working steamboat service along the river, charg-ing its small group of passengers 1,000 rupees for the privilege of taking one month instead of two to travel to Allahabad.

To begin with, ocean-going steamships that could connect London and India were pushed by an assorted band of engineers and speculators.[39] But it was Lord Elphinestone and Sir John Malcolm, the two authoritarian administrators who succeeded one another as Governors of Bombay who led the campaign. Elphinstone's effort to persuade the Court of Directors to back a pilot voyage through the Red Sea was rebuffed in 1824. The first journey began six years later, when Malcolm decided to spend the Bombay government's own money on an experimental journey.[40]

The vessel used was a 124-foot-long, 411-ton 'armed steam vessel' which had been commissioned from the Parsi shipbuilder Naoroji Jamsetjee initially to check piracy along India's west coast. Launched in October 1829 it was named, ironically, the *Hugh Lindsay* after the Chairman of the Court of Directors who had refused to back the venture to start with. On its first journey it carried government despatches, 366 private letters and a single passenger, Colonial Campbell of the Bombay artillery. Able to store only five days' worth of fuel, the ship was delayed at Aden, Jedda and then Cossar, the Ottoman ports where it needed to stop to load coal. The *Hugh Lindsay*'s final destination was Suez where Colonel Campbell and the letters of lonely British civil servants were shifted onto camel-drawn carriages for a quick and safe journey to Alexandria and then on to Marseilles and London. The vessel took thirty-one days there and thirty-seven back for a journey it was initially thought would take ten. Over the next two years, the *Hugh Lindsay* shuttled back and forth between Bombay and Egypt. A second, smaller and weaker vessel left Calcutta a few months after the *Hugh Lindsay*, but failed to make its way around the south coast of Ceylon. The British officer who had been sent with letters to reach it at Suez was left stranded, and limped his way slowly back to India by sail.[41]

Despite limited success, Malcolm's successor as Governor of Bombay believed the 'experiment' of connecting London and India by steam had 'succeeded beyond the most sanguine expectations of those who were well aware of the difficulties attending its navigation'. Steam was pushed by one committee after another in London, becoming a parliamentary obsession by the mid-1830s. Far more than an interest in commercial profit, the desire to create a more effective system of command drove their interest. Men far removed from India imagined vessels that were fuelled by hot air would help their rhetoric reach Asia more quickly and be obeyed more diligently than before.[42]

Historians often impute commercial motives to the East India Company's effort to assert greater power in India in the 1830s. After all, this is often regarded as the era of free-trade imperialism, when Britons used their proconsuls and gunboats to crack open closed markets in other parts of Asia and elsewhere. The decade ended with the first Opium War, when Britain responded violently to Chinese efforts to regulate the East India Company-sponsored narcotics industry.[43] Merchants in Calcutta and Bombay (some involved in the opium trade) initially supported steamboats, but commercial support ebbed away as the real costs were more than imagined and speeds far slower. The steam services that began to operate in the 1830s were far too expensive to be useful for trade. The coal needed to keep the *Hugh Lindsay*'s paddles turning alone cost almost 75,000 rupees (£393,000 in 2016 prices), and cheaper boats were too weak to make their way through the Arabian Sea. These high costs did not bring correspondingly huge revenues. On the *Hugh Lindsay*, postal charges for the letters brought in only 1404 rupees, with little more to carry passengers. To spend a month being conveyed in a cramped, noisy cabin on the Ganges from Calcutta to Allahabad, a Company officer would have to pay the same amount. Even if traders could pay there was no space for anything but the lightest 'light cargo'. The purpose of steam was not to transport goods to be bought and sold, or to improve trade.[44]

Instead, steamboats and steamships were designed to give greater security to Britain's fragile imperial power in India. Rather than being used to transport goods to be brought and sold, expensive steam engines were put into motion to accelerate the circulation of the small objects of empire, the silver coins and printed papers that the imperial hierarchy relied on. The quicker treasure and paperwork could be exchanged, the more secure officers felt about the deference of subordinates to their commands. A steam 'communication' 'between India and the mother country' would 'entirely change the relation between the two'; the Company would 'derive full indemnification for any expense which you might incur in the speedy transmission of your instructions', Elphinstone wrote. The advantages were 'incalculable', Malcolm argued: just as well given the exorbitant cost of steam transport.

Steam communication was intended to create a more enduring and regular physical connection between the scattered sites of British power, linking the imperial capital in London, the presidency towns, district capitals and cantonments. But it could not assert authority over the spaces in between. The report by H. T. Prinsep, secretary of the government in Calcutta, on the Ganges noted that steamboats offered a safe way to transport treasure, because the mechanical pace of a steam vessel meant it could outrun the human or wind powered vehicles which raiders used. Prinsep noted that a battalion of soldiers was needed to defend 38 million rupees' worth of treasure brought down by river from Agra to Calcutta. A steamboat would need only a small guard, 'for no band of robbers could follow it or waylay it'. In the 1830s new technology allowed the British to escape, avoid and ignore violence rather than suppress it.[45]

Ten years later the same argument was made when the 'experiment' of creating a steamboat connection between Calcutta and Dhaka was being assessed. The service had run at a huge loss because merchants did not want to pay a higher price for marginally quicker access to markets with a service they believed would not endure. '[F]ew of the native merchants have as yet overcome their prejudices against the new,' the controller of steam vessels condescendingly explained. At Dhaka imperial technology did not transform Indian ways of doing business. Its purpose instead was to make the loose frame of British power more secure. Private steam ventures were impossible the admittedly self-interested controller of steam conceded in 1847. But, '[w]ith a government very different considerations suggest themselves' than making an immediate profit. The greatest justification for steam was the need to find a safe and stable way of shipping money collected from landholders in the countryside to the imperial treasury at Calcutta.[46]

The 1830s saw the proliferation of many other projects intended to create a more uniform and systematic structure of power in India. Law and steam took up much of senior Company officers' time, but there were other schemes. There was the attempt, for example, to map Indian territory, resulting in the Great Trigonometric Survey. These years saw the growth of an increasingly systematized process of revenue collection based on the detailed surveyance of land. They witnessed, too, the emergence of the Post Office in India, as the East India Company attempted to suppress the thousands of courier (*dak*) services and then, in 1837, insist all correspondence was carried by its own system of collecting and delivering mail. They saw debate over ways of educating Indian officers so that the Company's law courts and revenue offices worked more efficiently, in the process creating more standardized forms of instruction.

Historians sometimes argue that these efforts were part of a systematic effort to improve Indian society, signs that the 1830s were an era of 'liberal imperialism' when Britain's despotic power in India was deployed with the intention of doing good.[47] In fact, they were driven by far more mundane concerns. Each project was driven by the attempt to create an ordered system of rule, and so to protect the Company's power in India from challenge. The ideal was to replace the haphazard scattering of institutions the Company's conquests had created with a single structure that operated with the same mechanical regularity as one of Mawdsley's steam engines. Notably, the 1830s saw an increase in the use of mechanical metaphors to describe the operation of the British regime in India.[48]

Summon no zamindars

The dispersed institutions of imperial power in India were anything but a machine. The project of creating a systematic structure of government was not successful in the way its authors intended. But these projects marked a change in the relationship between British power and Indian society. The 1830s saw the growth of a style of government that engaged with people through abstract systems and general categories. A steamship, a rational code of law or a revenue map did not need to pay attention to the particularities of specific places, or the circumstances of particular men and women. That, indeed, was their purpose. The aim of these institutions was to consolidate a regime suspended above the lives of its subjects, able to sustain itself while having only the thinnest connection with the people it was supposed to rule. At its crudest, that meant governing without the need for talking to Indians.

The practice of surveying provides a good example of the extension of government through forms and records rather than speech. The first half of the nineteenth century saw the expansion of the British effort to map India. These were the years of the aforementioned Great Trigonometric Survey of India, in which hundreds of surveyors measured every part of the Indian landmass, calculating the height of South Asia's great mountains while doing so. Mount Everest was named after British India's second Surveyor-General. Extensively studied by historians, such grand projects made no impact on British administration. The Great Trigonometric Survey had no connection to the far more prosaic but more important project of surveying land to aid the collection of taxes. British officers were permanently stationed in each district to produce maps that were supposed to delineate the boundaries of villages and define the limits of each landed estate. To do so, though, they were supposed only to use documents in the district offices. The Survey Department strongly discouraged their surveyors from interrogating potentially untrustworthy locals. '[H]e is to summon no zemindars [sic] and make no enquiries from any party,' the Board of Revenue ordered. If confusion arose or something was contested, the surveyor was to talk only to the amin, or Indian revenue official.[49]

Whether it was from the bridge of a steamship or from behind a theodolite, there was no room either for picturesque detail or for extensive inquiries about local practice in the mid-nineteenth-century British officers' view of India. 'The steamer goes boring on without the slightest regard for our love of sketching,' Emily Eden complained in 1837. Indian terrain was to be crossed at speed or drawn with the regular, homogeneous pen of the imperial map-maker; there was no place for complexity or care. The British government worked by creating a form of rule which was suspended, as if in mid-air, with nothing but the most perfunctory engagement with local society.[50]

Yet the detached institutions of British power created their own life, and in the process subtly changed Indian ways of doing things. The systems the British introduced to bolster their rule dispersed new procedures throughout India's cities, towns and villages, interposing the authority of the state where it had not existed before, in the process moulding the conduct of Indians to abstract, depersonalized forms. Taxation, for example, was no longer about negotiating with particular local authorities, but a matter of paying the appropriate rate for a particular size plot of land. The East India Company's new postal service asked letter-writers to send and receive their mail from fixed addresses, rather than relying on local knowledge about the identity of an individual. Litigants shaped the stories they told before the court so that their actions fitted the categories of the Company's law; it was no use simply telling the facts of the case and then appealing to the Company 'for justice'. A case could only be won if it conformed to the rules, whether enacted in regulations or distributed in privately produced manuals. Britain's empire began to be asserted through Indian acquiescence to mundane, routine procedures and forms of paperwork.

The circulation of stamped paper is a good example of this process. From the very end of the eighteenth century, the East India Company insisted that various different documents, deeds, contracts, and most controversially newspapers, had a stamp on them bought from the Company. This was a classic colonial tactic for 'raising a revenue for the support of the State', as one regulation put it. Opposition to the Stamp Act in Britain's North American colonies had, of course, helped bring about the American Revolution. Fifty years after American independence a much more intrusive regime was imposed on India. From 1824 no document without a pre-paid government stamp could be presented in court. The range of documents that had to be so certified expanded as enforcement intensified, as contracts, deeds, conveyances, leases, powers of attorney, insurance policies, and receipts and, after 1824, newspapers were all brought under the scope of the law. By the mid-1820s, perhaps 5 per cent of the time and resources of each District Collector's office was spent dealing with stamped paper, ensuring supplies, distributing stashes to the shopkeepers who sold them on, keeping registers, ensuring local merchants used them in transactions. The Collector of Rangpur in northern Bengal toured the offices of city merchants in November 1825 and found many were still writing on plain paper and that no one knew anything about the stamp laws. Five years later traders were coming to the Collector's office asking to buy stamps to fix to old documents, in order to make them legal.[51]

Through time these stamps developed their own, seemingly free-floating authority. People imagined they could guarantee a promise even when far removed from the state's effective command. A British lawyer in the early twentieth century recorded the story of an elderly Marwari man who used stamped paper to certify the chastity of his wife. He was worried his nephew was flirting with her, and forced the boy to promise and sign across a stamp 'such as would have been affixed to a demand promissory note'.[52]

After the 1824 regulation, millions of stamped documents went into circulation. At points of friction, Indians resisted their use. Occasionally, stores of stamped paper were ransacked by rebels and criminals. The enforcement of stamp regulations was named as one of the grievances that contributed to the rebellion of 1857–8 that briefly eradicated British power in north India. In that period the distribution of stamped paper was read by insurgents as a sign of the infinite desire of the British state to penetrate and transform every corner of Indian social life. But before and after the great storm of rebellion the British imagined that the distribution of these small objects of imperial power marked their effective dominance of Indian society. It was seen as a sign of their power to limit fraud, for example. A document stamped and registered could not be easily copied or altered, or so it was thought. The circulation of stamped paper connected with a British idea of empire as a system of ordered government, which had replaced the supposedly chaotic and arbitrary systems of pre-British rule.

It is hard to say what kind of power this vast network of circulating paper actually exercised. Stamped paper did not reduce corruption; it merely created a new field for deception, as forgers tried to copy the stamps themselves. Officers had no use for the information they collected about the transactions they were trying to regulate. There was no way of ensuring transactions certified were not themselves coerced.

The neat registers kept in the Company's officers allowed British officials to imagine they had created an effective, unitary structure of rule; they fostered a delusion of power. In fact, all stamped paper did was to force Indians to use paper money and write on paper emblazoned with the word 'Government'; it did not imply submission to British rule. Cash payment could as easily be made to another state. The paper produced by the 'native states' that surrounded British-ruled territory used almost identical forms, yet many had a tense relationship with British power. In many places, the rebel governments of 1857 tried to keep up the Company's stamp paper rules. The British governed by representing their power in an abstract, disembodied form, avoiding the need to ask for the consent of the people they ruled. But their very abstraction meant British institutions could be taken up and used to achieve very different purposes, sometimes to challenge British power.[53]

8

FEAR AND TREMBLING

In April 1857 fires broke out in the soldiers' quarters at Lucknow, capital of the newly conquered province of Awadh. The bungalow of the regimental surgeon was torched. A second incendiary wave began at the beginning of the next month. On 2 May one regiment of Indian infantry protested against using rifle cartridges they believed were contaminated with pig and cow fat. Another regiment, the 48th Native Infantry, was ordered to fire on the rebels. The following night the huts of the 48th were set alight in retribution for their suppression of the demonstration. Sir Henry Lawrence had arrived two months before as Chief Commissioner of Awadh, and walked through the lines that night. The men were, he said, 'very civil' though downcast at the loss of their homes and property to the fire.

Eventually Lawrence came across an Indian artillery officer, a forty-something Brahmin 'of excellent character'. The two men talked for an hour. Lawrence was surprised by 'the dogged persistence' with which the soldier argued the British government was trying to convert the natives to Christianity. The British had conquered India by fraud, defeating princes at Bharatpur, Punjab and Awadh, the officer said. They wanted to turn Indian soldiers into an obedient force that would do as they were commanded. European soldiers were too expensive. Instead, the British 'wished to take Hindoos to sea to conquer the world' and could only do that if Indians ate what Europeans ate and did what Europeans did. This, the soldier said, was 'what everybody says'. Another soldier wondered if the aim of the British was 'to join London to Bengal'. Lawrence said he had heard similar views for a long while.[1]

Two days later and 280 miles away Indian soldiers at the garrison of Meerut rose up and killed their British officers. They then marched forty miles to Delhi, where they enlisted the support of the city's mob and Bahadur Shah Zafar, the 82-year-old Mughal sovereign. Until that moment the Mughal empire possessed theoretical sovereignty over the whole of India, but its practical force extended no further than the outer limits of Delhi's Red Fort. Illuminated with the lustre of Zafar's authority the 300 Meerut mutineers became the core of an insurrection that overturned the East India Company's government throughout north India and restored some kind of Mughal power throughout the empire's old heartland. Lucknow and the surrounding province fell to insurgents on 30 June. The city's 2,000 British inhabitants barricaded themselves into a sixty-acre plot of land centred on the Lucknow residency, where they were besieged until 27 November. The city itself was only recaptured in March 1858. Henry Lawrence did not last anywhere near that long. He was killed by shellfire on 4 July.

Ever-present precariousness

The insurrection of 1857–8 is often seen as an abrupt punctuation in the history of British power in India. Early commentators compared it to a natural rather than a human catastrophe: 1857 was described as a forest fire, a crashing wave, a bursting storm. 'Little, I am certain, did any man there', a Collector from Bihar suggested, 'dream of the wild storm about to burst over us.'

To begin with, Britons were not sure how to explain it, or even how to describe it. An immediate response was to describe each individual garrison's revolt as a series of 'mutinies', but the insurrection as a whole was described with different words, sometimes as a rebellion or revolt, but more frequently simply a crisis or calamity. From the mid-1860s, Britons began to talk about the events of 1857 as 'the mutiny' and to attribute it to human causes.

By then one explanation began to gain prominence. The insurrection, British writers argued, was sparked by British efforts to impose modern European practices and values. India began to be described as a traditional society which violently resisted the change overeager Britons had forced on it. This version of events spread particularly with John Kaye's *History of the Sepoy War*, a work published in a series of volumes from 1864 onwards. Kaye argued that 'it was the vehement self-assertion of the Englishman that produced this conflagration'. Indians, he argued, rose in resistance against English education, against British efforts to impose the rule of law, against modern forms of communication and the attempt to abolish 'barbarous' rituals such sati and to proselytize Christianity. Critical of the East India Company in many places, Kaye nonetheless excused the British from causing the mutiny because their actions were intended to do good. Such an interpretation has more or less prevailed in the 150 years since.[2]

Kaye's story was an attempt to justify the great crisis by extolling the virtues of its cause. In fact, though, there is little evidence to suggest the East India Company attempted to transform Indian society before 1857; nor is there any evidence that Indians rose up against efforts at reform. Rather, insurgents like Sir Henry Lawrence's artillery officer fought against the increasingly authoritarian way the British clung to power. The rebellion of 1857–8 was created by Britons' fearful over-attention to dissent rather than their blithe efforts at reform.[3]

The 1857 rebellion was not a revolt against a confident regime intent on spreading capitalism, civilization and modernity throughout the world. It was an insurgency against an anxious regime's counter-productive efforts to hold on to power. It was driven by the East India Company's fearful effort to destroy any centres of authority in India that displayed the smallest flicker of independence, whether self-governing states, little kings, landholders or in its own army. It was led by the lower-middle-class men whose status and livelihood were most severely corroded by the tactics the British used to protect their rule. Uneven in its spread, the insurrection was concentrated in the regions of north India where the East India Company had recently imposed itself with greatest force but then left too little military manpower to hold onto its power.

A few British commentators understood the causes of the rebellion very well. The Protestant Irish doctor Montgomery Martin was one of them. Martin championed a vision of empire ruled by free trade and self-government rather than Britain's monopolistic power. Serving in Ceylon, East Africa and Australia before working in Calcutta, Martin became friendly with the reformist circle around Rammohan Roy and Dwarkanath Tagore in Bengal. Informed by these liberal Indian connections, Martin's account of the 1857 rebellion was critical of the way the East India Company exercised power in India. As he put it:

> The constant preponderance of expenditure over income, and an ever-present precariousness, have been probably the chief reasons why the energies of the Anglo-Indian government have, of late years, been most mischievously directed to degrading kings, chiefs, nobles, gentry, priests and landholders of various degrees.

In Martin's account, the mutiny was caused by the perennial British sense of danger in India, not self-confidence. Their anxiety, Martin argued, led them to act out of character in India. A people who developed a flexible form of government in their own country became rigid and paranoid in Asia. An elite which respected tradition in Britain had 'rolled, by sheer brute force, an iron grinder over the face of Hindoo society' in the subcontinent, intent on 'crush[ing] every lineament into a disfigured mass' in order to sustain 'a small white oligarchy and an immense army of mercenary troops'. In fact, this description massively overstated the extent of British force before 1857, but it conveys a good sense of the kind of regime Indian insurgents thought they needed to challenge. It also explains why the violence was so brutal. Each side thought it was fighting for its survival.[4]

The idea of a homogeneous Indian peninsula

Montgomery Martin was also right about the effects of financial insecurity and political vulnerability on British policy. After the fiscal crises of the late 1820s, Governor-General Bentinck had reduced posts and salaries to create a short period of fiscal stability. But the cutbacks in spending together with the agricultural depression of the late 1830s weakened India's economy, and shrank the Company's income from land tax. Bentinck's fiscal discipline was not followed by his successors, and spending on steamships and roads did not bring any financial return. From the late 1830s, the Company's expenditure grew more quickly than its revenue, and debt was expanding once again. By 1846, the annual deficit of expenditure over income peaked at £2.58 million. In 1850 the total debt hit £50 million, more than twice the Company's annual income, and the Company was forced to borrow at the relatively high rate of 5 per cent. The consequence was an effort to find additional sources of cash, and to do so by squeezing existing Indian hierarchies.[5]

Revenue and Expenditure, 1830–1874.[6]

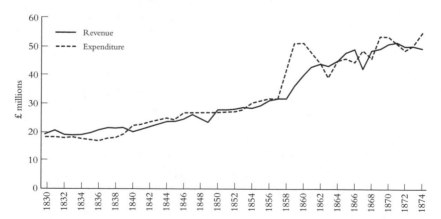

The decade before 1857 saw an intensification of the British effort
to extract revenue from rural India. Teams of surveyors were sent
into territories to be settled, measuring every field and assessing
how much they were due to pay. In north Indian villages two-thirds
of the total produce of the land was supposed to be taken by the
government. Trying to collect that money directly from villagers,
British officers dismissed zamindars and other local lords as 'a host
of unproductives'. Many were dispossessed and pensioned off with
sums far smaller than their previous income. Those who survived
saw a serious cut in their living standards. The result was the suppression of a class of individuals who were occasionally rapacious,
but usually essential to the flow of local resources needed to maintain the living standards of rural society.[7]

Even where they could not dispossess local lords, Company
officers attacked other sources of mutual dependence between landholders and peasants. Privileged, low-rent forms of land tenure had
long been essential to the management of rural society, allowing
local figures to pay low rents or none at all and redistribute resources
to the poor and lower middle class. Rent-free land allowed local
leaders to fund institutions essential for the functioning of local
society: schools, religious institutions, village officials. As historian David Washbrook argues, they provided a safety vent which
allowed people to subsist in times of economic crisis, supporting
India's squeezed lower middle classes. But in the cash-strapped
1840s, the British saw these land grants as fraudulent devices which
nefarious native elites used to undermine the Company's power.
Commissions and inquiries were set up to look into supposedly
corrupt land claims, and taxes increased where the legitimacy of a
claim to revenue-free land could not be proved.[8]

In western India a commission was set up to look into landhold-
ing around Dharwad, near Hubli, in the southern Maratha lands
in 1843, and later extended to the whole of Bombay presidency.
Thirty-five thousand plots of land were investigated by a tribunal
of three European officers, sitting day after day making quick

judgment about who owned what and how much they should pay in taxes. By 1847, 20,000 plots were declared to be held illegally. The government did not have the power to put these paper decisions into practice. Only 23,334 rupees was ordered for immediate resumption, half of the total sum identified as fraudulently lost to the public coffers. But the effect on local opinion was profound. By 1856, a visiting British officer found the district 'in a very excitable and discontented frame of mind' because of the commission's work. The following year the landholders of Dharwad were still angry. Most stayed nominally loyal to the East India Company throughout the rebellion, but their submission was extracted by fear not affection, particularly by the presence of a detachment of European troops and the brutal, exemplary execution of a small number of men suspected of plotting insurrection. Outside Dharwad town the region was in open revolt, as bands of insurgent leaders toured the countryside enlisting soldiers in the rebel army. The first Indian commentator on the causes of the revolt argued that the resumption of revenue-free land was the insurrection's greatest cause.[9]

The Company did not only attempt to dispossess potential challengers in British-ruled territory. It also affected the British attitude to 'native states' throughout South Asia. The conquests of the 1800s and 1810s had not completed the East India Company's subordination of Indian territory. Well into the 1840s a third of India was still governed by sovereigns who retained their independence, but had to suffer the close attention of a British Resident, constantly looking out for any sign for conspiracies to undermine the Company's power. Potentially disloyal regimes were dispossessed, and neighbouring land occupied. Punjab, Sindh and Awadh were the most prominent threats. British officers were particularly concerned when a monarch died, and the loyalty of the new incumbent could not be assured. They worried that the death of a prince without a natural heir gave groups of people opposed to British rule an opportunity to conspire. These moments offered the British the chance to remove the source of threat and consolidate their power. In 1834 the Court of Directors had allowed the Company in India to annex the territories of heirless rulers, a process accelerated after 1847 when a new, more aggressive Governor-General, Lord Dalhousie, took charge. Dalhousie talked about 'the idea of a homogeneous Indian peninsula'. He imagined the British would only be safe if they were the sole sovereign power. In the eight years he was in charge, Dalhousie annexed more than any other single Governor-General, a quarter of a million square miles.[10]

Maratha states were particularly vulnerable to the rigid application of what became known as 'the doctrine of lapse'. The reduced regime of Satara was the last possession of the direct heirs of the Maratha warrior-king Shivaji. Given its historic prestige, the British always saw Satara as a centre of possible opposition. Reports about its raja manoeuvring against the Company had inspired John Malcolm's fear of the collapse of British power in 1828, at the time of the Moro Raghunath case. Twenty years later the death of the last king of Satara was followed by a minor rebellion and the Company decided to take over, sending the king's family into exile. The same thing happened at Jhansi five years later, when Raja Gangadhar Rao died childless. His wife, Rani Lakshmibhai, was given a pension of 60,000 rupees but evicted from her husband's ancestral fort along with the young boy she had adopted. Lakshmibhai became one of the most notable rebel leaders. As famous was Nana Sahib, the adopted son of the last Peshwa. Despite frantic lobbying in Calcutta and London Nana Sahib was denied a pension by the Company, and went on to lead the fight against the British in the northern city of Kanpur.

The same kind of paranoia drove the British desire to consolidate power on the frontiers of Company territory. The invasions of Sikh-ruled Punjab in the west and Burma in the east were promulgated by fears about neighbouring states plotting ferment in British-ruled lands. Tension grew in Punjab during the succession struggle that followed the death of the founder of the Sikh empire, Maharaja Ranjit Singh, in 1839. Conflict had broken out between Punjab's

Persian-speaking royal court and middle-class Punjabi-speaking soldiers who claimed to act on behalf of the collective body of armed Sikh men, the *khalsa*. The British thought the rise of the *khalsa* threatened their own territories. Sikh soldiers thought the British were planning to invade Punjab. The first Anglo-Sikh war of 1845–6 ended with British victory, the Sikh state's partial dismemberment and growing resentment at British involvement in Punjab's affairs. The second Anglo-Sikh war began when British officers were attacked by anxious troops in Multan. Company soldiers began to seize forts in Punjab, Sikh soldiers starting fighting in response and local chiefs supported heavily armed locals instead of an alien power. Dalhousie described what happened: '[t]he question was for us no longer one of policy or expediency, but one of national safety. Accordingly, the Government put forward its power.' British power was asserted in a 'struggle severe and anxious', a short and brutal war in which few prisoners were taken on either side. Punjab became a British province in March 1849, and Dalhousie was promoted to the British peerage, from Earl to Marquess.[11]

Three years after the annexation of Punjab, Dalhousie's government went to war with Burma. Again, conflict grew as a neighbouring state showed signs of hostility to the expansion of British power. When merchants were harassed and the Burmese government did not demonstrate appropriate respect, the British invaded in 1852. Echoing the language of the British participants at Plassey in 1757 or the Maratha wars of the early 1800s, Dalhousie argued that 'dread is the only real security we can ever have . . . for stable peace with the Burman state.' The Company wanted to fight until 'the Burman Court and the Burman people alike have shown that they now dread our power'. War led to the assimilation of the southern half of Burma into Britain's Indian empire. It also sparked bitter condemnation from liberals in Britain.

The Manchester industrialist and MP Richard Cobden ridiculed Dalhousie's belief that war against such a puny power was necessary. Cobden thought British public opinion was driven by the desire to

seek revenge against previous humiliation. Britons supported conquest in India 'so long as [it was] believed to be profitable'. His 1853
pamphlet *How Wars Are Got Up in India* proved it wasn't, and ended
with a prediction. '[D]eeds of violence, fraud and injustice' would be
repaid with a violent penalty. Cobden recognized something later
historians have missed, that violence in India was driven by passion
as much as reason, by a sense of the need for retribution against past
wrongs as much as a desire to advance clearly calculated interests.
His aim was to rouse 'the national conscience', to avert 'by timely
atonement and reparation, the punishment due for imperial crimes'.[12]

There was no such atonement. The final annexation took
place in Awadh in 1856, in the last days of Dalhousie's years as
Governor-General. Awadh occupied a rough square of territory 250 miles across centred on Lucknow, the city where Sir
Henry Lawrence was to lose his life. Since the late eighteenth
century, Awadh's practical autonomy had been steadily restricted
in the interests of the East India Company's security. An army
was imposed and revenue demanded to pay for it. When rulers
resisted, as Nawab Wazir Ali did in 1798, territory was occupied
by the British. In 1801, the half of Awadh which lay between the
Jamuna and Ganges rivers was annexed by the Company. For the
next fifty-five years this shrunken province stayed intact, but its
government was trapped between increasingly powerful local
landholders and British networks of power. Awadh became a major
source of soldiers for the East India Company's army, as 40,000
troops were recruited from the province. And the province bought
an increasingly large quantity of British goods. Hemmed in by
these imperial networks, Nawab Wajid Ali Shah, sovereign from
1847, ended up with little room for political manoeuvre. Instead
of exercising governmental power, he retreated into the world
of culture and sought to construct an autonomous life in music,
poetry and theatre. Seen as an overly sensuous lush by his British
critics, Wajid Ali Shah was one of nineteenth-century India's most
important artistic innovators, reviving the *khatak* style of Indian

dance, founding a music school and writing some of the first plays in the Urdu language.[13]

All but a few British officers were unsympathetic. William Sleeman, appointed as Resident to Awadh in 1848, described the province as 'a scene of intrigue, corruption, depravity, neglect of duty and abuse of authority'. Lucknow, he argued, was 'an over-grown city, surrounding an overgrown court, which has, for the last half century, exhausted all the resources of this fine country'. Sleeman believed Wajid Ali Shah's court had 'alienated the feel-ings of the great body of the people'. Before his appointment to Awadh, Sleeman had been in charge of the government department concerned with catching dacoits and 'thugs': the word originally referred to criminals the British believed were members of a reli-gious cult. There, he developed a particularly suspicious frame of mind. He 'was ever on the look-out to capture a thief'. A British critic described him as an 'able and zealous officer', but also 'the emissary of a foregone conclusion'. Those words were written by Captain Robert Bird, a refined and well-connected officer in the Bengal army whose fluent Persian led to his appointment as Sleeman's assistant. Sleeman accused Bird of spending too much time buying and selling horses, and being too friendly with the Nawab, and had him transferred to Punjab. Bird felt Sleeman's investigation was prejudiced. He collected evidence to prove that Sleeman's portrayal of social breakdown could not be accurate. If British-ruled districts were so much better off than Awadh, why did peasants not move there, he asked? If they had become so badly alienated from their rulers people would have fled Awadh, and there was no evidence they had.[14]

Sleeman's biggest criticism was that the King of Awadh presided over a state of war and anarchy which threatened to spill out into British lands. The level of violence in Awadh was certainly high. In the 1850s an average of 628 people were killed each year, a murder rate comparable to that of present-day South Africa. But most of this violence occurred in the process of tax collection, as Awadh's government tried to collect land revenue needed to pay money demanded by the Company. As Sleeman's successor admitted, death had not arisen from ordinary crime or disorder, but from 'faction fights' and 'collisions' between revenue collectors and landholders. The scale of violence does not show that Wajid Ali Shah's court had abandoned order for the sake of drunken revelry, quite the reverse in fact. Awadh's government was trying to assert its own authority over the province's society by violent means. Because its power had become so closely entangled with the Company it lost the capacity to persuade powerful social groups to submit to its authority without using force.

The last annexation took place on 30 January 1856. Wajib Ali Shah was asked to sign over his state to the East India Company, he refused, and it was forcefully taken away. But the king did not rebel. Worried about the consequences of resistance, he asked his subjects to stay loyal to the British. Instead, he travelled to Calcutta with the intention of going on to London to plead his case before Queen Victoria. Wajid Ali Shah persuaded Robert Bird to leave the East India Company's service and become his agent, with a view to sending him to London to lobby Parliament and the British press for the return of his lands. Bird arrived in London, but only a senior queen and one son accompanied him from the Nawab's family. The British incarcerated Wajid Ali Shah until six months after the rebellion ended. Once they had deposed him, the Company tried to impose their authority on the war-torn countryside more emphatically than even Wajid Ali's government had done. Awadh's landholders were dispossessed and a revenue survey started to collect tax directly from peasants. Throughout 1856 and the first half of the next year, British officers suffered constant attacks, and the Company found revenue impossible to collect until, in June 1857, the scale of rebel violence forced them to flee the countryside entirely.[15]

The governed not the governing class

British commentators on the events of 1857–8 sometimes imagined the rebellion was driven by the rage of recently dispossessed kings and aristocrats, whether Maratha princes or Awadhi *taluqdars* (landlords). It is easy to misunderstand the impact of these evictions and annexations. As the 'loyalist' Indian Muslim leader Sayyid Ahmad Khan argued, it was 'the governed not the governing class' who rebelled. Sayyid Ahmad Khan's perspective is worth paying attention to. From a Pathan family of Mughal officials, he grew up around the Mughal court and was employed as a government officer from 1838. He lived through the rebellion itself in rebel-held Bijnor. A historian and poet, Sayyid Ahmed's writings before 1857 barely acknowledged the British. It was possible to live as a member of the northern Indian gentry without paying much attention to British power. The insurrection changed that, making Sayyid Ahmed believe he had no choice but to deal with the British. His pamphlet *The Causes of the Indian Revolt*, published in Urdu from Agra in 1858, was the first Indian account of the rebellion. Sayyid Ahmed went on to become an advocate of Indian Muslim engagement with western science and a supporter of British rule, for which he received a knighthood, becoming Sir Sayyid. His loyalty, though, was complicated and partial. It was a strategy for coping with the defeat of Muslim power in India rather than a decision born from active love for British rule. Some of his relatives joined the insurgency, as many of his colleagues in the Company's service did. But Sayyid Ahmad thought rebellion was the work of a disorderly mob who could not create a stable regime. Perhaps he also recognized that though rebel victory would not dent his chances of continuing in government service, joining the insurgency would end his career if the British won. 'The mutineers were for the most part men who had nothing to lose,' he wrote, and Sayyid Ahmed himself had a lot.[16]

Sayyid Ahmed argued that the insurrection was not a campaign by feudal magnates to restore their lost principalities. After all, the King of Awadh thought that appealing to Queen Victoria was a better way to restore his control of Awadh than a full-scale revolt. Most large landholders equivocated before joining the insurrection. Some of the greatest rebel leaders, Rani Lakshmibhai of Jhansi, for example, only turned into rebels very later in the revolt, when their loyalty was challenged by the British. The insurrection was led by north India's dislocated lower middle classes. The proclamations of rebel leaders particularly called upon soldiers, clerics, artisans, petty officers, minor landlords and merchants to join the revolt. These were not the Mughal elite, but men who benefited from the institutions the Mughal regime and its successors sustained. Before 1857 they flourished in the spaces which India's pre-colonial regimes left open for self-rule. Few had been hostile to the British to begin with. As Sayyid Ahmed argued, the revolt was not an effort 'to throw off the yoke of foreigners'.

In the northern Indian provinces where the revolt was eventually fiercest, the British had begun their rule by promising to be impartial, not taxing too much, offering security for trade during troubled times and providing a major source of employment for soldiers and officials. They did not introduce peace and stability and were too arrogant to listen to their subjects well enough, but north India's middle classes imagined the British might be taught how better to exercise their power. But as the Company's sway expanded across the whole of the subcontinent, British paranoia grew and power was asserted with ever-greater force. Lord Dalhousie's annexations and wars of conquest made belief in British benevolence impossible to sustain. As the historian F. W. Buckler argued almost a century ago, the insurgents of 1857 believed the British, not they, had overturned legitimate political order.[17]

Soldiers faced the power of the British most directly. That is why they were the first to revolt. According to Sayyid Ahmad Khan, the pride of Indian troops had grown as the Company acquired more and more land. 'It is we', an early soldiers' proclamation declared, 'who have conquered the whole territory extending from Calcutta to Kabul for the English, because they did not bring any English army with them from England.' But these soldiers felt humiliated just as their pride grew. As British territory expanded so pay shrank, as troops had less opportunity to earn the allowance for working in foreign territory they had previously been entitled to. Army discipline became more severe. And since January 1857, a rumour had started to circulate that the cartridges used to fill their rifles contained cow and pig fat. In fact, animal grease was quickly withdrawn. Soldiers were allowed to buy their own grease and test the paper in water to ensure it did not contain oil. As Kim Wagner notes, 'not a single greased cartridge was ever distributed to the sepoys'. But the soldiers saw the British response to their anxieties as irrationally violent, proof perhaps that there was a conspiracy to undermine their way of life. Protests in Bengal in April led to the hanging of isolated rebels, and the disbanding of regiments. On 4 May, fires began to be lit at the cantonment in Ambala in Punjab, and the regiment there was instantly disarmed. When a section of the Meerut garrison refused to use the new cartridges at the end of April, eighty-five of them were court-martialled and sentenced to ten years' hard labour. On 9 May, their comrades were forced to watch as the reluctant soldiers were stripped, shackled and marched off in chains to begin their sentences. Prostitutes in the marketplace taunted those soldiers still under British orders: 'If you had an atom of manhood in you, go and release them,' they are reported to have said. In another story, respectable women asked the soldiers for their arms: 'we shall fight and liberate the brave officers [instead]', they said. The cowardly troops were asked to 'keep inside the home and put on bangles'. Humiliation of this kind could not be borne for long.[18]

On the morning of 10 May, rumours circulated that the garrison at Meerut would mutiny. Indian servants insisted their European masters stay at home. At dusk a cavalry regiment rode out to free imprisoned comrades. One of the infantry regiments followed. A third regiment was agitated but wavered. Colonel Finnis, their

British commander, implored them to put down their arms. A shot, perhaps fired by accident, went off, which injured his horse. Finnis was then blasted at close range by a soldier from one of the regiments that had already mutinied. Frightened they would be hanged for murder, the rest of the garrison believed they had no choice but to join the rebellion. Finnis's death was followed by the killing of three other British officers, eight women and eight children. Mutineers on horseback rode to Delhi. Others rode into the countryside, spreading violence into the villages around Meerut. Soldiers had talked for weeks beforehand about resisting the cartridges. But the first spark of rebellion was not the product of a long-term plan. It was sparked by soldiers' fears about the brutal consequences of British power.[19]

For eleven days Meerut and Delhi were the only garrisons that mutinied, creating a short-lived belief among the British that the uprising would quickly be quelled. After all, plenty of similar mutinies had been suppressed quickly in the past. The difference now was that thousands of civilians in the surrounding towns and countryside quickly took up arms. At Meerut, the *kotwal*, or head of the city police, sided with the rebels, and quickly freed a small number of prisoners in the gaol before fleeing himself. The remaining 839 prisoners were liberated later by the crowd, 'yelling and shouting, and vociferating savage denunciations of vengeance on all Europeans', as one observer put it. Those Britons who could barricaded themselves into the garrison's ammunition storehouse, but forty Europeans were killed at Meerut in a night of violence and panic. The mutinying soldiers were mostly Brahmins, but urban celebrations involved large numbers of Muslims, particularly Shia, as groups roamed the streets chanting 'Ali, Ali, our religion has revived'. This was an uprising of butchers and weavers, cooks and grass cutters, aided by the almost instant defection of the police to the mutineers' side, with a large number of liberated prisoners joining in, too. The same social groups participated in the revolt once it reached Delhi. Rebel cavalrymen arrived from Meerut early in the morning of 11 May, burning the city's eastern toll-house and the telegraph office. Within hours, crowds of lower-middle-class Delhi residents had formed a mob. Delhi's elite had a disdainful attitude to this band of *badmashes*, or ruffians. 'No person from a decent family was a part of this crowd of rioters,' one Mughal courtier wrote. '[T]he respectable people were all locked inside their houses.'[20]

The mutiny of 1857 quickly turned into a peasants' revolt as well. As Eric Stokes wrote, 'rural disturbance at first outpaced military mutiny'. At Meerut most of the police were Gujars, belonging to a community of cattle herders who had a reputation for their war-like behaviour but particularly suffered from the Company's high taxation. Gujar leaders organized bands of men to attack centres of prosperity and power, creating what British observers described as 'anarchy'. The British presence at Sikrandabad, forty miles south of Meerut, was attacked on 12 May. By that date, Sayyid Ahmad Khan reported that it was impossible to travel on the roads of Bijnor, forty-five miles north-west of the rebellion's epicentre, without being attacked.

Amid this growing insurgency of soldiers, peasants and artisans, the revolt did have one very significant noble backer. Emperor Bahadur Shah Zafar had long felt humiliated by the British effort to limit his power and to snuff out the last traces of Mughal authority. When the mutineers arrived in Delhi, they sought Bahadur Shah Zafar's support, which was quickly offered. In doing so Zafar did not seek political power as we would normally understand it. A philosopher and poet rather than a political leader, Zafar saw the insurrection as an opportunity to restore a Mughal system of government and exact retribution for the dishonourable way he had been treated by the British. His purpose was not to augment his own capacity to command. Bahadur Shah Zafar shaped the rebel government, making sure sepoy leaders were not displaced by nobles, but he did not direct it. Instead, he provided moral sanction for the new regime, then tried to use his authority to direct it away from excessive violence.[21]

With Zafar's support, the circulation of insurgents between towns in northern India intensified. A second wave of garrison uprisings occurred in late May and early June. On 20 May part of the army rebelled at Agra, the capital of the North Western Provinces, but was quickly disarmed by European soldiers. Soldiers in the cantonments of Lucknow and Muttra rose up on 30 May. The garrison at Bareilly, capital of the Afghan-dominated region of Rohilkhand, revolted the following day. Kanpur (called Cawnpore by the British at the time) mutinied on 5 June, and British soldiers took refuge in an entrenchment at the north of the town. Nana Sahib, the adopted son of the last Maratha Peshwa, lived at Bithoor, fifteen miles away. The day after the Kanpur mutiny he declared his support for the uprising and sought the backing of the Emperor Bahadur Shah Zafar.

After two weeks of sustained bombardment, Nana Sahib offered safe passage to the British at Kanpur on 25 June, but the British men were massacred as they boarded boats onto the Ganges two days later, probably because the sepoys had become increasingly frightened about being attacked themselves. On 15 July, 200 British women and children were shot and butchered as a British army led by General Henry Havelock approached in an effort to recapture Kanpur. It was this 'Cawnpore massacre' that defined the horror of 1857 for generations of Britons afterwards. 'Remember Cawnpore!' became the cry during the war of reconquest. The massacres occurred at the lowest point of British power. With the exception of a few besieged residencies and cantonments, the East India Company's authority had been extinguished from a vast swathe of territory between Patna in the east and Patiala in the west. Beyond that territory, British survival relied on embattled garrisons surrounded by people happy to submit to a rebel regime.

These massacres show that 1857 was far more than a political conflict for the insurgents. It was a struggle for survival. As historian Faisal Devji argues, the rebels were concerned above all to protect the distinctions that constituted Indian social life. At the core of Indians' sense of self in the eighteenth and early nineteenth centuries was their membership of groups which distinguished them from their neighbours. These groups were defined in different ways, by caste, occupation, gender and geography. For many of the rebels, though, religion provided a common denominator, a way to articulate the sense an individual had of belonging to a particular way of life they would fight to protect. Religious belonging depended on shared practices rather than beliefs. Friendship across community divisions depended on respect for different customs. Culinary habits were particularly important. North Indian society held together because everyone respected that Brahmins refused to eat food that was not cooked by other Brahmins, Hindus refused beef and Muslims rejected pork. Forcing everyone to eat the same foodstuffs would annihilate the distinctions that each individual's status and honour relied on, and in doing so erode the very fabric of Indian social life.

The one element that cut through all rebel statements was the fear that the Company was making everyone eat the same food together, and so corrode the most fundamental character of Indian life. Joint messing, in prison or the army, was a particular target of criticism in rebel proclamations. The rebels rose up seeking autonomy from a domineering power which they thought wanted to turn them into an undifferentiated, statusless mass. This was certainly a war fought for independence, but it was fought in fervent opposition to the idea that Indians shared a common culture or nationality. Against the supposed British attempt to flatten difference and create unity, rebel proclamations emphasized Indian plurality, in the name of 'the Hindus and Musalmans of Hindustan'.[22]

British officers thought the concern about animal fat was ridiculous. But Indian fears reflected an accurate understanding of British desires, if not the practical realities of Company rule. Take religion, for example. Among Britons in India, evangelical Christianity was on the rise in the 1840s and 1850s. Most British officers probably did think India's Muslims and Hindus were infidels who would suffer eternal damnation if they did not convert. Proselytizing pamphlets had been circulated with greater frequency, even in cantonments. European religion and the British government seemed to occupy the same space, as the 1830s and 1840s saw new churches built in cantonments, often bringing the centres of British worship and British power within a few yards of each other. The British did talk about subjugating the whole of India to a single, unitary form of power, even if they saw the East India Company as a decidedly secular kind of authority. The Company wanted to introduce a single set of laws and create a system of communications, steamships, telegraph, roads and railways which would make their government more secure by annihilating distance and difference.

The British did not try to convert Indians to one religion. Most officials were extremely anxious about any hint of official support for evangelism. A story circulated that the Governor-General, Dalhousie contributed money to missionary organizations in India. Lord Ellenborough, President of the Board of Control, described the news as 'one of the most dangerous things which could have happened to the security of our government in India', a rumour that could be the cause of 'the most bloody revolution which has at any time occurred in India'. In the minds of most Britons, the conquest of territory or imposition of new laws was a separate matter from the conversion of Indians to Christianity. But with no place for conversation with Europeans, lower middle-class Indians did not know that.[23]

Sayyid Ahmad Khan knew there was no government plan to Christianize India, but his account of the revolt was a damning indictment of a regime whose way of working allowed such misunderstandings to grow. The British, he said, had no regard for the 'characteristics' or 'daily habits' of the people they ruled. 'Our Government never knew what troubles each succeeding sun might bring with it to its subjects, or what sorrow might fall upon them with the night.' The consequence was that 'Hindustanees fell

into the habit of thinking that all laws were passed with a view
to degrade and ruin them, and to deprive them and their fellows
of their religion.' The 'real cause' of the revolt was the absence of
conversation between the Company and its subjects. In particular,
Sayyid Ahmed blamed the fact that the 'people do not have a voice
in Government's councils'.

Sayyid Ahmed was not talking about the flow of abstract information through official inquiries and surveys, nor did he think a
free press made any difference. For him, politics was personal. Good
government relied on face-to-face conversation between people
who were not afraid of each other. It depended on the existence
of 'common friendship ... which springs from the heart' between
ruler and ruled. Sayyid Ahmed repeated the complaint that men
and women familiar with Mughal idioms of government had made
against the Company for a long time. The British did not cultivate
the friendship of Indians. They kept themselves apart. They refused
to live among the people they ruled. They spoke with contempt and
ill temper to their subjects. Even the most senior Indian officials were
abused. It was 'well-known to Government [that] even natives of
the highest rank never come into the presence of officials, but with
an inward fear and trembling'. The disastrous result of this was that
Indians connected law, religion and conquest with a single image of
British force intent on subjugating every distinction of Indian society
under British power. As one Muslim in Sayyid Ahmed's town of
Bijnor asked, 'what ease have we, they are always inventing new laws
to trouble us, and to overturn our religion'. If British rule continued,
'there would be no difference between Mahomedans and Hindoos,
and whatever they said, we should have to do'.[24]

Badshahi Sarkar

The rebels sought relief in the restoration of a Mughal empire.
Despite British efforts to diminish the prestige of the descendants
of Timur, Mughal allegiances remained strong through most of the

subcontinent. Up to 1857, soldiers fighting for the British had been commanded by a Company that, nominally in its own eyes, was a vassal of the emperor. The sovereignty of the empire was proclaimed in the *qasbah* towns of north India as the mantra *khalq khuda ka / mulk badshahi ka / hukm kampani bahadur ka* (creation belongs to God, the country is the emperor's and administration the Company's) was shouted to beating drums. As Meerut's cavalrymen put it in their first message to the emperor, 'the English have been ruling on your behalf'.

Once the insurrection spread, petty lords and great kings rose up alike claiming they were vassals of Bahadur Shah, sending anxious letters to Delhi asking to be confirmed in their possessions, often using the moment to dispossess local rivals. This was as true for Hindu Rajputs and Marathas as much as former Mughal officials, even for kings who had thrown off Mughal authority before 1857. The rulers of Awadh had declared their independence from Mughal power in an elaborate ceremony held in 1819, where the Nawab was converted into a Padshah, or emperor: the British merely called him King. But when the Lucknow garrison revolted and returned power to the old court, the mutineers demanded the new Awadh regime declare its allegiance to the Mughal emperor once again. The new rebel Nawab, Wajid Ali Shah's young son Qadir Birjis, declared he ruled merely as a provincial governor of the Mughal empire. With the submission of both the Nawab of Awadh and the man claiming to be Peshwa to the emperor's authority, the rebellion tried to recreate the exact constitutional form of the Mughal empire as it existed in the early eighteenth century.[25]

This return of Mughal authority was supposed to replace the aloof British regime with an empire based on friendship and conversation. In many places, those conversations took new forms. Old Mughal officers like the *kotwal* and *kazi* returned alongside new, more plebeian councils and courts, where troops particularly had a voice. The insurrection began with fierce debates between soldiers in garrisons, and the restored Mughal regime was not going to suppress the conversation its existence relied on. In Delhi, the rebels created a court of administration, 'a sort of military junta', where six elected soldiers met with four representatives of the palace to talk and decide about the life of the city. To begin with, the court's president was Bakht Khan, an officer (like the man Henry Lawrence had spoken to in May 1857) from the artillery corps who had served in the Company's army for forty years. In practice the court was constantly harassed by Delhi's princes, and found it impossible to speak with a single common voice. In Lucknow, the mutineers decided to elect a new king, but two factions, which divided the infantry and cavalry regiments from one another, backed different claimants. Eventually, Birjis Qadir, the twelve-year-old son of Wajid Ali Shah, was chosen. But Lucknow's military council retained effective control. The democratic sentiments of the mutineers meant a clear line of command only came into being when the approach of General Henry Havelock's army created a mood of urgency.[26]

Throughout the months in which the Badshahi Sarkar (the emperor's government), ruled, the Mughal regime existed as an ideal more than a political reality. In Delhi itself the Emperor Bahadur Shah Zafar tried to put the Mughal idea of ensuring a balance between different communities and interests into practice. He attempted to protect Europeans from massacre, ensured Muslims did not kill cows and insisted that both soldiers and nobles were represented on the government's council. The emperor asserted that the Mughal regime was not fighting an Islamic war. When a group of Sufi Maulvis tried to fly the green standard of holy war on Delhi's largest mosque, the Jama Masjid, Bahadur had it taken down, saying that 'such a jehad was quite impossible and an act of extreme folly, for the majority of the Purbea [ex-Company] soldiers were Hindus'. But these efforts to balance and incorporate depended on the moral aura of Zafar's physical presence, not the emperor's construction of an effective form of conciliatory practice. The emperor could not insist on any kind of order or hierarchy beyond the city walls of

Delhi. Outside the capital the Badshahi government was a system of independent franchises. Leaders who fought in the name of the emperor were driven by different motivations, and put very different styles of political rule into practice. The history of the rebellion showed the enduring power of the ideal of Mughal sovereignty. But it also demonstrated that a century of war and Company government had destroyed the practical authority of Mughal institutions. With their demise, the memory of how the different communities and interests of India could coexist without serious social fracture had been annihilated. Eighteen fifty-seven brought together groups of armed men to fight against the same enemy with radically different political visions.[27]

One vision, articulated by a significant minority of rebels, saw the war as an attempt to eradicate the rule of infidels and create a polity able to sustain a regenerated version of Islam. In the early nineteenth century this kind of politics was nurtured on the fringes of British power, in kingdoms beyond the borders of the East India Company's regime such as Afghanistan or in princely states under British 'protection' such as Tonk, Hyderabad or even Hindu-ruled Gwalior. Here, political radicals linked up with sufi saints to offer an ethical alternative to British power.

The most famous sufi radical of 1857 was Maulavi Ahmadullah. A tall, muscular man with 'beetle brows' and an aquiline nose, Ahmadullah was the son of a south Indian nobleman who was educated in Hyderabad and spent some time in London as a young man. After studying the arts of war Ahmadullah became a disciple of a sufi master near Amir Khan's old centre of power at Tonk, in Rajasthan. In the 1830s and 1840s Ahmadullah lived in the princely state of Gwalior, a centre of anti-British organization. He was present when British security concerns forced Gwalior to disband its army, a moment of humiliation which may have strengthened his desire to challenge British power. From the early 1850s, Ahmadullah began to travel throughout northern India to preach holy war to evict the British from India. At Agra he lived in a palace but wore the clothes of a faqir, a Muslim holy man, meditating and holding his breath to demonstrate his physical prowess at prayer meetings. Ahmadullah used music to attract support, holding parties in the evening where members of the town's Muslim middle classes would gather to hear *qawwali*, or sufi devotional songs, to build support for jihad. 'He is a dervish only in name, actually he is a prince and is preparing the masses to wage a war against the government,' one British officer asserted.[28]

Ahmadullah's move from nobleman to sufi warlord marked a more fundamental transition, particularly in his relationship to authority. The power of Sufi leaders was based on popular support rather than government patronage. They acquired money and recruited followers from the people who listened to them rather than relying on official backing. Consequently, they were less vulnerable to the corrosion of India's Muslim political hierarchy than other religious leaders. During the uprising, Ahmadullah thought his purpose was to lead a popular uprising that would renew Islam, not restore a political order he thought was decaying. His style was prophetic rather than authoritarian, based on a passionate denunciation of British crimes, a reputation for invincibility and a wariness, verging on paranoia, about aristocratic plots which might derail the uprising.

The relatives of the last Nawab of Awadh saw the rebellion in a different light, using it as a way to restore the authority of the region's time-honoured rulers. The conflict between the two groups in Awadh was a battle between demagoguery and aristocratic authority, a clash between a movement that renounced worldly goods in the name of moral renewal and a form of statecraft wanting to re-establish a traditional political order based on wealth and patronage. After a particularly impressive victory against the British, the prince offered his spiritual allegiance to Ahmadullah, agreeing that the whole army should be placed in the Maulvi's hands. But Ahmadullah demanded the prince's officers only join his army if they renounced their wealth. The two sides went their separate ways again. It was not the last time a leader who had freed himself from worldly possessions would claim to lead India's masses against British power.

Relying on nothing more than his ability to persuade men to follow him, Ahmadullah survived far longer than other rebel rulers. Once both Bahadur Shah Zafar in Delhi and Birjis Qadir in Lucknow were defeated, Ahmadullah retreated in March 1858 to the rebel heartland of Rohilkhand, 200 miles north-west of Lucknow. He was captured in July 1858 after a local raja betrayed him. The raja had Ahmadullah blown up by a cannon, then cut his head from the remains of his body to hand to the British Collector in exchange for a reward of 50,000 rupees. The head was put on a stick and displayed outside the newly restored British government's office.[29]

Pragmatic radicals

Maulvi Ahmadullah's prophetic visions were very different from the reasons which drove Nawab Mahmud Khan to take part in the uprising, although the story had a similar end for both. Mahmud Khan was leader of the insurgency at Najibabad, a small town 120 miles or four days' ride north-east of Delhi in the district of Bijnor where Sayyid Ahmad Khan was stationed. Like Sayyid Ahmad Khan, Mahmud Khan was a descendant of Afghans who had come to north India with the Persian conqueror Nader Shah and then settled in the area where the north Indian plain meets the foothills of the Himalayas. If Ahmadullah was an enthusiastic opponent of British power, Mahmud Khan was a reluctant rebel.

When mutinous soldiers first sought his support, Mahmud Khan sent them away, telling them they could 'make trouble' near the district capital of Bijnor as long as they left him alone. The first weeks of June saw the East India Company's authority in the district challenged by gangs of rebels throughout the countryside. When he decided to leave Bijnor, the British Collector chose to hand the government's buildings and property, including 109,430 rupees in cash and 38,000 in stamped paper, to Mahmud for safekeeping. Mahmud arrived to meet the British collector 'wringing his hands and making a very sad face' at the growing power of the insurgents, according to Sayyid Ahmad. By the end of the month he had plumped for the rebels' side and used it to strengthen his power. He moved money from the Company's treasury to his own fort twenty miles away, and replaced British-appointed officers with his own staff. By the middle of July, the Mughal emperor formally invested Mahmud Khan with the title of Nawab, and the town criers of Bijnor had begun to cry *Khalq khoda ka, mulk badshah ka, hukm Nawab Mahmud Khan ka*: the people belong to God, the country to the king and administration to Mahmud Khan.[30]

Mahmud Khan's regime tried emphatically to return to Mughal patterns of rule. Sayyid Ahmad Khan reported that he had developed an 'obsession with displaying at least some of signs of royal rule, and wiping out the chief symbols of the Government's authority', altering the weights and measures ordered by the Company's government, for example. But the formal trappings of Mughal administration did not give Mahmud unbridled power. His regime alienated local landlords, and these men began to challenge him. Mahmud's troops started to raid and ransack the forts of 'troublemakers'. As it escalated, violence polarized along religious lines, as Mahmud's largely Muslim officers fought largely Hindu rural elites. Fear and a desire for revenge grew, as retaliatory violence intensified. 'This hatred', Sayyid Ahmad Khan noted, 'became so bitter that no one could put any credence in what Muslims said about Hindus, and vice versa.' What began as a political battle turned into a religious war with Hindus massacring Muslim confectioners and cloth-printers in the town of Haldaur, and Muslims ransacking and killing anyone they could find in Hindu temples. Mahmud Khan ended up fighting beneath a Muslim flag. Sayyid Ahmad Khan believed this was mere opportunistic pragmatism. The Nawab's men, he said, chose to leave Muslims unharmed as a 'matter of political expediency, for the wretches were only interested in keeping the Muslims on their side'.

Calcutta is quite safe

Despite the often limited coherence of rebel forces, the British response to any threat of insurgency was usually to retreat to their few fortified citadels. Europeans abandoned their collectorates and business houses for the nearest fort, seeking protection behind thick walls and guns commanded by soldiers with white skins. The summer of 1857 saw British officials and their entourages packing up their instruments of government and abandoning the courts and revenue offices scattered around the small European settlements of India's dispersed district capitals, often long before rebels arrived. The British retreat from Bijnor on 7 June was one of the earliest flights. Had the Collector stayed, Mahmud Khan might have remained on the British side. At Tirhoot, at the other, eastern, end of the zone under insurgent control, indigo planters fled their estates in early July, moving to the East India Company's station at Muzaffarnagar. Eighty men, thirty women and forty children crammed themselves into two houses. All but two of the British civil stations in Bihar had been abandoned by the beginning of August even though the province saw very little fighting. Gorakhpur, near the border with Nepal, was abandoned on 13 August, despite the only sign of insurrection being a small 'poorly armed rabble'. The speed of British retreat turned ambivalent leaders into rebels and hastened the spread of the revolt.[31]

Panic was rife even in places far from the main centres of revolt. Indian soldiers refused to use the new cartridges at two garrisons near Calcutta, Barrackpore and Berhampore, but they were quickly disarmed. Pro-British Indian observers were sure there were sufficient European soldiers to protect the city's European inhabitants. But Calcutta's British residents imagined conspiracies were being hatched at every corner to overthrow their power. The exiled Emperor of Awadh, Wajid Ali Shah, living by then in an unarmed palace in Calcutta's southern suburb of Metiya Burg, was the favourite demon figure of British fantasy. Once rebellion broke out in Lucknow, Europeans imagined him to be conspiring with disbanded soldiers to murder them in their beds. 'Calcutta is quite safe – although the magnates of Chowringhee don't think so,' the Indian liberal journalist Girish Chunder Ghose wrote. On 9 June Ghose noted that the 'ladies and gentlemen' in the British suburb of Ballygunge were so scared they had 'started from their beds at midnight' in a state of panic. In fact, the noise came from 'the festive glee and pyrotechnic wonders' of a wedding party. Five days later Calcutta was affected by more serious panic. Europeans fled to Fort William or took refuge on steamships in response to a rumour that the garrison had revolted again. Late into the night the house belonging to the major in charge of Calcutta's defence was 'besieged by all sorts of people wishing to obtain shelter in the Fort'.[32]

The limits of the insurrection were defined by the distribution of European soldiers. Indian troops mutinied throughout India and beyond, not only in north India but also at Peshawar and Ambala in Punjab, Barrackpore near Calcutta and Chittagong in far south-eastern Bengal, at Madras, Karachi and Bombay, even in the Indian garrison at Singapore. Where the British presence was protected by large detachments of European troops, these garrison mutinies did not spark a broader revolt. Calcutta was defended by two European battalions, with perhaps 2,500 soldiers in total, more than 10 per cent of the total of 22,698 European soldiers in the Company's north Indian army. There was a strong garrison at Dinapur, on the outskirts of Patna, to protect the western frontier of Bengal. At the far north-west of India, in Punjab, soldiers were concentrated to keep the population of a newly conquered and supposedly warlike province in check. Punjab was occupied by eleven battalions of British troops, dispersed between eight garrisons. Because Punjab was seen as the most dangerous place in India it was defended with enough troops to defend British power. By contrast, the Mughal

empire's old Hindustani heartland had scant European troops, with
only one infantry regiment apiece at Lucknow, Meerut and Agra.
Even if the British had responded more quickly to rebellion, these
scattered detachments of about 4,000 soldiers would have been no
match for the perhaps 100,000 sepoys who took up arms against
their employers on north India's plain.

By the end of July 1857 many British officers started to believe
that they could only survive by abandoning the stretch of territory
between Bihar and Punjab where the rebellion was most intense.
The priority was for the Company to keep its capacity to collect
revenue from the fields of eastern India's profitable rivers and deltas.
'For the moment,' the newly appointed Governor-General Charles,
Earl Canning wrote on 8 August, 'everything must give way to the
necessity of arresting rebellion or general disorder below Benares. If
this is not done our slender remains of revenue will be in jeopardy.'
This strategy left embattled enclaves of Britons stranded at Lucknow
and Delhi. British opinion in London demanded that Europeans
besieged in the midst of the insurgency be rescued. Between defence
and rescue, British policy vacillated. Small forces were sent to capture Delhi, Kanpur and Lucknow, but most troops were forced to
sit and wait for the arrival of reinforcements.[33]

The greatest early British triumph happened at Delhi, but this
was an equivocal victory. A small British force pushed its way
from Ambala in Punjab to Delhi soon after the Mughal capital was
captured by rebels. It was joined by a second detachment on 14
August, led by the brutal Ulsterman John Nicholson, a man who
liked to keep the head of a chief he had executed on his desk. In
the years soon after the revolt, the British imagined their assault
was the victory of Nicholson's 'gallant few' fighting against hordes
of zealous 'fanatics'. In *Self-Help*, his 1859 post-mutiny celebration
of British national character, the journalist Samuel Smiles spoke
of 3,700 British-led 'bayonets' defeating an army of 75,000 crazed
Muslim insurgents.

In reality, the victory was much less impressive. The Company possessed 6,800 troops, mostly Indian or Nepali, and there were not many more Mughal soldiers in Delhi. A few Muslim jihadis had arrived throughout July, but they came in small numbers, the last and largest contingent of only 600 coming from Amir Khan's old state of Tonk on 21 July. For the most part Delhi's rebel army had begun to dissipate in the month before the attack, as soldiers went unpaid and supply routes had been blocked by British forces. By the end of July, there were only 10,000 badly equipped, hungry Mughal soldiers left in the old capital. When the British started to shell Delhi six weeks later, many troops and most of Delhi's administrators fled, including the last Mughal chief of police, Gangadhar Nehru, grandfather of independent India's first Prime Minister. By the time the British army marched to the city walls, they probably had a small numerical advantage over the forces they challenged. As usual, the idea of a tiny number of morally superior Britons holding massive Indian forces at bay was a myth. The battle for Delhi was a fight between two starving, demoralized and badly disciplined armies.

The British started to march from their ridge-top position in the middle of the night of 13 September, but their movement was disordered and far slower than planned. To begin with the emperor's troops retained control of Delhi's key sites, the Jama Masjid, Chandni Chowk and the main police station. John Nicholson was fatally wounded. The British lost more than 1,100 men and 60 officers in the first few hours of fighting. Exhausted and disheartened, large numbers of British soldiers broke into liquor shops, absenting themselves from the fight by getting drunk on looted alcohol.

Samuel Smiles described the storming of Delhi as 'the most illustrious event' to occur during the mutiny. He wrote that every member of the 'English race' had been a hero and quoted Captain William Hodson, 'one of the bravest', saying that no other nation would have stood its ground so doggedly. The passage Smiles quoted was written in Hodson's diary before the fighting had even started, when Hodson imagined a great, noble victory was possible.

The reality of war transformed his opinion. After the battle Hodson wrote that it was the first time he saw 'English soldiers refuse repeatedly to follow their officers'. '[T]he troops are utterly demoralized by hard work and hard drink.' Thirty-eight per cent of the British infantry were killed or wounded, with more than half the officers also lost in the fighting. After the first day, the Mughal army could easily have driven the British out of Delhi if an order had been given to counter-attack, but the emperor's forces were themselves fractured. They did not have a single leader, did not share a strong enough sense of common purpose and, unlike the British, had homes in India to return to. After days of street fighting the rebel soldiers retreated in waves, some to fight on elsewhere, others to their families. Only a small contingent surrounding the man who had no home but this defeated city, the Emperor Bahadur Shah Zafar was left to surrender to the British army. Delhi was under British control by 21 September.[34]

The conquest of Delhi created an island of British power at the western end of the rebel-controlled zone. It also ended the rebels' claim to be the heirs of Mughal power. But it did not end the revolt. Awadh remained a rebel stronghold. A force led by Sir Henry Havelock eventually reached Lucknow, but was besieged itself until liberated by an army led by Sir Colin Campbell which arrived on 15 September 1857. Campbell's army relieved the Europeans stranded at the residency but was then forced to retreat, leaving the rebels in charge of Awadh's capital city until March the following year. The human cost of these limited gains was extraordinary. A third of the original Lucknow garrison had died, in addition to 256 soldiers within the relieving force losing their lives.

The reconquest of India only began once 40,000 soldiers arrived from Europe to give the British numerical superiority. As it marched up from Calcutta, the British army gained the support of groups of Indians who had fallen out of favour with rebel forces in each place. In Sayyid Ahmad Khan's Bijnor, for example, the predominantly Hindu landholders whom Mahmud Khan had tried to tax quickly rallied to the British standard. Landlords in Awadh worried about the radicalism of the rebel army and thought the British were more likely to protect their property and supported the Company to.

Despite gathering some degree of elite Indian support, the British reconquest was marked by massive, indiscriminate violence. This violence was not a fine-tuned effort by the British to rebuild power. It had the character of a forward panic, caused by the sudden release of fear and the quick appearance of passive targets on which to take out pent-up feelings of anger.[35]

The desire for vengeance was shared by high officials and junior soldiers, from India to Britain. Exaggerated reports had been transmitted to London about terrible violations and atrocities committed by Indian insurgents, as false tales were circulated about European women 'turned naked into the streets' and 'abandoned to the beastly lusts of the blood-stained rabble', as one early book put it. There was, missionary Alexander Duff wrote, 'some species of hallucination respecting the real condition of affairs here'. The passion these stories excited was extreme. 'I wish I were commander-in-chief in India,' Charles Dickens wrote, 'I should do my utmost to exterminate the Race upon whom the stain of the late cruelties rested.' Thomas Macaulay was unusually reflective about his state of mind. He noted the British nation's 'one terrible cry for revenge' but was, he felt, 'half ashamed only half ashamed, for the craving for vengeance which I feel'. 'I could be very cruel just now if I had power,' Macaulay wrote. He wondered whether 'the severity which springs from a great sensitivity to human suffering' was better than 'lenity which springs from indifference'. As Macaulay debated the intellectual case for and against brutality as a response to rebellion, British officers and soldiers in India were acting out countless varieties of genuine cruelty.[36]

Delhi was one of the most brutal sites of revenge. In the days that followed its capture, 200 suspected rebels were hanged from gallows in the centre of the city without trial. The Emperor Bahadur Shah Zafar had been promised that his life would be saved if he gave himself up. He was captured, found guilty of treason and then exiled to Burma for the rest of his life. His two sons were summarily shot to prevent them being the subjects of a new wave of rebellion. The entire population of Delhi was evicted, and British officials debated demolishing the whole city. In fact, only the structures inside Delhi's Mughal Red Fort were knocked down. But the city was ransacked and plunder given official sanction by the appointment of British prize agents whose job was to collect wealth and divide it in exact proportions among the conquering army. A few notables, able to provide clear evidence of continued loyalty to the British through the short-lived Mughal regime, were given protection tickets and left alone. Without that evidence, dispossession was severe.

The merchant Umed Singh claimed he had suffered during the uprising for the crime of being able to read English and remaining a 'partisan' of the East India Company. After the reconquest, his house was demolished and land dug up to recover buried gold and jewels to the value of 60,000 rupees. This was a personal catastrophe. 'The labour of a whole life, the accumulation of many long years of all of us, is thus knocked on the head,' he said. Already an old man, he was left with nothing to live on in retirement. An Indian observer from nearby Mhow thought the violence of the British reconquest was worse than Nadir Shah's sacking of Delhi 118 years before. 'No one ever thought that the capture of Delhie by Englishmen would be attended with more cruelty to the general population, than that by a Nadir,' wrote Sannat Nana. Trade bounced back, but the dislocation of 1857 permanently killed off Delhi's cultural life. As their sources of patronage were annihilated, musicians and musical connoisseurs, poets and calligraphers went elsewhere seeking work and Delhi's 300-year history as the cultural capital of Mughal India came to a quick end. After 1857 Delhi was a very different city.[37]

British violence was driven by the 'anguish' of humiliation, as John Kaye put it, motivated by a visceral desire to undo 'the degradation of fearing those whom we had taught to fear us'. Kaye thought British brutality dissipated as passions subsided, but violence seems often to have become routine, something to which initially anxious soldiers became desensitized. The 47-year old Scottish Brigadier General James Neill was author of some of the earliest, most brutal violence at Allahabad and Kanpur. Early in the war he hanged six supporters of Maulvi Ahmadullah on thin evidence, nervously writing about carrying out 'a duty I never contemplated having to perform'. 'I have', he went on, 'done all for the good of my country, to re-establish its prestige and power.' But on his march upcountry Neill killed indiscriminately, gunning down bystanders on the banks of the Ganges from his steamship and burning entire villages. Like other British soldiers, Neill justified cruelty with cruelty, believing that barbarity could only be stopped by reciprocal acts. As time passed Neill would deliberately offend Indian religious sensibilities. At the site of the Bibighur massacre he forced the men accused of rebellion to clean the blood of Europeans with their tongues before hanging them.[38]

Amid these cruel, cathartic acts of reconquest, the need to rebuild British authority created a countervailing set of arguments. Governor-General Charles Canning worried that British vengeance would incite further opposition and create news cycle of violence. Canning famously offered clemency to rebels who switched sides in July 1857. 'There is a rapid and indiscriminate vindictiveness abroad ... which it is impossible to contemplate without a feeling of shame for one's own countrymen,' he wrote to Queen Victoria. Canning's approach was dominated by an effort to rein in British passions in the interests of British power. 'I will not', he insisted in December, 'govern in anger.'

These sentiments were vigorously lampooned in the British press. The satirical magazine *Punch*, for example, published cartoons which stoked up 'the British Lion's Vengeance on the Bengal Tiger'. It celebrated the noble deeds of previous conquerors like Robert Clive and urged its readers to 'Cry Havelock! And let slip the dogs of war'. In response to similar pressure from Europeans in India, Canning himself equivocated, issuing a proclamation in March 1858 which insisted that the property of north Indian landholders would be confiscated. But politicians, if not the rabid sections of the press, came increasingly to see that conciliation was the only way to end the war.

Dominated more by battles between different groups of politicians than public opinion, the British Parliament seems to have been largely immune from the cry for revenge. When the uprising took place, a Whig ministry led by Lord Palmerston was desperately trying to cling to power. In Parliament Palmerston minimized the scale of the crisis. When details of the rebellion began to arrive in July and August 1857, Palmerston's government denied it was anything other than a minor military mutiny, which a detachment of additional troops would quickly suppress. The government sent reinforcements by slow steamship rather than using quicker vessels equipped with new screw propellers. Amid growing public clamour for retaliation, Whig ministers left London for their country estates in one of the hottest summers in living memory. Palmerston's government was splitting into rival factions. The only way to keep it together was to minimize the scope for argument.

The Conservative MP Benjamin Disraeli was one of the few politicians to challenge the ministry's inaction, and it was his approach which shaped the new order created to rule India after 1858. Once rebel strongholds there had been defeated the biggest question was how to encourage India's elites to submit to British power and what to do with the East India Company. Disraeli's argument was that the revolt had been sparked by the dispossession of India's great landed magnates. The British state, he said, needed to stand forth as the protector of the subcontinent's ruling classes, guaranteeing their security in return for their submission not merely to the East India Company, but to the British Crown. To begin with, this was simply clever rhetoric to humiliate the Palmerston administration. But Disraeli quickly found himself in power, appointed Chancellor

of the Exchequer in the Conservative administration led by Lord
Derby once the Whig government had collapsed. As a minister
Disraeli worked closely with Queen Victoria and Prince Albert
to create a new political order in India based on the conservative
principles he had used to attack Palmerston.

The East India Company was finally abolished as the institution
for governing India in October 1858. Day-to-day direction of
the Britain's government in India would be carried out by a new
Secretary of State, advised by a council of old imperial bureaucrats.
Formal sovereignty lay with the monarch. Officially, Victoria was
merely declared India's Queen. But as historian Miles Taylor shows,
in practice she used the title of Empress long before this was formally
granted in 1877, particularly when she was standing with the monarchs who used imperial titles on the European continent. The royal
couple wanted to create a style of regime in India which emulated
the absolutist monarchies with which Prince Albert was familiar in
Austria and Germany. Before his death in 1852, the foremost British
influence on royal thinking about India was Arthur Wellesley, Duke
of Wellington, a man who always insisted on the need to uphold
centralized, authoritarian and military power. Before and during the
rebellion Victoria tried to present herself as warrior-queen, harassing and cajoling her ministers to send more troops, trying to impose
the forceful authority of a single homogeneous British army. Once
the war was over, the Queen was presented as Victoria Beatrix, the
peacemaking despot who would heal the wounds of a fractured
society once Britain's absolute authority had been restored.[39]

The British government's post-mutiny strategy was to suppress
opposition, try and assert absolute authority, then conciliate the
Indian elites whose reasons for loyalty critics like Disraeli doubted.
Conciliation occurred partly through symbolism, partly through
practical shifts in policy. The first move was a proclamation from
Queen Victoria in November 1858 asserting that India would be
ruled with the same sense of obligation as 'all our other subjects'
and that the British state had no desire to alter Indian ways of life.

Positions in Britain's imperial bureaucracy would, Victoria promised, be 'admitted to offices in our service'. The next move was not, of course, a massive opening up of the civil service to Indian talent but the creation of a new Indian order of chivalry. In the early 1860s, the Queen, the Prince and the new Chancellor of the Exchequer created the order of the Star of India which Albert envisaged as a kind of aristocratic Indian parliament in which ancient rulers were represented in the same fashion as the imperial German diet. More pragmatically, landholders in northern India were allowed to return to their landed estates, as long as they submitted to the authority of the new Royal British Raj. The Government of India recognized it could not rule without the acquiescence of a large proportion of the country's regional magnates. Massive violence had eradicated the idea that large-scale opposition to British power had any chance of success. But the government's purpose was to ensure the submission of Indian nobles was not as humiliating as it might otherwise have been.

For large numbers of northern India's landed elites, submission to British authority was the only way to end the chaos and violence which had raged over the previous eighteen months. There does not seem to have been great enthusiasm for British power. In most cases India's elites simply saw that India's new Queen and her local officers were on the side of order and peace. An address submitted by landholders to British officers in the war-torn province of Awadh in October 1859 drew no great moral distinction between British and rebel violence. The British as much their opponents had initially been authors of disorder. '[I]n one direction', they narrated,

> the pile of the fire of rebellion blazed high and consumed the plain of the citizens. On the other side, the storm of the water of the swords of the troops of the Commander-in-Chief, coming in waves to extinguish the fire, turned the whole kingdom into chaos.

The peace-loving subjects of the province had been squeezed between the destruction of both rival armies, the *taluqdars* and ordinary people 'overwhelmed by destruction' until Victoria's new government 'drew the reins of the horse of anger, and spread the carpet of [the] counsel of friendship'. The nobles of Awadh ended their comments with optimism about their future under the British. The British had undoubtedly conquered India. Their 'house' was emphatically 'founded by the sword'. But, at last, with the proclamation declaring that Queen Victoria would rule by seeking the friendship of her subjects, the British seemed to have recognized that 'the perpetual stability of that house depends on the love of the people', and that 'The basis of empire is strengthened by the ties of affection.' Explicitly placing British rule within the lineage of good Mughal governance, the *taluqdars* noted that the Emperor Akbar had 'followed that course'. By returning the estates of landholders, involving *talqudars* in maintaining local law and order and opening the imperial bureaucracy to Indians, the 're-established English power' acted upon the same foundations.[40]

With their talk of consolidating conquest by seeking the affection of subjects, the *taluqdars* spoke a long-standing political language which emphasized the importance of conciliation and balance, sometimes even affection and love, in maintaining the bonds between ruler and ruled. The petition intended to offer counsel to India's British rule, suggesting that their regime would only thrive if they gave up the arrogant and high-handed ways that had caused the mutiny. Some British officers, Lord Canning among them, tried to follow this advice. But over the next few decades, the same language of love and affection was spoken by Indian interlocutors with greater despair, as negotiation between the imperial bureaucracy and its Indian subjects proved to be impossible.

The great rebellion of 1857 created what historian Francis Hutchins described as 'an illusion of permanence', an idea that British power in India could withstand a challenge on any scale.[41] For many Indians, it killed off the idea that this strange, aloof régime was a temporary anomaly. It forced serious thinking about how practically to cooperate, accommodate or resist it. But one of its most important effects was on the psychology of the British practitioners of empire in India. Eighteen fifty-seven was followed by new efforts to justify the exercise of British power in the Indian subcontinent, by the first serious efforts to seek legitimacy through 'improvement'. Most of these efforts were directed at a British public, particularly British parliamentarians, who wondered whether the attention, lives and money of their compatriots should be spent governing a society that so obviously did not want British rule. But for the cadre of imperial bureaucrats themselves, many of whom came from families whose Indian careers stretched back three or four generations, 1857 removed the need for any kind of justification at all. For official families, the 'mutiny' was simply the most extreme moment in the continual cycle of resistance and conquest, of humiliation and then vindication, which governed Britain's empire in India. After 1858 British power was asserted, violently and permanently, not to benefit Indians nor to pragmatically advance British interests, but to undo the dishonour of 1857's tragic defeat.

9

THE MAKING OF
MODERN INDIA

Looking across Bombay harbour before the fog of industry clouded the view, a nineteenth-century observer would have seen a wall of mountains thirty miles to the east. Rising from sea level to 800 metres in a few miles, this landscape of forts and forests, with its narrow plateaus and steep canyons, was described by an 1859 travel guide as 'the most picturesque and beautiful in the world'. These, the northernmost hills of Western Ghats, are rich with historical associations. One peak is supposed to have been the Maratha leader Shivaji's lookout. Another is named after the Duke of Wellington. But for a group of British men in the middle of the nineteenth century they were simply an engineering challenge.[1]

Starting during the early 1840s, merchants, engineers and entrepreneurs in Calcutta, Bombay and Britain cajoled and lobbied the East India Company to let them lay railway lines throughout India. These were men with interests in cotton manufacturing, connections to business throughout the British empire and an often evangelical enthusiasm for machine-building. By the early 1850s they had built an experimental line and secured the provisional backing of the Governor-General to lay tracks elsewhere. Their toughest challenge was to force railways through the hills that acted as the west coast of India's retaining wall, to link the Arabian Sea with the cotton-producing Deccan plateau and eventually Calcutta and Madras. The route they chose, through the Bhor Ghat, needed a fifteen-mile track to be driven through mountains, in some places built on the edge of vertical slopes, in others blasted through solid rock. Eight viaducts and twenty-five tunnels needed to be constructed. The cost of the two routes through the Western Ghats was £2 million, nearly one-tenth of the total amount spent on railways in India before 1870.[2]

The construction of the Bhor Ghat incline marked a new kind of modern mass enterprise in India. Europeans hired Indian workers in unprecedented numbers. An average of 25,000 men worked on the ghat with the workforce peaking in January 1861 at 42,000. These numbers included 2,500 skilled masons and tens of thousands of unskilled earth carriers alongside trumpet players to call people to work and interpreters to explain what they had to do. Railway works also saw the arrival of a new class of British overseer, as hundreds of civil engineers and construction contractors on short-term contracts shuttled back and forth from Britain to direct construction. Work for Europeans in India was no longer reserved for a tiny elite of government officers, a scattering of merchants and working-class soldiers. The Bhor Ghat incline marked the incorporation of Britain's empire in India into the lives of middle-class Britons, as artisans, mechanics, contractors and 'the gentlemen of the engineering staff' came to India, together making up what the Governor of Bombay called 'a small army of Englishmen' no longer bound 'to the mere dictates of authority' as their predecessors had been. For these new arrivals, Britain's Indian empire was a physical landscape which needed to be mastered, not a place with a people and history.[3] James Berkley, the engineer who mapped the railway route through the Bhor Ghat, returned to Britain with nothing but a series of geological specimens. George Clark, the first engineer on the Great Indian Peninsula Railway, published numerous books on the castles in his adopted South Wales but the Maratha fortresses he built his railway lines around elicited not a flicker of interest.[4]

The decades that straddled the great Indian rebellion of 1857 saw the emergence of a new kind of British power in India, based not on violence against people but the capacity to shape the physical environment of the subcontinent. These were years when men like James Berkley and George Clark were given large amounts of money to spend on public works. They saw the construction of irrigation canals and dams, telegraph lines, roads and eventually railways, all attempts to impose British authority on Indian rock and soil with brick, stone and steel. Later imperial bureaucrats and historians suggested this kind of geological imperialism was driven by the effort to improve a society they believed was backward. Others see it as part of the integration of India into global markets, to create what the historian John Darwin calls 'the British World-System'. In fact, it began as little more than the limited British attempt to shore up their shaky grip on power.[5]

The assertion of the empire's infrastructural power in India was driven by zealous advocates of technological improvement in close contact with the rapidly growing engineering culture in Britain. The second quarter of the nineteenth century saw 'progress' become a rallying cry for large sections of Britain's upper and middle classes, and was associated with the physical sciences, with engineering and commerce. The Institute of Civil Engineers had been founded in 1818. The first university engineering department opened at King's College London in 1838, and had James Berkley, the engineer who laid out the route through the Bhor Ghat, among its first students. Enthusiasm for engineering was celebrated in public at the Great Exhibition of 1851. Technological modernity had its critics, of course. Thomas Carlyle scornfully castigated Britain's new 'metallurgic cities' and believed the railway and extension of the franchise undermined the valves which civilisation relied on. But these were years when many argued that the spread of industry and machinery demonstrated 'man's triumph over the great physical forces by which the conditions of the universe are determined', as one celebratory catalogue for the Great Exhibition put it.[6]

The technological vision of modernity propogated by the new British prophets of improvement allowed them to imagine they could sweep away existing patterns of Indian life. India was seen as an unpeopled landscape to be reshaped by low-paid India labour. This was the first time Britons thought they could work in India without enlisting the support of anything other than Indian muscle. James Berkley initially thought it was possible to build India's first railway line with only British contractors. Scientific measurements, universal rules for assessing how different materials acted under pressure and the possibility of British engineers arriving on quick steamships made local knowledge redundant, he believed. The British vision of an economy built on profitable public works threatened to sweep away the complicated networks of Asian enterprise, and replace centuries-old commercial relationships based on friendship and trust with an economy driven by steel and machines.

Of course it did no such thing. As ever, the power of British officers was limited. India's landscape and population offered resistance to the imperial designs of British engineering. The most important force shaping the pattern of public works in imperial India was not British capital or Indian collaboration, but the political sensibilities of the imperial regime. Imperial bureaucrats were concerned most of all to protect their authority in India as cheaply as possible. Financial security and political safety were the greatest priorities. The men who ruled India were often willing to give their rhetorical support to physical 'improvement', but in practice they only supported public works when they were persuaded they were an effective response to some kind of crisis.

In the 1840s, physical infrastructure was only supported when it could mitigate the loss of revenue caused by famine. In the 1850s, public works were only backed when they could strengthen the British military position in times of possible war. After the great rebellion of 1857–8, public works became an indelible part of a new story about the power of British rule. Instead of asserting violence against people, power was asserted by imposing British authority in inert materials, proving the strength of the Raj by manipulating stone and iron. The story officials told was directed at the British themselves as much as their Indian subjects, offering self-justification to an anxious imperial hierarchy and a worried public that their recently humiliated regime was efficient and powerful. Funding of public works edged up in the early 1850s. It jumped dramatically in the years after 1857, up by a quarter to 1860, then doubling again by 1870. But despite new resources to put the vision of engineers and construction contractors into practice, the coalition between Victorian Britain's prophets of technological progress and the imperial regime was always wary and fractious. The pervasive political anxieties of the imperial regime shaped the direction of the Raj's technological enthusiasm in practice.

Evangelical irrigation

British India's craze for public works began with the succession of famines that hit north and south-eastern India during the 1830s. The two worst famines of the 1830s saw the East India Company's first great irrigation projects. The first, the south Indian famine of 1832–3, particularly affected the coastal Telugu-speaking region around Rajahmundry. It took a decade for famine to bring about any serious action. The year 1832 saw unusually high rainfall in the area. One of the country's worst ever hurricanes hit the south-east coast in May 1833, destroying crops and cattle. Existing systems of distribution collapsed. By July, 5,000 people were being fed daily with food paid for by charities or private individuals, but the money quickly ran out. When grain was transported from one place to another, small acts of violence were common. British officers were surprised that 'such personal anguish' produced 'no *jacquerie*, no fanatical outburst against their rulers'. The region returned to some kind of calm soon after the worst months. But persistently bad weather and the weakness of local institutions meant there was no recovery, and most people in this once prosperous region lived on at the edge of subsistence.[7]

British action was not sparked by mortality but by the collapse of the Company's revenues. The tax collected in Rajahmundry district had fallen from 1.9 million rupees in 1812 to an average of 1.5 million in the early 1840s. In March 1843, a commissioner was sent to inquire 'into the cause of the rapid decline'. Submitting his report a year later, Henry Montgomery offered a complex account of political breakdown, particularly blaming famine on the demise of a locally accountable elite who had once protected and nurtured the fortunes of the district. Montgomery's 206-page report was complex and nuanced, and included improving the work of the local bureaucracy as one of its many recommendations. Montgomery argued that the famine was caused by the collapse of a social system and offered a complex set of solutions. The Board of Revenue found it impossible to frame a clear plan in response.[8]

But the following year the 41-year-old army officer, irrigation engineer and evangelical Christian Arthur Cotton sent them a much more straightforward report. Cotton treated the famine as a crisis caused by the uneven flow of water to cultivated land, and believed that the solution was physical, technical and therefore simple. A new 'system of irrigation' would 'provide means of counteracting the irregularity of the natural supplies of water' and increase both the productivity of the soil and the British government's revenue by four times.[9]

Later in his long life Arthur Cotton described himself as 'a man with one idea': irrigation. But his early years were about war not water. Born in 1803, the tenth son of an Oxfordshire officer from the army's mail corps, Cotton was enlisted in the East India Company's military college at Addiscombe, near Croydon, as a fifteen-year-old. Three years later he was sent as a military engineer to Madras. War between Britain and Burma broke out soon after he arrived in India, and Cotton helped to blow up enemy forts. Then, one evening while gazing up at the stars when sailing back across the Bay of Bengal, Cotton had a moment of religious conversion. Thereafter he read the

Bible every day and, as his daughter later put it, ensured 'his hours, both of toil and pleasure, were marked by a sense of the presence of the Unseen Saviour'. Arguments about irrigation were underwritten by the certain belief that he was working 'for the glory of God ... and the benefit of men', and that British Christians had a peculiar destiny to improve the world. The British were, he wrote in 1854, 'a powerful, intelligent, well instructed, and energetic European people, with unbounded means at their disposal and above all the principles of truth and righteousness taught them in the Bible'. Cotton's commitment earned him the nickname *sanyasi*, or devotee, among some of the Indians who worked for him. Compared to fellow officials it gave him a rare confidence in the capacity of his work to transform India.[10]

Returning from a period of convalescence in Australia, Cotton was sent to build a church and a breakwater at the port city of Vizagapatnam, 500 miles north along the coast from Madras. The work was light, so Cotton spent much of his time exploring on horseback around the coastal Telugu-speaking region. Three days' ride south-east of Vizagapatnam he came across water flowing through a region struggling to recover from famine, and began to think about the redemptive possibilities of British power on a scale never before imagined.[11]

Rising in hills seventy miles north-east of Bombay, the Godavari weaves its way nearly a thousand miles through the Deccan plateau, eventually watering the land over which Mangapati Devi and Benjamin Branfill fought in the 1790s and then falling into the Bay of Bengal in a twenty-mile-wide delta that branches out from the town of Rajahmundry. The river drains water from a 115,000-square-mile basin, once discharging three times the volume of the Nile at Cairo. Cotton saw the unpredictability of the river's flow as both a waste of water and a test of his ingenuity. An abundance of water destroyed crops in some places and a deficiency of water caused drought elsewhere. Cotton thought God had designed the Indian landscape to cause suffering unless virtuous men acted to mitigate it.[12] For the first forty years of British rule, the East India Company had presided over 'grievous neglect', bringing 'disgrace to a civilised country' through their inaction. Now, Cotton argued, they had the obligation to redeem themselves, by building dams and channels to spread the flow of water evenly throughout the countryside.[13]

The East India Company in Madras was more interested in saving money than atoning for the sins of man. They commissioned Cotton to take charge of public works in the district but gave him far fewer resources than he thought were needed. Cotton estimated the work would need six officer engineers, eight sappers (junior military engineers) and 2,000 masons. He was allocated one newly arrived 'young hand' to teach, two apprentice surveyors and a handful of stoneworkers. These limited resources forced him to rely on old Indian techniques. To save on masonry work he copied the method of construction used in the grand ancient anicut (the word was the transliteration of the Tamil *anaikkattu*, or dam work) on the River Cauvery at Tanjore. Cotton created a loose pile of mud and stone on the riverbed which he then covered in lime and plastered with concrete, instead of building up entirely with stone. The Godavari anicut cost a third of his original projection, a total of £47,500. Aside from the steel in the sluice gates, everything in his waterworks would have been familiar to the labourers who first built dams in the region 1700 years earlier.

But Arthur Cotton was trying to employ these old techniques within a grand design to transform India's landscape that was unprecedented in scale. Pre-British irrigation systems diverted the flow of running water. Cotton's plan was to store water and then move it across far larger distances, transporting it to places that had never seen water even in the wet season. His prophetic style of engineering led him to argue that the natural environment could be radically reshaped by divinely inspired men.

These arguments about the scale of change under British rule influenced British policy, particularly helping shape the institutions that led the new interest in public works during the 1850s. Arthur Cotton's most compelling critique was that the East India Company commissioned roads, irrigation schemes and railways in a haphazard fashion, losing money as a consequence. Cotton's arguments were contained in a series of letters to senior government officers which culminated in a privately printed volume, *Public Works in India*, circulated in London in 1853. This book was as fierce an attack on the priorities of the imperial regime as James Mill's *History of British India* had been thirty-six years earlier. Like Mill, Cotton criticized the British for being seduced by Indian ways of doing things, and thought a cadre of men who knew nothing about the subcontinent could drive forward change. The British 'Civil Service' had, he argued, succumbed to what he called 'the Hindu view' that the purpose of government was merely to collect revenue. Instead, Cotton wanted to place a new, centralized public works administration at the core of the British regime, staffed by young, energetic men who had little experience of the subcontinent. A single Board of Public Works would systematically drive forward the creation of an India-wide network of canals and roads and would be cheap. Each member of the board should have a paper stand with the words 'Do it, do it, do it' written on it. Out in India's districts, the central government figure would no longer be the Collector but the engineer.[14]

Cotton's hectoring led to the creation of the Public Works Department, a body which brought together the various strands of the imperial government concerned with physical infrastructure into a single organization. With a single secretariat, headed by powerful new government official to make the case for public works in the Governor-General's Council, expenditure on roads and canals, new buildings and, eventually, railways grew. Revenue collection remained the British regime's main priority until 1947. The Collector continued to be the supreme government official in many parts of India, and a fraction of government revenue was spent on 'improvement' compared to the military, for example. But physical infrastructure took up by far the largest proportion of this still relatively small sum, accounting for 9.5 per cent (or £3 million) of total government expenditure in 1854. By comparison, spending on all forms of education, from primary to university, hovered at between 0.5 and 0.7 per cent of government outgoings until the mid-1860s.[15]

By 1854, three years before northern India was engulfed in a real all-out war Arthur Cotton described himself as a tired, victorious warrior. 'The tide of Indian improvement has now fairly set in,' he wrote in the preface to the first public edition of *Public Works in India*, 'the battle has been fought and won.' Cotton described himself as 'an old soldier after a long battle, sitting down quietly ... to eat his rice and talk over the incidents of the day, in the full assurance that the enemy are irrecoverably overthrown' The danger now was not that the government did nothing, but that it funded the wrong kind of thing, railways, for example or the wrong sort of irrigation. Officials mistakenly envisaged railways 'as a sort of infallible means of improvement'. Now that everyone had become an advocate of public works, 'the chief difficulty is discerning friend from foe', he said.[16]

One of these foes was Sir Proby Cautley, the engineer who designed the British irrigation system on the Ganges river. From a family of wealthy clergymen, Cautley was in the same class as Cotton at the East India Company's military school at Addiscombe. His first engineering job was to renovate the old Mughal-era canals that irrigated the doab, or triangle of land between the Ganges and Jamuna upstream from their confluence at Allahabad. Here, like Cotton, Cautley was responding to famine. These were years when northern India's Gangetic plain seemed hotter than ever, as declining forest cover led to soil erosion and water evaporation. One observing official, Donald Butter, thought the jungles had all been 'dried up'. Ecological decline had caused a catastrophic drought to sweep through the area from Allahabad to Delhi in 1837–8, and engendered a powerful mood in favour of a grand new scheme of waterworks. Cautley created a massive network of canals, more than 350 miles in total, which eventually opened in April 1855.

The opening ceremony was a grand affair with water flooding into the channels to the crash of cannon fire. But like Cotton, Cautley had struggled with an imperial government which adequately funded his plans. Construction was slow, limited by a lack of materials and the absence of staff.[17]

The government's limited support had consequences, most importantly the foundation of India's first institution for technical education. Cautley couldn't afford to recruit technicians from England. His solution was to train men based in India, British and Indian, to do the engineering work. He established an engineering class at Roorkee, near the head of the Ganges canal, in 1845. Two years later the class became a college, teaching twenty students a year. The earliest Indian student, Munnoo Lal, graduated in 1849 and was immediately appointed as a teacher-translator of engineering textbooks into Hindustani. The college quickly became the centre for diffusing and developing engineering knowledge throughout India, inculcating the technical know-how needed to measure land and build bridges, canals and railways into its mixed-race classes of Indian and British students and producing the standard reference works on civil engineering in India. In 1851 there were fifty students studying at the college, twenty-one in Indian languages, and forty-two students had passed through 'furnished to the service of the state', as the college prospectus put it. In that year it was renamed the Thomason College of Civil Engineering, housed in a grand new neoclassical building, which survives today as the administrative block of Roorkee's Indian Institute of Technology. By the mid-1850s fifty students were graduating each year.[18]

The civil engineering college at Roorkee was the oldest educational institution built to introduce Western knowledge of any kind to Indian students. The few British-supported colleges built beforehand were founded to cultivate Indian forms of scholarship, and most were paid for by Indian not imperial funds. Roorkee shows us the kind of education that mid-Victorian Britons thought was most important to make their government in India work. It was technical and prosaically practical. It treated India as a physical landscape that could be remoulded by the mechanical power of the British, not a country populated by communities whose differences needed to be understood. But most importantly, this institution was created as a result of the failures and limitations of the imperial regime. The college at Roorkee came into being because the British government in India did not devote the resources to public works which Victorian engineers demanded.

Despite their similar careers, Sir Arthur Cotton and Sir Proby Cautley argued vehemently about the direction of irrigation in India. Both men shared an evangelical belief in the capacity of British engineering to improve the subcontinent, but they also had different opinions as to how that expertise should be applied. Cautley's schemes tapped surplus water from high up a river system, drawing it into an entirely new system of irrigation canals, leaving the main river flow diminished in force but otherwise unaffected. Cotton's approach was cheaper but more fundamental, building massive mud and stone dams at a river's point of greatest flow, and then effectively creating a new river system downstream. The two men made the case for their different approach in the supposedly universal language of science. In fact, the difference was a product of the different ecological conditions of the regions in which they began their careers. Cautley worked in India's dry northern plain, where the only way to move large volumes of water was by creating a new network of canals. Cotton began his career as an irrigation engineer among India's eastern deltas, in places where water flowed across land naturally during much of the year. Cotton's irrigation system on the Godavari was a success, helping revive the region's economy. Failing to understand the local context to his work, Cotton hubristically projected his approach as a universal solution to the hydrological challenges of the whole of India. His projects in drier regions, to connect rivers between Kurnool and Kadapa for example, failed badly.[19]

British irrigation in mid-nineteenth-century India began with an ecological crisis and ended in only very limited success. But the history of stone dams and brick canals, of evangelical engineers like Cotton and Cautley and their intemperate antagonisms, also mark the beginning of a new notion of the power of the state in imperial India.

In mid-Victorian Britain politicians did not see the support of public works as the responsibility of central government. Infrastructure, whether roads, railways, bridges or schools were commissioned and paid for by philanthropy or fees. Engineers like Isambard Kingdom Brunel were vociferously hostile to the idea that the state should do anything other than let them get on with their privately funded profit-making ventures. Until well into the late nineteenth century, central authority licensed private and local initiative, but it did not drive forward 'improvement' itself.

In India the succession of crises which seemed to challenge the British presence in in the second quarter of the nineteenth century produced a different idea of the proper power of government. There engineers demanded that public works be funded from state expenditure. Particularly after the great crisis of 1857–8, the men who governed the state agreed. Paradoxically though, the exaggerated idea of the power of government in India was produced by the absence of political leadership. The imperial state in India had a far weaker social foundation and far more limited revenue base than the government in Britain. The imperial state continually jumped from one crisis to the next. It was very poor at managing its relationship with Indian society, and increasingly anxious after the rebellion. In practice, it could do nothing that required the consent of established Indian elites and political communities. Its solution, instead, was hiring low-paid, often lower caste labour to manipulate steel and stone. But that practice allowed the 'state' to project an unprecedented and false idea of its power upon Indian society.

Alice and the engineers

Railways only became a vehicle for asserting imperial power haphazardly and belatedly. To begin with, the imperial regime shared the views of Arthur Cotton, and thought that blasting dry metal lines

Shaista Khan, Mughal Governor of
Bengal, 1664–1688)

Company ships ready to sail at
Deptford, London, painted in 1683, the
year William Hedges sailed to Bengal

The pepper fort of
Anjengo, 1772

The conqueror of India and – briefly – Mughal emperor, Nader Shah

East India Company soldier posing in the decade of conquest, c.1760

Crowds pack into Westminster Hall to watch the trial of Warren Hastings, 1789

The Afghan warlord and eventual
subject of British power, Amir Khan

Skulls and bodies at the Bada Imambara
at Lucknow after the 1857–8 rebellion

Masons working on
a bridge section of
Bhore ghat incline,
between Bombay and
Pune, 1855

Bellary town centre from Bellary fort, taken in the 1860s, the decade before the famine

Labourers at a relief camp during famine, Allahabad 1900

King George V processing through Delhi on the way to Coronation Park, 1911

India's empty new capital,
New Delhi from the air in 1935

Indian terrorism sensationalised, a
French picture of the assassination
attempt on Lord Hardinge, 1913

Moving Curzon's statue of Clive
of India, King Charles Street
London, 1916

A picket of British soldiers in Amritsar, 1919, defending imperial institutions in the wake of the Jallianwalagh Bagh massacre

Workers at the Birla Jute Mill, Calcutta, 1929

Nationalist crowds gather on the streets of Peshawar, May 1930

Riot Police in Peshawar,
May 1930

New Wealth.
Imported cars outside
Bombay races, 1932

US Air Force base at Sadiya in the far north-east of India, 1944

Congress Interim Government, August 1946

Muslim refugee camps in Delhi, 1947

Monuments to the Raj and the Indian nation-state, Coronation Park, Delhi, 2015

onto the Indian landscape was a wasteful enterprise. The driving force behind India's first railway projects were private enthusiasts, but the absence of government support made the spread of railway lines slow.

The first train routes opened in Britain, the USA and France between 1825 and 1828. Commercial lines were laid throughout the world, from Australia to Russia to Cuba, over the next twenty years. By 1845, all that had happened in India was the speculative gathering of rival groups of merchants, engineers and former officials to propagate a series of rival railway plans. In Calcutta, the Anglo-Indian agency houses led the campaign. The landholder and mine-owner Dwarkanath Tagore played a central role in founding the Great Western Railway Company of Bengal. The company was created to build railways to transport indigo and sugar from the lower Ganges valley to steamboats waiting at Calcutta. It did not build a single foot of track.

At the same time, the Great Eastern Railway Company was created in Bombay by a group of merchants and former officers, some Indian and some British, many of whom had made their money shipping cotton and then opium from central India through Bombay to China. Exports to China boomed through the 1830s, and capitalists looked to diversify their investments into other sources of revenue, including infrastructure. The most prominent figure was Jeejeebhoy Jamsetjee, the Parsi son-in-law of a bottle seller who built nineteenth-century Bombay's greatest commercial empire. Jamsetjee ran a fleet of ships between western India and Canton, and then ploughed his profits into philanthropic projects in Bombay and Pune when the parsimonious British government refused to invest in local infrastructure. The railway was just one of the many institutions Jamsetjee hoped to divert his wealth into, alongside bridges linking Bombay to neighbouring islands, hospitals, schools and an architectural college. Despite the success of his other ventures Jamsetjee's railway company went nowhere.[20]

These India-based, commercially oriented outfits were challenged by firms that raised all their capital in London, and had closer connections to British political power. Unsurprisingly, these British firms won the battle for the first railways contracts. In Bengal the East Indian Railway Company hoped to construct a railway line upcountry from Calcutta as far as Punjab. Its founder did not begin life with any connection to engineering or India but his career tells us something about the early Victorian lure of both. It also illustrates how British organizations were displacing Indian commerce. Rowland Stephenson (no relationship to the famous Stephenson railway family) was born in Bloomsbury, London. He was educated at Harrow and initially seemed destined for a banking career. The financial collapse of 1828 caused the failure of the firm Stephenson worked for, and forced this twenty-year-old to turn to the more financially viable field of engineering. By 1838, he had become secretary of the steamship company which became the Peninsular and Oriental Steam Navigation Company two years later, and which had begun to threaten Indian-owned shipping concerns. Using the connections to the East India Company that he had developed working for P&O, he began to lobby for the construction of railways in India, visiting Calcutta in 1843.

The line Stephenson planned would transport cotton down from the fields of Awadh to Calcutta to be shipped by sea to feed the factories of Manchester. Stephenson's arguments were designed to appeal to northern English industrialists, and to anti-slave campaigners looking for a source of cotton which did not rely on American slave labour. Stephenson also played on British fears of Indian corruption and chaos by claiming that Indian-based companies could not be trusted. Merchants in India did not engage in 'wilful or intentional malpractice', he said, but their interests were too widely spread for them to pay enough 'personal attention' to any one enterprise. 'No undertaking of magnitude' should be allowed to go ahead if 'the sole and irresponsible control is placed under Calcutta management'.

The London-based Great Indian Peninsula Railway Company similarly undermined the claims of Jeejeebhoy's Great Eastern firm in Bombay. The Peninsula Railway Company was brought together by John Chapman, another man who had turned to engineering after a personal crisis. Chapman was a radical Baptist lace machine-maker from the East Midlands town of Loughborough, whose firm had gone bankrupt in 1834. After taking a series of odd jobs, including editor of *The Mechanics' Magazine*, Chapman was hired first by Joseph Hansom to redesign his two-seater horse-drawn carriage, and then by the free trading abolitionist George Thompson to consider how to expand India's trade. His answer was to found a train company, persuading the luminaries of the British railway world to back a railway line that cut from Bombay through to central India and then on to Calcutta and Madras.[21]

The early 1840s saw railway mania in Britain but little interest from officials about railways in India. Lord Ellenborough, Governor-General of India between 1842 and 1844, believed that mechanical transportation was a distraction from his sole purpose of imposing political order on the subcontinent. As investors were uncertain about the prospects of investing so much money so far from home without state backing, capital was not forthcoming. The debate over railways was similar to the arguments made about the spice trade in the 1600s. Money would only be made available in the East with state support. Describing himself as the lone champion of railways in India, John Chapman mournfully complained that his 'solitary efforts' were laughed at by investors and officials alike. It was a near impossible task to raise the small sum of £2,500 to pay for a trip to Bombay to research the route in 1845. When the Bombay railway company asked the government to consider their proposals, the response was polite inaction. A committee of officials was asked to investigate, but after five months the railway company had still heard nothing. When it did report, government officers were sceptical that a railway line even to the foot of the Western Ghats would be profitable. The imperial regime was initially even anxious about giving railway companies access to the data they needed to make their case, preventing Chapman from looking at the police office's records about people passing through particular places. By the autumn of 1846, Chapman's firm was exasperated.

'We are not now seeking unconditional sanction,' they wrote, but needed to know 'what is the proper course of proceeding.'[22]

The breakthrough came when the railway companies began to argue that railway lines were a military necessity, and to make this argument in London. Rowland Stephenson suggested that a grand railway network could link Calcutta, Delhi, Bombay and Madras in order to ensure the 'better security ... of the entire country'. In his book *Indian Railways: as Connected with the power and stability of the British Empire in the East*, the Scottish soldier and engineer William Andrew suggested that a network of railway lines stretching from Calcutta and Bombay to Punjab would have prevented supply and ammunition shortages during the Anglo-Sikh war and 'spare[d] the health and save[d] the lives of European troops' who otherwise were forced to march in difficult weather.[23] These arguments portrayed the railway as a tool of conquest not an instrument of economic expansion. They led the Company in Britain to give permission to the two London-based firms to build experimental lines, and to offer to guarantee their investors a fixed return of 5 per cent per annum, however much profit railway lines actually made. The first railway line, covering the twenty-one miles from Bombay north to Thane in fifty-seven minutes, opened on 16 April 1853. After the first steam trains were sent to the wrong port, the first line twenty-four miles from Hughli in Bengal opened a year later, on 15 August 1854.[24]

The men who planned the railways thought they would only have to confront technical difficulties. But nature was not the only obstacle; managing people was the most difficult challenge. The railway route from Bombay to Pune through the Western Ghats only opened after a major strike, a riot and the murder of a European engineer. The contract to build the line was first given to William Faviell, the son of a Yorkshire canal builder who had worked on railways throughout the east of England before being employed to build the first experimental stretch of Indian railway, from Bombay ten miles north to Thane, in 1850. The line was funded by the Great Indian Peninsula Railway Company, an organization managed by

London bankers, army officers and retired East India Company officers. They thought Faviell had done a good job, so he was given a second contract to build the Bhor Ghat incline in 1855. But work was interrupted by the uprising of 1857.[25]

The investors and politicians who funded the railway line insisted on low rates of pay for labourers, but the rebellion made it much harder to encourage workers to abandon their villages for little return. Railway work was tough. Labourers carried earth twenty miles a day, then slept outdoors on wet, cholera-ridden hillsides. Once the 1857 insurrection broke out, one engineer noted that labourers 'would not leave their homes until they were sure their small Tenements would be safe from the mutineers'. Others found they could earn more money in the British army. A few probably refused to work for British engineers while a rival Indian regime was gaining power. Some left the Bhor Ghat incline for more remunerative work, where contractors with greater capital could pay them more money. Unlike Faviell, Parsi merchant Jeejeebhoy Jamsetjee had links with Bombay-based commercial networks which allowed him to pay twenty-five rupees a month for skilled masons, twice the rate Faviell paid, and his sections of the line were in easier, less precipitous country than the Bhor Ghat. It is hardly surprising that Faviell's subcontractors detected a 'mutinous spirit' among workers by the end of 1857.[26]

The limited British commitment to the railway created a crisis at the top of the incline in January 1858. Worried about having enough money to complete their section and angry at the slow pace of work, British engineers starting paying workers half the specified rate. The labourers protested. As one engineer described it, a mob 'commenced crushing around' the Britons' tent, and only fell back when they were promised more money. The disturbance subsided, but the engineers were still angry and resolved 'to go with all the arms they could muster along the lines of the huts' to arrest the ringleaders of the 'outbreak'. The incident ended badly. After a series of skirmishes with labourers the engineers were forced to retreat but discovered that one of their number, Mr Curran, was missing.

He was found injured and died shortly afterwards, bludgeoned to death by an angry labourer. Officers of the railway company asked to investigate learnt that many of the masons and subcontractors working on the Bhor Ghat incline had not been paid for months. William Faviell complained about the monsoon, the impact of the mutiny on the cost of labour and the 'native character', but above all he blamed the railway company's refusal to increase labourers' rates of pay. Caught between parsimonious investors, a reluctant imperial regime and an insurgent workforce, Faviell decided to break his contract, quit India and return to England. The rest of his long career was spent building railways elsewhere in the British empire, in Ceylon and South Africa, but not India.[27]

Faviell's successor lasted less than a month. Solomon Tredwell was the son of a canal digger who worked his way up to be a major contractor on Isambard Kingdom Brunel's great but doomed ship the *Great Eastern*. By 1859 and in his mid-thirties, Tredwell had become a man of 'means, experience, energy and liberal and able management'. The Great Indian Peninsula Railway Company imagined he would be a safe pair of hands to complete the Bhor Ghat, and quickly appointed him. Tredwell started shipping the machinery he needed to build the incline, arriving in Bombay with his wife, Alice, on 29 October 1859. Within a month he was dead, killed by an 'alarming' but unnamed illness. Most probably Tredwell died of cholera, the disease which killed something like a third of the workforce on the Bhor Ghat, 'carrying off' two European contractors and reducing the number of labourers on the lower half of the Bhor Ghat incline from 10,000 to 1,000 in January 1860 alone. Unlike these men, Tredwell died a rich man, leaving his estate of £70,000 to his wife. Alice took over the management of the Bhor Ghat contract 'with a degree of spirit and judgment' that government officers in Bombay thought remarkable, given her sex and her recent loss. The project was duly completed by 1863, eight years after the contract was first awarded.

The official story was that Alice relied on the railway company's own managers, and they were more skilled at 'handling' Indian labour than William Faviell's men had been. In reality, two decisions ensured the construction of the railway route was finished with less friction than before. First, the railway company increased the rates of pay for masons and labourers. Second, the government sent a large contingent of police to 'preserve the public peace' on the ghat works, as well as deputing additional magistrates to provide summary justice. These actions were a response to the danger of Indian violence, evident both in the riots on the hillside and the insurrection of 1857 more widely. The insurrection of 1857 brought a more serious commitment by the British state in India to public works.

That commitment was evident in the speech given by the Governor of Bombay, Sir Bartle Frere, on the opening of the route from Bombay to Pune. On the evening of 21 April 1863, after a day spent travelling up and down the new railway track, Frere stood in a banqueting hall in Bombay to announce to a gathering of grandees that India had entered the 'railway age'. He said nothing about the difficulties engineers and labourers had faced. His words flattened the true, unsteady history of infrastructure in India into a celebratory account of British progress. Big public works were the way Queen Victoria's new Indian Raj would project its power. But the speech was riven with all the contradictions that marked British attitudes to their presence in India in the years which followed the Indian mutiny. Frere talked about the apparent improvement of India under British rule, predicting the quick transformation of the country from a society of bullock carts to one of steam locomotives. He wondered if one day British engineering would be worshipped in the place of the Hindu gods sat in ancient temple caves. Yet his celebration of the positive effects of public works was incredibly vague. Frere's speech praised the scale and power of the British presence for its own sake, not for its consequences. The viaducts on the Bhor Ghat were bigger than all the bridges of London, he said, and more stone had been quarried than for the breakwaters of Plymouth and Portland, or the pyramids of Giza for that matter. Nothing specific was said about the commercial advantages of the new route. More vital was the use of railways to protect and project British power, allowing military supplies and manpower to be transported quickly to sites of conflict. Frere argued that the railway would 'quadruple the available military strength of India'. The greatest benefits for Indians would come, he suggested, not from travelling in but working on the railways, particularly from the close proximity between supposedly 'indolent' Indian workers and their newly arrived middle–class British masters who had 'habits of method and punctuality'. For this imperial bureaucrat, railways were not a means for economic or social transformation. They were a vehicle to project British power and character.[28]

Moral and material progress

In February 1858 the great Victorian liberal John Stuart Mill drafted a crucial piece of East India Company propaganda. War was raging in India. Company officials in London felt impotent, and frightened, fearful that violence in India would undermine their institution. Mill was the senior examiner of correspondence for the Company in London, a position that gave him an income and a field of public activity, but also left him enough time for liberal journalism and political activism. In the first half of 1858, Mill was the main advocate of the East India Company's survival. Mill lost that argument, and the Company was abolished in October 1858. Yet the case for the Company he made in 1858 became the staple argument justifying British authority in Asia.

Mill's essay, the 'Memorandum of the Improvements of the Administration of India during the Last Thirty Years' was circulated to British Members of Parliament. It was perfunctory and inelegantly written, replete with long sentences and double negatives. The overall story Mill conveyed was, though, clear. British power had been exercised steadily and firmly over India's social fabric and physical landscape in order to bring 'improvement' to 'the physical and mental condition of the inhabitants', he claimed. The British regime in India had achieved good, Mill argued, in three main ways. First, through low and fair taxes, by limiting the government's capacity to extract resources from India society. Second, by maintaining law and order. And, third, 'through improvement of the country by public works'. Mill afforded ten pages to each of these themes, with the final few pages of his essay dedicated to other sources of change, including two pages on education, and a few paragraphs on plans to introduce superior kinds of cotton and tea.

Mill framed his argument in classical laissez-faire language, but he argued that India needed to be treated differently. Low taxes and law and order were necessary for 'securing to every one the full fruits of his industry', providing an incentive for people to work. In England sufficient energy and capital existed for irrigation or railways to be built through private enterprise. But the relative poverty of India, Mill argued, meant that 'direct aid of Government to industry' was needed. India's difference meant it was peculiarly suited to the direct imposition of state power. Expenditure on public works should not be extravagant, Mill thought. But in India it was to be the state, not private enterprise, which provided the main impetus to economic growth.

John Stuart Mill's emphasis on infrastructure marked the peculiar form of liberalism which he and other mid-Victorians wanted to introduce to India. Mill thought the state in Britain and India needed to do very different things in each place. In Britain, he emphasized the regenerative power of the free human intellect. In his metropolitan political visions, education was the most important public service, as it cultivated the capacity for freedom. Mill's most famous tract, *On Liberty*, written in the summer of 1857 while news kept flashing into England of the outbreak of the Indian mutiny, argued that the progress of any people depended on their capacity to educate one another in open debate. Mill thought progress in the west depended on a nation's common sense of purpose, and on the exchange of views between free, educated citizens. 'The only unfailing and permanent source of improvement is liberty,' Mill said, 'since by it there are as many possible independent centres of improvement as there are individuals.'[29]

Mill's account of progress in the subcontinent was based on drier, narrower principles. There, the fact of Britain's despotic power made it impossible for Mill to imagine people could have any say in their own government. Without the energizing language of liberty, improvement was reduced to a function of people's automatic responses to physical incentives, to the rule of law and to irrigation works. In Britain, Mill was sure that progress came from an argumentative public spirit, from the clash of opinions he described in *On Liberty*. In India, it was about the lonely calculation of a peasant thinking how much extra land he could plough if he had access to more water.

Mill's post-mutiny Memorandum laid the foundation for the approach to empire adopted by imperial bureaucrats and British politicians over the next half-century and more. From 1858, the imperial regime began to actively propagate a story about its physical 'improvement' of India. Beginning in 1861, the Government of India published annual 'Moral and Material Progress' reports that took and expanded John Stuart Mill's Memorandum as a model. Each began with a list of laws passed, then discussed finance, the Post Office, telegraphs, steamships, public works and the Indian geological department. This was a vision of the state as commander and builder, not a nurturer of human capacity and talent. Reports concentrated on law first, then physical infrastructure and public works, only then education. The documents from each province listed the funding going to universities and schools; in 1859–60, education took the modest sum of 1,032,021 rupees, or £68,800, in Bengal, roughly the same as the amount spent rebuilding army barracks that year.

With limited capacity to quantify India's productive activity, and no means at all to gauge Indian opinion, the country's 'progress' was measured by the increase in official transactions which could be counted. Improvement was assessed by expenditure on roads, irrigation and barracks, by the pace at which railway lines lengthened or the increase in the number of letters passing through British India's Post Office (from 224,000 in 1855 to 556,000 in 1860). The imperial state's proudest boast was having the cheapest postage rates in the world.

The expansion of public works brought with it a heavily calculating approach to the power of the British state in India. Immediately after the rebellion was suppressed in 1858, the Government of India started to minutely classify public works. The physical infrastructure needed to keep the imperial regime working from day to day, things like barracks and law courts, was to be funded from the government's ordinary revenue collection without any concern for remuneration. Beyond this limited core, central and provincial governments only authorized expenditure they thought would lead to a direct return, most importantly in increased revenue payment. Works needed to be '*profitable* in a pecuniary point of view ... to the entire body politic of the State'. Anything 'not profitable in this sense, should not be undertaken'.[30]

The imperial regime experimented with different ways of directing investment into the most remunerative kind of works. In the 1860s, engineers and officials imagined that state-guaranteed private companies were the best vehicle. That decade saw the birth of irrigation companies and the expansion of railway firms, each of which built public works without placing their costs on public accounts. But their narrow revenue base meant these companies quickly sank into financial difficulty. By the 1870s, the British political mood was more emphatically in favour of the direct assertion of state power over waterways and railway lines. The 1870s were a decade when British governments were newly confident about their ability to direct the course of large enterprise. In 1869, the Suez Canal had been completed through the collaboration of French engineers and bankers and Ottoman Egypt; initially, the British government opposed the project, and argued that infrastructure was best completed through the initiative of private finance. Even though the canal did not shorten the time of the journey between

Britain and India, Benjamin Disraeli's Conservative government bought £4 million worth of shares in the Suez Canal Company in 1874. His purpose was to ensure an increasingly vital transport link could not be used against British interests.

The motivation for taking over the government-backed irrigation and railway companies in India was similar: a desire to ensure the continued viability of politically important assets, and a belief that only government control would ensure they operated in the interests of the British state. The imperial regime argued it would be better able to control costs and could ensure benefits to the broader community were factored into pricing. From 1869, railway lines started to be built by the government itself. In 1878, the government bought the Madras Irrigation Company; a year later, it purchased Rowland Stephenson's East India Railway Company, and took over the remaining private firms over the next few years. Instead of relying on investors to support private initiatives, public works were funded from the government's own revenues or from loans.

With more emphatic government backing, public works expanded and brought with them a greater demand for professional engineers. The 836 miles of railway line that existed in 1860 grew to 15,806 by 1890, then doubled again to 35,327 in 1921. By 1867, nineteen out of India's twenty most populous cities were linked by steam locomotive. The acreage of Indian land irrigated steadily increased, as barrages were built on the River Krishna, Thomas Cautley's Ganges canal was expanded and large new irrigation systems constructed in Sind and Punjab. Momentum finally lay with the advocates of technological progress. *The Engineer*, Britain's first journal for the engineering profession, noted in 1869 that 'India appears likely, for some time to come, to create the greatest demand on the energies of our profession.' The Public Works Department tried to recruit engineers from Britain quickly, but first found demand for trained professionals exceeded supply. In the late 1860s, it was recruiting fifty engineers a year, but still had vacancies. By 1879, the Government of India employed 1,004 men (only seventy-four Indian, the rest

European or mixed race) in its engineering service, and recruited roughly thirty engineers a year. These figures remained stable over the next few decades, with 938 in India's engineering services in 1913. Throughout these years, there were almost as many profession als in the Government of India's engineering service as there were members of the Indian Civil Service.[31]

By the 1880s public works had become an integral part of the landscape of British power in India. Infrastructure was central to the argument Britons used to justify their presence in India. As well as a thousand middle-class British engineers employed directly by the imperial government, public works provided employment for thousands more contractors and workers in British engineering firms that built everything from steam engines to sluice gates. These individuals had interests firmly outside of British authority in India. In the eighteenth century, trading outposts, forts, barracks and law courts had created a commitment to political domination in India which had been hard to abandon in previous years. In the same way, the physical intervention of the British in India's landscape, the construction of steel tracks and stone channels, created a practical, emotional attachment to the institutions of imperial power which Britons found difficult to give up.

These commitments existed despite the very limited tangible advantages public works bestowed on Indian society. For India's residents themselves, the lure of new technology was limited until well into the twentieth century. The rhetoric of British India's evangelical engineers obscured the very limited real demand which existed among Indians for water transported through irrigation canals or for rail transit. In many places, irrigation increased the marginal cost of production beyond subsistence levels for peasants. Often, it was more efficient to cultivate crops which used less water than to pay for the new waterways. Only a small number of rich farmers benefited, most of whom were cultivating cash crops for European markets, and there were not enough of those to fund big irrigation projects. Gains on investment in new irrigation projects were minimal – 0.57

per cent per year for the decade preceding 1876. New waterworks transformed life in some places, creating new settlements, the 'canal colonies', in central Punjab for example. Even here, a quick boom was followed by a long decline in agricultural productivity. But the only really cost-effective British irrigation works were those which repaired existing, pre-imperial dams and canals.

Similarly, the most important technological change for the transportation of heavy goods in nineteenth-century India was not the arrival of the quick, expensive railway: it was the move from pack animals to carts pulled by two or four beasts in the first half of the century. This was the process historian Amalendu Guha calls 'the bullock cart revolution'. Throughout the 1860s and 1870s railways found it impossible to compete not only with bullock carts, but also with human-powered river transport. Rowing boats along the Ganges and Jamuna won a price war with the railways over the cost of transporting heavy goods. Vessels powered by human beings were able to undercut steam vessels elsewhere.[32]

Eventually, of course, railways changed social conditions, allowing large numbers of workers to congregate in centres of production as never before, speeding up the flow of commodities and creating new settlements. They intensified the flow of primary produce from India's hinterland to the great port cities. They also allowed Indian enterprise to disperse out from these increasingly European-dominated cities into small towns and settlements on railway lines. But these changes were slow, and did not work out in the way British officers imagined. Neither railways nor irrigation systems had much of an impact on the livelihood of most Indian workers for some time. Most importantly, they did not prevent famine. Canal-building didn't prevent some of the world's worst famines occurring in India during the 1870s and 1890s. Without the kind of political leadership able to coordinate the productive activity of Indians for the benefit of society as a whole, the dreams of 'improvement' projected by the prophets of modernity in the 1840s and 1850s ended up as illusory fantasies.[33]

10

THE LEGALIZATION OF INDIA

Albert Edward, Prince of Wales, visited India in 1875. With a retinue of a dozen doctors, journalists, churchmen and lords, he hunted and dined through every part of India with splendid self-confidence. A year later Queen Victoria had herself officially declared *Kaisar-e-Hind*, Empress of India. In 1877, an elaborate ceremony was held in the old Mughal capital of Delhi to confirm the new title. With these acts, officials said, 'the union of India with England has been asserted to be indissoluble'.

Motivated more by Britain's status in Europe than the administration of India, the new pageantry was very shallow. Beneath their new elaborate costumes, the British officers charged with the day-to-day administration of India were still gripped by panic. Twenty years after Britain had reconquered the northern provinces of India, the imperial bureaucrats who ruled India were newly fearful about the security of their regime.

There was paranoia on India's borders, which led to war against assertive neighbours in Afghanistan and Burma. There were new concerns about internal resistance, where memories of the mutiny gave imperial officials a heightened sense of their insecurity. The murder of two British judges in the late 1860s persuaded British officers that 'sources of anxiety' were very real. Bureaucrats saw seditious conspiracies everywhere, blaming them on the 'fanaticism' of Muslims and the hostile 'national sentiment' of Hindus. Muslim radicals were incarcerated, tortured and convicted of waging war against the Queen, despite thin evidence. At the same time, British officers started to note the emergence of new political associations organizing in the urban centres of the subcontinent from Lahore and Dhaka to Madras.

Western India was the area of greatest worry. Two developments particularly concerned the British.

The first was the birth of the Pune Sarvajanik Sabha, an organization founded in 1870 by a group of men who wanted to voice criticism within the institutions of the imperial regime, led by the judicial officer and social reformer Mahadev Govind Ranade. Born in 1842 to a family of Brahmin government officials, Ranade was one of the first students to be educated at the University of Bombay. He started off as a fervent critic of British rule. Ranade's scholarship was suspended after he wrote an essay saying India was better off before the British conquest. Throughout his life, he sought to revive the 'national' spirit of self-rule he saw in Shivaji's Maratha state; Ranade wrote a history, the *Rise of the Maratha Power,* which attributed its growth and survival to popular patriotic sentiment. But Ranade's celebration of India's past was increasingly coupled with a clear sense of the opportunities that lay open in modern, British-ruled India. If they were 'roused' by institutions articulating their voice and left for the most part to rule themselves, Ranade thought there was scope for 'the mass of the people' to flourish under British sovereignty. He compared the British conquest in India to what he saw as William the Conqueror's beneficial invasion of England in 1066.[1]

His style of critical loyalism did not prevent British officers from suspecting that Ranade supported violent opposition to British power. Appointed to the government's judicial service in his mid-20s, Ranade progressed quickly through the junior ranks of British India's judicial service to start with. In 1879, however, to prevent seditious activity, he was posted to one of Bombay presidency's most remote districts. Even in the remotest part of Gujarat he was tracked by the secret police.

Ranade's exile was sparked by the second event that increased British suspicion, an insurgency which briefly gained support in the countryside around Pune. The uprising was led by a former official in the British government's military accounts department, Vasudev Balwant Phadke. There were, as government officers suspected, connections between the Pune Sarvajanik Sabha and the revolt, but their leaders had very different objectives. Phadke had attended the lectures which Ranade gave criticizing the economic record of the British regime in India. But unlike members of the Sabha, Phadke began to believe that violence was the only way to change the situation. He began making incendiary speeches in 1875. In 1878, at the age of thirty-three, he left his wife, retreated to the forests of Maharashtra and began building a revolutionary army. Phadke linked up with gangs of low-caste jungle-dwellers, people who had once been an integral part of every Indian army but were marginalized by the extension of British power. His band raided villages around Pune announcing that unless the salaries of imperial bureaucrats were cut and the money redistributed to poor peasants, Europeans would be attacked and assassinated. Eventually parts of the city of Pune were captured for a few days and two old Maratha palaces burnt down in the chaos.[2]

As the elite leader of a movement to mobilize India's poor masses, which had the sympathies of many middle-class Indians, Phadke might be said to have inaugurated the modern history of anti-imperial protest. When they wrote about the uprising, the British belittled the campaign and its supporters, describing Phadke's actions as a series of mere 'gang robberies'.[3] But the uprising was not suppressed until July 1879, when Phadke was captured, tried and transported to Aden. Brought before the court at Pune for trial, British officers were shocked when middle-class Pune residents applauded Phadke from the gallery. 'Sympathy', one judge said, 'was on the side of the accused in spite of the injuries which he had done to his countrymen.'[4]

The rise of the Pune Sarvajanik Sabha together with Phadke's revolt coincided with a resurgence of criticism in Britain itself towards policy in India. The idea of Britain as an Asiatic power was important to Benjamin Disraeli's Conservative government, in power from 1874 to 1880. Disraeli imagined that exotic pageantry would be popular in Britain and the subcontinent, but by 1879 the costs and violence of imperial war were being vigorously condemned throughout the UK. In the run-up to the 1880 general election, William Gladstone campaigned against the Tories' 'dangerous' and 'impractical' imperial policy. His Liberal Party won a landslide. Gladstone argued that Britain had pushed its power in Asia beyond the limits of safety. Wars in Afghanistan and Burma were signs of imperial overstretch. Events like Phadke's revolt demonstrated the fragility of British power. There were, he argued, 'a multitude of unsolved problems connected with the administration of our Indian Empire'.[5]

For the men who staffed the highest positions in the imperial bureaucracy, 1879–80 was a time of crisis for Britain's Indian empire. The result was a new spate of propaganda justifying the exercise of British power. This was the period when the idea of the British empire as *Pax Britannica* was invented and popularized. Mistakenly interpreted by historians as showing British confidence during the high noon of empire, the texts which extolled the virtues of British power drip with anxiety, sometimes even panic. For example: Sir Richard Temple's *India in 1880* conveyed a sharp sense of the 'grave responsibilities' and 'recondite problems' faced by the British in India. The first edition was written on his retirement, as Temple journeyed back to Britain to begin a career as a Conservative politician. Worried that readers had not understood his message properly, the third edition of his work began by outlining fifty-three specific 'troubles' which threatened British power, listing everything from bad ventilation to cyclones, but focusing on the different forms of Indian 'disaffection', 'discontent' and 'hostility' towards the British took. The Indian government's statistician Sir William Hunter noted 'British rule in India is on trial again' in his book *England's Work in India*. Temple and Hunter were joined by dozens more imperial judges, council members and district officers, publishing books that defended the practice of British power in the subcontinent.[6]

If public works provided the main justification for British rule in the propaganda which immediately followed the 1857 uprising, law was the main ideological prop for imperial power two decades later. Sir William Hunter celebrated British officers for the 'splendid and difficult task' of introducing 'order in place of anarchy'. The British had, Hunter claimed, ordered India so successfully that 'the modern Englishman 'complains that he can seldom get a shot at a tiger'. Sir John Strachey, Lytton Strachey's uncle and Richard Temple's successor as finance member of the Viceroy's council, told how '[t]he energies of the Government' had first been applied to the consolidation of British power, then to the 'evolution of an ordered system of administration out of the chaos bequeathed to us by the old rulers of the country'. For these men, British power was no longer characterised by the soldier and tax collector but the police officer and judge. By the 1880s, 'conquest' was no longer solely about military power. It also involved the paradoxical process of forcing Indians to regulate their conduct by contracts and rules rather than brute force. The purpose of British violence was to introduce the peaceful rule of law.[7]

Until well into the twentieth century, law in imperial India retained the mark of it having been created by a conquering power: it was a system of rules imposed without consulting the people to which it applied. But the law also reflected the chaotic and limited capacity of British authority, always needing to involve Indian's in practice. In order to work, imperial India's legal system relied on the cooperation of a vast spectrum of Indian staff, from peons to puisne judges, who had their own ideas and their own ways of doing things. This involvement meant some, particularly middle-class Indians, thought the imperial legal system was a place where they could build their own spheres of authority and self-governing ways of life. The supposed neutrality of the law also gave Indians scope to criticize and challenge what they did not like about British power. But for Indian authority to grow within the structures of imperial law, a state whose basic purpose was to protect conquered power would need to be converted into a very different kind of regime, which ruled through dialogue with its subjects rather than domination. Unsurprisingly, efforts to limit the conquering command of the British caused those whose lives were bound up with the fact of European dominion in India considerable anxiety.

The final fate and consequences of Vasudev Balwant Phadke's rebellion illustrates some of these tensions. For the upper-middle classes of the western Indian city of Pune, Phadke's uprising demonstrated that Britain's conquest of Indian could not be reversed. Even those who thought the use of force could be justified against the British ruled it out until mass support for an anti-British war was peacefully organized. Phadke's fate proved that Indian violence would be outgunned by British imperial soldiers for the foreseeable future. Phadke's example was celebrated in the pages of the Calcutta newspaper *Ananda Bazar Patrika* but the newspaper did not call on its readers to pick up arms. Closer to home it inspired the Pune-based radical Bal Gangadhar Tilak. Tilak thought the British would eventually need to be evicted from India through a violent struggle, but he was careful throughout his political career never to urge violence, only supporting measures which stayed within his interpretation of imperial legality. That, however, was not enough to prevent him from spending two periods in gaol.

For others, Phadke's revolt confirmed that British power could not be relied on to create order, peace and prosperity in India. More conservative figures than Tilak thought the uprising proved that imperial institutions would only protect British power and could not be trusted to maintain the security of Indian property. Indians needed to take the law into their own hands in the wake of the Phadke revolt, the Pune Sarvajanik Sabha proposed that its members stand in for incompetent British authorities by acting as a volunteer police force. The revolt was, they said, merely the work of 'a few misguided hare-brained spirits', who had taken advantage of 'the diseased state of the body politic' to stir up 'professional robbers' and 'dacoits'. It got out of hand because poverty lured thousands into crime and the British had not trusted India's elites to defend order and authority. Of course, their proposal was rejected. Sir Richard Temple, Governor of Bombay, thought the Sabha was made up of members of India's permanently 'disaffected class', who could not be trusted. But despite being suspected by the imperial authorities the Sabha enlisted a band of volunteers to hunt Phadke down and reassert order in the region. Phadke himself was detained by British soldiers, but members of the Sabha successfully acted to enforce law and order by discovering and arresting the perpetrators of the Pune fires which followed Phadke's outbreak.[8]

Legislative reconstruction

The history of modern Indian law begins in the 1860s. Before the great struggle of 1857–8, imperial bureaucrats had talked about extending a coherent and systematic rule of law evenly across British Indian territories but did little to put this into practice. Thomas Macaulay's Code of Criminal Law had not been enacted. Until the great rebellion, the uneven power of Britain's empire was upheld by soldiers and armed tax collectors rather the East India Company's network of judges and courts. Privately printed handbooks had given judges a guide for some kind of standards to apply in cases. Otherwise there were no codes, few regulations and precedent did not apply. Writing in 1862, the lawyer John Norton complained that judges had been left with nothing but their personal sense of justice with which to decide cases. A few officers anxiously 'endeavoured, by private reading, to supply their unavoidable deficiencies' but they never knew if their opinions about what was and was not law were correct. The less studious were left 'to the devices of their own imagination'. Until 1857, law in India was noted for 'its confusion [and] utter want of principle and unity', as the English lawyer James FitzJames Stephen wrote.[9]

'The effect of the Mutiny on the Statute-book was unmistakable', Stephen suggested in his *A History of the Criminal Law of England*. It was 'practically a principle of British government ... that serious disaster in any department of public affairs should be followed by large legislative or administrative reconstruction', his friend Sir Henry Sumner Maine wrote. It was Britain's defeat by and then decisive victory against the brief attempt to revive the Mughal regime in 1857–8 which spurred the creation of a new legal system in India. The imposition of new law, like the spread of public works, was an extension of Britain's reconquest of the Indian subcontinent.

India's conquest by imperial law occurred most of all through the quick enactment of a succession of law codes. As successive law members of the Governor-General's Council, Sir Henry Maine and Sir James FitzJames Stephen were the primary agents of this legislative refounding of empire. Born in 1822 and 1829 respectively, the two men became friends at Cambridge when Maine was appointed Professor of Civil Law at the age of twenty-five and Stephen was an undergraduate. They shared a liberal but authoritarian sensibility. They believed in the progress of society, in modern commerce and social mobility. But they thought progressive change relied on an elite with intellectual self-confidence, which had the ability and right to write laws to apply to millions of people in a society they knew nothing about. They argued, as one obituary of Stephen put it, 'that discipline is absolutely necessary for mankind'; thus that 'compulsion was ... perhaps the most necessary ingredient, in the progress of human society'.

This attitude conformed to the spirit of conquering authority which followed the great insurrection throughout the British regime in India. Suspicious of democracy and hostile to unnecessary conversation with the subjects of government, Maine and Stephen were happy to impose laws founded on philosophical principles alien to Indian society where they could. But they also perceived the need to preserve Indian customs where change would be 'unsafe', as they put it. More so than earlier generations, Maine and Stephen thought law reflected the character of a civilization, and its imposition on another society was capable of diffusing 'a new set of moral ideas'. Yet the security of Britain's power in India always came before any project of moral reform.[10]

The legal revolution began when the Code of Civil Procedure finally eradicated the need for imperial lawyers to consult experts in Hindu and Muslim law in 1858, and a modified version of Macaulay's Penal Code was introduced two years later. These texts placed the security and efficiency of the British regime before every other concern.

The Penal Code, still today the foundation of criminal law in South Asia, was designed to be carried 'as easily as a pocket bible', Stephen noted. Covering the entire criminal law in 511 short chapters, the whole text was shorter than the entry for murder in the most widely used English criminal law textbooks. The Code's priority was the smooth and safe functioning of the imperial regime not the punishment of crimes against individuals. Ten sections dealt with 'offences against the state'. Another nineteen covered actions contemptuous of public servants, proposing a series of draconian penalties for petty acts of insubordination. The refusal to answer an official 'authorized to question' was punishable by imprisonment for up to six months, for example. Crimes against objects essential to imperial power, coins and stamps, for example, were punished severely. The Code gave functionaries of the state a status far greater than they possessed in the UK. '[T]he official body in India', Stephen noted, 'was charged with more important functions than the officials of any other country in the world except absolutist

Russia.' In contrast to the proliferation of strictures that projected the authority of government, the bodies of Indians were poorly protected. Only three sections dealt with murder, and four covered other forms of culpable homicide.[11]

In the decade after the Penal Code was passed, Henry Maine and James FitzJames Stephen added hundreds of new measures. Codes were passed covering almost every area of law, from contract to civil procedure, carriers to companies. The telegraph and the steamship allowed the rapid passage of drafts and minutes between Calcutta or Simla and London, letting India be viewed as a scene of English law-making as it had not been before. A few of these new laws introduced slightly modified versions of English statutes to India, the 1866 Indian Companies Act, for example. Many, though, relied on nothing more than the abstract reason of their authors. The codes were produced by a small group of men, ranged between London and India, who believed in their ability to make law for millions without consulting its subjects. Discussion in the legislative council was technical and perfunctory. The council was 'emphatically a body which meant business', and wasn't willing to be delayed by listening to the voice of people, British or Indian, outside the official hierarchy. By the early 1870s, the only areas left untouched by codification were the Hindu and Muslim law dealing with inheritance and family matters, and the law of wrongful liability.[12]

If one dominant trend ran through this vast and disparate collection of new laws it was the expansion of the imperial state's effort to monitor and regulate the small-scale transactions that sustained British power. The decades after 1858 saw a large increase in the scale of the government's ambition to collect information, for example. Data about a few transactions, wills, a few forms of landed tenure, companies and stamped paper had been recorded before 1858. But from the 1860s, law after law was passed insisting the protagonists in an ever-increasing list of dealings travelled to government offices to transcribe their names and the basic details of particular transactions. To give a few examples: in 1860, an income

tax was created for India, and a network of bureaucrats appointed
to enforce it in the presidency towns. From 1862, a more rigorous
effort was made to regulate the sale of stamped paper. In 1863 the
personal details of every minor servant in government offices was
registered. Two years later, an India-wide infrastructure was inaugurated for registering property transactions, creating new registry
offices in every district town. In the same year, an Act was introduced for regulating joint stock companies, and the limited liability
corporation was created in India for the first time. The 1860s saw
the birth of India's registration state, obsessed with transcribing
information about hundreds of transactions in large ledger books.
Unlike today though, the late nineteenth-century regime was more
interested in recording the fate of things than people. It was only
after the registration of property and corporations began that the
state started to take an interest in the births and deaths of human
beings, first in Calcutta in 1866, in Madras in 1867, and Bombay in
1872. Registration still was not compulsory throughout India until
well into the 1880s.[13]

To an extent imperial legislation mirrored the process of legal
change in Britain. There, too, the government's power expanded
through the creation of new forms of regulation and the construction of new registry offices. But there were important differences.
In Britain, regulation was about defining people's rights over events
which everyone knew about, but where legal obligations seemed
unclear. The registration of births and deaths was driven by uncertainty about the inheritance of land. Companies were registered
to determine clearly who was liable in cases of bankruptcy. State
regulation grew as a way of classifying people's rights and liabilities
in a society where transactions were public, but where new forms
of business meant legal responsibility was not precisely defined.[14]

In India, the avalanche of new regulation was shaped by the fact
that lawmakers did not know what was going on in the society
they governed. Registration was about bringing invisible activities
into view for the first time. Unlike the British Parliament, imperial

bureaucrats were not making laws to govern activities they were involved in themselves. The transcription of information about contracts and land deals, stamped paper and new companies was an effort to understand a society otherwise considered inscrutable. Instead of defining rights over transactions in public view, the power of the state was used to make public what was otherwise unknown.

This effort to make Indian life visible to the imperial state brought with it new and intensive forms of surveillance. Groups of people seen as posing a danger to British power were marked out and required to inform the state about themselves in special ways. The prostitutes who worked near army bases were forced to register with the government: venereal disease was a major threat to the fighting capacity of the army, with 18 per cent of British soldiers admitted to hospital with the condition in Madras in the 1870s, 45 per cent in some other garrisons. Tribes considered to contain criminal elements, as well as bands of eunuchs, were compelled to give detailed information about themselves. Communities with a reputation for killing female children at birth were targeted with special population counts before the decennial census of Indians began in 1871.[15]

In each case, the imperial regime's effort to count and to list, to write yet more information down on the ruled lines of official ledgers, was a sign of its inability to otherwise know anything about the people it ruled. The government did not think it could trust local informants. The knowledge of its district officers was insufficient. The transcription of key facts and figures at a single moment was rarely an effective way to contain intelligent, mobile people; at best it offered a snapshot of a rapidly changing society. But it allowed the government to believe it could do something to assuage its fears about not knowing what was happening.

The classic case of using these impersonal techniques to rule an otherwise ungovernable people was the use of the fingerprint, pioneered in British India. Indians had long used hand marks as signatures. It was William Herschel, an English magistrate in

Bengal, who first employed prints as unique identifiers, using them to monitor the compliance of public works contractors. In 1858, when the man who supplied the raw materials to metal a road in the district gave a handprint in lieu of a signature, Herschel noticed the distinctive swirls on his fingerprints. Taking a print of these seemed a useful way of tracking otherwise anonymous, untraceable contractors who might make off with advance payment before finishing their work.

Over the next twenty-five years, Herschel was stationed in a succession of troubled districts. In Arrah, at the far western end of the province of Bihar, he said 'the mutiny still left work to do'; at Nadia in northern Bengal '[t]hings were so bad that the administration of Civil Justice had unusual difficulty in preserving its dignity.' Herschel thought fingerprinting was the only way to keep track of a mobile and violent population in these fractious places. Through the 1870s, a flood of new documents arriving in British-ruled districts needed individuals' identities to be verified and Herschel made sure every one of them was certified with fingerprints.

Only in the late 1890s did fingerprinting move from being a tool of bureaucratic regulation to a technique for crime-solving; there, too, its use was based on British ideas about the unknowable nature of India's population. The first person to be convicted with fingerprint evidence was a cook accused of killing a tea planter in Bengal in 1902, but he was only prosecuted for theft because the judge was not willing to hang a man on fingerprint evidence alone. The first execution for murder based on such evidence occurred, again in India, four years later.[16]

Fingerprinting provided a rare moment of real connection between the physical reality of Indian life and the British administration of imperial India. Most of the time, the British effort to collect information used new kinds of abstract and anonymous techniques which created an artificial world, distant from the real processes that drove social and commercial life. Concerned primarily to make visible activities which seemed invisible to the imperial regime, in fact official categories created a world of shadow institutions and paper structures, whose real existence was very different from the forms conjured up in official documentation. Hundreds of joint stock corporations were created, for example, which seemed to be a public shell for corruption and fraud. The Indian Companies Act allowed the proliferation of speculative British-run ventures in Bombay and Calcutta which attracted the capital of trading groups such as Banias and Marwaris and then collapsed, their founders absconding with the cash. Bombay's registrar of companies complained that 62 out of the 172 companies created after the passing of the Act had not informed the government of the address from which they traded in their first year of operation; seventy-two had not submitted their accounts. The British justified their rule by claiming to have introduced certain laws to a land of anarchy, but in practice imperial law offered an uncertain foundation for the sustenance of a viable and stable form of economic activity.[17]

The massive expansion of legislation in the two decades which followed the Indian rebellion asserted the power of the imperial regime, and defined Indian society as one in which the state could interfere. But it also posed questions about the limits of British power. The law relied on Indian staff. The growth of the imperial regime's system of paperwork needed tens of thousands of assistant magistrates and record-keepers, police officers and peons. The gigantic scale of this Indian organization overseen by a tiny number of Europeans raised in British minds the possibility of non-compliance, of orders not being followed properly, of things being done in ways which did nothing for British power. It also posed questions about whether it was accountable to the people who administered it and whom it was supposed to serve.

Friends and fellow subjects

In the months of 1879 when Vasudev Balwant Phadke's revolt against British power was raging around Pune, an article questioning the

British rule of law in India was published in the *Calcutta Review*. Written by the 29-year-old north Indian lawyer Sayyid Mahmood, the piece asked whether British rule in India 'owe[s] its origin to conquest, and its maintenance to physical force'. Phadke, like James FitzJames Stephen and Henry Maine, would have definitively answered yes; the Maratha revolutionary thought the British regime was founded on violence and could only be held to account by countervailing forces. Sayyid Mahmood disagreed. But his argument was no less of a challenge to British power than Phadke's.

Mahmood argued that the British were not the sole rulers of India. British authority depended on 'native agency, native friendship, native counsels, native valour'. '[T]he vast majority of Englishmen', he argued, 'take delight in the fallacious idea of being "the conquerors of India".' In fact, he argued, India had not been conquered at all. Turning British stories about conquest on their head, Mahmood argued that British pride in 'the glory and rights of conquest' underestimated the virtue of British rule. A Muslim himself, Mahmood castigated the 'Muhammaden [i.e. Mughal] period [as] one long narrative of assassinations and cold-blooded butcheries'. The British had been invited to rule by Indians frustrated by anarchy and violence, bringing 'order and good government, peace and civilization'; their power rested not on force or technological superiority but Indian will. Mahmood's belief that the empire was founded on consent not force led him to argue Indians had rights, and that the British had the duty to share power. There was a time, he imagined, 'when laws will be framed with the consent of the country', and whole districts 'administered by native efficiency'.

In his essay, Mahmood made the same argument the Regius Professor of History Sir John R. Seeley would expound four years later in perhaps the most famous nineteenth-century rationalization of Britain's empire, *The Expansion of England*. Seeley was friends with British officials who had recently returned to pen their own justifications of British rule, most notably Sir John Strachey. Much of Seeley's work offered a typically imperial defence of the pacifying, civilising effect of British rule empire at a time of crisis. The difference was that Seeley played down the importance of violence to Britain's government throughout the world. Seeley's empire was based on migration and consent, not force. Like Mahmood but unlike most of his British compatriots, Seeley argued that the British empire relied on Indian cooperation.

The similarity between Seeley and Mahmood's arguments was probably more than a coincidence, for the two men spent two years in close proximity at the same Cambridge college, when Seeley had just been appointed Regius Professor of Modern History and Mahmood was a young student. Like Seeley, Mahmood argued that the East India Company had 'brought order and good government'. Seeley, however, was barely interested in the consequences of his arguments for the nature of British rule; his point was only that it was largely pacific and good. Mahmood, by contrast, used it to vehemently condemn the arrogance of India's purported 'conquerors', and thought it meant the British were not entitled to rule India alone.

Born in 1850, the son of the Muslim political leader Sir Sayyid Ahmad Khan, Mahmood was sent to England to study English to enable him to argue persuasively against what his father regarded as false views of Islam being propagated by Europeans. Mahmood's sociable personality inclined him towards public life and perhaps also public glory. While reading Latin, Greek and Arabic at Cambridge, Mahmood studied law and was called to the Bar in April 1872.

Having experienced the 1857 uprising first-hand, Mahmood's father thought India's elites needed to accept the fact of British domination. But Sir Sayyid did not think there could be a close connection between the two peoples. His son was more optimistic, developing a conception of an Anglo-Indian political order which exceeded the limited bounds for collaboration laid out by his father. At a dinner for British officers hosted in Allahabad to celebrate his return in 1872, the 22-year-old Mahmood made the case for a liberal empire based on a common conviviality as well as shared ideals. His aim, he said, was 'to unite England and India socially even more than politically'. Unlike his father, Mahmood argued that Anglo-Indian sociability could create the foundation for a virtuous form of political power. 'English rule in India' could create an ethical state. But this state, he said, 'in order to be good, must promise to be eternal'. Mahmood argued that such a regime was impossible 'until the English people are known to us more as friends and fellow subjects, than as rulers and foreign conquerors'.[18]

In 1879, when he published his *Calcutta Review* article, Mahmood had just been appointed a district judge, a position usually given to European civil servants. Over the following years, he was asked to officiate on the bench of the Allahabad High Court, before being appointed to the permanent position of puisne judge in 1887. Mahmood's rise was part of the broader involvement of Indians in the institutions of British rule occurring during the 1870s and 1880s.

This was a moment when 'the administrative grid', as historian Anil Seal calls it, 'was pressed down more firmly' on Indian society than ever before, and the extension of governmental power could not rely on expensive and unenthusiastic British bureaucrats alone. During the last thirty years of the nineteenth century new institutions were created to enlist Indian elites to work for imperial ends. Municipal corporations were formed for local notables to deliberate and fund apparently low-level improvements like waterworks and roads, usually with the District Collector in the chair. District boards were instituted with a similar function in rural areas. Indians were increasingly involved in teaching and management in universities. Small numbers of Indians were being recruited into the Indian Civil Service, with the government primed to appoint Indians to one-sixth of each year's positions from 1879. But it was the law that saw the greatest Indian involvement. The legal profession was dominated by Indians soon after 1857, and a few judges were appointed from the late 1870s. The law was attractive partly because income

was independent of the whim of imperial paymasters, and partly
because its abstraction and neutrality allowed Indians to think they
could find places within it exempt from the British effort to dominate Indian society. But none of these changes gave Indians any
great executive power. Indians could be judges but not lawmakers,
and they always earned less than Europeans.[19]

Despite the limits of Indian involvement, tensions became
increasingly apparent. With their ever-embattled sense of unease
about being a tiny minority in an alien society, Europeans in India
insisted the law was a tool for asserting their violent dominance over
Indian society. The legal system was, for example, used to protect
their ability to inflict violence on employees and subordinates with
more or less impunity. The killing of servants was not rare, but the
murder of a 'native' was always treated far more lightly than the
murder of a European. The greatest perpetrators were European
men using violence to direct Indian labour hundreds of miles from
the nearest town or cantonment, plantation owners and other managers scattered throughout the countryside. Judges acquitted killers
by claiming that Indians had naturally frail bodies. Lord Lytton,
Viceroy between 1876 and 1880, claimed that 'Asiatics are subject
to internal disease which often renders fatal to life even a slight
external shock.' The 'diseased spleen' was a classic defence, used to
suggest that death was caused by the failure of internal organs not a
kick from a metal-capped boot. A tea planter talking to the writer
Wilfrid Scawen Blunt in 1882 claimed that 'natives', when struck,
were 'capable without any exaggeration of dying to spite you'.[20]

These were men and women who, to Sayyid Ahmed's frustration, did indeed celebrate Britain's conquest of India, and thought
conquest gave them the right to resist the involvement of Indians
in the judicial system. Until the early 1880s, they were reassured by
the fact that only Europeans could try Europeans in the countryside,
even though, 'by a strange anomaly', Indians could sit in judgment
of Europeans in the presidency towns. In 1882 an Indian judge in
Bengal was promoted to a position in the countryside and so lost

his jurisdiction over Europeans, and had his complaint passed on to the government by Maharaja Sir Jotindra Mohun Tagore, one of the most 'eminent' of Calcutta's Bengali upper class. The complaint led Lord Lytton's successor as Viceroy, the liberal Lord Ripon, to propose to abolish such an anomaly. Ripon's argument was that it was too expensive to try all Europeans in the High Court, and that Indians would not apply to join the civil service if they did not have the same powers as Europeans.

This minor administrative move led to a 'storm of passion' in both India and Britain. Mass meetings were held in every Indian town with a sizeable European population, and a campaign in Britain was led by *The Times*. In London Tory British newspapers complained of the onset of 'anarchy in India'. James FitzJames Stephen used the debate to reiterate his belief that British rule was founded on the violence of conquest, and that empire meant nothing without the will to impose British ways of doing things on an alien society. When the liberal anti-imperial Blunt travelled to India in 1882, he found himself journeying with people who held similar opinions and recorded their outrage. Apart from the Muslim crew and a man appointed to run the Calcutta mint, Blunt's companions on the crowded, disease-ridden steamship *Gurkha* were a 'rough set of Colonial English and planters' who angrily complained about the measure. One 'intelligent young planter' thought there was 'a new rebellion brewing in India'. Indians had started to curse and throw stones at the British, he said. 'India would be lost' if the bill was passed, as it would prevent Europeans from suppressing Indian dissent with violence. Blunt himself believed the Ilbert Bill was 'a very poor instalment' in the equality that successive British governments had promised between the Queen's English and Indian subjects. But the men on the *Gurkha* all thought it was a 'revolutionary measure, which would put every Englishman and every Englishwoman at the mercy of native intrigue and native fanaticism'. The oldest and rudest planter told Blunt that India 'was a conquered country, and the niggers were all rogues from the first to the last'.[21]

In 1883, the year he returned to India to work for an English newspaper in Lahore, Rudyard Kipling wrote that 'old stagers say that race feeling has never been so high since the mutiny'. Kipling would go on to become the most popular poet of Britain's late imperial age. He was eighteen during the Ilbert Bill controversy. The debate shaped Kipling's attitude to empire for the rest of his life, helping him forge an idea of the English in India as an embattled but chosen people, whose 'dominion' over 'lesser breeds without the Law' was always endangered by Indian plots and weak-willed British politicians. The law was central to Kipling's conception of British rule, but his idea of law was racial and spiritual, not based on any actual judicial process. Sometimes, he thought it needed to be imposed by lawless violence. Kipling's rule of law was about action not reason and logic. It was run by officers who were 'neither saint and sage / But only men who did the work', as he wrote in his poem 'Wage-Slaves'. 'Self-exiled from our gross delights' their peculiar predilection for efficiency and order gave the British the right to rule the world. Here, Kipling was not reproducing the official view of viceroys and council members. His writing connected with the feelings of embattled minor administrators, merchants and plantation managers who felt they performed the labours of empire for insufficient reward.[22]

It was this British understanding of the law as a practical system of European domination which Indians in the imperial legal system came up against. The official ideology of imperial justice allowed plenty of space for Indians to officiate as lawyers and judges, as long as they swore allegiance to the Queen and were educated in British India's rules and codes. But there was much more than the official view, far more to law than obeying written orders. The practice of imperial law was governed by tacit conventions which Indian justices were not part of. Racial social hierarchies cut across the supposed equality of the court room. Business was discussed at European-only gatherings; many Britons resented any suggestion Indians could be their social equals. The Bengali nationalist leader

Surendranath Banerjea was dismissed as a magistrate in Sylhet after claiming an equal position in the civil lines he shared with European officials. Indian judges took more time and wrote longer opinions than their British colleagues, and were criticized for not being efficient or impartial when they did so. It seemed that the law was governed by double standards, where subscription to formal rules was never enough to make one part of the system.

Sayyid Mahmood was appointed a judge in the wake of the Ilbert Bill controversy. Unable to resist the storm of protest, Lord Ripon backed down, giving Europeans the right to be tried by a jury of Europeans; the measure in fact meant they were more likely to be acquitted in cases involving violence against Indians. Indian opinion was universally outraged. In an attempt at pacification, the government decided the next vacant High Court seat would go to a 'native' lawyer, and in 1886 Sayyid Mahmood was appointed puisne judge at Allahabad. He lasted seven years in a position which was intended to be permanent. His relationship with his 'brother judges' gradually deteriorated until he was dismissed after being accused by the Chief Justice for being drunk and late in submitting his judgments. Mahmood himself thought he was the victim of a chain of events that proved that his 'brother judges' were not willing to treat him as an equal member of the court.[23]

Throughout his time on the bench, Mahmood became increasingly frustrated with his British colleagues' lack of serious interest in the law. Their judgments were cursory and short, based on the quickest route to a secure decision rather than detailed contemplation of the law on a particular point. They often relied on British statutes rather than traditions of pre–British Indian jurisprudence. Mahmood riled his colleagues by criticizing their translation of Arabic, Persian or Sanskrit sources. He often argued that their clumsiness caused them to 'import foreign ideas', and illegitimately interfere in areas of life supposed to be governed by indigenous norms.

For example, in a case heard in February 1885, Mahmood

defended the right of a neighbour to purchase land from a Muslim landlord instead of an outsider using a complex set of arguments drawn from Islamic law. He argued that Muslim law was rooted in 'Republican' principles, and was concerned to ensure the maintenance of peace among a society of equal small proprietors. One principle was that members of a particular community should have the right to resist 'the intrusion of a stranger' if they were able to buy land put up for sale instead. Mahmood's judgment in the case was a 15,000-word essay on the history of Islamic law and ethics. His 'brother judge' John Oldfield agreed with Mahmood's decision, but for very different reasons. In a 200-word text he dismissed his colleague's references to Islamic history, arguing that imperial statutes allowed European judges to decide such cases with their sense of 'equity' or common sense. Instead of being bound by Indian principles which he did not trust or understand, Oldfield wanted to rely purely on the efficient, rational British imperial mind.

Mahmood thought these attitudes were bound up with the British belief that they were India's conquerors. Mahmood's painstaking effort to explain India's indigenous legal principles began as an effort to undo conquest, and create the friendly, collaborative kind of Anglo-Indian political order he had proposed in his 1879 *Calcutta Review* piece. In fact, his experience in the court played out in precisely the way he discussed the emotional breakdown between Britain and Indian in that article: 'Under the influence of supposed grievances on the one hand, and the effect of injured pride on the other, the political and social relation of the Englishman with the people of this country becomes a matter of national insult or of personal insult and provocation.' Against Mahmood's seeming insolence, the British asserted their wounded pride by refusing to let him decide criminal cases, excluding him from decision-making meetings, sneering at him for his legal nit-picking and then, when he complained about not being involved, drowning him under a deluge of petty paperwork. Mahmood was attacked by English lawyers for obsessing over the meaning of ancient texts and accused of introducing 'new rules of law' as he did. Mahmood himself became prickly and hostile, and probably started to drink more and more. By 1892, both sides were engaged in a hostile exchange of letters. The Chief Justice should, Mahmood wrote in October 1892, 'have allowed himself enough time to understand the Indian laws and the facts of Indian life, before assuming the position of *veni, vidi, vici*'. Eventually, the Governor of the United Provinces recommended he not be allowed to return to the court after an extended period of leave. His argument was that Mahmood had slowed down the Allahabad court's efficiency; there would be no hope of working through its huge backlog if Mahmood was allowed to return to work. North India's only Muslim High Court judge had been sacked.[24]

British-ruled India's legal system relied on Indian participants to function; judges often claimed Indians were treated fairly within it. Yet the law's British functionaries found it difficult to practically acknowledge Indians as equal partners within the law. Events at the Allahabad court, just like the Ilbert Bill controversy, demonstrated that British administrators saw British rule very differently from the way Mahmood imagined it. It was not a system of global governance in which Britons and Indians worked to maintain peace and justice under the imperial authority of the British Queen Empress. It was, they thought, a system based on the forceful subjugation of one people, one race even, by another.

Mahmood's father, the one-time Bijnor district officer Sir Sayyid Ahmad Khan, was very clear about that. It was impossible for an Indian to claim equal status within an institution so vital for maintaining British authority, he thought. In a newspaper article written soon after his son departed from the Allahabad court Sir Sayyid noted that the British might 'brag about their impartiality', but it was impossible for 'the *conquerors* of this country' to sit 'together on the same bench' in 'equal terms of respect of honour' with members of a conquered nation. As Sir Sayyid argued,

If an Indian in such a position tries to preserve his self-respect which is concomitant to nobility and uprightness, the relations between him and his European colleagues get embittered. On the other hand, if utterly regardless of self-respect he makes himself quite subservient to the wishes of his European colleague, who because he belongs to a conquering race, *naturally* believes in his superiority, he is able to pull on pretty well. But this can never be expected from a man who wishes to remain true to his conscience, and in whose veins runs the blood of his (noble) ancestors. It is no secret that there is as much difference between the Englishman's treatment of his own countryman and that of others as there is between *black* and *white*.

For Sir Sayyid, tension in the court was the unavoidable after-effect of the violence that underpinned British sovereignty in India. He had not wanted his son to be a judge in the first place, or occupy any position involving proximity to Europeans. Mahmood was supposed to become friends with Europeans, but should not seek to exercise governmental power jointly with them. Echoing a long-standing Indian critique of British bureaucracy, Sir Sayyid was glad that Mahmood had been liberated from the demeaning clock-watching of the court and was now 'the master of his own time'.

Sir Sayyid Ahmad Khan is often described as the foremost Muslim 'loyalist' in late nineteenth-century India, and seen as a fervent supporter of British rule. He was, after all, emphatically on the side of the British in 1857. But as historian Faisal Devji notes, Sir Sayyid's politics were governed above all by the pragmatic sense that the Mughal regime's former ruling class needed to acknowledge they had been defeated by Britain's conquering violence.[25] Sir Sayyid thought that resistance was futile, and that British power was the only possible source of stability and order. But Sir Sayyid's argument was that defeat could be borne with dignity if Indians developed and renewed their own ways of doing things in walks of life which did not challenge British power. Indians could not jointly exercise judicial or executive authority. But they could work in the distant, subordinate offices of state power where contact with Europeans was minimal; and they could carve out a space for civilized life in religious, educational and cultural spheres. While Sayyid Mahmood believed Indians could participate as equals in the authority of the state, Sir Sayyid thought their regeneration would come through a retreat into spaces and institutions where they could have more autonomous power. Over the following decades the different positions taken by Sir Sayyid and his son were reflected in debates about the course of action Indians should take to recover their liberty, and act with a sense of autonomy and self-reliance.[26]

The decisions of his antagonists have been forgotten, but Mahmood's lengthy judgments are some of the few which continue to be cited in the legal practice of post-imperial South Asia. Nonetheless, the conflict in Allahabad seems to have broken him. For a few years he helped to run the college he and his father set up, the Muhammadan Anglo-Oriental College at Aligarh. Against his father's better judgement, he tried to begin his legal practice again. But Sayyid Mahmood was by now drinking heavily, and becoming increasingly paranoid and often violently angry. At Aligarh, students were reported to have had to put up with 'the degraded spectacle of a drunkard wandering around and shouting at them & everybody.' Mahmood's friends worried that he might be violent towards his wife, and called in the local magistrate. Mahmood never recovered. His drinking estranged him from his father before the old man died in 1898. Sayyid Mahmood himself was dead five years later at the age of fifty-three, broken, perhaps, by the contradiction between his faith in an Anglo-Indian legal order and his exclusion from the institutions of imperial power.[27]

11

THE GREAT DEPRESSION

Between twelve and thirty million people were killed by starvation or famine-related diseases in India in the last quarter of the nineteenth century. Millions died in the great famine years 1876–8, 1896–7 and 1900–1901, hundreds of thousands in smaller famines in between. Famine occurred when people found it impossible to 'command the means by which grain may be purchased', as a group of Indian famine observers put it in 1896. When famine hit, entire districts emptied as people left home looking for any way to earn money they could. When rains failed in 1876 in Indapur, an area ninety miles east of Pune, 10,000 of its 67,000 population left, and the same number deserted the same place twenty years later. Hundreds of villages throughout north, west and south India were left without a soul. Sometimes only local elites who had stores of grain stayed. Before mass migration between the new independent states of India and Pakistan in 1947, these famine years saw the greatest movement of people in Indian history.

To begin with, people on the verge of starvation left their villages on long-established routes. Some went overseas. Hundreds of thousands moved to work in the plantations of Ceylon during the 1870s and 1880s. Others travelled to Mauritius or even the Caribbean. But most people walked to wetter, more prosperous parts of the Indian subcontinent. The Gujarat coast and the wooded region around Nagpur were common destinations, where coastal trade might provide work or forests provide fruits to forage.

But as famine conditions grew worse, the destitute found a new destination: British-run work camps. In the 1860s and 1870s, district officers opened work schemes in a haphazard fashion. As famine became a definite reality in the minds of the British regime, famine relief became another way of life governed by imperial rules and regularities. Starting from the early 1880s, each provincial government wrote famine codes that calibrated exactly how much work each person was supposed to do and how much pay they should receive. The codes included details about where to dig latrine ditches (too far away for people to use them); where to bury the dead (in deep mass graves); what to do with children too young to work (put them in big nurseries with two overseers for every sixty children). Huts were to be laid out to make sure, as one observer put it, 'the encampment has the appearance of a well ordered village'.

Photography had become an obsession for many Britons in India during the late nineteenth century, and the famine camps became an early subject. The spread of the handheld Kodak No. 1 camera after 1888 allowed everyday scenes to be captured on film. Photographs were taken of clusters of the starving, queues of people receiving food or pay and neat lines of tents where they were accommodated. Bombay governor Sir Richard Temple wrote in 1877 that '[t]here is only one possible mode of escape [from famine], namely *labour*,'[1] yet very few photographs of famine work survives in the public record. One of them, taken by Frederick Lechmere-Oertel, shows hundreds of bodies, squatting and leaning forward, the men clothed in nothing but plain waist cloths and the women in worn saris, with an overseer standing with a large stick in the foreground. The photograph was taken at a famine relief camp near Allahabad, probably in 1900, but the scene might have been anywhere in India during the last quarter of the nineteenth century. The women and men sit in front of piles of small stones, breaking rocks.

Born in Germany before moving to India to study at the engineering college at Roorkee which Thomas Cautley founded, Lechmere-Oertel wrote some of the textbooks used to train engineers. His photographs were, though, a record of the poor employment of late nineteenth-century India's labour force. At the worst moments of famine in 1897 and 1900, six million were being fed by British relief, more than half in return for the kind of work depicted in the photograph. In these years, the imperial state employed eight times more people than all the factories of the subcontinent combined. Given the unmet needs of late nineteenth-century Indian society, this massive workforce was put to use very badly. India's railway network was growing and in need of labourers; heavy industry was expanding and demanded workers. But instead of increasing India's production or prosperity, the British government forced workers to sit on the ground, just as in Lechmere-Oertel's photograph, breaking stone. Their task was to make gravel to lay roads, but the roads they made rarely went anywhere useful and were usually washed away with a few weeks' monsoon rain.[2]

These famine camps transformed the way Indians interacted with the British state. Before the late 1850s, ordinary Indian civilians encountered the imperial regime in brief moments, in court or revenue offices where officials made perfunctory decisions that were then poorly enforced. In the years after the rebellion of 1857–8 interaction increased, as the reconquest of north India placed more people in contact with British violence, and then labour was hired in larger numbers on public works. But still, in most places, the British regime was very distant.

The famine camps that opened in the late nineteenth century initiated a direct encounter between British officers and unprecedented numbers of their subjects. This new style of mass imperial contact was partly stimulated by British compassion for India's poor. But imperial bureaucrats treated famine victims neither as people whose welfare needed to be secured, nor as workers whose creative labour could be put to productive use. Instead, the poor were dealt with as potential trouble-makers and a possible drain on the imperial regime's resources. Even confronted with mass death, the imperial regime's instincts were to project British power and protect the livelihood of its agents. The purpose, as ever, was to ensure lines of control were sustained and imperial institutions not left open to challenge.

The dramatic history of the world

Famine occurred when there was not enough work for people to earn the money to feed themselves when climatic conditions turned bad. That breakdown happened as India's workforce was exposed to greater competition from overseas, and India's rulers were unable or unwilling to support alternative ways for people to earn money to buy food.

The middle of the nineteenth century was a period of global economic dislocation. This was the world's first era of globalization, when goods people used every day (food, ordinary clothes, household consumables) were shipped across continents for the first time. A global mass market emerged for wheat, opium, sugar and meat but above all for cotton. Indian consumers began to buy the cloth produced in Lancashire's cotton mills in massive quantities. British-made textiles then flooded into India to clothe the empire's expanding army from 1857 to 1858, and followed the re-establishment of British power. In the 1830s there were only sixty million yards of cotton goods exported to India each year. In 1858 the figure had grown to 968 million yards. Exports pushed a billion yards in 1870, three yards a year for every man, woman and child resident in the Indian subcontinent.

The importing of British textiles did not simply annihilate the Indian manufacture of cloth and clothes. New products and expanded transport links created new opportunities for work. India's connection to global markets was devastating in many places. But it had complicated effects, affecting districts which were well connected as much, often worse, than the isolated countryside.

Take Bellary, for example, a town called 'the capital of the famine districts' by one observer in the early 1880s, at the centre of the district which saw the greatest mortality through India's great famine years. Lying in the dry centre of the southern Indian peninsula, 130 miles from the west coast at Goa, 180 miles north of Bangalore and 240 miles south-west of Hyderabad, Bellary was never remote or isolated. Throughout the famine years in the second half of the nineteenth century, Bellary's middle-class inhabitants saw it as the cultural centre of southern India, with vibrant theatres and a thriving literary scene. The lawyer and playwright Kolachalam Srinivasa Rao imagined Bellary as the place from which the cultural life of India could be regenerated. Rao's *Dramatic History of the World*, written in Telugu in the 1890s and translated and printed in 1908, drew from a dizzying range of dramatic traditions, from ancient Greece to aboriginal Australia, to inspire a rebirth of Indian drama. In what one might call India's middle south, the district was on the border between the Mughal-ruled provinces of the north and India's far southern provinces. In the centre of the Indian peninsula, it stood at the junction of the Telugu-speaking east and Kannada-speaking west. Bellary's cultural role grew from both its central place in global trade and from famine. It was the buying and selling of cotton over decades which linked Bellary to India's coasts and then Europe, allowing Srinivasa Rao to think about the town in relationship not just to Asia and the Middle East, but the rest of the world. But the first modern theatrical groups in the town emerged out of charities created to provide relief during the 1876–7 crisis.

Bellary town grew around granite rocks that provided a platform for armies defending the surrounding land. Coming under British rule in 1801, Bellary became an important cantonment town, the site of southern India's largest army base. The town's military role helped it grow to become India's forty-first most populous settlement by 1871, with 51,766 inhabitants and, according to military surgeons, the greatest number of venereal disease cases in the Indian army. The military base supported the growth of imperial institutions: a church, a courthouse and a tax office were built around the fort in the early nineteenth century, as well as a market named the Cowl Bazaar, after the *qaul*, or promise, which soldiers made when they enlisted in the Company's army. British officers focused on the needs of this urban settlement, but only a small fraction of the district's population was drawn to the town. In the 1870s, the surrounding district had 912,000 inhabitants.

The black, hard soil around Bellary town was bad for growing grain but good for cotton. For centuries, cotton from these fields had been shipped 130 miles directly west to Hubli and then on to the rest of the world from Karwar, the port where two of Katherine Cooke's husbands had died, or to Bombay. But its greatest use was in clothing for local people to wear. Scattered throughout the region, villagers manufactured thread on spinning wheels or simply twirled cotton onto iron bars. This thread was woven into cloth on looms which were 'in all essential points exactly similar to the common hand-loom of England', except the shuttle was not moved by any 'mechanical contrivance'. Perhaps a third of the income of most peasant households was earned by women spinning in their homes.

This was hand-powered industry, diffused throughout the villages of India, but it existed alongside the beginnings of steam-powered manufacturing. Around 1865, Daniel Abraham, a Catholic Tamil whose family had moved from Madras in the 1820s, opened a cotton mill. A decade later, Sabapathy Muliyar, a Hindu merchant, opened twelve cotton steam presses, three ginning factories and a weaving factory. Part of the capital for both the Abraham and Muliyar enterprises came from the money each man's family had respectively earned by selling goods to the army at Bellary: Abraham's father had been a distiller who sold liquor to soldiers. Sabapathy Muliyar's grandfather had been the cantonment's commissariat. But both men also had British trading partners.[3]

In the 1840s and 1850s, European-manufactured textiles were reaching Bellary by bullock cart. Over the next decades goods started to come by rail, as lines were opened in 1871 which linked

Bellary to Madras and through the Bhor Ghat incline to Bombay. Although yarn, cloth and clothes came in great quantities from Lancashire, work in the local cotton industry did not disappear. Bellary's highly skilled weavers concentrated on expensive patterned cotton and silk saris, with particular towns developing a reputation for specific colours and styles. Poorer weavers adjusted by making white, coarse *khadi* cloth that Lancashire mill-owners could not make cheaply enough. British officials still counted 23,293 looms in Bellary in 1869–70, one for every forty-three men, women and children in the district.

Yet to survive against European products, spinning and weaving became more specialized, more of a male occupation and more urban. The textile industry was no longer scattered throughout villages. To cut costs it was concentrated in towns like Bellary, in narrow alleyways where groups of men specialized in particular styles or colours of sari, or in the Abraham or Sabapathy factories. Global competition forced Indian textile manufactures to stop employing women who spun and wove in their homes while their husbands tilled the fields. The result was that peasants had fewer sources of income when the weather cut their agricultural work. Middle-class consumers could still buy Indian-made cotton and silk goods in the bazaars; but many of the people who had once produced them starved.

New global connections opened up the possibility of other forms of work. There was a brief moment when a more balanced relationship between Britain and India's producers and consumers seemed possible, but such moments did not last. In 1860, 80 per cent of Britain's cotton industry's raw materials came from America, but these supplies were cut by the civil war. Factory owners started to look to cotton-producing districts in India like Bellary to fill the gap in supply. 'To India', the radical liberal politician and inspector of public works Arthur Arnold wrote in his *History of the Cotton Famine*, 'belongs the origin of cotton manufacture.' The British mechanization of cotton-making had been spurred 'by our envy and cupidity' at the fabrics made by skilled Indian weavers, Arnold said. It would be a 'strange, but a happy instance of redistributive justice' if India became the main supplier for British looms. Men like Arnold imagined India would prosper by growing and processing primary products for industrial societies, as Australia, Canada and New Zealand did at the same time.

But there wasn't enough investment in the capital needed to allow cotton-growing to thrive. In the 1860s, factory owners and MPs in Britain lobbied for investment in India that would increase the supply of raw cotton. A railway line cutting directly from Bellary to Karwar was mooted but never built. Canals stretching from Bellary to India's east coast were projected but, again, there was no funding. The possibility of shipping cotton to Britain encouraged Abraham and Sabapathy to invest their limited capital in opening cotton-processing factories but, relatively speaking, these were tiny enterprises. The Government of India failed to seize the moment, and refused to invest in the infrastructure needed to develop the country's cotton supply. The Secretary of State for India found the demands of British mill-owners infuriating. They 'talk more like fools than any set of men I have come across for a long time', Charles Wood complained in February 1861.[4]

Towns connected with the growth and export of cotton boomed during the American Civil War, from Bellary to Bombay, but when supplies resumed from the southern states of the United States to Britain in 1865, India's cotton boom turned into bust. Workers moved back to the countryside where there was less demand for the crop, and were forced to make a living growing poor grain crops like jowar. The population of Bombay itself shrank from 800,000 to 644,000 by the time the first census was compiled in 1871. The revival of Britain's cotton industry in the years that immediately followed the American Civil War took place with little Indian competition and with Indian supplies. Ever greater quantities of cheap cloth and clothes were sold throughout India. India was an increasingly important market for British goods, taking 8.2 per cent of British exports in 1870–1922 and 16 per cent in 1913. But as late as the 1890s, cotton was only cultivated on 346,000 acres of the district of Bellary, 16 per cent of the total land under the plough.

When other parts of Britain's empire prospered, India's incorporation into global markets increased the country's poverty. The expansion of markets in everyday necessities made it harder for Indian workers to make a living from agriculture as well as from manufacturing textiles. Once railways were built, the British imagined improvements in transport would increase living standards, by increasing the demand for crops and reducing the price of food needed for labourers to survive. In fact the effect was often reversed. Higher prices for food had always been charged in places where crops were lost to natural catastrophe, such as a drought or flooding. But poor transport links meant prices could stay low in neighbouring areas. As railway lines stretched into every part of India, merchants across larger distances were able to increase prices to match the price in the area of greatest dearth, and there was always a dearth somewhere.

Take Bellary again. The soil of Bellary was owned by small chieftains, the kind of men who, seventy-five years earlier, Thomas Munro had imagined would form a peaceful yeoman class to underpin British rule. Bellary was, after all, the capital of the Ceded Districts where Munro had finessed his system of land management. The fantasy was that British rule would encourage the growth of a class of independent peasant proprietors, who would labour and thrive without support from any indigenous hierarchy. In practice, though, Bellary's 992 villages were divided between a few thousand magnates each of whom employed between ten and fifty men to work their grain and cotton fields. The big village houses were built on top of grain pits. Ploughing and sowing were traditionally paid for with grain given from the chief's store. Even in difficult times, enough grain was kept to be distributed to keep poor labourers alive.

But the sharp increase in grain prices in the early 1870s

encouraged local lords to sell their grain supplies on the open market. Local systems of entitlement began to unravel. Instead of working for a lord in exchange for subsistence in good times or bad, labourers were forced to eke out whatever livelihood they could. They were compelled to sell their muscle power by the hour to buy more expensive grain, or to scrabble on the dry Deccan soil to cultivate their own tiny plots of land. When crops were destroyed by drought, there was no work. The decline in traditional systems of subsistence occurred alongside the loss of weaving work, and together undermined a poor family's chances of survival.

In an 1872 report on the condition of the district, a British revenue official described Bellary's population of 912,000 as 'a quiet and well-disposed set of men'. Its author, the Madras officer John Kelsall, imagined cultivators had done well from increases in the price of grain and cotton brought by the extension of the railway lines. But Kelsall's sight was limited. He misread the energy and money concentrated in the small garrison town of Bellary itself for the condition of the district as a whole. After the rebellion of 1857–8, British officers had strengthened the cantonment, built a new arsenal and a new hospital for Europeans. In the early 1870s a new courthouse and tax office were added, together with a grand railway station at a cost of 100,000 rupees a few years later. Beyond the district capital, Kelsall noted local government offices were in a ruined state. He did not notice the collapse in living conditions for most of Bellary's inhabitants beyond.[5]

Bellary's population did not passively submit to its worsening situation. Many resisted, most of them unsuccessfully. The sale of grain by local landlords sparked riots. Labourers protested against their landlords' decision to abandon their obligations, and with it the collapse of the principle of reciprocity supposed to bind rural society together. As one sub-collector put it in September 1876, 'the poor ryots [peasants] consider that, as they have helped enrich the sowcar [landlord], the latter should not fail them in their time of need.' Crime and disorder also soared. In 1876 and 1877 respectively there were 159 and 273 large robberies in the previously peaceful district of Bellary. In the whole of Madras presidency, these years saw the highest crime rates for the entire period of British rule.[6]

In years gone by, riot and crime would have forced great magnates to concede. But in the 1870s, rural leaders were less vulnerable to protests than they had been before because they had new support from British forces of violence. In the aftermath of the 1857–8 revolt, the imperial army was on anxious standby for opposition capable of undermining British power. Bellary was home to the largest garrison in British-ruled territory in south India, with between 800 and 1000 soldiers through the 1870s, 1880s and 1890s. When hardship grew in the early 1870s, more armed police were drafted in, 300 in total to the three worst famine affected districts of Bellary, Kurnool and Kadapah. As violence even failed to register their protest against the collapse of the system which secured their survival, peasants had little chance when the weather turned bad. In 1874, crops were destroyed by heavy rains. The next two seasons saw a serious drought, causing the price of staple foodstuffs to increase even further, to four times their 1873 level. Death in Bellary came for hundreds of thousands, and through the whole of southern India millions more.[7]

Twenty thousand famine victims walked into Bellary town in the summer of 1876. British officers encouraged them to leave by offering work. By October, the Collector and district engineer had opened 330 relief works in Bellary district alone. To start with, workers were given a variety of tasks, clearing prickly pear, digging out water storage tanks as well as collecting stones for roads. The aim was to move people away from areas of European settlement: only three work camps were opened in the district town, when this had by far the largest congregation of the poor. At the end of 1876, just over half of the population of Bellary district's 912,000 people were receiving some kind of relief, 324,506 of them in return for work in labour schemes: one third of the district's men, women and children was a paid labourer for the British state.[8]

The local government's haphazard relief efforts saved some lives. But by the beginning of 1877, senior government officers in Bombay and Calcutta were anxious that the proliferation of local relief projects threatened to plunge India into chaos and push the regime into debt. Sir Richard Temple was sent to restore order and financial probity. Temple was concerned that local relief works uprooted millions from their villages without concentrating them in any other place, allowing them to wander the countryside in mobs that threatened violence and endangered British power. Temple's answer was to limit and contain, to restrict the poor to a small number of camps where they could be better surveyed. Village works were closed. The able-bodied starving were told they needed to walk to larger public works projects, 'on which large bodies of men could be concentrated, supplied with food, and properly organized and controlled', as the officer in charge of famine works in Bombay presidency put it. Labourers were strung out in a single controllable line of workers instead of being scattered throughout the countryside. A. K. Connell, an Irish critic of the bureaucracy in India, wrote in 1883 that the policy turned the imperial government into a great 'taskmaster' directing 'a gigantic population of slaves', but Temple and Strachey saw it as a way to turn Indians into diligent labourers and build public works. Also at the same time the rations given to famine victims were reduced. In the interests of 'financial economy', Temple initiated an 'experiment', to see whether famine victims could survive on the cash equivalent of one pound of rice a day, plus a small sum in money. The figure had been calculated as the amount needed to allow prisoners in Madras's jails barely to subsist. It did not take into account the fact that famine victims used up calories working to get their food.[9]

In the two years of the famine, the average number working on relief projects throughout southern India was 877,000, with those ill or too frail to work fed in unhealthy relief camps. With cholera and dysentery rife, the chief surgeon of Madras presidency calculated that there were 918 deaths for every 1000 people in relief camps in his province. Despite large-scale relief efforts, the great south Indian famine of 1876–8 caused the death of over five million Indians, 2 per cent of the subcontinent's population. It spread from Madras and Bombay to parts of Awadh and Punjab, but the epicentre was the central south, the region Temple visited in 1877.[10] In Madras presidency, two million, or 10 per cent of the population, died. In the districts of Bellary and Kurnool one-fifth were killed, and the population over the next decade was a quarter below what it would have been had these deaths not occurred.[11]

Senior British officers argued that death on this scale was an act of God. India, particularly the dry Deccan, was simply prone to famine, or so officials like Sir Richard Temple believed. Massive mortality was inevitable unless Indians worked harder and saved their money to tide them over in bad times. The task of British rule was to give the starving work in exchange for food, trying to teach men and women whose bodies and minds had been weakened by years of destitution the virtue of labour and thrift. Most Indians, by contrast, blamed the British. It was the duty of political leaders to stop massive starvation, and the British regime failed badly.

When he travelled to the famine-affected areas in 1883, Wilfrid Scawen Blunt noted that precisely the people he expected to support British rule were hostile to British power. On 26 November, Blunt visited the mill-owner Daniel Abraham. The same evening he was invited to a dinner party hosted by C. Sabapathy Iyer and his wife, newly converted Christians who drank wine but wore Indian jewellery and entertained their guest with a Telegu dance. These people had racial and religious affinities with the British, yet they were angry at the government's response to economic crisis and then famine. They spoke of the chaos of relief, of a million and a half rupees wasted because there was no communication with the people the government were trying to save, of people given money with nowhere to buy grain and railway lines shipping food that stood in depots without distribution. Charity, collected by the British Mansion House Fund or by private individuals in India, tended to be well spent, as Bellary's local political hierarchy were in charge of it. But, Abraham, Iyer and others argued, government money was wasted. One officer had a travelling allowance of 3,000 rupees for twenty-two days (£30,000 in 2016 prices), but did nothing because he could not speak the language. Blunt's new friends said famine was caused by high taxation and 'the extinction of the larger landowners, who used to keep grain in store for bad years'.

The greatest problem was the British government's failure to listen to the people they ruled. C. Sabapathy Iyer told Blunt that he had visited England, toured the country estates of liberal aristocrats, spent time with the British radical statesmen John Bright and Charles Dilke and 'been feted everywhere'. But in Bellary 'the collector's wife is too proud to call upon his wife'. 'There was no real sympathy anywhere,' Iyer complained. Blunt spent time with the district's Collector and its police chief, but thought the most intelligent Englishman was Mr Hanna, the railway superintendent. Even he knew nothing about Indian opinion 'as the English live in a world of their own'. '[G]ood had been done in the past', but 'evil was being done now', the men and women who Blunt met complained.[12]

Friendly intercourse

Just short of two years after Wilfrid Blunt's visit, a good friend of C. Sabapathy Iyer set out on a journey from Bellary. Then forty-eight, Sabapathy Mudeliar was Bellary's most prominent man. From a family of merchants and military contractors, he had begun his career in Bellary's British revenue office in the years after the great rebellion. He worked there for fifteen years before setting up his own firm, first acting as cotton-buying agent for a London merchant, then building a succession of cotton presses and weaving factories near Bellary. Mudeliar's business enterprise was a part of the process of economic change that pushed the district into famine, as his factories drew work away from women scattered through the countryside, even though, during the crisis itself, he was a major philanthropist, feeding 4,000 men and women throughout the famine.

Mudeliar was a central figure in the civic as well as commercial life of Bellary and beyond. Often the convenor of public meetings in his home town, he was an active member of the Madras Native Association. The 1870s and 1880s was the age of petitions and memorials, and of the town and regional associations that produced them. In the Madras presidency alone, a hundred local associations were formed in the decade after the great famine. Throughout India, these organizations differed in style according to the political culture of each place. The British Indian Association of Awadh was dominated by conservative landholders, the Pune Sarvajanik Sabha by mathematics teachers, the People's Association of Allahabad by bankers and traders. These new organizations were led by urban notables who were willing to take part in the government of their own communities where there was an opportunity to do so. Mudeliar, for example, was elected as first Indian chairman of the Bellary municipal corporation in the months before he left for Pune. His career had been bound up with the military, bureaucratic and commercial life of empire, and he was certainly no opponent of British rule itself. But he was a fervent critic of the aloof and absolutist way British power was exercised. In 1885 he travelled to challenge and critique British power, taking part in one of India's first 'national' gatherings. He had been invited to the first meeting of the Indian National Union at Pune. While he was travelling the venue was moved to Bombay, and the name changed to the Indian National Congress.[13]

The seventy-two delegates who attended the first meeting of the Indian National Congress were men from a similar kind of background to Mudeliar. They were not aristocrats or landholders. They were the creators and leaders of self-consciously modern institutions which had been founded during the previous generation. These men were lawyers and newspaper proprietors, schoolmasters and merchants, active members of the hundreds of local political societies which had grown up in the cities and district towns of India since the great rebellion like the Madras Association and more informal series of gatherings in Bellary. The founders of the Indian National Congress came from a diverse and scattered political class that had decided engagement with imperial institutions, including imperial markets, was the best way to further the development of their own societies. But in 1885 these men came together in a mood of disappointment with the intention to criticize.

The imperative to organize came from the sense that Britain's despotic hold over India had intensified since 1857–8, and that British liberalism was not interested or powerful enough to challenge the influence of the imperial bureaucracy. For liberal Indians Lord Lytton, Viceroy from 1876 to 1880, epitomized the worst of British authoritarianism. Lytton thought that the only people in India's hierarchy who should have any place in the Queen Empress's regime were aristocrats, and these would remain splendid but largely silent figures. Otherwise, Lytton's policy was exemplified by his government's aloof and devastating approach to the 1876–7 famine. The Tory Lytton was followed by the liberal Ripon, who turned out to be a major disappointment. There was a brief moment of possibility in 1880, as the new Viceroy tried to increase the role of elite Indians in courts and municipal corporations. 'We shall not', Ripon's right-hand man Evelyn Baring wrote, 'subvert the British Empire by allowing the Bengali Baboo to discuss his own schools and drains.' But reforms were quickly challenged by mid-level bureaucrats, merchants and planters. The venomous white opposition to the Ilbert Bill illustrated the limits of benign British leadership. 'We must agitate', argued the prominent Bengali newspaper *Amrita Bazar Patrika*. 'We can never hope or deserve success if we foolishly rely upon the personal magnanimity of those who rule India.'[14]

Famine and India's poverty more broadly were the driving forces of discussions in the early Congress. The very location of the first meeting was shaped by the aftermath of mass starvation. The plan was originally for the first conference to be held at Pune, the city with India's most vibrant culture of critical political discussion. Pune had been the site of riots in 1875, of Sathe's revolt in 1878 and the growing 'loyal' critique articulated by M. G. Ranade's Pune Sarvajanik Sabha. Announcements were sent out in March 1885. The meeting was supposed to begin on Christmas Day, and to last for six days. The Sabha was to act as host for delegates from every part of India. The old Peshwa's palace had been bought by the organization and would act as the venue. By the middle of December, delegates had already started to gather. But years of famine followed by years of dearth had depleted Pune's residents, and December 1885 saw a serious cholera outbreak. The organizers were worried that the weakened bodies of incoming delegates, tired after long travel, would make them susceptible to the disease. The meeting was therefore moved at the last minute to the Goculdas Tejpal Sanskrit College in Bombay, and reduced to three days.

Discussions in the early Congress did not challenge British imperial sovereignty. The loyal delegate from Masulipatam called its English-educated attendees 'the children of our beloved mother Empress'. But they did demand the inclusion of Indian voices within imperial institutions. '[P]assing through a long minority', it was time for Indians to be treated like adults, and given a say in their own government, the man from Masulipatam stated. The institutional reforms which Congress proposed would have radically challenged the character of British rule. The first meeting called for the abolition of the London-based Council of India, for the inclusion of 'a considerable number' of elected Indians within the Raj's legislative councils, for the opening of the Indian Civil Service to Indian talent and the creation of a Royal Commission, 'the people of India being adequately represented thereon', to reform the workings of British power. Representation was the central issue.

Later radicals and historians accused the early Congress of being a group of self-serving public apparatchiks, desperate to do no more than secure their own advancement. It was certainly an elite body. But delegates argued that they needed to be represented not only for their own good but in order to articulate the voice of the poor. They were able to compare the fate of other parts of the British empire — Australia or Canada as well as British India — where the fact that large sections of the population had a voice in political institutions ensured that governments responded quickly to economic hardship. When the American civil war brought the Lancashire cotton industry to a standstill for example, the local journalist Edwin Waugh published stories of the 'home life of the Lancashire cotton folk', with local dialects, individual characteristics and names: Ann, Sarah, Martha, John. *The Times* published letters from 'a Lancashire lad' in the same idiom. The result was a nationwide campaign for action. In the late 1870s, the Pune Sarvajanik Sabha had started to print records of the plight of different districts under famine conditions, trying to use the experience of India's masses to put pressure on the government. But the Sabha recognized that something more forceful than publishing reports in journals was required.

At the first meetings of the Congress, the delegates were united by a common critique of the poverty of India, and a common sense that British rule was at fault. During the second half of the nineteenth century the leading figure in articulating this challenge was the statesman Dadabhai Naoroji, perhaps the best known figure at the Bombay gathering. Born near Bombay in 1825, Naoroji was the son of a poor Parsi priest. In his early career he mixed a long-standing western Indian interest in mathematics with both commerce and the British regime's obsession with counting things. Naoroji started a newspaper at the age of twenty-six, helped found a political association in Bombay at twenty-seven, and was then appointed to a chair in mathematics and philosophy at the age of twenty-nine. A year later he left for London to set up the English branch of the Indian firm he worked for. Like Sabapathy Mudeliar he quickly set up his own cotton-trading firm, but supplemented his income with the salary of Gujarati Professor at University College London. Naoroji lived in England for thirty years with only 'transient . . . sojourns in India'.

Naoroji's main argument was that 'the present system of British administration' sucked resources from India to Britain. His style of analysis owed much to a long-standing tradition of statistical inquiry in western India, which began when a Major Vans Kennedy calculated that India was less crime prone than Britain in the 1820s, and Naoroji Furdonjee surveyed Kabul Bazaar a decade later. During the first years of India's great depression and famine Naoroji used his mathematical background to build a statistical model of the total production and consumption of India's population, creating the subcontinent's first ever numbers for national income. He argued that India's poverty was caused by the annual transfer of resources from India to Britain. This 'drain of wealth' had, he argued, deprived India of the capital required for it to thrive.[15]

Naoroji argued that British rule was a system that redistributed wealth from poor Indian peasants to prosperous sections of the British elite. Indians worked for poor wages to produce crops sold cheaply to the rest of the world. Between 1835 and 1872, he argued, India had exported an average of £13 million goods each year with no corresponding return. The labour of Indian taxpayers was also used to pay different groups of British notables, from railway company shareholder to retired imperial civil servants, making up a total loss of £30 million annually. The limited investment that returned to India benefited imperial rather than Indian interests, Naoroji maintained. His own wealth came from the cotton industry, and like other cotton capitalists Naoroji was initially a supporter of investment in infrastructure which would speed raw cotton from fields in places like Bellary in exchange from British manufactured goods. In the early 1870s Naoroji was enthusiastic about the railways. A decade later, he joined the growing chorus of Indian political leaders critical of the way India's railways were used to protect Britain's power and military might rather than India's prosperity, arguing that a system which should have diffused prosperity in fact spread hardship.[16]

With a keen eye for historical comparisons, Naoroji suggested

Britain's drain of wealth was far worse than anything that had happened before in Indian history, worse than the plunder of India by Mahmud of Ghazni or Nader Shah. Its most important effect, Naoroji argued, was to deprive India of the resources needed to maintain its resilience in different conditions and grow. India was 'depleted', 'exhausted' and 'bled', so Indians found themselves pushed to the edge of subsistence when flood or drought came. The drain meant there was a continuous, 'chronic state of famine'.

Naoroji felt the imperial regime was too tightly bureaucratic to listen to Indian opinion in India itself. In the more open and argumentative political context of the metropole, he believed the British public would respond to the arguments, and could be persuaded to reform their country's financial relationship with India and staunch the flow. It was to achieve that purpose, and to act as the 'representative of India', that this 'man of strange name and race', as he described himself to his voters, stood three times for Parliament. Naoroji was elected as the Liberal MP for Finsbury on the second occasion in 1892. In Parliament, the white-haired, gold-bespectacled Naoroji spoke wittily in favour of Irish Home rule, as much as India.

During his thirty English years Naoroji's money, charisma and connections allowed him to become the nodal point in a network of Indians coming to London to study or practise law. Many of the leaders who travelled to the first gathering of the Indian National Congress had been introduced to each other by Naoroji in London. Brought together by the Grand Old Man's personality, the meeting's purpose nonetheless departed from Naoroji's political strategy. Naoroji thought the only opening for Indian representation lay in London. Most of the rest of the leaders who gathered in 1885 doubted whether lobbying in the metropolis was capable of changing anything in the subcontinent. If there was an overarching argument in the delegates' speeches it was that 'the centre of the practical work of Indian administration should be shifted from England to India', as Bombay's K. T. Telang put it; and that localizing power would undo India's poverty. Sabapathy Mudeliar fiercely condemned the Famine Commission's British-appointed members for their inability to understand local conditions. He criticized British administration for being top-heavy and British-based, and for wasting money that could have been spent on famine relief. The Council of India, the body of retired bureaucrats that guided Indian policy from London, would have the 'advantage of making the government more local than now'.[17]

The early Congress did little to mitigate famine or poverty in India. British responses to the motions it submitted were curt, or nonexistent. There was no grand parliamentary inquiry into the iniquities of British rule. The Indian empire's councils were not opened up to large numbers of Indian voices, at least not until the 1920s. The army, rather than the economic development of the country, continued to be the main drain on imperial finances. The imperial regime did not officially or publicly concede to the demands of early nationalists, but Indian political organization did have an impact on both the direction of British policy and, as we shall see in the next chapter, Indian enterprise. But on its own Congress did nothing.

The country is ruined by treachery

The annual meetings of the Indian National Congress were the result of the growth of new urban political associations during the late nineteenth century. At the same time, new forms of organization and protest began to emerge in the countryside. From the 1860s, peasant campaigns struggled against the dislocation of rural society caused by the complicated impact of India's connection into newly global markets. These movements had different causes, and took different forms, leading campaigners to make very different kinds of alliances with other social groups.

Some campaigns, like the Indigo Riots in eastern India in 1859, occurred in response to the effort by British investors to extend the cultivation of cash crops for export to Europe by force. With British power as a target, the 'Blue Mutiny' became a popular cause for Calcutta's middle-class critics of the Raj, as well as British radicals. The event was dramatized by the Bengali postmaster and then railway inspector Dinabandhu Mitra in the play *Nil Darpan* ('the blue mirror'), one of the first great productions of modern Bengali theatre. The Irish missionary James Long printed the work in English and spent a month in prison for slandering plantation owners. Despite their victory against the supporters of the revolt, the government was too worried about the spread of insurgency to back their compatriots wholeheartedly. The result was the Indigo Act of 1860, which outlawed the British planters' attempts to force peasants to grow indigo.[18]

Others, like the Pabna rebellion in the same region of northern India in 1873, saw protest directed against local Indian landholders. As a result, the response of middle-class Indian opinion was more complex. The Pabna uprising was sparked when landlords increased rents dramatically in line with rises in the price of grain. In years gone by, peasants would have mobilized through caste councils and clan groups, gathering in large numbers with lathis to force land-holders to negotiate. At Pabna, buffalo horns and drums were still beaten to summon villagers to meet. But old techniques were trans-lated from sound into print and developed for the age of litigation and circulars, 'So and so *projas* [peasants]!!', one printed paper said in Pabna, 'as soon as you see this circular hasten over to the side of the insurgent party. If you fail to come over within a day, we will hasten to fish in the pond by your lake.'

The biggest change, though, was the creation of permanent asso-ciations for rural workers to assert their rights. Peasants claimed to be part of the imperial constitutional order, responding to the effort to increase rent by declaring 'themselves to be ryots [subjects] only of the queen'. To assert this status, cultivators started to organize, collecting money to fund court cases when peasants were faced with large increases, so peasants could outspend their landlords in lawyers' fees in many cases. At the same time, alliances were made with leaders in the cities, particularly Calcutta. The imperial officer Sir William Hunter, a man considered by many to embody the official British mindset, described the rebels as having 'fought with keen persistence but with few ebullitions of violence', 'conducting before our eyes an agrarian revolution by due course of law'.[19]

The 1873 protests opened up sharp divisions in rural Indian society. 'Class feeling' extended as far as people's dress. A British officer noted that wearing a *chaddar* (shawl) and carrying an umbrella was a sign that someone was 'a landlord's man'. A man 'merely clad in a *dhoti* and *gamcha* ... was at heart a unionist'. Middle-class urban opinion was divided as well. Many owners of rural property lived in imperial India's capital, and were anxious when their domination of the countryside – and hence their livelihood – was challenged. Calcutta's *Ananda Bazar Patrika*, a paper set up 'to give voice to the growing sense of irritation of the English-educated community of the province', enthusiastically backed the Indian National Congress and sided with landholders. The newspapers compared rioters to Genghiz Khan. The aim of the rioters, the paper said, was 'to insult and destroy the caste of respectable men, to violate the chastity of females of gentle blood, to break into pieces the images of idols'.

Other leaders, whose incomes were less dependent on landed estates, supported the peasants' cause. R. C. Dutt, the second Indian to be appointed to the Indian Civil Service, championed the peasant cause, as did Bengal's leading novelist, Bankim Chandra Chattopadhyay. Both men's argument was that the hands-off approach of British authorities had allowed landholders to become local despots, wreaking chaos in rural Bengali society. The police were too weak to restrain local notables; the courts did not guarantee peasants their rights; the state simply collected useless paperwork. 'The country is ruined by treachery, tenants die due to exploitation. What to do with reports', *Grambarta Prakashika*, a paper which focused on rural matters, wrote in 1880.[20]

These claims were not only repeated in print, but led urban

associations to make links in the countryside. In the early 1880s, Bengal's most powerful political association, the Indian Association, sent agents into the rural provinces to convene meetings and 'inaugurate' new Ryot's Unions. In years of dearth and near-famine in Bengal, 1884, 1886–7 and 1889, for example, surveyors travelled around linking up with local activists, recording details of agrarian conditions and pressuring landholders and district officers for relief. By 1888 these campaigns meant the Association had 124 branches throughout India, most in Bengal. Yet in eastern India the connection between rural political and city leaders was limited by class differences. A position that emphatically sided with peasants against their landholders would undermine the livelihood and status of too many members of Calcutta's upper middle class. In the west and south of India, things were different. In Bengal, the umbrella carriers and dhoti wearers were often in conflict. In Bombay and Madras, in the lands hit most badly by famine, they claimed to be on the same side.[21]

The people should be made to understand

On the afternoon of 13 December 1896 a meeting was held in the public square of the coastal village of Khattalwada, a hundred miles north of Bombay. Two thousand anxious men listened to a speech surrounded by police officers with loaded guns. The meeting had been called by the Pune Sarvajanik Sabha to inform peasants about their rights in another year of devastating famine. Since its role in calling the first meeting of the Indian National Congress, the Sabha had shifted in a more radical direction, especially since 1890 when the nationalist leader Bal Gangadhar Tilak took over the organization. Like Bengal's Indian Association, the Sabha had moved beyond writing reports of famine conditions and holding meetings of regional notables, and begun to draw large crowds to protest against the British failure to mitigate famine. In places like Khattalwada, the Sabha managed to mobilize peasants on a large scale only by connecting to the surge of rural political association. Tilak's local agents befriended the leaders of rural societies where peasants and minor landlords united to campaign against high taxes and the exorbitant rates of interests charged by moneylenders.[20]

The speaker at the meeting was Achyut Sitaram Sathe, a 22-year-old law student sent from Pune to gather information about conditions in the countryside and help peasants organize the prevention of mass death. Since the last great famine in 1876–8, the government had published its famine code, a set of rules theoretically supposed to prevent starvation. These promised to reduce taxes and to employ the poor in public works when times were hard. At Khattalwada, Sathe was teaching this crowd of peasants the rights they had under the code, explaining how to apply to the Collector for a discount on their revenue payment. The crowd were 'awed', according to newspaper reports, by the imperial regime's firepower. Sathe reassured them that 'they were engaged in a loyal proceeding and need fear nothing'. But the English officers at the scene thought he was teetering on the verge of subversion.

Throughout the long meeting, Sathe asked the Assistant Collector to take a seat on the stage. The British officer in charge, James Houssemayne Du Boulay, insisted on standing mute, aloof, with a 'severe' expression on his face. Aged only twenty-eight Du Boulay was a third of the way through his career in India. He came from a family that started off in the Church and the City of London, and came late but emphatically to empire. Du Boulay's father was a housemaster at Winchester College; his brothers and sisters were scattered through every part of the empire, from China to South Africa. James himself joined the Indian Civil Service in 1888, eventually rising to become private secretary to the Viceroy of India Lord Hardinge. His career throughout these years was dominated by a concern for keeping the machinery of British rule going, avoiding unnecessary commitment but acting with force where necessary. Du Boulay was 'straight and taciturn', a man of reserve embarrassed by a handshake that lasted too long, who even wrote home to his children in a reserved style. At Khattalwada, such distance was a tactic of rule.

At one point in the meeting an audience member suggested the people gathered 'should demand redress of their grievances' from 'the Sirkar's representative'. According to old Indian political idioms Du Boulay should have done exactly that, to listen to complaints, then use his personal authority to mitigate distress himself. But both Sathe and Du Boulay shared a more abstract and bureaucratic concept of political power. Sathe recommended peasants wait a few days before submitting a request for a rent reduction on an official form, the Bombay government complained about being flooded with identical documents, blaming the avalanche of paperwork on cunning Brahmin agitators corrupting the minds of the rural masses. At Khattalwada, there was certainly no question of negotiation. The senior government officer present at the meeting thought his job was to ensure order was preserved and British power maintained safely, not to listen to complaints. If anyone in the British government had responsibility for the subsistence of the poor it was not him. 'Mr Du Boulay had attended the meeting that day with quite a different object,' Sathe told his audience. At the end, the Assistant Collector 'bade a polite, though conventional adieu' to the speaker and left with his armed guard.

British guns stayed silent at Khattalwada, but they were used fifty miles south against Indian protesters. In the 1890s, the strip of land along the coast north of Bombay quickly becomes heavily wooded, and its forests had long been a refuge for Indian peasants in times of crisis. A place for foraging for fruit, collecting wood or making alcohol from tree sap, the natural, lush resources of India's woodlands offered subsistence in times of drought. In the late nineteenth century, commercial forestry created profits for Indian timber merchants but undermined the livelihood of forest-dwellers and peasants who saw the forest as a haven in times of tribulation.

Conflict between famine victims and forest managers grew from November 1896, when 5,000 people gathered at Bassein, near

Bombay, to protest against rules banning the fermentation of toddy and the collection of wood. A riot occurred in early December at Kelve-Mahim, when peasants broke into the forestry department's office and burnt government records. Their aim was to make sure British regulations banning toddy manufacture could not be implemented. Even though the attack was on buildings and records rather than people, frightened imperial officers ordered the crowd to be dispersed by firepower. 'The attempt to rule on the strength of the force of arms only ill becomes a civilized Government of the nineteenth century,' the liberal *Indian Spectator* said in response.

The sensitivity of the imperial state to any small sign of disaffection drove the suppression of all efforts to criticize the British policy towards the famine. The imperial regime carefully monitored the language and actions of Indian political associations, ready to act forcefully if there was any hint that 'agitators' were 'attempting [to] incite disaffection'. Contrary to the intention of the Indian National Congress and its allies, there was no attempt to create a conversation, still less to countenance any kind of negotiation. Arrests and prosecutions happened quickly if there was any hint of illegality. Achyut Sitaram Sathe, the young lecturer who had spoken at Khattalwada, was briefly arrested for suggesting forest-dwellers should cut wood or tap palm trees to brew toddy in violation of increasingly stringent forest rules. Sathe was released, but his colleague Govind Vinayak Apte was imprisoned for a year, and the Pune Sarvajanik Sabha ceased 'to be recognized as a body which has any claim to address Government on questions of public policy'. From then onwards its petitions were not even answered. The Pune Sarvajanik Sabha attributed this response to the anger of the British authorities, and castigated the 'curt replies; abuse and threats' it was subject to. This was, the Sabha's journal noted, the inevitable response whenever 'official high-handedness meets with popular opposition'.[23]

The government's high-handedness ended up putting the dominant nationalist figure in western India, Bal Gangadhar Tilak, behind bars. The 1896–7 famine was followed by a devastating plague in the Sabha's stronghold of Pune. When half the population deserted the town, the British employed draconian measures, forcing entry into private houses and destroying personal property. The officer in charge of anti-plague measures, W. C. Rand, quickly became a figure of hate in the town. While they were travelling to celebrate Queen Victoria's diamond jubilee, he and his military guard were assassinated by members of a secret society founded to protect the Hindu religion from alien attack. The Bombay government thought Tilak was behind the killings. 'There is', it stated, 'the clearest possible connection . . . between the continual incitement to disaffection' in Tilak's writings and meetings, and the killings. Tilak was charged with inciting disaffection. In a hasty trial, he was convicted by a split, mixed-race jury and sentenced to eighteen months in prison in Burma (after a campaign by British officials in London, his sentence was reduced to eleven months). The prosecution's case rested on no more than Tilak printing a modern Marathi poem in which the great leader Shivaji awoke from death to complain about the ruin of the country under British rule. Tilak's conviction depended on the British judge reinterpreting the word 'disaffection' in the penal code to mean 'absence of affection'. Tilak himself insisted that he had cooperated with the government throughout the famine and plague in a manner 'wholly inconsistent with the charge of sedition'. He would never have been convicted, he said, if the judge or any of the jurors had been able to read the poem in its original language.[24]

Throughout the famine, the Sabha spoke a language that the imperial authorities did understand though. In these years, the Sabha drew from their network of local informants to publish reports that mirrored the imperial regime's own inquiries. These texts noted the state of each village, the price of grain, the number of people who had fled and the sources of income. Their aim was to collect information about 'things which subordinate Government officers cannot know or will not report to their superiors', which the agents of 'a popular body like the *Sabha* who move and work among the people alone can observe'. They then politely badgered every outpost of the imperial regime to put its explicit commitments into practice. They proposed that roads, railway lines and bridges be built with unemployed labour, grain shops opened, revenue remitted, orphanages started, government forests be thrown open. 'Relief works need to be started for 1000 people. ... Suggest the construction of a bridge on the Sukee river,' the reporter from the village of Kerhala in Khandesh wrote. The purpose was to channel the 'general cry for relief', as the Pune Sarvajanik Sabha put it, into specific pressure points, based on very particular information.[25]

Even in the midst of famine, British officers thought visible concessions to Indian criticism was a sign of weakness. The most important demands of rural leaders and urban radicals were fiercely resisted: there were few reductions in revenue, even when remissions were permitted under the famine code. The 'very small suspensions and remissions of land revenue' which occurred were 'the most questionable feature of the scheme of relief' according to even the imperial regime's own report into the famine operations during 1896–7. The report explained the reason for the regime's harshness in this way: 'the Government felt it necessary to be rather harder in the matter than it would have otherwise been in consequence of an agitation originating in Poona'.

Yet where they could act without seeming to negotiate, where a response to Indian pressure could be interpreted as the consolidation of imperial power not a concession, British bureaucrats did respond. The action of those responsible for shaping policy was – without them being willing to admit it – guided by the comments of their Indian critics. In its journal in January 1897, the Sabha was 'glad to note that its influence is felt even in the dark chambers of the Council'. The hope that its work would 'silently mould the future policy of Government' was not entirely groundless.[26]

Pressure from the Sabha and others meant the government's response to the famine of 1896–7 was quicker and more effective than it had been twenty years before. A hundred and sixty-seven thousand people were employed on relief works in the worst affected areas as early as November 1896. Six and a half million people were given relief at the peak of the crisis throughout India, 4.6 million receiving money in exchange for work. In Bombay presidency, the principle that relief should only be given to able-bodied people who would work was followed through, with work only offered at large-scale residential relief camps from March 1897. But policies to reduce the dependence of the supposedly 'undeserving' poor were quickly abandoned. The government found it impossible to apply a 'distance test' that refused relief for anyone who lived within ten miles of a work site. Attempts at introducing piecework were quickly dropped. After pressure from campaigners, kitchens were opened at famine camps to feed children and immobile dependants of the working poor.

The result of the British regime's silent recognition of Indian criticism was that death occurred on a smaller scale than two decades before. The famine of 1896–7 was still catastrophic, and was followed by another great famine in 1900–1901. The extension of railway lines and the improvement of roads meant famine prices and famine conditions spread more quickly to regions where crops had not badly failed, but as demographer Arup Maharatna notes, famine mortality was lower in these later crises than in previous years. In Bombay presidency's famine-affected districts, there was an average 250 per cent increase in the number of deaths in 1877 compared to non-famine years. In 1897, the same famine districts saw an increase of 'only' 148 per cent in mortality. Throughout the whole of India, there were at least a million deaths that would not have occurred without famine in each of the crises of 1896–7 and 1900–1901, and death came in the largest numbers where protest was the least. But those numbers were probably a fifth of the total killed by the far less serious ecological and economic crisis of 1876–8.[27]

The famines of these years set the pattern for the British response to Indian political action over the next half-century. Dissent was vigorously suppressed, but concessions were made as long as the

British could persuade themselves that they were augmenting the power of the imperial state. The British government failed to reduce India's poverty – it did not even try to – but its aim was to ensure the very poorest did not die in large numbers. For the first time, the imperial government was serious about ensuring the survival of the people it ruled. The changing pattern of famine relief shows the beginning of what might be described as India's welfare state, a system of rule which presupposed that the state had a responsibility to act to protect and improve society.[28]

This was a strange and peculiarly hands-off approach to state intervention. For the most part, the government refused to ensure the local economy was capable of sustaining a decent livelihood for people through bad times, by reducing taxation or providing loans to tide people over, for example. Suffused with an attitude of anxiety, imperial bureaucrats worried that subtle interventions would hand power to people it could not trust. There was, for example, nothing to ensure loans went to the right place; or that reductions in revenue would help the poor. Instead, the government created its own centres, which it could control entirely on its own terms, to ensure people's survival. The British built a feeding machine which, for the most part, was physically distant from the homes of the people it tried to help, dependent on the massive migration of the destitute from their homes. As some of its critics argued, when this most laissez-faire of states intervened in Indian society, it acted with the most bureaucratic form of 'state socialist' power.

Progressives must not be given their heads

As centres for the employment of poor Indian workers, the famine camps were rivalled only by India's great cities, but these grew slowly and sporadically compared to the changes taking place in the rest of the world. The years after the great rebellion of 1857–8 saw village-dwellers move to and from India's metropolitan centres according to the staccato rhythm of India's globalizing economy.

The total population of India's ten largest cities grew from three to four million people in the last thirty years of the nineteenth century. Calcutta, easily India's largest city, expanded by almost 250,000 people to reach a population of a million in 1901. But urbanization was uneven, sporadic compared to what was happening in Europe, America or Japan. The overall numbers of people moving to India's cities were a fraction of the population moving to urban centres elsewhere in the world. During the same years, London grew by 2.3 million, greater New York by 2.5 million, Berlin by one million and Tokyo by more than 500,000. When much of the rest of the world was rapidly urbanizing, Indian remained a largely agricultural society. In Britain in 1900, 45 per cent of the population lived in settlements of more than 50,000 people. Britain was exceptionally urbanized; but perhaps 15 per cent of the world's people lived in cities. Only 3.5 per cent, or eight million of India's population of 283 million, lived in towns, making India perhaps the most rural society in the world.

In India, the fastest growing cities were places where yarn was spun and cloth woven: Calcutta, Bombay, Kanpur, Ahmedabad and, outside the area of direct British control, Hyderabad. Yet in 1901 there were still only half a million factory workers in the whole subcontinent. Even by 1917 that figure had only doubled, leaving more than 90 per cent of the population directly dependent on agriculture for their livelihood. Most of the world's demand for manufactured goods was met from Europe and America. The puzzle is why India's cheap, often starving labour force was not put to use on a large enough scale to industrialize Indian society.

One important answer is a lack of capital. Dadabhai Naoroji was right to argue that India's producers were starved of resources, but his precise line of argument is not convincing. The problem was not that Britain sucked resources from India to Britain. In reality, the amount transferred in pensions and 'home charges' was relatively small, and money sent from India to Britain was returned in capital investment from the UK. The problem, rather, was that

the institutions which governed India's economic life were geared
to support a narrow range of industrial activities, mainly those
focused on processing primary produce for export. There were
long-established lines of financial support for managers of businesses
in European-managed enclaves; but these European firms were
not interested in expanding to produce goods for India's domestic
markets or employ large numbers of Indian workers. Beyond those
enclaves, large-scale industry was too risky for most Indian entrepreneurs to contemplate.[29]

In the commercial life of the British empire in India, the
European-owned managing agency house held sway. These grew
out of the shipping companies and railway contractors that supported the mid-nineteenth-century East India Company. After
British domination was emphatically asserted in 1858, these firms
developed a sprawling web of interests, taking over coal mines and
tea plantations, steamship companies, paper factories and jute mills.
Between 1885 and 1895, agency houses even controlled a swathe of
territory in East Africa, including the Arab-dominated port city of
Mombasa. By 1900, European firms owned three-quarters of the
industrial capital of India, perhaps £200 million in total.

These were businesses concerned with maintaining British status
and order, not with maximizing profits in the long term. Ruled by
a class of perhaps a thousand British managers, the agency houses
saw themselves as the commercial equivalent of the Indian Civil
Service, maintaining British power and profitability in what they
saw as a hostile economic environment. They had limited interest
in the economy beyond India's big port cities and a few European-
dominated commercial towns. They emphasized the importance
of personal networks and status instead of knowledge or ambition.
'Engineers and specialists must not be allowed to run away with
themselves,' one manager wrote in the 1920s. 'Optimists and pro-
gressives must not be given their heads.'

The agency houses oversaw a pessimistic and fearful business
culture, which was reluctant to invest in new ventures. With no

knowledge of India's domestic markets, agency houses stuck to the old export staples of jute or tea, or relied on government contracts. The great missed opportunity was the development of products to sell in India's domestic market. Yet they were wary even of investing enough to ensure existing industries remained profitable. Even in the export trade, machinery was not replaced, the skills of employees uncared for and premises dilapidated. An observer of Calcutta's jute mills at the beginning of the long depression in the 1870s was appalled by the run-down state of the factories, 'large repairs and replacements were urgently needed . . . the words "depreciation" and "wear and tear" not finding their place in the Indian mill-owners vocabulary'. In 1880, six out of eleven Calcutta jute mills had no reserve funds to pay for the replacement of worn-out equipment.[30]

More so than imperial bureaucrats, the agency houses insisted on maintaining racial barriers. Astonishingly, there was only a single case of an agency house creating a formal partnership with an Indian manager, in 1892. The agency houses blocked the route for Indian entrepreneurs to access capital in global money markets. The only way to access money from outside India was for entrepreneurs to work with lone European investors, working beyond the agency house system, as Daniel Abraham did in Bellary. But the sources of overseas capital were limited and sporadic.[31]

British business leaders blamed India's poverty on the supposed absence of a spirit of industry among the country's population, thinking Indian entrepreneurs were 'wanting in enterprise', as E. W. Collin, author of the *Report on the Existing Industries in Bengal*, wrote in 1890. More accurate was the comment by the Bombay mill-owner Manmohandas Ramji in 1916. The problem, Ramji said, was an absence of capital; 'many a commercial and industrial enterprise is nipped in the bud just because there is no bank to foster and develop it'. Until the twentieth century at least, the rigid racial hierarchies of the agency houses blocked Indian access to global capital markets. Many Indians saved money, but the British-dominated banking sector did not invest in Indian enterprise.

Even if capital could be found, large-scale investment seemed poorly protected. Imperial law was more interested in asserting the power and status of the British government than protecting private property rights. Judges made what from the outside seemed arbitrary decisions, and had little capacity to enforce their judgments. As a result, even if capital could be found, large-scale investments seemed unsafe. Taxes were low, but those which were levied seemed arbitrary. There was, above all, no trust between Indian entrepreneurs and the British officers who managed the economic system they worked within.

As a result, in the late nineteenth century Indian businessmen hedged their bets, limiting their risks, making sure they could afford to survive fluctuation in global prices. Their behaviour looked narrow and conservative to outsiders. They relied on sources of money and trade they knew they could trust. Indian trade relied on financial institutions which survived from pre-British days, or long-lasting local, ethnic and religious solidarities. Those few pockets where Indian entrepreneurs and workers created industrial prosperity were the result of a complicated relationship between long-standing Indian institutions and forces coming from outside.

Manchesters of the East

The two Indian cities which grew the fastest during these years of famine were Kanpur and Ahmedabad. Each had a population of around 100,000 at the end of the great Indian rebellion. Both expanded as centres of textile production, with the growth of spinning mills and cloth factories pushing them to grow by 60 per cent in the thirty years between 1871 and 1901, making Kanpur and Ahmedabad India's third and fourth largest industrial cities after Bombay and Calcutta. Both were described as the 'Manchester of the East', along with Osaka in Japan and Singapore. Yet their stories could not be more different.

Kanpur, in the centre of northern India's Gangetic plain, began the 1860s as a cantonment town and a sacred site for Britons wishing to keep alive the gory memory of the Indian rebellion's most famous massacre of Europeans. The city's industrial growth was driven by the strong relationship between the city's British traders and the nearby imperial army. The first large enterprise, Elgin Mills, opened in 1861 and made the cloth for woollen blankets. Three more huge textile mills and hundreds of shoe factories opened during the next decades, drawing labourers from the neighbouring countryside to make uniforms and boots for imperial troops. Kanpur boomed when war quickly increased the number of soldiers needing the goods it produced; 70,000 workers moved there during the First World War, another 110,000 during the Second. Until long after independence in 1947, this was a British city. The first Indian-owned factory was only opened in 1921, but Kanpur stayed a citadel of European capital until the early 1960s.[32]

Ahmedabad, 250 miles due north of Bombay, and four days by horse from the port of Surat, had a far longer history as a centre of commerce. In the days of the Mughal empire it was the capital of the province of Gujarat. One European visitor described it in 1695 as 'the greatest city in India, and nothing inferior to Venice for this trade; tho' its houses are low and made of mud and bamboo'. The city's wealth prevented it from being sacked by the Marathas then allowed it to survive as a commercial hub after the British took over in 1818. At the centre of its prosperity were hundreds of Jain and Vaisnava Hindu banking families and moneylenders, who took deposits from savers and lent money to merchants and weavers.

It was these men who eventually financed the growth of Ahmedabad's cotton mills, but it took a peculiar moment of risk-taking for the city's cotton industry to take off. In the uncertain commercial climate of mid-nineteenth-century western India, there was little incentive for new enterprises. Local bankers could make good money from lending to cottage weavers or jewellery makers; they even started to offer credit so that small-scale manu-facturers could use imported European yarn. Investing in factories producing yarn or cloth would have opened Ahmedabad to highly volatile worldwide prices, with no secure return. Change came a small distance from the ordinary patterns of money-making, from a Brahmin whose family were not merchants but government clerks.

Ranchhodlal Chhotalal's great-grandfather had been the chief minister of the Mughal governor of the province of Gujarat. His father was paymaster of Baroda state, and a close friend of the British Resident's chief administrator. Born in 1823, Ranchhodlal was an intelligent child, a brilliant chess player from the age of eight and quickly fluent in the Persian, Marathi and English used in government offices. Through his family connection, Ranchhodlal began work as a clerk to the British collector of customs as a nineteen-year-old in 1842. In his mid-twenties, still a government servant, Ranchhodlal was writing about why, if it was cost-effective for English entrepreneurs to carry cotton back and forth 7,000 miles between Europe and India, 'should not the manufacture of cotton in India pay'? In 1850, before a single cotton factory had opened in the west of India, Ranchhodlal approached the region's bankers. He published a prospectus in a Gujarati weekly newspaper, and started to lobby the banks in Baroda. But the money did not materialize, and the factories were not built.

Ranchhodlal's career as a mill-owner depended on the fortunate coincidence of his dismissal from office shortly before the American Civil War briefly spurred on India's cotton industry. By 1854, he had become chief officer of a large tranche of territory to the east of the city of Ahmedabad. He was suspected of taking a bribe from one side in a property dispute, and then accused of forging documents to prove his innocence. The local British political establishment was divided on his fate. He was eventually acquitted of any wrongdoing, but never reappointed. After his dismissal, Ranchhodlal was employed to manage one of Ahmedabad's big banking houses, in the well-established and trusted role of Brahmin clerk. There, Ranchhodlal connected with two worlds. His confidence that money could be made by competing with British cotton manufacturers came from his government connections, the money to channel into his new enterprise came from his links to Ahmedabad's traditional banking families. Ranchhodlal himself put up 10 per cent of the capital, his new employer Maganbhai Karamchand provided the same again, and the rest came from friends among Ahmedabad's merchants and bankers.

Ahmedabad's first mill opened after a fraught process. Ranchhodlal ordered spinning and weaving machinery from London through the nationalist merchant-politician Dadabhai Naoroji, but the ship carrying it was lost at sea going around the Cape of Good Hope. The first engineer, an Englishman called Mr Dall, died before the plant arrived. When it finally arrived, the mill's plant needed to be transported from the port of Cambay by bullock cart. Dall was succeeded by four more European engineers all of whom failed to get the mill running. Eventually, it took the collaborative effort of Ranchhodlal, a mechanically minded astrologer called Sankleshwar Joshi and a sixth European engineer, Mr Edlington, to get the mill's 2,500 spindles turning.

On 30 May 1861, eighteenth months later than planned, the leading citizens of Ahmedabad gathered at the new mill. Mrs Edlington, wife of the British engineer who completed the plant, smashed a bottle of wine on the machinery and the crowd cheered as the plant started working, manufacturing yarn for the first time. Spinning was soon followed by steam-powered looms which wove white cotton into material for sheets and dhotis. By the time Ranchchodlal's Ahmedabad Spinning and Weaving Company opened for business, the American Civil War had briefly interrupted the supply of cotton to British mills and created an opportunity for Indian manufacturers.[33]

A second mill at Ahmedabad opened in 1867. By 1900 there were twenty-seven in the city, directly employing 15,943 workers. Just like Ranchhodlal's first factory enterprise, these mills were financed as entrepreneurs pieced together small amounts of Indian capital. Described by Sunil Khilnani as 'the first modern city created by

Indians', Ahmedabad's growth was fuelled by Indian capital and coordinated by Indian leadership. Once Ranchhodlal's success set a profitable example, the city's existing commercial families, its Jain and Vaisnava merchants, moved into steam-powered textile manufacture and started investing in cotton factories. Reliant on new connections to the global economy, the mills were nonetheless managed in the old way, through face-to-face contact with large numbers of small investors. Ahmedabad's old banking firms connected every part of the industry. Brokers not just capitalists, they bought raw cotton from farmers as well as providing capital, and then linked up with merchants selling yarn and cloth. Control over every element of the cotton trade was the only way Ahmedabad's merchants felt they could avoid being exposed to abrupt shifts in global prices and demand.

But Ahmedabad's cotton magnates straddled trade and politics, easily stepping from their factories into the local government institutions which played a greater role in managing life in the city from the 1880s onwards. As the first Indian chairman of Ahmedabad's municipal corporation after 1883, Ranchhodlal Chhotalal led the construction of one of India's first underground sewage systems, lobbying British officials and harrying influential figures in Britain – including Florence Nightingale – for support. The city's mercantile leadership funded Gujarat College, an institution to develop local arts and sciences which opened in 1879. It built schools and hospitals, and promoted organizations which supported Gujarati language and culture.

Ahmedabad's late-nineteenth-century civic leaders were proud of their city and their region, using the word *swadeshbhakti*, devotion to one's land, to describe their actions. But theirs was the pragmatic politics of self-government. The British government was seen as inefficient and unreliable, a force which needed to be kept at arm's length but not directly challenged. Trade unionists and capitalists in Britain started to lobby for regulations in India to improve factory conditions – and to increase the costs of their

competitors. Ahmedabad's mill-owners argued they should set up
an association to monitor matters for themselves because interference by bureaucrats would be 'injurious'. 'He knew from experience
what correspondence with Government on any subjects means', the
Ahmedabad mill-owner Bechardas Lashkari argued. '[T]he dilatory
nature of the correspondence that would take place between the
Government and the millowners, would in many instances prove
detrimental to the regular working of the Mills.'[34]

This self-governing Indian city hosted the eighteenth meeting
of the Indian National Congress, in December 1902. The chairman of the Ahmedabad reception committee was the mill-owner
Ambalal Sakarlal. He opened the session by pointing to the threat
to Ahmedabad's cotton industry from British power. 'Gentleman,
as you entered the city, you must have noticed the tall chimneys on
both sides of the railway tracks. These are our textile mills,' Sakarlal
said. Despite their expansion, Ahmedabad's factories had suffered
from recent efforts by the imperial government to give an advantage
to British manufacturers, duties having been imposed on Indian
cotton. Beyond these particularly malign measures, Sakarlal talked
about India suffering from the drain of wealth through pensions
and home charges, and the British government's 'inelastic revenue
demand', which made it hard for peasants to survive. Having seen
two terrible famines, which had killed a quarter of Gujarat's population, 'all asked "Why are we so poor?"'

Sakarlal was proud of the growth of his city, but he thought it
was not enough for Indian merchants to create an island of self-
governing enterprise in Ahmedabad. The 'inferior political position'
of India's leaders 'hampered their trade,' he argued. 'Commercial
pursuits without political action were suicidal.' The profitability
of business and the prosperity of the country relied on more than
laissez-faire. It needed a new kind of political leadership able to put
Indian interests first. In these famine years, India's destitution could
only be undone by political agitation.[35]

12

GOVERNMENTS WITHIN GOVERNMENTS

I n March 1906, Haji Abdulla Haji Kasim started south-west India's first modern bank. Abdulla was a wealthy merchant from the burgeoning coastal town of Udupi, 190 miles south of Goa and thirty miles north of Mangalore, the largest town in the Kanara region. He made his money buying and selling fish, fruit and matches. Haji Abdulla's business linked him to both Britain and the Middle East. Abdulla was a cosmopolitan patriot. He was the first person to buy a car in Udupi, and the first to drink coffee at breakfast time. But the money he made was invested in his home town.[1]

The bank Abdulla began was his response to India's first great nationalist campaign, the Swadeshi movement. Literally meaning 'our country', Swadeshi was sparked by Viceroy George Curzon's decision to split the province of Bengal, 1300 miles north-east of Udupi, an act seen as an attempt to emasculate India's most articulate political leaders, proof that the British had no intention of involving Indians in their own rule. 'We felt', one Bengali leader wrote, 'that we had been insulted, humiliated, and tricked.'

Humiliation would be met by boycotting British goods and shunning all contact with the imperial regime. In Bengal, the boycott led to a 22 per cent drop in the purchase of British cotton, a near-total collapse in the consumption of foreign cigarettes and a shift in drinking habits from English dark ale to German light beer. The sale of most British goods quickly bounced back. More important was the spur Swadeshi provided to domestic institution-building throughout India. The movement led to the creation of new institutions, from schools to businesses. The idea, as the Bengali poet Rabindranath Tagore put it in 1905, was to fulfil 'the country's needs by the efforts of the people themselves'. In Mangalore, Abdulla Haji Kasim's aim was moral transformation. The banks would help 'not only to cultivate habits of thrift among all classes of people, without distinction of caste or creed, but also habits of cooperation among all classes'. Abdulla argued that '[t]his is Swadeshism pure and simple.'[2]

On its first day of operation the Canara Banking Corporation, the bank Abdulla Haji Kasim created, occupied one room, had a single member of staff and took deposits of thirty-eight rupees (equivalent to £384 in 2016 prices). Two years later it had 2,648 subscribers, with a good cross-section of the region's most prosperous classes depositing money, particularly Brahmins, Muslims and Christians. By then it had been joined by a second local bank, the Canara Hindu Permanent Fund. More followed over the next two decades. The banks of Kanara grew steadily, weathering the succession of banking crises which killed off most of India's new banks in the 1910s, staving off competition from a growing number of local rivals. Today, 110 years on from its foundation, the renamed Corporation Bank has 3,200 branches and the Indian banking profession is dominated by men and women from Kanara.

The rapid burgeoning of Kanara's banking industry was one sign of the emergence of a new form of political action, designed to challenge the conquering force of the imperial state. From Mangalore to Bengal, Punjab to Madras, political leaders throughout the cities and small towns of the subcontinent talked of nationality and autonomy, of the need for people to cast off their subordination to

British institutions and do things for themselves. Swadeshi politics was about the people who lived in India shaping their own destiny. But it was about them doing so by creating new social and economic institutions, not seizing sovereign power. Its slogan was 'self-reliance not mendicancy'. Most hoped to construct a national social and political order without the need for a full-scale onslaught against British authority. Abdulla Haji Kasim was no great enemy of British power. The Madras newspaper *Swadesamitram* was genuine in protesting against imperial journalists who said political activists were 'prompted by the desire to subvert the British sovereignty and to establish a purely Indian ascendancy'. Some did believe Indian society could only be regenerated if British power was challenged directly. But the priority throughout was to deny the conquering force of the British empire through self-help or 'constructive work', as Mohandas Gandhi later called it. It was an approach which would shape Indian politics for a generation.

Frontier revivalism

The effort to create self-reliance independent of British institutions began decades before Curzon's partition of Bengal. It had roots in many different regions. Punjab, in the north-west, was particularly fertile ground. Here, the new politics of self-reliance coalesced around a group of political leaders influenced by currents of religious revivalism, particularly by the effort to reform Hinduism. One such catalyst was the ascetic leader Saraswati Dayananda.

Dayananda was born in 1823. His father was a Brahmin tax collector from Gujarat. He left home in his early twenties and became a wandering mendicant, eventually preaching to large crowds throughout India. His message was that Hindus needed to purify their society by returning to the Vedas, Hinduism's earliest scriptures. Dayananda believed these texts defined a rational religion which had a clear creed and a single god. Hindus needed to abandon idolatry, elaborate rituals and their reliance on priests. Renewing the pure core of Hinduism would help the Hindu inhabitants of India free themselves from foreign influence and achieve self-mastery, or what he called *swarajya*.

Dayananda died in 1883, poisoned by a dancing girl in the household of a Maharaja he dared to criticize. His followers created congregations and built meeting houses throughout north India. Dayananda's story had particular resonance in Punjab, where he spent fifteen months in 1878 and 1879. The new teaching connected with the remarkable effervescence of political and religious debate occurring in the province during these years. Punjab was a 'newly emerging frontier society' as C. A. Bayly put it. Cultivation and trade were expanding. Canal settlements were attracting settlers, providing a source of men and wheat for the armies policing the continually violent border with Afghanistan to the west. Punjab's prosperity was, though, uncertain, with bouts of famine. Migration, insecurity and economic change fuelled political and religious debate, and helped a plethora of Sikh and Muslim organizations to grow alongside the Hindu organization which Dayananda founded, the Arya Samaj.

The followers of Dayananda who joined the Arya Samaj included a large proportion of the Hindu middle classes of Punjab. Ambitious and concerned for their children's careers, they quickly founded a school in Lahore. One of many new educational institutions created to regenerate indigenous society in the second half of the nineteenth century, the Dayananda Anglo-Vedic College offered an English education and the prospect of an official career safe from Christian influence; there were no European teachers. By the early twentieth century the school had 900 students. Punjab's Arya Samaj branches had 250,000 members. Their aim was to build self-reliance by creating a powerful national force in the midst of imperial institutions. British observers noted that the majority of the 'active citizens' of the province, minor civil servants, lawyers, schoolmasters, belonged to 'this modern movement'. In some districts 90 per cent of Indian government officials were members.[3]

The worldly orientation of the Arya Samaj's leadership created a backlash in the 1890s. A rival group, nicknamed the 'Mahatmas', wanted greater focus on personal conduct even if that meant withdrawing from the 'bodily comfort' of the city. The greatest point of controversy was whether Arya Samaj members could eat meat, the Mahatmas insisting on strict vegetarianism. Eventually, they withdrew to set up their own residential school, or Gurukul, at Kangri in the foothills of the Himalayas. In an austere set of buildings, boys from seven to twenty-one years old lived in seclusion and self-discipline, learning ancient Indian philosophy and literature and training as Vedic preachers. The founders of the Gurukul did not intend to isolate their pupils from Western influence. They wanted to incorporate 'the best' of 'Occidental thought', as the first principal put it, into the Hindu curriculum. But self-reliance and 'independence of character' needed to be developed in places the conquering imperial state could not reach.[4]

The debate between the two sides reflected many of the tensions and oppositions created from the attempt of people in India to assert their autonomous power in a conquered society. The violence of the imperial state had destroyed most of India's political institutions, in Punjab as elsewhere. The 1857 rebellion demonstrated the futility of rallying to pre-British, Mughal or Maratha authority. If people were to restore a sense of their dignity, power needed restoring on a new basis, in spheres of life which would not constantly be challenged by the imperial state. But where so many walks of life were now influenced by imperial systems and regulations, knowing where to draw the line was hard. 'Public work' to raise living standards or nurture self-respect was impossible without compromises with imperial power. Self-affirming asceticism allowed the soul to stay pure but had little immediate impact.

Even though both factions of the Arya Samaj tried to build Indian self-reliance without directly confronting British power, they still faced British hostility. 'The foreign rulers of India have never been happy about the Arya Samaj', the political leader Lala Lajpat Rai noted. 'They have always disliked its independence of tone and its propaganda of self-confidence, self-help and self-reliance.' Lajpat Rai had no doubt the Arya Samaj was creating a rival form of power. He went on: '[the British] cannot look with favour on an indigenous movement which, according to them, can do big things without their help and guidance, and which has established a sort of Government within the Government.'[5]

Lajpat Rai was one important architect of the 'government within the government' created by Indian patriots in Punjab and beyond. The son of a Hindu teacher of Urdu, he was born in a small town between Delhi and Lahore in 1865, and became a successful lawyer while also helping to organize the Arya Samaj. In his mid-twenties, Lajpat Rai was part of the group that built the Dayananda Anglo-Vedic College. He then worked on a range of projects, founding orphanages to rescue destitute Hindu children from the grip of famine and Christian missionaries, working to relieve hill-dwellers made homeless by earthquake, and helping create India's earliest nationalist insurance company and bank.

This latter work of 'co-operative endeavour', as he called it, was Lajpat Rai's most enduring legacy. Like other political leaders in late nineteenth-century Punjab, Lajpat Rai noted that money earned from the province's expanding agricultural society 'was being used to run English banks', instead of being ploughed into Indian enterprise. The solution was to create Indian-run financial institutions which would encourage moral regeneration as well as support the wealth of the province. At the insistence of a friend, Lajpat Rai sent a memorandum to a group of leading men in Punjab – lawyers, educationalists and government officers, Sikhs, Parsis and members of the religious organization founded by Rammohan Roy in Bengal, the Brahmo Samaj, as well as Arya Samajists – urging them to deposit capital with a new financial institution. The Punjab National Bank started business on 19 May 1894, with Lajpat Rai's brother as its first manager. Its name expressed the complicated relationship between nation and region in

the politics of late-nineteenth-century self-reliance; national work
should be directed to develop one's own region or community first;
creating a bank just for Punjab was work that would benefit the
whole Indian nation. The result was an institution that has endured
to the present day and is now India's third largest bank.

Lajpat Rai believed this peaceful style of institution-building
would supersede the violent, warmongering politics he associated with the British regime in particular and the west in general.
'Europe was in constant war right up to the nineteenth century,'
Lajpat Rai thought. Europe had exported its violent 'men of genius',
its 'men of daring and dash' who 'cared little for the wrongs which
they thereby inflict on others' to India. In contrast to the cathartic
violence unleashed by the British, Lajpat Rai thought India needed
to celebrate its history of peaceful 'civilization' and rational social
development. Long before M. K. Gandhi had begun to dominate
the public stage, nationalists like Lajpat Rai based their arguments
for Indian self-reliance on a critique of the place of force in politics.
'Their general spirit', Lajpat Rai said of his compatriots, 'is opposed
to all kinds of violence.' In place of the aggressive sovereign power
of the British regime, Lajpat Rai celebrated the peaceful self-
organizing capacity of India's many different societies.[6]

This critique of the logic of conquest led Lajpat Rai to sharply
challenge Indians who celebrated the martial prowess of their
own communities, including Sir Sayyid Ahmad Khan. Sir Sayyid
criticized the newly founded India National Congress for its lack
of martial honour. Mughals and Rajputs, he said, 'who had not
forgotten the swords of their ancestors', were being encouraged to
submit to Bengali clerks 'who at the sight of a table knife would
crawl under [their] chair'. Sir Sayyid thought the warrior aristocracy of north India needed to acknowledge its defeat by British
armies and submit to British authority, but should still be proud
of their martial history. By contrast, Lajpat Rai argued that the
literature, philosophy and science of the Mughal past needed to be
celebrated, not war. India was the land of peaceful improvement,

of reason rather than passion and conflict, he thought. 'No race ever complained of its having been ruined by a Rajput invasion.' 'It is time', he argued, 'that the followers of the Prophet should be proud of their ancestors, not on account of their conquests, but on account of their great efforts in the dissemination of knowledge in the world.'

Paradoxically, these criticisms of the self-appointed guardian of the Mughal empire's martial glory might have been influenced by Mughal traditions of thought. There is a direct line of influence. Lajpat Rai's father taught the language of Mughal government. His ancestors worked as Mughal officials. Lajpat Rai himself was always himself more comfortable writing in Persian characters rather than in the Devanagari script now used for Hindi. Like Mughal writers, Lajpat Rai saw India as a community of communities. His thinking linked up with the idea of preserving the distinction between different communities so central to the resistance of 1857's rebels to British power. But he stressed the importance of compromise and balance between the interests of different groups.

Unlike the rebels of 1857, Lajpat Rai thought India's plural communities could form a single nation. Centuries of peaceful co-existence meant India's different societies collectively formed a single 'geographical, cultural and historical entity', he said. But Lajpat Rai's nation was a composite entity, made up of the half-merged aspirations of different sub-nations. Each needed to develop on its own terms. A country, he wrote, 'consisting of Hindus, Mahomedans, Christians and others cannot be said to be progressing unless all the component parts of it contribute to the progress of the whole.'

What mattered was that the moral and social life of each part of the nation grew in their own way together. Solidarity should not be forced by the coercive powers of the state. Like many early nationalists, Lajpat Rai was far more interested in social organization than state power. He was very flexible about the type of government which should rule India. Until the end of the First World

War Lajpat Rai thought India's national regeneration could occur within the British empire, although imperial power needed to be radically transformed so Indians had more autonomy. After the war, he became an early advocate of a total break with Britain. When religious violence wracked the subcontinent during the 1920s, Lajpat Rai was the first prominent nationalist to call for India to be split up, arguing that the division of India into four or five states would allow India's different communities to co-exist and develop together. Peaceful separation could create more lasting unity than enforced homogeneity. The important thing was to work to uplift one's own community, not to seize control of the state.

Self-reliance

Lajpat Rai's practical work and writing reflected the dominant mood of Indian nationalism in the thirty years before the Swadeshi movement. Throughout India, leaders shared a common critique of the conquering power of the British state. They tried to displace it by building the self-reliance of different communities rather than capturing the machinery of government. In this politics of self-reliance, 'community' was defined in thousands of different ways. Sometimes it coincided with the geographical borders of British India or was even larger. Sometimes it was tiny. The work of regeneration occurred in different styles. Sometimes it took a political form. Most commonly it focused on social, economic, cultural or religious renewal. In some times and places, assertion by one group occurred in peace with others; otherwise it led to conflict.[7]

These were decades that saw currents of religious revivalism become more intense, as Indians latched onto religion as one sign of their autonomy. These efforts often involved an attempt to purify religious customs, as in the Arya Samaj's effort to give greater definition to a core of Hindu belief. In the process, private, family or neighbourhood-based rituals were pushed into the public domain. In Pune and Bombay, a group of nationalists including

Bal Gangadhar Tilak took up local, family-based rituals which celebrated the Hindu elephant god Ganesh, turning them into a major public ceremony. Ganesh was chosen because he could unite Hindus from different backgrounds and stand as a symbol of the Hindu Indian nation. Parading the figure through the centre of British-ruled cities asserted indigenous ownership of public space.[8]

Religion provided a focus for the assertion of autonomy among Muslims, too. Here, domestic religious revivalism connected with opposition to the expansion of European power in Arab-speaking Muslim lands, with the French occupation of Tunisia in 1881 and British occupation of Egypt the year after. The call for Islam to strengthen itself was global, often linking to a new-found belief in the leading role of the Ottoman Turkish sultan, or *khalifa*, as leader of global Islam. The late 1880s and early 1890s saw the apotheosis of pan-Islamism, as figures such as the cosmopolitan radical Jamal Ud-din al-Afghani travelled between India, Persia and the Middle East encouraging Muslims to unite in opposition to British power. But global movements had a local life. Pan-Islamism inspired riots on the border with Afghanistan in the 1890s, and strikes among Muslim jute mill-workers in Calcutta.[9]

In practice, pan-Islamism did little more than heighten British anxieties about plots to expel them from Asia. A more significant response came from Muslims trying to create autonomous pockets of Islamic authority within British-ruled India. Many leaders criticized Sir Sayyid Ahmad Khan's emphasis on the need for Muslims to submit before Britain's conquering power. Sir Sayyid wanted to educate Muslims to occupy junior positions in the imperial hierarchy, arguing they could serve and protect the Muslim community while collaborating with the British. His critics saw cooperation with the British as corrosive and advocated seclusion and the regeneration of Islamic customs with little Western participation. In doing so, they nonetheless transformed Islamic forms of education and religious practice.[10]

That was the approach adopted by the founders of the institution that grew into one of the world's most important centre of Islamic learning. Founded in 1867 in a small north Indian town, the Darul Uloom ('house of knowledge') at Deoband aimed to renew Islamic traditions of learning and offer a modern education for religious leaders. It replaced the informal relationship between master and pupil that had previously characterized Islamic learning with the bureaucratic style of the European classroom. Deoband had printed curricula, ranks of desks and chairs, timetables and rule-based systems of decision-making and fund-raising. By the end of the nineteenth century, Deoband had become the most important centre of Muslim scholarship in the world after Cairo's Al-Azhar. But this impressive instance of institution-building did not only try to replace Western education, it tried to displace imperial justice. Deoband produced legal opinions, or *fatawa*, offering authoritative opinions on legal matters for India's Muslims. Just like the institutions that grew from the Arya Samaj, Deoband created a 'government within a government'. It built a new form of power based not on the sovereignty of the conquering state but the shared energies and feelings of members of the same community.[11]

The assertion of this new kind of communal power created tension. Active hostility to members of other communities was rare. But conflict emerged as rival groups acted out their communal loyalties in public spaces, and came across others with different allegiances. Tilak's cross-neighbourhood Ganesh festival sharpened religious dividing lines in Pune and Bombay, with riots breaking out between 1893 and 1895. Campaigns organized by Hindus to protect the holy cow had a similar impact, causing fifteen major riots in Punjab between 1883 and 1891. A major wave of violence occurred in Awadh and Bihar in 1893. In each case, fighting escalated because British authorities were too distant and disengaged to negotiate a settlement between rival groups. Without political representation in public institutions, differences could only be negotiated by force on the streets. But in the 1890s violence did not represent deep-rooted antagonisms between communities. One hundred and seven people were killed in riots in 1893, a fraction of the number who died in the riots which accompanied the partition of India half a century later. Nonetheless, killing on this scale frightened the organizers of cow-protection campaigns and led them to pull back from actions that might create more conflict.[12]

There was much more to the Indian politics of self-reliance than conflict between Hindus and Muslims. The growth of nationwide organizations such as the Arya Samaj and Darul Uloom at Deoband occurred alongside the creation of institutions to support the life of much smaller groups; the residents of a town, the members of a caste or sub-caste, the followers of a particular profession. In each case, the community mindedness of the late nineteenth century did not aim to seize control of the state for the benefit of a particular group. Its purpose was to regenerate South Asian society from within its own divisions and categories on many different scales.

Looking at what happened town by town, district by district allows one to see the importance of local efforts to build the self-reliance of particularly communities beyond the power of the imperial state. Along the Andhra coastline, for example, the 1890s saw the growth of district associations, concerned with social reform and the development of the Telegu language. In this, a region which had seen a British presence since the 1740s, there was no English-language newspaper until 1920 but plenty printed in the vernacular. In Mangalore, on India's west coast, a leading member of the Gaudi Saraswati Brahmin community opened a high school to challenge the dominance of missionary education in 1891. A hostel for Bunts, the warrior-peasant community which dominated village life in the region, was opened a few years later to house students from the countryside staying in the district capital, and became a centre for Bunt culture. In Bengal in the east of India, intellectuals created a sense of the province's autonomous cultural identity; but they did so by founding societies which reconstructed the distinct history of particular sub-regions. An assembly to study the history of the town of Murshidabad was established in 1887, for example. In south-east

Bengal, revivalism was more practical. There, in the town of Barisal deep in the Bengal delta, Ashwinikumar Dutta sent 40,000 signatures to the House of Commons in London demanding India be governed by an elected legislature in 1887. But his volunteers also created a 'government within a government' in the region, complete with schools, arbitration courts and financial support for the poor. Their aim was to develop what Dutta called *atma-sakti*, or self-reliance. These efforts, just like nationwide institutions created by the Arya Samaj or Darul Uloom, were designed to assert a kind of practical autonomy against Indian's imperial conquerors.[13]

This late-nineteenth-century politics of self-reliance was not necessarily incompatible with loyalty to British power. Sometimes loyalism was actively professed. The largest cow-protection rally of 1892, of 10,000 people at Benares, ended with three cheers being given for the true Hindu religion and for Queen Victoria. Even where leaders resisted submission to British power, the challenge was limited. The 1890s saw the creation of a few secret societies which offered physical training and whispered vaguely about armed uprising. But violence was very rare. In practice, critics of empire were reluctant to confront British power.

Administrative division

The events of the first five years of the twentieth century changed that. Then, the Indian politics of self-reliance came into conflict with the last incarnation of Tory imperialism in India, with its effort to impose and celebrate the violent power of the British state on Indian society. The official British attitude in these years agreed that India was made up of a multiplicity of communities. But it tried to deny Indians any but the smallest capacity to govern themselves. In place of local initiative and organization the imperial regime projected the power of India's supreme ruler, the Viceroy.

Between 1898 and 1905, it was Lord George Curzon who occupied that role. Curzon celebrated both British ways of doing things and his personal capacity to put them into practice. '[T]he highest ideal of truth', he said before an Indian university audience in 1905, 'is to a large extent a western conception.' During his seven years in India, Curzon tightened up British power over one institution after another, starting with Calcutta Corporation in 1899 and ending up with its universities in 1904. Described by the historian David Cannadine as a 'ceremonial impresario', Curzon thought Indians would not resist the consolidation of imperial authority if they were dazzled by spectacular displays of British sovereign majesty. His government was ruled by a catastrophically unrealistic idea about the capacity of the British regime to rearrange Indian society.[14]

Curzon's idea of British power was displayed in 1903 at the Delhi Durbar. To celebrate the coronation of Edward VII as Emperor of India, Curzon gathered the princes and senior British officials of the Raj in Delhi. On 1 January, after marching with a line of elephants and thousands of troops through the city's centre, the Viceroy arrived in the midst of a sixty-square-mile park. Laid out in front of him was a spatial representation of the way he thought power worked in India. The Viceroy, representing the Crown, was at the centre, with his council of British officers and the rulers of large native states close at hand and lesser princes radiating out. India's middle classes were nowhere, peasants and workers only present as soldiers and camp followers. The reporter Valentia Steer called it 'a panorama of Eastern splendor and of Western might'. Just like the Mughal *darbars* which it partially emulated, the ritual was supposed to bind the subjects of a ruler into his polity. 'I want to make it a celebration not of officials alone but of the public,' Curzon said. The Viceroy even talked about Indian 'citizenship' within the empire. But unlike noisy pre-British courtly gatherings, Indian participation occurred in silent ritual. In Curzon's vision of empire there was no space for the kind of negotiation between ruler and subjects that had sustained Mughal power.

This was imperial order projected for the age of the photograph and silent film. Curzon's display was captured and propagated using the very latest technology. The durbar ground was connected with electricity and festooned with lights. Photographers, amateur and professional, snapped pictures everywhere. Four film crews, two British, two Indian, worked at the site. Obsessed with detail, Curzon met with film crews and directed them to places where the event could be filmed to the best effect. Cinema presented a spectacular, moving image of the event, with no possibility of a response: the ideal medium of communication to convey Curzon's idea of power. Staged only seven years after the Lumière brothers presented the first moving pictures in Paris, the durbar was India's first film event. Films of the durbar were shown at makeshift screenings throughout the subcontinent. In reality, audiences thought the display demonstrated little more than the Viceoy's own 'inordinate love of pomp and show'. Less than two years after the end of a devastating famine the Indian press castigated the durbar as a vain and wasteful form of entertainment.[15]

A few nationalist leaders – Surendranath Banerjea was one – wondered in public whether the great show might be accompanied by a reconstitution of Britain's empire in India based on Indian leaders having a more active role. In fact, exactly the reverse occurred. The supposedly unifying effect of the durbar was followed by the announcement of the British government's decision to divide India's most active, patriotic community exactly a year later. The partition of Bengal created the greatest anti-British upsurge in India since 1857.

The partition proposal began deep in the bowels of the British bureaucracy, in a series of trivial exchanges between bureaucrats engaged in the arcane detail of trying to rationalize provincial boundaries. The process by which it emerged tells us something about the nature of British power in India. A scheme with a big impact developed from a set of small-scale efforts to mitigate imperial anxieties. There was no unifying philosophy or ideology other than the effort to maintain British power. Decisions were made with no negotiation with the people they affected.

The initial impulse for partition came from the idea of moving all the districts populated by people who spoke the Oriya language into a single province, to save the costs of language-training. Different options were debated for months. Curzon was furious that plans were being developed without him hearing about it. In his most famous minute, the Viceroy complained about British officials 'calmly carving about and rearranging provinces on paper, colouring and recolouring the map of India' without anyone consulting India's supreme ruler: himself. 'Round and round like the diurnal revolution of the earth went the file, stately, solemn, sure, and slow' before at the last stage Curzon was supposed to register his assent.

By the time Curzon imposed his authority on the scheme, it had developed into a plan governed by exactly the opposite principle from that which the discussion began with. A province where people spoke a single language was divided, and its eastern half merged with a region where people spoke a different language. Bengal would be split in half and merged with Assam to the northeast. The measure was justified with the claim that the boundaries of government units did not reflect the boundaries of real communities: 'Mere administrative division does not produce social division, any more than administrative unity produces social union,' the government said in public. But the desire to weaken the political voice of Bengal was one major factor behind the measure. As the author of the partition plan put it, 'Bengal united is a power; Bengal divided will pull in several different ways.' Herbert Risley, the official who masterminded partition, understood the need to keep the public and private arguments separate. When he was asked to explain his reasoning in one exchange of letters he wrote, 'it is not altogether easy to reply in a dispatch which is sure to be published', because 'one of our main objects is to split up and thereby weaken a solid body of opponents to our rule'.[16]

Patriotic spirit

Soon after the partition plan was announced in January 1904, Curzon visited the city intended as the capital of eastern Bengal, Dhaka. There, he persuaded the area's largest landlord, Khwaja Salimullah Khan, to support his scheme. Salimullah had initially been sceptical. A loan of 100,000 rupees (almost £1 million in 2016 prices) together with alterations in the plan to make the new province of Eastern Bengal bigger persuaded him to support partition. Like many aristocratic Muslims, Salimullah thought he could stop the decline in his influence by playing a leading role in a more emphatically Muslim-dominated province. But Dhaka, the planned capital of Eastern Bengal, was in 1904 a mixed city, home to a large Hindu population, whose economic and cultural life was closely tied to Calcutta and other centres further west. The response to Lord Curzon was vehement. The Viceroy was followed around by boys with placards lobbying him to abandon the idea of splitting Bengal. '[D]o not turn us into Assamese', some said, articulating the fear many in eastern Bengal had about being united with people they saw as less civilized and inferior.

Throughout Bengal, partition created resistance on an unpredicted and unprecedented scale. Huge meetings were held at Calcutta town hall in February 1904 and then January 1905, uniting every part of Hindu Bengali society. Dozens of pamphlets were published within weeks of the announcement. Sixty-nine petitions were received from Dhaka alone within a month. Seventy thousand signatures were sent to London in July 1905.

Protest quickly turned from lobbying to non-cooperation, and expanded beyond Bengal. A motion to boycott British goods was passed at a public meeting near Khulna in eastern Bengal on 13 July 1905; a similar motion was passed three weeks later in Calcutta. Two thousand public meetings were held in every part of Bengal, with European products burnt at many. At Durga Puja, in October 1905, 50,000 gathered at Calcutta's Kali temple, vowing not to buy foreign goods. A province-wide conference was held at Barisal in April 1906. Thousands of volunteers marched through the streets shouting nationalist slogans against police orders. Meetings at Khulna had been dispersed by force in December 1905, but British violence was stronger at Barisal, where students, sometimes school-children, were beaten. The Indian-managed press condemned the 'tyranny' of the police and army, although no protesters were killed. Lajpat Rai condemned a government 'commanding 260,000 or 500,000 soldiers, stooping to strike us by striking our boys'. British rule had adopted 'Russian models' and 'frightful' tactics. The British empire had established 'a reign of military terrorism'. Even the British-edited press worried that these 'blunders' would 'only have the effect of manufacturing an army of martyrs'.

British violence helped protests spread far beyond Bengal, with meetings across India from the far south to Punjab in 1906 and 1907. Assemblies were held in district capitals throughout the subcontinent, from Madras to Punjab. Tens of thousands gathered to hear the Bengali radical Bipin Chandra Pal give lectures at Rajahmundry and then on the beach at Madras when he toured along south India's coastline. Pal argued that the partition of Bengal proved the British had no intention of sharing power with Indians. Their government would always remain 'despotic'. Pal talked of a 'new movement' and mass 'upsurge'. Mohandas Karamchand Gandhi began his first political pamphlet, *Hind Swaraj*, written in 1908, by noting the 'new spirit' that had swept through the whole of India. 'The spirit generated in Bengal has spread in the North to the Punjab, and in the South, to Cape Comorin.'[17]

Wherever they spoke or wrote, opponents of partition contrasted the distant violence of the imperial state with the natural unities they saw in local society. Opposition to Curzon's 'administrative division' was based on the community-minded approach to politics which had emerged during the previous years, with its focus on nation building and self-reliance. From this standpoint, nations were not made by the bureaucratic measures of government; they grew from the 'common impulse' which came from people living together. As Bipin Chandra Pal put it in his Madras lectures, '[a] nation is not a mere collection of individuals. . . . it has organic life'.

Some wealthy Indians opposed partition because it corroded their economic interests; the merchant Nalinbihari Sircar was worried that the development of the port at Chittagong would weaken trade in Calcutta. But few Swadeshi activists saw Curzon's partition as simply an act which endangered their interests in a calculable way. It was seen as a moment of violence against an organic entity which had its own autonomous life. In Bengal the national community was often described in human, feminine terms, usually as the mother. 'Let us turn', the radical Aurobindo Ghosh urged his compatriots, 'from these pale and alien phantoms (the instruments of British rule) to the true reality of our Mother as she rises from the living death of a century.'[18]

The apparent violence of this act of dismemberment pushed Indian political leaders towards new forms of political argument and action they could barely countenance before 1904. Some expected petitioning and public meetings to force the government to back down; others wanted to focus on non-confrontational 'self-development'. But for the majority caught up in the movement of 1905–7, lobbying and institution-building needed to be combined with an active effort to undermine the sources of British power. 'After the Partition', Gandhi wrote, 'people saw that petitions must be backed up by force, and that they must be capable of suffering.' 'People, young and old, used to run away at the sight of an English face; it now no longer awed them.'[19]

The year 1905 saw the first clear articulation of Indian arguments in favour of an independent national Indian state. These arguments were made most starkly outside India, among a diaspora of Indians in Germany, the USA, Britain, Japan and France. One important centre was India House, a student residence in Highgate, north London, organized by the Sanskritist and lawyer Shyamji Krishnavarma in 1905. Born to a petty merchant family in Gujarat during the 1857 rebellion, Krishnavarma was inspired by the Arya Samaj's emphasis on the need to return to the principles of ancient Hindu society. After meeting Dayananda in his early twenties, Krishnavarma became the Arya Samaj's key Sanskrit intellectual and head of its publishing house. To begin with, this did not lead to a direct contest with British power. Krishnavarma studied Sanskrit at Oxford in the early 1880s, then trained as a barrister, returning to India with letters of introduction to a collection of British officers including the Viceroy. Back in India, he helped the Arya Samaj grow while working as a minister in Indian-ruled states and developing an increasingly strong critique of British power. But his career was blocked by opposition from British bureaucrats. In 1897 Krishnavarma returned to London to counter imperial power through 'a relentless propaganda effort directed at its imperial centre', as historian Shruti Kapila notes.[20]

Like his contemporaries at home, Krishnavarma argued that Indian nationalism was an organic movement driven by unconscious spiritual forces which could not be marshalled by the violent forces of the state. But Krishnavarma's location in London led him to develop a positive view of the benefits of sovereign political power. Some of his close allies embraced anarchism, arguing that nationalists needed to oppose all governments, not only the imperial government, with bombs and guns. Krishnavarma himself advocated 'the ethics of dynamite'. He paid for lessons in bomb-making from a Russian revolutionary. But he was no anarchist, arguing instead that India needed its own form of national state power. Thinking only a few miles distant from the centre of imperial authority, the only form of national freedom Krishnavarma could imagine was an 'absolutely free and independent form of national government'. India could only achieve self-reliance if it was a sovereign geopolitical entity, with its own bureaucracy, army and police, possessing 'the same form of Government as now obtains in England'.[21]

Krishnavarma claimed to have coined the term *swaraj*, or self-rule, although the first public use of the term was variously attributed to

Dayananda and to Dadabhai Naoroji as well. Whatever its origin, the meaning of *swaraj* was fiercely debated. Many argued that *swaraj* was about social renewal not the seizure of governmental authority. For political leaders engaged in the practical struggle with imperial power, Krishnavarma's vision of independent state power was too abstract, and had too little to offer the practical challenges which faced Indian society.

Gandhi's *Hind Swaraj* offered one version of this argument. Gandhi was born in the same province as Krishnavarma two years later. Both were from relatively humble backgrounds, but had made their way to London to study law at the Inner Temple. But soon after leaving London Gandhi took a job as a lawyer in South Africa, starting his political life protesting against discrimination against Indian migrants in Cape and Natal province. Gandhi wrote *Hind Swaraj* on the ship from London to South Africa after a visit to the imperial capital had failed to persuade the British government to grant Indians in South Africa citizenship rights. Gandhi's argument was influenced by this failure, but also by the Swadeshi movement. Gandhi had kept in touch with events in India, and was excited by the expansion of Indian political ambitions which followed the partition of Bengal. 'All our countrymen appear to be pining for National Independence', Gandhi noted.

Hind Swaraj had the same urgent desire for self-rule which drove advocates of revolutionary violence like Krishnavarma. But the pamphlet challenged both their creed of violence and their desire to emulate British political institutions. Violence lay at the heart of the modern state, Gandhi said. He thought its lawyers, railway systems and armies prevented people from having control over their own lives, creating counter-productive, self-destructive instincts. Violence had caused Indians to be overtaken by the same unbridled passions which drove British imperial power. It pulled its perpe-trators into retaliatory spirals of fear and revenge that led them to be no better than the people they opposed. For Gandhi, *swaraj* was about moral and social regeneration in contrast to the modern system of power. It needed to start with individuals having mastery over themselves, 'over our mind and our passions', as Gandhi wrote. It was not about communities asserting power on a large geopolitical scale. '[T]he Government of England is not desirable,' Gandhi argued. In its place Gandhi proposed a commonwealth of self-governing villages where individuals could take full, rational responsibility for their action.

With their focus on self-reliance rather than the capture of state power, Gandhi's arguments connected to the mainstream of nationalist argument. Before 1905 the dispersed forces of India's nationalisms had worked to renew the life of particular communities without confronting British authority. Afterwards, nationalist institution-building became a way to directly challenge the power of an imperial state seen as violent and immoral, to forcefully relocate power in Indian institutions in Indian hands. Institution-building was coupled with 'passive resistance', the positive correlation to a programme of 'organized and relentless boycott', as the Bengali-born radical Aurobindo Ghosh put it.

Nationalists repeated the argument Sayyid Mahmood had made thirty years earlier; that Britain's 'conquest' of India had in fact relied on Indian collaboration. But while Mahmood used this argument to insist the British open their courts and councils to Indians, Swadeshi activists saw it as the basis of an anti-imperial political tactic. Withdrawing support for the institutions which conquest had created would force the Raj to collapse. As the journal *Sandhya* wrote in November 1906, if 'the chowkidar, the constable, the deputy and the muniff and the clerk, not to speak of the sepoy, all resign their respective functions, feringhee [foreign] rule in the country may come to an end in a moment'. Speaking at Madras in 1907, Bipin Chandra Pal argued that the 'new movement' would not be able to force the British to leave India. But it could radically shrink the scope the imperial regime had for exercising its power. 'By restricting the Government to its narrowest possible limits', Indians would develop 'the spirit of self-reliance'.[22]

In Bengal, the work of creating this alternative system of power was conducted through a network of local societies which spread throughout the province's countryside. The model was outlined by the poet Rabindranath Tagore in a lecture given at Calcutta's Minerva theatre in July 1904. Entitled *swadeshi samaj* ('our own society'), Tagore's address urged Bengal's middle classes to abandon English-style urban politics. Instead, they should tour the villages to revive traditional Indian festivals and folk dramas, songs and talks illustrated with magic lantern slides. Village life would be regenerated by activating old symbols, and using them to drive a range of local self-help initiatives.[23]

Tagore's lecture was so popular it needed to be delivered again eleven days later in, ironically enough, the Curzon theatre. It encouraged a flood of volunteers to put these principles into practice, some from Calcutta, others from district capitals scattered throughout Bengal. The societies they created offered physical and moral training, helped those in distress, organized craft production and arbitrated disputes. Swadeshi leaders tried to revive the village industries; the idea was that boycotted Western cloth would be replaced by traditional artisan crafts like handloom or silk weaving, not great industrial factories. A diary from the town of Pabna discovered by the historian Sumit Sarkar noted that in 1905 and 1906, the bazaars were full of Swadeshi goods, and the 'town is busy with the medieval charka'.[24]

By April 1907 about a thousand village *samitis* (societies) were working in Bengal; in the area around Barisal alone, the *samitis* claimed to have set up eighty-nine arbitration committees which settled 523 disputes in their first phase of activity. The police estimated that there were over 8,000 volunteers in eastern Bengal. By May of that year, the government had started to regulate public meetings, banning any large gathering. In many places, open-air folk entertainments like *jatras* and *kathakalis* took their place. The district magistrate of Bakarganj worried that these events 'reache[d] all classes and spread seditious doctrines among them. At the same time, unlike a public meeting which could easily be banned, osten sibly cultural events were 'very difficult to deal with'.[25]

The nationalist campaign of 1904–8 was not, though, a move-ment of the masses; few peasants were involved. Most volunteers came from landed or local official classes. But the style of these middle-class-led 'governments within governments' varied dra-matically. Some were led by prominent landholders, and were keen to push social change without disturbing the local social structure. Others were led by radical lawyers, teachers and clerks with less at stake in the rural hierarchy; a few were covers for revolutionary activity, and occasionally engaged in violence. Samiti members at Santipur, a small town sixty miles north of Calcutta, assaulted two missionaries in June 1906. A series of armed robberies were organ-ized by Swadeshi activists from the same place two years later.[26]

Educational initiatives briefly flourished alongside the samitis. Swadeshi volunteers opened schools throughout Bengal, the first in Rangpur in northern Bengal, the town where Rammohan Roy spent most of his career. In November 1905, a group of schoolboys from the government school were expelled for attending a Swadeshi meeting. Radical students from Calcutta University sped to the town to organize a rival school, which opened with 300 pupils within days. Hundreds of local schools opened in the following months. British authorities were particularly frightened about the movement's attempt to 'get hold of primary education', and mould the minds of young children to take a hostile stance to British power. Some British officers worried that technical education would be used as a cover for bomb-making. But national schools grew less because of their ideological stance than because they met demand for a practical education among Bengal's lower middle class; in some areas they educated lower castes, too. Hundreds of nationalist schools endured into the 1910s.[27]

By contrast, the attempt to build nationalist colleges collapsed fast. A National College in Calcutta was founded under a National Council of Education, but no other colleges affiliated, and student numbers declined quickly. In a job market dominated by British capital, students worried about finding employment with a 'national' degree.

As important in explaining the failure of the new colleges, government-funded institutions like Calcutta University had started to support efforts at exactly the kind of national regeneration Swadeshi campaigners called for. Successive Viceroys had failed to impose their authority against nationalist 'sedition'. Universities had become the first imperial institutions in which Indian voices dominated. Teaching staff and governing bodies were predominantly Indian from the 1890s. After 1892, Bombay University only had a European Vice-Chancellor for three years, between 1912 and 1915. Calcutta University had an Indian Vice-Chancellor in the 1890s, and was then led by Indians from 1905 onwards. During the Swadeshi years Calcutta University's Vice-Chancellor Ashutosh Mukerjee was a hostile opponent of the 'national' movement, criticizing its schools and colleges as 'hotbeds of sedition'. But he introduced a compulsory paper in the Bengali language, and built a set of research centres in disciplines seen as essential for national renewal, particularly ancient history, applied psychology and industrial chemistry. Other institutions, Allahabad University, for example, became centres for nationalist history writing and political science. To many, it seemed that self-reliance could be developed in the loose structures of institutions created, initially at least, by the imperial state.

Swadeshi capitalism

The complicated relationship between nationalist institution-building and imperial power was most apparent in the world of business. The 1890s and 1900s saw the emergence of ideas about economic self-reliance, which encouraged the growth of Indian businesses to meet Indian consumer demand. But these firms rarely cut themselves off entirely from imperial structures.

Explicitly nationalist businesses were founded in the decade before Swadeshi. The Punjab National Bank began trading in 1894. Bharat Life Insurance was founded in Punjab two years later to challenge the fact that Indians were charged '10% extra' than Europeans for life cover. India's first drug company, the Bengal Chemical and Pharmaceutical Works, was created in 1893 by the Edinburgh-educated chemist Prafulla Chandra Ray. But the Swadeshi years gave business a big impetus. The mood to buy Indian goods helped Bengal Chemicals increase its sales tenfold, allowing one British observer to describe it as 'an object lesson to capitalism in the province'. Bengal Chemicals was joined by the Calcutta Pottery Works, which sold 'swadeshi teacups, saucers, teapots' after its manager returned from Japan in 1906 with training in glazing ceramics. New firms made cotton, soap, matches, cigarettes, cycles, cutlery and pen nibs. In Bombay the Cooperative Swadeshi Stores sold Indian-made goods to the western metropolis's middle classes. In Madras, the Swadeshi Steamship Company challenged the British monopoly on coastal shipping, engaging in a price war with its rivals that dramatically cut the cost of transport during these years.[28]

In Madras, too, a few months before Abdulla Haji Kasim opened his bank in Mangalore the Indian Bank was founded. Its creation was driven by a combination of Swadeshi sentiment and the rage of South Indian merchants at the collapse of British financial institutions amid scandal and suicide. The two British business partners in Madras's largest agency house, Arbuthnot's, had become over-exposed to bad investments in London. They then lied about the scale of their debts. One killed himself, the other was sentenced to eighteen months in prison. The lawyer representing the house's Indian creditors decided British businesses could not be trusted, and that local businesses needed their own bank.[29]

The most powerful and enduring business to benefit from the Swadeshi upsurge was the Tata Steel Company, the firm that dominated (and still dominates today) the Indian metals industry. The Tatas were Parsi priests from the small town of Navsari in Gujarat. They moved into business and made money from trading opium and then cotton in the middle of the nineteenth century. The names of the mills which Jamsetji Tata first built indicate his hope for imperial patronage: first Alexandra (after the Prince of Wales's new bride) then Empress Mills. But by 1905, the Tatas had turned to other forms of capital.

Aware of India's massive iron ore deposits, Jamsetji noted the country's total dependence on British steel and wanted India to be more self-sufficient. Continuously after 1883, Tata petitioned the British government to be allowed to open an Indian steel factory. Tata was continuously blocked by the India Office which had placed a firm 'interdict on a legitimate Indian industry', ensuring that every single rail or sheet of steel in India needed to be shipped from Europe. But by the turn of the century the government in India was coming under relentless pressure from Indian political leaders to support domestic business. Britain's steel industry could not cope with the demand coming from the continued growth of Indian infrastructure, particularly railways. The government was happier for the deficit to be supplied 'by one of her own dependencies' than from a competitor like Belgium or the USA.

The strength of Indian opinion and competition from rival imperial states caused the ban on Indian-made steel to be lifted in 1899, and restrictions on coal and iron ore mining to be eased too. To begin with, imperial officials and likely Indian industrialists assumed the capital for Indian steel would come from Britain, so company law was changed to allow Indian firms to register on the London stock exchange. But British financiers were reluctant to invest. '[O]ld and tried industries were offered as more favourable and safer investment,' as the businessman V. B. Godrej noted. Railways and agency houses soaked up capital available for investment in the subcontinent, with the City having no imagination to seek out other ventures. Indian steel was seen as too risky.[30]

Jamsetji Tata died in 1904. To open India's first modern steel factory, his son turned to a different source of money. Instead of relying on the London stock market, Dorabji Tata sought investment from middle-class Indians. Frustrated by their dependence on British power, enthused by the idea of supporting indigenous enterprise, thousands of small investments flooded in. The Tata Steel Company was launched in August 1907. It rolled its first steel in 1912, making train rails and the fishplates that link them together. In 1916, it diversified into making cases for explosive shells.

Tata's first major customer was the imperial state. Without a large domestic industrial sector, the only institution which had demand for heavy metals was the government. Yet Tata grew as the weakness of British imperial power coincided with Indian enthusiasm about creating self-reliant institutions. To meet the imperial regime's demand for steel, Tata created a series of settlements and institutions beyond the reach of imperial power. With help from American geologists and steelmakers, Tata located India's first modern steel plant in the Chota Nagpur plateau in eastern India, building the new town of Jamshedpur between 1908 and 1912. From the beginning, the town was administered by an Indian company not the government. It saw one of India's earliest instances of national urban planning, with streets laid out in tree-lined boulevards, parks and recreation grounds.

Economic growth and institutional dynamism occurred in the places that were furthest from the rule of British bureaucrats. India's 'native states', where large areas of territory were ruled with minimal British involvement, pioneered research in science, technology and the growth of banking, for example. It was the Maharaja of Mysore, Sir Krishnaraja Wodeyar, not one of the Raj's British provincial governors, whom Jamestji Tata persuaded to open India's first Indian Institute of Science in 1909. India's first large-scale electricity generating plant was built in Mysore, too. The state of Baroda launched one of India's most successful nationalist banks.

Before Swadeshi, large-scale Indian capital was restricted to a small number of industries and a small number of cities, particularly textiles in Ahmedabad and then Bombay. Coinciding with a moment of relative prosperity for India's economy, energized by the spirit of national self-reliance, the second half of the 1910s saw the dispersal of Indian capital and the growth of Indian-managed organization in small towns and cities; in places like the new steel settlement of Jamshedpur, but also throughout small towns like Mangalore or Rajahmundry, with their new banks, industries and civic institutions. The local capitalists and political leaders who drove the expansion of Indian business in small-town India adopted a variety of different and shifting attitudes to British power. The founder of Corporation Bank Haji Abdulla Haji Kasim was a moderate supporter of the Swadeshi movement, but that did not stop him from taking the title of Rai Bahadur; nor did his imperial title stop him from hosting a visit by M. K. Gandhi in 1922. But their actions created a network of businesses independent of empire which did not rely on the formal assertion of British imperial power.

Imperial recess

In December 1911 King George V visited India. His main function was to preside over another massive display of imperial pageantry, the second Delhi Durbar. But while Curzon's 1903 assembly had been designed to celebrate the intensity of imperial power, the King was in India to preside over a moment of retreat. By 1911, the mood among British decision-makers in London and Calcutta was against Curzon's style of autocratic meddling. Under Indian pressure, the British government had decided to revoke the partition of Bengal. More importantly, the King announced that the Raj was moving its capital from Calcutta to Delhi, from a commercial metropolis with a vibrant and critical public sphere to a deserted city full of decaying monuments. Delhi's entire population had been evacuated in 1857; its cultural and political life had been annihilated. Hundreds of miles away from centres of political activity, it was seen by officials as the safest place for the imperial state to rule India in dangerous times.

The years before the outbreak of the First World War were a time of imperial recess. At a moment when they worried more about social reform in Britain and the possibility of war in continental Europe, British politicians imagined they could disentangle themselves from the commitments which administration involved while retaining some semblance of sovereign power. 'It is certain', the Viceroy, Lord Hardinge, grudgingly wrote in the introduction to the report that transferred power to Delhi, 'that the just demands of Indians for a larger share in the Government of the country will have to be satisfied.' Hardinge thought India would end up being governed by Indian-run provincial administrations, 'with the Government of India above all [of] them and possessing power to interfere in cases of misgovernment' but otherwise having a vague coordinating role.

This was a vision of the British government having a similar role as the eighteenth-century Mughal emperor: a distant, symbolically important authority with little role in the details of administration. Appropriately, the original plans for the new capital linked New Delhi to the old Mughal city of Shahjahanabad, through a long avenue that had the Jama Masjid at the northern end, Connaught Place in the centre and the Purana Qila in the south. Even this scheme was a victim of imperial retreat. To reduce budgets and prevent opposition from Delhi's residents, the new city stopped abruptly to the north of the new railway station, leaving old Delhi unchanged. The government did not even have the will to shape the urban life of its own capital city.[31]

This recessive mood was sharply criticized by Tory imperialists and retired imperial officers who thought empire could only be sustained by the forthright assertion of Britain's conquering authority in India. Lord Curzon led the charge against the creation of the new capital. Calcutta was 'English built'. It was the place from which 'English statesmen, administrators and generals ha[d] built up to its present commanding height the fabric of British rule'. Delhi was 'a mass of deserted ruins and graves', a place 'shut off from the main currents of public life' where the government would become 'immersed in a sort of bureaucratic self-satisfaction'. Curzon believed this decision to move from an 'English city' to 'the dead capital of Mahomedan Kings' was the sign of an empire in decline.[32]

Obsessed as ever with image, Curzon tried to push forth the conquering power of the British state through his own symbolism. As Viceroy, he built monuments which celebrated the rupturing violence of imperial conquest. In the 'English city' of Calcutta, Curzon commissioned a great memorial to Queen Victoria which had a belligerent angel of victory on its top. At the Plassey battle-field in northern Bengal, he commissioned an obelisk in tribute to the soldiers who fought Siraj-ad-Daula. He also ordered a statue of Robert Clive at Plassey to sit outside the India Office (now Foreign and Commonwealth Office) in London. This last figure is the only depiction of Clive as the direct author of violence: bronze panels around the base show cannons exploding into the Nawab's army.

After Curzon resigned as Viceroy in 1905, these projects slowed drastically, becoming increasingly distant from the official story which the government in London and India tried to tell about its empire. Curzon harried and cajoled over two decades, having to fundraise privately, and with the support of assorted retired colonels and Collectors eventually got his monuments built. He particularly drew upon the resources of disgruntled former Indian officials, including one or two related to people close to Clive. 'We English', one correspondent wrote, 'seem to have a genius for injuring those who have done us great service abroad.' Contributors to the Clive statue included Viscount Milner, two former Viceroys and Sir John Edge, the judge who had dismissed Sayyid Mahmood from the Allahabad bench. But beyond this community of retired imperial officers, there was no public enthusiasm in these efforts to celebrate conquest, or Britain's empire in India at all, in fact. John Morley, Secretary of State between 1906 and 1911, wanted a statue of Garibaldi where Curzon wanted to put Clive, and to name the row outside the India Office Milton Street. None of Curzon's memorial projects was completed until after the First World War.[33]

The slow pace of Curzon's imperial monumentalization was a

sign of British pessimism about their empire in India. The Swadeshi agitation was followed by years when plots appeared to be everywhere. British officers were murdered and conspiracies to kill Governor Generals seemed commonplace. Imperial bureaucrats and politicians were paranoid about Indians linking up with India's archenemy, Germany. An attack on the judge of Muzaffarpur killed two British women in 1908; the Collector of Tirunelveli was killed in June 1911; Lord Hardinge himself was badly hurt by a bomb blast in 1912. Worried texts were once again published from British presses with titles such as *Indian Unrest* (1910), *England's Problem in India* (1912), and *India in Travail* (1918), each proposing measures to sustain the endangered power of the British that ranged from granting full self-government to massive coercion. But beyond Curzon's band of supporters, imperialism had few allies.

For the first time since 1858, some Britons even started to doubt the physical possibility of sustaining British domination in India. The 1910s saw the high point of official racism, but it was more often used to explain Britain's imperial failures than to justify the empire's spread across the globe. Medical experts imagined that Europeans were biologically superior to Indians, but thought they were incapable of sustaining their 'brain power, or the civilization due to it' in Indian's tropical climate for long. Sir Richard Havelock Charles, the Irish-born Professor of Anatomy at Lahore Medical College, then chief medical officer of the Government of India between 1913 and 1923, argued that 'white races cannot permanently colonize the tropics and remain white'. Charles believed the sun and heat caused European men and women to develop a 'congeries of mental and sensory disturbances' and morally to degenerate. In time they became irritable, short-tempered, overly introspective and unable to sustain the confidence and clarity of mind he believed marked the superiority of the 'white race'. More likely caused by the 'monotony of life in remote stations' or their anxiety about challenges to their power, the mental condition of 'tropical neurasthenia' was frequently diagnosed among Europeans.

Often, the condition was used as an excuse by perfectly fit men and women to escape the worsening political conditions for Europeans in India and go home. But complete mental breakdowns were not rare. 'Brain fog' was commonplace. Fear of the collapse of British authority was compounded by a belief that Britons were losing the psychological character to hold on to power.[34]

Before 1914, India played little significant role in Britain's projection of power overseas. Neither economically nor militarily did Britain rely on the subcontinent. After the failure of efforts to increase supplies of raw cotton in the 1860s, India exported few useful raw materials for Britain's manufacturing industry. India was (just about) the largest market for Lancashire cotton, but textiles did not dominate the British economy. Indian saltpetre exports had been eclipsed by Chilean sodium nitrate in the 1860s and then chemically made explosives in the 1890s. From then to 1914 India was the supplier of very little military hardware. The purpose of the Indian army was to suppress internal opposition and protect British India from external powers, not extend British interests outside India. The only large involvement of Indian troops outside South Asia before 1914 was against Chinese forces in the first Opium War of 1839–40. After then, in all but a few minor skirmishes, Indian troops only fought in India or on its borders. Despite Curzon's repeated offers, Indian soldiers were not used in the conflict in South Africa between 1898 and 1901 as generals and politicians tried to keep the fight with Transvaal 'a white man's war'. 'The primary job of India's soldiers was the defence of India', as military historian Hew Strachan puts it. The 'possession' of India was a source of pride and a place for Tory imperialists to play out their fantasies about hierarchy and absolute power. It provided a livelihood for thousands of British officers, soldiers and ancillary staff. But beyond this narrow spectrum of the population, Britain's domination of India had little practical use to Britain itself.[35]

In India by 1914, British power was being subtly challenged by thousands of institutions through which people exercised their will to shape their own social, economic and sometimes even political lives. Sometimes the growth of these institutions was resisted, sometimes they were grumpily accepted by the British regime; occasionally they were co-opted by imperial officers to help the British maintain power. But throughout the subcontinent the Indian energy for institution-building contrasted with the recessive mood of Britons in government. India's early twentieth-century nationalist enthusiasms diminished the British state's commitment to empire. Many in India imagined that with little interest or zeal, British power would fade away. That is not, of course, what happened. The surprising importance of India to the First World War effort wrought dramatic change to Britain's imperial ambitions and created a powerful indian backlash.

13

MILITARY LIBERALISM AND THE INDIAN CROWD

Sometime in the early 1820s a sailor from Devon in south-west England arrived in Calcutta to work as a river pilot. He met an English girl and they married in Calcutta Cathedral. John and Julia started a family that stayed in India until Indian opposition to British rule forced them to leave. The Indian careers of its members allowed the Dyer family to climb the social ladder. The couple's three sons became technicians and surveyors. Their four daughters married into East India Company service families. Their second son was on track to become an engineer before he noticed the demand for beer from European soldiers. At Kassauli, a military town in the foot-hills of the Himalayas, Edward Dyer founded India's first modern brewery, two years before the great insurrection of 1857. There, he made the beer that would be India's bestseller for a century, naming it 'Lion' after the animal which symbolized British power. Edward's children continued the pattern of becoming ancillary staff in the imperial regime, building careers based on positions of small-scale domination over local Indian populations. Some became engineers. Most joined the army. So, when John Dyer's grandson Reginald arrived to violent protests in Amritsar on 11 April 1919, he faced a challenge to his family's way of life, not just a movement resisting the British state.

The First World War had left India in a state of economic crisis and political upheaval. To suppress dissent, the government extended wartime restrictions on civil liberties. The Indian National Congress declared a general strike. Indian leaders called for protests to be peaceful, but, as demonstrators were killed and arrested, rioting started to spread. Imperial troops fired on crowds in Delhi on 30 March. Aircraft machine-gunned people from the air at Gujranwala the following week. At Ahmedabad rioters killed European officers and crowds were fired on.

Dyerism

The worst violence, on both sides, occurred in the city of Amritsar in Punjab. Motivated by economic hardship and the government's anxious suppression of dissent, crowds gathered to protest against everything from the refusal of the railways to allow platform tickets to the dismemberment of the Ottoman empire. At the beginning of April 1919, the imperial authorities accused Congress activists of bringing 'the Government established by law in British India into hatred and contempt'. Police arrested two of the most prominent Congress leaders. The newly famous political leader M. K. Gandhi was blocked from travelling to Punjab. Violent protests spread through the city. On 10 April public buildings were stormed and gutted. Two banks and a missionary school were looted. Five Englishmen and ten Indian protesters were killed. A crowd pushed a female missionary off her bicycle, beat her and left her for dead. Europeans retreated to the enclaves of the city's fort and cantonment but enemies of British rule ran riot in the rest of the city. On the evening of 11 April, hundreds gathered at a public meeting declaring that 'the British Government had been overthrown', and decided to cut the railway line. Posters appeared calling on 'the Indian nation' to 'Kill and be killed' and 'Conquer the English monkeys with bravery'.[1]

Reginald Dyer was born near his father's brewery in Punjab. Dyer spent the first eleven years of his life in India, but was sent to school in Ireland to preserve a sense of his separateness from Indian society. From there, he joined the army, helped suppress riots in Belfast and ended up back in India in 1887. By 1919 he had risen to become a temporary brigadier general, and had charge of the Jalandhar division of the imperial army. On 11 April the city's civilian Deputy Commissioner authorized General Dyer to use whatever force was needed to impose British order on a city which had been taken over by crowds. Two days later, just before noon, Dyer's troops marched around the city announcing by drumbeat that all public meetings were banned.

Early the same afternoon, Dyer learnt that a crowd had gathered at the public waste ground where many of the 'seditious' public meetings of the past few months had been held, the Jallianwala Bagh. It was a mixed crowd of between 10,000 and 20,000. Some were there for a protest meeting, others for the Sikh festival of Baisakhi. General Dyer entered the ground with fifty Indian soldiers carrying .303 rifles, forty Gurkhas armed only with swords, and the European chief of police. With no warning, his troops started shooting, firing 1,650 rounds into the crowd. Official figures said 379 people died. The Congress inquiry into the shootings counted more than 1,000. By a long way, this was the worst use of military force against a civilian crowd in British history.

Dyer was briefly lauded by his superiors in Punjab for quickly stopping the collapse of imperial power, and was sent to command troops in Afghanistan. 'Your action correct and Lieutenant-Governor approves,' Dyer was told when he first reported his action to the head of Punjab's government. But as news of the Amritsar killings spread to London his conduct began to be criticized by his compatriots. The British government's liberal Secretary of State for India, Edwin Montagu, insisted on a public investigation into the Punjab violence. Within months, Dyer was summoned to appear before a Disorders Inquiry Committee in the Punjab capital of Lahore.

The committee consisted of a mild-mannered Scottish judge, Lord William Hunter, four other Britons and three Indian lawyers. The commission's proceedings were irritable and anxious. Dyer and its British members agreed that coercion was needed in Punjab. The arrest of 3,200 'rebels', the shooting of massed gatherings and bombing from the air were seen as 'difficult' but necessary nonetheless to 'hold on' to British imperial power if done in the right way. The committee approved of thirty-seven cases of firing and censured only one. Their belief in the use of violence to preserve British power placed the Britons at odds with their Indian colleagues, eventually leading to a total breakdown between the two sides. 'You people want to drive the British out of the country,' Hunter shouted at C. H. Setalvad, a moderate lawyer on the inquiry committee, in one particularly tense exchange.

The Hunter inquiry marked the arrival of a new force in Indian politics: the crowd. Up until 1919, British officers thought about Indian politics in terms of potentially seditious political leaders. The mass of India's population existed off-stage. As passive subjects, they were the occasional target of government action. In government reports, the 'mob' was sometimes described as being brought into play by scheming political leaders, sporadically excited by religious passion, but the masses had no political life of their own. From the events in Punjab in 1919 onwards, 'the crowd' began to be seen as a political actor in its own right. The Indian government's report on the disturbances used the word 'crowd' 150 times in seventy pages; the Hunter report 280 times in 175 pages, and the text's narrative began with a mass 'outbreak'. The fear, throughout, was that the escalation of crowd violence might cause the collapse of the Raj's power. Hunter was not sure middle-class revolutionaries were a great threat, but the report's authors feared that 'a movement which had started in rioting and become a rebellion might have rapidly become a revolution'.

Dyer and his British critics disagreed about the best response to this new politics of spontaneous crowd violence. The government in London and the Viceroy believed the quick and firm use of force against rioting needed to be accompanied by concessions to India's political elites. They wanted Indian nationalists to help them control the crowd. They had started to believe that British sovereignty in India relied on conceding pockets of power to Indians in an otherwise despotic regime. By 1919, the British government had started to frame reforms to include a liberal element in India's autocratic constitution.

Dyer, by contrast, thought any act of retreat would quickly cause the Raj to unravel. For him, British power in India was based on conquest, and conquest could only be maintained if violence was continually asserted against a population which could quickly turn into a mob. Any kind of equality entailed a dangerous lack of respect for India's conquerors. After a crisis, such as those of 1857 or 1919, authority could only be restored if Indians were forced to submit themselves, sometimes humiliatingly, before their masters. So, after the initial disorders in Punjab, barristers in Amritsar were forced to do menial work. Every resident of Gujranwala was ordered to salute and salaam when they passed a British officer. Any Indian passing along the street where the missionary Miss Sherwood had been attacked was commanded by Dyer to crawl on their bellies.

Given in a packed Lahore assembly hall in November 1919, Dyer's testimony before the Hunter Commission used the language of personal triumph and humiliation. Dyer treated his cross-examination as a series of insults and slights. He often lost his temper. The 'rebel' meeting at the Jallianwala Bagh was, he argued, an act of 'defiance' against his authority that needed to be 'punished'. 'It was', Dyer famously argued, 'no longer a question of merely dispersing the crowd.' The shooting was calculated to produce 'a moral effect', to reduce 'the morale of the rebels', and in the process, force Indian subjects to submit.

Dyer's response to riots in Amritsar was a retaliation to an existential challenge. The way of life he had been brought up in was wrapped up with the idea of Indian obedience to British commands.

If those commands were not obeyed, Dyer would not be able to consider himself a dignified human being. When asked why he did not just shoot to disperse the crowd, Dyer said the people who gathered 'would all come back and laugh at me'. Without the killing, he said, 'I considered I would be making myself a fool'.[2]

Dismissed quickly by his Commander-in-Chief, in poor physical and mental health, Dyer travelled to Bombay without a hotel reservation and was forced to stay in a dirty dormitory before taking a troopship back to England. The Army Council banned him from any further employment in the armed forces. Back in Britain support for him grew in some quarters, and his actions at Amritsar were debated in Parliament. There Dyer became a political *cause célèbre* for die-hard Tory and Unionist politicians who believed Britain's global power was acquired and retained by conquest not partnership; they saw every act of concession as a humiliating desertion of the embattled bastions of imperial power before the insurgent crowd. The Irish Unionist, one-time First Lord of the Admiralty and staunch opponent of Irish nationalism, Sir Edward Carson, was Dyer's most fervent advocate. In his speech before the House of Commons, Carson portrayed Dyer as the defender of English values and imperial power against the international revolutionaries manipulating crowd violence in Egypt, Ireland, Russia and India. 'It is all one conspiracy, it is all engineered in the same way, it all has the same object – to destroy our sea power and drive us out of Asia.'[3]

Dyer's British defenders and critics were united in their desire to sustain British sovereignty in India against new forces of resistance and rebellion. Theirs was a passionate, sometimes vicious debate: some of Dyer's critics accused him of being 'unBritish' and on the verge of insanity; some of his defenders accused the Jewish Secretary of State of being part of a global conspiracy of Jews against British power.

The intensity of these arguments was partially caused by the deep-rooted commitment which the everyday operators of imperial power had long felt towards empire. But it was partly caused, too, by the fact that empire in India had recently become important to Britain in a new way. In 1919, India was no longer merely a self-sustaining, self-justifying outpost of British power that mattered only to families like the Dyers who ruled it. The First World War briefly turned British India into a vital source of British geopolitical power, a recruiting ground for soldiers and a base for materials and cash. World war forced Britain's political leaders to adopt a more liberal attitude towards the Government of India. But it also created forces that ensured liberal imperialism could not last.

Military liberalism

The First World War transformed Britain's purposeless imperial sovereignty in India into a vital source of global power, in the process mutating the ideas Britons had about how to hold onto the Raj. The Raj's liberal moment was caused by the anxieties of war.

When George V declared war in August 1914, few imagined India would play a big role in the conflict. But within weeks politicians in London ordered a mixed division of Europeans and Indians to East Africa, and two divisions to be sent to the Western Front. Two more of India's nine divisions were sent to Mesopotamia and Egypt. Indian soldiers sailed abroad and quickly died in battle: 525 Indian men were lost in one week on the Western Front in October 1914; 3,889 were killed in a single night at Ypres in April 1915, many from poison gas; 1,700 Indians died in the eight-month struggle at 1915 at Gallipoli. By the end of 1915, the two Indian infantry divisions in France were moved to the Middle East, where they besieged the Kut-al-Amara, and then captured Baghdad. For two and a half years, the Middle East was an exclusively Indian theatre. By 1918 there were a quarter of a million Indian troops in the Mesopotamian Command. Sixty-two thousand Indians were killed in total. To fill the rosters, the pace of recruitment increased. In 1914 the Indian army had been made up of 80,000 Britons and 230,000

Indians. During the war, an additional 800,000 Indian soldiers were recruited, and were joined by 400,000 non-fighting men.

War increased British concern about their security in India. The insurrection of 1857–8 still cast its shadow. British soldiers based in India were sent to Europe, too, but 'natives' were sent more quickly to avoid the chance of their mutinying. '[T]he more that go to war the less danger there is at home,' the Viceroy Lord Hardinge suggested when war broke out. In every other society, the nationalist leader Lala Lajpat Rai complained, people were being trained to defend their homeland, even African Americans and Indians in the United States. '[B]ut the Indians of India cannot keep arms.' British paranoia was so extreme that a thirteen-year-old boy was 'marched off' and sent to trial for showing his five-year-old friend how a cap gun worked.[4]

Underlying this paranoia was the fact that India had become, briefly and uniquely, vital to Britain's global geopolitical power. Britain itself massively outnumbered the rest of the empire in supplying troops to war. But 60 per cent of all non-British imperial soldiers fighting during the conflict were recruited from India. India became a source of money and materiel as well as men. India, with a tiny pre-war manufacturing industry, supplied 60,000 rifles and seventy million rounds of small arms ammunition. Large parts of India's railway network were broken up and shipped to Iraq and rebuilt there to transport troops. In 1917–18 alone, 1,800 miles of track, 13,000 feet of bridging, 200 engines and 6,000 other rail vehicles left India. The sandbags that walled the trenches on the Western Front were made of Bengal jute. Annual military expenditure quickly grew from £20 to £30 million. Indian taxpayers provided the British government a 'war gift' of £100 million, almost twice the Indian government's annual revenue. In addition, the British Indian regime subscribed to £100 million in war loans from American banks. Even the Viceroy complained of India being 'exploited by the war office'.[5]

The experience of war for most Indian soldiers was grim. Life on the Western Front tended to be better than the Middle East. But even in Europe, soldiers lived in wet trenches, ate poor food and were not trusted with machine guns for fear of mutiny. Better treatment occurred when they were wounded, when they were sent first to Southampton, then Brighton. There, a few injured Indian soldiers were treated in the luxurious surroundings of Prince Albert's orientalist architectural concoction, the Pavilion. Most were housed in a converted workhouse. In the Middle East, work often consisted of hard physical labour, supplies were poor, and even the injured were badly cared for. Most importantly, troops saw mass death and injury close at hand, when soldiering in India in the years before had rarely exposed troops to violence. In letters that were increasingly censored, soldiers wrote home expressing their rage at the horror of war. 'For God's sake', one Punjabi Muslim wrote to a friend, 'don't come, don't come, don't come to this war in Europe.' Some letter-writers accused the British of putting Indians in the front line before Europeans. News of bad conditions spread, making recruitment in some places difficult. In Amritsar, for example, women followed recruiters for miles trying to persuade recruits not to fight.[6]

The war changed the shape of British rule in India. It quickly led to a crisis in the recruitment of Britons into the imperial civil service, as young men destined for India were drafted as officers to command troops on the Western Front. As historian David Potter puts it, '1914 broke for ever the measured regularity of previous ICS recruitment. Others already in post left to fight. The result was a quick promotion of Indians to act as collectors, magistrates, police inspectors to fill the gap.'[7]

British officers believed they had no choice but to involve Indians more in day-to-day administration. In Punjab, where 60 per cent of soldiers were recruited, British officers conceded authority in the countryside to local aristocrats who acted as recruiting sergeants. War committees involved landholders, the leaders of local institutions and Indian government officers in the coordination of recruitment efforts. In many cases, these turned into local *panchayats*, taking on responsibility for welfare and dispute resolution. In the west of the province near the frontier with Afghanistan, local saints, or *pirs*, were enlisted to persuade tribal Muslims to support the war effort. Expanding the scope for 'Indian initiative' helped the recruitment of troops, and reduced support for anti-British revolutionaries.[8]

These local forms of cooperation overlapped with moves by senior officials and British politicians to allow more involvement of Indians in government. These moves were driven by fear, particularly that opposition to British rule might spread throughout India and dent the war effort. British officers were always frightened by revolutionary violence. A short-lived campaign of Indian terrorism in Punjab was suppressed in 1915, with forty-two people executed. But peaceful protest grew in 1916, as organizations campaigning for 'Home Rule' held meetings and sold pamphlets in every part of the subcontinent. In November, a joint meeting of the Indian National Congress and the Muslim League in the city of Lucknow proposed a programme of constitutional reform, which would have handed the government of India's provinces to elected Indian representatives. Officers in their cantonments and collectorates were scared of marches and petitions, and saw Indians campaigning for constitutional reform as seditious extremists, intent on causing revolution. Provincial governments and district officials urged repression. Sir Michael O'Dwyer, Governor of Punjab, wanted widespread arrests. Some Home Rule campaigners were interned, but the central government in Simla and Delhi did not think Home Rule campaigners were intent on revolution; and they did not believe they had the capacity to suppress a revolt even if there was an all-India plot, particularly not during war. The Viceroy urgently pressed the government in London to make quick concessions to prevent protest from escalating.

British fear culminated in a liberal moment. On 20 August 1917, the Secretary of State, Edwin Montagu, declared to the House of Commons that the government wanted the 'increasing association

of Indians in every branch of the administration', with the long-term
aim of India possessing 'responsible government within the British
empire'. By 1917, Britain was governed by a coalition between
Liberals and Conservatives. The precise words that Montagu spoke
were written by the arch-imperialist Curzon, who had come to
believe the empire would only be safe if power was given to Indian
elites in the provinces. Nonetheless, Curzon's text insisted that
the power of determining the pace of change lay with the British
Parliament. This was 'the language of the schoolmaster', as one
British critic of the imperial bureaucracy put it, willing to 'loosen
the bonds of discipline', but insistent that further progress depended
on 'good behaviour'. The words 'liberty' and 'self-government'
were carefully avoided in the final text. Motivated by an imperial
government in India desperate to uphold its authority but realistic
about its capacity, the empire's liberal moment was part of an effort
to bolster Britain's sovereignty in the subcontinent. As India's new
Viceroy, Lord Chelmsford, wrote to O'Dwyer, the declaration was
made 'for the purpose of allaying the political situation existing in
the country'. Its intention, Chelmsford said, was to create 'a political
truce'.[9]

The declaration connected to the increasingly liberal language
British politicians used to talk about their aims in fighting the war.
In August 1914, Britain had entered a war to defend its position
as the world's greatest imperial power. By 1916, it had begun to
justify its involvement with the language of liberty and justice.
Joining the war in 1917, the American President Woodrow Wilson
claimed the U.S.A was fighting 'against autocratic power' throughout the world, and for the 'liberation of its peoples'. As Lala Lajpat
Rai noted, Wilson's pronouncements 'raised hopes in the minds of
Indian Nationalists of justice being done to India in case the Allies
came out victorious'. The southern democrat's ideas of liberation
and democracy were highly racialized; Wilson certainly did not
imagine Asians or Africans would be able to govern themselves. In
reality, the last year of the conflict had expanded empire massively,

extending British domination throughout the Middle East and Africa. But once the war was over, Britain had no choice but to put some of its rhetoric of liberty into practice in its autocratically ruled dominions, or else face a crisis that could threaten its existence. The Russian revolution in 1917 seemed to presage the fate of regimes which tried to eradicate dissent by coercion alone. British regimes were challenged in Egypt, Palestine and Ireland as well as India. 'There is', the reform paper noted, 'a spirit of liberty in Asia, and India cannot be left behind.' Unbridled autocracy was dead.[10]

Something like revolution

This liberal moment created a brief sense of optimism among many Indian political leaders. It instilled in them the possibility that imperial institutions might not be incompatible with Indian efforts to create self-reliance and self-rule. In doing so, it created strange allies and challenging ideas. For a short period, for example, Mohandas K. Gandhi became both a supporter of imperial power and military force.

Gandhi had returned from South Africa in 1915. His first political work in India was to investigate increases in rent and land tax in two distant parts of the subcontinent, Champaran in Bihar and Kheda in Gujarat. In both places, Gandhi helped channel 'upward pressure from the rural masses themselves', as historian Jacques Pouchedepass puts it, into campaigns to improve living standards. Seen first by many nationalists as a strange religious crank, Gandhi gained a reputation for courage after refusing to leave Champaran when the British ordered him to do so in April 1917. A British officer wrote of him 'daily transfiguring the imaginations of ignorant men with visions of an early millennium'. But Gandhi's power did not come from his religious aura. It was based on an ability to persuade landlords and British officers as well as peasants to negotiate settlements; rent increases were cancelled in both districts. Gandhian politics involved 'a constant process of mediation' between groups of people who were antagonistic to one another, but who Gandhi and his fellow workers treated as friends or even brothers.

By the end of 1917, Gandhi's relationship with the British had been strengthened through his assistance in recruiting men for the war effort. To help his work in Champaran, Gandhi offered to recruit a corps of labourers from the local railway depot at Ranchi to build railways in Mesopotamia. Then, when he had moved back to Gujarat in early 1918, he volunteered as a recruiting agent for the British army, attending the British government's war conferences in Delhi in April and May. Gandhi wrote to the Viceroy saying that he would 'make India offer all her able-bodied sons as a sacrifice to the Empire at its critical moment' if he could. By that act, he thought 'racial distinctions would become a thing of the past'. Gandhi believed enlistment would teach nationalist volunteers the courage they would need in non-violent protest. 'Swaraj', he said, 'is not for lawyers and doctors but only for those who possess strength of arms.' 'Fight unconditionally unto death with the Briton for the victory and agitate simultaneously unto death, if we must, for the reforms that we deserve.' Reluctant to alienate their most popular recruiting sergeant, district officers agreed a compromise, and let peasants make reduced revenue payments in Gujarat.[11]

Towards the end of 1917 Edwin Montagu was quickly called to India, and there, jointly with the Viceroy Lord Chelmsford, wrote a set of reform proposals intended to stave off nationalist protest. The British cabinet debated the proposals five months before the war was over, in June 1918. Parliament passed them into law in December 1919. The 1919 Government of India Act introduced a 'democratic' element into every level of India's government, from local boards to the Viceroy's council. At the smallest scale, India's urban and rural councils became elected bodies, with Indian chairmen. In Delhi, a two-chamber imperial legislature was created to debate the actions of the central government. The Viceroy retained a veto and the power to push forward rejected bills. The architects of India's new constitution thought power was going to be concentrated at the provincial level. Here, a system of 'dyarchy' was established, where some matters became the responsibility of ministers accountable to elected provincial assemblies, and others of imperial bureaucrats ultimately accountable only to the Viceroy and British government. The idea was to replicate the relationship between the imperial Parliament in London and the white self-governing dominions in a miniature form. 'Local' issues like education, health and agriculture would be administered by elected politicians while 'imperial' questions such as taxation and defence were governed by central bureaucratic power.

The reforms were fiercely criticized by many nationalists. The electorate was small and had a say over limited matters; only 5.5 million property-holders were able to vote in the provincial assembly elections, one-tenth of the male population. Indian politicians had no real power because they did not control the budget. Many felt the reforms demonstrated that 'the bureaucrats were not prepared to give up materially any fraction of the power which they have enjoyed', as one Bombay newspaper complained. But before the brutality of the Amritsar killings started to sink in, most elite nationalist leaders were willing to think seriously about working within the new structure. Gandhi argued that the reforms could be 'considerably improved', but needed 'a sympathetic handling rather than a summary rejection'. In particular, he saw the reforms as the British abandonment of the right to rule India by force. The only case Britons had to stop Indians from taking over the government was the 'right of conquest', Gandhi said. But the reforms' authors had abandoned 'any claim' by that right. To begin with, Gandhi thought 'the old spirit of fear, distrust and consequent terrorism was about to give place to the new spirit of respect, trust and goodwill'.[12]

Gandhi's optimism was misplaced. Montagu and Chelmsford's new constitution introduced a 'democratic' element to government without challenging the instincts of a conquest state. Their constitution did not challenge the authoritarian instincts of the imperial bureaucracy. There was no revision of the structure of administration; no attempt to alter the mentality of the Raj's functionaries, with its emphasis on protecting British enclaves of power first, by force if need be. Indeed, elections and responsible ministers were introduced while the power of the imperial regime to coerce in times of crisis expanded. The Viceroy, the surprisingly radical soldier and cricketer Lord Chelmsford, only managed to persuade the hardcore of British provincial governors and district officers to support the reform scheme by continuing wartime coercive legislation into the peace. The Anarchical and Revolutionary Crimes Act of 1919 extended the government's right to detain suspected terrorists for two years without trial, and allowed the police to arrest anyone they wanted without a warrant. It was this piece of legislation that sparked the political campaign that ended up with army violence in Punjab, including the Amritsar massacre.

The fate of India's new constitution was shaped by the actions of its potential Indian participants, in particular their response to two forces: to government coercion and the economic crisis which followed the war. British violence in Punjab created widespread scepticism about the government's desire to involve Indians in the structure of power. It was Gandhi who went to Punjab to lead the Indian National Congress's inquiry into the Punjab disorders. To begin with, the prospect of an official inquiry into disorders gave Gandhi hope that the British government was willing to recognize and atone for its wrongs. But Gandhi, like the rest of Congress, saw the Hunter Commission's report as a shameful whitewash. The government's failure to prosecute and dismiss anyone other than Dyer for the 'misdeeds' in Punjab convinced him the goverment had become 'dishonest and unscrupulous'. The government's actions in Punjab were 'humiliating', and India's honour needed to be restored Gandhi agreed.

Nationalist frustration at the 'abominable despotism of the bureaucracy', as Tilak called it, was coupled with distrust of the British government's autocratic actions in the Middle East. There, the scale of British attempts to rearrange the borders of the Muslim world were slowly becoming apparent in India. Britain was supporting the dismemberment of the Ottoman empire and creation of an independent, secular Turkey as well as a separate monarchy in the Arabian peninsula. Britain was secretly carving the rest of the Middle East between its own French imperial power. For many Muslims, the Ottoman Sultan was the *khilafah*, ruler of the Turkish empire, but also spiritual leader of global Islam; many were outraged by his demise. A campaign against the partition of the sultan's lands had emerged among young Muslims in India during the war. Gandhi saw the abolition of the *khilafat* as an act of 'humiliation' for Muslims throughout the world. Joined to the Punjab atrocities, it was the issue on which he could build unity between Hindus and Muslims in India. 'I can no longer retain affection for a Government so evilly manned,' he said.[13]

Late in 1919, the Indian National Congress was still intent on participating in the new councils. Within a year, Gandhi had successfully persuaded his nationalist colleagues that they needed to restore their honour against a government that had acted dishonourably, and pull out. From maintaining 'friendly' terms with British officers in the districts he worked in in 1917, Gandhi had become the leader of nationwide mass protest against British rule. A general strike was called for 1 August 1920. People were urged to withdraw from government schools and law courts, to refuse to stand or vote in India's new constitution, and to court arrest. Gandhi's plan was to 'deliberately oppose the Government to the extent of trying to put its existence in jeopardy'. At the December 1920 meeting of Congress, Gandhi argued that a disciplined, India-wide campaign of non-cooperation would lead to *swaraj*, self-rule, within a year, whether within or outside the British empire.

Many, Britons and Indians, experienced 1921 as a year of revolution. The Governor of the United Provinces described the year's strikes, anti-rent campaigns and riots as 'the beginnings of something like revolution'. The socialist leader Jayaprakash Narayan spoke throughout his life of 'the tradition of 1921', calling it 'the most glorious page in the living history of our national revolution'.

Nineteen twenty-one saw the national emergence of many figures who would lead Indian politics for the next generation: Rajendra Prasad, Abul Kalam Azad and, most of all, Jawaharlal Nehru, to name three. Thousands of young men and women abandoned the prospect of an education or a good career for the sake of the national movement. Some were from elite backgrounds; Jawaharlal's father was a wealthy nationalist lawyer who could provide an income if he didn't have a job. Others were not. Jayaprakash Narayan was a recently married nineteen-year-old, the son of a minor clerk in the canal department, when he left Patna College to join the nationalist movement twenty days before his exams. He had no resources to fall back on if the revolution failed.[14]

But in many places, peasants and workers, not lawyers and clerks, drove the uprising. Their protest was fuelled by the declining economic condition of India in the years after the end of the First World War. The war expanded the demand for crops and other consumer goods while decreasing production for everything not directly connected with the war effort. India's £100 million war loan needed to be paid for by Indian peasants. In many places, landlords keen to ingratiate themselves with the authorities pressured peasants to subscribe. Crops were exported to feed men and horses in the Middle East, and these exports put pressure on agriculture. '[F]odder is being exported while the Deccan starves,' the Governor of Bombay candidly admitted to the Governor-General in private. If there was ever a moment when wealth was drained out of India, this was it.

As a result, the cost of consumer goods spiralled during the war, with the price of rice trebling between 1911 and 1920 in many places, for example. Famine returned in some places, and, coupled with influenza, killed millions in 1918–19 and 1920–21. Demographers calculate that there were eleven to thirteen million excess deaths in these years compared with the average. Hardship came late to India's cities, but hit in 1921. *Investors' India Year Book* described it as 'the greatest and most widespread period of depression that has ever been experienced'. A rapid decline in both rural and urban living standards created anger directed both at landlords and British power. As one British intelligence officer put it, peasants thought 'that they supplied the men and the money and [the Government] issued them with bits of paper instead'.[15]

Congress's 1921 non-cooperation movement was a 'chameleon campaign' as Judith Brown calls it, channelling thousands of different local campaigns and approaches into an onslaught against the British on a scale not seen since 1857. It linked with the grievances of tea garden workers in Assam, cattle grazers in Bihar, Sikhs trying to re-establish control of temples from unorthodox factions, prosperous peasants protesting against increasing taxes in coastal Andhra, poor Muslim peasants in Kerala. The rural area between Lucknow and Benares in Gangetic north India was a strong centre for the movement. There, peasant associations had been organizing from the end of the war in far greater numbers than ever before; 100,000 joined the peasant associations in the first months of 1920, before nationalists from outside the region arrived, with tens of thousands at demonstrations. Peasant leaders thought their protests would have more chance of success if they linked up with Congress's campaigns. As one organizer in Awadh put it, 'if we could link our Kisan [peasant] movement with some established organization, or gain the support of well-to do groups and lawyers, then this movement would become the future of India.'

The non-cooperation movement involved some of the wealthy and powerful. Ahmedabad industrialists and rich Calcutta lawyers were reluctant to quit their expensive clubs and abandon their imported whiskies but took part. Many of the latter were worried that 'the country is running amuck after the Sainthood of Mr. Gandhi', as a pro-nationalist British observer put it, but performed token acts of sacrifice for the sake of appearances. Gandhi was aware of the different shades of opinion the campaign needed to incorporate and adjusted his message depending on the audience. On 19 August 1920, on a journey which ended up in Kerala, Gandhi visited Mangalore, speaking at a meeting chaired by the merchant and founder of Corporation Bank, Haji Abdulla Haji Kasim. By then Haji Abdulla was a member of the Madras legislative council and had accepted the imperial title of Bahadur Khan. Gandhi gave a speech challenging the chairman's willingness to accept imperial trophies. It would take 'only a little self-sacrifice', he suggested, if 'your Khan Bahadurs and other title-holders were to renounce their titles'. Men like Haji Abdulla could take a stand while surrendering 'no earthly riches'. In fact, the resignation of titles was the least successful component of the non-cooperation movement. Rabindranath Tagore famously renounced his knighthood in the aftermath of the Jallianwala Bagh massacre, refusing a badge of honour 'in the incongruous context of humiliation'. But by January 1921, only twenty-four out of 5,186 Indian titleholders had resigned. The government chronicler of the movement suggested that those honoured 'were not the kind of people to be carried away by the Non-Cooperation agitation'.[16]

The movement was most successful where it connected with people's interests, or where campaigns were linked to prior patterns of nationalist institution building. The boycott of British cotton was championed by small-scale Indian traders and manufacturers, and saw the import of cloth almost halve between 1920–21 and 1921–2. Bonfires of foreign cloth were lit in every city. *Khadi*, the homespun white cotton championed by Gandhi, became the uniform of politicians; the campaign saw a surge in retailers branding themselves as *khadi*-sellers, as well as the resurgence of Swadeshi manufacturing. Support for the non-payment of taxes was overwhelming, in the small number of districts where Gandhi approved this most dramatic form of civil disobedience. School and college students quit government teaching institutions in large numbers although most eventually returned. In Bengal alone, 24,000 students left them. As in 1906, national schools, colleges and local volunteer associations flourished. Non-cooperation created a massive, nationwide body of nationalist political organizers for the first time, with thousands of volunteers and money to finance its work. Some 14,582 delegates attended the annual Congress at Nagpur in November 1920, the session where the full non-cooperation programme was agreed. Ten million rupees (£129 million in 2016 prices) were collected in the three months between April and June 1921.[17]

But the non-cooperation movement did not see India's middle classes abandon the institutions which upheld British power. The number of resignations by Indian government officers was 'infinitesimal', as the Viceroy put it, with scattered resignations of police officers and honorary magistrates. A hundred and eighty lawyers quit, but most returned to their practices after a few months. Very few academics left government universities.

This failure of elite non-cooperation partly occurred because middle-class government workers were worried about the breakdown of law and order which might accompany an administrative collapse. A few were actively loyal to the Raj, but many were loyal to the effective working of modern governmental authority, whoever happened to be in command. In some spheres, employees did not leave because government institutions were already Indianized. By the 1920s, the judiciary was largely Indian. There were only a tiny number of non-Indian teachers and administrators in Indian universities. Indian universities were part of worldwide research networks. Physicists and chemists were denied political citizenship in their own society, but participated as equal members of the global enterprise of science. University departments of history and political science were free to construct narratives about India's sophisticated and self-governing national future and past. The new universities of Allahabad and Dhaka saw a flourishing of research on ancient and medieval Indian history showing how the prosperity and political order of a plural society were maintained before the British conquest. Nationalist leaders who built autonomous organizations within the often loose matrix of imperial power were equally sceptical. Lala Lajpat Pai criticized the movement, for example, because students at his Dayananda Anglo-Vedic College

in Lahore were asked to join the boycott. The institution taught
boys in order to renew Indian skill and honour, but it was affiliated
to the University of Punjab and received government funding. For
many lawyers, academics and educationalists, the scope for nation-
building in nominally imperial institutions made non-cooperation
seem a futile enterprise.

The government's story depicted the non-cooperation movement as a battle between order and chaos. In their narrative, the
rational order represented by the British government was overcome
by the irrational passions of India's illiterate masses. One version
of this narrative, commissioned by Parliament and approved by
the Secretary of State for India, was written by the imperial government's Director of Public Information and fellow of All Souls
College, Oxford, Rushbrook Williams. Williams described Gandhi
as a charismatic but naïve idealist, caught up in a movement he
could not control. He noted that Gandhi himself saw *swaraj* as 'the
government of the self', and aimed at the creation of a society where
individuals had far greater self-mastery, not political independence.
Williams thought his aims were laudable. But Gandhi's vagueness
about his political goals, and his refusal to exclude anyone from
his political coalition, 'sowed the seeds of disruption within his
movement'.

Williams narrated the events of 1921–2 as a 'tale of anarchy and
disorder'. Chaos spread throughout northern India, with sporadic
instances of arson, looting and riot. Most seriously, '[t]he terrible
Moplah Outbreak' in Kerala saw largely Muslim peasants attack the
British government and Hindu landlords on a massive scale. Riots
broke out in Bombay when the Prince of Wales visited in November;
a city-wide strike brought Calcutta to a standstill. By November
1921, the Government of Bengal wrote that the non-cooperation
movement 'has built an organization of very real power'; 'this it will
be necessary to break if decent administration is to be restored'. The
government 'found themselves obliged' to institute a more repressive approach. The Congress's volunteer organizations were banned;

volunteers in large numbers were arrested. Baton charges became common. The greatest violence occurred when the Kerala uprising was suppressed by a full-scale military occupation by Gurkha soldiers, with forty-three imperial troops and 2,000 rebels killed. In the most savage incident, not mentioned in Williams's account, sixty-seven prisoners died of suffocation when they were crammed into a train wagon on their way to gaol.[18]

Like other British and some Indian observers, Rushbrook Williams thought violence was naturally present in the Indian crowd. Gandhi and other senior Congress leaders told a different story. Their version of events placed the violent forces of British imperialism squarely as a protagonist. For Gandhi, it was the forceful passions of imperial power which elicited the undisciplined response of Indian protesters. Violence was, for him, linked to the passionate desire of people to achieve instant emotional gratification. But Gandhi thought a regime based on conquest was peculiarly prone to create violent situations: 'Let it be remembered', he wrote in an article in July 1921, 'that violence is the keystone of the Government edifice.' Gandhi thought violence occurred in cycles, as one act created a more violent retaliation and events spun out of control. The July article criticized a moment at Aligarh in north India when a crowd committed arson. Their fault, though, lay in responding to the provocation of British force, a failing which led to greater repression. The same process took place in Kerala. The Moplah rebellion began as a response to the police raiding a mosque; the Indian failure to eschew violence when responding to repression led to a massive government crackdown. Events such as these proved that the imperial state 'had rendered itself almost immune from violence on our side', as acts of violent protest would be used as an excuse for imperial authorities to assert greater force.

This was the logic which led Gandhi to suspend the non-cooperation movement in February 1922. Gandhi's decision came in the midst of another cycle of violence, which began in the small town of Chauri Chaura near the border between Indian and Nepal.

On 2 February, a crowd gathered in the marketplace demanding a reduction in high meat prices. They were beaten by the local police, and several leaders locked up in the police station. A well-organized protest was instigated; the police fired shots in the air and beat up a Congress volunteer; protesters threw stones; police retaliated by shooting into the crowds, killing three and then, disastrously, retreated into their station. This retreat led an impassioned crowd to burn the building down, killing the twenty-three policemen trapped inside. Within two days, a cycle of protest that began with shouts in the marketplace against the cost of mutton had escalated into a massive military clampdown. The government imposed martial law and raided houses throughout the town. Two hundred and twenty-eight people were tried. One hundred and seventy-two people were initially sentenced to death, although eventually only nineteen were hanged.

Gandhi thought the cycle could only be broken by stopping the campaign and performing an act of penance. He fasted for five days and announced the suspension of all activities which challenged British authority. By February 1922, the imperial government faced a clamour of criticism from officers and Conservative politicians demanded a crackdown. The nationalist decision to call off the non-cooperation movement gave the imperial government the opportunity to respond to its overenthusiastic allies. With no nationwide organized challenge to British power, the government finally had the courage to arrest Gandhi. On 10 March he was sentenced to six years for sedition, but was released after eighteen months when his health made the British authorities fear he might die in gaol.[19]

Some of Gandhi's more radical colleagues complained that the suspension of the non-cooperation campaign saved the British Raj. It is impossible to predict what would have happened if the campaign had not been brought to a quick end. One scenario is that escalating violence on both sides would have pushed potential nationalists to side with the British. Until the 1920s, the empire's anonymous systems of modern power, its law courts and irrigation canals and railway lines involved many of India's middle classes without forcing them to choose sides for or against the British empire. Many were quiet nationalists, who wanted to see Indians ruling every tier of government in the subcontinent before too long. But a protest movement that to many would have looked increasingly like a chaotic mob might have caused substantial numbers to side with imperial order. Congress's campaign had made only a small dent in the submission of Indian soldiers to imperial command; after the Bombay riots of November 1921 industrialists in that city backed off from confrontation. Even at the height of the movement, British authorities had enough Indian tax collectors and police officers, railway guards and sub-magistrates to maintain their limited but functioning command over Indian society. If violence continued, many more middle-class Indians would have reluctantly chosen to side with imperial forces they associated with order rather than anarchy. A regime whose force always lay in its capacity to assert violence would have had an opportunity to shore up its fragile administration. Perhaps the relative peace of the years after 1922 allowed imperial power to collapse quietly but more emphatically than it might have done otherwise.

The decline of the Collector

C. S. Venkatachar arrived at Fatehgarh, a district capital situated on the Ganges eighty miles to the north of Kanpur, in January 1923, eleven months after Gandhi's suspension of non-cooperation. Then twenty-two years old, Venkatachar had recently returned to India after two years in Britain. Born in Bangalore, he studied at Madras University and had been offered a place at Manchester University to study the new science of chemical engineering. While in London he chose instead to sit for the Indian Civil Service examinations. Venkatachar's year saw the wartime slump in British recruitment into the ICS continue. Talented British university graduates were put off by the diminished prospects of needing to share authority with Indians, together with the loss of purchasing power caused by Indian inflation. A hundred and fifty candidates sat the ICS exams in London, with thirteen Indians and only three British passing. The heavy Indian bias of Venkatachar's batch led to a flurry of imperial hand-wringing among the Tory defenders of empire in Britain. These criticisms culminated in David Lloyd George's speech in the House of Commons celebrating the permanence of India's 'steel frame'. Venkatachar noted in his memoir that Lloyd George's words were a sign that 'the imperialist legend' of the Indian Civil Service 'had abruptly come to an end'. As the report commissioned by a worried British government in 1924 into the mood of the 'superior civil services' put it, 'an Indian career occupies a position in popular estimation in England decidedly inferior to the position it occupied in 1902.'[20]

On the last stage of his journey to Fatehgarh, Venkatachar shared a carriage with a man who had resigned as superintendent of the local post office, in belated response to Gandhi's call to boycott imperial institutions. 'Here I was,' he wrote in his memoir, 'entering the portals of the Raj; this odd fellow was leaving it.' At Fatehgarh the new imperial official found a British regime in a state of unease, fearful that the actions of men like Venkatachar's travelling companion would force them to quit India.

British civil servants were nostalgic for the authority and calm they supposedly enjoyed in days gone by. The Collector whom Venkatachar first worked with 'reminisced of the idyllic life he had led as a junior officer, playing polo'; but having weathered the 'Gandhian storm', he was desperately trying to leave India. Arthur Collett his second Collector, was from a family of British officers who had served in southern India, but chose himself a posting in the United Provinces because he was fond of pig-sticking. Collett had been the Collector of the district where the burning of Chauri Chaura had taken place. The revolution of 1921 caused him to leave India, too; he was persuaded back by the governor of the province to hold the British line, but retired early. These men were nostalgic for 'a wholly bureaucratic system, unexposed to criticism or inter-ference on the part of representatives of the people', as a 1924 report into the conditions of the civil service put it. What they did not notice was the quiet erosion of British power in the countryside, as peasants and small landlords increasingly supported leaders hostile to imperial authority.[21]

Venkatachar was being trained to occupy the post of District Collector, the central figure in the imperial iconography of power. The position of Collector began with Lord Cornwallis's reforms of the 1790s, when East India Company officials were sent into India's district capitals. By the late nineteenth century the district officer had accumulated the titles of Collector and Magistrate, and was the conduit for every form of imperial power at the lowest scale of government ruled by European officials. He was the chief magistrate, head revenue collector and primary coordinator of all functions of government in the district he presided over. British bureaucrats were used to thinking that the silent and largely unac-countable working of imperial chains of command was the epitome of efficiency. As a district official – he first acted as Collector at the age of twenty-nine, in 1927 – Venkatachar described his time being taken up by routine scrutiny. The main job was to make sure the work of myriad local functionaries, from the village accountant to the keeper of arms licences to the local irrigation officer, was being done according to rules passed down from the apex of imperial power. British rule did little that was active; there was no 'devel-opment' work in the 1920s. In its local work the British regime 'possessed a remarkable uniformity of procedure, forms, technique and thought'. Ultimately, the administration worked through a 'show of force', and the ability to bribe and bludgeon enough local notables to support British power.

The Montagu–Chelmsford reforms created new, official struc-tures of authority to rival this imperial hierarchy. Much of the district officers' work was now directed by Indian ministers who held power at a provincial level. Policing and finance were 'reserved' for imperial bureaucrats; but most public works, education and agriculture were administered by elected politicians, based not in the district but the provincial capital. Collectors were no longer the sole point of visible power in a district. 'The politician now stood forth as the mediator and had displaced the district officer,' as Venkatachar put it; 'the decline in the influence of the collector's position was visible.'

Before 1923, Congress was unanimous in boycotting elections to the new provincial and all-Indian councils so the British needed to rely on other political groups. After the first election to the new provincial councils, in 1921, ministerial office was occupied by a mix of local aristocrats and liberal political leaders put off by Congress's radical turn. Irritated by the corrosion of their authority, British officials almost universally castigated the actions of these newly elected Indian leaders. Officials in one province noted that 'great strain was thrown on the permanent officials by the tendency on the part of Ministers to carry out popular wishes (based on ignorance) without careful consideration.' British officers criticized Indian representatives for failing to 'properly' connect with voters, for refusing to 'educate' the electorate about the realities of power, for their 'mediocre' intellect together with their 'fanatical views'.[22]

In practice, in many places newly elected politicians pushed the expansion of publicly funded services as quickly as provincial finances would allow. After decades during which publicly funded primary education was extended very slowly, Indian ministers passed laws which made school attendance compulsory for the first time. Primary school was mandatory in Bombay province in 1923 (excluding Bombay city, where mill-owners did not want children to go to school) and Bengal in 1930. In the United Provinces, where Venkatachar was posted, the decision was left to the newly elected district boards; most made primary school compulsory in 1926. Even before these legal changes, the number of children attending school grew quickly throughout India: 2.9 million pupils were enrolled in the first year of primary school in 1916–17; 5.3 million in 1926–7. Alongside schools, the new ministers built irrigation projects and hydro-electric schemes, land banks and agricultural cooperatives.

The clash between British officers and Indian political leaders within and outside the new institutions meant the capacity of imperial administration collapsed in the early 1920s. British India's governments were vulnerable to financial crises, as peasant protesters and nationalist campaigners blocked the collection of revenue. Land revenue and excise duties were controlled by British finance officers in provincial governments, so their payment was often resisted. If an area 'can organise itself sufficiently it can resist the introduction of a revised settlement', the Governor of Bombay admitted in 1929.[23] Congress-backed temperance campaigns cut the collection of taxes levied on the sale of alcohol. In Madras, these had a devastating impact, cutting the province's income by eight million rupees in 1921–2 (8 per cent of the province's total expenditure that year). When the provincial assembly refused to increase other taxes, the government needed to cut personnel: 4,765 constables and 7,000 village staff lost their jobs. British control of the commanding heights of the imperial state meant the incomes of Europeans were kept safe, but officials in Madras complained that the crisis 'contributed not a little to the sense of alarm and insecurity which has pervaded the services'.[24]

In many cases, it was local councils in towns and districts, not the new provincial government which most aggressively pushed public improvement. Many of the mundane functions of government had been administered by these institutions from the 1860s. By the 1920s India had 752 urban municipalities, and an elected board in every district. Imperial bureaucrats initially saw 'local self-government' as a way for the imperial government to offload the costs of things like roads and municipal waterworks onto local elites. As long as the enclaves of European power – the cantonments and civil lines – remained in the hands of the military, the authors of the Montagu–Chelmsford reforms were happy to hand these local resources over to 'popular control'. Beyond the places where they themselves resided, British administrators thought the destiny of imperial power was not to be determined by who ran the sewage system.

Congress's boycott of imperial institutions did not extend to local government. In many parts of India during the 1920s and early 1930s, local government became a nationalist stronghold. In Calcutta directly elected mayors controlled a budget of more than twenty million rupees after 1923. Calcutta's voters chose radical critics of British rule, first Chittaranjan Das, then Subhas Chandra Bose, to run their city. In Fatehgarh, Venkatachar noted that nationalist political leaders 'took a great interest' in local elections even when other institutions were boycotted. In many towns and districts, public offices flew Congress flags and ensured that government-funded schools taught anti-British curricula. When the imperial regime introduced new rules banning teachers from 'political agitation', they were often simply ignored. It was, after all, the local elected district board which had responsibility for the discipline of school employees.

The result was a renaissance of local Indian power in the cities and districts of India, and the creation of another organizing centre for nationalist practice and ideas. Even the British hierarchy admitted the productive effect of local Indian political leadership. 'There has been a very general and very marked growth in the interest taken in the extension of education and of medical facilities', the British government's 1929 report into the working of the new constitution noted. The report's authors thought the extension of elections to the province of Bihar and Orissa's district boards led to a fall in 'efficiency' but had no choice but to report a big expansion in the province's medical infrastructure; since the reforms had come into effect, the number of medical dispensaries increased from 178 to 319, 'a substantial achievement'.[25]

While more institutionally-minded Congress politicians spread throughout local government, Gandhi's allies concentrated on 'constructive work' instead, focusing on the practical task of 'nation-building'. The Gandhians placed particular emphasis on encouraging everyone to spin their own cotton. Spinning, weaving and wearing plain, rough, white *khadi* cloth was a rejection both of Western dress and the idea of India as a collection of communities separated by their own sartorial traditions. Unlike election to imperial or local assemblies, this allowed women to work as equal participants in the creation of the nation. As Gandhi wrote, *khadi* 'binds all brothers and sisters into one'. In the five years which followed the massacre at Amritsar, white cotton and the Gandhi *topi* (hat) became a uniform for nationalists and a visible but peaceful sign of confrontation with British power.

Lost Dominion

The various confrontations and crises which seemed to beset imperial power in the early 1920s led British men interested in the continuity of their regime to pressure for tough, forceful action to restore imperial authority. Anxious British officers and their backers in London called for a return to the spirit of conquest in order to undo the weakening of British power they had seen since the end of the war. In Fatehgarh, C. S. Venkatachar noted the circulation of one such call, a book published in 1924 in the name of A. L. Carthill. *The Lost Dominion* was a publishing 'sensation', according to Lala Lajpat Rai. The book stood in a long line of imperial texts lamenting the contemporary weakness of the Raj and urging Britons in India to stand forth as benevolent, violent despots.

Carthill was a pseudonym for Bennet Christian Calcraft-Kennedy, the son of a clergyman who served as Collector, magistrate and judicial commissioner in western India, and retired as a judge in 1926. Calcraft-Kennedy's experience in government led him to believe in the centrality of force to sustain British rule. He criticized the British government for handing power to 'literary

Indians', and 'clever politicians' whose rule, he thought, would bring down stable government and order. Britain's 'mission' in India was 'high and holy', he argued, but could only be maintained by a policy of 'constructive repression', which denied the Indian public any role in their own rule. Calcraft-Kennedy's book caught the imagination of a good proportion of British officers. Sir Michael O'Dwyer, the hardline governor of Punjab and supporter of General Dyer, liked it so much that he structured the last chapter of his own, 1926, memoir around the argument of the book. India was not 'lost' to Britain, O'Dwyer argued, but it could only be preserved by 'broad, firm and consistent statesmanship', backed up by physical force.

From the small outpost of British rule at Fatehgarh, Venkatachar thought the book expressed the 'doubts and misgivings' of the British about the future of British rule. The book was the catalyst for the newly appointed Indian civil servant to discuss the philosophy of imperial power with his disillusioned English superior. The English Collector Arthur Collett thought that men like Calcraft-Kennedy and O'Dwyer were right in thinking violence could keep India under some kind of British rule. For Venkatachar as much as British officers, the working of the British regime depended on the display of violence from day to day. Force was displayed in different ways; by the placing of gangs of armed soldiers in visible places to prevent 'trouble'; by the arrest of political leaders who challenged imperial power; or by officers dashing off on their motorbikes to shoot dangerous wild animals, as Collett's replacement the 'dare-devil' Michael Nethersole did. But 'the whole concept of government by force had been metamorphosed by the Amritsar massacre', Collett thought. Extreme acts of violence were difficult to justify in the eyes of the British or Indian public. Coercion was continually criticized by a range of official and non-official bodies, from local Congress committees and town bar councils to speeches made in the House of Commons. The Montagu–Chelmsford reforms had helped to create pockets of official power which directly challenged the will of the imperial hierarchy.[26]

The result was that the contradictions present within India's post-war political settlement became even more marked. British sovereignty could only be retained if more power was handed away. But coercion was also intensified. To avoid the humiliating spectacle of set-piece battles with Congress politicians in court, the imperial regime tried to avoid using the regular justice system to suppress its opponents. The government became a more actively political force, trying to enlist allies and punish its enemies, turning district towns into battlegrounds between the supporters and opponents of British power. When its critics displayed themselves in public, it used its police and soldiers to move protesters away from public spaces. Mass arrests, the tactic used in the early 1920s, treated protesters as individuals, but opened the imperial state to public humiliation in court. Instead, the police and army treated protesters as nameless members of crowds, trying to restrain and move masses of people away from places associated with British power. In place of the mass arrest, the lathi charge became the most common coercive strategy.[27]

The game we have to play

By the mid-1920s, the failure of India's new constitution to create a stable form of imperial power led to a spate of parliamentary reports and inquiries; the Lee Commission reported into the Raj's failure to recruit enough British officers; the Mudiman Commission into deadlock within India's diarchic constitution; the Linlithgow Commission into the crisis of Indian agriculture. The crisis was bad enough for Stanley Baldwin's Conservative government in Britain to appoint a full inquiry into the working of the Montagu–Chelmsford constitution. The original act insisted a review take place within ten years, but in November 1927 King George V issued a royal warrant to a committee of seven men to inquire into 'the development of representative institutions in India'. The commission was led by the liberal Sir John Simon, and included three soldiers, two lords and representatives from all the main British political parties, including Labour's Clement Attlee. But it was an all-British body. To ensure British interests were protected, perhaps to ensure unanimity, no Indian was asked to deliberate on his or her own country's future. When they saw the scale of hostility to the appointment of this all-white body, the commissioners tried to compensate with the idea of Indian politicians electing a committee of their own, and then holding a 'joint free conference' in Delhi to shape India's political destiny. That did not stop the Simon Commission from facing uproar when it arrived in India for the first of its two visits, in February 1928.

One response came with the appointment of a rival, Indian committee. Faced with Indian hostility, the Secretary of State for India had encouraged the 'malcontents to produce their own proposals'. Motivated by the provocation that they would be unable to agree a constitution, political leaders from widely different perspectives came together to try to frame the political future of India. Deliberations were led by the liberal, one-time loyalist leader Tej Bahadur Sapru and the Congress lawyer Motilal Nehru. Nehru's son, the then 38-year-old Jawaharlal, acted as secretary. Defying Lord Birkenhead's taunts, the Nehru committee quickly framed a constitution for a self-governing India. The document included a bill of rights, a declaration that all authority lay with the people, and a reconfiguration of administration so that power lay not with India's communities and provinces but with central government.

Written with the aim of gaining the widest Indian support, the Nehru report was a conservative document. It emphatically refused to discuss the dispossession of propertied elites, for example. It was also clear in retaining the imperial distribution of authority between different tiers of government, in many cases merely replacing British command with Indian deliberation. In that sense, the report marked an important shift in the politics of Indian nationalism. Its structure was a sign that leading figures within the nationalist movement were moving away from the politics of bottom-up nation building and community self-reliance. Since the late nineteenth century, an important source of political energy lay in local institution building; it was this kind of politics which dominated the regional movements of the late nineteenth century, the practical work of the Swadeshi movement, even non-cooperation with its emphasis on spinning as a counterpart to the boycott of British cloth. The Nehru report showed that this style was being eclipsed by a politics which had elections, law making and the ability to command the bureaucratic machinery of state as its end goal. The aim was to take over instruments of imperial state power and use them for nationalist ends.

That shift transformed Gandhi's role from that of a major figure shaping the direction of Congress politics into a symbol of and talisman for a movement whose purpose was shaped by others. Gandhi initially refused to attend the deliberations of the Nehru committee, and then asked to 'be excused' from presiding at the conference held to 'uphold and popularise' the report. In a letter replying to Motilal Nehru's plea for Gandhi to attend, he asked, 'what shall I do there?' Instead of 'constitution-building', Gandhi wanted to concentrate on 'constructive work'; not only spinning and weaving, but working to quell the violence between Muslims and Hindus which was increasingly breaking out. The end of the non-cooperation movement saw the emergence of a different kind of crowd, about whose potential for violence Gandhi was equally concerned. A serious riot occurred in Calcutta in April 1926; during the next twelve months forty riots caused 197 deaths and injuries to 1,600. Riots occurred as economic dislocation increased stress, local religious assertion increased tension and a foreign government offered no cross-communal leadership. Gandhi tried friendship, fasting, writing and a peace conference to stop the violence. In September 1928, the aftermath of riots at Godhra in Gujarat attracted his attention more than a conversation among liberals and lawyers about how to operate state power.[28]

The response to the Nehru report was structured by this growing mistrust and fear of violence. Muslim political leaders helped to write the report, but many felt that its focus on the authority of the

central Indian state did not pay enough attention to the interests of
minorities. Too much room was left open for the Hindu majority to
elect politicians who would oppress Muslims, they thought. Many
in the Muslim League thought that giving more power to India's
provinces, some of which had Muslim majorities, would ensure
India's diversity was taken into account in post-imperial decision-
making. But these were years when organizations representing the
rival interests of different religious communities quickly grew. The
Hindu Mahasabha, for example, founded in 1915, developed into
a major political force. Lobbied by increasingly vocal Hindu politicians, the Nehru committee was reluctant to concede to Muslim
arguments, refusing to recommend the separate representation of
minorities throughout India. According to Muslim League leader
Muhammad Ali Jinnah, India's putative constitution-makers had
adopted 'a narrow-minded policy' which would 'ruin the political
future of the Muslims'.

Later on, Muhammad Ali Jinnah described the Nehru report as
the 'parting of the ways' between Congress and the Muslim League.
But in 1928, the cycles of Indian protest and British reaction were
more significant than Hindu–Muslim tension in shaping the political life of the subcontinent. The all-white Simon Commission
did not have any trouble recruiting committees of Indian political leaders to offer it advice in every province. But its arrival saw
the return of organized street protests, and the politics of boycott
and non-cooperation. When they arrived at Bombay in February
1928, the committee members were greeted by a national strike.
Thousands lined their route with black flags. When the committee
toured again in October 1928, it was met by throngs of nationalist
volunteers protesting in the streets of every city it visited. At Lahore
in Punjab, protests were led by Lala Lajpat Rai. These were years
when elite political leaders and British officials alike were gripped by
fear of the 'Indian mob'. Lajpat Rai was a figure described as having
'a soothing effect [o]n the fury of the crowd' by an Indian political
scientist a few years later. 'Even crowds', Ilyas Ahmad wrote in 1940,

echoing the view of the Indian members of the Hunter Commission twenty-one years before, 'can be influenced to discipline and to the idea of consequences.'[28]

After playing a central role in the Swadeshi movement, Lajpat Rai had been deported in 1907, then went into voluntary exile to the United States during the First World War. There, he built up an India Information Bureau, read political philosophy and increased support for Indian nationalist causes. Initially denied permission to return to India in the aftermath of the Amritsar massacre, he was granted a passport in February 1920 and, like Gandhi, returned to be greeted by crowds. Lajpat Rai led the walkout of students from government institutions in Punjab and was then jailed during the non-cooperation movement in 1921. He was elected to the Imperial Legislative Assembly once non-cooperation was suspended in 1923. It was Lajpat Rai who moved the motion in the assembly urging a boycott of the Simon Commission.

Even in the late 1920s, Lajpat Rai's politics were still concerned with undoing the 'fact of conquest', as he called it, by building Indian organization and self-reliance. His continual aim was to force the imperial state to hand power over to the institutions of Indian society. 'The duty of every Indian patriot', he wrote in 1922, 'consists in educating his people to formulate their will and to acquire the training, the discipline and the power of imposing it on their foreign masters.' But, like many of his compatriots, Lajpat Rai's thinking had taken a more statist turn. 'It is', he wrote in the months before the Simon Commission protests, 'the duty of the State to see that its people are not illiterate'; it was 'the responsibility of the State in equipping the citizen properly for the race of life'. While Gandhi always saw the state as an institution founded on violence, for Lajpat Rai it was something far greater than the capacity of the government to tax and coerce. According to the latest political philosophy, Lajpat Rai argued, '[t]he state is no longer a sovereign power issuing commands'; it was made up of the collective duties which citizens who shared some kind of common feeling owed to one another. A regime which tried to issue commands based on the threat of violence had no effective power, he argued.[29]

Leading protesters against the Simon Commission on 30 October 1928, Lajpat Rai came up against British officers who believed the power of the imperial state would only survive through the use of force. Congress organized a strike in Lahore for the day the commission would arrive in the city. British officials were worried that crowds would stop the committee from stepping off their train, so set up a barricade around the railway station. Lajpat Rai led a march to confront the blockade. Seriously outnumbered, police commanders responded by ordering their men to march forward beating protesters with lathis. There were no arrests. The idea was simply to drive protesters away, and avoid the public and laborious process of being confronted by nationalists in court. Lajpat Rai was surrounded by minders, but police broke through and injured him on the left chest and shoulder. Hearing about the attack, Gandhi's response was to telegram immediate congratulations to the Punjabi leader. Lajpat Rai's injuries were a moment of 'good fortune'. By demonstrating courage against force, the attack held out the prospect of a 'full transformation of authority' and the conversion of 'government by the sword' into government 'based on popular will and confidence'. The 'assault', Gandhi said, was 'part of the game we have to play'. 'Swaraj' would only come when Indians were willing to die.

Lajpat Rai did die of a heart attack eighteen days after his beating, his doctor claiming the sixty-three-year-old's death was brought on by the assault. He became Indian nationalism's greatest martyr. His death brought 100,000 silent mourners onto the streets of Lahore for his funeral; in his death at least, Lajpat Rai did have a restraining effect on the crowd. But it also catalysed calls for a more aggressive campaign to break British power. Pressure mounted from Bombay and Bengal as well as Punjab for a return to civil disobedience. The talk beforehand had been of India becoming a self-governing dominion within Britain's empire. After Lajpat Rai's death, it was

increasingly about the complete renunciation of any form of imperial sovereignty and independence. Gandhi tried to be a restraining
force, arguing that Congress needed to confine itself to 'constructive work', boycott and the redress of 'specific grievances', thinking
independence was unimaginable if the divisions between different
groups of Indians were healed. But the mood was for a complete
break, and an unprecedented onslaught on the institutions of British
state power.

14

CYCLES OF VIOLENCE

As the great fascist powers conquered mainland Europe, a mild-mannered academic gave a speech looking forward to a time when public life would be 'dominated not by passion but by reason'. Beni Prasad was still only forty-five in December 1940, but had been head of the Allahabad University politics department for over a decade. As one of India's best-regarded observers of politics he had been asked to give the presidential address to the third session of the newly formed Indian Political Science Association. Prasad argued that the self-governing future of India lay in a regional federation. For Prasad, fusing the passions of national identity with the power of the state was the kind of outdated politics which had caused the outbreak of the Second World War. The war proved it was impossible to shoehorn the world's 'divergent languages, religions and cultures' into a series of absolutely independent nation-states. Instead, Indians would choose to govern themselves in a 'composite state'.

Prasad's talk expressed a view common among India's thinkers and politicians about the future of India. 'Federalism' was the buzzword. From M. K. Gandhi to the Maharaja of Mysore, observers spoke of India as a coordinated series of self-governing communities, not a nation-state. For Gandhi, the village was the basic unit of self-government; India, he thought, was a 'congeries of village republics' each of which was the centre of 'a series of ever-widening circles' with little power imposed from above. For Prasad, as for others, religion and region provided the basic units. The focus, though, was on creating a form of politics which ensured that the relationship between India's plural groups was maintained by 'reason' and 'balance'. Most Indian observers shared a common critique of British rule as a system driven by forceful, acquisitive passions. They thought India could produce a form of politics to better reconcile potentially violent antagonisms.[1]

Prasad did not live to see his hopes and predictions so dramatically contradicted by the turn of events. He died in 1945, two years before Britain's Indian empire collapsed amid the kind of violent passions he lamented throughout the rest of the world. In August 1947 a single realm was split into two states, each of which claimed to rule on behalf of homogeneous, unified nations. For a few awful months everything – land, houses, movable property, culture and people – was defined as the property of Hindus and Sikhs or Muslims, imagined to belong either to the state of India or Pakistan. This division drove millions away from their homes, dispossessing them from their ways of life and memories. Hundreds of thousands died in partition violence. The first war between India and Pakistan quickly followed, when 7,500 soldiers were killed fighting opponents who weeks earlier had been members of the same imperial army.

Few expected a catastrophe on this scale. Why did events so emphatically contradict the predictions of so many? By 1947, a series of overlapping crises made millions of people destitute. Used as a buffer for the British economy in the 1920s, India had not recovered from the downturn after the First World War when the global depression struck in 1929. Then, after 1939, India was confronted with the unprecedented mobilization needed to fight a world war. But India's domination by a distant, fragile and quickly collapsing imperial power meant there was no force capable of coordinating production and holding society together. Nationalists articulated

ideas of unity, of course, but amid the ruins of empire they failed
to provide unity in practice. Depression and war led to political
fragmentation, and saw the failure of any single organization to offer
effective leadership. They led a frightened population to retreat so as
to be with others they thought were their own kind. By the 1940s,
the cycles of embittered and embattled violence which had shaped
imperial power extended throughout many sections of Indian society. Large numbers of Hindu, Sikh and Muslim men believed they
needed to conquer or suffer the humiliation of conquest themselves.

The devastation of the post-war subcontinent and the failure
of its political institutions means the scale of violence should not
surprise us. What is remarkable is the speed with which the actions
of ordinary citizens and political leaders made sure it came to an
end. In 1946, most observers predicted British India would descend
into a civil war which could last decades. In 1950, the Raj seemed
to have been succeeded by two poor but democratic and quickly
developing successor states.

Burning money

Imperial India's last catastrophe started with the onset of the world's
worst economic crisis. The crash of the New York stock market in
October 1929 sparked a loss of confidence in global credit. It was felt
in India immediately. By 1929 even the poorest Indian peasant had
become enmeshed in a global chain of lending, and was vulnerable to
the actions of distant bankers. The production of wheat, rice or millet
relied on local grain traders borrowing from moneylenders in small
towns, who borrowed from city bankers. The crunch of 1929–30
pulled money back to the centres of global banking, New York and
London. A similar chain of events took place from the wheat prairies
of the American Midwest to the millet fields of the Indian Deccan:
farmers had crops but their usual buyers did not have cash. The prices
which peasants were paid for their crop collapsed, first wheat and
millet, then rice, but village dwellers faced the same tax demand.

Poverty was compounded by the government's decision to restrict the supply of money in India's economy. Bankers and civil servants in London were worried that any devaluation of India's currency would lead to the quick decline in the value of British assets in India. London insisted the rupee stay at one shilling and sixpence in sterling, and forced the government in New Delhi to take coinage and paper money out of circulation to keep the value of the currency high. The Viceroy and his chief finance officer resisted, knowing that restricting the money supply would make the economic crisis worse and reduce their own quickly shrinking tax take. The Viceroy's entire council threatened to resign unless the rupee was allowed to float freely on the currency markets. But in this last great moment of metropolitan imperial power, it was London not Delhi or Simla which controlled the currency; and the psychology of embattled defence reached imperial finance. Sir Montagu Norman, Governor of the Bank of England, told the Raj's government to have a bit of backbone, insisting devaluation would be an act of 'defeatism' in the face of the 'enemy'. Following Norman's orders, the Indian government secretly melted down silver rupees and burnt paper notes and treasury bills. The total amount of cash circulating fell, from five billion rupees in the late 1920s, to four billion in 1930, to three billion by 1938. Sir Homi Mody, chairman of the Bombay Millowners Association, suggested British policy would 'leave them without a friend in the country'. He was not wrong.[2]

The global economic crisis caused India's connections to the rest of the world to shrink back. The fall in Indian prices allowed wages to drop, and made Indian products more competitive than overseas goods. British goods and money were withdrawn from India. They were given an added push by the resurgence of swadeshi sentiment, and the return of campaigns to boycott European goods in the early 1930s. The unexpected result was that the total output of Indian industry increased, with textile mills upping production by 23 per cent, for example. It was British industry which suffered, as the export of cotton piece goods from the UK fell dramatically, from 1.25 billion yards in 1930 to 376 million two years later, ending up at 145 million yards in 1939–40. As well as cotton, by the late 1930s India had become largely self-sufficient in steel (less than 30 per cent of its requirements were imported in 1936) and entirely self-reliant in sugar. The only way European industrialists could make money from South Asian markets was by opening factories in India themselves. Where India did consume goods from overseas, they increasingly came from Asia – particularly Japan – not Europe, further disconnecting Indian business from empire.[3]

The collapse of agriculture and the expansion of Indian industry drove hundreds of thousands into India's cities. Calcutta grew from 1.2 to 2.1 million between the censuses of 1931 and 1941; Ahmedabad from 270,000 to 590,000. India's largest ten cities saw the arrival of three million people. These largely male and poorly paid workers were forced to make a home for themselves in cities which did not have the infrastructure to accommodate them. British and elite Indian efforts to improve living conditions ended up creating pristine new enclaves for the better off. They were concerned more to protect the middle classes from the supposedly disordered, disease-ridden mob than to improve living standards for all. Perceived as dangerous, the poor were governed through coercion. Hardly surprisingly, they themselves were quick to resort to violence when they felt under attack.[4]

But political opposition to British rule in these depression years tended to come from the countryside not the town. The collapse in agricultural prices particularly affected more prosperous usually upper-caste peasants who sold a significant proportion of their crop on the open market. These groups, often imagined by the Raj to be supporters of British rule, turned to Congress, becoming the core of the organization's political base for a generation.

Country-wide protests had begun to escalate once again since the arrival of the all-white Simon Commission to India and the death of Lajpat Rai. The agrarian crisis gave them added fuel. As ever,

Congress tried to channel existing local protests into a single movement. In the forested areas of Gujarat and central India hundreds
of thousands flouted laws restricting pasturage and gleaning in forests. In the south and west millions refused to pay land revenue. In
Punjab, foreign cloth was boycotted particularly successfully in cities
and small towns. In many places protest merged into social banditry,
and crops were seized from landlords by the poor. But north India's
Gangetic plain was the heartland of protest, where day-to-day life
was dominated by the political battle between Congress and the
government for the support of local peasant leaders. Congress won
the battle for support in most places, creating an infrastructure often
more effective than the British state's.[5] In one district, Rae Bareli,
the Congress had 8,040 members, 13,081 volunteers, 32 offices and
1,019 villages which publicly flew Congress's flag even when the
organization was banned.[6]

The early 1930s saw the return of oscillation between crowd
protest and repressive violence, both sides believing they needed to
show their strength, but both also reluctant to let violence spiral out
of control. Thoughtful political strategist as ever, Gandhi tried to
channel protest by encouraging defiance against the government's
salt laws. Salt was a commodity everyone used. The government
had a monopoly and refused to reduce the price. Gandhi himself
spent three weeks marching from Sabarmati in Gujarat to the coast
at Dandi, where he symbolically boiled a beaker of sea water and
was then quietly arrested. Following Gandhi's lead, nationalists
marched to beaches across India, fighting with the police to keep the
Congress flag flying on Calicut beach and suffered lathi charges in
Madras. Despite Gandhi's emphasis on non-violence, the campaign
'thrived upon the violent eruption of the masses and the violent
repression of the police', as historian David Arnold puts it. By the
beginning of 1931, Gandhi was once again concerned that crowds
were being provoked to act violently by police brutality.[7]

The Viceroy was worried about the escalation of violence, too.
Concerned that British officers might respond to riots with another

Amritsar, Lord Irwin wanted to entice Congress to support law and order with a further wave of liberal reforms. In February, a group of Indian businessmen engineered negotiations between the two sides. The result was a pact, and a short visit by Gandhi to London to negotiate with British politicians. But having successfully gaining the support of millions of peasants in the countryside, Congress activists saw little reason for compromise. The mood among many British officers was similarly against anything which could be considered 'surrender'. Gandhi and Irwin conceded too much as far as their foot soldiers were concerned.

The 'backbone' of imperials officials was particular strengthened by the stand of die-hard Conservative Members of Parliament in London, now led by the perennially opportunistic Winston Churchill. In the middle of Gandhi's negotiations in March 1931 Churchill famously raged that there should be no surrender to this one-time 'Inner Temple lawyer, now become a seditious fakir of a type well known in the East'. 'The truth is,' Churchill said to the West Essex Unionist Association, 'Gandhi-ism and all that it stands for will have to be grappled with and finally crushed.'[8]

Gandhism was indeed crushed, temporarily. Pressure from the nationalist and imperialist rank and file led peace to break down. Congress resumed its campaign of civil disobedience at the beginning of 1932. Gandhi was gaoled, and government officials were given tacit permission to use force to preserve British authority. This time, there was no question of the kind of embarrassing inquiries which had caused Reginald Dyer's downfall. Congress's organization was smashed by lathi charges and mass arrests. The Indian Civil Service officer C.S. Venkatachar, by now Deputy Commissioner of the Gonda district, noted that it seemed as if 'the Civil Disobedience movement had been crushed. Repression and reaction were in the ascendant. The bureaucracy was on top.'[9]

But even in the midst of the last great assertion of conquering violence against Indian protest, the imperial bureaucracy knew it could not govern alone. The protests in 1930–32 made clear how much damage Indian resistance could do to the financial position of the Raj. The fiscal consequences of depression, particularly the rapid collapse of British India's tax take, led ministers in London to see that India's business leaders and middle classes needed to be involved in making policy for the Raj to survive.

Between 1931 and 1934, a succession of round table conferences, perambulating committees and joint sessions of the houses of parliament slowly and fractiously sketched out a new constitution for India. Churchill and the Tory die-hards opposed the formation of this constitution every step of the way. They wanted the massive reassertion of Britain's conquering despotism instead. Their argument was based on a passionate commitment to a vague idea of British sovereignty across the globe, not a realistic assessment of Britain's effective power throughout the world. But Stanley Baldwin, the steel manufacturer turned Conservative politician who had been appointed Prime Minister in 1935, did make the calculations. Baldwin saw that, in strained economic times, the British state's capacity to marshal human and material resources would collapse without Indian involvement.[10]

Midway through the joint-parliamentary committee on Indian reforms, a group of Conservative peers complained that if Britain gave up control of Indian finance, the creditworthiness of the Government of India would be corroded. The government's riposte cut to the core of a more pressing interest: unless India controlled its own tax policy there would not be enough money to pay the pensions of retired Indian civil servants. In August 1935, in the longest piece of legislation ever passed by Parliament, a new constitution was created which gave elected politicians full control of governments in India's provinces and created a power-sharing executive at the centre. This was, though, no great strategic realignment. The reforms of 1935 were another compromised effort to stave off crisis.[11]

No peace with the conqueror

The depression provoked a turn to the left for many Congress leaders, as a need for stronger collective action to tackle India's growing inequality became paramount. By the time the Government of India Act was passed in 1935, Jawaharlal Nehru had become the most prominent member of the socialist grouping within Congress. His rise was partly based on his role channelling the campaigns of north Indian peasants into anti-British protest, but partly also on Gandhi's patronage. Gandhi was critical of Nehru's belief that social change could be led by a potentially coercive state. But he thought the younger man's instincts led him towards consensus rather than conflict. Radical in rhetoric, Nehru developed a more accommodating political style under the patronage of Gandhi. Nehru thought Congress needed to be the sole organization speaking for the Indian nation; in practice this meant it should incorporate conservative as well as radical opinion.[12]

Nehru's wife, Kamala, was being treated in Europe for tuberculosis. He was released early from a two-year prison sentence in September 1935 to visit her. He spent a few weeks in Lausanne, and, when he was not sitting with his wife, chatted to communist intellectuals who happened to be passing through. Nehru was not allowed to return to India before the expiry of his sentence in February 1936, so he visited London meanwhile. There, the British spies who trailed him were disappointed by the Congress leader's lack of radicalism. Nehru appeared alongside socialists and communists, speaking on platforms with Victor Gollancz, Paul Robeson and Erskine Caldwell, but his speeches were 'dull', 'colourless' and even to left-wing audiences 'moderate in tone'.

Nehru's demeanour was partly influenced by his wife's illness – Kamala died on 26 February – but his gloom was also provoked by a sense of the impossibility of meaningful conversation with India's imperial rulers in London. On 6 February 1936, Nehru was persuaded to speak to members of both Houses of Parliament.

He began by explaining his reluctance to come. 'Our premises . . . are so utterly different,' he said. '[I]t would be impossible to discover a common ground on which we can understand each other.' Indians and the Britons who ran the Raj had an 'entirely different appreciation of India's present and past', Nehru said. What's more, 'the forced and unhappy union' between the two countries 'left a background of hostility between India and England'. 'There can be no peace with the conqueror and the way of the conqueror must always create conflict.'[13]

In his speech, Nehru condemned the new constitution as a conservative effort to keep the vested interests which ran India in power. The 1935 Government of India Act handed the functions of government to politicians accountable to Indian voters for the first time. But it fragmented the actions of the state between provincial ministries, ensuring there was no single focus for nationalist power. At the centre, the reforms proposed that power would be shared by elected politicians, British officials and the rulers of India's 500 'native states'. But because India's princes were reluctant to participate in the new system even this element of self-government never started. Nehru and the Congress left saw the reforms as a device to block the creation of any nationalist state power capable of challenging British interests.[14]

Nehru's constant theme was that this imperial effort to fragment the subcontinent contradicted the historic fact of the unity of India. India was a plural society which nonetheless had a single culture and civilization, and only thrived when ruled by a single power he believed. India's problems now, Nehru argued, were 'fundamentally economic'. A strong, centralized state government was needed to redistribute land, stimulate industrial development and ensure every citizen had a good education.

Nehru talked about 'the decay of British imperialism', and thought the British regime would not last long. Protecting their last embattled bastions of power, the British had developed 'over-sensitive skin' and responded to criticism with the 'fiercest repression'. 'British imperialism' had reached a final vicious stage, and needed a small push to shove it out altogether. All this meant Nehru thought there was no point in nationalists participating in the flawed constitution. In the winter and spring of 1936, he wanted Congress to fight on until the British were forced to hand over full independence.[15]

Nehru returned to India in March 1936 'like a tired child', as he put it, 'yearning for solace in the bosom of our common mother, India'. But instead of peace he found argument and crisis. The Bengali radical Subhas Chandra Bose was captivating urban lower-middle-class audiences with his call for a socialist transformation of India. But the rise of socialism was challenged also by a resurgent Congress right wing, fuelled particularly by the increasing involvement of big business in nationalist politics.

Small merchants and factory owners had supported Congress from the early 1920s, setting up a nationalist commercial organization, the Federation of Indian Chambers of Commerce and Industry, in 1927. But India's growing cadre of large factory owners had been wary of publicly opposing British power. Tata Steel and the big Bombay mill-owners had been too worried about losing government orders to support Gandhi's civil disobedience campaign, for example. But these were men who had done well out of India's disconnection from the global economy during the depression. They were angry with Britain for financial policies which kept domestic demand low. As a result, they began to think of the economic possibilities of a nationalist government interested in expanding consumer spending. Despite his hostility to industrialization, Gandhi's belief that the rich held their wealth as trustees of the community as a whole legitimized business involvement in Congress. Business leaders were a vital source of money for nationalist campaigns, but the price of their support was that the left's anti-capitalist rhetoric needed to be toned down, and that Congress participate in the new constitution. Unlike Nehru, Congress's pro-business right wing thought the organization should form ministries in India's soon to be self-governing provinces.

In the spring and early summer of 1936, a war for the soul of India's leading nationalist organization raged in the meeting halls and committee rooms of India. Nehru and his socialist allies urged Congress to support radical social change. It should, they argued, refuse to participate in provincial ministries which didn't give them enough power. In particular, Nehru argued that national, central state planning of the economy was essential. Congress-supporting urban business leaders were frightened that meant the Soviet-style nationalization of private assets. Similarly, the dominant farmers encouraged to support Congress by the depression in the countryside worried that the leftward turn would cause their private property to be collectivized. In a movement the *Times of India* called a 'revolt of Congressmen against their President's socialistic views', moderates called for unity, stood up for the defence of property and argued that Congress ministries under the imperial constitution could assist in a peaceful transfer of power.[16]

With opposition to their platform from such powerful forces, the socialists were forced to compromise. Unwilling to let the organization split, Nehru did indeed tone down his rhetoric, and reluctantly agreed Congress should stand candidates in the provincial elections and form ministries if elected. By 1939, he supported the right-wing candidate for Congress's presidency to ensure the organization did not split. For their part, business leaders were willing to accept central planning, as long as it did not mean the mass expropriation of private capital.

Conscious central control

The idea of central state planning had become the unifying concept around which the different ideological strands of Congress could unite; it also played a critical role alienating Congress from other political forces in the subcontinent, particularly those representing Muslims. Socialists focused on the use of planning to reduce poverty and inequality, and believed it needed the government to take over the ownership of large firms. The Congress right thought it involved the regulation of production and the distribution of goods, ownership of assets, not nationalization. For them, planning was about controlling the flow of money and encouraging business to coordinate better. Despite these differences, planning came to dominate the language which almost all Indian politicians used to think about political power. As a committee full of industrialists put it in a letter to Nehru, 'with the present accepted conception of a modern state, some form of state control regarding all industries is now necessary'. But the idea of planning made Congress believe it needed to possess exclusive power over every facet of government. If it needed to engage in messy negotiations with other parties, it would not be able to coordinate the economy with a single rational mind.[17]

These arguments were made in response to the chaos and disorder observers saw in the world around them, as much as they were a reaction to poverty. In the 1930s and early 1940s, figures from across the political spectrum saw planning as the only way to stave off the collapse of society, on an international scale, into anarchy. Speaking to an audience at Madras University in 1933 the liberal economist Nanjangud Subba Rao thought that the turn to planning was stimulated 'by the disorders and maladjustments in the economic life of the world' which led to depression and war. Like Beni Prasad in his presidential lecture at Mysore, commentators associated global crisis with the pursuit of irrational passions throughout the world. Even socialists emphasized the importance of structure above anarchy. Jawaharlal Nehru professed that 'my own predilection is entirely for order'. 'I dislike a mess,' he wrote to a British friend in 1941. From right to left, planning purported to replace chaos with order, passion with the calm effort of reasonable beings to rationally shape their world.[18]

This new emphasis on central state planning changed thinking about the relationship between the Indian nation and the state. Before the 1930s, political leaders had urged their compatriots to regenerate national life through social action. Figures from Lajpat Rai to Rabindranath Tagore, Bipin Chandra Pal to M. K. Gandhi associated the effort of the state to intervene and unify with empire and despotism. But speaking in 1933, Subba Rao thought that democratic elections meant there was 'no longer any terror of the State'. As ideas about planning spread, the apparent need for a single 'collective mind' to coordinate economic life allowed India to be reimagined as a 'single whole' with a single 'unifying centre'; not as set of different communities loosely coordinated in a federal structure. Planning required a single force which could act, as Subba Rao put it, 'as the agent of the community at large'.

The new emphasis on a government acting as the voice of a supposedly homogeneous community made those who did not feel part of that 'single whole' anxious. New ideas about the state emerged alongside the increasingly centralized management of the organization most likely to run an independent Indian state, the Indian National Congress. In the mid-1930s commentators began to speak of 'the Congress High Command', an entity one political scientist called 'the Leviathan of [the] Indian freedom movement' associated with 'just a few individuals or families'. Congress was by far India's most popular political body, with the support of a majority of voters in most provinces. But its claim to incorporate all Indian communities and act on behalf of everyone was unrealistic; its opponents saw these claims as an instance of tyranny paralleled only by the 'despotic' British regime.

Lower caste leaders, in particular the untouchable politician B. R. Ambedkar, argued that Congress merely wanted to institutionalize rule by India's upper castes. Ambedkar tried to persuade the British government to introduce separate electorates for the 'depressed classes' in the new constitution. In 1932, he compromised after Gandhi fasted against an attempt to fragment the Hindu community; Ambedkar agreeed that a certain number of places should be reserved for untouchables in seats voted for by the general population, but the criticism of Congress as an upper caste body continued long after 1947. Muslims similarly felt frightened by Congress's claim to speak on behalf of a homogeneous Indian society. Convinced of the rational need to centralize, Congress leaders had no conception of the fearful passions their attempt to monopolize power stoked in their rivals.[19]

Hindu Raj

The first elections to form entirely Indian-run provincial ministries were held in January and February 1937. A quarter of the adult male population of India was entitled to vote, and roughly half of those did so. Congress won by a landslide, winning 62 per cent of the seats it contested, taking 716 out of 1,585 seats in total. In the remaining seats a scattering of parties were victorious, representing a fragmented variety of groups which thought Congress did not represent their interests: Muslim Bengali peasants; Punjabi landlords; low castes in the south. Congress's success and the fragmentation of its rivals meant it was able to form ministries in nine out of eleven provinces in British India, six alone, three as the dominant partner in a coalition with other parties.

Congress's decision to rule alone in the old Mughal heartland of the United Provinces created the greatest resentment. With its massive volunteer network and highly organized system for engaging with voters, Congress won 134 seats in India's most populous province, giving it a majority of twenty. During the elections, Congress worked with the Muslim League to defeat candidates backed by the British. But the League in north India was largely a body made up of the region's old urban Muslim gentry. Nehru and his socialist allies worried that forming a coalition with aristocrats would block their socialist plans. Led by Nehru's close ally Govind Ballabh Pant, the United Provinces' new Congress government claimed its majority gave it a mandate to govern on behalf of every group in the province, Muslims included. Pant called for 'complete organic unity' between all nationalist forces, arguing that the reduction of social inequality needed the province to be ruled by a strong, united political will. Pant was particularly enthusiastic about Congress adopting central state planning.

The consequence was that the largely Hindu Congress was castigated for wanting to create a 'Hindu Raj'. There was a grain of truth in those claims. Some Congress politicians had long flirted with Hindu nationalism. In a few towns and villages, Congress used Hindu religious imagery to mobilize support during the elections. In Bengal, Congress tried to win over the Hindu Mahasabha, which claimed the mantle of being the only true nationalist organization in the province; they also talked of a common Hindu identity to include lower castes. By 1938 Congress leaders emphatically asserted their secularism. Worried about alienating Muslims, Nehru insisted Congress banned members of Hindu nationalist organizations from playing any role in its activities. In the United Provinces, Congress did connect with some strands of Muslim opinion, trying to recruit Muslim members en masse, but none of this helped undo the alienation most Muslims felt from the still largely Hindu body. Congress's attempt to incorporate different groups into their own structures looked like an effort to assimilate rivals and annihilate the different religion and identity of Muslims. As one critic wrote, Congress's aim was 'that the Muslims should walk into the parlour of Hinduism and be swallowed up'.

As Indian-run ministries were formed, British officials withdrew from positions of executive authority in India's provinces. The British retreat to Delhi or Simla after 1937 led to the de facto partition of India between regions ruled by representatives of the Congress high command and regions ruled by other parties. The division occurred, more or less, between the central mass of the Indian subcontinent and its peripheries to the east and west; between areas populated mostly by Hindus and those peopled mainly by Muslims. This split was not, however, a straightforward one between Hindu and Muslim communities. Congress did not claim to be a Hindu organization and the leading 'Muslim' organization, the Muslim League, had performed catastrophically in the 1937 elections. None of the parties elected to power in the non-Congress provinces claimed to speak on behalf of a single Muslim community. The politics of non-Congress India was dominated by organizations claiming to represent the distinctive circumstances of different regions, not an all-Indian identity.[20]

But in protest at Congress's effort to centralize power, Muslim leaders began to conjure up a rival political entity. If Congress insisted on national, centralized state power, Muslim politicians increasingly thought they needed to speak the same language. Congress's victory in 1937 led Muslim leaders in the Muslim-majority provinces of Punjab and Bengal to authorize the leader of the All-India Muslim League, Muhammad Ali Jinnah, to negotiate on their behalf at an all-India level for example. Central Muslim representatives such as Jinnah argued that if Congress would not dismantle its 'Hindu Raj', they needed to push for the creation of a Muslim state to exist alongside it.

That state was spoken of in a vague and abstract way. To give it definition would have alienated too many potential supporters. There was no sense here that Muslims had a shared history or common institutions, little reference to India's Mughal heritage, for example. As historian Faisal Devji argues, there was no effort to link Muslim nationhood to ethnicity or land. For Jinnah 'Muslim' was an almost totally empty political category. When a Muslim state was first proposed at the Muslim League's Lahore conference in 1940, its backers could not even agree whether it would be one or many sovereign entities. For most of the men who supported it, a Muslim state was merely a device to force Congress and the British to concede to Muslims significant power throughout India. But the new state had a name, which began to be shouted by crowds at political meetings with increasing intensity after 1940: Pakistan.[21]

Historians interested in the division of India and the creation of Pakistan often tend to focus on the high politics leading to the split. Partition is seen as the tragic result of negotiations between the leaders of governments and political parties, resulting in the 'Transfer of Power' of the unified sovereignty of the British over India to two states at a single point of time. But a claim to sovereignty is not the same as the reality of being able to rule. The process of partition was shaped as much by the anxious facts of political power on the ground as negotiations in Viceregal drawing rooms. In fact, long before August 1947, governmental power had already begun to be practically divided.

Losing their heads

The Second World War accelerated this process of division. War forced the British government to cede the practical self government of Indians in more spheres of life than ever before, as mobilization without Indian support was impossible; but mobilization occurred through a complicated mix of powers that often ended up creating divisions and antagonism. As importantly, resources were mobilized in a way that meant the economic troubles of the depression intensified. War created insecurity. It pushed many parts of India into famine. In the process, it created populations that saw themselves less as members of a nation on the verge of independence than as members of communities under attack.

Indian politicians were not sure how to respond when war broke out in September 1939. Congress's nine provincial ministries resigned in protest at the Viceroy's decision to declare India at war without consulting them, and were replaced by the direct but weak rule of provincial governors. A few nationalists on the state-socialist end of the political spectrum were sympathetic to Britain's fascist antagonists, but the most vociferous campaign in the early days of the conflict protested against nothing more formidable than a monument commemorating the Black Hole in Calcutta. In 1940 the Bengali leader Subhas Chandra Bose organized a demonstration to pull down a memorial justifying British conquest, was put in gaol and then escaped and fled to Germany. Bose turned up in Berlin to ask the Nazis for help leading an insurrection against the Raj. At the other end of the political spectrum, the Indian Communist Party pledged its support for the imperial state once Hitler invaded the Soviet Union and Russia was an ally. Most political leaders were not so clearly for or against Britain's war effort. The bulk of Congress socialists saw the war as a fight between rival imperialist powers and wanted to stay out. Others pledged a vague loyalty to the allies while insisting that India be recognized as 'fully independent' to properly fight. In any case, until the last weeks of 1941, the war seemed a long way off. The greatest official fear was that Russia or Germany would invade through the Khyber Pass. As historian Indivar Kamtekar puts it, 'the Second World War caught the colonial state looking the wrong way.'[22]

But the Japanese army's lightning march through South East Asia to the frontiers of eastern India from December 1941 exposed the fragility of the Raj. Garrisoned by Indian soldiers, Singapore was supposed to have been an impregnable bastion. It fell, though, in less than a week's fighting, and set off a wave of hysterical panic throughout the subcontinent. Diarist Nirad C. Chaudhuri remembered that everyone in Bengal thought the Japanese would occupy all of the province by March 1942. Arrangements were made to destroy anything militarily useful in the city of Calcutta. Boats throughout Bengal which might have assisted Japanese invaders were burnt, destroying the usual means by which food was supplied throughout the province. British government officers sent their families to the hills; Indian officers moved them in with families elsewhere in India. In Madras, the prospect of invasion seemed so imminent that government offices were moved to towns scattered throughout the interior, and the big cats in the city's zoo killed to stop them rampaging after the inevitable attack. When the city's Indian chief officer complained that 'everyone seemed to have lost their head', the British chief of police sent a platoon to the zoo who 'ruthlessly did their job in minutes'. By the middle of 1942, the government was drawing up plans to retreat from India and lead the fighting against Japan from Australia. Indians withdrew their savings from British-run banks and could not even trust paper money so started to collect small coins.[23]

The Raj's greatest failure was the rapid collapse of British rule in Burma. India's eastern neighbour had been under British government since the late nineteenth century, governed separately from the rest of the subcontinent only since 1937. The imperial regime in Burma was based on isolated European outposts, weakly connected by Burmese 'collaborators' and a dense network of Indian merchants. This structure collapsed quickly when faced with Japan's military machine. In the monsoon of 1942, British and Indian troops trudged back through the highlands of Arakan and Assam, along with perhaps 140,000 civilian refugees. Army drivers were so weak from starvation many could not manoeuvre heavy Chevrolet trucks, and dozens fell into ravines. The British government's relief policy was heavily biased in favour of Europeans. As in Malaya, once Europeans were evacuated British officers thought there was no one left to defend. All vehicles in Malaya, Singapore and Burma were commandeered by white Britons. Wounded soldiers were left without treatment. Between 50,000 and 100,000 people died of disease while trekking slowly through the mosquito-infested tracts on India's eastern frontier.

More than any other event, this moment of British state failure enraged millions of Indians, turning the attitude of many towards the Raj from 'sullen passivity', as Nehru put it, 'to a pitch of excitement'. Wounded soldiers returning from the front spread news about their treatment and escalated the mood of anger. Political leaders challenged the empire's hypocrisy, claiming to fight in the name of freedom while refusing to let Indians rule themselves. August 1942 saw the greatest upsurge of anti-British sentiment in India since 1857. In his weekly newspaper column Gandhi was apoplectic. 'Hundreds, if not thousands, on their way from Burma perished without food or drink, and the wretched discrimination stared even these miserable people in the face. One route for whites, another for blacks! Provision of food and shelter for the whites, none for the blacks! India is being ground down to the dust and humiliated even before the Japanese advent.' It was time, Gandhi said in May 1942, 'for the British and the Indians to be reconciled to complete separation from each other'. A month later his message was even clearer: 'For God's sake leave India alone!'[24]

'Every Indian who desires freedom and strives for it must be his own guide,' Gandhi said while launching the 'Quit India' movement on 8 August 1946. Gandhi's idea was that every Indian should take freedom for themselves, and create their own self-government in the chaos of wartime. Congress's entire leadership was arrested on 9 August before a plan could be communicated to Congress volunteers, so the campaign which followed was indeed shaped by the local ideas of activists. In fact, its course was probably directed most of all by the public articulation of imperial anxieties. The British government's Secretary of State for India, Leo Amery, justified mass arrests by listing the outrages he imagined Congress were planning: 'strikes, not only in administration and commerce, but in the administration and law courts, the interruption of traffic and public utility services, the cutting of telegraph wires, the picketing of troops and recruiting stations'. Nationalist activists thought these activities had indeed been planned, so put the imperial government's worst fears into practice.[25]

Over the following two months, imperial institutions faced a rebellion in a large swathe of territory stretching from the eastern United Provinces to south-west Bengal, as well as isolated pockets of insurrection in western India. The 'August rebellion' was fiercest in areas of the eastern United Provinces and Bihar where large numbers had migrated to South East Asia, and had experience of Britain's collapse. With the Congress high command in prison, leadership came from students and young people, peasants and factory workers. Expecting British rule to quickly fall, rebels blew up government offices and cut telegraph lines. In most cases, sabotage occurred with the least possible damage to property; Congress volunteers consulted engineers about how to disrupt British communications without damaging infrastructure which they hoped would soon be in national hands. In some areas violence was more visceral, trains were stopped and Europeans dragged out and killed. British power did totally vanish in some districts, as 'national governments' were established in Maharashtra, Bihar and south-west Bengal, the latter surviving until 1944. 'I am engaged here in meeting by far the most serious rebellion since that of 1857,' the Viceroy wrote to Winston Churchill.[26]

As historian Yasmin Khan puts it, 'the ghosts of mutiny floated everywhere in the air.' Like the rebellion of 1857, the Quit India movement was only suppressed with massive force. As one British officer wrote home, 'the police were completely demoralised and we were given a free hand, pretty well, to use force where necessary without the usual rigmarole of getting a magistrate's written sanction.' Between 1,060 and 2,500 protesters were killed and 60,000 to 90,000 imprisoned, with the conditions in gaol for most volunteers appalling. An American observer compared the state of prisons to concentration camps.[27]

A nation in arms

The movement was a sign of revulsion against British power at a moment when it seemed on the verge of collapse. But revulsion was not accompanied by universal opposition to the war effort. A few nationalists did want to assist the Axis powers. Having travelled from Germany to Japan and then reached Japanese-occupied Singapore, Subhas Chandra Bose gathered an Indian National Army, a force which eventually included 43,000 men but played no significant role in the war. Always with an eye for a good conspiracy, British officials imagined the whole of Congress was an organization of fifth columnists, plotting with their opponents to help the Germans and Japanese to victory. But the anger of Congress leaders was based on their being dragged into a brutal conflict they thought the sclerotic systems of imperialism in India could not win, not opposition to the war itself. Many Congress leaders wanted to evict Britain from India quickly so that they could better resist fascism. Japan was recognized as a potential Asian ally, but its own imperial conquests were castigated and feared. Even when angriest at the British empire, Gandhi assured the British and, particularly, their American, Chinese and Russian allies, that an independent India would allow the 'United Nations' (the term the Allies used to describe themselves) to use India as a military base to drive Japan out of South East Asia and China. 'I do not want to be the instrument of Russia's defeat nor of China's', Gandhi said. Privately, he even admitted that Subhas Chandra Bose, with his active support for the Axis powers, 'will have to be resisted'.[28]

In the midst of a violent campaign against the atrophied structures of British sovereign power, some offered more active support. India's bureaucratic and commercial elites were unwilling to throw their lot in with the chaos promised by Congress's struggle. Business leaders saw an expansion of wartime production as a potential source of profit. Small-scale landholders and local aristocrats feared that Britain's quick exit would break down order and hierarchy. Many feared that a Japanese invasion would be more violent than the continuation of British sovereignty. Conservative Muslim leaders in Punjab and the north-west went so far as declaring jihad against the Japanese for treating Muslims in South East Asia badly. Non-Congress leaders saw the war as an opportunity to consolidate power and 'colonise the attenuated public sphere', as C. A. Bayly put it. The Muslim League joined Lord Linlithgow's war cabinet. Jinnah condemned the Quit India movement as 'Gandhi and his Hindu Congress blackmailing the British' to create a 'Hindu Raj'. Right-wing Hindu nationalists called on their supporters to enlist in the imperial army to turn their mythical homogeneous Hindu national community into a 'nation in arms'.[29]

These allegiances were limited and complicated. But, together with a transformation in the institutions of British power, they allowed the state in India to recover after the multiple disasters of 1942. Two developments particularly pushed a restructuring of the Raj. First, in 1943, what C. A. Bayly called a 'quiet military coup' occurred. The government in London dismissed British India's stuffy civilian bureaucracy and placed military men in charge. The Commander-in-Chief of the Indian army, Lord Archibald Wavell, replaced the aloof Lord Linlithgow as Viceroy; a general noted for his logistical skills, Claude Auchinleck became chief military officer. Auchinleck and Wavell restructured the government to focus exclusively on victory against Japan. These were two intellectually ambitious men who understood the importance of technology and logistics to modern warfare, and believed British victory required key institutions to be controlled by Indian leaders.

As significantly, American involvement in the war put pressure on the British regime to organize the war effort more efficiently and inclusively. The Japanese attack on Pearl Harbor was followed by the quick flood of American government officials, military officers and technical experts into the subcontinent. India had been a destination for supplies under the Anglo-US Lend-Lease agreement since late 1941, but shipments increased dramatically in 1943, with 125,000 tons of goods arriving every month from the beginning of that year. American military hardware transformed the Indian army; the number of anti-tank guns increased from twenty to more than 2,000 between 1941 and 1944, for example.[30]

Despite their physical investment in the war effort, American visitors worried that Indian opposition to British authority would cause the country to fall to the Japanese. 'India is about to Fall. The uncomprehending philosophy of England is meeting its reward,' the US Assistant Secretary of State Breckenbridge Long wrote in April 1942. Britain in India was 'blind, self-centered and tenacious of the phantoms of the past'. The American President Franklin D. Roosevelt demanded Britain grant India full self governing dominion status. With the die-hard Winston Churchill now Prime Minister, the British government refused to grant India independence. But the importance of American money and soldiers forced the Raj, finally, to promise self-government after the war, and take the United States' demands seriously in the meantime. By 1944, American soldiers and engineers had taken large sections of Indian infrastructure. They were running the 800-mile Bengal and Assam Railway, doubling the amount of freight shipped to eastern India's front line. They were also building a network of landing strips to allow planes to take off to bomb Japanese territories.[31]

The last three years of war saw a massive increase in Indian mobilization, with the Indian army growing from 900,000 in December 1941 to 2.3 million by the end of the war. It also saw the creation of an administrative infrastructure which tried to impose the government's will on the Indian economy to a degree never before imagined. The manufacture and supply of the 60,000 different items needed to keep soldiers in battle was organized with greater central control. From 1941, government orders fixed the quantity and price of everything from steel rail and cotton shirts to cigarettes and geometry protractors. Government spending expanded five times. The government's supply department increased its staff from twenty to 17,000. New technologies were deployed to organize production. There was a rapid increase in the collection of statistics, in surveying and in the use of scientific managerial techniques such as operational research. India's scientific infrastructure expanded quickly, too, with the creation of the Council of Scientific and Industrial Research in July 1942. The CSIR was founded to develop the chemistry and physics needed to ensure military hardware kept working; it still exists today as the organization which coordinates India's system of national laboratories.[32]

This new state infrastructure tried to put Indian calls for a nationally planned economy into practice. It created unprecedented structures to involve Indian business leaders in decision-making for example, as panels of industrialists were appointed to coordinate production throughout India. Alongside the massive expansion of the army the state also recruited millions of workers from hitherto unmobilized groups into India's industrial economy. Hindu and Sikh peasants from Punjab refused to sacrifice their growing income from rising wheat prices to fight the Japanese and stayed to defend their homeland. The military had no choice but to enlist beyond its usual recruiting ground of Punjab, low-caste men from Madras presidency finding the army particularly attractive. Similarly, millions of 'tribal' and lower-caste men and women were recruited into factories, and then often also drafted into pioneer labour corps which laid roads. The civilian labour corps ended up with fifteen million members. Strikingly, it was the lower-caste leader B. R. Ambedkar who was appointed minister of labour in the executive council which Lord Wavell appointed in July 1942.

By 1944, the British began to present the war effort as a national project. British propaganda intensified, portraying the conflict as the united struggle of Britons and Indians to defend a self-governing India. Auchinleck, the Commander-in-Chief, created 'josh groups', where soldiers debated their pay and conditions as well as politics. Indian troops 'were empowered as thinking individuals who were capable of taking the initiative', as Bayly puts it. The military high command banned British officers from criticizing leaders like Nehru or Gandhi for fear of alienating Indian soldiers. Volunteers were encouraged to enlist not as subjects of empire, but as 'citizens of India'. Citizen militias were recruited to the defeated north-eastern regions. Air Raid Precaution volunteers signed pledges to 'face and defy every peril threatening India's national security' '[b]ecause I am proud to be a citizen of India'.[33]

The greatest changes occurred in the army itself. The worst forms of discrimination were outlawed. Training was much better organized, with Indian and African recruits spending nine months away from the front line developing the skills and attitude to fight, with every member of a division, from the British commander to the lowliest Indian private, attending lectures together. India Command created clear strategies focused on fighting in the conditions of South East Asia. Wavell recognized the futility of trying to drive

heavy trucks through jungles so infantry battalions were demech-
anized. As recruitment expanded, the army was forced to accept
recruits in poor physical condition. Military scientists conducted
experiments with different kinds of food. The change in diet was
so great that some emaciated recruits found it difficult to digest the
increase in the then usual two mealtimes, so the army added two
rounds of sweet milky tea with biscuits during the day. The effect of
these changes created an effective fighting machine that halted the
Japanese advance on the borders of north-east India. Better supply
networks and high morale allowed the Allied army to stop the
Japanese army in the battles of Imphal and Kohima in the spring of
1944, and then, in November 1944, drive on to reconquer Burma.[34]

But – and this is the important point – mobilization was patchy
and uneven. It occurred in separate institutions and enclaves, the
army being the largest and most important. Overall British political
leadership was weak and ridden with anxiety, incapable of creating
shared purpose or national will, and Indian political leaders were
unwilling to step in to help mobilize a war they did not feel was
their own. People supported the state when doing so suited their
particular interests.

Few who had the choice voluntarily contributed to the war effort.
Any shared sense of purpose did not extend far enough to encourage
wealthy Indians to limit their living standards, for example. With a
guaranteed market, the war was boom time for industrialists. The
Raj's desperation for Indian cooperation meant business leaders
were appointed to the committees responsible for setting the prices
at which their own goods were bought. But the imperial state did
not then increase taxes on corporate profits. Similarly, farmers able
to invest in producing surplus rice or wheat made big profits, and
the government's rural tax machinery was not capable of taking a
contribution from them. Unlike the national government in Britain,
the Raj's limited connection with Indian society made it too anxious about increasing taxes or investigating undeclared sources of
profits. The number of people paying income tax doubled between

1938 and 1945, but it was still less than half a million by the end of the war. The government could not even persuade wealthy Indians to sacrifice consumption in favour of buying government bonds. In 1947, the economic historian D. R. Gadgil wrote about the 'inability of the Government to take a firm stand against important interests'. The reason was explained by the Secretary of State in 1943: 'The Indian war effort . . . is pretty frankly a mercenary undertaking so far as the vast majority of Indians are concerned,' he said. Anxious as ever, the government thought it was too dangerous to squeeze people whose support it relied on.[35]

This lack of civilian support meant that the Raj was in financial difficulties throughout the war, despite the government's creation of an elaborate machinery to control the economy. Its solution was to print money. The war was financed by what economists at the time called a 'deficit-induced, fiat money inflation, the worst kind of inflation'. The massive expansion of the money supply did have a theoretical basis in real assets. The production of goods for the war effort had led to the accumulation of large but debts owed to the Indian government in pounds sterling; no one knew if they would ever be paid back. But they were treated as notional property against which rupees could be printed, much to the despair of Indian economists. As during the depression, the currency was the last tool that an imperial state with no capacity elsewhere could manipulate. But unlike the 1930s, the money supply was deliberately expanded, from 1.7 to 11.4 million rupees between 1938 and 1945, and prices rose accordingly, double or even treble in many cases.[36]

Inflation was good for rich farmers and factory owners, but most people suffered from an increase in the cost of living. Middle-class government employees struggled to make ends meet. Factory workers suffered, but the government's demand for industrial goods ensured there was some minimal assistance for them. Labourers starved in rural areas where there was no relief. Rural Bengal was worse hit. There, as we have seen, government-induced inflation was compounded by the destruction of the boats used to transport food, the unwillingness of the government to institute famine works and Winston Churchill's refusal to send grain despite Wavell's insistent requests. The Bengal famine of 1943 killed between two and three million people, but famine stalked the rest of India on a smaller scale. As in India's previous famines, millions left the countryside. In many places the source of a rural livelihood had completely broke down. Millions staggered, starving and, because of the price of clothes, naked into towns. People 'were moving towards towns in crowds', an observer noticed on the train journey between Cochin and Bombay in 1943. In Bengal local infrastructure totally collapsed, with schools and hospitals closing, and family ties being destroyed by death and migration.

Unlike previous famines, the war at least meant the destitute had a chance of finding work in munitions or textiles factories.[37] But the imperial home front in India was very different from the home front at the heart of the empire. Conditions in slums and workplaces were terrible. People were mobilized and classified, whether working, ill or dead, in narrowly defined communal groups, and the division and fragmentation of Indian society intensified. In Bengal, Hindu and Muslim organizations competed in their ability to save their own folk, and castigated their opponents for neglect. Muslims and Hindus were divided from each other by many means. Volunteer militias formed to help famine relief but also to defend through force. Different state organizations were dominated by different communities, with accusations and anxieties about being forced to submit to the dominance of others. In Calcutta, for example, the Muslim League ministry in Bengal appointed the firm of M. M. Ispahani to supply grain to relieve starving city-dwellers. Ispahani was a staunch support of the Muslim League, and a friend of Muhammad Ali Jinnah. His appointment was fiercely criticized by the Hindu Mahasabha as an effort to create 'Pakistan' by stealth. As Hindus complained about the provincial ministry of Bengal becoming a Muslim stronghold, Muslims criticized the institutions run by the central government for being dominated by Hindus. Calcutta's

Air Raid Precautions volunteer force was said to be 95 per cent Hindu. The system of shops selling commodities at controlled prices run by the Department of Supply was accused of being dominated by Hindus as well. Starkest of all was the fate of the famine dead. The police did not have the capacity to deal with corpses piling up in Calcutta. Where no relatives were quickly found bodies were labelled as Hindu or Muslim and handed over to respective private religious organizations. Long before 1947, the social and political fabric of India was being divided. Depression, war and the failings of the Raj, were doing their work.[38]

The transfer of power

A regime that had been recast to win the war had no purpose once the Japanese were defeated. A society mobilized, however haphazardly, to defend itself against an enemy had no need for foreign rule once it achieved victory. In the last years of the war, Wavell reported a south Indian liberal politician telling him 'the present régime could carry on quite comfortably till the end of the war . . . unless we get into serious difficulties over food'. But once wartime passions to defend the homeland had abated, the fragility of the British presence in India was obvious. Despite being armed and organized as never before, the imperial state could only project power overseas, not over India itself.

The British presence had been weakened first of all by an ever-shrinking number of Britons in India to sustain British power. After years in which small numbers of British candidates put themselves forward, and were usually beaten in examinations by Indians, the elite civil service stopped recruiting entirely in London in 1943. By the end of the war there were 510 Indians to 429 Europeans in the ICS. The Britons who led empire's everyday administration were 'tired and have lost heart', British cabinet members admitted in 1946. The senior Indian officials on whom the British relied often had nationalist sympathies. Jawaharlal Nehru had three close relations in the Indian Civil Service. When nationalist leaders were on the run from the British during the war, it was not unusual for them to stay with ICS officer friends or relatives.[39]

The decline in the numbers of British officers in India reduced the population with a direct interest in maintaining British power, but the commitment to the Raj was limited even among the British. Many British army officers were wartime conscripts, and had no family connection or ideological commitment to empire. British visitors worried that ordinary British soldiers were discontented and often themselves on the verge of mutiny; they could not be kept to hold India for long. The Labour politician Douglas Houghton gave a lecture tour of British barracks in early 1946, and found British soldiers angry, resentful and desperate to quit, complaining that 'they can't rule India, for God's sake stop India ruling us'. It also made it impossible for the British to impose power against wide-spread Indian resistance.[40]

The conditions in which this shrinking number was expected to hold on to power stayed bad. Rural protest movements spread. For the first time, there was evidence of communist organization in the countryside. Revolt was fuelled by the continuation of high prices, and the failure of living standards for the poorest to improve after the end of the war. 'The grim spectre of impending famine' once again caused the Viceroy to beg for Gandhi's help preserving peace and social order in February 1946. Gandhi was as hostile to class war as the British. To stave off social breakdown, he spoke against hoarding and urged the middle classes to make sacrifices so 'that the poor may live'. To stop crisis people needed to curb their needs and desires, he said. 'We must', Gandhi urged his countrymen after meeting the Viceroy's private secretary, 'economize like misers.'[41]

Most alarmingly for the British, protest grew once again, spreading now to significant parts of the imperial regime's armed forces for the first time. To the surprise of many British officers, the military stayed 'loyal' throughout the war, but that changed in 1946. In February, a revolt took place on board ships of the Royal

Indian Navy moored in Bombay harbour. The mutiny began in protest against poor food and the arrest of a rating for scrawling 'Quit India' on the side of one ship. As in 1857, violence escalated as men heard about the punishment of others. Rumours (which were untrue) circulated that sailors had been fired on. Using ships' radios to communicate, the rebellion spread to seventy-eight ships and twenty shore establishments, involving 20,000 sailors in total. Sailors hoisted the flags of Congress, the Muslim League and the Communist Party together, but only the communists supported the rebellion. It was not the guns of the imperial regime, but the words of nationalist leaders which encouraged the rebels to back down. Gandhi's great Gujarati ally Vallabhbhai Patel went to Bombay and persuaded the rebels that independence would happen more quickly if they submit. When residents of Bombay rioted in support, they were met by British soldiers from four regiments, aided by armoured cars. Two hundred and thirty-three demonstrators were killed in the violence. A socialist British soldier complained that the brutality was caused by British soldiers' frustration about not being demobilized. Many of the mutineers were arrested and dismissed from the navy, but not punished further.[42]

The prospect of famine again, the likelihood of India-wide revolt and the loss of British officers' 'heart' to rule, made the regime in Delhi desperate to hand over authority to an Indian government at the centre as soon as it could. The newly elected Labour government in London was committed to a quick transfer of power, too. In London, the new Foreign Secretary Ernest Bevin worried that the Labour Party would be perceived as weak if it transferred power too hastily. But the Prime Minister, Clement Attlee, had a long history of supporting Indian self-government. There was a significant body of Labour opinion in favour of 'the recognition of full Indian national rights', as one group of parliamentarians put it. The King's speech in July 1945 promised the 'early realisation of full self-government'. The question for the British government was not whether to go but how to exit with 'honour' and 'dignity'.

Elections were held in India in December 1945 and January 1946, and seemed to confirm the division of India between two camps. Congress won an overwhelming majority, with the Muslim League capturing 75 per cent of the Muslim vote, enough to rule two out of India's four Muslim majority regions, Bengal and Sind. The division occurred between radically different attitudes about how power should be configured in the future. Congress claimed to be the unified voice of a single, progressive India. It 'included in its fold the members of all religions and communities in India', the then Congress President Maulana Azad wrote in July 1946, and that meant it thought it had the right to rule alone. 'The link that has brought all these various groups and communities together ... is the passionate desire for national independence, economic advance, and social equality,' Azad went on. With a sense of the need for a strong coordinating power to plan India's 'progress' from poverty to prosperity, the majority of Congress politicians believed India needed a strong central government. Its 'passionate desire' to centralize national power was inconsistent with sharing authority at the centre. But its links to business leaders, and its deep-rooted organizational structures everywhere apart from Bengal and Punjab, meant its claims needed to be taken seriously.[43]

By 1946, the Muslim League had pulled together many different groups in India alienated from this Congress vision of centralized state power. Its coalition was disparate, made up of communities which otherwise would have been rivals. It brought together big rural landlords in Punjab, resentful of the way grain was requisitioned and rationed during the war; impoverished Muslim peasants in Bengal, hostile to the continued attempts at domination by largely Hindu zamindars; sufi saints in Sind, opposed to more orthodox, centralizing Islamic clergy who tended to support Congress. Unlike Congress with its central committee meetings and annual Congress, the League was incapable of mediating antagonisms between its different constituencies. It could not contain conflict between Shia and Sunni in north India, for example. All that united the League was a shared fear about 'the tyranny of the Hindu majority' if Congress came to power. But that was enough to allow its support to expand during and after the war. As a village headman from Punjab put it when interviewed in 1946, 'If there were no League, the Hindus would get the government and take away our land.'[44]

In opposition to Congress's vision of a centralized Indian state, the Muslim League insisted sovereignty lay with the provinces, which could then group themselves into more than one state, creating Pakistan if they chose. Rule by a government elected by India's Hindu majority would, the League argued, 'reduce Muslims, Christians and other minorities to the status of irredeemable helots'. Mohammad Ali Jinnah thought Muslims would be best protected if state power was divided into a federation of quasi-independent provinces, overseen by a weak central power where the interests of India's Muslim minority would be grouped together and well represented. By the end of the war Jinnah's public position was that a state of Pakistan should be created; but this notion of a separate Muslim state was a tactic designed to achieve a better deal for Muslims within a single federal state. Jinnah's ploy refused to acknowledge how intense the passion for separation had become between many Muslims and Hindus during the previous few years. The hyper-rational, London-trained lawyer continually overestimated the power and patience of his interlocutors. War, famine and the separation of Indian between Congress and League provinces had already encouraged communities to separate, and led the British to believe they needed to leave fast.

By the summer of 1946 the Viceroy was bleak about the prospects of any form of British authority continuing in India for long. As early as April that year, Wavell's priority had been to prevent India descending into chaos, irrespective of who was in charge. His 'chief concern was to get a body of efficient administrators whom India would recognize as representative leaders of Indian public opinion', as he put it. That meant transferring power to an entirely Indian regime as quickly as possible. Wavell proposed to hand day-to-day running of government to an Indian interim government. India would, at last, be treated 'like a Dominion Government', with the Viceroy doing nothing more than chairing meetings and overseeing the rapidly shrinking army. Wavell wanted the government to involve the Muslim League as well as Congress, but the League insisted on staying out until negotiations moved in their direction. At the beginning of September 1946, all the central Indian ministries were handed to Congress ministers. The Viceroy insisted Jawaharlal Nehru 'was not Prime Minister or Chief Minister', but only 'the head of the popular part of the Government'. But Nehru chose the ministers, decided the business of government and had a private secretary who doubled up as secretary to the new cabinet as a whole. He was, in effect, Prime Minister.

If there was a single moment when the British transferred power over the central machinery of government in India this, not India's independence in 1947, was it. From September 1946, the public language of rule subtly changed. From that date, Wavell called Congress ministers 'colleagues' in public at least. They governed as a 'cabinet', which made collective decisions. There were, the Viceroy noted, 'minor skirmishes', but 'we have got on well on the whole'. 'Our method of working', Nehru insisted later in the month, 'is for all of us to discuss common problems and to arrive at joint decisions for which we are jointly responsible.' There were to be no subjects reserved only for Europeans. The government in London praised Wavell's 'handling of [his] colleagues' in public at least, suggesting his 'liberal concessions' were a way the Viceroy could keep his new ministers 'straight on essentials'. As Wavell knew, the new language of collaboration reflected the fact that government in India could only now rely on Indian organization rather than British power.[45]

From the end of August 1946, Congress's high command behaved as if it was the central government of India. The interim government started to run its own foreign policy, independent of the British for example. As soon as the new ministers were appointed, the British Foreign Office in London appointed a High Commissioner to represent British interests in Delhi, treating India the same way as entirely self-governing members of the Commonwealth like Australia or Canada. Nehru started to establish diplomatic relations with other powers, particularly Soviet Russia. V. K. Krishna Menon, the London-based politician and co-founder of Penguin Books, was deputed as Nehru's personal emissary to tour European capitals with the Government of India paying the bill. One of his first actions was to ask the Soviet Union to ship wheat to India to ease the likelihood of famine. Both Nehru and Menon started a campaign to have India be given a seat on the United Nations security council. The Viceroy thought Menon's actions were 'ill-advised and ill-timed' but could do nothing to stop them.[46]

In August 1946, the only institution in British India still controlled by the British was the army; this was the subject of the only real conflict which developed in the interim cabinet. Two weeks after taking over, Nehru wrote to the Commander-in-Chief insisting that the army 'make it feel that it is the national army of India'. Auchinleck's response was not hostile to Nehru's proposals. In his reply, he pointed out that the army had only defeated Japan by putting them into practice already; 'national service' had already become a vital element in the rhetoric used to persuade Indian soldiers to defeat the Japanese; troops were being recruited from every part of India; after the war, Indian soldiers were being withdrawn from postings overseas. Instead of defending the authority of Britons in India, Auchinleck was concerned that the army was not Indian enough. India's middle classes were not coming forward in large enough numbers to staff the Indian army's officer cadres. The imperial Commander-in-Chief turned the table on Nehru, calling for the putative Prime Minister of India's help in nationalizing the army.

August 1946 was the moment when British officials made their final retreat from almost every corner of the Raj. From the end of the month, imperial secrets were safe nowhere other than in the inner core of the Viceroy's private office. To prevent it falling into

Indian hands 'top secret' imperial military correspondence was no longer sent even to the Viceroy or Commander-in-Chief.[47] The impending arrival of nationalist ministers sparked the destruction of embarrassing files. In July 1946 the Viceroy's secretary sent a note round the ministries, asking secretaries about documents 'which might be used as material for anti-British propaganda'. Anticipating the need to retreat quickly, some departments replied that they had 'been weeding documents out for upwards of a year'. Most were burnt. Four dispatch boxes full of files of 'historical interest' were sent to the Viceroy's private office in Government House in Simla, the last exclusively British space left in the Indian government. On 29 August 1946, these boxes were taken to Delhi airfield. Accompanied by a British secretary from the war department, Mr Dundas, they were flown on BOAC flight 10F82 to London's Heathrow airport, to eventually find their way into the India Office's library. The Indian government file tracing their journey makes it clear what happened. Its title referred to 'the disposal of old records . . . on the formation of a "National Government"' in September 1946.[48]

These files were the first things Vallabhbhai Patel looked for when he arrived as India's new Home Minister in the first week of September 1946. From Gandhi's home province of Gujarat, Patel had started his political career by being elected sanitation commissioner in Ahmedabad in 1917. In the early 1920s, he organized peasant proprietors in campaigns against the payment of imperial taxes, but had become Indian nationalism's greatest supporter of the use of strong, centralized state power to keep Indian united. It was Patel who persuaded Congress not to alter the structure and traditions of the Indian Civil Service once the British left the subcontinent. His robust willingness to talk about authority and efficiency helped him with Lord Wavell. 'We get on well,' Wavell wrote. The two men had a one-to-one dinner soon after Patel had taken over as Home Minister. Wavell asked him how he was getting on with the 'Intelligence Bureau'. 'They burned all the interesting secret records before I took over,' Patel replied. 'Oh yes, I told them to do that,' Wavell said, and they 'laughed in a friendly way'.[49]

The culmination of administration

In August 1946 it was not only paper that burnt. The impending creation of the Congress government sparked riots throughout India. Violence was worst in the increasingly divided city of Calcutta. The same day Wavell published the names of the interim administration, Mohammad Ali Jinnah announced that 16 August would be 'Direct Action Day', when Muslims would take to the streets to oppose Congress tyranny and support the creation of Pakistan. The Muslim League wanted their activists to target the British as much as Congress, to prove that the League needed to be taken as seriously as its rivals. But in India's cities the British state had little physical presence. Protest, particularly in Calcutta, merged with the fears different communities had developed of being dominated by Indian rivals.[50]

Bengal's Muslim League government called a one-day holiday and a mass demonstration, a sign for many Hindus it was intent on tyrannizing them. From first light, streams of Muslims walked from every part of the city to the maidan, the great open space in the centre of Calcutta. Skirmishes broke out from 7.30am as Muslim demonstrators tried to stop Hindu shopkeepers from opening their stores. The violence was driven by destitution and a desire for economic gain as much as communal anxieties. Some people smashed shops shouting, 'we'll fight and take Pakistan!' Others simply looted, taking goods they could not afford to buy, not worrying about the religious affiliation of the shopkeepers. In the middle of the morning groups of Muslims on their way from Howrah, on the western side of the River Hooghly, walking to the demonstration at the maidan started to turn back, drawn more by the prospect of looting near the city's railway station than the chance to demonstrate their support for Pakistan.

As looting spread, Hindus and Sikhs retaliated, resisting what they saw as their subordination to Muslim rule. Gopal Patha, one of the few killers whose words have been recorded, explained his actions like this: 'if we became a part of Pakistan we will be oppressed so I called my boys and said, this is the time we have to retaliate, and you have to answer brutality with brutality.' Patha was a butcher and a local boss, who had weapons and followers at his command; Patha himself went into the streets with two pistols he had bought from an American soldier. '[I]f we heard one murder has taken place, we committed ten more.' Overall, in three days of rioting, more than 4,000 people died.[51]

On both sides, violence was led by mobs who lived in a city not their own; watchmen, coachmen, loaders, boatmen, sweepers, taxi drivers, slum dwellers, men with no family nearby, often uprooted by poverty from their home village who had no sense of belonging other than their religious community. Calcutta in 1946 had been swollen by famine in the countryside. It was a city of hundreds of thousands of 'lone men' who eked out an insecure existence in textile mills and munitions factories, but whose prospects had got worse after the end of the war. Pushed to the edge of civility by the pressures of depression and war, these men had nothing in common but the precarious way they earned a living and their membership of one religious community or another.

But these conditions did not create violence on their own. In Bengal in 1946, mass killings were driven by the fact that members of India's two major religious communities both feared they were beleaguered minorities, facing destruction in the face of coercive state power unless they defended themselves with force. Muslims were frightened that unless they carved out an autonomous Pakistan they would be annihilated by a Congress-led, India-wide Hindu Raj. In Bengal, though, Hindus were only 45 per cent of the population, and had lived under a Muslim provincial government since 1937. Pakistan, or even an extension of provincial autonomy, would mean their being dominated by Muslims. Violence was not about religion or culture, but was driven by the fear communities had about other communities monopolizing state power. Weeks after the riots the Hindu nationalist leader Shyama Prasad Mookerjee noted accurately that '[w]hat happened in Calcutta was not the result of a sudden explosion. It was the culmination of an administration.' What he missed was the fact that fear of administration motivated both sides.[52]

Hindus 'got the better' of the fighting in Calcutta, as Vallabhbhai Patel put it. But Muslims fled to small-town Bengal and the cycle of violence continued. While riots in Calcutta only lasted a few days in August, fighting endured from October to December in Noakhali and Tippera, two districts where the famine had been particularly devastating, and where anti-Hindu rhetoric against landholders was particularly strong. Violence there was encouraged by leaflets saying the Muslim community was in grave danger and calling on Pakistan to be created by force: 'Our community is being hit by our enemies'; 'learn the scientific method of destroying Hindu properties'; 'with Pakistan established, the whole of India should be conquered'; 'all Congress leaders should be murdered one by one'. Violence was heavily organized, focusing on sites symbolically important to rival communities, with the destruction of almost all Hindu temples and the forced conversion of large numbers of men and women. Just as rioting divided cities into Hindu and Muslim neighbourhoods, violence partitioned the countryside by default, as those under attack fled to regions or relief camps where members of their community were in the majority. And as news spread quickly, riots in one place sparked fear in another, creating the strongest idea yet of religious communities which spread from one end of India to another. Hindus in Lahore held a 'Noakhali Day' to protest against violence against their co-religionists in Bengal; in Bombay, the stock exchange was quickly closed.[53]

As passions grew in the last quarter of 1946, the majority of political India thought the country was on the brink of civil war. Observers feared that millions on each side would be mobilized

into volunteer armies, and mutual resentment would sustain conflict for years. The British government's constitutional adviser
Nicholas Mansergh noted that 'ardent members of the Congress
and of the League both spoke freely about the possibility of civil
war'; both sides thought such a war could be won. Major General
Shahid Hamid, the private secretary to the Commander-in-Chief,
imagined that the Muslim League would recruit Muslims in the
army, and that Congress would be joined by volunteers from the
Hindu nationalist Rashtriya Sarvajanik Samaj. 'We are not yet in
the midst of civil war', Gandhi wrote on 15 September, 'but we are
nearing it.'54

Amid growing chaos, British officers in India imagined they
faced a choice between their two usual options: coercion or retreat.
Without a sustained commitment to maintain imperial power by
the Labour government in London, the first was impossible. In India
Lord Wavell thought 'one must either rule firmly or not at all', so
without 'a decision to rule India for fifteen or twenty years' there
was no choice but exit. The aim, as Wavell put it in a paper to the
British cabinet, should be 'to withdraw British authority with the
minimum disorder and loss to Her Majesty's Government and to
India'. Three weeks after the Calcutta riots, Wavell drafted a scheme
for the phased exit of all British personnel from India which he titled
'Plan Breakdown'. British officers were to leave India province by
province, starting with Madras, Bombay, Central Provinces and
Orissa where Congress had a stable, well-entrenched regime. It
was hoped that the 'shock' would force the Muslim League and
Congress to agree a settlement. If they did not, areas ruled by the
same party would presumably federate to form sovereign states. But
India would achieve self-government first of all as a collection of
independent provinces and principalities.

When it arrived in London, Wavell's plan created outrage. The
breakdown scheme was based on the Viceroy's assessment of the
facts of British power on the ground. As a soldier, Wavell was
interested in the physical occupation of territory. He recognized

where territory had been lost and where the pretence of power needed to be abandoned. But politicians in Britain were primarily interested in the formal display of sovereignty not the reality of local power. Their concern was the projection of power through the British manipulation of images of authority, which the age of the mass media allowed to be carefully controlled. Wavell's scheme for retreat abandoned the pretence of sovereignty that the British empire in its last phases in India relied on. The Prime Minister Clement Attlee and the Secretary of State Lord Pethick-Lawrence knew the British had no choice but to retreat. But they believed retreat could occur while maintaining the illusion of a conscious, planned transfer of sovereign power; they wanted to propagate myth, in other words, that the empire ruled until the last, that it had willingly transferred power of its own volition.

Wavell was recalled. In his place, the charming, media-conscious Lord Louis Mountbatten was appointed to stage-manage the 'transfer of power' and protect the image of British sovereign authority. Announcing his appointment in February 1947, Attlee also declared that Britain would leave India by June 1948. Mountbatten arrived on 24 March 1947, by which time fear and rioting had spread from Bengal much further west. In Bombay, Muslim League guards had started escorting fellow Muslims going out to the cinema back to Muslim 'zones'. In Amritsar, iron gates were erected separating Muslim from Hindu and Sikh streets.

The new Viceroy decided Britain's governing infrastructure could not last much more than a year. It was, he thought, safest for the British to leave as quickly as they could. Mountbatten also accepted that the only way to quit was to turn the de facto division of India between different communities into the partition of Britain's sovereignty into two states. The British were out in five, not fifteen months.

It was, ultimately the Congress leadership's reluctant decision to accept partition which forced Mountbatten's hand. 'The truth', Nehru admitted years later, 'is that we were tired men and we were getting on in years ... The plan for partition offered a way out and we took it.' India seemed to be on the brink of communal civil war. In addition, a peasant insurgency was growing in Bengal and the Deccan. In north and west Bengal's *tebhaga* (two-thirds) movement, sharecroppers made the moderate demand that no more than one third of their crop should go to the landlord. But the movement saw the growth of communist organization for the first time outside the cities which housed the industrial working class. The proliferation of red flags in Indian villages frightened Congress and the British. To prevent revolution or political breakdown, the Congress leadership sought the means to achieve the quickest transfer of power to a strong central state. A united independent India would have led to years of negotiation in the constituent assembly. Nehru thought this would have stopped the country getting on with the urgent use of central state power to make India less poor; Patel thought it risked civil war. In the end, Congress's obsession with central state planning trumped its desire to keep India united. The historian K. M. Panikkar used an appropriate metaphor to describe Congress's view: 'Hindustan is the elephant ... and Pakistan the two ears. The elephant can live without the ears.'[55]

But the Congress high command only agreed India could be partitioned if Bengal and Punjab were also divided in two on religious lines. Hindu and Sikh leaders particularly saw the removal of large Muslim populations in these two marginally Muslim-majority provinces as a chance to assert their own dominance. In the anxious atmosphere of the 1940s, Indian leaders preferred to exercise a monopoly of power over truncated spaces rather than risk sharing authority over larger swathes of land. Jinnah and the Muslim League initially insisted the two provinces form part of Pakistan intact. But once Congress accepted partition, the Muslim League had no momentum in negotiations. Jinnah, reluctantly, accepted what he called a 'moth-eaten' Pakistan at the final meeting in the Viceroy's residence with a sad, barely perceptible nod of the head. Z. H. Lari, a lawyer who had campaigned for partition, complained that what

Pakistan offered 'will be from every point of view so weak that we will find ourselves in serious difficulties'.

The fears of millions meant that India had become a divided society long before the summer of 1947. But those divisions did not have neat boundaries. They occurred within cities and in non-contiguous parts of the countryside. They could not be placed on either side of single lines and form international boundaries at the eastern and western end of the Indian subcontinent. The announcement of the plan that India would be partitioned occurred on 3 June, two months before the boundary of the two states was announced. In the meantime, Indians imagined thousands of other ways to reconfigure the sovereignty of the subcontinent. Muslim League leaders in Bombay urged the creation of pockets of Pakistan in Bombay province; Muslim politicians in Punjab and Bengal campaigned for their provinces to stay united, arguing that Hindus and Sikhs should be allowed to join Pakistan's constituent assembly; others thought India's largest conurbations could become city-states and achieve independence in their own right. The Nizam of Muslim-ruled Hyderabad in the south-centre of the subcontinent, initially wanted his state to join Pakistan, and then tried to assert its autonomy from both countries. Travancore, in the far south-west, made a bid for complete independence based on the higher than average levels of education in its population and the possession of rare metals vital for the construction of nuclear weapons beneath its soil.

Until the very date of independence in August 1947, Pakistan was nothing more than 'a fictive counter-nationalism to the Congress', as Yasmin Khan puts it. It was a fiction, nonetheless, which aroused passionate hopes and anxieties. In the months before independence, fear was fuelled by uncertainty, as no one knew where the boundaries of the new state would lie. Killings began in Punjab when gangs of Hindus and Sikhs attacked Muslims moving to make this fictional nation into a reality. Railway stations were attacked at the end of July. The first major act of sabotage occurred when the 'Pakistan special' carrying soon-to-be Pakistan officials from Delhi to Lahore was blown up five days before independence. Retaliation against Hindus and Sikhs occurred in Lahore, in particular, with some reports saying the station was a scene of constant gunfire on 14 and 15 August. Escalating fear of violence drove millions to trek one way or another across the border between India Pakistan. On their journey, hundreds of thousands were massacred. As in August 1946, frightened migrants brought with them a passion for revenge to their places of refuge. Violence escalated in mobile chains of retaliation. Muslims driven from northern India took their revenge when they moved to western Punjab. Hindus and Sikhs, angry about being driven from the land which had housed their families and shrines for centuries, arrived in Delhi and massacred the residents of the old city. Aggressors on both sides drew from professional techniques for inflicting violence they had learnt during the war. Mass death was not the work of mob frenzy. Partition killings were perpetrated by bands of disciplined, trained men using sophisticated weapons they had stolen from the army. A society mobilized to conquer outside itself had lost the capacity to live without fear, and entered into a brutal cycle of violence. Fractured into frightened, defensive enclaves, parts of India conquered themselves. The death toll has been estimated to be between 180,000 and 500,000.[56]

There are strange parallels between the violence which began and sustained British rule in India, and the violence which ended it. In both cases, small groups, fearful of attack, huddled in heavily defended safe spaces. They took revenge on those who caused their fear when they could gain the upper hand. In both cases, groups of people asserted a violent right to defend themselves without conversation with their opponents, and with no notion of how the cycle of violence was going to end. Violence escalated as people took responsibility for the survival of their own community, narrowly defined, without 'comprehending the working of other minds', as Beni Prasad put it. The difference was that the British concern with the acquisition of money and territory, and their lack of interest in control over people, meant the violence of conquest ended whenever Indians rendered nominal submission to it. Unlike the violence of imperial power, the violence of partition had a potentially unstoppable genocidal dynamic, because the existence of the living bodies of the enemy without one's own territory was a threat. In the history of political violence in India up to that point, the partition massacres were unique in being accompanied by rape and forced conversions. Many women who had been violated were not welcome back to their original families, however much India's new patriarchal states insisted that they were to be returned to their husbands and fathers. It was, perhaps, the intention of the perpetrators to force women – the potential mothers of children who could fight against them – to abandon the community of their rivals.

Historians often write about the violence of 1947–8 as the original trauma of India and Pakistan, as an unparalleled moment of tragedy which should always cloud our thinking about the creation of the subcontinent's new independent states. It was certainly tragic. But given the scale of social and political collapse, the violence which occurred in 1947–8 should be seen neither as surprising nor unique. The adjustment of the boundaries of Europe and the rest of Asia that followed the end of the Second World War was accompanied by mass migration, rape and death in many parts of the world. Proportional to their overall population, the transfer and massacre of Germans from Czechoslovakia were as devastating as India's partition violence. The civil wars that followed defeat of the Japanese in South East Asia were far longer and, again, led to greater loss of life. What is remarkable about the violence which accompanied India and Pakistan's independence is the speed with which it ended. Compared to the dreams of Indians before independence, partition was a disaster. But it could have been much worse.

Violence had been allowed to escalate because the British regime's priority before 15 August was to organize the safe retreat of soldiers and officers to ports and then on ships home. In the weeks before the handover of power, Mountbatten instructed the British army to avoid any operational situations unless British lives were at stake.

The only Indian soldiers the British deployed were members of the newly created Punjab Boundary Force, an organization which lasted only thirty-two days, and was so small it could only allot two men to every square mile in the border regions. It took three disastrous weeks for the new governments of India and Pakistan to act. In those first weeks, there was a moment of uncertainty about who the citizens of each of the new states actually were. For a brief moment, the government of Delhi seemed to have abandoned responsibility for Muslims, for example. Huge refugee camps for Muslims which sprang up the tombs of Mughal emperors in the city were deemed the responsibility of the distant Pakistani government. But by the middle of September, fast-acting emergency committees had been set up, soldiers from southern India had been deployed and political leaders were touring the worst affected districts.

In Delhi, it was Gandhi's tours of Muslim camps in the second week of September which made it clear to many that Muslims in India were Indian citizens. By November, Muslims started to move back to their homes, although only 150,000 out of 500,000 were left in the city. Still unhappy about the scale of violence, in January 1948 Gandhi decided to fast until violence ceased completely. The effect was massive. '[C]ontrition written on people's faces, a stoop in their walk, tears in their eyes,' wrote Begum Anees Qidwai, everyone's 'conversation was about Bapu's fast'. A hundred thousand government employees signed a pledge to work for peace, as did many political leaders, from the Hindu Mahasabha and various Muslim organizations who had long been critics of Gandhi. Peace committees were formed. Formerly antagonistic religious groups repaired each other's desecrated mosques and shrines.

Twelve days after he ended his fast, Gandhi was killed by a bullet fired by a Hindu nationalist frustrated at his 'concessions' to Muslims. Gandhi's death created a reaction against the cycles of violence he had struggled with throughout his life. As Gyan Pandey puts it, 'Gandhi achieved through his death even more than he had achieved through his fast.' His assassination stopped India from becoming an exclusively Hindu and Sikh space. Muslims in India and Hindus in Pakistan were still nervous, still ready to migrate at a moment's notice; many did move over the following years. The largest movement of Hindus from East Bengal, where there was little direct violence in 1947, occurred in the early 1950s. But with Gandhi's death, 'the world veritably changed', as the Urdu writer Ebadat Barelvi put it. 'Overnight, such calm was established, such a peace that one could not have dreamed of even a few days earlier.' Reason, briefly, seemed to have prevailed over chaos and passion.[57]

15

THE GREAT DELUSION

At the midnight hour of 15 August 1947 South Asia was bathed in darkness. If they were awake, most citizens in the newly independent dominions of India and Pakistan saw in the transfer of sovereignty by candle flame or paraffin lamp, without electricity able to power a wireless. From the parliament building in New Delhi, Jawaharlal Nehru announced India's awakening 'to life and freedom'. But Nehru's speech was heard by a fraction of India's population. More than 80 per cent of the people in the two countries which had just achieved independence lived in the countryside, and all but 1,500 (0.2 per cent) of India's half a million villages had no power.

The British left India a society of extremes. In pockets amid poverty South Asia was prosperous and modern. In the fifty years before 1947, cities had grown fast, British India going from one to six settlements with more than a million people. In India, 31.5 million (out of 370 million) people lived in settlements with a population of more than 100,000. These cities had electric streetlights and modern typewriters, railway stations and buses as well as slums and open drains. In the mid-1930s, 200,000 cars drove on the streets of India, every one imported from Europe or Japan. Bengal had one of the oldest Automobile Associations in the world. India had the highest rate of road accidents. University departments worked at the cutting edge of international science. By 1947, India was one of a small number of countries which conducted research in nuclear physics.[1]

The Second World War was a good time for some. Business boomed as shortages in every sector of the economy needed to be filled at any price. Rampant inflation was good for people living in the countryside able to tap the profits of production. This was boom time for rich peasants in places like Mysore and Punjab, where there were few agricultural labourers whose income would rise slower than the cost of living. But people paid in fixed wages suffered. Field labourers, factory workers and middle-class government employees all faced massively higher prices but no increase in income. Despite big industrial profits, one economist estimated that industrial wages fell by 30 per cent during the war. Agricultural labourers who did not own the land they worked on fared even worse. For many, it was a struggle to survive. Roughly the same amount of food was grown as in 1900, but the population was a fifth larger. Famine and serious scarcity had recently returned to parts of the subcontinent. The average new-born could expect to live only thirty-two years. In 1947, life for the vast majority of citizens in South Asia was rural, hard and short.[2]

Despite the century-long British effort to control the natural environment, millions were vulnerable to the vicissitudes of the seasons and the landscape. Two years after partition the 27-year old Pakistani writer Syed Waliullah wrote a description of rural Bengal in these years of chaos, emphasizing the brutal effects of nature on people's lives. From a family of minor government officials, Waliullah grew up during the depression in a village near Chittagong, before studying in the small town of Mymemsingh and then Calcutta University. At partition he chose Pakistan and became a news editor on Pakistan Radio. His novel *Lal Shalu* (translated later as *Tree Without Roots*) described the collapse of sociable norms in rural Bengal during years of famine and war, and was brutally unsentimental about life in the countryside. Waliullah was writing about a region which had once been one of India's most productive places. His home district was where the East India Company had hoped to conquer in the 1680s to profit from local agriculture and trade. By 1947, it was home to a struggling population left exposed to storms, floods and drought. To survive, land needed to be ploughed and reploughed to the point of exhaustion with 'no rest, no peace and what is worse, no nourishment, at least not from the ravenous ones who suck it dry'.

Waliullah described a rootless society in constant motion. Millions searched for something to eat or a place to make their home. People were ruled by 'a great restlessness', yet 'go hungry and starve'. Everyone dreamed of 'leaving their homes'. But the rivers, the trains, the paths were all crammed full of people on the same search. '[T]hey sweat and they swear, they solemnly pray for the infliction of God's curse on their neighbours and then they pray, equally solemnly, for their own safety,' Waliullah wrote. The political institutions which might have protected the vulnerable had long broken down. The forces which once ensured the poor were looked after had long collapsed. This was a description of a chaotic society in which everyone sought a refuge or an enclave just to survive.[3]

Enclaves

India's later British rulers and their post-imperial chroniclers liked to propagate the view that imperial rule in India was a systematic form of power driven by coherent ideas. 'The Raj' is a phrase which embodies a certain kind of authoritarian high-mindedness. On television or in fiction it is now associated with unbending, stiff-lipped men capable of imposing their visions of order and hierarchy and on an otherwise chaotic society. Historians of empire spend much of their time discussing those visions, tracing the British belief in the inferiority of Indian society, their rhetoric about 'civilization' and 'development', their arguments about property and the rule of law. Too often the context of those visions is absent, and texts are read with no reference to the situations they were written in. In reality, the British proclaimed their strength and purpose when their authority seemed the most fragile. In fact, as we have seen in this book, British power in India was exercised sporadically. It was driven by a succession of short-term visceral passions. It did not have a systematic vision of peace and stability, nor a way of working able to produce order. It created chaos.[4]

Rather than a coherent political vision, British rule in India was based on a peculiar form of power. Fearful and prickly from the start, the British saw themselves as virtuous but embattled conquerors whose capacity to act was continually under attack. From the seventeenth to the twentieth centuries, they found it difficult to trust anyone outside the areas they controlled. Their response to challenge was to retreat or attack rather than to negotiate. The result was an anxious, paranoid regime. The British state was desperate to control the spaces where Europeans lived. Elsewhere it insisted on formal submission to the image of British authority. But it did not create alliances with its subjects, nor build institutions that secured good living standards. The British were concerned to maintain the fiction of absolute sovereignty rather than to exercise any real power.

The result was that the British left South Asia a fragmented society. In theory, they transferred authority to new governments which possessed the power to protect everyone in the territories they ruled. In reality they left an uneven mess of enclaves and ghettoes, in which people were divided from each other by a jumble of different authorities, institutions and economic forces. The political institutions which the British left protected some people; institutions nationalists had built supported a few more. But most people were left unprotected from whoever or whatever forces had the greatest clout in mid-twentieth-century South Asia, whether the weather, rapacious landlords or powerful local political bosses. The British empire's greatest legacy was to create some of the most disjointed and chaotically ruled societies in the world.

To start with, the British transferred supreme authority to more than two states. When they announced their rapid timetable for departure in June 1947, the British declared that their supreme authority over India's 565 'native states' would simply lapse. By the date of partition, only 114 of these half-independent regimes had been cajoled into joining the Union of India and none to join Pakistan. For a brief period after August 1947 the world's list of independent sovereign regimes was swelled by hundreds of new absolute monarchies. Amir Khan's old principality of Tonk, with 2,500 square miles and 300,000 people, was formally independent for seven months until its Nawab signed up for his state to be incorporated into the Indian state of Rajasthan.

A few of these autonomous monarchies tried to resist the subcontinent's new political geography. Kashmir in the far north stayed independent for two months, until its Hindu Maharaja decided to take his Muslim-majority province into the Union of India and sparked the first war between India and Pakistan. Travancore in the south-west briefly declared its intention to 'recover' independence.

Last of all was Hyderabad, the largest native state 'situated in India's belly', as the minister in charge of state integration Vallabhbhai Patel put it. This Muslim monarchy was still a massive sovereign enclave a year after partition, intent on maintaining its independence from India and Pakistan. In the spring and summer of 1948 the Nizam's regime was fighting against a massive communist insurgency and Congress activists. The conflict drove tens of thousands of refugees into makeshift camps set up in neighbouring territories.

The new independent Indian government invaded in September 1948. Its aim was to dissolve the enclave of Hyderabad into the national Indian state, abolishing monarchical power by forcing it to accept the supposedly undivided sovereignty of the Indian people. But the Nizam's resistance led to four days of war and a communal massacre, as more than 50,000 Muslim supporters of the Hyderabad regime were killed by the army and Hindu soldiers.

Hyderabad began its life in free and democratic India under

military rule, with 17,550 of its citizens imprisoned by the invading army. The ensuing peace was caused by the prospect of elections, by the fact that the subjects of Hyderabad had become voting citizens of a new nation. Without conciliation, 'those who are down and out and full of fear' might vote against Congress at the polls. As a result, leaders in New Delhi decided that those 'who sinned so grievously' needed to be forgiven.[5]

Between the two new sovereign states of India and Pakistan, powers were incompletely defined and borders were not well demarcated. Passports took years to emerge; to begin with it was unclear who was entitled to which, and what should be written on their pages. The responsibilities of the two legal systems were not well understood. Well into the 1950s, judges in Calcutta were writing to Pakistani citizens explaining that were not entitled to sue in an Indian court. Many did not realize the creation of two states meant claims for lost property across India and Pakistan's new frontiers now needed to be handled by diplomats not lawyers.

Some people were simply stranded by partition. Nineteen forty-seven left some of South Asia's poorest people living in enclaves along the northern border between the Indian state of West Bengal and first Pakistan and then Bangladesh. One hundred and seventy-three small islands of land were entirely enclosed by the territory of a neighbouring state. The confused boundaries of the two states in northern Bengal date back to poorly defined peace treaties between the Mughal empire and its far neighbours in the early 1700s; one story says the enclaves were used as stakes in chess games between north-east India's regional kings. Until a deal was finally struck in 2015, the enclaves' 80,000 people were immobile and stateless, with no electricity and very few public amenities.

These border territories are a rare case of enclaves making people worse off. Mostly, enclaves are used as they were under the British Raj, to protect the powerful and wealthy from the rest of society. Post-imperial South Asia is still dotted with spaces where better living conditions are protected against poorer people living outside.

The urban map of the independent subcontinent was speckled with military cantonments, for example. Here, large swathes of often green and spacious land are divided off and protected from the city beyond by soldiers, remaining centres of military power in the midst of ostensibly democratic societies. Cantonments were first carved out by the British to create places where European military and civil officers could live without fear of a potentially insurgent population. Since 1947 these they have become cities within cities, offering a feeling of order for middle-class civilians as well as for the army and government. Army-ruled enclaves make up large areas of the centre of many South Asian cities: Lahore, Dhaka, Kanpur, Bangalore, Hyderabad. Added together, the area of India's cantonments would today make up a city bigger than India's most populous city, Mumbai. They remain more or less under military rule. The cantonment of Secunderabad in Hyderabad, which Indian soldiers fought to control in 1948, is one of the biggest. The majority of its population of more than 200,000 are civilians. Even though recent reforms mean half of its board are now elected, the army's commanding officer is still in overall charge. Residents complain that only roads in areas where soldiers live are maintained to a pristine standard.

In less heavily militarized places, middle-class South Asians use this imperial model of separation and defence to partition themselves from the 'chaos' and 'dysfunction' believed to rule the rest of society. Middle-class refugees from Pakistan settled in well-organized 'colonies' in Delhi, where living standards have been protected by community associations and, increasingly, security guards. Many public and private institutions follow the British-era pattern of putting residences and workplaces in isolated compounds. Universities, research institutes and large corporations provide accommodation as well as supporting a social life for their employees. These institutions foster a sense of common purpose, but they also reproduce the imperial idea that home is somewhere distant from the place people reside. Within the heavily guarded spaces of South Asia's bureaucracy, business and media, elites have cultivated their own exclusive communities, creating social norms which separate themselves from the rest of society.

Recently, these enclaves have been privatized, and take physical form in private gated communities, where the capacity to pay for property is the sole criterion for entrance. These new forts (some even with mock crenuellations) are scattered around the fringes of South Asia's quickest growing cities: Bangalore, Pune, Lahore, Delhi. Money buys an idea of safety and defence by providing closed-circuit cameras and security guards.

Gated communities are often marketed to lure expatriates back to the subcontinent with a safe, luxurious lifestyle. They have, for the most part, dropped any reference to the subcontinent's history in the seventy years since independence, creating distance between the green, pristine, generic forms inside and the supposedly characteristic South Asian mess outside. 'It's not like Pakistan, it's like a new country. You can get everything,' said a manual worker interviewed in 2013 who commutes to Bahria Town on the edge of Islamabad. Anuraag Chowfla, an architect who has planned some of the largest communities in India, reports that he 'sometimes joke[s] with the developer that now you should design your own flag and passport'.[6]

Popular sovereignty

The enclaves of well-defended prosperity which pepper India, Pakistan and Bangladesh exist in defiance of the idea supposed to justify the exercise of political power throughout the subcontinent: popular sovereignty.

Almost to a man, the British thought their sovereignty in the subcontinent originated with the violence of conquest. The difference between legitimate authority and violence was blurred; the fact of domination needed no other justification than its capacity to exercise brute force. But the imperial state's story about conquest was contested by Indian commentators, who argued that power should and could only be exercised with the consent of the people being ruled. From Sayyid Mahmood to M. K. Gandhi to B. R. Ambedkar, critics argued that the Indian people not the European army were sovereign. The British only governed because Indians let them, and that meant Britain had obligations to the people it ruled.

First used to try to persuade India's foreign rulers to govern in partnership with the people they ruled, the idea of popular sovereignty became the basis for Indian nationalism's effort to evict the British from power. This principle marked the difference, for both India and Pakistan, between the sovereignty of the empire's conquest state and the post-imperial regime. For Jinnah and Nehru alike, it was the people, not a party, an elite or a state, which had the authority to rule once the British disappeared. In contrast to British attitudes which they argued emphasized division and hierarchy, nationalists thought the people of their respective nations possessed a single voice or soul. There was, in this vision, no room for enclaves or imperial demarcations. Popular sovereignty meant the state's power needed to be exercised evenly, for the sake of all sections of society.

Since independence, ideas about popular sovereignty have been used to assert the break with the imperial past. A notion of shared citizenship has shaped polities supposed to be based on the will of the people not force. Constitutions have given people rights they can defend in court. Ballot boxes have allowed ordinary people to challenge elites who claim to exercise power on their behalf. In India, the idea of popular sovereignty has meant undemocratic forms of rule have never been sustained for long. Indira Gandhi's attempt to suspend India's constitution in 1975 lasted two years. Pakistan and, since 1971, Bangladesh have faced half of their post-imperial life under different forms of authoritarian rule yet even here the idea of popular sovereignty has force, too. Military dictators have always claimed (however implausibly) some kind of popular mandate. In neither Pakistan nor Bangladesh have military rulers survived more than five years without being forced to hold some kind of election. They have not lasted more than ten before multi-party democracy returned. Pakistan's most violent military crackdown, in East Bengal in 1971, sparked a war which broke South Asia's Muslim state in half. Throughout the subcontinent, the sovereignty of 'the people' has been routinely used to oppose privileged bastions of dominance and to challenge elites when they hoard money and power in their forts and enclaves.[7]

From long before independence and partition, these ideas of popular sovereignty drove the practical process of institution-building. The belief that power should be exercised by the people not a distant, violent state drove Indians to create schools, universities, banks, volunteer organizations, even businesses: when the City of London failed to invest in his steel business, Dorabji Tata appealed to the Indian people for capital. But before the end of the Second World War Indian institution-building was blocked by the coercive anxieties of the British regime. Independence allowed the energies of South Asia's institution builders to be unblocked and dispersed. In the name of democracy and popular political power, newly independent India and Pakistan created education and community uplift programmes, invested in science and technical education, built heavy industrial plants, founded new colleges and universities and dug hundreds of thousands of tube wells. As far as their limited capacity allowed South Asia's new states helped coordinate the expansion of production and the improvement of living standards. The path to economic development was fraught, fiercely contested and often patchy – but growth happened.

Compared to the stagnant chaos of the last years of British rule, living standards improved. In the first decade and a half after independence, agriculture became more productive. Much more land was cultivated. Thousands of new factories were built. Industrial output expanded. Middle-class jobs in service industries and the public sector grew even more rapidly.

South Asia's growth occurred while its societies avoided the catastrophic social upheaval which happened elsewhere. The organizations which ruled post-imperial India and Pakistan were committed to the reconstruction of their societies without violent revolution. Living through the turbulent years of partition, their leaders emphasized growth through stability rather than dramatic social upheaval, and more or less achieved it. In practice, this emphasis on consensus entrenched elite hierarchies. In India there was no major challenge to the dominance of upper castes until the 1970s. In Pakistan, the military and bureaucracy retained the upper hand.

This consensual approach was widely condemned from the late 1960s for allowing unaccountable elites to dominate. But it allowed stability to follow the turmoil of war and partition, and supported a period of relatively prosperity. South Asia did not take a dramatically different path from other non-communist post-war societies where the idea of popular sovereignty was combined with the effort by pre-war elites to retain power. The greatest contrast was between South Asia's aristocratic democracies and the revolutionary upheaval of China. In the 1950s revolutionary China was living through the world's most devastating famine, which caused the death of at least twenty million. In the subcontinent, living standards improved as India and Pakistan's economies increased at a respectable 4 per cent. Not as quick as recent decades, this was only very slightly slower than the contemporary 'miracle' of France. It was only exceeded in Asia by Cold War societies artificially stimulated by the United States such as South Korea and Taiwan.[8]

South Asia's post-imperial choice of consensus and stability stopped civil war and prevented socially catastrophic upheaval. But it meant that, in the seventy years since independence, ideas of democracy, citizenship and popular sovereignty have not been strong enough to overcome the chaotic legacy of imperial geography. Democracy has forced governments to ensure that the poor survive; citizens have demanded the right to receive enough food to live from their governments. But democracy has not created a common public realm in which people from different social groups have a sense they can shape society as a whole. Instead, advantage is gained as different groups claim they have a right to access the prosperous enclaves which offer wealth and power. Different castes improve their position by claiming they are entitled to government jobs or seats in parliament. Used for dramatically different purposes, with much greater ambition, ideas about what the state is capable of doing have changed little since the days of the Raj. Governments rule by classification and division; poverty, for example, is a bureaucratic category which separates the poor from the rest of society. Governments claim to be able to act on their own, often without dialogue. They are poor at acting in concert with others.

The result is that people mitigate their poverty the same way they did seventy or a hundred years ago; through their restlessness and migration, by bringing themselves near to the prosperous enclaves of South Asia's highly uneven economic landscape. In many parts of the subcontinent now, it is impossible for a family of rural workers to make ends meet unless they have a child earning in the city. Despite two generations of popular sovereignty, South Asia's societies retain one characteristic from the days of the Raj which has endured long after the end of imperial rule. Famine and the most extreme forms of poverty have largely gone. But most people are still very poorly paid for a day's work.

Labour-saving devices

In 1947, the 28,000 Britons who returned home after the evaporation of British sovereignty in South Asia arrived to a society on the verge of an economic boom. Britain in 1947 had been badly bombed. It only managed to stave off bankruptcy with austerity and loans from the United States. But by contrast with India and Pakistan, people in Britain who earned their living though manual work had relatively good living conditions. The collapse of Britain's empire in India happened at the same time as a quick increase in wages and living standards.

'Old Indians' who returned home experienced this difference in the difficulty of employing servants. Officials and their wives complained about fighting for a seat on the London Underground or bus, about the boredom of being relatively young with little to do, about the weather; but above all about the cost of labour. After living in households that teemed with staff, the families of ex-officials could rarely afford to employ more than a single maid, sometimes not even that. The manuals which guided returned officers about how to live back in England suggested the purchase of labour-saving devices. Women had no choice but to do housework.[9]

The disparity between living standards in British-conquered India and metropolitan Britain had many causes. The most important, though, was the different way these two societies were ruled. Living standards were so much better in Britain in 1947 for a simple reason: labour had a stake in the direction of British society it did not have in South Asia under British rule.

The disparity was clear during the Second World War, when social differences widened in India but narrowed in the UK. The war did not cause Britain's class divisions to crumble nor did it invent the welfare state. For long after 1945 Britain was a highly militarized, class-ridden, fiercely hierarchical society. But union membership increased, social benefits expanded, women were enticed from their homes to armaments factories with relatively good pay as well as the chance to contribute to the war effort.

During the war, labour was a vital interest in the accommodation which had shaped the direction of Britain's polity. It did not run Britain. But, unlike India, organized labour had a seat at the table. Britain's foremost trade union organizer, Ernest Bevin, was Minister for Labour in Winston Churchill's cabinet. The involvement of labour helped the creation of the national military-industrial complex which transformed the British state into such an effective fighting force during the Second World War. But it also created the conditions for the sustained economic growth which lasted until the mid-1960s. The loss of India did not mark the beginning of Britain's decline but the start of an economic boom.

In the years when the men who governed British India were uncomfortably adjusting themselves to life after empire, Britain's high-technology, highly industrialized factories spun out a quickly increasing quantity of export goods. British exports grew from £1.6 billion in 1948 to £2.8 billion in 1954 and then £3.8 billion in 1960 (£61 billion in 2016 prices). In 1950 Britain had a 24.6 per cent share of the world's manufactured goods (compared to the USA's 26.6 per cent), with 52 per cent share of world motor vehicle exports.

Demand for British goods came from across the world. To buy them, Britain relied most on the now long self-governing 'white' empire. In the 1950s Australia was the UK's largest trading partner. But the Commonwealth took less than half of British exports in total, with demand from the United States and Western Europe growing the quickest. By contrast empire in India left little economic legacy. Exports to India and Pakistan were comparatively tiny. In the middle of the twentieth century, Britain's prosperity relied on the relative productivity of its well-paid workforce, not on global imperial power.

The coincidence of Britain's economic prosperity with imperial decline shows how disconnected British India had been from the main currents of British life. For much of its existence, Britain's empire in India contributed little of value to Britain itself. English merchants had initially been interested in the subcontinent as a source of commercial gain; the East India Company's first wars were fought to defend the factories and forts it thought it needed to make a profit. But imperial power quickly created its own logic, which had little to do with economics.

The exception occurred during the twentieth century's two world wars. But then India was only turned into a source of Britain's global power by corroding the basis of imperial power in the subcontinent itself. The First World War was followed by the first phase of India-wide mass nationalist agitation. Britain's financing of India's role in the Second World War cracked the Raj for good, pushing British rule into a final phase of famine and violence.

Outside these destructive, aberrant moments, British rule was sustained by an elite whose lives were focused on nothing more than the survival of Britain's sovereignty in the subcontinent. For them, the logic of empire was circular; the purpose of imperial power was to do nothing more than maintain imperial power, and with it their pensions and sense of personal authority. That logic aroused passionate commitment from British India's white ruling class. But it meant that once the Union flag had been hauled down from the last citadels of British sovereignty there was nothing to do but pack up and go home.

From a financial or strategic point of view there were good reasons why the British might have stayed on. By 1947, there were few British business interests in India. But Asia still mattered to Britain. Commercial interests existed in Malaya and Singapore, and Australia was still a vital trading partner. The public rhetoric of empire claimed that the job of officials was to maintain 'good governance', and that still needed to be sustained in order to prevent the subcontinent falling under communist rule. The subcontinent's states had borders which needed protecting from malign powers. Both India and Pakistan were concerned to maintain a stable, centralized form of government in the midst of the crises of the late 1940s, so they offered those who chose to stay good terms.

A few did stay. Fifty civil servants and senior police officers and a few more soldiers were hired on temporary contracts by the Pakistani government. They made up one-third of Pakistan's civil service until the early 1950s. The country's mint, railways, telegraph, army and civil service college remained under British control, the latter until the 1960s. A handful of civil servants remained in the Republic of India, together with dozens of soldiers and European businessmen. Kanpur's textile factories were owned by a British capitalist until the early 1960s, for example.

But given Britain's long history of involvement in India, these numbers were tiny. Remarkably few stayed on. Out of 608 European ICS officers working in India in December 1946, only

429 were still in India on the day of independence; sixty-two were
left by the end of 1947, no more than fifteen by 1952, only three of
those in the Republic of India. Those few who stayed took the jobs
which the transfer of power altered the least. Officers in charge of
border districts were less likely to quit. Men working in revenue
collection were also most likely to stay. The last British bureaucrat to leave India was J. W. Orr, who retired from his position of
Inspector for Customs and Excise in Delhi at the age of forty-five in
1955, to become director of a gold mining firm. Compared to the
last days of other empires, the British left the subcontinent quickly
and completely.[10]

Coming back home

This quick departure helps us to see what British rule in India was
about. British officers and soldiers were in India to maintain British
sovereignty. Once that had gone there was no point staying on. 'No
longer ... serving under the ultimate control of the Parliament of
their own country', as one government officer put it, remaining
in the subcontinent was seen as pointless, even possibly risky. The
government's 'absolute priority' was to ensure a quick and safe
return for its European staff. Five thousand British civilians were
shipped back at a rate of 1,000 a month. Twenty-two thousand eight
hundred soldiers, mostly wartime conscripts, took only a few more
months to return home.

Officers returning home had two options. They could take up
pensionable opportunities in 'another civil service' with a grant of
£500 (equivalent to £17,470 in 2016 prices). Or they were given a
'severance allowance' equivalent to full pay to the usual retirement
ago of sixty with the prospect of a good pension afterwards.

'Old Indians' who did not take other jobs could maintain the
same living standards as dentists or doctors without having to
work, but the vast majority put their experience in the machinery
of administration to work. Many were employed by other branches

of Britain's bureaucracy, the largest number becoming diplomats or officials in Britain's African empire, quickly moving to other places where their job was to look after another outpost of British sovereignty overseas. Nineteen out of sixty-one ICS men who took part in a study in the 1970s joined either the foreign or colonial service; ten became civil servants in the UK. One or two became farmers or businessmen. Whatever role they took up, most of these men, used to exercising governmental power, found a small realm of administrative life to dominate. If they did not become civil servants they became college bursars or school administrators, managed lobby groups or became town clerks or local councillors.[11]

For these men, British rule in India had been about the Viceroy and the Union flag. It involved absolute control over a network of citadels and enclaves large enough to give them a delusory sense that they had real authority. It was also about the theoretical capacity of the British state to act without needing to negotiate with other powers. Sharing power was anathema; working for another regime impossible. As the Punjab officer Edward Wakefield wrote when courted by both the Indian and Pakistani governments to stay, 'I had spent my life in the service of the Crown and did not feel disposed to serve another master.'

By 1947, British power was understood by talking about 'duty', 'responsibility' and 'service', words that conveyed the trappings of sovereignty rather than any real kind of authority. If these were impossible in India, if the slim possibility of power required too many messy compromises, there were plenty of other spheres where it could be exercised. The British state did not give up the idea of ruling Africa until the late 1950s. And there was Britain itself.[12]

In the United Kingdom, the collapse of British power in India was marked by remarkable little stress or anxiety. The point, again, is that empire in India was not about influence or interest, but about sovereignty. When the British left India there was little lament about the loss of markets or prospect of reduced profits. The fact that the Union flag no longer flew was embarrassing, but even those parts of Britain's political hierarchy most attached to it quickly adjusted. The most important legacy of empire was not the British desire to control other lands. It was the peculiar form of power which British rule embodied in India and that, after 1947, was transported home.

The strongest British support for British rule in India existed in the Conservative Party, but even Conservative politicians adjusted to the end of the Raj quickly. Many were former ICS or army officers, or had relatives who had served in the subcontinent. When they thought about India they tended to use a romantic conception of British sovereignty rather than a realistic assessment of Britain's power in the world. While negotiations were ongoing in India, most of them doggedly resisted the unravelling of British sovereignty. But when its passing was obvious, they accepted the demise of British power quickly. There was no interest in influence, in 'informal empire' as some historians have called it, if there was to be no Union flag.

By 1947 the upper ranks of the Conservative Party thought Britain had no interest in remaining in India. Winston Churchill noted that 'modern air squadrons are worth more than overseas territories'. When he visited India in January 1947, Harold Macmillan was told by the Indian representative of his family publishing firm that a rapid transfer of power to Congress would be good for profits, particularly if the new government invested in schools and universities. But to begin with, both men fervently resisted the way in which the Labour government 'allowed British administration to run down', particularly fighting the renunciation of sovereignty over the princely states. Macmillan's worry was that retreat would leave 'absolute chaos'. Early in 1947, he argued that national servicemen should be sent to reimpose British power.[13]

By May 1947, Churchill, Macmillan and the rest of the Conservative leadership were willing to support the Labour government's bill to transfer power to two independent dominions in the subcontinent. By then, the prospect of retaining sovereign power in India had gone. The only choice was rapid retreat. The Tory high command's decision to acknowledge independence brought anger from local Conservative associations, many sending motions to the 1947 annual conference affirming that they were still 'the great imperial party'. But even rank and file Conservatives recognized that retreat was inevitable. There were other bastions of British sovereignty which needed protecting.

This quick volte-face on India had the greatest impact on the career of perhaps the most important post-war Conservative politician not to become Prime Minister, Enoch Powell. Powell was a romantic conservative, a man who saw violence as potentially virtuous, and who believed in the importance of constructing myths about power in order to maintain order and civilized life. He spent three years as a fellow in classics at Trinity College, Cambridge, eighteen months as Professor of Greek at the University of Sydney and then enlisted in the army in the first months of the Second World War. Desperate to fight, he was continually frustrated by being appointed to a succession of jobs planning and organizing the war effort. Between 1943 and 1946 he spent two and a half years working in military intelligence in Delhi. He ended his army career writing the last British report into the post-war shape of the Indian military, suggesting, unrealistically, the army increase its proportion of white officers.

In February 1946 Powell was offered the chance to stay on as head of the Indian army's college for training Indian officers. But at thirty-four he too decided to quit India. Anxious about the imminent prospect of a handover of power, he thought London, Parliament and the Conservative Party would be the most effective place to campaign for the continuance of British rule.

In the summer of 1946, while British institutions were collapsing throughout the subcontinent, Brigadier Powell wrote a report for the Conservative Party explaining how the British could reconquer the Indian subcontinent. Then, as through the rest of his career, his concern was to stave off chaos and anarchy. Powell saw uniform, united sovereign power as the only way to prevent it. '[T]he forces

ot disorder are endemic,' he wrote in May 1946. Indians would
'look to British order as a welcome salvation from chaos and strife',
he imagined. 'India', Powell believed, 'would need direct British
control of one kind or another for at least 50 years more.'[14]

These fantasies meant Enoch Powell was one of the few Britons
to be shaken by the independence of India and Pakistan in 1947.
Reportedly, he walked all night through the streets of London in a
state of disbelief when he heard that the transfer of sovereignty had
been announced. But Powell quickly, famously, reconciled himself
to the sudden collapse of imperial sovereignty. Once British power
in India was gone, he recognized empire was over and castigated the
idea of a Commonwealth of independent nations as a meaningless
fraud.

Powell could relatively easily reconcile himself to post-imperial
Britain because he was not interested in spreading British culture or
civilization overseas. Unlike America's global power, Powell argued,
the British had no 'missionary enterprise' of making everyone like
them. What mattered was the British state retaining its sovereign
power to command and not be commanded. The important fact was
not the power Britain had over other places but that it ruled itself,
and was a haven of civilization and order against the chaos which
Powell thought raged elsewhere.

Powell's imperial conception of Britain's unitary, absolute sovereign power influenced his lifelong opposition to both the European
Economic Community and to alliance with the United States. It
also shaped his approach to race and immigration in the UK. Enoch
Powell was the most famous opponent of Asian and Caribbean
migration to Britain after the Second World War. His was a conception of England as a culturally and racially homogeneous society,
an idea which belied the realities of post-imperial Britain. His
idea of a single community with a unitary undivided will drew
from his experience of the enclaves of British power in India. Like
British officers within the nineteenth- and early twentieth-century
Government of India, Powell always thought unity was necessary

to prevent anarchy. Like them, he believed order relied on the existence of a homogeneous group which could act consistently, and which was bound together by common race, a common set of myths and a willingness to make sacrifices for the 'generation interest'. The united power of the English state had once extended throughout the world. Looking back later in life, Powell saw that the idea of British power over India was a fantasy. 'The Raj' itself, he said, 'was a mirage'; a belief in British authority in India his 'grand delusion'. Since 1947 Britain's claim to sovereignty had shrunk back to encompass just Britain itself. '[I]t was', he said when looking back on these years of 'colonial disentanglements' twenty years later, 'as if the nation and the monarchy had come back home again.' Enoch Powell's nationalism repatriated the logic of imperial sovereignty to the narrower confines of 'home'.[15]

This book has shown that the idea of strong, consistent, effective British power in India was indeed a delusion. From the start of Britain's presence in the subcontinent, Britons were fractious and anxious, governed by chaotic passions as much as the rational effort to calculate their advantage. The British were driven by profit and the desire for a secure income; but their anxieties often led them to behave in ways which undermined their own interests. *Pax Britannica* only existed in the safe havens British India's small number of European administrators created for themselves. Otherwise, the idea of British rule as the source of peace, order and secure property rights was a fantasy, projected by anxious administrators to persuade themselves and their British public they were in the right. In practice, British actions prolonged and fostered chaos far more than they cultivated security and prosperity.

But the grand delusion is not just that British India was not what its propagandists claimed it to be. It is that absolute sovereignty is ever an effective form of power. Power, as the German-American philosopher Hannah Arendt argued, is the experience of 'action in concert', the remarkable achievement of many different wills acting together. The British in India were capable of deploying violence, also of shaping the material world; they certainly had an impact. But they never created real power in this sense. The history of British rule in India shows how, in the long term, the desire to establish a unitary and absolute form of power is self-defeating. Obsessed only with their own position and security, British officials were never the political leaders of the Indian subcontinent. British administrators could not shape South Asian society in their own interests let alone for its own good. Two hundred years of government in India could not even create a secure foundation for their rule. Constantly made vulnerable by the chaos they themselves helped to create, the British who conquered India were always one step away from defeat and humiliation.[16]

In Britain now, traces of empire in India are few and far between. Politicians and foreign office officials are embarrassed to mention the years of conquest and domination when they discuss the UK's relationship with the subcontinent. Statues to imperial heroes can still be found in urban centres, with Curzon's figure of Clive perhaps the nearest sculpture to the centre of British executive power at No. 10 Downing Street, and Sir Henry Havelock and Sir Charles Napier just up the road in Trafalgar Square. But the British public are more likely to see these figures as the object of bewilderment than support or anger. When people suggest they might be removed, no one defends empire. Instead, critics are challenged for 'doing Britain down', for wanting to undermine Britain's sovereignty over itself in the name of foreign interests and ideas. It is as if Enoch Powell's efforts to make the 'nation and the monarch ... come back home' have been successful. Wherever it is invoked, the idea of Britain's absolute sovereign control over anything, including just itself, conveys a sense of the country as embattled and isolated, surrounded by chaotic forces it cannot deal with, imbued with the idea it can only survive by building defensive walls to protect and defend itself. As in India, it is an idea based on delusion. In fact, Britain has never done anything alone. The history of Britain itself has been shaped by global trade, and by friendship and conflict beyond the places its empire dominated. Britain itself is made up of different interests, towns and counties and identities; it has been most successful when authority has been exercised far from Westminster, and then coordinated by an inclusive form of political leadership. In practice, the absolute sovereignty of the monarch and Parliament is not the same thing as effective power. There are better ways Britain can engage with itself and with the world.

Colonel's retreat

Powell shared with most recent historians the idea that Britain's empire was a coherent force in the world. In the last few decades, for radical critics of global capitalism and defenders of global Western power alike, the history of Britain's empire in India has become a metaphor and a political football. In the process empire is seen to represent a straightforward set of ideas about global domination which have endured from the days of the Raj to the present day. This book has challenged these myths of imperial purpose and power propagated on both the political left and the right. Looking at empire from the bottom-up, through the real lives of its functionaries and subjects, we see how imperial power was rarely exercised to put grand purposes into practice. Its operation was driven instead by narrow interests and visceral passions, most importantly the desire to maintain British sovereign institutions in India for its own sake. That desire created structures and institutions in the subcontinent, as well as those thousands of cemeteries which mark the resting place of Britons who died and were buried in Indian soil. But it left no purpose, culture or ideology.

We get a sense of this by looking at the fate of the monuments the British built to commemorate their rule in the subcontinent. The total, sudden British retreat from South Asia in 1947 meant there was little impetus to pull imperial monuments down. British observers in the 1950s and early 1960s were surprised to find 'there were still many streets named after English viceroys', even statues of

the British army's most brutal commanders in place. British visitors
imagined this was because of the high opinion South Asia's 'leaders
of opinion' placed on their connections with Britain. After his wife
sat opposite a portrait of her grandfather, the one-time Viceroy
Lord Dufferin at a dinner in Delhi in 1958, Harold Macmillan was
'impressed by the respect in which the British people were now
held'. More important was the fact that political elites wanted to
maintain stability and continuity, and that the rapid departure of
the British made them quickly irrelevant to South Asian life. When
politicians thought about removing a statue of Queen Victoria in
Bombay, the Indian Home Minister Vallabhbhai Patel sharply criticized them 'for bothering about the question of monuments when
they had far more urgent business on hand'. Patel's point was that
because the statues embodied a form of power which had disappeared there was no point in pulling them down. The absence of
enduring imperial purposes or ideologies meant the British were
quickly irrelevant to South Asia.[17]

The statues started to tumble in the 1960s. By then, images of
long-dead British officers had begun to symbolize something new
and different. For the left, particularly, in South Asia, they came to
embody a far more expansive form of power than the British had
ever claimed in India. They came to represent the West's cultural
and economic domination of the 'third world', a kind of power
summed up by the word 'imperialism' but which critics thought
had been continued into their own present time. The United
States was the state seen to embody this malign force most of all,
regarded as extending its influence not merely through military
might but through the economic clout of US-owned companies.
But as Britain tried to mitigate its loss of imperial sovereignty by
deepening its partnership with the United States in the 1960s, the
UK increasingly became a target, too. A movement grew calling for
economic ties with Britain and the US to be cut, for English to be
replaced with Hindi and for old imperial statues to be pulled down.
These campaigns were driven by a kind of vernacular north Indian

populism concerned to challenge Anglicized Indian elites who had retained power after independence; their target was domestic more than global. They had little traction in southern India, where imperial statues stayed longer than elsewhere. But the consequence was that state and city governments started to move figures of kings, queens and viceroys into disused exhibition grounds, junk yards and parks. For the most part, that is where they have stayed, replaced in their original location by new figures of regional and national heroes.

But in the last decade India has seen the emergence of a new attitude towards the imperial past. Many statues have been uncovered and washed; the grass around them has been cut, and their sites have been added to India's tourist maps. Old imperial monuments have been cleaned and renovated. In 2016, Victoria Memorial Hall in Kolkata was in the process of being renovated. Delhi is to have a 'heritage corridor', which will connect a series of monuments from pre-Mughal to British times by underground railway. Throughout India, British-era buildings have been opened up as resorts for the delight of India's middle classes. Hotel chains market British governors' residences and hill station retreats alongside Mughal monuments and rajas' palaces as part of India's single seamless 'heritage'. The chaos and fragility of British rule are passed over. For Indian consumers British rule is associated with a 'colonial' style of solid wood, high ceilings and leather armchairs, which evokes escape from India's fraught present into 'old-world charm', power and luxury.

For some, then, British rule seems to represent a form of power that newly connects to the ambitions of a modern, outward-looking global India. For others it denotes a systematic form of oppression, a site of devastating cultural and economic oppression. In either case British memorials can be assimilated into stories about the exercise of political power in the past running up to the present. In the process, British rule has become an almost infinitely manipulable set of images and symbols, few of which connect back to the realities of British power.

As an example, one might take the fate of Coronation Park in New Delhi, the site of the 1877, 1903 and 1911 Durbars but also the dumping ground for some of the Indian capital's largest imperial monuments. The park will have an underground station and a new visitors' centre. The statues of Queen Victoria and George V have been cleaned, but placed alongside new large red stone edifices which have Ashoka's circle, the symbol of the Indian nation, carved into them. In the process, British monarchs have been assimilated into a story about Indian institutions and power. Renovation was begun to commemorate the 100th anniversary of the decision to move the capital of British India from Calcutta (as it was called then) to Delhi in 1911. Now, that moment might be seen as the start of Delhi's growth into a sprawling metropolis of more than twenty million people, the centre of political power but also the largest lure in India for rural migrants. In 2011, it was celebrated as the point when the British finally recognized Delhi's centrality to the Indian nation, an instant which 'return[ed] to the historic city its lost glory', but which also signalled the beginning of their city's rise to prominence. The history of empire has been appropriated into a narrative about Indian national life.

But the contrast with the moment when Delhi became British India's capital could not be more extreme. Nineteen eleven was the only time a British monarch stood as sovereign on Indian soil. The durbar was held to celebrate British sovereign power over India; the decision to announce the new capital was a minor part of proceedings. In fact, the British government decided to shift their capital because they did not think Delhi mattered. The move was the attempt by a regime in recess to protect its power through retreat, from the vibrant site of political opposition to a city they thought was dead and empty. The point is that unlike Indian governments now, British officers in India were not concerned with their practical power to do things throughout India. They had no outcomes to deliver, no objectives to implement, and no way to be held to account. They were interested merely in defending themselves and maintaining the trappings of authority, and that could happen distant from the scenes of real political action. As perhaps we too often forget, they belonged to a world which was very different from ours.[18]

NOTES

Preface

1 John Burnell, *Bombay in the Days of Queen Anne*, ed. Samuel Townsend Sheppard (London, 1933), 25, 62.

2 Calculated from Julian J. Cotton, *List of European Tombs in the Bellary District with Inscriptions Thereon* (Bellary, 1894).

3 Peter Robb, 'Memory, Place and British Memorials in Early Calcutta', in Ezra Rashkow, Sanjukta Ghosh, and Upal Chakrabarti, *Memory, Identity and the Colonial Encounter in India. Essays in Honour of Petter Robb* (New Delhi, 2016); Ralph Waldo Emerson, *English Traits* (London, 1866), 56.

4 Graveyards calculated from British Association of South Asian Cemeteries records, India Office Records, (hereafter abbreviated as IOR) Mss Eur F/370/1.

5 Public Works Department, Government of India, *Central Public Works Department Manual* (New Delhi, 2012), v.

6 Ministry of Personnel, Public Grievances and Pensions, Government of India, *Central Secretariat, Manual of Office Procedure* (New Delhi, 2010).

7 Ranajit Guha, 'Not at Home in Empire', *Critical Inquiry*, xxiii (London, 1997), 488.

8 Benjamin Disraeli, *Tancred: Or, The New Crusade* (1847), 268; in a famous reference to this passage Edward Said, *Orientalism. Western Conceptions of the Orient* (Harmondsworth, 1978), xiii, 5 rightly criticizes Disraeli's assumption of a homogeneous 'East', but misinterprets it to suggest Asia mattered in British political life.

9 Lytton Strachey, 'Warren Hastings. An Essay for the Grieves Prize', 1901–7, BL Add Mss 81930; Michael Holroyd, *Lytton Strachey. The New Biography* (1980), 190 [ch.4]; S. P. Rosenbaum, 'Strachey, (Giles) Lytton (1880–1932)', *Oxford Dictionary of National Biography*, Oxford, 2004.

1. Societies of Societies

1 David W. Anthony, *The Horse, the Wheel, and Language: How Bronze–Age Riders from the Eurasian Steppes Shaped the Modern World* (2010), 454; Romila Thapar,

The Penguin History of Early India: From the Origins to AD 1300 (2003), 37–98.

2 Muzaffar Alam and Sanjay Subrahmanyam, 'The Deccan Frontier and Mughal Expansion, Ca. 1600: Contemporary Perspectives', *Journal of the Economic and Social History of the Orient*, xlvii (2004), 357–89; Richard M. Eaton, *A Social History of the Deccan, 1300–1761: Eight Indian Lives* (2005), 1–9.

3 Rosalind O'Hanlon and Christopher Minkowski, 'What Makes People Who They Are? Pandit Networks and the Problem of Livelihoods in Early Modern Western India', *Indian Economic & Social History Review*, xlv (2008), 382; Dilip M. Menon, 'Houses by the Sea. State Experimentation on the Southwest Coast of India 1760–1800', in Neera Chandhoke (ed.), *Mapping Histories: Essays Presented to Ravinder Kumar* (2000), 161–87.

4 For Bengal's fluvial ecology, see Iftekhar Iqbal, *The Bengal Delta: Ecology, State and Social Change, 1840–1943* (Basingstoke, 2010); Richard M. Eaton, *The Rise of Islam and the Bengal Frontier, 1204–1760* (Berkeley, CA, 1993).

5 N. B. Dirks, *Castes of Mind. Colonialism and the Making of Modern India* (Princeton, NJ, 2001), 13; R. B. Inden, *Imagining India* (Oxford, 1990).

6 Ghulam Hossein Khan, *The Seir Mutaquerin, or Review of Modern Times* (Delhi, 1926) iii, 189.

7 Muzaffar Alam, *The Languages of Political Islam: India, 1200–1800* (London, 2004); Mouez Khalfoui, 'Together but Separate: How Muslim Scholars Conceived of Religious Plurality in South Asia in the Seventeenth Century', *Bulletin of the School of Oriental and African Studies*, lxxiv (2011), 87–96; Nandini Chatterjee, 'Reflections on Religious Difference and Permissive Inclusion in Mughal Law', *Journal of Law and Religion*, xxix (2014), 396–415.

8 Farhat Hasan, *State and Locality in Mughal India: Power Relations in Western India, c. 1572–1730* (Cambridge; New York, 2004), 58–61; Farhat Hasan, 'Forms of Civility and Publicness in Pre-British India', in Rajeev Bhargava and Helmut Reifeld, *Civil Society, Public Sphere, and Citizenship. Dialogues and Perceptions* (New Delhi, 2005), 84–106.

9 Rosalind O'Hanlon, 'The Social Worth of Scribes: Brahmins, Ka⁻yasthas and the Social Order in Early Modern India', *Indian Economic & Social History Review*, xlvii (2010), 563–95; David L. Curley, 'Kings and Commerce on an Agrarian Frontier: Kalketu's Story in Mukunda's Candimangal', *Indian Economic & Social History Review*, xxxviii (2001), 299–324.

10 'Case of the Rani of Rajshahi', 26 September 1780, IOR H/215, 353–66.

11 M. J. Akbar, *The Administration of Justice by the Mughals* (Lahore, 1948), 13; Stewart Gordon, ed., *Robes of Honour: Khil'at in Pre-colonial and Colonial India* (Delhi, 2003).

12 Stewart Gordon, *The Marathas 1600–1818* (Cambridge, 1993), 32.

13 Stewart Gordon, 'The Slow Conquest: Administrative Integration of Malwa into the Maratha Empire, 1720–1760', *Modern Asian Studies*, xi (1977), 1–40; Gordon, *The Marathas* 76–78.

14 Gordon, *The Marathas* 70–79.

15 M. N. Pearson, *The Portuguese in India* (Cambridge, 1987), 13; Ranajit Guha, *Dominance Without Hegemony: History and Power in Colonial India* (1997), 64.

16 Sanjay Subrahmanyam, *The Career and Legend of Vasco Da Gama* (Cambridge, 1997), 50–56.

17 Pearson, *The Portuguese in India*, 55.
18 David Armitage, *The Ideological Origins of the British Empire*, (Cambridge, 2000), 8.

2. Trading with Ghosts

1 Sushil Chandra Dutta, *The North East and the Mughals, 1661–1714* (New Delhi,1984), 154–6.
2 William Hedges, *The Diary of William Hedges, Esq. during His Agency in Bengal (1681–1687)*, ed. Henry Yule (London, 1887), i, 43–4.
3 Ibid., i, 133–4.
4 'His Majesty's Commission to the Commander of the Beaufort and 18 other ships', 14 Jan 1686, IOR E/3/91, 56.
5 Phil Withington, *The Politics of Commonwealth: Citizens and Freemen in Early Modern England* (Cambridge, 2009), 11 & passim; Philip Stern, 'Corporate Virtue: The Languages of Empire in Early Modern British Asia', *Renaissance Studies*, xxvi (2012), 512.
6 Philip Lawson, *The East India Company. A History, 1600–1857* (London, 1993), 9–52.
7 Basil Morgan, 'Smythe, Sir Thomas (c.1558–1625)', *Oxford Dictionary of National Biography* (Oxford, 2004).
8 For a detailed account of the trial see Philip J. Stern, *The Company-State: Corporate Sovereignty and the Early Modern Foundations of the British Empire in India* (New York, 2011), 41–61.
9 T. B. Howell, *A Complete Collection of State Trials* (London, 1816), x, 430–1; Henry Pollexfen, *The Argument of a Learned Counsel* (London, 1696).
10 Howell, *A Complete Collection of State Trials x*, 484–6.
11 Ibid., 386–94; Pollexfen, *Argument of a Learned Counsel*, 54; Stern, *The Company-State*, 43.
12 'His Majesty's Commission to the Commander of the Beaufort and 18 other ships', 14 Jan 1686, IOR E/3/91, 59.
13 John Evelyn, *Diary and Correspondence of John Evelyn*, ed. William Bray (London, 1850), 173.
14 Gary S. De Krey, 'Hedges, Sir William (1632–1701)', *Oxford Dictionary of National Biography*, (2004).
15 Hedges, *Diary of William Hedges*, i, 30, 15; Stern, *The Company-State*, (New York, 2011), 46.
16 Hedges, *Diary of William Hedges*, i, 52, 81–2; Charles Fawcett and William Foster, *The English Factories in India, 1678–1684*, 4 vols (Oxford, 1954), IV, 308; Kasimbazar Factory Records, IOR G/23/4.
17 Hedges, *Diary of William Hedges*, i, 33; K. N. Chaudhuri, *The Trading World of Asia and the English East India Company: 1660–1760* (Cambridge, 1978).
18 Hedges, *Diary of William Hedges*, 35–42.
19 Fawcett and Foster, *The English Factories in India, 1678–1684*, iv, 230; Hent de Vries, 'Connecting Europe and Asia. A Quantitative Analysis of the Cape Route Trade, 1497–1795', in Dennis O. Flynn et al. (eds.), *Global Connections and Monetary History 1470–1800* (Burlington, VT, 2003), 35–106; Farhat Hasan, 'Indigenous Cooperation and the Birth of a Colonial City: Calcutta, c. 1698–1750', *Modern Asian Studies*, xxvi (1992), 65–82.

20 Hedges, *Diary of William Hedges*, i, 64.
21 Hedges, *Diary of William Hedges*, i, 165.
22 'Transactions of the Committee of Secrecy', 14 January 1686, IOR E/3/91, 70–82.
23 John Bruce, *Annals of the Honorable East-India Company* (London, 1810), ii, 646–653.
24 Dacca Diary, August–Dec 1690, IOR G/15/1.
25 Ray Strachey and Oliver Strachey, *Keigwin's Rebellion (1683–4), an Episode in the History of Bombay* (Oxford, 1916); Stern, *The Company-State*, 62–4.
26 John Ovington, *A Voyage to Surat, in the Year 1689* (Oxford, 1929), 150; Alexander Hamilton and Carl Bridenbaugh, *Gentleman's Progress: The Itinerarium of Dr. Alexander Hamilton, 1744* (Chapel Hill, NC, 1948), 219.
27 Bombay Diary Book, Feb 1689–June 1690, IOR G/3/3.
28 Edward Barlow, *Barlow's Journal of His Life at Sea in King's Ships, 1659 to 1703* (London, 1934), ii, 433; Stern, *The Company-State*, 123.
29 Chaudhuri, *The Trading World of Asia*, 509–511.
30 Lawson, *The East India Company*.
31 Ramesh Chandra Majumdar, *The History of Bengal* (Bengal, 1948), 384–90.
32 Alexander Hamilton, *A New Account of the East Indies* (London, 1744), ii, 4–5.
33 Aniruddha Ray, *Adventurers, Landowners and Rebels: Bengal c. 1575–c. 1715* (New Delhi, 1998).
34 'Native Legend of Job Charnock and the Founding of Fort William', *Calcutta Review*, cxx (old series) (1905).

3. Forgotten Wars

1   John Biddulph, *The Pirates of Malabar, and an Englishwoman in India Two Hundred Years Ago* (London, 1907), 253–67.
2   Philip MacDougall, *Naval Resistance to Britain's Growing Power in India, 1660– 1800: The Saffron Banner and the Tiger of Mysore* (Wodbridge, 2014), 90–94.
3   Manohar Malgonkar, *The Sea Hawk: Life and Battles of Kanoji Angrey* (New Delhi, 1959), 163.
4   Stewart Gordon, *The Marathas* (Cambridge: 1993), 109–110.
5   Biddulph, *The Pirates of Malabar, and an Englishwoman in India Two Hundred Years Ago*, 266; Bombay Proceedings, Nov 12, Dec 28, Dec 9, 1712, IOR 131–4.
6   J. F. Richards, 'Norms of Comportment among Mughal Imperial Officers', in B. D. Metcalf, *Moral Conduct and Authority. Place of Adab in South Asian Islam* (Berkeley, CA, 1984), 285.
7   Muzaffar Alam and Sanjay Subrahmanyam, *The Mughal State, 1526–1750* (Delhi, 1998), 23–40.
8   K. N. Chitnis, *The Nawabs of Savanur* (New Delhi, 2000), 192.
9   Alam and Subrahmanyam, *The Mughal State,* 46–8.
10 Yusuf Ali Khan, *Tarikh-i-Bangla Mahabat Jangi*, trans. Abdus Subhan (Calcutta, 1982); Jadunath Sarkar, 'Murshid Quli Khan', *Bengal Past and Present*, xvi (1946); Abdul Karim, *Murshid Quli Khan and His Times* (Dacca, 1963), 163; A. Karim, 'Murshid Quli Khan's Relations with the English East India Company from 1700–1707', *Journal of the Economic and Social History of the Orient*, iv (1961), 264–88.

11 Muzaffar Alam and Sanjay Subrahmanyam, 'Trade and Politics in the Arcot Nizamat (1700–1732)', *Writing the Mughal World: Studies on Culture and Politics* (2012), 339–80.

12 *Despatches From England, 1730-1733. Records of Fort St George*, Madras (1930), 4 Dec 1730, 31; Alam and Sabrahmanyam, 'Trade and Politics'.

13 Gordon, *The Marathas, 1600-1818*, 110–112. Surendra Nath Sen, 'The Early Career of Kanhoji Angre', *Early Career of Kanhoji Angre and Other Papers* (Calcutta, 1941), 1–19.

14 Bombay Public Consultation, 5 & 9 May, June 17, 1718, 22 Oct, 1718, IOR, P/341/4; Addison logbook, IOR L/MAR/301A.

15 Surendra Nath Sen, 'The Khanderi Expedition of Charles Boone', *Early Career of Kanhoji Angria and Other Papers*, 12–19.

16 G. W. Forrest (ed.), *Selections from the Bombay Diaries, 1722–1788*, Bombay Secretariat, Home Series (Bombay, 1887), ii, 25; Fawcett and Foster, *The English Factories in India, 1678–1684*, 184.

17 G. W. Forrest, *Selections from the Letters, Despatches and Other State Papers Preserved in the Bombay Secretariat*, ii, 28.

18 Chaudhuri, *The Trading World of Asia*, 178.

19 Gyfford's career can be traced in William Gyfford to Charles Boone, 20 August 1719, IOR G/40/21, 13–20, and other documents in the same file.

20 K. M. Panikkar, '*Some Aspects of Nayar Life*', *Journal of Royal Anthropological Institute*, xlviii (1918), 255.

21 Menon, 'Houses by the Sea', 161–87.

22 For the history of Anjengo, see Leena More, *The English East India Company and the Native Rulers of Kerala* (Tellicherry, 2003).

23 *Diary and Consultation Book, 1719–1723. Records of Fort St. George* (Madras, 1910), June 1721, 91.

24 *Diary and Consultation Book, 1719–1723*, 4 May 1721, 73.

25 V. Nagam Aiya, *The Travancore State Manual* (Trivandrum, 1906), 325–7.

26 Mrs Gyfford to Bengal Council, 26 April 1722, IOR G/40/21, 196; Bengal Council to Thomas Matthews, 22 September 1722, IOR G/40/21 203; Ft St George Council to Anjengo, 199; Mrs Gyfford to Court of Directors, 6 Jan 1743, IOR E/1/32, 10.

4. Passions at Plassey

1 Michael Axworthy, *The Sword of Persia: Nader Shah, from Tribal Warrior to Conquering Tyrant* (London, 2010), 6–8; Sanjay Subrahmanyam, 'Un Grand Dérangement: Dreaming an Indo-Persian Empire in South Asia, 1740–1800', *Journal of Early Modern History*, iv (2000), 337–78.

2 Ananda Ranga Pillai, *Private Diary of Ananda Ranga Pillai*, ed. Henry Dodwell (Madras, 1922), i, 94; Ashin Das Gupta, 'Trade and Politics in 18th Century India' in D. S. Richards, ed., *Islam and the Trade of Asia* (Oxford 1970), 184-5.

3 Nirad C. Chaudhuri, *Clive of India* (London, 1975); An example of the importance of Plassey and Clive for modern Indian historiography is the textbook Sekhar Bandyopadhyay, *From Plassey to Partition: A History of Modern India* (New Delhi, 2004).

4 Quoted in Munis D. Faruqui, 'At Empire's End: The Nizam, Hyderabad and

Eighteenth-Century India', in Richard M. Eaton et al., *Expanding Frontiers in South Asian and World History: Essays in Honour of John F. Richards* (Cambridge, 2013), 22; John Malcolm, *The Life of Robert, Lord Clive* (London, 1836), i, 16.

5   For the political narrative see N. S. Ramaswami, *Political History of Carnatic Under the Nawabs* (New Delhi, 1984), 86–114.

6   Saunders to Court of Directors, 30 Sept, 1751 in *Despatches to England, 1743–1751. Records of Fort St. George* (Madras, 1933), 144.

7   Consultation in *Diary and Consultation Book, 1751. Records of Fort St. George*, 4 Nov 1751, 130.

8   Sarojini Regani, *Nizam-British Relations, 1724–1857* (New Delhi, 1963), 121–44.

9   André Wink, 'Maratha Revenue Farming', *Modern Asian Studies*, xvii (1983), 591–628.

10 Khan, *Tarikh-I-Bangla Mahabat Jangi*, 42–7.

11 P. J. Marshall, *Bengal: The British Bridgehead. Eastern India, 1740-1828* (Cambridge, 1987), 70–72; Gangarama, *The Maharashta Purana: An Eighteenth-Century Bengali Historical Text* (Honolulu, HA, 1965).

12 Marshall, *Bengal: The British Bridgehead.* 72.

13 Orme to Clive, 25 Aug 1752, IOR Mss Orme/19, 1–2.

14 William Tooke, Narrative of the Capture of Calcutta, 10 Apr–10 Nov 1756 in Samuel Charles Hill, *Bengal in 1756–1757:* (Calcutta, 1905), i, 268; Brijen Kishore Gupta, *Sirajuddaullah and the East India Company, 1756–1757:* (Leiden, 1962), 50.

15 Khan, *Tarikh-i-Bangla Mahabat Jangi*, 118–1199.

16 Nawab to Coja Wajid, 28 May 1756 in Hill, *Bengal in 1756–1757*, i, 3.

17 Jadunath Sarkar and Karim Ali (eds.), 'Muzzafarnamah', *Bengal Nawabs* (Calcutta, 1952), 63; Gupta, *Sirajuddaullah and the East India Company, 1756–1757*, 52.

18 Lenman, 'Clive, the 'black jagir' and British Politics', *Historical Journal* 26, 4 (1983), 801-829.

19 Letters from Clive to William Mabbot [January 1756], & 6 Oct 1756, CR1/1, 6 & 16, Clive Papers, National Library of Wales.

20 Clive to William Mabbot, 6 Oct 1756 in Hill, *Bengal in 1756–1757*, i, 228.

21 Council at Fulta to Court of Directors, 17 Sept 1756 in Hill, *Bengal in 1756–1757*, i, 214.

22 Clive to his Father, 9 Oct 1756, Hill, *Bengal in 1756–1757*, i, 227.

23 Hill, i, 242, 248, 227; Pigot to Nawab, 14 Oct 1756 in Hill, *Bengal in 1756–1757*, i, 241.

24 John Corneille, *Journal of My Service in India* (London, 1966), 66.

25 Corneille, *Journal of My Service in India*, 23, 88, 126.

26 Ibid., 109.

27 Watson to Nawab, 4 Feb 1757 in Hill, *Bengal in 1756–1757*, ii, 273. G. J. Bryant, *The Emergence of British Power in India, 1600–1784* (Woodbridge, 2013), 131.

28 Corneille, *Journal of My Service in India*, 115.

29 Hill, *Bengal in 1756–1757*, ii, 240; ii, 163; ii, 203, 76; Khan, *The Transition in Bengal, 1756–75*, 5.

30 Manik Chandra to Clive, 23 Dec 1756 & Clive to Manik Chandra, 25 Dec 1756, IOR H/193, nos.4–5.

31 Kumkum Chatterjee, *Merchants, Politics, and Society in Early Modern India :*
    Bihar, 1733–1820 (Leiden, 1996), 102–6.

32 Corneille, *Journal of My Service in India*, 113.

33 Journal of Captain Eyre Coote in Hill, *Bengal in 1756–1757*, i, 54; Clive's
    Narrative in Hill, *Bengal in 1756–1757*, ii, 420–3.

34 A. Mervyn Davies, *Clive of Plassey. A Biography* (London, 1939), 215–216;
    Mark Bence-Jones, *Clive of India* (London, 1974), 137.

35 Hill, *Bengal in 1756–1757*, i, cxcix–cci; Journal of Captain Eyre Coote Hill,
    Bengal in 1756–1757, iv, 55.

36 Percival Spear, *Master of Bengal. Clive and His India* (London, 1975), 91;
    compare with John Keegan, *The Face of Battle. A Study of Agincourt, Waterloo*
    and the Somme (Harmondsworth, 1983) and Randall Collins, *Violence: A Micro-*
    Sociological Theory (Princeton, NJ, 2009).

37 Bryant, *The Emergence of British Power in India, 1600–1784*, 153; Malcolm, *The*
    Life of Robert, Lord Clive, 271.

38 Letter from Clive to Luke Scrafton, January 1757, IOR H/808, 65.

39 Brenda J. Buchanan, *Gunpowder, Explosives and the State: A Technological History*
    (2006), 68–87; John William James Stephenson, *Treatise on the Manufacture of*
    Saltpetre (1835), 88–96.

40 Kumkum Chatterjee, *Merchants, Politics, and Society in Early Modern India*, 168–76.

41 Khan, *The Transition in Bengal, 1756–75*, 28; Henry Vansittart, *A Narrative of*
    the Transactions in Bengal, from the Year 1760, to the Year 1764 (1766), 35.

42 Khan, *The Transition in Bengal, 1756–75*, 32–5.

43 Ibid., 32–45.

44 Ishrat Haque, *Glimpses of Mughal Society and Culture: A Study Based on Urdu*
    Literature, in the 2nd Half of the 18th Century (1992), 58.

45 Jos J. L. Gommans, *The Rise of the Indo-Afghan Empire: c. 1710–1780* (1995), 57,
    Bryant, *The Emergence of British Power in India, 1600–1784*, 161; Mountstuart
    Elphinstone, *The Rise of British Power in India* (London, 1887), 400–417.

46 Khan, *Seir Mutaquerin*, iii, 9.

47 Bryant, *The Emergence of British Power in India, 1600–1784*, 179.

48 Trends calculated from John F. Richards, 'The Finances of the East India
    Company in India, c.1766–1859', *LSE Economic History Working Papers*, (2011);
    Khan, *Seir Mutaquerin*, iii, 9.

49 Chart source: Richards, 'The Finances of the East India Company'.

50 Robert Travers, *Ideology and Empire in Eighteenth-Century India. The British in*
    Bengal (Cambridge, 2007), 75.

51 'Account of the Late Famine in India', *Gentleman's Magazine and Historical*
    Review, xli (1771), 402–5; William Wilson Hunter, *The Annals of Rural Bengal*
    (London, 1868), 19–20.

52 Rajat Datta, *Society, Economy, and the Market: Commercialization in Rural Bengal,*
    c. 1760–1800 (New Delhi, 2000), 238–50.

53 'Account of the Late Famine in India', 403; J.R. McLane, *Land and Local*
    Kingship in 18th Century Bengal (Cambridge, 1993), 194.

54 'Grosely's Tour to London', *The Monthly Review, Or, Literary Journal*, xlvii
    (1772), 173; David Coke, *Vauxhall Gardens: A History* (New Haven, ConnCT;
    London, 2011).

55 William Maskelyne to Mrs Clive, Mss Eur, G37/24, 68.

56 H.V. Bowen, *Revenue and Reform: The Indian Problem in British Politics 1757–1773* (Cambridge, 1991), 13.
57 Alan Ramsay, *An Essay on the Right of Conquest*, (Florencem 1783), 9; David Hume, *Treatise of Human Nature*, ed. L. A. Selby-Digge (Oxford, 1896), 600.

5. New Systems

 1 Gabriel B. Paquette, *Enlightenment, Governance, and Reform in Spain and Its Empire, 1759–1808* (Basingstoke, 2008); C. A. Bayly, *The Birth of the Modern World, 1780–1914* (Oxford, 2004).
 2 Jon E. Wilson, *The Domination of Strangers: Modern Governance in Eastern India, 1780–1835* (Basingstoke, 2008), 19–44; Numbers calculated from *East India Register* (London, 1773) and *East India Kalendar* (London, 1800).
 3 Henry Morris, *A Descriptive and Historical Account of the Godavery District* (London, 1878), 20–21, 70–71, 258–60.
 4 Mallikarjuna Rao, 'Native Revolts in the West Godavari District, 1785–1805' (Andhra University PhD, 2000), 42–50; Jon E. Wilson, '"A Thousand Countries To Go To": Peasants and Rulers in Late Eighteenth-Century Bengal', *Past & Present*, clxxxix (2005), 81–109; Jon Wilson, 'How Modernity Arrived to Godavari', *Modern Asian Studies*, ii (2016).
 5 Branfill to Madras Board of Revenue, 17 Oct 1799, IOR F/4/170, 443.
 6 Branfill to Captain John English, 30 Mar 1800; Branfill to Col. Vigors, 31 Mar 1800; Branfill to Board of Revenue, April 1800, Andhara Pradesh Sate archives, Godvari District Records, vol. 856, 109–112 & 130.
 7 Kindersley to Board of Revenue, 13 May 1824, Andhara Pradesh Sate Archives, Godvari District Records, vol. 4638, 103–110.
 8 Bentinck to Court of Directors, 28 August 1804, IOR E/4/894, 381–3.
 9 Madras Despatch, 27 June 1804, IOR E/4/892, 571.
10 John Stuart Mill, Speech on East India Company Revenue Accounts, *Hansard, House of Commons*, 12 August 1867, §1384.
11 Bowen, *Revenue and Reform: The Indian Problem in British Politics 1757–1773*, 184–6.
12 Travers, *Ideology and Empire in Eighteenth-Century India*.
13 Fanny Burney, *Diaries and Letters of Madame D'Arblay*, ed. Charlotte Barrett (1796), iii, 411; P. J. Marshall, 'The Personal Fortune of Warren Hastings', *The Economic History Review*, xvii (1964), 293.
14 Edmund Burke, *The Writings and Speeches of Edmund Burke*, ed. P. J. Marshall (Oxford, 1991), vi, 381–3; Richard Bourke, 'Liberty, Authority, and Trust in Burke's Idea of Empire', *Journal of the History of Ideas*, lxi (2000).
15 Richard Bourke, *Empire and Revolution: The Political Life of Edmund Burke* (Princeton, NJ, 2015), 16–25, 339.
16 Wilson, *The Domination of Strangers*, 53.
17 Wilson, *The Domination of Strangers*, 58–76; D. H. A. Kolff, *Grass in Their Mouths: The Upper Doab of India Under the Company's Magna Charta, 1793–1830* (Leiden, 2010), 20.
18 John Francis Davis, *Vizier Ali Khan: Or, The Massacre of Benares*, (London, 1871), 12.
19 Thomas Williamson, *The East India Vade-Mecum; Or, Complete Guide to Gentlemen Intended for the Civil, Military, or Naval Service of the Hon. East India Company* (1810); M. S. Islam, 'Life in the Mufassal Towns of

Nineteenth-Century Bengal', in Kenneth Ballhatchet and John Harrison (eds.), *The City in South Asia: Pre-Modern and Modern* (London, 1980); Tania Sengupta, 'Living in the Periphery: Provinciality and Domestic Space in Colonial Bengal', *The Journal of Architecture*, xviii (2013) 905-943.

20 Mountstuart Elphinstone to Anne Elphinstone, 20 Nov 1796, IOR Mss Eur F88/59/21.

21 Anand A. Yang, *The Limited Raj: Agrarian Relations in Colonial India, Saran District, 1793–1920* (New Delhi, 1989), 94–5.

22 Julia Maitland, *Letters from Madras: During the Years 1836–1839* (London, 1846), 61–3; Joy Wang, 'Maitland, Julia Charlotte (1808–1864)', *Oxford Dictionary of National Biography* (Oxford, 2004) www.oxforddnb.com/index/101048645/Julia-Maitland, accessed 23 April 2016.

23 Maitland, *Letters from Madras*, 46–7.

24 'Abstract of Regulations of the Bengal Government', *Parliamentary Papers* 1831–2 (735–IV), iv, Appendix, 638–817.

25 H. T. Colebrooke, *A Digest of Hindu Law on Contracts and Successions, with a Commentary* (Calcutta, 1798).

26 Rammohan Roy, 'Questions and Answers on the Judicial System of India', *Parliamentary Papers*, 1831 (320A), 726.

27 Hossein Khan Tabatabai, *The Seir Mutaquerin, or Review of Modern Times*, III, 200.

28 Sudder Dewanny Adawlut, 19 Sept 1793, no.5, IOR P/154.

29 Chittabrata Palit, *Tensions in Bengal Rural Society: Landlord, Planters, and Colonial Rule, 1830–1860* (1975).

30 James Wordsworth, 'Police Report, District of Rangpur', (1799); J.D. Paterson to Police Committee, 30 Aug 1799, NAB, Faridpur District Records, vol. 62, 8.

31 Bernard S. Cohn, 'The British in Benares: A Nineteenth Century Colonial Society', *Comparative Studies in Society and History*, iv (1962).

32 R. K. Gupta, *The Economic Life of a Bengal District, Birbhum, 1770–1857* (Burdwan, 1984).

33 Petition of Alexander Paniotty, 4 April 1800, National Archives of Bangladesh, Dhaka District Records, vol.135, 268–80

34 Rammohan Roy, 'Questions', *Parliamentary Papers*, 1831 (320A), 718.

35 Ratnalekha Ray, *Change in Bengal Agrarian Society, c.1760–1850* (New Delhi, 1979); Eric Stokes, 'The First Century of British Colonial Rule in India: Social Revolution or Social Stagnation?', *Past and Present*, viii (1973).

36 McLane, *Land and Local Kingship in 18th Century Bengal*.

37 Iqbal, *The Bengal Delta*; C. A. Bayly, *Rulers, Townsmen and Bazaars: North Indian Society in the Age of British Expansion 1770–1870* (Cambridge, 1983).

38 Petition of Raja of Diviseema, 10 Jan 1812, Andhra Pradesh State Archives, Godavari District Records, vol. 873, 15–18.

39 Prasannan Parthasarathi, 'Deindustrialisation in Nineteenth-Century South India' in Giorgio Riello and Tirthankar Roy, *How India Clothed the World: The World of South Asian Textiles, 1500–1850* (Leiden, 2009), 426. Henry Montgomery, 'Report on Rajahmundry District,' 18 Mar 1844, IOR P/230/49, 2090-2192; Henry Morris, A Descriptive Account of the Godaveri District (London, 1878), 279-292.

40 Amales Tripathi, *Trade and Finance in the Bengal Presidency, 1793–1833*, (Calcutta, 1979), 211.

41 Calculated from tables in Montgomery, 'Report on Rajahmundry District', 2099–2100.

42 B. B. Kling, *Partner in Empire: Dwarkanath Tagore and the Age of Enterprise in Eastern India* (Berkeley, CA, 1976), 56; H. V. Bowen, *The Business of Empire: The East India Company and Imperial Britain, 1756–1833* (Cambridge, 2006), 278.

43 Wilson, *The Domination of Strangers*, 104–33.

44 Yang, *The Limited Raj*.

45 Bourke, *Empire and Revolution*, 672–3.

46 Dutta, *The North-East and the Mughals, 1661–1714*; Ray, *Change in Bengal Agrarian Society, c.1760–1850*.

47 E. G. Glazier, *A Report on the District of Rungpore* (Calcutta, 1873), 1–48.

48 National Archives of Bangladesh, Rangpur District Records, vol. 290, 65, vol. 298, 30.

49 Palit, *Tensions in Bengal Rural Society*, 38; Kling, *Partner in Empire: Dwarkanath Tagore and the Age of Enterprise in Eastern India*; Ray, *Change in Bengal Agrarian Society, c.1760–1850*.

50 William Digby to Board of Revenue, National Archives of Bangladesh, Rangpur District Records, vol. 306B, 271.

51 Shomik Dasgupta, 'Ethics, Accountability and Distance: The Political Thought Rommohun Roy (King's College London, PhD thesis, 2016).

52 C. A. Bayly, *Recovering Liberties: Indian Thought in the Age of Liberalism and Empire* (Cambridge, 2011).

53 Kling, *Partner in Empire*, 78.

54 Lyn Zastoupil, *Rammohun Roy and the Making of Victorian Britain* (Basingstoke, 2010), 121–150.

55 S. D. Collet, *Life and Letters of Raja Rammohun Roy* (Calcutta, 1913), 2d, 178–81.

56 'Revenue and Judicial System of India', *Parliamentary Papers*, 1831 (320A), 716–41.

57 Kling, *Partner in Empire: Dwarkanath Tagore and the Age of Enterprise in Eastern India*, 74.

58 Rammohun Roy (Raja), *The Essential Writings of Raja Rammohan Ray* (1999), 268–71; Bruce Carlisle Robertson, 'The English Writings of Raja Rammohan Roy', in Arvind Krishna Mehrotra, *A History of Indian Literature in English* (2003), 29–31.

6. Theatres of Anarchy

1 For the background of Manjeshwar temple, see P. Gururaja Bhatt, *Studies in Tuluva History and Culture: From the Pre-Historic Times Upto [sic] the Modern* (Kallianpur, 1975), 134.

2 Thomas Munro to Richard Wellesley, Dec 1799, BL Add Mss 13,679, 2–5.

3 Thomas Munro to William Petrie, 16 June 1800, IOR P/254/59, 6306–14; John G. Ravenshaw to G. Garrow, 27 Aug 1801, IOR P/254/77, 448–9.

4 Wellesley to Dundas, 28 July 1798, in Edward Ingram (ed.), *Two Views of British India: The Private Correspondence of Mr. Dundas and Lord Wellesley, 1798–1801* (1970), 55; B. Surendra Rao, *Bunts in History and Culture* (Udupi, 2010), 176.

5   N. Shyam Bhat, *South Kanara, 1799 1860: A Study in Colonial Administration and Regional Response* (New Delhi, 1998), 57–9.

6   C. A. Bayly, 'Wellesley, Richard, Marquess Wellesley (1760–1842)', *The Oxford Dictionary of National Biography* (Oxford, 2004) [www.oxforddnb.com/view/article/29008, accessed 31 July 2014].

7   Sir John Malcolm, *The Government of India* (London, 1833), 187.

8   Mark Wilks, *History of Mysore* (London, 1810), 660; Kate Brittlebank, 'The White Raja Of Srirangapattana: Was Arthur Wellesley Tipu Sultan's True Successor?', *South Asia*, xxvi (2003), 23–35; Penderel Moon, *The British Conquest and Dominion of India* (London, 1989), 278.

9   Arthur Wellelsey to Barry Close, 15 Dec 1799, in Lt. Col. John Gurwood, *The Dispatches of the Duke of Wellington, on His Various Campaigns* (London, 1837), xiii, 4–7.

10 Arthur Wellesley to Barry Close, 8 Feb 1800, in ibid., xiii, 35 Meerob Vartavarias, 'Pacification and Patronage in the Maratha Deccan, 1803-1818', Modern Asian Studies 51, i (2017), 1-43.

11 C. A. Bayly, 'The British Military-Fiscal State and Indigenous Resistance in India, 1750–1820', in Lawrence Stone, *An Imperial State at War: Britain From 1689–1815* (London, 1994), 344–6.

12 Burton Stein, *Thomas Munro. The Origins of the Colonial State and His Vision of Empire* (Delhi, 1989), 87–9.

13 Stein, *Thomas Munro*, 89–91; *History of the Madras Army* (1883), iii, 25–31.

14 For the career of the concept see Clive Dewey, 'Images of the Village Community: A Study in Anglo-Indian Ideology', *Modern Asian Studies*, vi (1972), 296–97; Thomas R. Metcalf, *Ideologies of the Raj* (Cambridge, 1997), 70; Ronald B. Inden, *Imagining India* (Oxford, 2000), 137–42; Richard Fox, *Gandhian Utopia: Experiments with Culture* (1989); Karuna Mantena, *Alibis of Empire: Henry Maine and the Ends of Liberal Imperialism* (Princeton, NJ, 2010), 126–66.

15 Kenneth Ballhatchet, *Social Policy and Social Change in Western India 1817–1830* (London, 1961), 33; David Washbrook, 'South India 1770–1840: The Colonial Transition', *Modern Asian Studies*, xxxviii (2004), 479–516.

16 Arthur Wellesley to Barry Close, 1 Jan 1803, in Gurwood, *The Dispatches of the Duke of Wellington*, 391–400; Randolf G. S. Cooper, *The Anglo-Maratha Campaigns and the Contest for India: The Struggle for Control of the South Asian Military Economy* (Cambridge, 2003), 284–313.

17 Munro to Lord Wellesley, 11 Dec 1802, in George Robert Gleig, *The Life of Major-General Sir Thomas Munro* (1831), 367.

18 John Malcolm to Lord Clive, 3 April 1803, in Gurwood, *The Dispatches of the Duke of Wellington*, i, 466; Henry Thoby Prinsep, *Memoirs of the Puthan Soldier of Fortune: The Nuwab Ameer-Ood-Doulah Mohummud Ameer Khan, Chief of Seronj, Tonk, Rampoora, Neemahera, and Other Places in Hindoostan*, trans. Basavan Lal Shadan (Calcutta, 1832), 180.

19 Cooper, *The Anglo-Maratha Campaigns and the Contest for India*, 141–212.

20 John Blakiston, *Twelve Years' Military Adventure in Three Quarters of the Globe* (London, 1829), i, 125; Prinsep, *Memoirs of the Puthan Soldier of Fortune*, 195.

21 Bowen, *The Business of Empire*, 231; C. A. Bayly, *Rulers, Townsmen and Bazaars: North Indian Society in the Age of British Expansion, 1770–1870* (Cambridge,

1983), 231–2; D. M. Peers, *Between Mars and Mammon. Colonial Armies and the Garrison State in India 1819–1835* (London, 1995), 202.

22 Bayly, 'Wellesley, Richard, Marquess Wellesley (1760–1842)'; N. Kasturi, *History of the British Occupation of India* (Calcutta, 1926), i, 139.

23 Arthur Wellesley to Lord Wellesley, 30 Dec 1804, in Gurwood, *The Dispatches of the Duke of Wellington*, iii, 882.

24 Bayly, *Rulers, Townsmen and Bazaars*, 120–1.

25 Prinsep, *Memoirs of the Puthan Soldier of Fortune*, 347, 188, 184 & 339; John Malcolm, *A Memoir of Central India, including Malwa and adjoining Provinces* (London, 1824), 325–249; James Baillie Fraser, *Military Memoir of Lieut. Col. James Skinner* (1851), 115 & 139.

26 Memoranda of 3 April 1814 and 1 Dec 1815, in S. V. Desika Char, *Readings in the Constitutional History of India, 1757–1947* (Delhi, 1983), 193–7.

27 Roland Thorne, 'Hastings, Francis Rawdon, First Marquess of Hastings and Second Earl of Moira (1754–1826)', *The Oxford Dictionary of National Biography* (Oxford, 2004).

28 Gordon, *The Marathas 1600–1818*, 175–8.

29 A.P. Coleman, 'Ochterlony, Sir David, First Baronet (1758–1825)', *The Oxford Dictionary of National Biography* (Oxford, 2004).

30 Henry Thoby Prinsep (ed.), *A Narrative of the Political and Military Transactions of British India, under the administration of the Marquess of Hastings, 1813 to 1818* (London, 1820), 334; Prinsep, *Memoirs of the Puthan Soldier of Fortune*, 460–6.

31 Regani, *Nizam-British Relations, 1724–1857*, 255.

32 Prinsep, *Memoirs of the Puthan Soldier of Fortune*, v.

33 On Afghan warriors, see Gommans, *The Rise of the Indo-Afghan Empire*. On the Pindaris, see Stewart N. Gordon, 'Scarf and Sword: Thugs, Marauders, and State-Formation in 18th Century Malwa', *Indian Economic & Social History Review*, vi (1969), 403–29, and Birendra Kumar Sinha, *The Pindaris, 1798–1818* (Calcutta, 1971).

34 Amar Farooqui, *Sindias and the Raj: Princely Gwalior c.1800–1850* (New Delhi, 2011), 17–25.

35 Farooqui, *Sindias and the Raj*, 25–35.

36 Captain Sydenham, 'Memorandum on the Pindarries', *Parliamentary Papers* 1818 (370), 8; 'Correspondence regarding the Pindaris', Jan–May 1815, IOR, H/600.

37 John Malcolm, *A Memoir of Central India, including Malwa and adjoining Provinces*, i, 427–62.

38 Sir William Henry Sleeman, *Report on Budhuk Alias Bagree Decoits, and Other Gang Robbers by Hereditary Profession* (Calcutta, 1849), 268; Adam White, *Considerations on the State of British India* (Edinburgh, 1822), 216.

39 Radhika Singha, '"Providential" Circumstances: The Thuggee Campaign of the 1830s and Legal Innovation', *Modern Asian Studies*, xxvii (1993), 94; Kim A. Wagner, *Thuggee: Banditry and the British in Early Nineteenth-Century India* (Basingstoke, 2007).

40 Eric Stokes, *The English Utilitarians and India* (Oxford, 1959).

41 Numbers calculated from Richards, 'The Finances of the East India Company in India, c.1766–1859'.

42 'Synopsis of evidence', *Parliamentary Papers* 1831–2 (370–IV), IV, appendix, vii.

43 Edward West, *A Memoir of the States of the Southern Maratha Country* (Bombay, 1869), 195–205.

44 Letters from Thomas Munro to Lord Elphinstone, 26 July–10 Aug 1817, Dharwar Collector's Diary, Maharashtra State Archives, 804/1818–19, 5.

45 West, *A Memoir of the States of the Southern Maratha Country*, 202.

46 D. H. A. Kolff, 'Rumours of the Company's Collapse. The Mood of Dasahra 1824 in the Punjab and Hindustand', in Crispin Bates, *Mutiny at the Margins: New Perspectives on the Indian Uprising of 1857*, 6 vols (New Delhi), ii, 25–42; James Mill, *The History of British India with Notes and Continuation, by Horace Hayman Wilson*, (London, 1858), iii, 114–142; Frederick John Shore, *Notes on Indian Affairs* (London, 1837), i, 158–61.

47 John Briggs, *Letters Addressed to a Young Person in India* (1828), 48.

48 C. A. Bayly, *Indian Society and the Making of the British Empire* (Cambridge, 1988), 144.

49 Personal visit, April 2015.

7. The Idea of Empire

1 Malcolm to Bentinck, 13 Sept 1828, in John William Kaye, *The Life and Correspondence of Major-General Sir John Malcolm* (1856), ii, 511.

2 Bayly, *Rulers, Townsmen and Bazaars*, 105, 136; C. A. Bayly, 'Town Building in North India, 1790–1830', *Modern Asian Studies*, ix (1975) 483–504.

3 My discussion of the Moro Raghunath case is heavily indebted to Haruki Inagaki, 'The Rule of Law and Emergency in Colonial India: the Conflict between the King's Court and the Government in Bombay in the 1820s', PhD thesis, King's College London, 2016; the court's judgment is transcribed at 'The Case of Habeas Corpus in India', *Oriental Herald*, xxix (1829), 41–91.

4 Boyd Hilton, *A Mad, Bad and Dangerous People?: England 1783–1846* (Oxford, 2006), 324–476.

5 Herbert Cowell, *The History and Constitution of the Courts and Legislative Authorities in India*. (London, 1872).

6 Note from Calcutta Supreme Court, *Parliamentary Papers*, 1831 (320E), 112.

7 For this process in Bengal see Wilson, *The Domination of Strangers*, 133–60.

8 John Malcolm to Charles Metcalfe, 30 Nov 30 1827, in Kaye, *The Life and Correspondence of Major-General Sir John Malcolm*, ii, 503.

9 For a general discussion of the court, see Gagan D. S. Sood, 'Sovereign Justice in Precolonial Maritime Asia: The Case of the Mayor's Court of Bombay, 1726–1798', *Itinerario*, xxxvii (2013); for a detailed discussion of the operation of the court see Inagaki, 'The Rule of Law and Emergency in Colonial India', 10–41.

10 *Oriental Herald* ix (April 1826), 127 & xii (April 1829), 1–92; Kaye, *The Life and Correspondence of Major-General Sir John Malcolm*, ii, 505, 522.

11 Frederick Drewitt, *Bombay in the Days of George IV: Memoirs of Sir Edward West* (London, 1907), 305–6.

12 Charles Metcalfe, Minute, 15 April 1829, *Parliamentary Papers*, 1831 (320E), 13–25.

13 Charles Grey and Edward Ryan, 'On a suggestion by the Governor-General in Council to the formation of a Code of Laws', *Parliamentary Papers*, 1831 (320E), 112.

14 Eric Stokes, *The English Utilitarians and India* (Oxford, 1959), xii.

15 David Lieberman, *The Province of Legislation Determined: Legal Theory in Eighteenth-Century Britain* (Cambridge, 1989), 241–76.

16 John Bowring (ed.), *The Works of Jeremy Bentham*, 11 vols (London, 1838), ix, 62 & ii, 314.

17 Terence Ball, 'Mill, James (1773–1836), Political Philosopher', *The Oxford Dictionary of National Biography* (Oxford, 2004).

18 Charles Knight, *The English Cyclopedia. A New Dictionary of Useful Knowledge* (London, 1854), iv, 231; James Mill, *The History of British India* (London, 1826), i, 177 & i, 332.

19 Mill, *The History of British India*, i, 264, 404.

20 See Stokes, *The English Utilitarians and India* for link between conservative imperial officers and utilitarianism.

21 T. E. Colebrooke, *Life of the Honourable Mountstuart Elphinstone* (London, 1884), 38 & 55; Kumar, *Western India in the Nineteenth Century*; Stokes, *The English Utilitarians and India*, 149.

22 For example the debate on 'Vote of Thanks for Marquis Hastings, *Hansard, House of Commons*, 4 March 1819, vol. 39, §869 & §891.

23 John Crawford, 'The Indian Taxation of Englishmen', *Edinburgh Review*, xlvii (1828), 144; 'The Institution of Caste', *The Edinburgh Review*, xlviii (1828), 32–4; Stokes, *The English Utilitarians and India*, 63–5.

24 Nicholas Dimsdale and Anthony Hotson, 'Financial Crisis and Economic Activity since 1825', *British Financial Crises Since 1825* (Oxford, 2014), 33–5.

25 Alexander Dick, *Romanticism and the Gold Standard* (Basingstoke, 2013); P. J. Thomas and B. Natarajan, 'Economic Depression in the Madras Presidency (1825–54)', *The Economic History Review*, vii (1936), 67–75; Bayly, *Indian Society and the Making of the British Empire*, 124–5.

26 Thomas Macaulay, 'East India Company's Charter Bill', 10 July 1833, *Hansard, House of Commons* xix, §535.

27 J. Lively and J. C. Rees, *Utilitarian Logic and Politics: James Mill's 'Essay on Government', Macaulay's Critique, and the Ensuing Debate* (Oxford, 1978).

28 Thomas Macaulay, 'East India Company's Charter Bill', §504–45.

29 Robert E. Sullivan, *Macaulay: The Tragedy of Power* (Cambridge, MA, 2009), 7.

30 Robert Eric Frykenberg, 'Malcolm, Sir John (1769–1833)', *The Oxford Dictionary of National Biography* (Oxford, 2004).

31 Metcalf, *Ideologies of the Raj*, 28–43; Jennifer Pitts, *A Turn to Empire: The Rise of Imperial Liberalism in Britain and France* (Princeton, NJ, 2005), 123–62.

32 Thomas Macaulay, 'East India Company's Charter Bill', §532–4.

33 Catherine Hall, *Macaulay and Son: Architects of Imperial Britain* (Yale, New Haven, 2012), 234.

34 Hall, *Macaulay and Son*, 214–238; Kartik Kalyan Raman, 'Utilitarianism and the Criminal Law in Colonial India: A Study of the Practical Limits of Utilitarian Jurisprudence', *Modern Asian Studies*, xxviii (1994), 760.

35 Different calculations are offered by W. H. Sykes, 'Expenditure in India on Public Works from 1837–8 to 1845–6', *Journal of the Statistical Society of London*, xiv (1851); Nitin Sinha, *Communication and Colonialism in Eastern India: Bihar, 1760s–1880s* (London, 2014), 165; and Richards, 'The Finances of the East India Company in India, c.1766–1859'; it is particularly difficult to isolate road-building from military expenditure.

36 Sinha, *Communication and Colonialism in Eastern India*, 155–64.

37 'First Steamboat of India', *Bulletin of the Victoria Memorial*, ix (1975), 33.

38 Lt.Col. Wilkie, 'The British Colonies Considered as Military Posts', *The United Service Magazine* (1841), II, 215; Daniel R. Headrick, *The Tools of Empire: Technology and European Imperialism in the Nineteenth Century* (1981).

39 Capt J. E. Johnson, 'Steam Navigation to India', *Kaleidoscope, Or, Literary and Scientific Mirror*, v (1824), 13–4.

40 Evidence of P. Malcolm to Select Committee on Steam Navigation, *Parliamentary Papers*, 1834 (478), 241.

41 Evidence of Thomas Peacock, McGregor Laird and Joshua Field to Select Committee on Steam Navigation to India, Jun 1834, *Parliamentary Papers*, 1834 (478), 1–80; 'Voyage of the Hugh Lindsay to the Red Sea', *ibid.*, Appendix, 112–124.

42 John Malcolm to Court of Directors, 10 May 1832, *Parliamentary Papers*, 1831–2 (735–II), ii, Appendix, 760.

43 John Gallagher and Ronald Robinson, 'The Imperialism of Free Trade', *Economic History Review*, vi (1953); Julia Lovell, *The Opium War: Drugs, Dreams, and the Making of Modern China* (London, 2011); Robert A. Bickers, *The Scramble for China: Foreign Devils in the Qing Empire, 1832–1914* (2011), 77–87.

44 Gallagher and Robinson, 'The Imperialism of Free Trade'; Lovell, *The Opium War*.

45 H. T. Prinsep, 'Note on the Introduction of Steam Navigation', *Parliamentary Papers*, 1831–2 (735–II), ii, Appendix, 680.

46 H. T. Prinsep, *Parliamentary Papers*, 1831–2 (735–ii), 677–85; J.H. Johnston, Controller of Government Steam Vessels to J.C.Sutherland, 16 February 1847, National Archives of Bangladesh, Dhaka Collectorate Records, vol. 554.

47 Uday Singh Mehta, *Liberalism and Empire: A Study in Nineteenth-Century British Liberal Thought* (Chicago, IL, 1999); Pitts, *A Turn to Empire*.

48 Wilson, *The Domination of Strangers*, 148–150.

49 Secretary, Board of Revenue to Superintendant of Survey Department, 25 June 1850, National Archives of Bangladesh, Dhaka Collectorate Records, vol. 280, 10.

50 Quoted in Sinha, *Communication and Colonialism in Eastern India*, 51.

51 Bengal Despatch, 18 Nov 1835, IOR E/4/746, 346; L. Magniac to Board of Revenue, 24 March 1825, Rangpur District Records, National Archives of Bangladesh, vol. 164, 23–7; L. Magniac to Board of Revenue, 26 April 1831, *ibid.*, vol. 170, 106–7.

52 Radhika Singha, 'Colonial Law and Infrastructural Power: Reconstructing Community, Locating the Female Subject', *Studies in History*, xix (2003), 89.

53 C. A. Bayly, *Empire and Information. Intelligence Gathering and Social*

Communication in India, 1780–1870 (Cambridge, 1996), 219; M. H. Fisher, 'The East India Company's "Suppression of the Native Dak"', *Indian Economic & Social History Review*, xxxi (1994), 311–348.

8. Fear and Trembling

1   Herman Merivale, *Life of Sir Henry Lawrence*, 2 vols (London, 1872), ii, 318, 322–3; William Hodson, *Twelve Years of a Soldier's Life in India* (London, 1859), 296.

2   'The Sepoy Rebellion', *London Quarterly Review*, ix (1857); John William Kaye, *A History of the Sepoy War In India* (London, 1872).

3   Kaye, *A History of the Sepoy War In India*, i, xii.

4   Robert Montgomery Martin, *The Indian Empire*, 8 vols (London, 1858), ii, 89; Walter Scott Seton-Karr, *A Short Account of Events during the Sepoy Mutiny of 1857–8* (London, 1894), 9; For a good discussion of British and Indian arguments about 1857 see Peter Robb, 'On the Rebellion of 1857: A Brief History of an Idea', *Economic and Political Weekly*, xlii (2007), 1696–1702.

5   Figures calculated from Richards, 'The Finances of the East India Company in India, c.1766–1859'; Romesh Chunder Dutt, *India in the Victorian Age; an Economic History of the People* (London, 1904), 210–222; Bayly, *Rulers, Townsmen and Bazaars*.

6   Chart Source: John F. Richards, 'The Finances of the East India Company in India, c.1766–1859'; 'Statistical Abstract Relating to British in India, from 1840–1865, *Parliamentary Papers*, 1867 (3817), 3–5; 'Statistical Abstract Relating to the British in India, 1865–1874', *Parliamentary Papers* 1875 (1350), 7–10.

7   Thomas Metcalf, *Land, Landlords and the British Raj: Northern India in the Nineteenth Century* (Berkeley, CA, 1992), 122; Rudrangshu Mukherjee, *Awadh in Revolt, 1857–1858: A Study of Popular Resistance* (New Delhi, 1984), 51.

8   Washbrook, 'South India 1770–1840', 479–516.

9   Mukherjee, *Awadh in Revolt, 1857–1858*, 51.

10 Michael H. Fisher (ed.), *The Politics of the British Annexation of India 1757–1857* (Oxford, 1997), 22.

11 Lord Dalhousie, 'Minute Reviewing his Administration', 28 Feb 1856, *Parliamentary Papers* 1856 (245), 4.

12 Richard Cobden, *How Wars Are Got Up in India: The Origin of the Burmese War* (London, 1853), 59.

13 Richard Williams, 'Hindustani Music between Awadh and Bengal, c.1758–1905, King's College London PhD Thesis, 2015.

14 Robert Bird, *Dacoitee in Excelsis: Or, The Spoliation of Oude* (London, 1857), 110; W. H. Sleeman, *A Journey through the Kingdom of Oude, in 1849–1850* (London, 1858), ii, 382.

15 Rosie Llewellyn-Jones, *Last King in India: Wajid Ali Shah* (London, 2014), 20–24.

16 Sir Sayyid Ahmad Khan⁻, *The Causes of the Indian Revolt* (Patna, 1995); Faisal Devji, 'Apologetic Modernity', *Modern Intellectual History* iv (2007): 61–76.

17 F. W. Buckler, 'The Political Theory of the Indian Mutiny', *Transactions of the Royal Historical Society*, v (1922) 71-100.

18 S. A. A. Rizvi and M. L. Bhargava (eds.), *Freedom Struggle in Uttar Pradesh,*

6 vols (Lucknow, 1957), i, 406; Kim A. Wagner, *The Great Fear of 1857: Rumours, Conspiracies and the Making of the Indian Uprising* (Oxford, 2010), 219.

19 Wagner, *The Great Fear of 1857*, 133–9.

20 Clare Anderson, *The Indian Uprising of 1857–8*, 57–8; William Dalrymple, *The Last Mughal: The Fall of Delhi, 1857* (London, 2009), 156–7.

21 Dalrymple, *The Last Mughal*, 27–58.

22 Faisal Devji, *The Impossible Indian: Gandhi and the Temptations of Violence* (London, 2012), 16–40.

23 Sebastian Pender, 'The Commemoration and Memorialisation of 1857' (Cambridge University PhD Thesis, 2015), 47; Khan, *The Causes of the Indian Revolt*, 117.

24 Khan, *The Causes of the Indian Revolt*, 14, 44; Wagner, *The Great Fear of 1857*, 21, 110.

25 Michael H. Fisher, 'The Imperial Coronation of 1819: Awadh, the British and the Mughals', *Modern Asian Studies*, xix (1985), 239–77.

26 Iqbal Husain, 'The Rebel Administration of Delhi', *Social Scientist*, xxvi (1998), 25–38; Rizvi and Bhargava (eds.), *Freedom Struggle in Uttar Pradesh*, i, 139.

27 Eric Stokes, *The Peasant Armed: The Indian Revolt of 1857* (Oxford, 1986), 87.

28 George Malleson, *The Indian Mutiny of 1857* (London, 1891), 17; Saiyid Zaheer Husain Jafri, 'The Profile of a Saintly Rebel: Maulavi Ahmadullah Shah', *Social Scientist*, xxvi (1998), 41.

29 Francis Robinson, 'Strategies of Authority in Muslim South Asia in the Nineteenth and Twentieth Centuries', *Modern Asian Studies*, xlvii (2013); Ayesha Jalal, *Partisans of Allah: Jihad in South Asia* (2009), 120–22; Jafri, 'The Profile of a Saintly Rebel'; Saiyid Zaheer Husain Jafri, 'Indigenous Discourse and Modern Historiography of 1857. The Case Study of Maulvi Ahmadullah Shah', in Sabyasachi Bhattacharya (ed.), *Rethinking 1857* (New Delhi, 2007); Gautum Bhadra, 'Four Rebels of 1857', in Ranajit Guha (ed.), *Subaltern Studies IV* (New Delhi, 1985), 270; Farooqui, *Sindias and the Raj*.

30 Tapti Roy, 'Rereading the Text. Rebel Writings in 1857–8', in Bhattacharya (ed.), *Rethinking 1857*.

31 George Dodd, *The History of the Indian Revolt and of the Expeditions to Persia, China, and Japan, 1856–7–8* (London, 1859), 155; Stokes, *The Peasant Armed*, 48.

32 Dodd, *The History of the Indian Revolt*, 153; Rizvi and Bhargava (eds.), *Freedom Struggle in Uttar Pradesh*, 293; Manmathanath Ghose, *The Life of Grish Chunder Ghose* (Calcutta, 1911), 200; Basudeb Chattopadhyay, 'Panic Sunday in Calcutta. 14 June 1857', in Bhattacharya (ed.), *Rethinking 1857*, 170–8.

33 Stokes, *The Peasant Armed*, 31.

34 Dalrymple, The Last Mughal, 350–8; Samuel Smiles, *Self-Help; with Illustrations of Character and Conduct* (London, 1859), 164; Stokes, *The Peasant Armed*, 93–6; Hodson, *Twelve Years of a Soldier's Life in India*, 243, 296.

35 Collins, *Violence*, 83–134.

36 Hall, *Macaulay and Son*, 326; Don Randall, 'Autumn 1857: The Making of the Indian "Mutiny"', *Victorian Literature and Culture*, xxxi (2003), 3–17.

37 Rosie Llewellyn-Jones, *The Great Uprising in India, 1857–58* (Woodbridge, 2007), 241–4, 130.

38 Kaye, *A History of the Sepoy War In India*, ii, 268–9. James Neill papers, IOR
    Mss Eur Photo 422/1–15.
39 Miles Taylor, 'Queen Victoria and India, 1837–61', *Victorian Studies*, xlvi
    (2004), 264–74.
40 'Address of the Talookdars of Oudh', *Parliamentary Papers*, 1862 (2985–I),
    256–8.
41 Francis G. Hutchins, *The Illusion of Permanence: British Imperialism in India*
    (Princeton, NJ, 1967).

9. The Making of Modern India

 1 Edward B. Eastwick, *A Handbook for India* (London, 1859), 317.
 2 Daniel Headrick, *The Tentacles of Progress. Technology Transfer in the Age of
    Imperialism, 1850–1940* (Oxford, 1988), 70.
 3 Bartle Frere, 'Proceedings at Official Opening of Bhore Ghaut Incline', 21
    April 1863, *Parliamentary Papers* 1863 (3168), 26.
 4 Ian J. Kerr, 'Berkley, James John (1819–1862)', *The Oxford Dictionary of National
    Biography* (Oxford, 2004) B. Ll. James, 'Clark, George Thomas (1809–1898)',
    The Oxford Dictionary of National Biography (Oxford, 2004) Joan Couniham,
    'Mrs Ella Armitage, John Horace Round, G.T. Clark and Early Norman
    Castles', *Anglo-Norman Studies VIII* (London, 1986), 74–87.
 5 John Darwin, *The Empire Project: The Rise and Fall of the British World-System,
    1830–1970* (Cambridge, 2011), 180–217.
 6 Thomas Carlyle, *Latter-Day Pamphlets* (London, 1850), 226.
 7 Morris, A Deceptive and Historical Account of the *Godavery District*, 304.
 8 Henry Montgomery, Report on Rajahmundry District, IOR P/280/48,
    2090–2192 & P/280/49, 2193–2296.
 9 Arthur Cotton, 'First Report on the Irrigation of Rajahmundry District', 22
    Aug 1844, *Parliamentary Papers*, 1850 (127), 3–16.
10 Lady Elizabeth Hope, *General Sir Arthur Cotton, His Life and Work* (London,
    1900), vii; Sir Arthur Cotton, *Public Works in India* (London, 1854), 36.
11 Hope, *General Sir Arthur Cotton, His Life and Work*, 50–5.
12 Cotton's theology drew from the ideas about atonement discussed in Boyd
    Hilton, *The Age of Atonement: The Influence of Evangelicalism on Social And
    Economic Thought 1785–1865* (Oxford, 1988).
13 Arthur Cotton, Second Report on the Irrigation of Rajahmundry District, 17
    April 1845, *Parliamentary Papers* 1850 (127), 39.
14 Cotton, *Public Works in India*, 297.
15 Robin James Moore, *Sir Charles Wood's Indian Policy, 1853–66* (Manchester,
    1966), 129–32.
16 Cotton, *Public Works in India*, viii.
17 Ian Stone, *Canal Irrigation in British India. Perspectives on Technological Change in
    a Peasant Economy* (Cambridge, 1984), 42; Sanjay Sharma, *Famine, Philanthropy
    and the Colonial State: North India in the Early Nineteenth Century* (Oxford,
    2001), 224; Joyce Brown, 'A Memoir of Colonel Sir Proby Cautley', *Notes and
    Records of the Royal Society of London*, xxxiv (1980), 185–97.
18 *Account of Roorkee College: Established for the Instruction of Civil Engineers, with a
    Scheme for Its Enlargement* (1851).

19 Hope and William Digby, *General Sir Arthur Cotton, His Life and Work*, 93–110; C. F. Brackenbury, *District Gazetteer, Cuddapah* (Madras, 1915), 84; For a critique of recent river inter-linking plans see Jayanta Bandyopadhyay, 'Water Science in India. Hydrological Obscurantism', *Economic and Political Weekly*, 1 (2012), 7–8.

20 Kling, *Partner in Empire: Dwarkanath Tagore and the Age of Enterprise in Eastern India*, 35; Lakshmi Subramanian, *Three Merchants of Bombay* (Gurgaon, 2012); Asiya Siddiqi, 'The Business World of Jamsetjee Jejeebhoy', *Indian Economic & Social History Review*, xix (1982), 301–24.

21 Daniel Thorner, *Investment in Empire: British Railway and Steam Shipping Enterprise in India, 1825–1849* (1977), 30–45.

22 Chairman of GIPR to Government of Bombay, 22 August 1846, Maharashtra State Archives, Public Works Department (Railways), i, 334.

23 Sir William Patrick Andrew, *Indian Railways; as Connected with the Power and Stability of British Empire in the East* (London, 1884).

24 J. P. Kennedy, Memorandum Relative to Railway Undertakings, 20 April 1853, *Parliamentary Papers* 1854 (131), 3–5.

25 Crawford to Young, 4 Dec 1855, Maharashtra State Archives, Public Works Department (Railways), iv, 339.

26 William Faviell to James Berkley, 18 Nov 1858, Maharashtra State Archives, Public Works Department (Railways), xxv, 39.

27 Frederick Appleby to William Faviell, 31 October 1858 and 'Report on serious disturbances', 26 January 1859, Maharashtra State Archives, Public Works Department (Railway), 1859 no. 206, 45–58 & 252–70.

28 Bartle Frere, 'Proceedings at Official Opening of Bhore Ghaut Incline', 21 April 1863, *Parliamentary Papers* 1863 (3168), 24–6.

29 John Stuart Mill, *On Liberty and Other Writings*, ed. Stefan Collini (Cambridge, 1989), 70.

30 Elizabeth Whitcombe, in Dharma Kumar (ed.), *Cambridge Economic History of India*, ii (Cambridge, 1983), p.693.

31 *The Engineer*, 19 March 1869, 205.

32 N. Charlesworth, *Peasants and Imperial Rule : Agriculture and Agrarian Society in the Bombay Presidency, 1850–1935* (Cambridge, 1985), 72; Clive Dewey, *Steamboats on the Indus: The Limits of Western Technological Superiority in South Asia* (Delhi, 2014).

33 Amalendu Guha, 'Raw Cotton of Western India : 1750–1850', *Indian Economic & Social History Review*, ix (1972).

10. The Legalization of India

1 Details of the Prince's tour are narrated in *Report on the Administration of the Bombay Presidency, for the Year 1875–6* (Bombay, 1876), i–xv.

2 Rosalind O'Hanlon, *Caste, Conflict, and Ideology: Mahatma Jotirao Phule and Low Caste Protest in Nineteenth-Century Western India* (Cambridge, 1985), 189–92; Mahadev Govind Ranade, *Rise of the Maratha Power* (1900), 1–22.

3 *Poona. Gazetteer of the Bombay Presidency* (Bombay, 1885); 'East India. Jurisdiction of Natives over European British Subjects'; V. S. Joshi, *Vasudeo Balvant Phadke : First Indian Rebel against British Rule* (Bombay, 1959).

4 Acting Judge, Ratnagiri, to Bombay Government, 19 March 1882, *Parliamentary Papers*, 1884 [C.3877] [C.3952], 100

5 *The Times* (London), 26 Nov, 1879, 10.

6 For the resurgence of anti-imperialism see Bernard Porter, *Critics of Empire: British Radicals and the Imperial Challenge* (London, 2007); Mira Matikkala, *Empire and Imperial Ambition: Liberty, Englishness and Anti-Imperialism in Late Victorian Britain* (London, 2010).

7 William Wilson Hunter, *England's Work in India* (London, 1881), 2, 19, 25; John Strachey and Richard Strachey, *The Finances and Public Works of India from 1869 to 1881* (London, 1882), 2.

8 Richard I. Cashman, *The Myth of the Lokamanya: Tilak and Mass Politics in Maharashtra* (Berkeley, CA, 1975), 28–30; *Quarterly Journal of the Poona Sarvajanik Sabha* xciv (July 1879).

9 John Bruce Norton, *Topics of Jurisprudence: Or Aids to the Office of the Indian Judge* (Madras, 1862); Sir James FitzJames Stephen, *A History of the Criminal Law of England* (London, 1883), 302.

10 'Sir James Stephen', *The Spectator*, lxx (Mar 17,1894), 366.

11 Sir James FitzJames Stephen, *A History of the Criminal Law of England* (London, 1883), 308. W. W. Hunter, *Seven Years of Indian Legislation* (1870), 5.

12 Leslie Stephen, *The Life of Sir James Fitzjames Stephen, Bart., K.C.S.I., a Judge of the High Court of Justice* (London, 1895), 255.

13 Ritu Birla, *Stages of Capital: Law, Culture, and Market Governance in Late Colonial India* (Durham, NC, 2009), 38–45; Mahabir Prashad Jain, *Outlines of Indian Legal History* (New Delhi, 1990), 499–555; Radhika Singha, 'Colonial Law and Infrastructural Power: Reconstructing Community, Locating the Female Subject', *Studies in History*, xix (2003) 87–*126*.

14 William Cornish et al., *The Oxford History of the Laws of England* (Oxford, 2010), xii, Public Law.

15 Philippa Levine, 'Venereal Disease, Prostitution, and the Politics of Empire: The Case of British India', *Journal of the History of Sexuality*, iv (1994), 579–602; Radhika Singha, 'Settle, Mobilize, Verify: Identification Practices in Colonial India', *Studies in History*, xvi (2000), 151–98.

16 Singha, 'Settle, Mobilize, Verify', 151–98; Chandak Sengoopta, *Imprint of the Raj: How Fingerprinting Was Born in Colonial India* (London, 2003).

17 Birla, *Stages of Capital*, 40–2.

18 Syed Mahmud, 'British Rule in India. Does It Owe Its Origin to Conquest, and Its Maintenance to Physical Force?', *Calcutta Review*, lxviii (1879), 1–19.

19 John Gallagher, Gordon Johnson and Anil Seal, *Locality, Province and Nation: Essays on Indian Politics 1870 to 1940* (Cambridge, 1973), 10; Sarvepalli Gopal, *British Policy in India, 1858–1905* (Oxford, 1965).

20 Elizabeth Kolsky, *Colonial Justice in British India: White Violence and the Rule of Law* (Cambridge, 2009), 140–2.

21 Wilfred Scawen Blunt, *India under Ripon; a Private Diary* (London, 1909), 16.

22 Quoted in E. M. Forster, 'Kipling's Poems', *Journal of Modern Literature*, xxx (2007), 24.

23 Alan M. Guenther, 'Syed Mahmood and the Transformation of Muslim Law in British India', McGill University PhD Thesis, 2004.

24 Gregory C. Kozlowski, *Muslim Endowments and Society in British India*.

(Cambridge, 1985), 119, Guenther, 'Syed Mahmood and the Transformation of Muslim Law in British India', 172–199, 212.

25 Devji, 'Apologetic Modernity', 61–76.
26 *Aligarh Institute Gazette*, 31 Oct 1893, reported in IOR L/R/5/70, 465, no. 6.
27 Guenther, 'Syed Mahmood and the Transformation of Muslim Law in British India', 109–111.

11. The Great Depression

1 Richard Temple, 'On the Physical Causes of Indian Famines', 18 May 1877, IOR L/E/5/65, 17.
2 Lechmere-Oertel Collection, IOR Photo 261(527); see also Jefferson Ellsworth Scott, *In Famine Land. Observations and Experiences in India during the Great Drought of 1899–1900* (New York, NY, 1904), 50.
3 Chandra Mallampalli, 'Meet the Abrahams: Colonial Law and a Mixed Race Family from Bellary, South India, 1810–63', *Modern Asian Studies*, xlii (2008), 929–970.
4 Arthur W. Silver, *Manchester Men and Indian Cotton, 1847–1872* (Manchester, 1966), 122, 198.
5 John Kelsall, *Manual of the Bellary District* (Madras, 1872), 238, 330.
6 David Arnold, 'Famine in Peasant Consciousness and Peasant Action: Madras, 1876–8', *Subaltern Studies III* (Delhi, 1984), 62–115.
7 *Army Medical Department Reports*, 1877, 1880, 1890, Parliamentary Papers 1878 [c.2169], 1882 [c.3272], 1892 [c.6697].
8 'Appendix to Report of Famine Commission, 1898', *Parliamentary Papers*, 1899, [C.9253], 145.
9 Arthur Knatchbull Connell, *The Economic Revolution of India and the Public Works Policy* (London, 1883), 139.
10 Richard Temple, Tour Notes, 1876, IOR Mss Eur F86/180, 111.
11 Mike Davis, *Late Victorian Holocausts: El Nino Famines and the Making of the Third World* (2002), 23–116. Tim Dyson, 'On the Demography of South Asian Famines: Part I', *Population Studies*, xlv (1991), 5–25; Tim Dyson, 'On the Demography of South Asian Famines Part II', *Population Studies*, xlv (1991), 279–97.
12 Blunt, *India under Ripon*, 52.
13 Anil Seal, *The Emergence of Indian Nationalism: Competition and Collaboration in the Later Nineteenth Century* (Cambridge, 1968), 194–245 & 263.
14 Quoted in *Seal, Emergence of Indian Nationalism*, 259.
15 Bayly, Recovering Liberties, 121, 196-7.
16 Dadabhai Naoraji, Poverty and un-British Rule in India (London, 1901); Manu Goswami, Producing India. From Colonial Economy to National Space (Chicago, IL, 2004), 224-226.
17 *Proceedings of the First Indian National Congress, Held at Bombay on the 28th, 29th, and 30th December, 1885* (1905), 27.
18 B. B. Kling, *The Blue Mutiny: The Indigo Disturbances in Bengal, 1859–1862* (Philadelphia, PA, 1966), 197–218.
19 Kalyan Kumar Sen Gupta, 'The Agrarian League of Pabna, 1873', *Indian Economic & Social History Review*, vii (1970), 253–69; Bipasha Raha, 'Harinath Majumdar and the Bengal Peasantry', *Indian Historical Review*, xl (2013),

331–53; Kalyan Kumar Sengupta, *Pabna Disturbances and the Politics of Rent, 1873–1885* (New Delhi, 1974), 50.

20 Uma Dasgupta, *Rise of an Indian Public: Impact of Official Policy, 1870–1880* (Calcutta, 1977).

21 Jogesh Chandra Bagal, *History of the Indian Association, 1876–1951* (Calcutta, 1953); Raha, 'Harinath Majumdar and the Bengal Peasantry', 341.

22 Extracts from Reports of Native Papers & Note by Secretary in Famine Department, Famine Department, Maharashtra State Archives (1897), no. 279.

23 Cashman, *The Myth of the Lokamanya*, 136–8.

24 Government Solicitor to Chief Secretary, Government of Bombay, 9 February 1897, Maharashtra State Archives, Revenue (Famine), vol. 122, Maharashtra State Archives; *Quarterly Journal of the Poona Sarvajanik Sabha* xix, 3 (1897), 15; Stanley A. Wolpert, *Tilak and Gokhale: Revolution and Reform in the Making of Modern India* (Berkeley, CA, 1962), 101; Gordon Johnson's Provincial Politics and Indian Nationalism: Bombay and the Indian National Congress 1880 to 1915, (*Cambridge*, 1973), 99.

25 *Quarterly Journal of the Poona Sarvajanik Sabha* xix, July & Oct 1896, 1 & 2, 6–10.

26 'Report of the Indian Famine Commission', *Parliamentary Papers* 1898 (Cmd 9178), 186.

27 Arup Maharatna, 'Regional Variation in Demographic Consequences of Famines in Late 19th and Early 20th Century India', *Economic and Political Weekly*, 29, 23 (June 4, 1994), 1399-1410.

28 Henrik Aspengren, 'Empire: A Question of Hearts? The Social Turn in Colonial Government, Bombay, c.1905–1925', in Mark Duffield and Vernon Hewitt, *Empire, Development and Colonialism* (London, 2009), 45–57.

29 For a summary of the arguments see K. N. Chaudhuri, 'India's International Economy in the Nineteenth Century: An Historical Survey', *Modern Asian Studies*, ii (1968), 35–50.

30 Dipesh Chakrabarty, *Rethinking Working-Class History: Bengal, 1890–1940* (Princeton, NJ, 1989), 17; Maria Misra, *Business, Race, and Politics in British India, c.1850–1960* (1999), 41–4.

31 Misra, *Business, Race, and Politics in British India, c.1850–1960*, 26–8.

32 Zoë Yalland, *Boxwallahs: The British in Cawnpore, 1857–1901* (Norwich, 1994).

33 S. M. Edwardes, *Memoir of Rao Bahadur Ranchhodlal Chhotalal* (Exeter, 1920), 15–23.

34 Sunil Khilnani, The Idea of India (London, 1977), 120. Achyut Yagnik, *Ahmedabad: From Royal City to Megacity* (New Delhi, 2011).

35 Annie Wood Besant, *How India Wrought for Freedom, the Story of the National Congress Told from Official Records* (Madras, 1915), 353–8.

12. Governments within Governments

1 N. K. Thingalaya, *The Banking Saga. The Story of South Kanara's Banks* (Mangalore, 1999); K. V. Kamath, *Corporation Bank. A Corporate Journey* (Mangalore, 1997).

2 Kamath, *Corporation Bank*, 5.

3 Henry Wood Nevinson, *The New Spirit in India* (1908), 294; Sidney Webb, 'Preface' in Lala Lajpat Rai, *The Arya Samaj; an Account of Its Origin, Doctrines, and Activities, with a Biographical Sketch of the Founder* (1915), xii.

4 Lala Lajpat Rai, 'The Story of My Life' in Dal Ram Nanda (ed.), *The Collected Works of Lala Lajpat Rai* (2003), v, 320–2.

5 Lajpat Rai, *The Arya Samaj; an Account of Its Origin, Doctrines, and Activities, with a Biographical Sketch of the Founder*, 155–6.

6 Lala Lajpat Rai, *The Political Future of India* (1919), 184; the argument here draws from Faisal Devji's discussion of Mughal politics in The Impossible Indian, 9–40.

7 The argument here draws in part from Partha Chatterjee, *The Nation and Its Fragments. Colonial and Postcolonial Histories* (Princeton, NJ, 1993).

8 Cashman, *The Myth of the Lokamanya*, 75–95.

9 Pankaj Mishra, *From the Ruins of Empire: The Revolt Against the West and the Remaking of Asia* (London, 2013), Nikki R. Keddie, *Sayyid Jamal Ad-Din Al-Afghani: A Political Biography* (Berkeley, CA, 1972).

10 David Lelyveld, *Aligarh's First Generation: Muslim Solidarity in British India* (Princeton, NJ, 1978); Barbara D. Metcalf, *Islamic Revival in British India: Deoband, 1860–1900* (Princeton, NJ, 2014) Devji, 'Apologetic Modernity'.

11 Metcalf, *Islamic Revival in British India*.

12 Gyan Pandey, 'Rallying Round the Cow: Sectarian Strife in the Bhojpur Region, c.1888–1917', in Ranajit Guha, *Subaltern Studies* II (1983), 60–130. Sandra Freitag, Collective Action and Community. Public Arenas and the Emergence of Communism in North India (Berkeley, CA, 1989).

13 Surendra Rao, *Bunts in History and Culture*; M. Venkateshwar Rao, 'District Associations and Their Contribution to the Political Development of Andhra, 1892–1920', PhD thesis, Osmania University, 1992; Swarupa Gupta, *Notions of Nationhood in Bengal: Perspectives on Samaj, c.1867–1905* (Delhi, 2009), 275.

14 Sumit Sarkar, *Modern India. 1885–1947* (New Delhi, 2014), 105.

15 Stephen Bottomore, '"An Amazing Quarter Mile of Moving Gold, Gems and Genealogy": Filming India's 1902/03 Delhi Durbar', *Historical Journal of Film, Radio and Television*, xv (1995), 495–515; Alan Trevithick, 'Some Structural and Sequential Aspects of the British Imperial Assemblages at Delhi: 1877–1911', *Modern Asian Studies*, xxiv (1990), 569.

16 Chris Fuller, 'Anthropology and Government in British India, 1881–1911: Ibbetson and Risley Reconsidered', Talk to Max Planck Institut, Göttingen (2014); Sumit Sarkar, *The Swadeshi Movement in Bengal, 1903–1908* (Delhi, 1973), 17.

17 B. R. Nanda, *Gokhale: The Indian Moderates and the British Raj* (Princeton, NJ, 1999), 243–4; Nanda, *The Collected Works of Lala Lajpat Rai*, I, 90; Anthony J. Parel (ed.), *Gandhi: 'Hind Swaraj' and Other Writings* (Cambridge, 2012), 20.

18 Quoted in Andrew Sartori, *Bengal in Global Concept History: Culturalism in the Age of Capital* (Chicago, 2008), 144; Sarkar, *The Swadeshi Movement in Bengal, 1903–1908*, 86–87.

19 Parel (ed.), *Gandhi*, 21; Karuna Mantena, 'Another Realism. The Politics of Gandhian Nonviolence', American Political Science Review 106, 2 (2012), 455–70.

20 Shruti Kapila, 'Self, Spencer and Swaraj. Nationalist Thought and Critiques of Liberalism, 1890–1920', *Modern Intellectual History*, iv (2007), 109–27.

21 Harald Fischer-Tiné, *Shyamji Krishnavarma: Sanskrit, Sociology and Anti-Imperialism* (New Delhi, 2015).

22 Pal, *Speeches*, 54

23   Rabindranath Tagore, 'Swadeshi Samaj', *Nabya Bharat,* xxiii (1905), 29–47; translated in Rabindranath Tagore, *Greater India* (Madras, 1921), 1–8.
24   Sarkar, *The Swadeshi Movement in Bengal, 1903–1908,* 379.
25   Sarkar, *Modern India. 1885–1947,* 120, 283–5, 302, 370–404.
26   Sarkar, *The Swadeshi Movement in Bengal, 1903–1908,* 375.
27   Ibid., 148–171.
28   P. A. S. Mani, *Life Assurance In India* (Bombay, 1950), 287.
29   Sarkar, *The Swadeshi Movement in Bengal, 1903–1908,* 124.
30   Vinay Bahl, 'The Emergence of Large-Scale Steel Industry in India under British Colonial Rule, 1880–1907', *Indian Economic & Social History Review,* xxxi (1994), 452–6.
31   Lucy Peck, 'Linking Histories: The Planning of New Delhi', *India International Centre Quarterly,* xxxiii (2006), 1–12; Marquess of Crewe, 'Local Autonomy in India', *Hansard,* House of Lords, 29 July 1912, §.742.
32   *Hansard,* House of Lords, 21 February 1912, §162.
33   Lord Curzon, Correspondence about Clive Statue, May 1909–Aug 1920, IOR Mss Eur F112/512.
34   Dane Kennedy, 'Diagnosing the Colonial Dilemma. Tropical Neurashthenia and the Alienated Briton', in Durba Ghosh and Dane Kennedy (eds.), *Decentring Empire. Britain, India and the Transcolonial World* (London, 2006), 151–181.
35   B. R. Tomlinson, 'India and the British Empire, 1880–1935', *Indian Economic & Social History Review,* xii (1975), 347; John Gallagher and Anil Seal, 'Britain and India between the Wars', *Modern Asian Studies,* xv (1981), 389.

13. Military Liberalism and the Indian Crowd

1   Report on the Punjab Disturbances, April 1919, *Parliamentary Papers,* 1920 (Cmd. 534), 933–6; Report of the committee appointed by the government of India to investigate the disturbances in the Punjab, *Parliamentary Papers,* 1920 (Cmd. 681), 38.
2   Nigel Collett, *The Butcher of Amritsar: General Reginald Dyer* (2006), 340.
3   Derek Sayer, 'British Reaction to the Amritsar Massacre 1919–1920', *Past & Present,* cxxxi (1991), 158.
4   Hew Strachan, *The First World War* (Oxford, 2003), I, 793; Tan Tai-Yong, 'An Imperial Home-Front: Punjab and the First World War', *The Journal of Military History,* lxiv (2000), 371–409; Lala Lajpat Rai, *Young India; an Interpretation and a History of the Nationalist Movement from within* (New York, NY, 1917), 36.
5   Ritika Prasad, *Tracks of Change. Railways and Everyday Life in Colonial India* (Cambridge, 2015), 215; David Lockwood, *The Indian Bourgeoisie: A Political History of the Indian Capitalist Class in the Early Twentieth Century* (London, 2012), 31.
6   Tai-Yong, 'An Imperial Home-Front', 382; David Omissi, 'Europe Through Indian Eyes: Indian Soldiers Encounter England and France, 1914–1918', *The English Historical Review,* cxxii (2007), 371–96.
7   David C. Potter, 'Manpower Shortage and the End of Colonialism: The Case of the Indian Civil Service', *Modern Asian Studies,* vii (1973), 49.
8   Tai-Yong, 'An Imperial Home-Front', 394, 398.

9   Tomlinson, 'India and the British Empire, 1880–1935'; 352; Peter Robb, 'The Government of India and Annie Besant', *Modern Asian Studies*, x (1976), 125; Bernard Houghton, 'Reform in India', *Political Science Quarterly*, (1920), 546.

10 Lala Lajpat Rai, *Unhappy India* (Calcutta, 1928), 442; Adam Tooze, *The Deluge: The Great War and the Remaking of Global Order 1916–1931* (London, 2014).

11 Speech at Surat, 1 Aug 1918 in Mohandas K Gandhi, *Collected Works of Mahatma Gandhi*, 100 vols (Delhi, 1958), xvii, 171; to S. Sastri in Gandhi, *Collected Works*, xvii, 135; Letter from E. L. L. Hammond, 18 Dec 1917 in Gandhi, *Collected Works*, xvi, 507; Tai-Yong, 'An Imperial Home-Front', 384, 397; David Hardiman, *Peasant Nationalists of Gujarat: Kheda District, 1917–34* (Delhi ; New York, 1982), 107.

12 Gandhi, Collected Works of Mahatma Gandhi, xvii, 17, 133.

13 Judith M. Brown, *Gandhi's Rise to Power. Indian Politics 1915–1922* (Cambridge, 1972), 246; Gail Minault, *The Khilafat Movement: Religious Symbolism and Political Mobilization in India* (New York, 1982); Gandhi, Collected Works of Mahatma Gandhi, xxi, 90.

14 Gyan Pandey, 'The Peasant Revolt and Indian Nationalism. The Peasant Movement in Awadh, 1919–1922', in Ranajit Guha, *Subaltern Studies I:* (New Delhi, 1986), 143; Daniel Kent Carrasco, 'Jayaprakahsan Narayan and Lok Niti. Socialism, Gandhism and Political Cultures of Protest in the XX Century' (King's College London PhD thesis, 2015), 39.

15 Brown, *Gandhi's Rise to Power*, 61; Sarkar, *Modern India. 1885–1947*, 169–170; Pandey, 'The Peasant Revolt and Indian Nationalism. The Peasant Movement in Awadh, 1919–1922', 193; Rajat Kanta Ray, *Social Conflict and Political Unrest in Bengal, 1875–1927* (Oxford, 1984), 344.

16 Judith Brown, *Modern India: The Origins of an Asian Democracy* (1994), 225, 309; Pandey, 'The Peasant Revolt and Indian Nationalism. The Peasant Movement in Awadh, 1919–1922', 189; Speech at Mangalore, August 1920, Gandhi, *Collected Works*, xxi, 187.

17 Brown, *Gandhi's Rise to Power*, 291.

18 Rajat K. Ray, 'Masses in Politics : The Non-Cooperation Movement in Bengal 1920–1922', *Indian Economic & Social History Review*, xi (1974), 388–91.

19 Shahid Amin, *Event, Metaphor, Memory: Chauri Chaura, 1922–1992* (Berkeley, CA, 1995) Mantena, 'Another Realism'.

20 C. S. Venkatachar, Narrative, April 25 1977, IOR Mss Eur F 180/85, 10-12; Report of the Reforms Enquiry Committee, *Parliamentary Papers* 1924–5 (Cmd. 2360), i, 94.

21 *Parliamentary Papers, 1924-5* (Cmd. 2360) i, 57.

22 Views of Local Governments, *Parliamentary Papers* 1924–5 (Cmd. 2362), iii, 311

23 Simon Epstein, 'District Officers in Decline: The Erosion of British Authority in the Bombay Countryside, 1919 to 1947', *Modern Asian Studies*, xvi (1982), 500–1; Alan W. Heston, 'Official Yields Per Acre in India, 1886–1947: Some Questions of Interpretation', *Indian Economic & Social History Review*, x (1973), 328.

24 Views of Local Governments, *Parliamentary Papers* 1924–5 (Cmd. 2362), iii, 8; Indian Financial Statement and Budget, 1921–2, *Parliamentary Papers* 1921(153), 36.

25 Indian Statutory Commission, *Parliamentary Papers* 1929–30 (Cmd. 3568), i, 312.

26   A. L. Carthill, *The Lost Dominion* (Edinburgh, 1924), 93, 238; A. L. Carthill, *Madampur* (Edinburgh, 1931), 327; Michael O'Dwyer, *India as I Know It* (London, 1926), 449-453; Venkatachar, Narrative, IOR Mss Eur F180/85, 18.
27   Taylor Sherman, *State Violence and Punishment in India, 1919-1956* (London, 2009), 64-72
28   Telegram to N. C. Kelkar, 18 Oct 1928 in Gandhi, *Collected Works*, xxxiii, 117; Brown, *Modern India*, 238.
29   Ayesha Jalal, Self and Sovereignty. Individual and Community in South Asian Islam since 1850 (London, 2000), 303; Ilyas Ahmad, 'The Crowd', *The Indian Journal of Political Science*, ii (1940), 21.
30   Lajpat Rai, *Unhappy India*, 9, 13.

14. Cycles of Violence

1   Beni Prasad, 'Presidential Address', *The Indian Journal of Political Science*, ii (1941), 435, 426; Beni Prasad, *History of Jahangir* (London, Bombay etc., 1922); Beni Prasad, *The State in Ancient India. A Study in the Structure and Practical Working of Political Institutions in North India in Ancient Times* (Allahabad, 1928); Harijan, 4 August 1946, Gandhi, *Collected Works*, lxxxv, 79.
 2   Dietmar Rothermund, *India in the Great Depression, 1929–1939* (Columbia, MO, 1992), 32–35, 41; Brown, *Modern India*, 254–261; Rajnarayan Chandavarkar, *The Origins of Industrial Capitalism in India. Business Strategies and the Working Classes in Bombay, 1900–1940* (Cambridge, 1994), 261.
 3   Chandavarkar, *The Origins of Industrial Capitalism in India*, 267; Claude Markovits, *Indian Business and Nationalist Politics 1931–39: The Indigenous Capitalist Class and the Rise of the Congress Party* (Cambridge, 1985), 239.
 4   Nandini Gooptu, *The Politics of the Urban Poor in Early Twentieth-Century India* (Cambridge, 2001), 98–110.
 5   David Arnold, *The Congress in Tamilnad: Nationalist Politics in South India, 1919–1937* (New Delhi, 1977).
 6   Sarkar, *Modern India*. 298–305; Judith M. Brown, *Gandhi and Civil Disobedience: The Mahatma in Indian Politics 1928–1934* (Cambridge, 2009), 101–8.
 7   Arnold, *The Congress in Tamilnad*.
 8   Martin Gilbert, *Churchill: A Life* (London, 1991), 498.
 9   C. S. Venkatachar, Narrative, IOR Mss Eur F180/85, 29.
10   B. R. Tomlinson, 'India and the British Empire, 1935–1947', *Indian Economic & Social History Review*, xiii (1976), 331–49.
11   Tomlinson, 'India and the British Empire, 1880–1935', 370.
12   Benjamin Zachariah, *Developing India: An Intellectual and Social History, c.1930–50* (New Delhi, 2005), 217.
13   Report on Nehru's activities in London, IOR L/PJ/12/293, 26–30.
14   Benjamin Zachariah, *Nehru* (London, 2004), 77.
15   'Proceedings of Congress, Lucknow Session, 12–14 April 1936', *Indian Annual Register* (1936), 261.
16   Markovits, *Indian Business and Nationalist Politics 1931–39*, 114.
17   Markovits, *Indian Business*, 143.
18   Zachariah, *Developing India*; Nanjangud S Subba Rao, *Some Aspects of Economic Planning. Sir William Meyer Lectures, 1932–3,* (Bangalore, 1935), 13, 99.

19 Benoy Sarkar, 'Demo-Despotcracy and Freedom', *Calcutta Review*, ixx (1939), 95; Christophe Jaffrelot, Dr. Ambedkar and Untouchability: Fighting the Indian Caste System (New York, NY, 2005) 52-73.

20 William Gould, *Hindu Nationalism and the Language of Politics in Late Colonial India* (Cambridge, 2004), 231. Haig to Linlithgow, 27 March 1939, quoted in Gould, *Hindu Nationalism* 207.

21 Ayesha Jalal, *The Sole Spokesman. Jinnah, the Muslim League and the Demand for Pakistan* (Cambridge, 1985), 36–50; Faisal Devji, *Muslim Zion: Pakistan as a Political Idea* (London, 2013).

22 Indivar Kamtekar, 'A Different War Dance: State and Class in India 1939– 1945', *Past & Present*, clxxvi (2002), 189.

23 Srinath Raghavan, *India's War. The Making of Modern South Asia, 1939–1945* (London, 2016), 271.

24 'Shiver of 1942', p.343, 345; Bayly, p.267; Hugh Tinker, 'Indian exodus'; *The Raj at War, 106.*

25 Paul Greenough, 'Political Mobilization and the Underground Literature of the Quit India Movement, 1942–44', *Modern Asian Studies*, xvii (1983), 45.

26 'Interview with V. R. Nimkar, Cambridge Centre for South Asian Studies, http://www.s-asian.cam.ac.uk/pdf/146.pdf last accessed 25 February 2016.

27 Yasmin Khan, *The Raj at War: A People's History of India's Second World War* (London, 2015), 191.

28 Sarkar, *Modern India. 1885–1947*, 390.

29 C. A. Bayly, '"The Nation Within": British India at War 1939–1947', *Proceedings of the British Academy*, cxxv (2004), 281; Raghavan, *India's War* 273.

30 Raghavan, *India's War*, 71, 243.

31 Christopher G. Thorne, *Allies of a Kind: The United States, Britain, and the War Against Japan, 1941–1945* (Oxford, 1979), 241; Raghavan, *India's War* 407.

32 Raghavan, *India's War*, 68; S. C. Aggarwal, *History of the Supply Department (1939–1946)* (Delhi, 1947), 1 & passim.

33 Bayly, '"The Nation Within"', 284.

34 Raghavan, *India's War*, 425.

35 Kamtekar, 'A Different War Dance'; Raghavan, 346.

36 Raghavan, *India's War*. S Iyengar, 'Economic Control in India During the War', *Indian Journal of Economics*, xxiv (1944), 258.

37 Raghavan, *India's War*, 351.

38 Janam Mukherjee, 'Hungry Bengal. War, Famine, Riots, and the End of Empire. 1939–1946' (University of Michican PhD thesis, 2011), 166, 200; Anwesha Roy, 'Making Riots, Making Peace. Communal Riots and Anti-Communal Resistance in Bengal, 1941–47' (Jawaharlal Nehru University, 2015), 115–130.

39 David C. Potter, *India's Political Administrators, 1919–1983* (Oxford, 1986), 129–31.

40 Wavell, 'Note on the Services', 29 June 1946, Nicholas Mansergh (ed.), *The Transfer of Power*, 12 vols (London, 1970–1983), viii, 1087; Douglas Houghton, 'Diary of Ten Weeks in India', Jan–Mar 1946, People's History Museum, Manchester.

41 Wavell to Amery', 25 February 1944, *The Transfer of Power*, iv, 760; Gandhi,

Collected Works of Mahatma Gandhi, 'Statement to the Press' and 'G.E.B. Abell's Note', both 11 February 1946, lxxxiii, 121 & 420.

42 Lawrence James, *Raj: The Making and Unmaking of British India* (London, 2000), 592.

43 Azad to Wavell, 25 June 1946, Nicholas Mansergh (ed.) *The Transfer of Power, 1942–7 (12 vols, London, 1970–83)*, viii, p.1033, 1037.

44 Ayesha Jalal, *The Sole Spokesman*; Yasmin Khan, *The Great Partition: The Making of India and Pakistan* (New Haven, CT, 2007), 11.

45 Wavell to Lord Pethwick-Lawrence, 10 Sept 1946; Nehru to Wavell, 18 September 1946; Pethwick-Lawrence to Wavell, 20 Sept 1946, *Transfer of Power*, viii, 482–4, 538–57.

46 Wavell to Pethwick Lawrence, 23 Sept 1946, *Transfer of Power*, viii, 573–6.

47 Shahid Hamid, *Disastrous Twilight: A Personal Record of the Partition of India by Major-General Shahid Hamid* (Barnsley, 1993), 98.

48 'Removal of Records from India', IOR R/3/1/149.

49 Wavell to Lord Pethwick-Lawrence, 10 September 1046, *Transfer of Power*, viii, 484.

50 The account of the Calcutta killings here particularly draws from Roy, 'Making Riots, Making Peace. Communal Riots and Anti-Communal Resistance in Bengal, 1941–47'; Mukherjee, 'Hungry Bengal. War, Famine, Riots, and the End of Empire. 1939–1946'.

51 Khan, *The Great Partition*, 66.

52 Harun-or-Rashid, *The Foreshadowing of Bangladesh: Bengal Muslim League and Muslim Politics, 1906–1947* (Dhaka, 2003), 245.

53 Roy, 'Making Riots, Making Peace', 252.

54 Ibid., 289.

55 Khan, *The Great Partition*.

56 Khan, *The Great Partition*; Swarna Aiyar, '"August Anarchy". The Partition Massacres in Punjab, 1947', in D. A. Low and Howard Brasted (eds.), *Freedom, Trauma, Continuities. Northern India and Independence* (Walnut Creek, CA, 1998), 15–39.

57 Gyanendra Pandey, *Remembering Partition: Violence, Nationalism and History in India* (Cambridge, 2001), 144–6; Yasmin Khan, 'Performing Peace. Gandhi's Assassination as a Critical Moment in the Consolidation of the Nehruvian State', *Modern Asian Studies*, xlv (2011), 57–80.

15. The Great Delusion

1 Jahnavi Phalkey, *Atomic State* (Ranikhet, 2013).

2 Kamtekar, 'A Different War Dance'.

3 Syed Waliullah, *Tree Without Roots* (London, 1967).

4 Classic texts in this literature on imperial ideas are Said, *Orientalism*; Inden, *Imagining India*; Metcalf, *Ideologies of the Raj*; Mehta, *Liberalism and Empire: A Study in Nineteenth-Century British Liberal Thought (Chicago, CA, 1999)*.

5 Taylor C. Sherman, 'The Integration of the Princely State of Hyderabad and the Making of the Postcolonial State in India, 1948–56', *Indian Economic & Social History Review*, xliv (2007), 501.

6 Inderpal Grewal, 'The Masculinities of Post-Colonial Governance:

Bureaucratic Memoirs of the Indian Civil Service', *Modern Asian Studies*, i (2016) 602–35; AFP news agency, *'Happiness for Some in Pakistan's Gated Communities'* (2013); Personal interview with Anuraag Chowlfa, 14 February 2014.

7 Niraja Jayal Gopal, *Citizenship and its Discontents. An Indian History* (Cambridge, MA, 2013); Karuna Mantena, 'Popular Sovereignty and anti-colonialism in Richard Bourke and Quentin Skinner, Popular Sovereignty in Historical Perspective (Cambridge, 2016), 296–309.

8 Data from http://populationcommission.nic.in/content/933_1_LiteracyRate.aspx, last accessed 1 May.

9 Elizabeth Buettner, *Empire Families: Britons and Late Imperial India* (Oxford, 2004), 221–40.

10 Roland Hunt and John Harrison, *The District Officer in India, 1930–1947* (London, 1980), xv.

11 Calculated from ibid., xi–xx.

12 Sir Edward Wakefield, *Past Imperative: My Life in India, 1927–1947* (London, 1966), 215–16; Potter, *India's Political Administrators, 1919–1983*, 131–3.

13 Nicholas Owen, 'The Conservative Party and Indian Independence, 1945–1947', *The Historical Journal*, xlvi (2003) 403–436.

14 Owen, 'The Conservative Party and Indian Independence, 1945–1947', 414; Camilla Schofield, *Enoch Powell and the Making of Postcolonial Britain* (2013), 66; Peter Brooke, 'India, Post-Imperialism and the Origins of Enoch Powell's "Rivers of Blood" Speech', *The Historical Journal*, l (2007).

15 Schofield, *Enoch Powell and the Making of Postcolonial Britain*, 73, 69.

16 Hannah Arendt, *On Violence* (San Diego, CA, 1970), 44.

17 Paul M. McGarr, '"The Viceroys Are Disappearing from the Roundabouts in Delhi": British Symbols of Power in Post-Colonial India', *Modern Asian Studies*, xlix (2015), 8, 15.

18 Jayanta Sengupta, 'Kolkata's Landmark Victoria Memorial Hall Getting Makeover', Kolkata, *Economic Times* (2015); 'Section of Metro's Heritage Corridor Tunnel Complete', *Economic Times* (2015); Jyoti Rai, '100 Yrs of History, Glory of Capital Delhi', Chandigarh, *The Tribune* (2011).

BIBLIOGRAPHY

MANUSCRIPT SOURCES

India Office Records

Mss Eur F86, Temple Papers
Mss Eur F88, Elphinstone Collection
Mss Eur F112, Curzon Papers
Mss Eur F180, ICS Officer Narratives
Mss Eur F370, British Association of South Asia Cemeteries
Mss Eur G37, Clive Papers
Mss Eur Photo 422, James Neill Papers
E/ Correspondence with India
F/ Board's Collections
G/ Factory Records
H/ Home Miscellaneous
L/E, Economic Department files, 1796–1950
L/MAR, East India Company ships' logbooks
L/PO, Viceroy's Private Office Papers, 1865–1948
L/PJ, India Office Records, Public and Judicial
L/PS, Political and Secret Department
L/R/, India Office Record Department Papers
P/ Bengal Proceedings
P/ Bombay Proceedings
V/ Official Publications

British Library, Manuscripts Collection

Add Mss 13,679, Wellesley Papers

National Library of Wales, Aberystwyth

Clive Papers

National Archives of Bangladesh

Bakarganj District Records
Barisal Collectorate Records
Dhaka Collectorate Records
Dhaka District Records
Faridpur District Records
Rangpur District Records

National Archives of India

Home, Establishments Department, 1921
Department of Information, 1942–1947

Andhra Pradesh State Archives, Hyderabad

Godavari District Records, 1790–1830
Madras, Local and Municipal Department, 1920–1930

Maharashtra State Archives, Mumbai

Dharwar Collector's Diary, 1818–1819
Ratnagiri Collector's Diary, 1817–1820
Bombay Public Works Department (Railways), 1844–1861
Revenue (Famine Department), 1897–1901

People's History Museum, Manchester

Douglas Houghton, 'Diary of Ten Weeks in India', Jan.–Mar. 1946

PUBLISHED PRIMARY SOURCES

Ahmad, Ilyas. 'The Crowd.' *The Indian Journal of Political Science* 2, no. 1 (1940): 11–22.

Aiya, V. Nagam. *The Travancore State Manual*. Trivandrum, 1906.

Ali, Karim. 'Muzzafarnamah' in *Bengal Nawabs*, ed. Jadunath Sarkar, Calcutta, 1952.

Andrew, Sir William Patrick. *Indian Railways as Connected with British Empire in the East*. London, 1884.

Anon. 'Account of the Late Famine in India.' *Gentleman's Magazine and Historical Review* 41 (1771).

Anon. 'Grosely's Tour to London.' *The Monthly Review, Or, Literary Journal* 47 (1772).

Anon. 'The Institution of Caste.' *The Edinburgh Review* 48 (September 1828).

Anon. *Account of Roorkee College, Established for the Instruction of Civil Engineers*. Secunderabad, 1851.

Anon. 'The Sepoy Rebellion.' *London Quarterly Review* IX (October 1857), 208–62.

Anon. 'Native Legend of Job Charnock and the Founding of Fort William.' *Calcutta Review* CXX (old series) (1905).

Anon. 'Proceedings of Congress, Lucknow Session, 12–14 April 1936.' *Indian Annual Register*, July 1936.

Bagal, Jogesh Chandra. *History of the Indian Association, 1876–1951*. Calcutta, 1953.

Barlow, Edward. *Barlow's Journal of His Life at Sea in King's Ships, 1659 to 1703*. London, 1934.

Besant, Annie Wood. *How India Wrought for Freedom, the Story of the National Congress*. Madras, 1915.

Bird, Robert. *Dacoitee in Excelsis: Or, The Spoliation of Oude*. London, 1857.

Blakiston, John. *Twelve Years' Military Adventure in Three Quarters of the Globe*. London, Henry Colburn, 1829.

Blunt, Wilfrid Scawen. *India under Ripon; a Private Diary*. London, 1909.

Bowring, John, ed. *The Works of Jeremy Bentham*. 11 vols. London, 1838.

Brackenbury, C. F. *District Gazetteer, Cuddapah*. Madras, 1915.

Briggs, John. *Letters Addressed to a Young Person in India*. London, 1828.

Brown, Joyce. 'A Memoir of Colonel Sir Proby Cautley.' *Notes and Records of the Royal Society of London* 34, no. 2 (1 March 1980): 185–225.

Bruce, John. *Annals of the Honorable East-India Company*. London, 1810.

Burke, Edmund. *The Writings and Speeches of Edmund Burke*. Ed. P. J. Marshall. Vol. 6. Oxford, 1991.

Burnell, John. *Bombay in the Days of Queen Anne*. Ed. Samuel Townsend Sheppard. London, 1933.

Burney, Fanny. *Diaries and Letters of Madame D'Arblay*. Ed. Charlotte Barrett. London, 1796.

Carlyle, Thomas. *Latter-Day Pamphlets*. London: Chapman, 1850.

Carthill, A. L. *The Lost Dominion*. Edinburgh, 1924.

Carthill, A. L. *Madampur*. Edinburgh, 1931.

Cobden, Richard. *How Wars Are Got Up in India: The Origin of the Burmese War*. London, 1853.

Colebrooke, H. T. *A Digest of Hindu Law on Contracts and Successions*. Calcutta, 1798.

Colebrooke, T. E. *Life of the Honourable Mountstuart Elphinstone*. London, 1884.

Collet, Sophia Dobson. *Life and Letters of Raja Rammohun Roy*. Calcutta, 1913.

Connell, Arthur Knatchbull. *The Economic Revolution of India and the Public Works Policy*. London, 1883.

Corneille, John. *Journal of My Service in India*. London, 1966.

Cotton, Julian J. *List of European Tombs in the Bellary District with Inscriptions Thereon*. Bellary, 1894.

Cotton, Sir Arthur. *Public Works in India*. London, 1854.

Cowell, Herbert. *The History and Constitution of the Courts and Legislative Authorities in India*. Calcutta, 1872.

Crawford, John. 'The Indian Taxation of Englishmen.' *The Edinburgh Review* 47 (January 1828).

Davis, John Francis. *Vizier Ali Khan: Or, The Massacre of Benares*. London, 1871.

Disraeli, Benjamin. *Tancred: Or, The New Crusade*. London, 1847.

Dodd, George. *The History of the Indian Revolt and of the Expeditions to Persia, China, and Japan, 1856–7–8*. London, 1859.

Drewitt, Frederick. *Bombay in the Days of George IV: Memoirs of Sir Edward West*. London, 1907.

Dutt, Romesh Chunder. *India in the Victorian Age; an Economic History of the People*. London, 1904.

Eastwick, Edward B. *A Handbook for India*. London, 1859.

Edwardes, S. M. *Memoir of Rao Bahadur Ranchhodlal Chhotalal*. Exeter, 1920.

Elphinstone, Mountstuart. *The Rise of British Power in India*. London, 1887.

Emerson, Ralph Waldo. *English Traits*. London: Ticknor and Fields, 1866.

Evelyn, John. *Diary and Correspondence of John Evelyn*. Ed. William Bray. London, 1850.

Fawcett, Charles, and William Foster. *The English Factories in India, 1678–1684*. 4 vols. Oxford, 1954.

Forrest, G. W., ed. *Selections from the Bombay Diaries, 1722–1788, Bombay Secretariat, Home Series*. Bombay, 1887.

Forster, E. M. 'Kipling's Poems.' *Journal of Modern Literature* 30, no. 3 (2007): 12–30.

Fraser, James Baillie. *Military Memoir of Lieut. Col. James Skinner*. London, 1851.

Gandhi, M. K. *Gandhi: 'Hind Swaraj' and Other Writings*. Ed. Anthony J. Parel. Cambridge, 2012.

Gandhi, Mohandas K. *Collected Works of Mahatma Gandhi*. 100 vols. Delhi, 1958. http://www.gandhiserve.org/e/cwmg/cwmg.htm, last accessed 1 February 2016.

Gangarama. *The Maharashta Purana: An Eighteenth-Century Bengali Historical Text*. Honolulu, HA: 1965.

Ghose, Manmathanath. *The Life of Grish Chunder Ghose*. Calcutta, 1911.

Glazier, E. G. *A Report on the District of Rungpore*. Calcutta, 1873.

Gleig, George Robert. *The Life of Major-General Sir Thomas Munro, Bart. and K. C. B., Late Governor of Madras*. London, 1831.

Government of Bombay. *Report on the Administration of the Bombay Presidency, for the Year 1875–6*. Bombay, 1876.

Government of India. *Central Secretariat, Manual of Office Procedure*. Thirteenth edition. New Delhi, 2010. http://cpwd.gov.in/publication/worksmanual2012.pdf, last accessed 2 April 2016.

Gurwood, Lt. Col. John. *The Dispatches of the Duke of Wellington, on His Various Campaigns*. London, 1837.

Hamid, Shahid. *Disastrous Twilight: A Personal Record of the Partition of India by Major-General Shahid Hamid*. Barnsley, 1993.

Hamilton, Alexander, and Carl Bridenbaugh. *Gentleman's Progress: The Itinerarium of Dr Alexander Hamilton, 1744*. Chapel Hill, NC, 1948.

Hamilton, Alexander. *A New Account of the East Indies*. London, 1744

Hedges, William. *The Diary of William Hedges, Esq. during His Agency in Bengal (1681–1687)*. London, 1887.

Hill, Samuel Charles. *Bengal in 1756–1757: a selection of public and private papers* dealing with the affairs of the British in Bengal during the reign of Siraj-Uddaula. Calcutta, 1905.

Hodson, William. *Twelve Years of a Soldier's Life in India*, London, 1859.

Hope, Lady Elizabeth. *General Sir Arthur Cotton, His Life and Work*. London, 1900.

Hossein Khan, Ghulam. *The Seir Mutaquerin, or Review of Modern Times*. Delhi, 1926.

Houghton, Bernard. 'Reform in India.' *Political Science Quarterly*, 34, no. 4 (1920): 545–55.

Howell, T. B. *A Complete Collection of State Trials and Proceedings for High Treason and Other Crimes and Misdemeanors*. London, 1816.

Hunter, W. W. *Seven Years of Indian Legislation*, London, 1870.

Hunter, W. W. *England's Work in India*. London, 1881.

Hunter, W. W. *The Annals of Rural Bengal*. New York, 1868.

Ingram, Edward, ed. *Two Views of British India: The Private Correspondence of Mr. Dundas and Lord Wellesley, 1798–1801*. London, 1970.

Johnson, J. E. 'Steam Navigation to India.' *Kaleidoscope, Or, Literary and Scientific Mirror*, 5 (13 July 1824).

Kaye, John William. *A History of the Sepoy War In India*. London, 1872.

Kaye, John William. *The Life and Correspondence of Major-General Sir John Malcolm*, London 1856.

Khan, Ameer-ood-doulah Mohummud, *Memoirs of the Puthan Soldier of Fortune*, ed. H. T. Prinsep, Calcutta, 1832.

Khan, Yusuf Ali. *Tarikh-I-Bangla Mahabat Jangi*. Translated by Abdus Subhan. Calcutta, 1982.

Khan, Sayyid Ahmad. *The Causes of the Indian Revolt*. Patna, 1995.

Knight, Charles. *The English Cyclopedia. A New Dictionary of Useful Knowledge*. London, 1854.

Knight, Robert. *The Imam Commission Unmasked*. London, 1859.

Lajpat Rai, Lala. *The Arya Samaj; an Account of Its Origin, Doctrines, and Activities, with a Biographical Sketch of the Founder*. London, 1915.

Lajpat Rai, Lala. *The Political Future of India*. New York, 1919.

Lajpat Rai, Lala. *Unhappy India*. Calcutta, 1928.

Lajpat Rai, Lala. *Young India: an Interpretation and a History of the Nationalist Movement from within*. New York, 1917.

Madras Record Office. *Despatches to England, 1743–1751. Records of Fort St. George*. Madras, 1933.

Madras Record Office. *Diary and Consultation Book, 1719–1723. Records of Fort St. George*. Madras, 1910.

Madras Record Office. *Diary and Consultation Book, 1751. Records of Fort St. George*. Madras, 1938.

Mahmood, Syed. 'British Rule in India. Does It Owe Its Origin to Conquest, and Its Maintenance to Physical Force?' *Calcutta Review* 68, no. 135 (1879).

Maitland, Julie. *Letters from Madras: During the Years 1836–1839*. John Murray, 1846.

Malcolm, Sir John. *A Memoir of Central India, including Malwa and adjoining Provinces*. London, 1824.

Malcolm, Sir John. *The Government of India*. London, 1833.

Malcolm, Sir John. *The Life of Robert, Lord Clive*. London, 1836.

Mansergh, Nicholas, ed. *The Transfer of Power, 1942–7*, 12 vols. London, 1970–1983.

Martin, Robert Montgomery. *The Indian Empire*. 3 vols. London, 1858.

Merivale, Herman. *Life of Sir Henry Lawrence*. 2 vols. London, 1872.

Mill, James. *The History of British India with Notes and Continuation, by Horace Hayman Wilson*. edition. London, 1858.

Mill, James. *The History of British India*. Third edition. London, 1826.

Mill, John Stuart. *On Liberty and Other Writings*. Ed. Stefan Collini. Cambridge, 1989.

Morris, Henry. *A Descriptive and Historical Account of the Godavery District*. London, 1878.

Nanda, Bal Ram, ed. *The Collected Works of Lala Lajpat Rai*. Delhi, 2003.

Nevinson, Henry Wood. *The New Spirit in India*. London, 1908.

Norton, John Bruce. *Topics of Jurisprudence: Or Aids to the Office of the Indian Judge*. London, 1862.

Orme, Robert. *A History of The Military Transactions of the British Nation In Indostan*. London, 1763.

Ovington, John. *A Voyage to Surat, in the Year 1689*. Oxford, 1929.

Pillai, Ananda Ranga. *Private Diary of Ananda Ranga Pillai*. Ed. Henry Dodwell. Madras, 1922.

Pollexfen, Henry, *The Argument of a Learned Counsel*. London, 1696.

Poona. Gazetteer of the Bombay Presidency. Bombay, 1885.

Prasad, Beni. 'Presidential Address.' *The Indian Journal of Political Science* 2, no. 4 (1941): 413–37.

Prasad, Beni. *History of Jahangir*. Bombay, 1922.

Prinsep, H. T. *A Narrative of the Political and Military Transactions of British India, under the administration of the Marquess of Hastings, 1813 to 1818*. London, 1820.

Proceedings of the First Indian National Congress, Held at Bombay on the 28th, 29th, and 30th December, 1885. Madras, 1905.

Quarterly Journal of the Poona Sarvajanik Sabha. Poona, 1870.

Rizvi, S. A. A., and M. L. Bhargava, eds. *Freedom Struggle in Uttar Pradesh*. 6 vols. Lucknow, 1957.

Roy, Rammohan. *The Essential Writings of Raja Rammohan Ray*. Oxford, 1999.

Scott, Jefferson Ellsworth. *In Famine Land. Observations and Experiences in India during the Great Drought of 1899–1900*. London, 1904.

Seton-Karr, Walter. *A Short Account of Events during the Sepoy Mutiny of 1857–8*. London, 1894.

Shore, Frederick John. *Notes on Indian Affairs*. London, 1837.

Sleeman, William H. *Report on Budhuk Alias Bagree Decoits, and Other Gang Robbers by Hereditary Profession*. Calcutta, 1849.

Sleeman, William. H. *A Journey through the Kingdom of Oude, in 1849–1850*. London, R. Bentley, 1858.

Smiles, Samuel. *Self-Help; with Illustrations of Character and Conduct*. London, 1859.

Stephen, Leslie. *The Life of Sir James Fitzjames Stephen*. London, 1895.

Stephen, Sir James FitzJames. *A History of the Criminal Law of England*. London, 1883.

Stephenson, John W. J. *Treatise on the Manufacture of Saltpetre, Descriptive of the Operations and Proper Plans to Be Used for the Manufacture of Culmee and Cooteah*. Calcutta, 1835.

Strachey, John, and Richard Strachey. *The Finances and Public Works of India from 1869 to 1881*. London, 1882.

Subba Rao, Nanjangud S. *Some Aspects of Economic Planning. Sir William Meyer Lectures, 1932–3*. Bangalore, 1935.

Sykes, W. H. 'Expenditure in India on Public Works from 1837–8 to 1845–6.' *Journal of the Statistical Society of London* 14, no. 1 (1851): 45–7.

Tagore, Rabindranath. 'Swadeshi Samaj.' *Nabya Bharat* 23, no. 1 (1905).

Vansittart, Henry. *A Narrative of the Transactions in Bengal, from the Year 1760, to the Year 1764*. London, 1766.

Wakefield, Sir Edward. *Past Imperative: My Life in India, 1927–1947*. London, 1966.

Waliullah, Syed. *Tree Without Roots*. London, 1967.

West, Edward. *A Memoir of the States of the Southern Maratha Country*. Bombay, 1869.

White, Adam. *Considerations on the State of British India*. Edinburgh, 1822.

Wilkie, Lt. Col. 'The British Colonies Considered as Military Posts.' *The United Service Magazine*, June 1841.

Wilks, Mark. *History of Mysore*. London, 1810.

Williamson, Thomas. *The East India Vade-Mecum*, London, 1810.

Wilson, W. J. *History of the Madras Army*. Madras, 1883.

SELECTED SECONDARY SOURCES

The following is a selection of secondary works used writing this book. For more detailed references, see the notes.

Aiyar, Swarna. '"August Anarchy". The Partition Massacres in Punjab, 1947.' In *Freedom, Trauma, Continuities. Northern India and Independence*, edited by D. A. Low and Howard Brasted. Walnut Creek, CA, 1998.

Alam, Muzaffar, and Sanjay Subrahmanyam. 'Trade and Politics in the Arcot Nizamat (1700–1732).' In *Writing the Mughal World: Studies on Culture and Politics*. New York, NY, 2012.

Alam, Muzaffar, and Sanjay Subrahmanyam. *The Mughal State, 1526–1750*. Delhi, 1998.

Amin, Shahid. *Event, Metaphor, Memory: Chauri Chaura, 1922–1992*. Berkeley, CA, 1995.

Bayly, C. A. '"The Nation Within": British India at War 1939–1947.' *Proceedings of the British Academy* 125 (2004): 265–85.

Bayly, C. A. *Recovering Liberties: Indian Thought in the Age of Liberalism and Empire*. Cambridge, 2011.

Bayly, C. A. *Rulers, Townsmen and Bazaars: North Indian Society in the Age of British Expansion, 1770–1870.* Cambridge, 1983.

Bhadra, Gautum. 'Four Rebels of 1857.' In *Subaltern Studies IV*, edited by Ranajit Guha. New Delhi, 1985.

Bhat, N. Shyam. *South Kanara, 1799–1860: A Study in Colonial Administration and Regional Response.* New Delhi, 1998.

Biddulph, John. *The Pirates of Malabar, and an Englishwoman in India Two Hundred Years Ago.* London, 1907.

Birla, Ritu. *Stages of Capital: Law, Culture, and Market Governance in Late Colonial India.* Durham, NC, 2008.

Bourke, Richard. *Empire and Revolution: The Political Life of Edmund Burke.* Princeton, NJ, 2015.

Bowen, H. V. *The Business of Empire. The East India Company and Imperial Britain, 1756–1833.* Cambridge, 2006.

Brown, Judith M. *Gandhi's Rise to Power: Indian Politics 1915–1922.* Cambridge, 1974.

Bryant, G. J. *The Emergence of British Power in India, 1600–1784.* Woodbridge, 2013.

Buckler, F. W. 'The Political Theory of the Indian Mutiny.' *Transactions of the Royal Historical Society*, Fourth Series, 5 (1 January 1922): 71–100.

Carrasco, Daniel Kent. 'Jayaprakahsan Narayan and Lok Niti. Socialism, Gandhism and Political Cultures of Protest in the XX Century.' PhD thesis, King's College London, 2015.

Cashman, Richard I. *The Myth of the Lokamanya: Tilak and Mass Politics in Maharashtra.* Berkeley, CA, 1975.

Chandavarkar, Rajnarayan. *The Origins of Industrial Capitalism in India. Business Strategies and the Working Classes in Bombay, 1900–1940.* Cambridge, 1994.

Chatterjee, Kumkum. *Merchants, Politics, and Society in Early Modern India: Bihar, 1733–1820.* Leiden, 1996.

Chatterjee, Nandini. 'Reflections on Religious Difference and Permissive Inclusion in Mughal Law.' *Journal of Law and Religion* 29, no. 3 (October 2014): 396–415.

Chatterjee, Partha. *The Nation and Its Fragments. Colonial and Postcolonial Histories.* Princeton, NJ, 1993.

Chaudhuri, K. N. *The Trading World of Asia and the English East India Company: 1660–1760.* Cambridge, 1978.

Cooper, Randolf G. S. *The Anglo-Maratha Campaigns and the Contest for India: The Struggle for Control of the South Asian Military Economy.* Cambridge, 2003.

Dalrymple, William. *The Last Mughal: The Fall of Delhi, 1857.* London, 2009.

Dasgupa, Shomik: 'Ethics, Accountability and Distance. The Political Thought of Rammohun Roy'. King's College London, PhD Thesis, 2016.

Datta, Rajat. *Society, Economy, and the Market: Commercialization in Rural Bengal, c. 1760–1800.* Delhi, 2000.

Devji, Faisal. 'Apologetic Modernity.' *Modern Intellectual History* 4, no. 1 (2007): 61–76.

Devji, Faisal. *The Impossible Indian: Gandhi and the Temptations of Violence.* London, 2012.

Dewey, Clive. 'Images of the Village Community: A Study in Anglo-Indian Ideology.' *Modern Asian Studies* 6, no. 3 (May 1972): 291–328.

Dirks, Nicholas B. *Castes of Mind. Colonialism and the Making of Modern India.* Princeton, NJ, 2001.

Dyson, Tim. 'On the Demography of South Asian Famines: Part I.' *Population Studies* 45, no. 1 (1991): 5–25.

Eaton, Richard M. *The Rise of Islam and the Bengal Frontier, 1204–1760.* Berkeley, CA, 1993.

Farooqui, Amar. *Sindias and the Raj: Princely Gwalior c. 1800–1850.* Delhi, 2011.

Fisher, Michael H. 'The Imperial Coronation of 1819: Awadh, the British and the Mughals.' *Modern Asian Studies* 19, no. 2 (April 1985): 239–77.

Gallagher, John, and Anil Seal. 'Britain and India between the Wars.' *Modern Asian Studies* 15, no. 3 (1981): 387–414.

Gallagher, John, and Ronald Robinson. 'The Imperialism of Free Trade.' *The Economic History Review* 6, no. 1 (1 August 1953): 1–15.

Gordon, Stewart. *The Marathas 1600–1818.* Cambridge, 1993.

Gould, William. *Hindu Nationalism and the Language of Politics in Late Colonial India.* Cambridge, 2004.

Guenther, Alan M. 'Syed Mahmood and the Transformation of Muslim Law in British India.' PhD thesis, McGill University, 2004.

Guha, Amalendu. 'Raw Cotton of Western India: 1750–1850.' *Indian Economic & Social History Review* 9, no. 1 (1972): 1–41.

Guha, Ranajit, 'Not at Home in Empire.' *Critical Inquiry* 23, no. 3 (1997): 482–93.

Guha, Ranajit. *Dominance Without Hegemony: History and Power in Colonial India.* Cambridge, MA, 1997.

Hardiman, David. *Peasant Nationalists of Gujarat: Kheda District, 1917–34.* Delhi; New York, 1982.

Hasan, Farhat. *State and Locality in Mughal India: Power Relations in Western India, c. 1572–1730.* Cambridge, 2004.

Headrick, Daniel R. *The Tools of Empire: Technology and European Imperialism in the Nineteenth Century.* Oxford, 1981.

Hunt, Roland, and John Harrison. *The District Officer in India, 1930–1947.* London, 1980.

Hutchins, Francis G. *The Illusion of Permanence: British Imperialism in India.* Princeton, NJ, 1967.

Inagaki, Haruki. 'The Rule of Law and Emergency in Colonial India: the Conflict between the King's Court and the Government in Bombay in the 1820s', PhD thesis, King's College London, 2016.

Iqbal, Iftekhar. *The Bengal Delta: Ecology, State and Social Change, 1840–1943.* Basingstoke, 2010.

Jalal, Ayesha. *The Sole Spokesman: Jinnah, the Muslim League, and the Demand for Pakistan.* Cambridge, 1985.

Kamtekar, Indivar. 'A Different War Dance: State and Class in India 1939–1945.' *Past & Present* 176, no. 1 (August 1, 2002): 187–221.

Kapila, Shruti. 'Self, Spencer and Swaraj. Nationalist Thought and Critiques of Liberalism, 1890–1920.' *Modern Intellectual History* 4, no. 1 (2007), 109–27.

Khan, Yasmin. *The Great Partition*. New Haven, CT, 2007.

Kling, B. B. *Partner in Empire: Dwarkanath Tagore and the Age of Enterprise in Eastern India*. Berkeley, CA, 1976.

Kolff, D. H. A. *Grass in Their Mouths: The Upper Doab of India Under the Company's Magna Charta, 1793–1830*. Leiden, 2010.

Lawson, Philip. *The East India Company. A History, 1600–1857*. London, 1993.

Lelyveld, David. *Aligarh's First Generation: Muslim Solidarity in British India*. Princeton, NJ, 1978.

Mantena, Karuna. 'Another Realism: The Politics of Gandhian Nonviolence.' *American Political Science Review* 106, no. 2 (2012): 455–70.

Markovits, Claude. *Indian Business and Nationalist Politics 1931–39: The Indigenous Capitalist Class and the Rise of the Congress Party*. Cambridge, 1985.

Marshall, P. J. *Bengal: The British Bridgehead. Eastern India, 1740–1828*. Cambridge, 1987.

Menon, Dilip M. 'Houses by the Sea. State Experimentation on the Southwest Coast of India 1760–1800.' in *Mapping Histories: Essays Presented to Ravinder Kumar*, edited by Neera Chandhoke. London, 2000.

More, Leena. *The English East India Company and the Native Rulers of Kerala: A Case Study of Attingal and Travancore*. Tellicherry, 2003.

Mukherjee, Janam. 'Hungry Bengal. War, Famine, Riots, and the End of Empire. 1939–1946.' PhD thesis, University of Michigan, 2011.

Palit, Chittabrata. *Tensions in Bengal Rural Society: Landlord, Planters, and Colonial Rule, 1830–1860*. New Delhi, 1975.

Pandey, Gyan. 'The Peasant Revolt and Indian Nationalism. The Peasant Movement in Awadh, 1919–1922.' In Ranajit Guha, ed., *Subaltern Studies I*, New Delhi, 1986: 143–97.

Pandey, Gyan. *Remembering Partition: Violence, Nationalism and History in India*. Cambridge, 2001.

Peers, D. M. *Between Mars and Mammon. Colonial Armies and the Garrison State in India 1819–1835*. London, 1995.

Phalkey, Jahnavi. *Atomic State. Big Science in Twentieth-Century India*. Ranikhet, 2013.

Potter, David C. *India's Political Administrators, 1919–1983*. Oxford, 1986.

Raghavan, Srinath. *India's War. The Making of Modern South Asia, 1939–1945*. London, 2016.

Rao, Mallikarjuna. 'Native Revolts in the West Godavari District, 1785–1805.' PhD thesis, Andhra University, 2000.

Ray, Ratnalekha. *Change in Bengal Agrarian Society, c. 1760–1850*. New Delhi, 1979.

Richards, John F. 'The Finances of the East India Company in India, c. 1766–1859.' *LSE Economic History Working Papers*, no. 153/11 (August 2011). http://eprints.lse.ac.uk/37829/1/WP153.pdf, last accessed 10 April 2016.

Robb, Peter. 'Memory, Place and British Memorials in Early Calcutta.' in Ezra Rashkow, Sanjukta Ghosh and Upal Chakrabarti, (eds). *Memory, Identity and the Colonial Encounter in India. Essays in Honour of Peter Robb*. New Delhi, 2016.

Rothermund, Dietmar. *India in the Great Depression, 1929–1939.* New Delhi, 1992.

Roy, Anwesha. 'Making Riots, Making Peace. Communal Riots and Anti-Communal Resistance in Bengal, 1941–47.' PhD thesis, Jawaharlal Nehru University, 2015.

Sarkar, Sumit, *The Swadeshi Movement in Bengal, 1903–1908.* Delhi, 1973.

Sen, Surendra Nath. 'The Early Career of Kanhoji Angria.' in *Early Career of Kanhoji Angria and Other Papers.* Calcutta, 1941.

Singha, Radhika. 'Colonial Law and Infrastructural Power: Reconstructing Community, Locating the Female Subject.' *Studies in History* 19, no. 1 (2003): 87–126.

Sinha, Nitin. *Communication and Colonialism in Eastern India: Bihar, 1760s–1880s.* London, 2014.

Stern, Philip J. *The Company-State: Corporate Sovereignty and the Early Modern Foundations of the British Empire in India.* New York NY, 2011.

Stokes, Eric. *The English Utilitarians and India.* Oxford, 1959.

Subrahmanyam, Sanjay. 'Un Grand Dérangement: Dreaming an Indo-Persian Empire in South Asia, 1740–1800.' *Journal of Early Modern History* 4, no. 3 (1 January 2000): 337–78.

Surendra Rao, B. *Bunts in History and Culture.* Udupi, 2010.

Tai-Yong, Tan. 'An Imperial Home-Front: Punjab and the First World War.' *The Journal of Military History* 64, no. 2 (1 April 2000): 371–410.

Tomlinson, B. R. 'India and the British Empire, 1880–1935.' *Indian Economic & Social History Review* 12, no. 4 (1 October 1975): 337–80.

Travers, Robert. *Ideology and Empire in Eighteenth-Century India. The British in Bengal.* Cambridge, 2007.

Venkateshwar Rao, M. 'District Associations and Their Contribution to the Political Development of Andhra, 1892–1920.' PhD thesis, Osmania University, Hyderabad, 1992.

Wagner, Kim A. *The Great Fear of 1857: Rumours, Conspiracies and the Making of the Indian Uprising.* Oxford, 2010.

Washbrook, D. A. 'South India 1770–1840: The Colonial Transition.' *Modern Asian Studies* 38, no. 3 (2004): 479–516.

Williams, Richard. 'Hindustani Music between Awadh and Bengal, c. 1758–1905.' PhD thesis, King's College London, 2015.

Wilson, Jon E. *The Domination of Strangers: Modern Governance in Eastern India, 1780–1835.* Basingstoke, 2008.

Withington, Phil. *The Politics of Commonwealth: Citizens and Freemen in Early Modern England.* Cambridge, 2009.

ACKNOWLEDGEMENTS

This book exists because of the belief and support of four people in particular: Richard Vinen encouraged me to write for a wider audience, Andrew Gordon helped marshal my ideas to persuade publishers to put it into print, Mike Jones enthusiastically supported it, then Iain MacGregor guided the book to publication with insight and efficiency when it was orphaned in the UK; Rahul Srivastava and his team were enthusiastic advocates in India; George Lucas and Clive Little offered creative, thoughtful and efficient support in the United States, Harriet Dobson assiduously arranged illustrations and managed the production process, Richard Collins copy edited to perfection, smoothing hundreds of ugly phrases and saving me from as many errors. All those which remain are my own.

The following archives and libraries in Britain and South Asia offered assistance in allowing access to material used in this book: King's College London Maughan Library; Asia, Africa and Pacific Reading Room at the British Library; the State Archives of Maharashtra in Mumbai and Andhra Pradesh in Hyderabad; the National Archives of India; Nehru Memorial Museum and Library; and National Archives of Bangladesh, which remains, due to the work of Sharif Uddin Ahmed, one of the most friendly and well-organized archives in the subcontinent. The argument expounded and stories told in *India Conquered* have developed through conversations with friends over the last decade, but particularly with Neeladri Bhattacharya, Jim Bjork, Upal Chakrabarti, Rajat Datta,

Faisal Devji, Andrew Dilley, David Edgerton, Maurice Glasman, Iftekar Iqbal, Niraja Gopal Jayal, Patrick Joyce, Mike Kenny, Elaine Lester, Karuna Mantena, Adnan Naseemullah, Thomas Newbold, Eleanor Newbiggin, Kriti Kapila, Shruti Kapila, Prashant Kidambi, Ben Page, Jahnavi Phalkey, Martin Plaut, Srinath Raghavan, Peter Robb, Katherine Schofield, Taylor Sherman, Bhrigupathi Singh, Nitin Sinha, Philip Stern, Sujit Sivasundaram, Louise Tillin, Robert Travers, Georgios Varouxakis, Richard Vinen, Rupa Viswanath, Kim Wagner and David Washbrook; in these pages I'm sure each will find something to disagree with, but will also find traces of our conversations, too. I'm grateful to Ronald Anil Fernandes for welcoming me to Mangalore and sharing his curiosity about his home town; and to Anuraj Chowfla for talking me through the landscape of India's new gated communities. Versions of different chapters have been presented at Yale University in New Haven, Presidency University in Kolkata, North South University in Dhaka, Jawaharlal Nehru University in Delhi, Goettingen University, York University, Oxford University, at numerous seminars at King's College London and the Institute for Historical Research; I'm grateful for insightful critique and comments at each. In an academic world which sometimes seems bereft of new ideas, King's College London's history department is a wonderful place to teach and research, where, best of all, there's space to think; I am grateful to my colleagues for making it such. The engagement of a group of PhD students interested in the Indian and British state in the nineteenth and twentieth centuries has been immensely stimulating; particular mention is due to Shomik Dasgupta, Bulbul Hasan, Kieran Hazzard, Haruki Inagaki, Cathryn Johnson, Amy Kavanagh, Tom Kelsey, Liam Morton and Kapil Subrahmanyam. I'd like to thank Leicester City Football Club and the Labour Party for offering very different kinds of distractions at different times. I'd particularly like to thank Andrew Dilley, David Egerton, Iftekar Iqbal, Patrick Joyce, Elaine Lester, Thomas Newbold, Simon Parker, Jahnavi Phalkey, Srinath Raghavan, Anwesha Roy, Jonathan Rutherford, Katherine Schofield, Philip

Stern, James Vernon, Richard Vinen, David Washbrook and Dorothy Wilson for taking the time to read and comment on chapters. Finally, and most importantly, I'd like to thank my brother Tim and parents Rod and Dot Wilson for their love and support: Delilah and Elsie for such love and entertainment, without whom this book would have been written more quickly but there'd have been no point writing it; and Elaine Lester, for whom thanks are unnecessary and love cannot be expressed in words.

INDEX

JON WILSON was educated at Oxford University and the New School for Social Research in New York, and has taught history at King's College London since 1999. He directs Historians in Residence and also comments in a range of media on contemporary British and South Asian politics and government.

Photo by Farhad Chowdhury